THE ART OF RHETORIC
IN THE ROMAN WORLD

A History of Rhetoric

Volume I: *The Art of Persuasion in Greece* (1963)

Volume II: *The Art of Rhetoric in the Roman World* (1972)

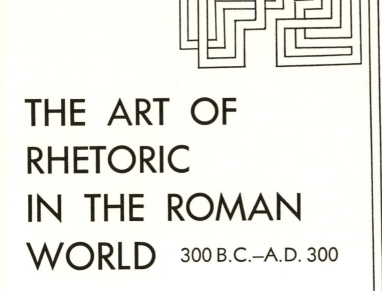

THE ART OF
RHETORIC
IN THE ROMAN
WORLD 300 B.C.–A.D. 300

BY GEORGE KENNEDY

PRINCETON UNIVERSITY PRESS
PRINCETON, NEW JERSEY · 1972

FOR CLAIRE

Contents

CONTENTS

CONTENTS

The following works are repeatedly referred to by the author's name alone, followed by volume and page, section, or column numbers. Abbreviations of journals are those used in *L'Année Philologique*. Abbreviations of authors and works are standard ones; when in doubt the reader may consult the introductory tables of the larger Greek and Latin dictionaries.

APG George Kennedy, *The Art of Persuasion in Greece*, Princeton, 1963.

Atkins J.W.H. Atkins, *Literary Criticism in Antiquity*, Cambridge, Eng., 1934, reprinted London and New York, 1952.

Bonner S. F. Bonner, *Roman Declamation in the Late Republic and Early Empire*, Liverpool, Berkeley, and Los Angeles, 1949.

CAH *The Cambridge Ancient History*, Cambridge, Eng., vol. 8, 1965; vol. 9, 1951; vol. 10, 1952; vol. 11, 1954.

Caplan Harry Caplan, *Ad C. Herennium De Ratione Dicendi* (Loeb Classical Library), Cambridge and London, 1954.

CIL *Corpus Inscriptionum Latinarum*, Berlin, 1862 and later.

Clarke M. L. Clarke, *Rhetoric at Rome: A Historical Survey*, London, 1953.

D'Alton J. F. D'Alton, *Roman Literary Theory and Criticism: A Study in Tenden-*

cies, London and New York, 1931, reprinted 1962.

Dessau   Hermann Dessau, *Inscriptiones Latinae Selectae*, Berlin, 1892-1916, reprinted 1954-55.

Gwynn   Aubrey O. Gwynn, *Roman Education from Cicero to Quintilian*, Oxford, 1926, reprinted New York, 1964.

Halm   Carolus Halm, *Rhetores Latini Minores*, Leipzig, 1863, reprinted, Frankfurt, 1964.

Kroll   W. Kroll, "Rhetorik," *Paulys Real-Encyclopädie der classischen Altertumwissenschaft, Supplementband* 7, Stuttgart, 1940.

Leeman   A. D. Leeman, *Orationis Ratio: The Stylistic Theories and Practice of the Roman Orators, Historians, and Philosophers*, Amsterdam, 1963.

Marrou   Henri Irénée Marrou, *A History of Education in Antiquity*, translated by George Lamb from the French edition originally published in 1948, New York, 1956, reprinted, 1964.

Marx   Fridericus Marx, *Incerti Auctoris De Ratione Dicendi ad C. Herennium libri IV*, Leipzig, 1894.

Michel   Alain Michel, *Rhétorique et philosophie chez Cicéron: Essai sur les fondements philosophiques de l'art de persuader*, Paris, 1960.

Norden   Eduard Norden, *Die antike Kunstprosa*, Leipzig and Berlin, 1923.

OCD   *The Oxford Classical Dictionary*, Oxford, edition of 1949.

ORF	Henrica Malcovati, *Oratorum Romanorum Fragmenta Liberae Rei Publicae*, Turin, 1955.
R-E	*Paulys Real-Encyclopädie der classischen Altertumswissenschaft.*
Schanz-Hosius	Martin Schanz and Carl Hosius, *Geschichte der Römischen Literatur bis zum Gesetzgebungswerk des Kaisers Justinian*, Munich, edition of 1959.
Schmid-Stählin	Wilhelm Christ, Wilhelm Schmid, and Otto Stählin, *Geschichte der Griechischen Literatur, zweiter Teil*, Munich, Band I, 1959; Band II, 1924.
Spengel	Leonardus Spengel, *Rhetores Graeci*, 3 volumes, Leipzig, 1853-56, reprinted Frankfurt, 1966.
Spengel-Hammer	Caspar Hammer, *Rhetores Graeci ex recognitione Leonardi Spengel*, Leipzig, 1894.
Stangl	Thomas Stangl, *Ciceronis Orationum Scholiastae*, vol. 2, Vienna and Leipzig, 1912.
Walz	Christianus Walz, *Rhetores Graeci*, 9 volumes, London and elsewhere, 1832-36, reprinted Osnabrück, 1968.
Warmington	E. H. Warmington, *Remains of Old Latin* (Loeb Classical Library), 4 volumes, London and Cambridge, 1961.

For definitions of rhetorical terms and references to discussions in ancient authors as well as the bibliography of ancient rhetoric cf. Heinrich Lausberg, *Handbuch der*

Literarischen Rhetorik: Eine Grundlegung der Literatur-wissenschaft, Munich, 1960. This largely replaces the long standard work of Richard Volkmann, *Die Rhetorik der Griechen und Römer in systematischer Uebersicht*, Leipzig, 1885.

Bibliography of rhetorical interest is carried regularly in *L'Année Philologique* under the various authors and also in the section *Histoire littéraire, Rhétorique*. A bibliography of rhetoric and public address is published annually in the August issue of *Speech Monographs*.

Foreword

This work is a companion volume to *The Art of Persuasion in Greece*, and though the nature of the subject has somewhat altered the form and increased the size, I hope it will be useful to a similar audience: students of classics and of speech seeking an overall picture of the history of rhetoric in the classical age of Rome. I have sought to present the main lines of development, to outline and perhaps occasionally to solve some problems, and to furnish a factual and bibliographical basis for further study. M. L. Clarke's *Rhetoric at Rome* has for nearly twenty years furnished a brief introduction to the subject: I have tried to give greater depth, particularly by adding a picture of Greek developments and by giving more historical background, and I have advanced some different hypotheses. My basic theme is that the Romans imitated from the Greeks an art of persuasion which gradually developed into an art often more concerned with what I call the secondary characteristics of rhetoric: not persuasion, but style and artistic effect. But in the empire an effort was made by a number of writers to recover some of the power of persuasion and some orators found new causes to plead in philosophy, Hellenism, and religion.

The book stops with the end of the classical period and purely pagan literature. The synthesis of classical and Christian elements in the fourth century and later seems to me a new and larger subject best reserved for another volume which I hope eventually to complete.

My studies have had the assistance of a summer grant from the Danforth Foundation (1963), a Fulbright to Italy (1964-65), a Guggenheim Fellowship (1964-65), and a grant from the University of North Carolina Research Council (1970). Completion has been delayed in part by my decision to write a book on Quintilian, published in 1969, and in part by administrative duties.

Chapel Hill
August 1, 1970

I would like to thank the following persons for help at various times: Dr. James F. Taylor compiled a great deal of preliminary bibliography for me in Haverford in the summer of 1963 and has maintained a steady encouraging interest in the work. Mr. R. Stanley Beaty helped put the finishing touches on the manuscript and scrupulously checked references in the summer of 1970 in Chapel Hill. Professor Douglas C. C. Young read a portion of the work in proof and saved me from a number of errors. My secretaries, Mrs. Erline Nipper, Mrs. Harriet Bonner, and in particular Miss Nancy J. Honeycutt have been of great assistance. Finally, I am much indebted to Mrs. Polly Hanford of Princeton University Press.

THE ART OF RHETORIC
IN THE ROMAN WORLD

CHAPTER ONE

Early Roman Rhetoric[1]

Rhetoric, defined in the strictest sense, is the art of persuasion as practiced by orators and described by theorists and teachers of speech. That basic meaning may be extended, however, to include the art of all who aim at some kind of attitude change on the part of their audience or readers, and then applied to what I shall call secondary rhetoric: critical or aesthetic theory not directly concerned with persuasion and the technique of works produced under the influence of these critical concepts. In all of these uses rhetoric is an abstraction; its concrete manifestations are principally oratory, but also other literary forms which share the purposes or tech-

* For abbreviations and bibliographic information not fully given in the notes see the table of abbreviations at the beginning of the book.

[1] For a general account of Roman rhetoric and oratory, esp. beginnings, cf. Victor Cucheval, *Histoire de l'éloquence latine depuis l'origine de Rome jusqu'à Cicéron*, Paris, 1892; Norden 156-81; Antonio Cima, *L'eloquenza Latina prima di Cicerone*, Rome, 1903; Gaston Boissier, "Introduction de la rhétorique grecque à Rome," *Melanges Perrot*, Paris, 1903; Friederich Leo, *Geschichte der römischen Literatur*, Berlin, 1913, 28-40 and 265-315; Schanz-Hosius 1.209-30; Wilhelm Kroll, *Studien zum Verständnis der römischen Literatur*, Stuttgart, 1924, esp. ch. 5 "Grammatische und rhetorische Sprachtheorien"; J. Wight Duff, *A Literary History of Rome from the Origins to the Close of the Golden Age*, reprint New York, 1960, 186-90; Enrica Malcovati, "L'eloquenza romana," *Annali della Università di Cagliari* 11 (1941) 137-61; Henry Bardon, *La littérature latine inconnue*, Paris, 1952; Clarke 10-49; S. F. Bonner, "Roman Oratory," *Fifty Years of Classical Scholarship* (ed. M. Platnauer), Oxford, 1954, 335-83 (2d ed. 416-64); Leeman 19-66. Tenney Frank, "The Prose of the Roman Statesmen," *Life and Literature in the Roman Republic*, Berkeley, 1930, 130-68 seems to me misleading.

niques of oratory, and it is even possible to speak of the rhetoric of sculpture or other plastic arts in so far as these aim at persuasion or attitude change.

The rhetoric seen in Latin literature is largely Greek. Romans first became conscious of methods of persuasion in the late third or early second centuries B.C. when their city had become not only the most powerful state of the Italian peninsula, but the greatest power in the Mediterranean, and they found themselves the object of every subtlety Greek rhetoricians could devise. Soon they began to imitate the technique themselves. Previously they had not consciously developed a theory of persuasion any more than they had taken a theoretical approach to other arts. Though certain aspects of Greek rhetoric were later sometimes treated as though they were native to Rome, it would be more accurate to say that these were congenial to Romans. The rhetoric taught by the Stoics,[2] for example, in so far as it put an emphasis on substance rather than style, seemed in the Roman spirit, and Cato's advice *rem tene, verba sequentur,* "Seize the subject, the words will follow," could pose as anti-Greek. The point of view which these words express became a part of the role of the noble Roman of the old school as played by Cato or Rutilius Rufus or many imitators. There were certainly many occasions when persuasion was needed in Rome before the arrival of Greek rhetoric and it would, of course, have been possible, if anyone had cared to try, to describe the acceptable techniques in use. It is characteristic of the Roman mind, however, that analysis was of no interest.

The early history of the Roman republic is filled with internal dissensions, especially strife between the "orders," the patrician aristocracy and the plebeian citi-

---

[2] Cf. APG 290-301. Other aspects of Stoic rhetoric such as its hairsplitting argumentation did not appeal to many Romans.

zenry, and this has sometimes been assumed to have involved a great deal of oratory.[3] The accounts which we have are certainly replete with speeches, but they were written many centuries later by rhetorically minded historians. The oratory is rarely, if ever, based on what was actually said, and there is no guarantee that any speeches at all were delivered in specific instances. This does not mean that there was no oratory in early Rome, only that it was less necessary and very probably less extensive than in Greek states like Athens. A number of points of evidence may be cited. First, Greek love of speeches can be seen in the very earliest compositions, the Homeric epics. Rome apparently lacked any counterpart to this expression, and its earliest literature was largely religious verse, legalistic prose, or very crude forms of comic drama.[4] Second, the Greek hero was from the start a speaker of words as well as a doer of deeds; the ideal Roman, according to the traditional picture, was austere and laconic, a man of action rather than words. Scipio Africanus, for example, if the story told by Aulus Gellius (4.18.3) has any foundation, played a Roman role in the defense he made before the people when charged with having accepted money from King Antiochus of Asia. "I recall," he said, "that this is the anniversary of the day on which I defeated Hannibal the Carthaginian, a man most hostile to your rule, in a great battle in the land of Africa and secured for you peace and glorious victory. Therefore, let us not be ungrateful to the gods, and, I suggest, let us leave this scoundrel and go from here straight to give thanks to Jupiter the Best and Greatest."

[3] Cf. Malcovati, *op.cit.* supra n. 1, 139-42.
[4] Cf. Schanz-Hosius 1.13-43, which attributes Roman failure to develop a native epic and tragedy in part to the absence of myth (p. 42); Duff, *op.cit.* supra n. 1, 47-67.

There are a number of objections to accepting this speech as historical,[5] but it gives a picture of what was thought appropriate to a noble Roman: strong ethos, an imperious manner, and brevity. When the people murmured against Scipio Nasica, consul in 138, he told them abruptly (Valerius Maximus 3.7.3): "Keep quiet please, citizens, for I know better than you what is to the best interest of the state." Another picture of a Roman attitude to oratory is found in the words which Cicero (*De or.* 1.35-66) attributes to Scaevola, a member of an old family long associated with the law. Scaevola objects to the encomium of oratory put in the mouth of Crassus, though partly adapted from Isocrates,[6] and thinks that many of the great deeds credited to oratory really belong to some other faculty. He asks (1.37), "Does Romulus really seem to you to have brought together shepherds and refugees, to have arranged marriages with the Sabines, or to have repressed the violence of neighboring peoples by eloquence rather than by his unique judgment and wisdom?"

Finally, the ancient sources date Roman oratory of artistic merit from no earlier than the end of the third or the early second century B.C. Cicero is certainly the best authority on these beginnings of great oratory at Rome, since he had studied the subject thoroughly and if he errs it is in the direction of overappreciation of his predecessors, but Cicero would not date its successes before Cethegus, consul in 204 (*Brutus* 57-60). Brutus (*Brutus* 293) is represented as regarding even the ora-

---

[5] Cicero did not know it (*De off.* 3.4), and Livy (38.56.1) reports that the information about the trial was confused. For a comparison of the versions in Gellius and in Livy, cf. J. Marouzeau, "Pour mieux comprendre les textes latins," *RPh* 45(1921) 165-66. Similar stories were told of the trial of Scaurus; cf. Val. Max. 3.7.8 and Quint. 5.12.10.

[6] Cf. APG 8-9.

tory of Cato in the second century as not worth noticing. We may conclude then, not only that rhetorical theory was lacking in early Rome, but that formal oratory did not play a predominant role until Greek influence became strong. Persuasion in Rome before the second century B.C. was relatively nonverbal and nonargumentative, and rested on family prestige, personal authority, and resources of power or money.

In order to understand Roman oratory better it is necessary to look more specifically at the categories and opportunities of rhetoric as they developed in the later Roman republic. The basic word for speech in Latin is *oratio*, which Cicero (*De off.* 1.132) subdivides into *contentio*, or debate, and *sermo*, or conversation. An *orator* originally was thought of as performing official religious or political functions, primarily as ambassador, but in the last two centuries of the republic the word took on a wider meaning.[7] Rhetoric in Latin is the Greek term *rhetorice*, or the more Latinized *rhetorica* (Quint. 2.14), though the more general *eloquentia* is sometimes used or a phrase like *ars dicendi*, "art of speaking," substituted. *Rhetorica* first appears in Latin in a fragment of Ennius (*Sotas* 4 Warmington) written sometime in the first half of the second century B.C.

Judicial Oratory

Oratory is divided by most authorities into three forms: judicial, deliberative, and epideictic. In Greek rhetoric, judicial oratory had a position of leadership. It was the first form to be written down, other than the imaginary oratory of the poets, and the first form to suggest the need for a systematic treatment of rhetorical

[7] Cf. Walter Neuhauser, *Patronus und Orator: eine Geschichte der Begriffe von ihren Anfängen bis in die Augusteische Zeit,* Innsbruck, 1958 and Michel 6-9.

technique. The development of Greek oratory into an art form seems to have been strongly influenced by the institution in the fifth century of large democratic juries before whom an artistically developed and uninterrupted speech was possible and even necessary. The writing of rhetorical handbooks seems to have been caused in turn by the requirement in Greece that litigants plead their own cases, rather than turn them over to advocates. Greek judicial oratory began at Syracuse in the fifth century, but was most fully developed at Athens in the fourth when both of these conditions prevailed.

At the time conscious rhetoric was beginning in Greece, Rome had only recently become a republic and was on the outer fringes of the civilized world. She developed legal procedures which were characteristically her own and which did not encourage the imitation of Greek rhetoric for some time. Furthermore, until the second century B.C. Romans showed little sign of being litigious.[8] Roman procedure[9] always required consider-

---

[8] Cf. Cic., *Brutus* 106. According to Gellius (4.3) the first suit involving a dowry took place as late as 231 B.C.

[9] Among many studies cf. Theodor Mommsen, *Römisches Strafrecht*, Leipzig, 1899; A.H.J. Greenidge, *The Legal Procedure of Cicero's Time*, Oxford, 1901; James L. Strachan-Davidson, *Problems of the Roman Criminal Law*, Oxford, 1912; Leopold Wenger (tr. by O. H. Fisk), *Institutes of the Roman Law of Civil Procedure*, New York, 1940; Fritz Schulz, *History of Roman Legal Science*, Oxford, 1946; H. F. Jolowicz, *Historical Introduction to the Study of Roman Law*, Cambridge, Eng., 1952; Wolfgang Kunkel (tr. by J. M. Kelly), *An Introduction to Roman Legal and Constitutional History*, Oxford, 1966; J. M. Kelly, *Roman Litigation*, Oxford, 1966; Max Kaser, *Das römische Zivilprozessrecht* (Müller's *Handbuch* 10.3.4), Munich, 1966. For a brief survey cf. *OCD* s.v. "Law and Procedure, Roman." A.H.M. Jones, "Imperial and Senatorial Jurisdiction in the Early Principate," *Historia* 3 (1955) 464-88 summarizes possibilities of appeal in both republic and empire. John Crook, *Law and Life of Rome*, Ithaca, 1967, 68-97, gives a general overview. A useful reference work is A. Berger, "Encyclopedic Dictionary of

able legal knowledge on the part of a litigant, far more than in Greece. Its most characteristic feature was the formula. The magistrate before whom a case was initiated, usually a praetor, drew up a precisely worded formula or legal definition of the wrong alleged ("if so and so proves to be the case, then let the defendant be condemned") and referred the case to a court whose function then became to decide whether or not the conditions of the formula were fulfilled. In early times there was no distinction between criminal and civil cases; charges usually had to be brought by an injured party. In the classical period this procedure was still applicable to private cases, and remained so throughout Roman history. The praetor, having set the formula, appointed a judge who was satisfactory to both litigants, and this judge, sometimes with some advisers (*concilium*), heard the case and rendered his decision, from which there was no appeal. In some cases a board of three or five *recuperatores* could be appointed instead. In either case the legal procedure did not encourage elaborate speechmaking and there was probably much interruption and questioning, though by Cicero's time, when set speeches were conventional in other kinds of courts, they had come to be used in private cases also. The very public setting, which we shall shortly consider, may have contributed to this development. Cicero's first speech, *Pro Quinctio*, is addressed to a single judge sitting with a small group of advisers, but is as much a piece of school rhetoric as anything he ever produced.

Although criminal charges were originally brought by an injured person, magistrates sometimes gave judgment against wrongdoers themselves, thus recognizing a pub-

Roman Law," *Trans. of the Amer. Philosophical Soc.* 43.2, Philadelphia, 1953.

lic interest in the case. Appeal could then be had to the
entire citizen body in the assembly on certain grounds:
if the defendant were a citizen, if the penalty enjoined
were death or scourging or a large fine, or if the defendant were a person who had held high office (Polybius
6.14.6-7). The assembly also tried cases involving offenses of a political or public character.[10] Only in such
trials would there seem to have been much opportunity
in the earlier republic for an orator to address a large
jury with a planned and uninterrupted speech. Though
virtues or vices of character and emotional appeal may
have been presented before magistrates, use of such
techniques had greater chance of success the greater the
audience. Trials before the assembly probably occurred
regularly in the early republic, but they were hardly daily
occurrences.

Most of the great trials of the late republic did not
take place in any of these courts, but in others which
supplemented them and tended to make obsolete the
trials before the assembly. If it had not been for the
procedural changes of the third and second centuries
B.C., which may themselves have resulted in part from
Greek influence, it is doubtful that Greek judicial rhetoric would ever have found much application at Rome. As
it was, the juries grew in size and eventually became
more democratic. In civil cases an important change was
the establishment of the centumviral court, which took
over jurisdiction of cases involving property and inherit-
ances[11] (Cic., De or. 1.173). The date is not definitely
known, but Festus (s.v. centumviri) says that the number of 105 jurymen, for which centumviri or 100 men is
an approximation, was arrived at by choosing three men

[10] Cf. George W. Botsford, *The Roman Assemblies*, New
York, 1901, 239-61 and 317-25.
[11] Cf. R-E 3.1935-51 and the works cited in n. 9, supra.

from each of the thirty-five tribes and there were not thirty-five until 241 B.C.; thus we have a *terminus post quem* for the establishment of the court. It seems likely enough that changes in Roman society, particularly increase in wealth and acquisition of property abroad after the first or second Punic war, led to increase in certain kinds of civil litigation and thus need for a new court. The jury, which was increased to 180 under the empire, was divided into three or four panels which could sit separately or together, according to the importance of the case. This centumviral court achieved its greatest height as a rhetorical arena in the early empire when the younger Pliny and other leading orators appeared before it in the Basilica Julia. The *decemviri stlitibus judicandis,* or juries of ten to deal with freedom cases, perhaps date from the same period as the centumviral court.

Up to the middle of the second century B.C. special judicial commissions (*quaestiones*) were occasionally appointed to deal with offenses not adequately covered by other procedures, and in the second half of the second and early first century these were gradually established as standing criminal courts. The earliest (149 B.C.) and most famous was the *quaestio de pecuniis repetundis,* the extortion court, the need for which became acute as Roman governors in the second century discovered the possibilities of enriching themselves at the expense of provincials.[12] The court subsequently became a political football between the conflicting interests of the aristocracy, which furnished the governors, and the knights, the financial class of citizens among whom be-

---

[12] Cf. William S. Ferguson, "The *Lex Calpurnia* of 149 B.C.," *JRS* 11 (1921) 86-100 and J.P.V.D. Balsdon, "The History of the Extortion Court in Rome, 123-70 B.C.," *PBSR* 14 (1938) 98-114; Erich S. Gruen, *Roman Politics and the Criminal Courts, 149-78 B.C.,* Cambridge, 1968.

longed the members of corporations to farm the provincial taxes. Many of the great cases of the late republic
and early empire were heard before this court. Other
quaestiones were established to deal with such charges
as murder, poisoning, treason, peculation, sacrilege,
bribery, violence, and adultery: in other words, all of
the major problems of the late republic. The size and
membership of the juries varied from time to time. We
have preserved in an inscription the text of the *Lex
Acilia* of 122 B.C., directed against extortion.[13] It provides
for a jury of 50 knights, and perhaps this number was a
norm for *quaestiones*, though in individual cases reduced
because of illness or disqualification. When Oppianicus
was tried for poisoning, there were thirty-two votes cast
in the final judgment (Cic., *Pro Cluentio* 74). In 70 B.C.
the size of the jury was probably increased to 75, 25 from
each of the three top census groups of senator, knight,
and tribune of the treasury. This number was also a
norm: in the trial of Scaurus in 54 B.C. 22 senators, 23
knights, and 25 tribunes voted (Asconius, *In Scaur.* 25).
The jurymen for every case were drawn from a panel
chosen for each court at the beginning of the year and
each *quaestio* was presided over by a praetor.

In Greece litigants or those accused of crime ordinarily pleaded their own cases, though they might have
some help from a professional speech writer. At Rome by
the time of the later republic most members of the upper
classes were prepared to speak in court, but they regularly got their more eloquent friends to help them, and
persons without rhetorical training almost necessarily
turned to a pleader. The purchase of a speech to be
memorized by the litigant, so common in Greece, was

[13] *CIL* I.2. Text, translation, and notes in E. H. Warmington
Remains of Old Latin, Cambridge, 1959, 4.316-31.

rare in Rome.[14] In practice major cases were pleaded by professional orators, called patrons. The system was an extension of the patron-client relationship of the earlier republic.[15] Originally a patron was a patrician who had certain responsibilities toward a number of clients who might be citizens or freedmen in Rome or in allied states. The clients looked to the patron primarily for legal help for the very specific reason that most of the law was not published or well known. The clients were ignorant of the *formulae* or legal procedures in cases in which they might be involved and they lacked the social prestige to defend their rights. Patrons were members of an inner and privileged circle. According to Dionysius of Halicarnassus (*Ant. Rom.* 2.9-11) the client's original duty to the patron was financial help, and this seems borne out by a speaker in Plautus (*Menaechmi* 571ff.), but it often involved political support or the status symbol of personal attendance upon the patron at his house in the morning or as he walked about the city. The patron-client relationship was permanent and inherited; though a client might acquire more than one patron, he could not free himself from a patron unless he were elected to one of the higher magistracies (Plut., *Marius* 5.5). This system continued to exist throughout Roman history and made it easy for the Romans to accept legal representation in trials. By the later republic "patron" is also used of anyone who undertook to plead a case for an-

[14] Cf. George Kennedy, "The Rhetoric of Advocacy in Greece and Rome," *AJPh* 89 (1968), n. 12, pp. 427-28. Relevant passages are Cic., *Brutus* 99-100, 169, and 205-7; Cic., *Ad Quint. Fr.* 3.8.5; Quint. 3.8.50; Suet., *De gramm.* 3 and 27.

[15] Cf. Neuhauser, *op.cit.* supra n. 7; Michel 35-38. On the use of advocates and patrons cf. Greenidge, *op.cit.* supra n. 9, 235-43. On the life of a patron, cf. Mary B. Parks, "Cicero and American Lawyers," *CJ* 22 (1926-27) 563-77.

other. Though the relationship here often involved some kind of social or political tie, it was not permanent. On the other hand, it was not supposed to be commercial either, though gifts were made in place of fees and as early as 204 B.C. it was necessary to pass the *Lex Cincia* to prohibit the payment of pleaders (Tac., *Ann.* 11.5; Cic., *De sen.* 10).

In the time of the elder Cato the patron was expected to have considerable legal knowledge, but this gradually changed, so that by the first century B.C. technical legal advice was secured by a patron or a client from a jurisconsult, a professional legal authority.[16] The patron determined the tactics and procedure of the case, and most important of all, its rhetorical presentation. His training for this had usually been study with a rhetorician followed by attendance upon other orators or men of affairs in the forum. In important cases it became the custom to have several patrons working in collaboration. Asconius (*In Scaur.* 18) says that four was the normal number in Cicero's time, but prominent cases often had more. Junior assistants called *subscriptores* were also used in some cases. Cicero often cooperated with other patrons, but he recognized many disadvantages to the system (*Brutus* 207-9). Throughout the late republic many of the chief men of the state, even when holding the consulship or other office, appeared frequently in court for clients, and in the empire leading senators continued to act as patrons. As a result the authority and prestige of the patron often greatly assisted the client's case (Cic., *Brutus* 111; Quint. 4.1.6-7).

The normal sequence of events at an extortion trial may be taken as an example of Roman court procedure in the later republic brought to its fullest development. At a preliminary hearing the defendant was summoned

[16] Cf. *R-E* 10.1164-67.

before the appropriate praetor by the patron chosen by the aggrieved provincials and the charge made. The praetor recognized the charge and then adjourned proceedings for a specified length of time so that evidence could be gathered and a defense prepared. A jury was chosen; the praetor acted as president. On the appointed day the prosecution opened its case, ordinarily with a set speech (*oratio perpetua*) in which the orator had a great deal to say in general about the wrongs committed, but in which he might well not reveal the evidence which he intended to use. If several patrons were collaborating, each might deliver a speech on some aspect of the case. The defense then had a chance to make a general opening reply, trying to anticipate the evidence which would be introduced. For example, Cicero, speaking in defense of Caelius before a *quaestio* considering a charge of aggravated assault, did not yet know who the witnesses for the prosecution would be (*Pro Cael.* 19 and esp. 63). Then came the presentation of the evidence, a chance at cross-examination, and an *altercatio,* or debate, between the patrons about the points in dispute (Quint. 6.4).[17]

We can get a picture of the presentation of evidence and cross-examination from passages like one in Cicero's *Pro Flacco* (10-11 and 22-23) and from the discussion in Quintilian (5.7). It appears that lengthy speeches were sometimes delivered by witnesses or patrons (Cic., *De or.* 2.48); Cicero's *In Vatinium* is such a speech and perhaps also Cato's lost speech against M'. Acilius Glabrio (Livy 37.57.13-15).[18] Some orators like Crassus were

---

[17] Cf. J. Poiret, *Essai sur l'éloquence judiciaire à Rome pendant la république,* Paris, 1887 and J. Humbert, *Les plaidoyers écrits et les plaidoiries réelles de Cicéron,* Paris, c. 1925. Cicero, *Ad Att.* 1.16.10, describes an altercation between himself and Clodius.

[18] Cf. *ORF* p. 30.

15

especially good at cross-examination (Cic., *De or.* 2.285). This part of the trial might take a number of days. Extortion cases were then adjourned for a second action. In other cases before *quaestiones* the court voted at this point, but if a majority of the jury was not convinced of either guilt or innocence, the procedures were adjourned and the patrons on each side tried again at a second action. The set speeches in first actions thus tended to take on the character of *exordia*, and only in those cases which proceeded to a second action was there an opportunity for an orator to deal with evidence already presented. This procedure was temporarily altered in 52 B.C. by a law of Pompey which required the evidence in cases of violence or bribery to be introduced before the speeches, as well as limiting the length of speeches and the number of patrons. From the vantage point of a hundred and fifty years Tacitus thought that the latter change, which may have been permanent, was the beginning of the end for Latin oratory (*Dial.* 38).

Roman law courts during the republic met out of doors, usually in the forum, where there stood in Cicero's time two large stone tribunals, the praetorium and the Aurelianum, and other temporary wooden tribunals were built as needed.[19] Cicero pleaded *Pro Flacco* at the Aurelian tribunal and *Pro Milone* at the praetorian. In one passage of the *Pro Scauro* (46-48) he points successively to the senate house, the temple of Castor, the capitol, all in sight, and in the direction of the temple of Vesta. The magistrate or judge was provided with a chair, the jury and important guests with benches on the tribunal, the patrons and their clients with benches on

[19] Cf. Greenidge, *op.cit.* supra n. 9, 133-34; Norman DeWitt, "Litigation in the Forum in Cicero's Time," *CPh* 21 (1926) 218-24; Harriet Dale Johnson, *The Roman Tribunal*, Baltimore, 1927.

the ground level. In the time of Augustus an awning was stretched across the forum, or part of it, to shield people from the August sun (Pliny, *Nat. hist.* 19.61). Porcius Latro once asked to have a case moved into a basilica (Quint. 10.5.18) and it is possible that this was done regularly in the rain and wind of winter; in Sicily, Verres moved under a covered portico to hold his hearings (Cic., *Verr.* 2.4.86). During the empire some courts seem always to have met in the basilicas, the centumviral court in the Basilica Julia, for example, but the proceedings remained very public.[20] Other courts remained outside even when the emperor himself presided (e.g. Suet., *Dom.* 8.1). Quintilian says (11.3.27) that the orator must be prepared to speak in the sun and on windy, damp, or hot days. The open nature of Roman trials doubtless had its effect not only on the orators, who sometimes pleaded with an eye on the crowd, called *corona* or "crown" in Latin, but on the popular attitude toward litigation and speech. In the words of Lily Ross Taylor:

"The people who came and went while the speaking was in progress could get a first hand contact with the proceedings such as is impossible in the limited space

[20] According to Livy 39.44.7, cf. also 26.27.3, the first basilica was the Porcia, built by Cato in 184 B.C. against considerable opposition. Flamininus alleged that Cato's public works were useless (Plut., *Cato Maior* 19.2). There followed the Basilica Fulvia or Aemilia in 179 (Livy 40.51.5) and the Sempronia on the site of the later Julia in 170 (Livy 44.16.11). Clearly they did fulfill some need, perhaps that of the *gallerie* of modern Italian cities: places for social and commercial congregation. On the plan of a basilica cf. Vitruvius 5.4-10. In general cf. Samuel Ball Platner and Thomas Ashby, A *Topographical Dictionary of Ancient Rome*, London, 1929. For an imaginative description of the centumviral court in session in the empire, based in part on Quint. 12.5.6, cf. Jerome Carcopino (tr. by E. O. Lorimer), *Daily Life in Ancient Rome*, New Haven, 1940, 187-89.

of the American courtroom. The trial was like a great drama in which the people crowding on the steps of the tribunal made Cicero think of the audience in the theatre to see a show. The very language of the law court has gone over into the theatre. The cases were divided into sections known as *actiones* and the prosecutor was known as an *actor*."[21]

Deliberative Oratory

In deliberative oratory the commonest Roman form was the *contio*. Basically *contio* meant a meeting, but the word was transferred to a speech delivered at a meeting other than a meeting of the senate. Addresses by a general to his troops, such as we find in historians, or to the people on the occasion of a triumph, campaign oratory such as there was,[22] and all kinds of speeches to the people in assemblies were called *contiones*.[23] For purposes of election of magistrates, ratification or rejection of laws, or hearing judicial appeals the Roman citizens met in assemblies (*comitia*), which bore different names depending on the voting procedure to be used.

[21] Cf. *Party Politics in the Age of Caesar*, Berkeley, 1949, 99.
[22] Campaign oratory in the modern sense did not play much role in Rome, and even less in Greece. Meetings were held in private Roman homes at which a candidate might speak (*contio domestica*, cf. Cic., *Pro Mur.* 30) and candidates seized pretexts for making speeches as Cicero did in the case of his oration *In toga candida*, known to us from Asconius' commentary. Most campaigning was a matter of personal solicitation of votes, cf. Taylor, *op.cit.* supra n. 21, 64.
[23] Cf. Theodor Mommsen, *Römische Staatsrecht*, Leipzig, 1887, 1.197-202; Botsford, *op.cit.* supra n. 10, 139ff.; R-E 4.1149-53; Dietrich Mack, *Senatsreden und Volksreden bei Cicero*, Keil, 1937, 7-10. On debate in the assemblies cf. Mommsen, *ibid.*, 3.1.392-96. Among the best pictures of the procedure are Cicero's account of the Rullan law (*De lege agraria* 2.13) and of the law recalling him from exile (*In Pisonem* 34-36) and Livy's account (34.1.8) of the attempt to repeal the *Lex Oppia*. Cf. also Livy 43.16.8; 45.36.1; Quint. 2.4.33.

Election assemblies, normally held in midsummer, proceeded directly to voting without speeches on behalf of the candidates. Most speeches to the people were delivered at informal meetings convoked by consuls, praetors, or tribunes to discuss some situation or proposed action, for example, Cicero's second and third *Catilinarians*. Such a meeting had to be convoked by a magistrate, but he might ask or allow others to speak, as Cicero was asked to speak on behalf of the Manilian law in 66 B.C. The magistrates could also convoke formal meetings of one or other of the assemblies to consider legislation, in which case the proposed bill usually had had prior senatorial approval and was posted publicly, so that it could be read and discussed. At these legislative assemblies private individuals were originally supposed to be invited to speak before the magistrates were given the floor in order to avoid intimidation and in order for the tribunes to hear some discussion before deciding whether or not to veto (Livy 45.21.6; Dio 39.35). In practice, however, much of the speaking was by the magistrates themselves, and general debate by ordinary citizens was probably almost unknown. An influential person could, however, demand to be heard, as for example the younger Cato did against the Trebonian law (Plutarch, *Cato the Younger* 43.1). He was allotted two hours, but resisted attempts to be silenced and consumed the whole day. After the speeches the assemblies sometimes voted immediately if the meeting had been called in a place where voting was sanctioned by religion, sometimes they adjourned and voted another day. When *contiones* were delivered in the forum area, the orator originally faced the adjacent comitium and senate house, but in the second century B.C., beginning with Licinius Crassus or with C. Gracchus, he turned instead toward the main rectangle of the forum, which was taken as a symbol of

19

the declining influence of the senate (Cic., *De amic.* 96; Plut., *C. Grach.* 5.2). Perhaps the change actually resulted from the need for a larger open space.

Although meetings of the assembly were of almost daily occurrence in some periods (*Brutus* 305), political foment in Rome was apparently conducted more behind the scenes than was the case in classical Athens, where proposals were often openly discussed, emended, and voted upon at the meetings of the people. The moments of crisis in the Roman assemblies were often legal clashes, such as occurred when a tribune interposed a veto or someone declared omens unfavorable for further action, but during the late second and early first century when some tribunes turned into demagogues there was a good deal of impassioned oratory in the assembly. Even at this time power remained in the hands of a comparatively small number of men, but they had to fight each other for the votes of the mob.

More extensive speechmaking prevailed in the senate. The greatest period of the senate's authority came in the seventy-five years or so after the second Punic war, the very period in which Greek rhetoric and Greek orators were first making an impression on the Romans. At this time the senate was certainly the chief scene of Roman eloquence, but even then there were limitations on the possibility of persuasion, for the senate was a highly oligarchic body whose decisions, though influenced by speeches, were also very much the result of ties of family or personal friendship and the prior decision of an inner group of senators.[24] The general procedure in the senate[25]

[24] "The senate was the least likely body in the world to be swayed by florid eloquence," A.H.J. Greenidge, *Roman Public Life*, London, 1901, 272.

[25] Procedures are known from references in the historians (e.g., Dion. Hal., *Rom. Ant.* 7.47) and in Cicero and from three passages in Aulus Gellius devoted to the subject (3.18;

was for the consul, praetor, or tribune who had convoked the session to state the business on which he wished advice, for the senate was in theory an advisory, not a law-making body. He then called upon individual senators for their opinions (*sententiae*) according to a roughly fixed order of rank. Once called upon, a senator could speak on any matter he wished (Gellius 4.10.8), and as long as he pleased—the younger Cato staged several filibusters—but he could not speak on his own initiative unless he were a magistrate in office.²⁶ In practice only the more prestigious members were usually called upon. Senators sometimes simply indicated their support for an opinion already stated or went and sat with a senator whose views they accepted. A senator who had spoken was allowed to rebut a subsequent speaker (*Scholia Bob.* 170 Stangl). If the matter came to a vote there was a division of the house and all senators present could participate.

Epideictic Oratory

Greek epideictic or demonstrative oratory was largely nonexistent in the Roman republic, and the only native Roman form of significance was the funeral eulogy, *laudatio funebris*.²⁷ The Greek funeral orations with

---

4.7; 4.10). Gellius made use of a handbook on senatorial procedure prepared by Varro for the use of Pompey. For modern discussions cf. Mommsen, *op.cit.* supra n. 23, 3.2.905-1003; Greenidge, *op.cit.* supra n. 24, 266-72; R-E *Suppl.* 6.700-719; Mack, *op.cit.* supra n. 23, 3-7.

²⁶ For Cato's filibustering cf. Caesar, *B.C.* 1.32.2; Plut., *Cato the Younger* 31.3; Gellius 4.10.8; *Scholia Bob., Pro Planc.* p. 157 Stangl. In form some of Cicero's *Philippics* are the best examples of senatorial speeches. *Phil.* 3.13 and 7.1 show how a senator could digress. *Phil.* 3,5,8,9,10,13, and 14 all deal with a specific *sententia*.

²⁷ Cicero, *De or.* 2.48-50, mentions other forms which are epideictic by nature, but says they have no special theory: rebuke, exhortation, and consolation.

which we are familiar[28] were delivered on the annual occasions at which the Athenian democracy mourned those
killed in war during the year. The speakers concerned
themselves with the state, not usually with individuals,
and they sometimes created significant literary monuments. Roman funeral orations were, in contrast, expressions of the virtues of the ruling oligarchy, the praise of
a distinguished man ordinarily by his closest agnate.[29]
The earliest one reported is that for Brutus the first
consul (Dion. Hal., *Ant. Rom.* 5.17.2-3) which may be
apocryphal, but funeral orations were common throughout the republic. The best account of the whole ceremony was written in the second century B.C. by the
Greek Polybius (6.53-54), who thought that Roman
funerals were admirable institutions for the education
of the young in the virtues of their elders. They were
certainly impressive. The deceased was borne on a couch
into the forum, accompanied by a procession of his family wearing masks to represent his ancestors and dressed
in gold and purple robes signifying the honors they had
earned, such as censorships, consulships, or triumphs.
The funeral orator spoke from the rostrum at the end
of the forum, first on the virtues of the departed, then
on the virtues of his ancestors, one by one. A mask was
made of the newest addition to the family's hall of fame,
and a record of the funeral speech was kept so that his
virtues and achievements could be recited at the funeral

[28] Cf. *APG* 154-66.
[29] On *laudationes funebres* cf. Fridericus Vollmer, "Laudationum funebrium Romanorum historia et reliquarum editio,"
Neue Jahrbücher für Philologie, Suppl. 18 (1891) 445-528; *R-E*
12.992-94; Donald R. Stuart, *Epochs of Greek and Latin Biography*, Berkeley, 1928, 209-20; O. C. Crawford, "Laudatio
funebris," *CJ* 37 (1941-42) 17-27; M. Durry, "*Laudatio funebris*
et rhétorique," *RPh* 16 (1942) 105-14. Occasionally a funeral
oration was written by someone other than the speaker, e.g.,
Laelius' speech for Fabius Maximus in honor of the younger
Scipio, cf. *ORF* p. 121.

of one of his worthy descendants. Cicero speaks scornfully (*De or.* 2.341) of the literary qualities of these speeches, and three examples preserved in inscriptions are not great works of art.[30] The speeches were often little more than a list of virtues, and the genre was apparently extremely conservative. There were, however, more literary examples such as Caesar's speech for his aunt (Plut., *Caes.* 5; Suet., *Jul.* 6). Roman rhetorical treatises largely ignore funeral orations, presumably because they were not part of the Greek tradition on which such treatises were built.[31] Speeches preserved by noble families were the oldest written Latin oratory, and thus a precedent for the preservation of a record of speeches. A very few, as we shall see, were perhaps given some circulation, but most could not be said to have been published in the usual sense of that word. They were generally not read for literary qualities and did little to foster an interest in oratory. Historians perhaps sometimes visited the family archives to draw on them, but Cicero (*Brutus* 62) and Livy (8.40.4) both point out that the records were filled with claims falsified in the interests of exalting the family's greatness.

The Earliest Latin Oratory

We have speeches, or summaries of speeches, attributed to almost all of the great statesmen of early Rome, even to the mythical or semimythical figures of remotest antiquity, in the historical works of Greek writers like Dionysius of Halicarnassus, Diodorus Siculus, Plutarch,

---

[30] *CIL* 6.1527,31670, and 37053 (Dessau 8392); *CIL* 6.10230 (Dessau 8394); *CIL* 14.3579. A Greek translation of a piece of a speech has recently been discovered on papyrus (P. Colon. 4701), cf. L. Koenen, "Die *laudatio funebris* des Augustus für Agrippa auf einem neuen Papyrus," *ZPE* 5 (1970) 217-83. Versions in historical works are of course more literary, cf. Appian, *Civil Wars* 2.20.143-47 and Dio Cassius 56.35-41.

[31] Cf. Durry, *op.cit.*, supra n. 29. There is occasional passing mention in rhetoricians, e.g., Quint. 3.7.2.

Dio Cassius, and in the work of the great Latin historian of Augustan times, Titus Livy. The early books of Livy are fitted out with oratory richly woven from the historical situation, the possible arguments available, and Livy's impression of the character of the speaker. The result is not very good evidence for early oratory, though it is an interesting product of the rhetoric of Livy's own day. To him it did not seem incongruous to project backward the rhetorical standards and tastes of the late republic and early empire to a much more simple time, for rhetoric was regarded as natural and necessary; moreover, verisimilitude was far less important than artistic creativity, and historicity less interesting than the organic portrayal of the growth of the Roman mystique toward its destined greatness. Livy, however, describes one speech in his history as "in that ancient and rough manner of speaking." This speech has become especially famous and was regarded by Livy's successors (cf., e.g., Tac., *Dial.* 17 and 21) as a typical oration by an early Roman. It is the address of Menenius Agrippa, ostensibly delivered in 494 B.C. when the entire plebeian body went on strike and refused to participate in the state until the poorer members were relieved of their crushing burden of debt. The outcome of this particular secession, according to tradition, was the appointment of the first tribunes to protect the persons of the plebeians against arrest. Menenius Agrippa was, Livy says, "an eloquent man and because he had risen from among them, dear to the plebs." He was sent by the patricians to address the plebs, which had taken up a position on a hill near Rome.

"After being admitted to the camp, all that he did was to tell this story in the old unpolished style of speech: once upon a time when all the parts of a man were not as now in harmony, but individual members had their own inclination and power of speech, the other parts were annoyed that the object of their duty, effort, and service was to supply the belly, while it sat quietly in their midst and did nothing but enjoy the pleasures offered. As a result they formed a plot by which the hand would not bring food to the mouth nor the mouth accept anything nor the teeth chew it. While in their anger they aimed to master the belly with famine, the members themselves and the whole body came as well to the final stages of starvation. From this it became clear that the belly also had no easy job and that it was not only fed but that in turn to all parts of the body it supplied blood, made rich from digested food, by which we live and have strength after it has been diffused through all the veins. Showing by comparison how this internal sedition of the body was like the anger of the people against the senators, he persuaded the minds of the men." (2.32.8-12)

According to Livy, Menenius spoke nothing more than this. Dionysius of Halicarnassus could not let slip an opportunity for oratory in his version of the incident (6.83-86) and wrote a much more elaborate speech for Menenius, ending however with the same fable. Is there any possibility that the fable is genuine? It is a bit of folk wisdom which also had appeared in Greek literature (Xen., *Mem.* 2.3.18), but that is not a reason to reject it here. One objection is that Cicero, our great authority on early Roman oratory, mentioning the incident of the secession in the *Brutus* (54), attributes conciliation of the plebs to the eloquence of M. Valerius and says nothing about the remarkable nature of what was said or that the contents of the speech were remembered.[32] Livy's

[32] Cf. R-E 15.841. The fable may come from a Greek sophistic source, cf. Wilhelm Nestle, "Die Fabel des Menenius Agrippa," *Klio* 21 (1927) 350-60, but something like it occurs in many

sources are largely the annalistic historians of the third, second, and early first centuries B.C., and their sources in turn were fairly reliable texts of laws and lists of magistrates, and less reliable oral tradition, particularly that passed down in noble houses, and funeral orations, whose errors and exaggerations have already been mentioned. The fact of a speech might be preserved by the tradition, but its contents are less likely to have been remembered over a span of two to four hundred years.

The only Latin speech dating from before the end of the second Punic war of which Cicero claimed knowledge was that by Appius Claudius Caecus[33] to the senate on the proposed peace with King Pyrrhus of Epirus about 280 B.C. Pyrrhus had invaded Italy out of personal ambition to equal the exploits of Alexander the Great fifty years before and at the behest of the people of Tarentum to help them against Rome. His ambassador was the Greek Cineas, the most eloquent man of his age, said to have been a follower of Demosthenes and to have approached him in manner and ability (Plut. *Pyr.* 14 and 18). He was a forecast of the many eloquent Greeks who were to wait upon the senate a century later. Appius Claudius Caecus was an old patrician with a long and distinguished career of public service, by this time quite blind (*caecus*). He had not even attended the senate for a long time (Livy, *Per.* 13), but shocked at the proposal

---

cultures, cf. Funk and Wagnall's *Standard Dictionary of Mythology and Legend*, s.v. "Belly and the Members."

[33] Cf. ORF 1.1-11; R-E 3.2681-85; Benedictus Niese, "Zur Geschichte des Pyrrhischen Krieges," *Hermes* 31 (1896), esp. 493-94; A. Cima, "Sull' orazione di Appio Claudio Cieco contro la pace con Pirro," *Bollettino di filologia classica* 11 (1904) 60-62; Paul Lejay, "Appius Claudius Caecus," *RPh* 44 (1920) 92-141; Malcovati, *op.cit.* supra n. 1, 145-46; Albino Garzetti, "Appio Claudio Cieco nella storia politica del suo tempo," *Athenaeum* 25 (1947) 175-224.

to deal on terms of an inferior with an invading king, he came to the senate and mustered his remaining strength to denounce his colleagues and bring them back to an awareness of the proper course for Romans. In this he succeeded, and the peace was rejected. Cicero says (*De sen.* 16; *Brutus* 61) that the speech was extant in his time, which would make it over a hundred years older than any other published oration, but in fact Cicero seems to mean that a version survived in Ennius' epic poem, the *Annals*, part of which he quotes: "Quo vobis mentes, rectae quae stare solebant/Antehac, dementes sese flexere viai?" "Whither have your minds, which used to stand firm in the past, now demented, turned away?" (fr. 194 Warmington). Cicero probably thought that Ennius was adequate authority for the historicity of the occasion and the general lines of the speech. Thus we cannot be certain that there ever was a published text.[34] Possibly a version of Appius' speech was written down by someone who heard it and then preserved by the family of the Claudii like a funeral oration, for Claudius' prevention of a treaty with Pyrrhus was one of the great events of a great life and is mentioned in the eulogy of him preserved on an inscription (Dessau 54); Cicero (*Brutus* 61-62) mentions this speech and funeral ora-

[34] Of the works cited in n. 33 Niese and Cima are skeptical of publication; Leo, *op.cit.* supra n. 1, 43 thinks the speech was preserved in family archives, as does Bardon, *op.cit.* supra n. 1, 22. Schanz-Hosius 1.41 accepts publication. Claudius' *sententiae* are said to have been preserved, cf. Cic., *Tusc. disp.* 4.4 and Pseudo-Sallust, *Ad Caes.* 1.2. Claudius also seems to have been connected in some way with the first publication of the judicial calendar, cf. Pliny, *Nat. hist.* 33.17 and Clyde Pharr, "Roman Legal Education," *CJ* 34 (1938-39) 257-70. It is unlikely that Appius' speech as known to Cicero was a rhetorical exercise, for there is no reference to the use of this theme for *suasoriae*. Claudius did, however, become a subject for *prosopopoeae* (Quint. 11.1.39) in imitation of Cic., *Pro Cael.* 34.

27

tions in the same breath. The most appealing version of the speech is that by Plutarch (*Pyr.* 19):

"In the past I was distressed at the misfortune to my eyes, Romans, but now I regret not being deaf as well as blind when I hear your shameful plans and recommendations for overturning Roman glory. Where is your usual boldness of speech in the face of all men to the effect that if the great Alexander himself had come to Italy and attacked us in our youth and our fathers in their prime he would not now be celebrated as undefeated, but either fleeing or dying somewhere here he would have left Rome more glorious? You surely show these words to be false pretense and empty boasting in your fear of Chaonians and Molossians,[35] though always the prey of Macedonians, while you tremble at Pyrrhus who used to pass his time following around and flattering one of Alexander's bodyguards. But now, instead of helping the Greeks in his own country, he flees from his enemies at home and wanders around Italy, proclaiming to us his authority and power, which was not adequate to secure for himself a small bit of Macedonia. Do not think that you are getting rid of him if you make him a friend, but that you are strengthening those who look down on you as easy for everybody to handle if Pyrrhus goes away without suffering for the insults he has given and even after taking pay for making the Romans a laughing stock of the Tarentines and Samnites."

This is certainly not quite what Claudius said, and does not agree with the two lines of Ennius' version or the short account of Appian (*Samn. fr.* 10.2). The thought of the first sentence may have some historical basis, since Appian has it, though in simpler form. Plutarch's use of the argument "we could have defeated

[35] People of Epirus of which Pyrrhus was king.

Alexander, and Pyrrhus is less than he" looks like the technique of a Greek rhetorician conjecturing something suitable to say out of Pyrrhus' known admiration for Alexander, and indeed the whole Alexander reference is a commonplace of the rhetorical schools, very probably introduced here as an amplification by Plutarch himself.[36] We can conclude little more about Appius Claudius' oratory than that it made a powerful effect which was long remembered.

Rhetorical Elements in Early Latin Literature

Latin literature as we know it began in the mid-third century B.C., first with translations and then imitations of Greek epic and drama. The Romans, who became masters of the Greek world of southern Italy and Sicily in the first half of the third century, decided that a great and triumphant state needed a great literature in its own language, even if the substance and form of that literature had to be largely Greek. This motive is clear from the fact that they turned first to the genres which could be conspicuously performed or which related to deeds of heroic proportions: tragedy, comedy, and epic. The first tragedy and first comedy on Greek models were produced by Livius Andronicus in 240 B.C. as part of a festival which followed the victorious end of the first Punic war. The first epic was Livius Andronicus' translation of the *Odyssey*, but before the end of the third century there appeared the first of a series of attempts to create a more Roman epic in Naevius' poem on the first Punic war in which he himself had fought. This search for a great national epic was continued in the second century by Ennius' *Annals* and eventually led in the first century to Virgil's *Aeneid*.

[36] Cf. also Plutarch's essay *On the Fortune of the Romans* 326c and the digression in Livy 9.17-19.

Naevius was also the first of a long line of Roman poets to use literature for invective and political attack,[37] principally against the powerful family of the Metelli, but also against Scipio Africanus (Gellius 7.8.5) in a fragment of a play which shows a fine sense of rhetorical amplification and climax and illustrates also the alliteration and assonance which were so characteristic of early Latin that it is not necessary to regard them as imitation of Greek technique:

> Etiam qui res magnas manu saepe gessit gloriose,
> Cuius facta viva nunc vigent, qui apud gentes
>   solus praestat,
> Eum suus pater cum pallio unod ab amica
>   abduxit.

> Even him whose hand often handsome deeds
>   wrought wondrously,
> Whose actions still now possess a vital vigor,
>   who stands out alone among all men,
> Him, hastily wrapped in a single frock, his
>   father dragged home from his girlfriend's!

There is also a fragment of Naevius on the evil influence of brash young orators in a state (Cic., *De sen.* 20).

The fragments of Livius and Naevius are very few in number. We have many more fragments from Ennius (239-169 B.C.), a south Italian who served in the Roman army, was "discovered" by Cato in Sardinia in 204, and subsequently was brought to Rome (Nepos, *Cato* 1.4). Cato's friendship apparently waned as Ennius' work became more and more Greek in spirit[38] and as his friend-

---

[37] Cf. A. Kurfess, "Die Anfänge der Invektive in Rom," *Jahresberichte des Philologischen Vereins* (1915) 103-12 and Tenney Frank, "Naevius and Free Speech," *AJPh* 48 (1927) 105-10.

[38] The *Annals* opened with a dream in which the poet claimed Homer spoke to him and told of the reincarnation of his soul

ship with Scipio Africanus grew. In addition to the epic *Annals*, Ennius composed about twenty tragedies and a number of other plays and poems. We have already noted that he was the first to use the word *rhetorica* in Latin, but the fragment is so short and the context so uncertain (*alii rhetorica tongent*, "others know the rules of rhetoric") that little can be deduced from it. Ennius' abandonment of the native Latin Saturnian meter for the Greek hexameter probably meant that greater attention had to be given to the quantity of syllables in Latin and this paved the way for imitation of Greek prose rhythm later in the century.

There is oratory, and a great deal of attempted persuasion, in the comedies of Plautus,[39] which are the earliest complete works of Latin literature and date from the late third and early second centuries. They helped introduce Romans to rhetoric as it had appeared in Greek New Comedy, but they are not very acceptable sources of information about Roman rhetoric since they are so closely modeled on the Greek originals. At most perhaps we can see occasional reflexion of Roman situations, for example of the patron-client relationship in the *Menaechmi* (571-97). Menaechmus happens to go to the forum in Epidamnus, where he lives, on the day of a law suit and finds himself trying to defend a poor (and guilty) client before the aediles who hold a preliminary examination of the case. He makes use of a *sponsio*, which was a quick way of settling a dispute by a legal

---

in Ennius, cf. Warmington, *op.cit.* supra n. 13, 1.4.13. On Ennius in general, cf. Warmington 1.2-465; Schanz-Hosius 1.86-100; H. D. Jocelyn, *The Tragedies of Ennius*, Cambridge, Eng., 1967; Otto Skutsch, *Studia Enniana*, London, 1968.

[39] Born in Umbria about 254 B.C., died in 184. Twenty complete comedies survive. Cf. George E. Duckworth, *The Nature of Roman Comedy*, Princeton, 1952, 49-56.

wager and is seen later in Cicero's orations for Quinctius and for Caecina: rather than exploring all facets of a case in a full trial it is agreed that if such and such specific facts are proved the defendant accepts defeat. Menaechmus proposed a very intricate set of conditions and apparently was planning to use bribes and false witnesses. He thinks he might have won, but his client insisted on going ahead with a trial and produced a bondsman who guaranteed his payment of the damages. The other side then introduced three witnesses who swore to all the allegations, and the client lost. There is no sign that either side delivered a set speech. Menaechmus is angry at the client's stupidity and even angrier that he has wasted a day in court, missing an engagement for dinner with his mistress. Though the legal procedure involved is Roman, the participants are Greeks, by birth Sicilian Greeks, and the setting is a Greek town on the eastern coast of the Adriatic where the Romans had recently sent some troops. The unscrupulous methods and shady characters are presumably intended to amuse a Roman audience which might not have found dishonest and philandering Romans so entertaining.

The Speeches in Polybius

Speeches in the historians are generally not good sources of information on Roman rhetoric because of the historians' attitude toward their art. There is, however, one partial exception, Polybius, whose distinguished history written in Greek in the mid-second century b.c. covered exactly the period of the late third and early second century when Latin oratory was coming into its own.[40] Polybius objected (12.25a and i) to the embel-

[40] On the speeches in Polybius cf. R-E 21.1524-27; Ragnar Ullmann, *La technique des discours dans Salluste, Tite Live, et Tacite*, Oslo, 1927, 16-19; F. W. Walbank, *A Historical Com-*

lished "tragic" history being written in his time and to the invention of speeches decked out with all the possible arguments as he found them, for example, in the Greek historian Timaeus. He insisted that an historian should report "what was truly said" (2.56.10; 12.25b1 and i8). In the extant portion of his work there are some speeches, mostly short, and the question therefore arises whether they can be regarded as faithful reports of "what was truly said." At the beginning of book 36 he comments on the procedure which he has been following. He uses the word *apangelo* "report," of his treatment of speeches, he again criticizes historians who like to make up their speeches, and he again says that it is proper for an historian to find out carefully "what was truly said," but to report only the most apt and telling parts. Certainly we should not try to use Polybius for information on Latin oratorical style, since all his speeches are reported in Greek and even in the case of Greek speeches the style seems to be his own.[41] On the other hand, the fact that Polybius' history covers only a relatively recent period makes it possible that he had heard or read unpublished descriptions of what was said on many occasions, as he points out himself (4.2.2). Both in Greece as a statesman of the Achaean League and in Rome, where he came as a hostage in 168 B.C. and lived as a close friend of Scipio Aemilianus, he knew personally the great and near great of the time. And his repeated

---

mentary on Polybius, Oxford 1 (1957) 13-14; 261-62; 2 (1967) 397-99; P. Pedech, *La méthode historique de Polybe*, Paris, 1964, 254-302. Pedech believes the speeches are often summaries of what was said, cf. esp. 275.

[41] The speeches, for example, show the same obsession with avoiding hiatus as does the rest of the work, though when Polybius quotes a document he preserves the hiatus, cf. Theodor Büttner-Wobst, "Der Hiatus nach dem Artikel bei Polybios," *Philologus* 16 (1903) 541-62.

assertion of the need to be true to events suggests that the substance of the speeches may be genuine.

An example of a passage which perhaps keeps close to what was actually said and on which Polybius could have heard the reports of eyewitnesses was the congress at Nicaea in Locris in 198 between Titus Flamininus, Philip V of Macedon, and others.[42] The personalities of the speakers, especially the mordant Philip and the calculating Flamininus, come through, as do the demands of all present, but Polybius has not worked the passage into a display of oratory. Of Polybius' more elaborate oratorical passages the longest are the speeches of Chlaeneas the Aetolian and Lyciscus the Acarnanian (9.28-39), each trying to win the support of the Spartans. Both speeches are much more emotional than the report of the congress at Nicaea—there are, for example, many rhetorical questions—and Chlaeneas' attack on Macedon reminds one of Demosthenes, but of course this treatment is suitable, and the speakers are Greeks with presumably Greek rhetorical educations. Polybius could easily have learned what was said even though the events occurred a few years before his birth.

The longest speech by a Roman in Polybius is that of the elder Scipio to his mutinous troops in 206 B.C. (11.28-29). Possibly some report of it was preserved or remembered and became known to Polybius through Laelius or someone in the family (cf. 10.3), but Polybius only claims that Scipio spoke something like this. It is a rather stiff speech, befitting an imperious Roman general to whom the speech from Gellius earlier in this chapter was attributed. The Roman to whom Polybius most frequently attributes words directly is the elder Scipio, the grandfather by adoption of his patron. He also quotes two members of the Aemilii Pauli house (3.108-9;

---

[42] Cf. Walbank, op.cit. supra n. 40, 1.13.

16.34) to which his patron belonged by birth, and Flamininus, the most important Roman commander in Greece in the days of his own youth (18.37).

Rhetorically the most interesting speeches in Polybius are the reports of embassies before the Roman senate. There are, for example, the speeches to the senate by King Eumenes of Pergamum and by the ambassadors from Rhodes (21.18-33) at the time when the senate was considering the disposition of Asia after the defeat of King Antiochus in 189 B.C. Both Eumenes and the Rhodian ambassadors show themselves to be highly skilled orators in the Greek tradition of argumentation, and the senators were clearly impressed. Eumenes begins by asserting that he wishes to avoid excessive pride, that he trusts the Romans entirely, and that he thus will say nothing about his own affairs. When brought before the senate again he persists in the claim that he will not discuss his personal desires, but he will warn the senate against the specious argument of the Rhodians. This is a form of *insinuatio,* or the subtle approach (*Rhet. ad Her.* 1.9-10), involving *prolepsis,* or anticipatory refutation, and also of *praeteritio,* the figure in which an orator details that which he will not discuss. For Eumenes really hopes to show the Romans that a course of action is in their interest when of course it is also very much in his own. Subsequently he deals almost as frankly with expediency as had the fifth century orators we know from Thucydides. His major point is that the Romans have a choice between acting in their own interest, which means giving much of the territory in Asia won from Antiochus to him, since he can be counted on to support Rome, or of being moved by the powerful words "liberty" and "autonomy" which the Rhodians will use and taking an action which will sound just, but will be inexpedient in that it will destroy his kingdom and thus deprive them

35

of their best friend in Asia. The Romans were to hear more about the conflicting merits of justice and self-interest from the Greek philosopher Carneades thirty-odd years later. Eumenes further introduces historical examples of the services of his house to the Romans and he argues that they should reward him *a fortiori* since they have well treated King Massinissa in Africa who has not done so much for them. The Rhodians reply by citing their own service to Rome, by trying to get the senate's good will in frankly admitting the virtues of Eumenes, but insisting that it was most honorable for Rome to set free the cities of Asia. Monarchy is everywhere hated. Since the Romans have power over the whole world, what they should seek now is praise and glory, and pursuit of that is their true advantage.

Before the first century B.C. all speeches in the senate had to be in Latin, delivered through interpreters if necessary,[43] and the translations of Greek orations, including the oratory of a king, must have been pretty heady stuff to some Romans. If the Latin diction was rough and the delivery halting, the organization, the argumentation, the figures of thought and general composition of the Greek original gave the senators first-hand models of sophisticated oratory. They saw especially the workings of enthymeme and example, of argument from probability, of topics of expediency, justice, and honor,

[43] Cf. Val. Max. 2.2.3, who says that Apollonius Molo was the first person to address the senate in Greek, probably in 81 B.C. Gellius 6.14.9 reports that C. Acilius translated for Carneades and the other ambassadors with him. In the second century many senators could have understood Greek, cf. Plut., *Cato Maior* 22.4, though governors usually had interpreters on their staffs, cf. Cic., *Verr.* 2.2.54. Cf. further *CAH* 8.458; Marrou 258. Postumus had addressed the people of Tarentum in Greek in 282 B.C. (Dion. Hal., *Ant. Rom.* 19.5.1) and Gracchus spoke Greek at Rhodes in 165 (Cic., *Brutus* 79). Cf. P. Boyancé, "La connaisance du grec à Rome," *REL* 34 (1956) 111-31.

and they began to imitate. If one reads through accounts of the early second century B.C. it is difficult not to be impressed with the number of embassies constantly sent to the senate on all manner of issues rising out of Rome's new role in the world's affairs since she had defeated Carthage and begun to intervene in Greece and Asia (cf., e.g., Polybius 23.1-5). It is surely no coincidence that Roman oratory achieved artistic form in the years when the Romans first heard in their own city, and partly at least in their own language, highly skilled and persuasive Greek orators. This influence of Greek orators is expressly recognized by Cicero in describing the beginnings of oratory at Rome:

"When with our empire established over all nations, lasting peace secured us leisure, there was no ambitious young man who did not believe that he should strive with all zeal for oratorical ability. At first, ignorant of all theory and not knowing any course of exercises or any rules of art, they attained what they could by native ability and wit. But later, *when they had heard Greek orators*, and became familiar with their writings, and studied with teachers, our countrymen burned with an unbelievable desire to speak." (*De or.*, 1.14)

The Beginning of Conscious Rhetoric

Even in the late third century, probably under the influence of what was seen in South Italy and Sicily, ability to speak began to be added to the list of traditional Roman virtues. In a funeral eulogy for his father delivered in 221 Q. Caecilius Metellus had said that he wished to be "a fighter in the first line, *the best orator*, the bravest general, to conduct affairs under his own command, to enjoy the greatest respect, to possess the greatest wisdom, to be counted the greatest senator, to

37

get much money in a good way, to leave many children, and to be the most famous man in the state" (Pliny, *Nat. hist.* 7.140); subsequently Cato said that the three most outstanding achievements were to be the "greatest orator, greatest general, greatest senator" (Pliny, *Nat. hist.* 7.100). In these passages an orator is perhaps thought of specifically as an ambassador, but speaking ability is the prime requisite. Fabius Maximus, the dictator whose delaying tactics held off Hannibal in 217, appreciated the importance of oratory (Plut., *Fab.* 1.4). M. Cornelius Cethegus, the consul of 204 B.C., is labeled by Cicero (*Brutus* 57) the first truly eloquent Roman, an opinion which he based not on an extant speech, but on the description of Cethegus in Ennius' *Annals* (fr. 300-305 Warmington) as *suaviloquens,* "sweet-speaking," *flos delibatus populi,* "the picked flower of the people," and *suadai medulla,* "the marrow of the goddess Persuasion." Ennius seems to have been influenced by Homer's description of Nestor and Eupolis' description of Pericles,[44] but as Cicero points out Ennius personally had heard Cethegus speak.

Cato the Elder

The first Roman orator of whom we can form a distinct impression is M. Porcius Cato, consul in 195, censor in 184 B.C.[45] We know Cato's speeches only from

---

[44] *Suaviloquens* is doubtless a translation of Homer's *hêduepês, Iliad* 1.248. Cicero (*Brutus* 57) compares Eupolis' remark of Pericles, that persuasion sat upon his lips. Aulus Gellius 12.2 reports ancient discussions of Ennius' line.

[45] Born in Tusculum 234 B.C., died 149. He was a "new man," that is, none of his ancestors had held high office in Rome. Principal sources are Livy, Polybius, Cornelius Nepos, Plutarch. Fragments in *ORF* and Dietmar Kienast, *Cato der Zensor: Seine Persönlichkeit und seine Zeit, mit den Redefragmente Catos,* Heidelberg, 1954. Cf. in general the works cited below and Leo, *op.cit.* supra n. 1, 283-90; Cima, *op.cit.* supra n. 1, Charles

quotations in later writers who often preserve only a few words, at most a few sentences. In a very few cases it is possible to grasp the organization or argument of a speech, but the fragments contribute mostly to our knowledge of Cato's prose style. Though it is difficult to be exact because of the varying titles under which speeches are cited, we seem to have bits of about eighty different speeches, the majority of them either *contiones* or speeches in the senate; there are, however, also a number of judicial speeches. Early in life Cato acquired a reputation as a patron (Plut., *Cato* 1.4), and throughout his career he seems to have been highly respected for his legal knowledge as well as for his oratorical ability (Nepos, *Cato* 3; Livy 39.40.5-7; Quint. 12.3.9), a combination which was common in Roman orators until the first century b.c. Cato's help and encouragement were available to those who wanted to undertake prosecution of corruption, decadence, or vice, and he himself, before, during, and after his censorship, repeatedly initiated prosecution to root out from the state anything which seemed a departure from traditional Roman austerity (Plut., *Cato* 15). He lived in a time of great change, when many Romans acquired wealth suddenly, when the allurement of Greek culture captivated not a few, and when Roman morals and mores were undergoing a revolution. Conservative Romans had almost always had great fear of the moral effects of luxury in private hands; from the Twelve Tables in the fifth century b.c. until the early empire there were repeated attempts to control

---

Knapp, "A Phase of the Development of Prose Writing among the Romans," *CPh* 13 (1918) 138-54; Marouzeau, *op.cit.* supra n. 5, 168-73; Schanz-Hosius 1.178-93; Francesco della Corte, *Catone censore: la vita e la fortuna*, Turin, 1949; H. H. Scullard, *Roman Politics 220-150 B.C.*, Oxford, 1951, esp. 256-72 and 288; Clarke 39-42; R-E 22. 108-65; Leeman 21-23 and 43-49.

luxury by legislation.[46] In the second century B.C. the Romans were sharply divided over the extent to which cultural changes should be welcomed or opposed.[47] Cato played his part in the extension of the empire into Greek-speaking countries, and he himself seems to have learned a good deal from Greeks (Plut., *Cato* 2.4). In general, however, he was the most outspoken opponent of Hellenization and thought that in the moral, and in many intellectual, fields Romans could only be corrupted (Plut., *Cato* 23). "I shall tell in its proper place," he wrote to his son Marcus, "what I found out at Athens about those Greeks, and I shall prove that it is a good thing to glance at their literature, not to study it thoroughly. Their race is quite worthless and unteachable, and I speak as a prophet in saying that when it gives us its literature it will ruin everything" (Pliny, *Nat. hist.* 29.14).

Of Cato's earlier accusations which we know, those in 190 B.C. against Q. Minucius Thermus are probably the most striking. Thermus was a supporter of Scipio Africanus, the leader of the faction to which Cato was opposed.[48] The speeches were apparently delivered in the senate when the question of granting Thermus a triumph was raised. Aulus Gellius quotes (10.3.14-17) a highly emotional invective where Cato speaks of Thermus' mistreatment of some native officials and compares it to

[46] Aulus Gellius 2.24 is a general survey of these. One of the most interesting was the *Lex Orchia* of Cato's time which limited the number of guests at a dinner. Cato tried to prevent its repeal, *ORF* 8.139-46.

[47] Cf. *CAH* 8.377-84 and Scullard, *op.cit.* supra n. 45.

[48] Cato is said (Livy 38.54.11; Gellius 4.18.7) to have instigated, though not to have conducted, the famous prosecution of L. Scipio, directed at P. Scipio Africanus in 187 B.C. and to have delivered a *suasio* (*ORF* 8.67) connected with the charges, but details are very confused, cf. Scullard, *op.cit.* supra n. 45, 290-303.

Cicero's attack on Verres. One bit, for example, reads: "who can bear this insult, who this power, who this servitude? No king dared to do this: could such things happen to noble men, born of noble stock, advisers of noble action? Where was the bond of alliance? Where the faithfulness of our fathers? . . ." The principal devices by which the emotional tone is heightened are anaphora, asyndeton, and rhetorical question, of which the first two at least are native to Latin. Cato may have been austere, but he felt no impropriety in expressing his stern views with emotional force. Ethos, vigorously expressed, produces pathos, and both of these elements came more easily to the Roman character than did extensive or intricate logical argument.

Naturally Cato's outspoken views and prosecutions brought him enemies, partly from those nobles who were drawn to Greek things, more perhaps from ambitious opportunists who found themselves frustrated by his watchfulness. In any event, he himself is said to have been brought to trial forty-four times on a variety of charges, but always acquitted (Pliny, *Nat. hist.* 7.100). Litigation was clearly a common political tool by the early second century.

Two of Cato's defenses which are better known to us than most are the speech which he gave about 190 B.C. in explanation of his activities as consul—the prosecutor and the specific charges made against him are not known —and the speech *On His Own Expenses*, probably made in 164 B.C. The earlier of these is known from a series of short quotations, mostly by grammarians interested in archaic diction, which give the impression that it was principally a narrative of his actions. He attributed the accusation to the machination of opponents: "Although my enemies have accomplished many new marvels, I never cease to marvel at their audacity and confidence."

41

He is not at all sparing in recounting his own virtues: "They praise me with the greatest praise: it was not supposed that any man could have prepared such a navy, such an army, so many supplies, nor that I could have prepared it so quickly."[49] Or "what I took I made (?) an everlasting monument to myself," a fragment where he is perhaps speaking of the number of towns he captured in Spain, greater than the number of days he spent there (Plut., *Cato* 10.3). The egotistical element seems stronger among Latin than in Greek orators. We have seen it in the speech attributed to Scipio, we will meet it again in Cicero; the declaimers described by the elder Seneca sometimes like to reflect upon their own cleverness, and even Pliny is not lacking in self-esteem. The attitude is a part of the strong element of character portrayal in Roman oratory: a Greek orator tends to argue his audience into believing something; a Roman by his authority convinces the audience that something should be believed because he says so, though of course the observation must not be pushed too far since there is some self-esteem in Demosthenes and much in Isocrates.[50] The quality of himself which Cato wants to stress is his frugality: when he went to Spain as consul he took but three servants; he drank the same wine as the rowers in the fleet; he left his horse in Spain to save the state the expense of bringing it back (*ORF* 8.51-54).

The speech *On His Own Expenses* seems to have resulted from charges made against him before the censors that he was privately living in greater luxury than the law allowed, the hope being that he could be made to seem a hypocrite. This speech too has great self-esteem

---

[49] *ORF* 8.22,28, and 40. Note how little effort Cato makes to avoid the repetition of similar words: marvels-marvels, praise-praise.

[50] Cf. *APG* 197 and 199.

and is noteworthy for the diabolical *praeteritio*, a figure which we have already met in Eumenes' Greek speech to the senate in 189 B.C. Whether learned from the Greeks or invented by Cato's own genius, it shows a mastery of dramatic technique requiring careful changes in the tone of voice and delivery, and producing stringent irony. Cato describes himself as seated in his study planning his speech and dictating to his slave:

"I ordered to be brought out the book in which my speech had been written on the matter of *sponsio* which I had made with M. Cornelius. The tablets were brought; the merits of my ancestors were read through; then the things which I had done for the state are read. In the passage which immediately follows these there was written in the speech 'I never lavished money, neither my own nor that of my associates, in canvassing for office.' Alas, don't, don't write that, I said, they don't want to hear. Then he read 'I never imposed commandants on the towns of your allies who ravaged their goods or their children.' That too delete, they don't want to hear. Read on. 'I never divided up the booty which had been captured from the enemy nor the proceeds from its sale among a few of my friends in order to keep it from those who had earned it.' That too erase; they certainly do not want this to be said; there is no need of its recital. 'I never gave free passage by the public post so that my friends might by their passes earn vast sums.' Go on and delete that entirely. 'I never distributed silver so that my servants and friends could drink my health, nor made them rich at the public cost.' You must scrape that out of the tablets right down to the wood. See I beg you where the state stands, in that the deeds which I meritoriously performed for the state, and for which I used to receive thanks, now I do not dare mention, lest I incur

43

ill will. Thus it has been brought about that it is possible to do harm with impunity, but not to do good with impunity" (Fronto 2 pp. 44-46 Haines; *ORF* 8.173).

Note that Cato does not pretend that his defense is extemporaneous, and that he expects his audience to have a certain interest in the process of composition, another sign of a growing rhetorical sophistication.

Of the magistracies he held, Cato was best known for his censorship in 184 B.C., even earning the cognomen *Censorius*. Twenty-one of his orations have with more or less probability been assigned to this year. Among the duties of the censors was to draw up the list of senators and knights, excluding those they regarded as unfit. Cato and his colleague Valerius expelled seven senators, the most famous being L. Quinctius Flamininus, brother of the great general Titus. According to Livy (39.42.6-7) Cato delivered speeches against the expelled senators, that against Flamininus being the most severe, but Plutarch (*Cato* 17.5) says that Titus appealed to the people in a legal action on behalf of his brother. The most famous part of the speech was that in which Cato described how Flamininus had had a Gaul put to death to amuse his young favorite who had missed the gladiatorial games.[51] In another celebrated action Cato deprived L. Veturius, a Roman knight, of his public horse on the ground that he was too fat to sit on it (*ORF* 8.78). Cato also attempted to check luxury by increasing

---

[51] Pederasty, like other Greek customs, became fashionable in some Roman circles, cf. Polybius 31.25.45, though referring to a slightly later period. Cato may not have opposed all pederasty. The one literal fragment of the speech (*ORF* 8.71) says: "Love is one thing, Philippus, lust is far different. The latter comes as quickly as the former goes; one is good, the other bad." *ORF* 8.60 and Plut., *Cato* 8.5 are critical.

taxes on women's jewelry and clothes and on carriages (Plut., *Cato* 18.2), a subject to which he devoted a speech (*ORF* 8.93).

The best-known phrase attributed to Cato's deliberative oratory is *censeo Carthaginem esse delendam,* "I think Carthage ought to be destroyed," a phrase which schoolboys have been told for generations was appended to every speech of Cato, though he did not live quite long enough to see its fulfillment at the end of the third Punic war, 146 B.C. It cannot be shown that he actually used these words, but something like them may have been said from time to time.[52] Plutarch says (*Cato* 27) that Scipio Aemilianus as assiduously asserted that Carthage should be saved, though he was in fact destined to destroy her! Cato's exhibition to the senate of a fresh fig, gathered a scant three days before in Carthage, is almost equally famous (Plut. *ibid.*), and shows a fine sense of drama in delivery.

Of Cato's deliberative speeches, indeed of all his speeches, the one which is best known as a whole is that delivered in 167 B.C. on behalf of the Rhodians who had sympathized with, but not actively aided Perseus of Macedon, just defeated by the Romans.[53] The Rhodians had sent to Rome ambassadors who were much cowed and did not speak very well when they appeared in the senate. Cato was the principal supporter of the Rhodians on this occasion and included his speech in his *Origines* (Livy 45.25.2). It is the first Roman speech in which we can see argumentation play a major role. The portions of the speech preserved in Aulus Gellius (6.3.1-50) may be translated as follows:

[52] Cf. Charles E. Little, "The Authenticity and Form of Cato's Saying: Carthago delenda est," *CJ* 29 (1933-34) 429-35.

[53] On the historical circumstances cf. *CAH* 8.287-90 and Scullard, *op.cit.* supra n. 45, 216-17.

45

"I know that it is customary when circumstances are favorable and expansive and prospering for the spirits of most men to exult and for their pride and boldness to grow and enlarge.[54] As a result, my great concern at present, since this matter has turned out so favorably, is that there be no mistake in deliberation which might check our good fortune and that this happiness may not turn out too unchecked. Adversity disciplines and teaches what needs to be done, prosperity is apt to turn men aside from right deliberation and understanding. Thus all the more earnestly I say and advise that this matter should be put off for some days until we return from our excessive joy to control of ourselves (ORF 8.163).

"For my part I do not think that the Rhodians wanted us to win the war as we won it, nor for King Perseus to be defeated. But the Rhodians were not the only ones who did not want us to win, for I believe many peoples and many nations had the same hope, and probably among them there were some who were not motivated by a desire for our disgrace, but were afraid that we would do whatever we wished if there was no one whom we feared and that they might be under our sole rule in servitude to us. It was for the sake of their own liberty, I think, that they adhered to this hope. Yet the Rhodians never publicly helped Perseus.

"Consider how much more suspicious we are in private affairs among ourselves. For each and every one of us, if he thinks something is being done against his own interest, strives with all his strength to prevent that ad-

---

[54] This appears to be the beginning of the speech, as ORF 8.196 appears to be the beginning of the speech *Against Galba*. Servius' observation (on *Aeneid* 11.301) that Cato and the Gracchi always invoked the gods at the beginning of their speeches is not borne out and may be derived from the opening of Pliny's *Panegyric*. But cf. Cic., *Div. in Caec.* 43!

verse thing from happening; but the Rhodians endured what they saw happening (164).

". . . These great advantages on both sides, this great friendship, shall we suddenly abandon? Shall we be the first to do what we charge them with wanting to have done? (165)

". . . He who speaks against them most strongly says, 'They wished to become our enemies.' Is there any one of you, I want to know, who, in a matter in which he himself is involved, thinks it right to be punished because he is accused of having *wished* to do wrong? No one, I think; for I would not in a matter which related to me (166). . . . What more? Is there, I want to know, any law so severe, which says 'If anyone *wishes* to do such and such a thing, let the fine be a thousand sesterces provided that is less than half his estate; if any one *wishes* to have more than five hundred acres, let the penalty be so much; if any one *wishes* to have a greater number of sheep, let him be fined so much?' Yet we all *wish* to have more of all of these, and we go unpunished for it (167). . . . But if it is not right for honor to be given because someone says that he *wanted* to do right but did not, will it be prejudicial to the Rhodians because they did not do harm, but because they say that they wished to do harm? (168)

". . . They say that the Rhodians are insolent, charging what I would not at all want said of me and my children. Let them be insolent. What business of ours is it? Are you angry if someone is more insolent than we are?" (169)

Cato's motive in defending the Rhodians may have been (cf. Gellius 6.3.7) the fear that their wealth would be plundered and confiscated by Romans whom he regarded as already too given to luxury,[55] but there is rather little of his usual moral indignation and character projection in the speech. Livy notes its mild tone (45.25.2). Cato is, if anything, sophistic.

The essay of Gellius (6.3) from which the fragments *On Behalf of the Rhodians* are quoted is an interesting piece of rhetorical criticism. Gellius, a writer of the second century A.D., had a special interest in early Latin literature, including Cato. He says that Cicero's secretary Tiro, perhaps after Cicero's death in 43 B.C., had written a letter to Quintus Axius in which he criticized Cato's rhetorical methods in this speech in a rather pedantic way: the opening was insolent, and Cato should have tried to win over the good will of his audience; the argument of the second fragment is a confession of guilt, not an acceptable defense; the third fragment is an invalid argument resembling one which Lucilius objected to in Euripides; the fourth, fifth, and sixth fragments are invidious sophistries, built on deceptive examples. The last fragment was not discussed by Tiro. Gellius answers each of these criticisms very well. He shows that Cato was not addressing an indifferent jury and there was thus little reason to seek good will. Cato was a senator speaking on public policy to others already much concerned. In each of the other parts Gellius tries to show that the arguments are in fact more valid than Tiro recognized. His view of the speech is summed up in these words (6.3.52-53):

[55] For other possible motives, cf. H. H. Schmitt, *Rom und Rhodos: Geschichte ihrer politischen Beziehungen seit der ersten Berührung bis zum Aufgehen des Inselstaates im römischen Weltreich*, Munich, 1957, 151-56. The thought of the speech is related to the development of Roman political ideals by H. Haffter, "Politisches Denken im alten Rom," *SIFC* 17 (1940) 97-121.

"It is to be noticed that throughout that speech of Cato all the arms and assistance of the rhetorical discipline are brought into play. But we do not see it done as we do in mock maneuvers or in battles simulated for entertainment. For, I repeat, the matter is not handled with excessive care and elegance and smoothness, but as in a contest where the outcome is in doubt, when the battle line has been scattered, and the fighting goes on in many places with varying success, so in this speech when that very well known arrogance of the Rhodians was stirred by the hatred and ill will of many, Cato employed every means at once of defense and offense, and one minute commends them as highly deserving, another acquits them as innocent, another charges that their possessions and riches should not be sought, another intercedes as though they had erred, another shows their friendship to the state, another appeals to mercy or to traditional Roman clemency or to the public interest. All of these things could perhaps be said in a more polished way or with greater rhythmical smoothness, but it does not seem possible for them to be said more strongly or vigorously."

Gellius probably goes too far in claiming that Cato's art escapes notice. He is thinking of Cato's technique in comparison with some products of the Roman empire, as he is also in speaking of the reality of the issue with which Cato is dealing and the resulting practical necessity of what he says. The contrast is significant as an indication of the direction in which Latin oratory was to move. It is clear that Gellius regarded Cato as acquainted with all the techniques of oratory as taught by rhetoricians (*omnia disciplinarum rhetoricarum arma*, 6.3.52) except for some fine points of style, which are a devel-

49

opment of subsequent ages. He agrees with Cicero (*Brutus* 68) that prose rhythm is lacking in Cato and it is true that the common clausulae of later prose are apparently not sought, though the dichoree, or double trochee ($-\cup-\cup$), characteristic of much Hellenistic literary prose, occurs three times. There is a decided accumulation of long syllables which would not have met with the approval of some rhetorical theorists but which to the modern ear gives the speech enormous weight. A good example is: "Advorsae res edomant et docent quid opus siet facto, secundae res laetitiae transvorsum tradere solent a recte consolendo atque intelligendo" (ending with a dichoree). The commonest rhythm at the end of a period is the thudding - - - - which occurs seven times. The passage is of course carefully organized into periods, though they are not long, and parallelism of sound and of sense are strongly marked. All of these factors contribute to the serious intensity which characterizes Cato's oratorial prose.

In comparison with the other fragments of Cato, with their ethical or narrative point of view, there is something remarkably Greek and argumentative about this speech: to this extent the comments of Tiro are right, though his evaluation of the arguments is not necessarily correct. It seems significant that there are a few points of contact between the Greek oratory of Eumenes and the Rhodian ambassadors in 189 B.C., as we saw it in Polybius, and this speech of Cato: the concern with hybris, the acceptance of the fact that states act in their own interest, the Rhodians' concern with the freedom of other cities, the wisdom of aiding Rome's friends, in general with the conflicting claims of the principles of justice or expediency as put into political practice. At the time of the embassy Cato had agreed with the Rhodians (Polybius 21.22.8) that a royal king could not be trusted (Plut., *Cato* 8.7-8). The similarities between the speeches are not close enough to allow the conclusion that Cato was intentionally imitating either of the earlier speeches, but it is quite probable that just as he exhausted the possible arguments in his attempt to appeal to many different senators, so he also composed a speech which by its very argumentative nature he hoped might appeal to senators attracted by Greek manners and learning. Cato's speech helped prevent a declaration of war against Rhodes, though the city was denied a treaty for the present and its power suffered.

Gellius' statement that Cato employed the arms of the rhetorical discipline raises the question of Cato's familiarity with rhetoric as taught in his time. Cicero thought that all oratorical virtues were to be found in Cato (*Brutus* 65), including excellent examples of the tropes and figures of speech which the Greek rhetoricians stressed (*ibid.* 69), though he felt also a roughness in Cato's composition, particularly because words, phrases, and sentences were not smoothly joined together, and he missed the rhythmical prose of his own day (*ibid.* 68).

The view has sometimes been taken that Cato was a natural orator untouched by Greek rhetorical theory, sometimes that he was very familiar, whether he admitted it or not, with Greek theoreticians.[56] These extremes are unrealistic and fail to consider the possibility to which the evidence, including the speech *On Behalf of the Rhodians*, clearly points, that actual oratory composed by Greeks was known in Rome. Although ancient authors sometimes alleged that Cato learned Greek only in old age (Cic., *De sen.* 26; Plut., *Cato* 2.4), these passages only mean that Cato found time in old age to study Greek literature in a way he had not done before. In the very passage cited, Plutarch says that Cato's writings

[56] Cf. Frank, *op.cit.* supra n. 1, 140-45.

were ornamented with Greek thoughts and anecdotes and contained many quotations and *sententiae* from the Greek.[57] After all, Cato spent a number of years with Greeks in southern Italy, in Sicily, and in Greece itself; he seems to have known Polybius when the latter was in Rome (Plut., *Cato* 9.2-3), and he employed a Greek grammarian named Chilo as a tutor to his son (*ibid.* 20.3). It was part of his old Roman pose to play down his debt to Greeks (*ibid.* 12.4) but this did not prevent him from utilizing Greek learning. Antonius a century later took a similar position (Cic., *De or.* 2.153). A number of other signs of probable Greek influence have been found in pieces of Cato's writing. One of the earliest speeches, that to his troops at Numantia (*ORF* 8.17), has an antitheses between *labor*, whose benefits long remain, and *voluptas*, or "pleasure," whose joys quickly flee, which is reminiscent of Prodicus of Ceos' *Choice of Heracles* (Xen., *Mem.* 2.1.21-34).[58] In the speech *On Behalf of the Rhodians*, as we saw, Tiro found sophistic arguments, in particular the use of *epagôgê*, or induction, and a modern critic has stressed the use of arguments from expediency, justice, and honor, the central concerns of oratory as taught by almost every Greek rhetorician since Aristotle.[59] None of these individual points is conclusive proof of familiarity with Greek rhetorical theory, but together they do seem to make it probable. On the other hand, many of the tropes and figures of speech in fragments of Cato, especially the repetition of words and sounds, are native features of Latin, even of

---

[57] Examples of these might be *ORF* 8.20 from Demosthenes, *Phil.* 1.30 and *ORF* 8.195 from *Phil.* 3.8 and 17. Cf. Rudolf Till, "Die Sprache Catos," *Philologus*, Suppl. 28.2 (1935) 24-25.
[58] Cf. Scullard, *op.cit.* supra n. 45, 257 and Benno Janzer, *Historische Untersuchungen zu den Redenfragmenten des M. Porcius Cato*, Würzburg, 1936, 2-4.
[59] Cf. Leeman 45.

colloquial Latin.[60] Figures of thought, like the *praeteritio* of the speech *On His Own Expenses*, are more sophisticated, and may have been suggested by Greek techniques.

Instruction in Greek rhetoric had begun at Rome in Cato's lifetime, but conservative Romans found formal education of the Greek type hard to accept. Cato himself grumbled (Plut., *Cato* 23.2) that Isocrates' students wasted their whole life on education and would have to use their knowledge to plead before Minos in the underworld. According to Suetonius (*De gramm. et rhet.* 25) in 161 B.C. the praetor Pomponius consulted the senate on the subject of philosophers and rhetoricians in Rome, and it was decided that he should have authority to expel them from the city. Two Epicurean philosophers had probably already been expelled in 173 B.C. (Athenaeus 12.547a). We do not know what incident set off the reaction of 161,[61] but one thing that was objected to can perhaps be seen in the events of 155 B.C. when three Athenian philosophers, Carneades the Academic, Critolaus the Peripatetic, and Diogenes the Stoic came on an embassy and attracted a great deal of attention, espe-

---

[60] Norden 164-69 saw Greek influence in most features of Cato's style, but this is excessive and has not been accepted, cf. Till, *op.cit.* supra n. 57, 21-25. Enzo V. Marmorale, *Cato Maior*, Bari, 1949, 199-224, viewed Cato as a "natural" orator, though he admitted some Greek influence. Kienast, *op.cit.* supra n. 45, 101-16, saw a synthesis of Greek and Latin elements. Leeman 22 and 45-46 makes a good distinction between native Latin devices of emphasis and Greek techniques, cf. also Clarke 41. On native features of rhetorical style in Latin, cf. Leo, *op.cit.* supra n. 1, 34-40.

[61] Attempts have been made to associate it with lectures on Stoicism by Crates of Mallos, cf. E. Vernon Arnold, *Roman Stoicism*, London, 1958, 100, and Ruth M. Brown, "A Study of the Scipionic Circle," *Iowa Studies in Classical Philology* 1 (1934) 161, but it is unlikely that Crates stayed from 169 to 161 or that his lectures, chiefly on grammar, were so obnoxious.

cially among the young, by the lectures which they delivered in the city (Cic., *De or.* 2.155; Gellius 6.14.8-10). Carneades lectured one day in praise of justice, but the next day, as was customary with Academics, with equal eloquence he argued against justice, "not out of serious philosophical belief, but in a kind of oratorical exercise of speaking on both sides of an issue" (Lactantius, *Div. inst.* 5.14.3-4).[62] Cato in particular was incensed (Pliny, *Nat. hist.* 7.112; Plut., *Cato* 22) and urged that the philosophers be sent packing, but they do not seem to have left under compulsion. Carneades himself was not sympathetic to rhetoric as a discipline of study (Cic., *De or.* 1.45-46), but his speeches were certainly more demonstrations of reasoning than they were moral lectures, and the Romans doubtless regarded him as equally philosopher and rhetorician, as did some Greeks (Diogenes Laertius 4.62). Very possibly the decree of 161 B.C. was directed against some less distinguished precursor of Carneades, though it was certainly not long enforced and it was perhaps never applied against philosophers who lived with a patron and did not publicly lecture. No further steps were taken against Greek rhetoricians and no steps were ever taken against grammarians, either famous ones like Crates of Mallos who visited Rome about 169 B.C. (Suet., *De gramm. et rhet.* 2) or the lesser ones like Cato's slave Chilo who were tutors in Roman families. The teachings of grammarians and rhetoricians overlapped at many points, but as long as they had influential patrons or did not indulge in offensive exhibitions they were tolerated. It was obviously the

[62] Cf. *APG* 300. The passage in Lactantius indicates that Carneades attacked justice with the argument that it led men to act against their own interest (cf. the speech of Eumenes against the Rhodians) and that Cicero imitated Carneades' discussion in a part of *De republica* not well preserved.

use of rhetoric in questioning received principles which most distressed Romans of the old school.

Knowledge of the Greek arts must have gradually become common during the second century B.C. Cato himself accelerated the process by writing for his son and then publishing the first Roman encyclopaedia of which we know.[63] His extant work *On Agriculture*, written except for the preface and a few special passages in a dry and technical style,[64] is perhaps a separate edition of part of this encyclopaedia. There was a section on medicine and also a discussion of rhetoric, so that Cato could be labeled not only the first major Roman orator, but the first Roman rhetorician (Quint. 3.1.19). Since he thought as little of Greek physicians as he did of Greek rhetoricians it seems likely that his objective was to make some of the technical knowledge of the Greeks available to Romans without endangering their souls by encouraging them to read much Greek or have contacts with Greeks who might question their beliefs: thus his remark that it is good to glance at Greek literature, but not to study it thoroughly (Pliny, *Nat. hist.* 29.14).

We know very little about Cato's discussion of rhetoric, not even for certain whether it contained discussions of the five parts of rhetoric: invention, arrangement, style, memory, and delivery, all of which would be expected in a Greek rhetorical treatise. Quintilian speaks (3.1.19) of the work as though it were in the Greek tradition. Three fragments attributed to Cato are perhaps from it: "orator est, Marce fili, vir bonus, dicendi peritus" ("An orator, son Marcus, is a good man skilled at speak-

---

[63] Cf. Schanz-Hosius 1.181-82 and Francesco della Corte, "Catone maggiore e i *Libri ad Marcum filium*," *RFIC* 69 (1941) 81-96.

[64] Cf. Alfred Kappelmacher, "Zum Stil Catos im *De re rustica*," *WS* 43 (1922-23) 168-72 and Leeman 21-24.

ing") (Seneca, *Contr.* 1. *pr.* 9); "Catonis praeceptum paene divinum, qui ait: rem tene, verba sequentur" ("the almost divine injunction of Cato, who says, 'seize the subject, the words will follow'") (Julius Victor 374 Halm), and the term *vires causae* ("the strong points of a case") (*De adtributis personae et negotio* 308 Halm) applied to a proposition supported by attributes both of person and of action. The latter subject is discussed by Cicero (*De inv.* 1.34) in connexion with the *conprobatio* or proof of an oration and may, therefore, be taken as some evidence that Cato discussed the different parts of a speech. It is hardly likely that he wrote on rhetoric in the second century without doing so. The second fragment is a declaration of Cato's preference for attention to matter rather than manner. We have already noted that it resembles rules of the Stoics. In Cato's time the *res* of a case would probably include legal knowledge as well as the immediate facts. *Verba* suggests a discussion of style, at least of diction, but figures and other ornamentation could have been omitted. It is remarkable that such striking words are quoted by no author before Julius, who lived in the fourth century A.D., but Cicero seems to paraphrase them in *De oratore* (1.20) and Horace too in *Ars poetica* (311). The first fragment is probably from the beginning of the discussion of rhetoric, since Marcus is addressed. There was a corresponding definition of (presumably) a farmer as *vir bonus colendi peritus* ("a good man, skilled at cultivating"; Servius, *Ad Georg.* 1.46). It too could be Stoic, but it is enough for it to be Roman and Catonic,[65] for

[65] Cf. Ludwig Radermacher, "Eine Schrift über den Redner als Quelle Ciceros und Quintilians," *RhM* 34 (1899) 286-92 and Fritz Schöll, "*Vir bonus, dicendi peritus,*" *RhM* 57 (1902) 312-14.

it couples ethos and hard work. The definition of the orator had great influence and is the first expression of a persistent ideal of Roman rhetoricians, the perfect orator, discussed in Cicero's *De oratore* and especially in Quintilian (e.g., 1. *pr.* 9), where the requirement that the orator be a good man is central.

In Cato's work, then, many of the features of Roman rhetoric and oratory are already evident: the adaptation of Greek argument and techniques to the Latin language and style, an emphasis on character even to the point of pathos, the concept of an orator as a person in whom morality was at least as important as intellect, a tendency to excerpt and compile rather than to speculate or invent. It also seems to have been Cato who first "published" a Latin speech. We have already seen that the text of funeral orations and of some similar works were *preserved* in family archives, but so far there has been no sign of deliberate publication. In *De senectute* (12) Cicero has Cato remark that the speech of Fabius Maximus at the funeral of his son is *in manibus*, but Cicero may have had no evidence for the words except a belief that the speech was preserved, and a single phrase in a dramatic context can hardly be pressed very hard. Cicero says (*Brutus* 65) that he has *found* and *read* more than 150 of Cato's speeches, which suggests that there was no general edition, though one may have been made later,[66] and that rather few copies existed of most of the speeches. According to Aulus Gellius (6.3.7; 13.25.15) two (at least) of Cato's speeches were preserved in the text of his historical work, *Origines*, written in Cato's old age (Nepos, *Cato* 3.3) and partly posthumous in publication. It is usually assumed that texts

[66] Cf. M. O. Baumgart, *Untersuchungen zu den Reden des M. Porcius Cato Censorius*, Breslau, 1905, and Leo, *op.cit.* supra n. 1, 284n.

of the other speeches were published from time to time after delivery as political pamphlets, but in fact there is no evidence for this and the probable course of events requires more careful examination.

In the speech *On His Own Expenses,* quoted above and probably composed in 164, Cato describes how he ordered his slave to bring out the *codex* in which he preserved the text of an earlier speech and read portions to him. We know from Quintilian (10.7.30) that an ancient orator often composed a *commentarius* in which he wrote out some portion of a projected speech and outlined the rest. *Commentarii* of Servius Sulpicius Rufus and of Cicero are mentioned by Quintilian, Cicero's having been edited by his secretary Tiro. It seems very possible that Cato's codex contained his *commentarii*. A *codex* was merely a series of tablets joined together, often used for notebooks or ledgers. In *De senectute* (38) Cato is shown the year before his death keeping his wits active by editorial work (*conficere*) on speeches in famous cases (*causarum illustrium quascumque defendi*). Cato is probably to be viewed as working within the tradition of the Roman noble who keeps a record of his family's illustrious achievements. Most speeches are not to be published, but are preserved. Publication of a few is planned in the *Origines.* Others were put in an intelligible form so that they could be consulted and after Cato's death were eventually given some circulation because of interest in them.

Posthumous publication was of course very common in antiquity. Not to mention the numerous works left incomplete by their authors, it is likely that some of the speeches of Demosthenes were posthumously published, as were the works of the elder Seneca, and there are other examples including Cicero's letters, probably *De*

legibus, and presumably those *commentarii* which Tiro
edited. If this picture is correct, Cato's objective in publication of speeches in the *Origines* and in preserving
texts of his other speeches was not political influence
at a particular time, nor advertisement of his legal abilities to prospective clients, as may have been the case
with some of the Attic orators, but a desire to preserve
knowledge of his life and point of view for posterity, and
thus the common literary motivation of antiquity, the
achievement of immortality: *non omnis moriar.*

If this picture is correct Cato first decided to publish
certain speeches by including them in the *Origines.* Do
we know of any particular reason which might have suggested the inclusion of a particular speech? We do know
one rather unusual circumstance. One of the two
speeches definitely known to have been included in the
Origines is that *On Behalf of the Rhodians.* On that
occasion danger of war had been averted principally by
Cato's speech, not by the efforts of the ambassadors. Yet
one of them, Astymedes, after going home, had the
effrontery to publish his own speech to the senate. It
is the first time that publication of a speech to the senate
by anybody is mentioned. The second speech in the
senate known to have been published is Cato's speech
on the same occasion. Polybius (30.4.6-17), the source
of the information about Astymedes, does not mention
that Cato published his speech too, which may be because it had not been published when Polybius left Rome
in 151 B.C. Polybius disliked the speech of Astymedes
and one may be certain that Cato liked it even less, since
he well knew how ineffective the Greek ambassadors had
been and how much he himself had played the crucial
role of preventing war. It was an excellent opportunity
to show the superiority of a Latin to a Greek orator,

59

and in all probability this, the earliest speech which we *know* Cato published, was in fact the earliest speech which he did publish. Subsequently he added his speech *Against Galba* (Gellius 13.25.15) to the *Origines* and perhaps other speeches.

Rhetoric in the Scipionic Circle

Cato's preference on moral grounds for a deliberately superficial knowledge of Greek culture is to be contrasted with the appreciation of Greek ideas and letters found among a group of authors of the second century B.C. who are collectively known as the Scipionic circle. The two attitudes persisted in Roman literary history and their later counterparts can be seen, for example, in the discussions of Cicero's *De oratore*, where Antonius' attitude toward Greek learning, and the liberal arts in general, is deliberately superficial (e.g., *De or.* 1.82). The principal activities of the Scipionic circle were in drama, history, philosophy, and satire, not in rhetoric, but Scipio, Laelius, and some others were statesmen and thus necessarily orators, and a number of concerns of the professional writers in the group have a relationship to the development of rhetoric, so that they need to be examined briefly.

The term Scipionic circle[67] is used to describe a very considerable number of people loosely associated, some as friends and equals, some as clients, with P. Cornelius

[67] The term was first used in the 19th century; its principal ancient authority is Cicero's *Scipionis in nostro, ut ita dicam, grege* (*De amic.* 69), in which *grege* means a rather large group, cf. Brown, *op.cit.* supra n. 61, esp. 14-15. This study deals chiefly with personnel. For general historical background cf. Pierre Grimal, *Le siècle des Scipions*, Paris, 1953, and Catherine Saunders, "The Nature of Rome's Early Appraisal of Greek Culture," *CPh* 39 (1944) 209-17.

Scipio Aemilianus Africanus, generally called the younger Scipio, who won the third Punic war for Rome. His grandfather by adoption, the elder Scipio, had been a patron of Ennius and others in his time, and his natural father, Aemilius Paulus, was an enthusiastic philhellene who claimed as his share of the booty after his defeat of Perseus only the Macedonian royal library, which he brought to Rome for his sons (Plut., *Aemilius Paulus* 28.6). The most important direct Greek influences in the Scipionic circle were the historian Polybius, brought to Rome as an Achaean hostage, and the Stoic philosopher Panaetius, who spent much of his time with Scipio in Rome (Cic., *Pro Mur.* 66; Vel. Pat. 1.13.3).[68] Laelius and probably others in the group had also studied with Panaetius' teacher, Diogenes of Babylon (Cic., *De fin.* 2.24). The principal philosophical influences on the circle were therefore Stoic, but as Cicero points out (*Pro Mur.* 66) it was not a narrow and austere Stoicism; certainly Scipio and his friends show little sign of having held the view of rhetoric which the Stoics Chrysippus and Cleanthes had taught, a kind of dry dialectical statement almost devoid of ornamentation.[69] If the various writers involved sought for logical subtlety, brevity, and directness of expression, which the Stoics approved, their style was also to be characterized by a simplicity and adroitness accompanied by grace and eloquence. They were not, however, attracted by the amplification and pomposity which came to be labeled Asianism and were

[68] On Panaetius, cf. Max Pohlenz, *Die Stoa*, Göttingen, 1948, 1.191-207.
[69] Cf. R. Reitzenstein, "Scipio Aemilianus und die stoische Rhetorik," *Strassburger Festschrift zur xlvi Versammlung deutscher Philologen und Schulmänner*, Strassburg, 1901, 143ff. and the reply of Wilhelm Kroll, "Rhetorica," *Philologus* 88 (1933) 457-62. Cf. APG 290-99.

common in some Greek authors of the time; at Rome
Asianism perhaps exercised some influence on orators like
Galba or the Gracchi and on the historian Coelius Antipater.[70] Polybius' objections to the flamboyant historiography of Timaeus must have been approved by his Roman
friends. The common bond which held together the Latin
writers in the group was a dedication to good writing, and
they naturally found the best models for this among Greek
authors. Though Greeks were far more welcome in the
house of Scipio than in the house of Cato (Cic., *De or.*
2.154), this did not mean a wholesale abandonment of
Roman traditions. Scipio was a Roman noble first and
always: for example, Greek political theory as imitated
by the Gracchi held little appeal for him.[71] Both tastes
were shared by his friends: Lucilius, for example, had a
keen interest in the Latin language, but also exhibits an
earthy devotion to Rome and Italy.

Of the interests of the Scipionic circle which relate to
rhetoric, the most important is a concern with diction,
the choice of words, their pronunciation, and even
their spelling. Writing a hundred years later Cicero calls
(*Brutus* 258) the mid-second century b.c. a time of pure
Latinity among all those who had not been corrupted
by some outside influence, but names as purest among
pure speakers Scipio and his friends Laelius and Philus.
It is logical to think that this interest owed much to
the Stoics, since they were leaders in the study of grammar at Pergamum and elsewhere. Crates of Mallos,
whose lectures in Rome in 169 b.c. have already been
mentioned, was head of the Pergamene school, and
Diogenes of Babylon, the Stoic among the ambassadors

---

[70] It is ordinarily assumed that Diophanes of Mytilene and
Menelaus of Marathus, the teachers of the Gracchi, were Asianists. They came from Asia, but we have no specific information
on their styles. Cf. Norden 171 and Leeman 75.

[71] Cf. Saunders, *op.cit.* supra n. 67.

of 155, was also interested in grammar.[72] Panaetius had studied with both men.

A grammarian's lectures probably took the form of reading and commenting on Greek poetry, especially Homer, discussing diction, including word coinage and etymology, the correct spelling, pronunciation, and inflexion of Greek words, the use of metaphors and other tropes, and labeling figures of thought and figures of speech.[73] From the Stoic grammarians the Romans learned about the contemporary controversy over anomaly, the doctrine supported in Pergamum that usage, not consistency, should determine the correct inflexional form of a word, and analogy, the doctrine that inflexional patterns should be consistent and free from exceptions, and more important they learned the concepts of barbarism, or the fault of choosing the wrong word for a context, and solecism, the fault of using a word ungrammatically. Of the virtues of style canonized by Theophrastus[74] (Hellenism or purity, clarity, propriety, and ornamentation) the last three could be taken over almost directly into Latin, while the first, which was the subject of most interest to the grammarians, was given a counterpart in the form of *Latinitas*.[75] We must not forget how difficult the creation of a work of literature was in Latin in the second century B.C. and even somewhat later, con-

---

[72] Cf. Diogenes Laertius 7.56-60; John E. Sandys, A *History of Classical Scholarship*, Cambridge, Eng., 1903, 1.144-64; R-E 11.1634-41 and 5. 773-77; APG 296-97; Rudolf Pfeiffer, *History of Classical Scholarship from the Beginnings to the End of the Hellenistic Age*, Oxford, 1968, 234-51.

[73] Cf. Dionysius Thrax 1; Suet., *De gramm.* 1-2; Marrou 160-72.

[74] Cf. APG 273-78. The Stoics added brevity to the list, cf. Diogenes Laertius 7.59.

[75] Cf. Charles N. Smiley, "*Latinitas* and *Hellenismos*," *Bulletin of the Univ. of Wisconsin, Philology and Literature Series* 3.3 (1906) 211-71.

sidering the lack of native literary traditions and the very limited vocabulary available.[76] A modern African writer might perhaps understand the problem better than a European or American. The Scipionic circle's greatest contribution to rhetoric and to Latin literature was linguistic self-consciousness: the introduction of the terms and categories of Greek grammar which could be used in creating and maintaining standards and developing new resources in Latin.

The younger Scipio himself had a thoroughly Greek education (Plut., *Aemilius Paulus* 6.5). His favorite author was Xenophon, whose works he always kept near him (Cic., *Tusc.* 2.62; *Ad Q. Fr* 1.1.23). Although he did not have an ambition to become a writer or advocate,[77] a few of his speeches were preserved or even published (Cic., *Brutus* 82). Cicero speaks of their gravity (*De or.* 3.28) and irony (*De or.* 2.270). Three of the fragments[78] employ the figure of speech called climax which shows a deliberate organization of the material to achieve emphasis. One of these (Gellius 6.12.5) is a spirited description of a depilated homosexual which may have some of the frankness the Stoics approved, but gets its bitterness from its detail and amplification, in other words from deliberate ornamentation.[79] The passage also shows a feeling for similarities of sound between contrasted words which the study of diction and grammar encouraged. In another fragment (Gellius 6.11.9) the

[76] The problem was greatest in philosophy and other theoretical studies because of the lack of abstractions in Latin, cf. J. Marouzeau, *Quelques aspects de la formation du Latin littéraire*, Paris, 1949.

[77] Cf. D. C. Earl, *The Political Thought of Sallust*, Cambridge, Eng., 1961, 24.

[78] ORF 21.17, 32, and 33.

[79] Cf. Leeman 51. Norden 170 pointed out as well periodicity, word play, and ethopoiia.

starting point is the distinction between *malitia*, or wickedness, and *nequitia*, or irresponsibility, while two other fragments show Scipio's interest in pronunciation and spelling.[80] None of the fragments gives a very clear impression of Scipio himself: to his successors and some of his contemporaries there was something superhuman about him: it is what led Cicero to idealize him in *De republica*, and an odd effect of it was the acquittal of L. Cotta when Scipio prosecuted him for extortion (Cic., *Pro Mur.* 58). The jury decided that it was not fair for anyone to be matched with the eloquence, virtue, and influence of Scipio. Here the ethos of authority, long so effective, received a check which was soon to be repeated on a larger scale in the challenge to the senate from the Gracchi. The transition from aristocratic orator to demagogue is about to begin.

The best-known Latin writer of the Scipionic circle is the comic dramatist Terence.[81] Like Plautus, his plays are so completely based on Greek works written a hundred or more years before, that not much can be learned from the speeches in them about Roman techniques of persuasion, but the Roman audience may have derived an increased awareness of Greek rhetoric from them. One example of this cited by Cicero (*De inv.* 1.33) is the technique of partition and narration in the *Andria* (49ff.). Another example is the section of the *Phormio* in which Antipho, Phaedria, and Geta consider what defense to use to Demipho, including practicing what expression to hold on the face. They decide to admit the "crime," a marriage without the father's permission, but show that it was done unwillingly under the order of a

[80] ORF 21.34 and 35.
[81] Publius Terentius Afer, c. 195-159 B.C. A few events of his life are known from the Suetonian-Donatan biography, which specifically mentions his friendship with Scipio and Laelius. In general cf. Duckworth, *op.cit.* supra n. 39, 56-61.

judge, which the contemporary Greek rhetorician would have called *stasis* of quality,[82] and Geta recalls that the case in court had been just, practicable, persuasive, and good (226), which looks like the parade of arguments of a Greek orator. The graceful Latin style in Terence's works has been admired from ancient to modern times and certainly reflects that interest in and feeling for words which Scipio and his friends shared.[83] Terence himself boasts (*Heauton. pr.* 46) of his *pura oratio*.

Most of Terence's plays are introduced by prologues which defend the author against criticism, for example the allegation that his plays were written by his powerful friends (*Heauton.* 22-26; *Adelphoe* 15-21), and especially the charge of *contaminatio*, which is an important concept in the history of Hellenism at Rome. *Contaminatio* is the use of two or more Greek originals in the composition of a single Latin play.[84] Terence does not deny having done this; his position is that he has produced a better play and that previous Roman writers have done the same thing (*Andria* 13-27). Terence's rival Luscius Lanuvinus seems to have taken a very purist attitude toward the work of a Latin playwright, regarding him solely as a translator.[85] *Contaminare* means to spoil by touching, but it is not entirely clear whether Luscius was more concerned that a classic Greek original was being "spoiled" by Terence, or whether he had a practical fear that if two plays, or parts of them, were combined in one the possible sources of plays would soon be exhausted, leaving dramatists no material. Some comedies

---

[82] Cf. APG 306-14.
[83] Cf. Leo, *op.cit.* supra n. 1, 251-55.
[84] Cf. Duckworth, *op.cit.* supra n. 39, 202-8.
[85] There were other complaints too, though not so openly expressed: the guild of poets seems to have been losing money because of Terence's success, cf. E. G. Sihler, "The *collegium poetarum* at Rome," *AJPh* 26 (1905) 1-21.

and tragedies were set in Roman scenes, but they had basically Greek plots and were apparently less successful than the more purely Greek plays. The most Roman poetry of the second century B.C. was satire, which had no formal Greek antecedent, though it borrowed Greek motifs from various genres. The development of the form need not be discussed here. The satiric spirit, unlike the comic or the tragic, was strong in Romans, and aspects of it appear both in the moral indignation of Cato and in the irony of Scipio. Ridicule, sarcasm, and vituperation were always a part of Roman oratory. Ennius had made a beginning in satire as in other forms, but the first great Roman satirist was Scipio's friend Lucilius,[86] whose work is known from references in Horace and other later writers and from a large number of fragments, mostly only a line or two, quoted by grammarians. Lucilius' interest for the history of rhetoric is his specific reference to the stylistic theory current among grammarians and rhetoricians. Book nine of his satires contained a poem on literary composition and spelling and listed a hundred kinds of solecism (fr. 397 Warmington). Book ten had a poem on style, mentioning the figure climax (fr. 416 Warmington), which we have noted in Scipio, and touching on laws of euphony (fr. 417-18 Warmington). The longest extant fragment on style comes from book five, where Lucilius is complaining about the failure of some friend to come to see him when he is sick:

> How I am, even though you don't ask, I will tell you,
> Since I have not joined the great majority. . . .

[86] C. Lucilius, c. 180-c. 102 B.C. He served under Scipio at Numantia and refers to him in his verse. Cf. Fridericus Marx, *C. Lucilii carminum reliquiae*, Leipzig, 1904-1905; George C. Fiske, *Lucilius and Horace: a Study of the Classical Theory of Imitation*, Madison, 1920; Warmington, *op.cit.* supra n. 13, vol. 3.

⟨I suspect⟩ that you want me, whom you *ought* to
    have *sought*,
to pass out of the picture. If you complain about this
"ought" and "sought" as artless or Isocratean
And entirely trashy and childish,
I won't waste my effort, if you are like that.
                                    (fr. 186-93 Warmington)

Aulus Gellius (18.8) quotes the passage as ridicule of
homoeoteleuta, the use of rhyming words. In the original
the words translated "artless," "trashy," and "childish"
are all Greek critical terms.[87]
    If we had all of Lucilius' work we would doubtless
have a great many more references to stylistic technical
terms and not only information on contemporary tragedy, which Lucilius criticized,[88] but a satiric picture of
contemporary rhetoric. It would especially be good to
have most of his second book which contained a parody
of the prosecution for extortion of Mucius Scaevola
Augur by Albucius about 119 B.C. Albucius was a philhel-
lenist who liked to pose as a Greek but hated Scaevola for
making fun of him by publicly addressing him in Greek
in Athens (Cic., *De fin.* 1.9; fr. 87-93 Warmington).
Lucilius often uses Greek words himself, especially when
talking about food, medicine, philosophy, or rhetoric
where no Latin word was available; sometimes his intention is to be funny, since he criticized excessive and constant borrowing.[89] Whereas Terence's contribution to
Latinity is largely a matter of the discovery of how to
express alien ideas in fine natural Latin, Lucilius' contribution to language, like Cicero's, involved the enrich-

---

[87] Cf. A. E. Housman, *"Luciliana,"* CQ 1 (1907) 149-51.
[88] Cf. D'Alton 48-51 and Warmington, *op.cit. supra* n. 12a,
3.xvii.
[89] Cf. W. C. Korfmacher, "Grecizing in Lucilian Satire," *CJ*
30 (1934-35) 453-62.

ment and enlargement of the language itself, something which could perhaps be less offensively done in the more Roman context of his work than in Terence's already highly Greek material.

Similarities between the style and critical position of writers of the Scipionic circle and some Latin writers of the next century make it tempting to apply some of the critical terminology of the later to the earlier period, and this tendency is encouraged by certain references in later authors. Cicero, for example, makes Scipio say (*De rep.* 3.42) that none of the Attic orators surpassed Laelius in sweetness or elegance, and Quintilian (12.10.39) calls Scipio, Laelius, and Cato *Attici Romanorum*, "the Attic orators among the Romans." These references, however, do not justify the use of the term Atticism of those second century writers who consciously aimed at a purity of style.[90] Cicero, on whom Quintilian depends, was interested, as we shall see, in turning some of the attention of orators of his own day away from imitation solely of Attic writers like Lysias or Xenophon and he tried to represent early Roman orators as counterparts to them, stressing at the same time the increase in subtlety and richness of Latin style since that time. Cicero does not say that the second century writers belonged to a school or group which deliberately imitated only the Attic orators, or even only classical Greek writers, which is what neo-Atticist orators of first century Rome did. Although they may have avoided the excesses of amplifica-

[90] Cf. Reitzenstein, *op.cit.* supra n. 69, and G. L. Hendrickson, "The *De analogia* of Julius Caesar: its Occasion, Nature, and Date, with Additional Fragments," *CPh* 1 (1906) 97-120. Henrickson admitted that the term Atticism was not in vogue much before the time of Cicero's *Brutus* and *Orator*, but he regarded Atticism as essentially identical with the earlier movement. Cf. also Ludwig Radermacher, "Ueber die Anfänge der Atticismus," *RhM* 54 (1899) 351-74.

tion or ornamentation or rhythm which came to be called
Asianism, there is no reason to believe that they thought
of themselves as Atticists in any sense. In many cases the
Greek models of which they were most conscious were
characteristically Hellenistic: Polybius, Panaetius, the
various Stoic writers, Carneades, perhaps Callimachus in
the case of Lucilius.[91] Scipio's love for Xenophon and
Terence's imitation of Menander were the best examples
of study of a model whom first century B.C. critics would
have admitted to be Attic. Neo-Atticism in rhetorical history should be reserved for the movement in Greek and
in Latin in the first century B.C. which imitated the simplicity in structure and composition of the Attic orators,
which in Latin generally avoided deliberate prose rhythms,
and which also aimed at purity of Greek or Latin diction.
If something is needed to describe the stylistic qualities of
purity and graceful simplicity seen in Terence and some
others of the Scipionic circle, and in the early first century
orator and poet Q. Lutatius Catulus,[92] as well as in the
poetry of Catullus and the prose of the admittedly neo-
Atticist Calvus, or of Brutus or Caesar, *Latinitas* is probably the most historically justified.[93]

A somewhat more acceptable, but not ideal, alternative
is "plain style," and it raises the question of the extent
to which the three stylistic characters, the categories of
grand, middle, and plain, were applied in second century Rome. These terms go back in some form to fourth

---

[91] Cf. M. Puelma Piwonka, *Lucilius und Kallimachos: zur
Geschichte einer Gattung der hellenistiche-römischen Poesie*,
Frankfurt, 1949.
[92] Cf. Richard Büttner, *Porcius Licinius und der literarische
Kreis des Q. Lutatius Catulus*, Leipzig, 1893, and D'Alton 58-62.
[93] Cf. Varro's definition of *Latinitas: est incorrupte loquendi
observatio secundum Romanam linguam* (fr. 41 Wilmanns).
Cf. Norden 183.

century B.C. Greek rhetoricians.[94] They first appear in Latin in the early first century B.C. in the *Rhetorica ad Herennium* (4.11-16). According to Aulus Gellius (6.14.8-10), Rutilius (possibly P. Rutilius Rufus) and Polybius described the three ambassadors of 155 B.C. as representing three styles of speaking. Carneades was violent and rapid, Critolaus clever and polished, Diogenes restrained and serious. The terms grand, middle, and plain are not used here, though Gellius clearly thought they were implied. The difficulty about these terms is that they are not absolutes in any sense.[95] The style of most authors varied with their subjects and the definition of the three labels varied from critic to critic. Perhaps some agreement could be reached about the grand style in extreme cases. The plain style was sometimes supposed to be simple and graceful, but sometimes equated with dialectic and ran the risk of being the absence of style. The middle style was to some an intermediate in ornamentation, to others it included the highly ornamented but characteristically smooth style of Isocrates. Terence was described as an example of the middle style by Varro (Gellius 6.14.6) but modern critics have seen in him principally the plain style. Plain style as applied to poets of the Scipionic circle is thus too vague to mean much. The chief utility of the stylistic characters was in allowing a teacher of rhetoric to show the variety which his students might need and to allow him to contrast qualities of which he approved or disapproved, roughly the way the terms are used by the author of the *Rhetorica ad Herennium* or by Cicero in the *Orator*.

[94] Cf. APG 278-82.
[95] Cf. Fiske, *op.cit.* supra n. 86, 70 and D'Alton 24, who note the problem.

71

Roman Orators of the Late Second Century B.C.

The greatest orator of the second century B.C. after the death of Cato was not Laelius or Scipio, but probably S. Sulpicius Galba, described by Cicero (*Brutus* 82) as the first Roman to aim at ornamentation, to try to charm his audience, or stir their feelings, and to amplify his subject with pathos or commonplaces. Galba was more effective extemporaneously than when judged by his published speeches (*ibid.* 93), but of these at least three were still known a hundred and fifty years later (Livy, *Per.* 49), all relating to his conduct as praetor in Spain. He seems at that time to have made himself the model of the perfidious Roman governor by accepting the surrender of Lusitanians, but subsequently massacring some and selling others into slavery. In 149 B.C. bills were introduced at Rome to undo his actions in so far as possible and perhaps to punish him personally. Cato, who had been a defender of Spaniards since the time of his own service in their country (Cic., *Div. in Caec.* 66), was a leader in the attack. Galba made little attempt at argumentation,[96] but relied on pathos and the feeling of Roman for Roman: with tears running down his face he commended to the care of the Romans his sons and dependents, about perhaps to be orphaned (Cic., *Brutus* 90; Livy, *Per.* 49; Valerius Maximus 8.1. *abs.* 2). The appeal succeeded, perhaps with the help of bribery (Appian, *Spanish Wars* 60) and Galba lived to become consul five years later. His escape had some influence in establishing the permanent *quaestio de repetundis*: though

---

[96] Cicero says (*Brutus* 89) that Galba made no defense, but according to the *Periocha* of Livy 49 he claimed that the Lusitanians were planning to attack him treacherously. What we know about the speech may come chiefly from Cato, cf. N. Scivoletto, "L'oratio *Contra Galbam* e le *Origines* di Catone," *GIF* 14 (1961) 63-68.

extortion does not seem to have been a charge against him, he had clearly made a great deal of money out of his actions (Appian, *ibid.*). His successful appeal to pathos seemed to Cicero (*Brutus* 89) a good indication that an orator who inflamed a judge could accomplish more than one who sought only to instruct. All of Galba's oratory was characterized by violent excitement (*ibid.* 93) and his rhetorical heirs were not his aristocratic friends, but the volatile demagogues.

Cicero (*Brutus* 95) makes M. Aemilius Lepidus Porcina, consul in 137 B.C., the next stage in the development of Latin oratorical style and the first to approach the Greeks in wit and in the use of periodic sentences. He apparently influenced Carbo and Tiberius Gracchus. Carbo is the earliest Roman orator said (*ibid.* 105) to have practiced oratorical exercises, which he did even in his tent while on military campaign (Quint. 10.7.27). One of the surviving fragments (Cic., *De or.* 2.106) seems to show a familiarity with the theory of the *stasis* of a legal action which was the principal obsession of Greek rhetorical theory in the second century B.C. Carbo anticipated orators of the next century like Antonius in his diligent activities as an advocate (*Brutus* 105). In Cicero's *De oratore* (1.40) Scaevola accuses Galba, Aemilius Lepidus Porcina, and Carbo of an utter ignorance of the law, but Scaevola's standards were clearly extreme and the accusation need not be taken at face value. Scribonius Curio was one of the first orators to introduce into a speech a large number of commonplaces, in this case on love, evidence under torture, and rumor. Cicero thought (*Brutus* 122) that they were tolerable at the time, though they seemed trite enough later. The old Roman manner and austere Stoic oratory is best represented in the late second and early first century by P. Rutilius Rufus (consul 105 B.C.) who would not compromise his principles even in his own defense, refused the aid of Antonius and Crassus, and was exiled about 92 B.C. after conviction on a drummed up charge of extortion (*Brutus* 115-16). He achieved immortality by retiring to live in honor among the provincials of Asia, whom he was accused of having fleeced (Val. Max. 2.10.5).[97]

The most important orators of the late second century B.C. were, however, the two brothers, Tiberius and Caius Sempronius Gracchus. With them begins that century of strife, reform, reaction, and war which brought the Roman republic to a close, certainly one of the awesome spectacles of history. Among the many elements which contributed to it were an unyielding traditionalism on the part of some, especially in the senate; a self-ambition on the part of others; a loss of a national sense of being Roman as the empire widened, citizenship was extended to new national groups, and a veneer of Greek culture was glued to Roman life; the waning of a need for solidarity as the last of the great foreign enemies were eliminated; a hesitation to invent, to improve, to speculate, which was endemic to Rome and which also afflicted the culturally exhausted Greeks, and probably many other tragic flaws. In the political changes which may conveniently be labeled the Roman revolution, oratory, now fully acclimated at Rome, initially played a leading role. A series of tribunes of whom the Gracchi, Saturninus, and Livius Drusus are the best known, attempted to use their office to alter the constitution in the direction of more popular government. They relied heavily upon the popular assemblies for support against the oligarchic and conservative senate, and the new oratory was a vital tool in inciting the assemblies to action. But the role of oratory in the Roman revolution steadily de-

[97] Cf. *ORF* 44.3-6, Michel 46-55.

clined as the military might of individual generals rose, and by the age of Caesar, Antony, and Octavian even the greatest Roman orator himself was powerless to control the course of events. In Greece the greatest oratory well known to us is that of the fourth century B.C., but the orators of the fifth century were in fact more significant and influential, though their speeches remained unpublished. Something similar is true in Rome, where the lost oratory of the late second and early first century B.C. probably played the greatest role in moving men's minds. Cicero's speeches down to his exile may be said to belong to the last part of this period, but the majority of his works, like the speeches of Demosthenes, are part of a splendid afterglow.

Special interest attaches to the oratory of the Gracchi because of their important role in Roman history. We have no true fragments of speeches of Tiberius Gracchus, the older of the two, who was tribune in 133 B.C. and whose major achievement was his bill to distribute public land among the urban proletariat. His mother, Cornelia, saw that he was given a Greek education and that he studied with the eloquent Diophanes of Mytilene (Cic., *Brutus* 104). He came under some influence of Greek political as well as rhetorical ideas.[98] Cicero has rather little to say about Tiberius' oratory, though he mentions that speeches survived and that they were distinguished more for their thought than their style (*ibid.*). Plutarch

[98] Cf. Plut., *Tib. Gracchus* 8.4-5; D. R. Dudley, "Blossius of Cumae," *JRS* 31 (1941) 94-99; Truesdell S. Brown, "Greek Influence on Tiberius Gracchus," *CJ* 42 (1946-47) 471-74. Leeman 52ff. probably goes too far in trying to associate philhellenism and popular politics during the next decades. Followers of the senatorial tradition could adopt many features of Greek life and thought, while popular leaders like Marius, Saturninus, and Glaucia remained untouched. Cicero (*De or.* 2.4) says Antonius pretended to be ignorant of Greek learning in order to be more persuasive to the people.

(*Tib. Gracchus* 2.2-5) elaborates an antithesis between the brothers in which Tiberius appears as quiet and sensible, restrained in delivery, with a sweet and subtle power of stealing into the heart. The speeches put in Tiberius' mouth by Plutarch (*Tib. Gracchus* 9.4-5) show a concern with justice or with expediency consistent with justice and honor (cf. Appian, *Civil Wars* 1.9 and 11).

Gaius, who ten years later followed his brother's path to the tribunate and assassination, was perhaps the greater and certainly the more impassioned orator.[99] In Plutarch's antithesis he figures as violent and emotional; his choice of word was colorful; he was the first Roman to adopt a delivery which included striding up and down and tearing his robe from his shoulder. Unintentionally, his anger and voice would rise in fever pitch, and he would lose control over what he was saying: we have reached the period of the demagogue. Feeling that his lack of control was a mistake, when he was going to speak he stationed a servant near him with a pitch pipe to sound if the pitch went beyond predetermined limits and thus to bring him back to a reasonable tone and order without interrupting the speech.[100] The most famous fragment of Gaius, spoken on the last day of his life, shows his emotionalism and according to Cicero (*De or.* 3.214) was so effectively delivered that even his enemies burst into tears: "Where can I flee in my mis-

[99] Cf. N. Haepke, *C. Semproni Gracchi oratoris Romani fragmenta collecta et illustrata*, Munich, 1915.

[100] The fullest account is Cic., *De or.* 3.225; cf. also Plut., *Tib. Gracchus* 2.5. In Dio's account (25.85.2) the servant (Licinius the grammarian?) has become a flute player offering a steady accompaniment. The point seems to have been the pitch and speed, not the maintenance of rhythm. Cf. Büttner, *op.cit.* supra n. 92, 81ff. For another instance of prompting cf. Seneca, *Contr.* 4. *pr.* 8.

ery? Where turn? To the capitol? It reeks with the blood
of my brother. To home? That I may see my mother
wretchedly crying and prostrate?"[101]

Gaius' teacher of rhetoric was Menelaus of Marathus,
whose help he was accused of using in writing his
speeches (Cic., *Brutus* 100). A couple of dozen of these
speeches have left fragments. When in 124 B.C. the senate tried to keep him in Sardinia as quaestor for a third
year, he acted with characteristic resolution and returned
to Rome unexpectedly where he defended his action,
apparently before the censors and also to the people.
Plutarch's account of the speech to the censors (*C. Gracchus* 2.5) agrees closely with the quotations in Aulus
Gellius (15.12) of the speech before the people; perhaps
the two were similar.[102] The line of argument was the
justice of his return, but it took the form of a simple
narrative of his more than adequate services to the state
and a presentation of his virtues of frugality and honesty,
reminiscent of those of Cato. The speech was thus of a
type familiar to the Romans, but it was brilliantly successful. The longest example of Gaius Gracchus' oratory
is a quotation, also preserved by Aulus Gellius (11.10),
from his speech against the Aufeian law. This was a bill
to turn over the recently acquired territory of Phrygia to
King Mithridates of Pontus. Nicomedes of Bithynia
also wanted it, and Gracchus seems to have thought it
ought to be held by Rome. He said in part:

"For however hard you seek, citizens, if you are wise
and honest with yourselves, you will find that none of
us comes forward to speak here without seeking some
reward. All of us who make speeches seek something,
and no one comes before you for any reason other than

---

[101] *ORF* 48.61. On the literary parallels, cf. Max Bonnet, "Le
dilemme de C. Gracchus," *REA* 8 (1906) 40-46.

[102] So Malcovati, *ORF* p. 181.

that he may get something. I myself who am telling you to enlarge your revenues and thus more easily direct your own interests and the state, do not come forward for nothing. The fact is that I seek from you not money, but a good name and honor. Others who come forward to urge that you not pass this law seek not honor from you, but money from Nicomedes; those who speak on behalf of the law, they too seek not a good name from you, but a price and reward for their own pockets from Mithridates. These, however, in the same rank and order of society who keep silent are perhaps the shrewdest, for they receive reward from all and deceive all. Since you think them set apart from these considerations, you bestow on them a good name. But envoys from the kings, since they believe them to be quiet in *their* interests, offer them much entertainment and money, just as in Greece, when a Greek tragedian thought it glorious that a whole talent was given him for one play, Demades, the most eloquent man in the state, is said to have answered him, 'Does it seem remarkable to you that you earn a talent by speaking? I got ten talents from a king for keeping quiet!' So now they too get the greatest reward for their silence."

The frank recognition that men are motivated by self-interest is slightly reminiscent of some of the realistic speeches of the Athenian democracy and is another sign of the acclimatization of Greek argumentation at Rome,[103] though the ethical element remains strong here: Gaius wants the audience to regard himself as superior to others. His choice of an anecdote is a sign of his familiarity with the history of Greek oratory.

[103] Cf. also the passage in *Rhet. ad Her.* 4.49 which has been attributed to C. Gracchus, ORF p. 191.

Prose rhythm was beginning to be sought in later second century oratory. It is not a very conspicuous feature of Gaius' style,[104] but he was regarded as giving more attention to composition than had other orators of the time (Gellius 11.13.2), though Cicero thought (*Brutus* 126) that his works lacked the final touch. Gaius' public career was lived in haste and ended in violence, and it is not surprising that he had little time for the revision that later became a prelude to publication. Leo was doubtless correct[105] in thinking that the speeches were published for practical political ends, much as were Demosthenes' *Olynthiacs* and *Philippics*.

Early Roman oratory means pre-Ciceronian oratory, and it may be said to come to an end with the distinguished group of speakers whom Cicero heard in his youth and who powerfully influenced him. We know them best from the dialogue *De oratore*, in which he represents them discussing the qualities of the ideal orator, and also from the *Brutus*. Cicero's picture of these orators in different works is fundamentally consistent and the fact that in *De oratore* he makes many references to specific incidents in their lives, the places they went, the people they met, and the things they did or said, increases the likelihood that even in that dialogue the portrayal is basically historically valid, though doubtless somewhat idealized. The greatest of the orators whom Cicero heard, and in his opinion the first to equal the Greeks (*Brutus* 138), were the moderate senatorial leaders Crassus and Antonius, and them he makes the central

---

[104] The most commonly cited early example of a rhythm learned from Greek rhetoricians is C. Fannius' *si, Quirites, minas illas* ($- \cup -/- \cup -/- -$), cf. Cic., *De or.* 3.183; Norden 172. In the fragment of C. Gracchus just quoted Leo, *op.cit.* supra n. 1,309, saw Asiatic dichorees.

[105] *Op.cit.* supra n. 1, 307.

characters in *De oratore*. He knew Crassus slightly better, studied in his house, and modeled himself after him (*De or.* 2.2). Third in ability, but far inferior to these two (*Brutus* 173), was L. Marcius Philippus.

Antonius

Marcus Antonius,[106] grandfather of the triumvir Mark Antony, is praised by Cicero for his invention, his arrangement, his memory, and his delivery (*Brutus* 139 and 141), in other words, his ability in all the parts of rhetoric except style. His greatest strength was in establishing belief in a fact in the minds of the audience or in arousing or allaying their suspicion (*Brutus* 144). Consequently, Cicero (*Brutus* 165) thought him more effective in judicial than in deliberative oratory, and with Crassus he became the most popular advocate of his day (*Brutus* 207). He was capable, if sincerely moved himself, of very powerful emotional appeals, as in the peroration of his speech for Manlius Aquilius on trial for extortion, when, so we are told, he not only ripped the toga from the scarred body of the old soldier to exhibit his wounds, as Marius sat sobbing in the first row, but implored the latter's help for his old colleague and evoked the jury's sympathy by calling upon the name "of every god[107] and man, citizen and ally" (*De or.* 2.194-96). This is perhaps only a more elaborate example of the emotional appeals which had been made before, but

[106] Born 143 B.C., consul 99, censor 97, put to death at Marius' order, 87. Cf. Augustus S. Wilkins, *M. Tulli Ciceronis De oratore*, Oxford, 1888, 1.13-17; *R-E* 1.2590-94; M. Krueger, *M. Antonii et L. Licinii Crassi oratorum Romanorum*, Breslau, 1909; Bardon, *op.cit.* supra n. 1, 169-71; Clarke 45-49; *ORF* pp. 221-37; Udo W. Scholz, *Der Redner M. Antonius*, Diss. Erlangen-Nürnberg, 1962; Leeman 58-59; Eric S. Gruen, "M. Antonius and the Trial of the Vestal Virgins," *RhM* 91 (1968) 59-63.

[107] As Cicero does at the end of the last Verrine.

there are other features of Antonius' advocacy which are more remarkable. First of all, unlike many of the earlier Roman orators, he had very little knowledge of law. Scaevola thought that Galba, Lepidus, and Carbo were ignorant of the law (*De or.* 1.40), but Antonius is represented as admitting his ignorance and claiming that he never felt the lack of such knowledge (*De or.* 1.172 and 248).[108] Rhetoric had thus come to seem adequate to deal with whatever challenges were offered, and Antonius, Crassus, and Philippus were regarded as able to accomplish almost anything by sheer eloquence (Cic., *Pro Quinc.* 80). Antonius was widely respected as a man of integrity: at the same time, he was passionately devoted to the interests of his case and client. Once he took on a case he worked as whole-heartedly, and perhaps even unscrupulously, for victory as had Greek logographers, more so in that they only wrote speeches for clients, whereas Antonius delivered them as well. One sign of his attitude was his refusal to publish any of his speeches, so that if taxed, as some orators were,[109] with inconsistency, he could flatly deny the charge whatever its truth (Cic., *Pro Cluentio* 140). "For," says Valerius Maximus (7.3.5), "on behalf of the life of those in danger he was prepared not only to use his eloquence, but to abuse his self-respect."

The best example of Antonius' oratory was his defense of Norbanus in 95 B.C. on a charge of *maiestas*, or treason. In Cicero's account (*De or.* 2.197-201) Antonius admits that all the facts of the case seemed to be against his client, who had acted with wanton violence, and Antonius himself, as a man who had recently been cen-

---

[108] On the separation of law and oratory, cf. Artur Steinwenter, "Rhetorik und römischer Zivilprocess," ZRG 65 (1947), esp. 105-11, and Schulz, *op.cit.* supra n. 9, 54-55.

[109] E.g., Crassus by Brutus, *De or.* 2.223.

sor, was under a cloud with his respectable friends for taking on the defense. Initially his one acceptable excuse was that Norbanus had been quaestor under him in Cilicia, for the Romans liked to think of a governor and quaestor as tied by a permanent loyalty.[110] In the defense, Antonius began[111] with that tie and made no concealment of his fears and doubts of success, but once he had acquired the sympathy of the jury for himself, if not for his client, he went on to his principal argument that the mob scene which had taken place could not be blamed on Norbanus, but was the responsibility of the Roman people at large (*De or.* 2.167), and further that it was in fact merited and just.[112] This he supported by historical examples of civil progress at the expense of disturbances between the nobles and the people: the expulsion of the kings, the creation of the tribunes, the sovereignty of the assembly, the right of summons. But if civil disturbance had so often produced good, surely Norbanus ought not to be charged with a capital crime. The legal question of what constituted *maiestas* Antonius glossed over as briefly as possible (*De or.* 2.201), much as Demosthenes played down the legal technicalities in his speech *On the Crown*. The disturbances had been set off by the prosecution of Caepio who was blamed for a disastrous defeat at Orange, and this gave Antonius an opportunity to expatiate in detail on the sins of Caepio. If anybody had diminished the majesty of Rome, the literal meaning of the charge against Nor-

[110] Cf. Cic., *Div. in Caec.* 61 and L. A. Thompson, "The Relationship between Provincial Quaestors and their Commanders-in-Chief," *Historia* 11 (1962) 339-55.

[111] In reconstructing the structure of the speech it is necessary to take into consideration the observation of Sulpicius, *De or.* 2.202-3.

[112] Antonius perhaps partly modeled his remarks on Carbo's defense of L. Opimius who killed C. Gracchus, cf. *De or.* 2.106-7.

banus, it was Caepio (*De or.* 2.164). This tactic helped
to divert anger from Norbanus to Caepio and his cowardice, and was effective also with the jury who were all
of the equestrian class and as a group hated Caepio for
his earlier proposal to take control of the juries away
from them. The crimes of Caepio also made a good
contrast with the modesty of Antonius himself and his
loyal friendship for Norbanus, to which he reverted at
the end of the speech. It was, all in all, very successful,
as even Norbanus' accuser, Sulpicius Rufus, had to admit (*De or.* 2.202-3), and it secured Norbanus' acquittal.
A moral philosopher or a constitutional historian could
easily find serious objection with the speech which could
well be described as sophistic. That Antonius was able
to produce it shows the degree to which oratory had developed at Rome; that the jury and popular opinion
found it acceptable shows the extent to which factionalism had already weakened Roman traditions of constitutional order and individual responsibility.

Cicero says (*De or.* 1.82) that Antonius had studied
Greek literature, but only late in life and superficially.
His superficiality here is analogous to his indifference to
legal knowledge, but perhaps more Roman, and like
Cato's scorn of Greek, it is perhaps open to the charge
of being something of a pose. Antonius was fearful that
too much Greek learning would render him suspect in
the eyes of juries. Like Cato he wrote a work on oratory:
Cicero (*Brutus* 163) calls it "meager enough" and has
Antonius claim (*De or.* 1.94) that it was published
against his will and that it dealt not with the art of
rhetoric as taught in schools, but with what he himself
had learned in practice (*De or.* 1.208). He seems, however, to be discussing an equivalent to Greek theories of
stasis in the quotation preserved by Quintilian (3.6.44),
though without technical vocabulary, "The matters are

few in number from which all speeches are born: a thing done or not done, a legal right or legal injury, a good thing or a bad one." That is to say, it can be argued in defense of a client that an act was not committed, or that it was done legally, or if it was done, and in violation of law, that it was morally justified, or necessary in some way. The other fragment of the treatise is the celebrated statement that the author had known many who were skilled speakers, but no one yet who was eloquent. Cicero (*De or.* 1.94) has Antonius explain this to mean that he had discovered no one who could "marvelously and magnificently amplify and ornament whatever he wished and who held within his own mind and memory every source of all those things which pertain to speaking." Discussing the matter in the *Orator* (18-19) he says that Antonius thought this achievement "scarcely granted to a god." All things considered, this statement is more important for Cicero's own goal in life and his ideal of the orator than for Antonius' views as seen elsewhere. Probably he meant little more than that every orator in his experience fell short of perfection and could learn something from others, thus justifying the writing of his little treatise.

Crassus

Antonius' slightly younger contemporary and friend, L. Licinius Crassus,[113] makes some contrast with him, though he is not a total antithesis. In Cicero's *De oratore* he is the spokesman for an orator with a wide and deep knowledge of almost all subjects. Although for practical purposes in court he pretended to look down on Greek

---

[113] Born 140 B.C., consul 95, censor 92, died 91. Cf. Wilkins, *op.cit.* supra n. 106, 8-13; Krueger, *op.cit.* supra n. 106; *R-E* 13.252-68; Bardon, *op.cit.* supra n. 1,171-74; Clarke 45-49; *ORF* pp. 237-59; Leeman 59-64.

learning (*De or.* 2.4), in fact he was thoroughly familiar with it and had in his youth not only studied Greek school rhetoric (*De or.* 1.137-47), but in imitation of Carbo had given a good deal of time to practice exercises (*De or.* 1.154-7). One of his teachers was the historian Coelius Antipater (*Brutus* 102), a writer of rather Asianist tastes. Crassus' literary interests were wide; he was an intelligent bystander at the discussions of philosophers and rhetoricians when he visited Greece, he had even read Plato's *Gorgias* with Charmadas the Academic (*De or.* 1.47), and in Asia he had had the instruction of Metrodorus of Scepsis (*De or.* 2.365). Cicero attributes (*Brutus* 143) two qualities to Crassus which Antonius lacked, one a knowledge of law, the other an accurate and elegant, but unaffected (*Brutus* 165) style which associates him with the tradition of *Latinitas*. It is thus not surprising to hear that he aimed at brevity, both in a general sense and in the composition of sentences,[114] and that his delivery was restrained (*Brutus* 158). His published speeches, to Cicero's regret (*De or.* 2.8), were few and brief, chiefly his own *commentarii* it would seem (*Brutus* 160-64), but some quotations from later speeches were also remembered, especially flashes of his famous wit (e.g., *De or.* 2.240-42).[115]

[114] Cicero says (*Brutus* 162) that his periods were contracted and short and that he preferred his composition to fall into short *membra* (Greek *kola*). He cites (*Orator* 223) as typical: *Missos faciant patronos; ipsi prodeant. Cur clandestinis consiliis nos oppugnant? Cur de perfugis nostris copias comparant contra nos?* The first two clauses Cicero calls *incisa* (Greek *kommata*). The other two are *membra* and make up a period. Cicero would have preferred *prodeant ipsi* on the ground that Crassus' word order creates a *senarius*, a verse form common in Roman comedy, but otherwise he admires the structure, including the spondaic *clausula* at the end.

[115] They are said (*De or.* 2.8) to date from his adolescence and (*Orat.* 132) not to be judicial, but neither statement is consistent with the references in the *Brutus*.

85

The most interesting of Crassus' speeches of which we can get much impression is that delivered about 93 B.C. before the centumviral court in the celebrated *causa Curiana*, the case of Manius Curius. An unnamed Roman had drawn a will leaving his estate in the first place to an as yet unborn child, or, if that child should die before coming of age, to Manius Curius, who was possibly a distant relative, possibly only a friend. Such a provision, called *substitutio pupillaris*, was common in Roman wills when a single child might be left an orphan. In this case the testator died almost immediately, but no heir was born, and ten months after the testator's death Curius claimed the estate. M. Coponius, a relative of some sort, objected and engaged the services of Q. Mucius Scaevola, later to be pontifex maximus and not to be confused with his father's cousin, Q. Mucius Scaevola the augur, though both were distinguished for their legal knowledge. Curius obtained Crassus for his advocate. Because of the fame of the advocates the court was thronged with an expectant crowd (*De or.* 1.180), and the proceedings took on something of the appearance of a test case. Scaevola in his speech naturally took the line that the literal requirements of the will had not been fulfilled. It was a matter of applying a formula: *pupillo non nato heredem esse non posse*, "no orphan being born, there could be no heir under the will." This he supported with extensive remarks on testamentary law and ancient formulas, with warnings about the dangers of trying to interpret the intent of a testator and subverting straightforward statement by clever interpretation, with appeals to the legal authority of his own father, and with much stress on the importance of preserving the civil law. The speech was learned, succinct, and polished (*Brutus* 195-97).

Crassus began his reply with a flash of wit, saying that

Scaevola reminded him of a boy who saw a thole pin and immediately wanted to build a whole boat; he had figured out [*excogitare; De or.* 1.243] that people were born before they died, but since here nobody was born, thus nobody died, and he thought by that tiny point to capture the centumviral court (*Brutus* 197). His argument naturally hinged on the intent of the testator, and he had much to say *pro aequo et bono*, "for what was equitable and good." As a Greek rhetorician would have urged, he overwhelmed the opposition with an exhaustive series of arguments and examples (*Brutus* 144-45). At the same time, he insisted that he was not attacking the civil law, but that Scaevola did not understand it, and he adduced learned legal opinions, including that of his father-in-law, Scaevola the augur (Cic., *Pro Caec.* 69). In his refutation of his opponent he proceeded to an ironic *reductio ad absurdum* from which comes the one literal quotation of the speech which we have: "For, Scaevola, if no will is rightly made unless you write it, all of us citizens [Crassus' inclusion of himself seems especially ironic] will come to you tablets in hand; you alone will write everybody's will. What will happen then? When will you have time for public business? Or your legal practice? Or your own affairs? When will you even find time to do nothing? A man does not seem to me to be free who does not sometimes do nothing!" (*De or.* 2.24). Cicero says (*Brutus* 256) that he would prefer to have written one of Crassus' barbs at Scaevola than to take two castles,[116] and Antonius, who of course had little interest in law, thought that the success of the speech was due largely to its humor.

The question of the word versus the intent of a testa-

---

[116] As General Wolfe is supposed to have said that he would rather have written a line of Gray's *Elegy* "than take Quebec tomorrow."

tor, or for that matter, of a law, had surely come to the attention of a Roman court before,[117] but this was perhaps the first case in which the full strength of a clever orator had been brought in direct conflict with the authority of one of the ablest jurisconsults in Rome. It was remarked that the most learned in law of the orators had met and triumphed over the most eloquent of those learned in the law.[118] Nothing perhaps better showed that Latin oratory had reached its maturity. For the history of oratory this is all that needs to be said; for the history of Roman law and the wider intellectual history of antiquity there arises the question to what extent oratory of this sort influenced the development in the law of principles of equity and a relaxation of rigid interpretation of word in favor of intent. No rhetorician of course, as rhetorician, favored one side rather than the other: he simply showed that arguments could be advanced in favor of either. We have some discussion of the topic in Aristotle (*Rhetoric* 1375a25-b25) and we know that it was touched on by Hermagoras, to cite only earlier authorities.[119] In practice an orator had to decide whether

[117] When the direct evidence was equal or unclear, Cato recommended choosing between litigants on the basis of their moral character, cf. Gellius 14.2.21 and 26. The characters of Curius and Coponius do not seem to have been important factors; perhaps they were virtuous nonentities. The extensive discussion of the word vs. the intent in Cicero's *De inv.* (2.122-44) written only a few years later seems to suggest that the topic was a familiar one in Rome.

[118] In *De or.* 1.180 Crassus calls Scaevola both most learned in law of the orators and most eloquent of those learned in law, but later, in *Brutus* 145, he could not resist making an antithesis of the two.

[119] Cf. *APG* 313. There is no good example in Attic oratory of a case involving the intent of a testator; it could have been argued in Isaeus 7, but Thrasyllus' right to call himself a son is

a case was worth undertaking for any reason, which nominally involved a moral decision on his part. In many actual cases there doubtless was something to be said on both sides: very likely Scaevola was sincerely alarmed at what he regarded an attempt to undermine the whole legal system which gave order and security to life in Rome. Crassus was as determined that Curius should not suffer injustice, and he did not believe that the legal system was in any real danger. In another case, however, he upheld a strict interpretation while Antonius argued for equity (Cic., *De or.* 1.178). Once an orator had decided that a case deserved pleading, for whatever reason, it was his duty to find the strongest possible argument and the most effective possible means of presentation. His opponent did likewise, and the court was then, ideally, presented with a fully developed and perfectly expressed statement of all the issues, with all their logical and ethical, institutional and human, individual and collective implications. This is how justice is achieved. Roman law, with its strongly traditional and formulary bias, would probably have taken only slow cognizance of its own injustices if left to itself. But the jurists of the first century B.C., like everybody else, studied rhetoric, and the contentious tradition of the Greeks brought to their attention positions and arguments which they would otherwise have been slow to consider. There was thus a general influence on the history of the law by effective rhetoric, but there was very little specific influence of rhetorical theory or techniques, even of the legalistic looking *stasis* system, on the theory or form of law. The clearest influence was probably in the actual courts

---

preferred. The Greeks thought family ties more important than testamentary intent.

of law, where the standards of acceptable argument,
evidence, or conduct were determined by the orators and
the usually nonprofessional judges, not by the jurisconsults.[120]

The Latin Rhetoricians

In 92 B.C. Crassus was censor with Domitius Ahenobarbus and the two of them, apparently in rare agreement, issued an edict (Suetonius, *De gramm. et rhet.*
25.2; Gellius 15.11.2):

"It has been reported to us that there are men who
have instituted a new kind of study, that youths are
going to school to them, that they have taken for themselves the name 'Latin rhetoricians,' and that young men
are wasting whole days there. Our ancestors arranged
what they wished their children to learn and to what
schools they wished them to go. These new ways, which
are a departure from custom and from the principles of

[120] Cf. Gellius 14.2 and Steinwenter, *op.cit.* supra n. 108. The
basic study alleging that rhetoricians exercised influence on the
development of concepts of equity and intent in Roman law is
Johannes Stroux, "*Summum ius, summa iniuria*," originally published in *Festschrift Speiser-Sarasin*, Leipzig, 1926, but reissued
as a part of *Römische Rechtswissenschaft und Rhetorik*, Potsdam, 1949. The general reaction has been that the claim is interesting, but probably not valid to a significant extent. For discussion cf. Fritz Schulz, *Principles of Roman Law*, Oxford, 1936,
129-31; Steinwenter, *op.cit.* supra n. 108; E. Meyer, "Die
Quaestionen der Rhetorik und die Anfänge juristischer Methodenlehre," ZRG 68 (1951) 30-73; Jolowicz, *op.cit.* supra n. 9,
576-77; Hildegard Kornhardt, "*Summum ius*," Hermes 81 (1953)
77-85; Harry Caplan, *Ad Herennium libri IV* (Loeb), Cambridge, 1954, 90-91; K. Büchner, "*Summum ius, summa iniuria*,"
HJ 73 (1954) 11ff.; J. Santa Cruz, "Die Einfluss der rhetorischen
Theorie der Status auf die römische Jurisprudenz insbesondere
auf die Auslegung der Gesetze und Rechtsgeshäfte," ZRG 75
(1958) 91-115.

our ancestors, neither please nor seem right. Wherefore both to them who hold those schools and to them who are accustomed to go there, it seems necessary to show our opinion: we do not approve."

Censorial disapproval carried a threat to the civil status of anyone who infringed the decree. The text is probably more or less genuine; the circumstances which produced it, however, are not entirely clear.[121] Suetonius goes on to say that rhetoric gradually became more acceptable, which he proves by evidence that Cicero and others declaimed in Latin. From the context it seems likely that he thought objections were against schools which taught rhetorical exercises in Latin.

Practical exercises in speaking were introduced into Rome in the later second century B.C.[122] We have seen that Carbo practiced by imitating judicial speeches, and Crassus imitated him. Suetonius speaking of the early first century (*De gramm. et rhet.* 25.8) mentions analysis of rhetorical texts and exercises in narration, translation, praise and blame, and in the evaluation of customs and myths. Cicero (*Brut.* 309-10) says that in his youth

---

[121] Fridericus Marx, *Incerti auctoris ad C. Herennium libri IV*, Leipzig, 1894, 144-45, thought the text, though not the fact of a decree, was a forgery. Most subsequent students have accepted the text, cf. G. Bloch, "De l'authenticité de l'édit censorial de 92 a.J.C. contre les *rhetores Latini*," *Klio* 3 (1903) 68-73. There is no need to conclude from the text that the Romans had laws establishing formal education along specific patterns. The word translated "arranged" is *instituerunt*, which can apply to the gradual formation of a tradition. On the problem of the *rhetores Latini* cf. Gaston Boissier," Introduction de la rhétorique grecque à Rome," *Mélanges Perrot*, Paris, 1903, 13-16; Corrado Barbagalla, "Stato, scuola, e politica in Roma repubblicana," *RFIC* 38 (1910) 481-514; Michel 64-70.

[122] Cf. Bonner 16-26 and M. L. Clarke, "The Thesis in the Roman Rhetorical Schools of the Republic," *CQ* 1 (1951) 159-66.

91

he let no day pass without oratorical exercises. "I planned and delivered declamations (*commentabar declamitans*), as they are now called, often with Marcus Piso and Quintus Pompeius or with someone else every day, doing it much in Latin but more often in Greek both because the Greek language, with its abundance of stylistic ornaments, gave me the habit of speaking similarly in Latin, and because unless I spoke in Greek I could not be corrected or taught by Greeks, who were the best teachers." The latter point is obviously important in understanding criticism of schools of Latin rhetoric, and the former remained true as well. A century and a half later Quintilian remarks on the importance of studying Greek exercises before Latin (1.1.12).

What exercises were like in the early first century B.C. can probably be inferred from Antonius' contemptuous reference to school exercises in Cicero's *De oratore* (2.100): "A law forbids a foreigner to ascend the wall. He ascends; he drives off the enemy; he is accused. There is nothing difficult in studying such a case. They rightly therefore give no directions for mastering it. This is more or less the form of cases in a school." This exercise is very similar to what later in the century came to be called declamation and specifically to a *controversia*, a declamation in the form of a judicial speech based on specified laws. The *Rhetorica ad Herennium* in discussing problems in judicial oratory uses examples which sound like themes for such exercises. A few of these are drawn from Greek tragedy (e.g., 1.17 and 18), more from fairly practical, though not always Roman, legal situations (e.g., 1.19; 1.23-25). There are also in *Ad Herennium* examples of themes of deliberative oratory, principally drawn from Roman history (e.g., 3.2). It is not specifically said in *Ad Herennium* that these themes

92

are to be used by students as exercises,[123] but the author repeatedly stresses the need for practice and the themes easily could be so used. Suetonius says (*De gramm. et rhet.* 25.9) that early declamations at Rome were drawn from history or from recent legal cases with specific references. The gradual abandonment of specific names and references was perhaps part of a deliberate attempt to make the exercise more universal and to suggest that the arguments might be applicable in a variety of individual cases. Antonius in *De oratore* (2.133ff., esp. 137-45) discusses the evil effects of separating theses and hypotheses and of making hypotheses too concrete. These are, respectively, Greek names for general and specific rhetorical exercises.

Although Carbo and Crassus had practiced exercises, they had done so privately, not in schools. Grammarians had probably taught some aspects of rhetoric in Latin. Opimius, for example, taught first philosophy, then rhetoric, and then grammar before going into exile with Rutilius Rufus in 92 B.C. (Suet., *De gramm. et rhet.* 26), but he may have done so only in private houses, or he may have restricted himself to theory, or his exercises may have been compositions like those of grammarians, not involving memory and delivery and the imitation of full judicial or deliberative speeches. Suetonius says (*De gramm. et rhet.* 25.5-6) that the earliest exercises did not involve debate, then came debates based upon actual occurrences, and finally debates on imaginary incidents. The first person to teach declamatory exercises in Latin, and presumably one of the teachers to whom the censors of 92 objected, was L. Plotius Gallus. Sue-

---

[123] The word *declamatio* appears in *Ad Herennium* (3.20) but refers to delivery rather than exercise in composition. Declamation of course put emphasis on delivery, cf. Cic., *De or.* 1.149.

tonius quotes (*De gramm. et rhet*. 26) a letter of Cicero (who would have been fourteen years old in 92, just the right age for a rhetorical school) saying that he wanted to join the crowds of young men who studied with Plotius Gallus, but was restrained by the authority of very learned men (he must mean Crassus and his friends) who thought that ability could better be nurtured by Greek exercises. This seems to confirm the suspicion that Latin declamation was an important characteristic of the new school (cf. also Quint. 2.4.42).

In *De oratore* (3.93-94), whose dramatic date is 91 B.C., Cicero has Crassus discuss his edict, which he treats as having been successful. His motive, he claims, was not (what had been alleged) that he did not want the abilities of the young to be sharpened, but rather he was afraid that their abilities would be blunted and their *impudentia*, or shameless self-confidence, be confirmed. "For among the Greeks, of whatever sort, I saw in addition to this exercise of the tongue some kind of learning and knowledge worthy of mankind, but these new teachers, I knew, could teach their students nothing but to be bold." The Latin schools had started in the first place, he says, because there was so much to learn in Greek rhetoric that many Romans had forgotten some of it before they learned the rest. The exercises were thus intended to be a short cut to rhetorical technique as a cultural veneer. A somewhat analogous problem may have existed in connection with Latin historical writing (*De legibus* 1.7). Quintilian (2.11.1) tells a story about a professor "of great reputation" who when asked what was a *schema* (figure) and *noema* (thought) said he didn't know but if they had anything to do with the subject they could be found in his declamation. The professor may not have been Plotius Gallus, but the position is similar.

It has often been assumed that Crassus' major concern was political.[124] Plotius Gallus was a friend and supporter of Marius (Cic., *Pro Archia* 20) and he might seem to be running a school for future demagogues. A word like *impudentia* certainly has a political ring when coming from a Roman aristocrat. Crassus' rejection of the notion that he opposes sharpening the wits of the young is probably intended to answer the charge of political motivation, though we need not necessarily believe him. In the context of Roman educational history, however, it is not likely that political considerations played more than a supporting role. Many Romans opposed innovations of any sort, and it was particularly a duty of the censors to make sure that traditions went unchanged. Crassus did his duty as censor, but not in quite the spirit that Cato would have approved, for it was not his desire to prevent change so much as his objection to superficiality that moved him to act, and this view Cato would not have shared. If the picture of Crassus in *De oratore* has validity, he claimed to believe not in a quick acquisition of useful bits of Greek culture, but in a wide and deep familiarity with liberal studies. He thought that the students of the Latin rhetoricians got a sense of education and superiority when in fact they had learned little or nothing. At the same time, this was not a sentiment which he wished to express too publicly, any more than he wished to seem too Greek in his oratory. He thus made use of his position to act within a Roman tradition, but in order to effect a non-Roman purpose.

Crassus was probably right about the Latin rhetoricians. As far as we can see, no theoretical instruction was offered at all, and the practical advantages of declama-

---

[124] Cf. Marx, *op.cit.* supra n. 121, 147-50; R. Pichon, "L'affaire des *rhetores Latini*," REA 6 (1904) 37-41; Gwynn, 58-69; Marrou 252-53; Michel 64-70.

tion were, at least in later years, often exaggerated at Rome. Latin rhetorical exercises were very soon again taught in Latin,[125] but side by side with Greek exercises and with the accompaniment of Greek theory. It may be partly due to Crassus that obsession with declamation, which he saw gaining ground, was put off until the end of the century, when it expanded to fill a vacuum, and that many Romans of the first century B.C. had a good knowledge of Greek literature and theory and an interest in the controversies of the Greek rhetoricians.

Hortensius

Crassus died in 91 B.C., Antonius in 87. Cicero did not begin to speak in public until the late 80's and was not an acknowledged orator of the first rank until his victory over Verres in 70. In the intervening years the greatest Roman orator was Q. Hortensius Hortalus.[126] To the ambitious young Cicero, Hortensius was the rival to be overcome, all the more because of a certain affinity of personality between them (*Brutus* 317). They clashed on several occasions: Hortensius spoke against Cicero's client Quinctius in 81 and was Verres' principal defense lawyer, but after his consulship (69 B.C.) he began to take life easy, and though he initially resented Cicero's election as consul, the two subsequently became good friends (*Brutus* 320-23). They appeared together in several cases, Cicero addressed a protreptic philosophical work to the

---

[125] According to Jerome (*Chronicles* on Olymp. 174.4 = 81 B.C.) Vultacilius Plotus, a learned freedman of Pompey, was a Latin rhetor and opened a school at Rome.

[126] Born 114 B.C., died 50. He wrote amatory poetry (Pliny, *Ep.* 5.3.5), a history of the Marsic war (Vel. Pat. 2.16), and a collection of rhetorical commonplaces (Quint. 2.1.11). Cf. ORF pp. 310-30; R-E 8.2470-81; Bardon, *op.cit.* supra n. 1,217-19; Leeman 92-95; J. Linderski, "Two Speeches of Q. Hortensius: a Contribution to the *Corpus oratorum* of the Roman Republic," *La parola del passato* 16 (1961) 304-11.

unphilosophically minded orator, and he lamented his death with apparent sincerity in the *Brutus.*

We know Hortensius' oratory almost solely from Cicero's descriptions of it and the references to Hortensius in his oration. Written versions of some of Hortensius' speeches were preserved, but they did not seem very impressive to later readers (Quint. 11.3.8), and Hortensius' involvement with Verres and the use of bribery in his defense of Terentius Varro (Ps.-Asconius, *Div. in Caec.* 193 Stangl) have reflected on his professional ethics in the opinion of many students.

Cicero calls Hortensius' style Asianist (*Brutus* 325) and says that the manner seemed appropriate in a young man, but not in later life.[127] This is the first time the term is used of an orator, Greek or Latin, and it is not certain that Hortensius would have understood what it meant. "Asianism" or "Asianist" does not occur in earlier Greek writers nor in *De inventione* or the *Rhetorica ad Herennium* or even in *De oratore* except in one passage (3.43) where *Asiatici* is used in the literal sense of orators from Asia. When Cicero wrote the *Brutus* in 46 B.C. *Asiaticus* was a novelty as a literary term and he is at pains to explain it. Early in the work (51) he speaks of eloquence as having sailed from the Peiraeus to all the islands and all of Asia and there losing the wealth of Attic diction. The language was presumably influenced by local dialects and even by barbaric tongues. But almost immediately the concept is enlarged from one of diction to a whole manner of speaking: "hence come the Asianist orators, not to be despised indeed either for

---

[127] "Asianist" rather than "Asian" or "Asiatic" is the preferable term since many orators so labeled were not from Asia. On the subject in general cf. Norden 126ff., 196ff., and 218-22; U. von Wilamowitz-Moellendorff, "Asianismus und Atticismus," *Hermes* 35 (1900) 1-52; Leeman 65 and 91-111.

quickness or abundance of speech, but too little compressed and too redundant. The Rhodians are sounder and more like Attic orators." Subsequently, in the discussion of Hortensius Cicero (325) explains that there are two kinds of Asianism: one epigrammatic and brilliant (*sententiosum et argutum*) with utterances not so much weighty and serious as neat and charming (*concinnis et venustis*). The other kind is swift and impetuous, characterized not only by a torrent of speech, but by ornamentation and fine language. The first kind is exemplified by the late fourth century historian Timaeus, who was a Sicilian and not an Asiatic, and by two orators of the early first century B.C., Hierocles and Menecles of Alabanda, which is a city in Caria in Asia. As examples of the other kind of Asianism, which Cicero says was current in Asia at the time he was writing, he cites two first century orators from Asia, Aeschylus of Cnidus and Aeschines of Meletus. Hortensius, he says (326), employed both kinds of Asianism.

In speaking of Asianism it is necessary to keep several things in mind. One is that Asianism had no theory and that Asianists were tied together only by imitation or instinct. Another is that the term is not used until the mid-first century B.C. In the *Brutus* Cicero thinks of it as a manner of speech used by certain orators and with certain weaknesses, but in itself it is not a term of reproach. It is, however, the counterpart of Atticism, and among the first century partisans of the latter it fast became a term of reproach. It is less approved already in Cicero's *Orator* (230-31). In the first century B.C. many Romans, like Cicero himself, went to study rhetoric in Asia and pointed or florid oratory, which may well have been common there, could be easily labeled Asianist.

At the same time, Asianism is a convenient term for the more artificial types of Hellenistic prose style, seen not only in writers from Asia, but in other Hellenistic stylists like Timaeus. As such it is a descendant of the artificialities of the sophists. The tinny jingles of Gorgias become the empty rhythmic epigrams of one type, the pompesities of Hippias become the elaborate verbiage of the other. Greek artificiality seems to have reached a peak in the third century B.C. and the orator Hegesias, who indeed did come from Magnesia in Asia, is the classic example of corrupted style (Cic., *Orator* 230; Dion. Hal. *On Lit. Comp.* 18). Such style flourished most with declamation or other oratory or composition which was not intended for practical purposes. Artificiality was probably less marked in the second century than it had been in the third, partly because of the discussions between philosophers and rhetoricians. Thus, Hermagoras does not seem to have been an Asianist and Carneades and Polybius certainly were not. Nor can they be labeled Atticists. Judging from Cicero's remarks, there may have been some revival of florid eloquence among Greek writers in the first century, though late in the century Dionysius of Halicarnassus regarded the battle as won by Atticism.

Asianism in this wider sense influenced Latin prose of the second and first centuries B.C. Some of the signs of such influence have already been remarked. The epigrammatic type may have helped to create that habit of speaking in *membra* which characterized Crassus. The dichoree, or double trochee, was regarded as the favorite Asianist rhythm (*Orator* 212), and we have noted some use of this in Cato and the Gracchi. The Asianists spoke, says Cicero (*Orator* 27), in a wild singing manner, and one is reminded of C. Gracchus on the rostra. Though Cicero connects Hortensius with both types of Asianism as he saw them in retrospect, it would seem that the second or florid type was the more congenial to him. Finally,

99

there can be no doubt that the mannerisms of florid
Asianism, including violent delivery, were exceedingly
conspicuous in the early speeches of Cicero himself.
Though he later came to exercise somewhat greater
stylistic judgment, he had good personal reasons for being gentle in treating inclination to Asianism and especially in regarding it as forgivable in the young.

This chapter has been chiefly an account of the Hellenization of Roman oratory: the appearance of conditions like those of Greek courts which made elaborate
pleadings more appropriate, the introduction of the
custom of publishing speeches reflecting an attitude that
they were an art form, the imitation of Greek techniques
of argumentation and style, signs of a familiarity with
Greek rhetorical theory, early attempts to create Latin
handbooks, the formation of a tradition of *Latinitas*,
the beginning of oratorical exercises, and the growth of
a feeling of the power and potential of oratory to accomplish a political or legal purpose, even when opposed by
the authority of specialized legal learning. Despite this
Hellenization, certain characteristics of Roman oratory
persist. They are matters of emphasis rather than complete departures from the Greek tradition. One is the
role of ethos in Roman oratory. The Greek orator tries
to get the good will and sympathy of his audience. If he
is writing a speech for somebody else he tries to suit the
speech to the speaker, who is often not a particularly
distinguished individual. In many speeches it is enough
if the character of the speaker does not impede the argumentation. Even when the orator has a well-known
Olympian character, as had Pericles or Demosthenes,
the position that something should be done or believed
because the great speaker says so is very rare. It is common in Rome. The orator brings into play all of his

ancestry, his services to the state, his Roman virtues. A good indication of the importance of ethos in Roman litigation is the partition of Cicero's *Pro Murena* (11). Cicero here says that the prosecution has had three parts: criticism of the way of life of the defendant, discussion of his merits for the consulship to which he has been elected, and the allegation of bribery made against him. Instead of remarking that only the last is really relevant, Cicero says that it is the first which ought to be most important, but has been treated by the prosecution as though it were only a legal formality! The most Roman of oratorical forms, the funeral speeches, carried emphasis on ethos the furthest. In political oratory, if a man did not have ancestors to give him a claim to good character he was allowed a good deal of freedom in dilating on his personal virtues. The lack of modesty which we sometimes think of as a peculiar weakness of Cicero was a permanent feature of Roman oratory, especially in the case of a new man like Cicero or Cato.

Aristotle and other Greek rhetoricians regarded pathos as the third ingredient of persuasion in addition to argument and ethos, but they usually thought of ethos and pathos as two quite separate things. As we shall see, the Roman critics come to view them as different degrees of the same thing, and from the point of view of Roman oratory they were quite correct. Much of a Greek speech is often not very emotional, and topics of pity or fear or indignation or whatever are most frequently woven into the epilogue, sometimes into the prooemium. Despite the austerity of the ideal Roman character, we have seen that Roman oratory was emotional almost from the start. This emotion arises from the character of the speaker or his opponent, and though it may reach its greatest intensity at the beginning or the end of a speech, it is often woven into the whole fabric, or more properly speaking, the speech is an expression of that character and never departs from it. This is clear enough in the orations of Cicero;[128] it was certainly true also, though we know them only in fragments, of speeches like Cato's *On His Own Expenses*, or of his censorial speeches, or the oratory of the Gracchi, or Antonius' speech for Norbanus. The best-known early Roman oration, Cato's speech *On Behalf of the Rhodians*, is partially an exception. If it has the ethos of the reasonable senator, it lacks the pathos which usually impelled him to action.[129]

[128] Cf. Friedrich Solmsen, "Cicero's First Speeches: a Rhetorical Analysis," *TAPhA* 69 (1938) 542-56.
[129] On the role of the orator cf. R. Schottlaender, "Der römische Redner und sein Publicum," *WS* 80 (1967) 125-46.

CHAPTER TWO

Cicero's "De Inventione" and the "Rhetorica ad Herennium"

M. Tullius Cicero was born at Arpinum, about seventy-five miles east-southeast of Rome, on January 3, 106 B.C.[1] Details of his early education at Arpinum and Rome are not recorded, but apparently he studied in a grammar school and then, in accordance with Roman custom, was installed in the house of a distinguished friend of the family to continue his studies and to learn to be a Roman by precept and example.[2] Though Cicero's paternal ancestors had not held public office, and he was thus strictly a *novus homo*, the family had important connexions. Cicero, his brother Quintus, his cousins, and an aunt all went to live with no less a person than the orator Crassus sometime in the late nineties. "We learned," Cicero later wrote (*De or.* 2.2), "what Crassus approved and were taught by the teachers whom he employed. In as much as we were at his home we observed often what was clear even to us boys, that he spoke Greek as though it were his native language, and we saw him propound topics for discussion to our teachers and treat other topics himself in his conversations so well that nothing seemed new or unheard of to him." Cicero goes on to say that he met at this time the other great orator of the age, Antonius, and had many talks with him. Not

---

[1] Details of Cicero's life are known principally from his own writings, esp. letters and the *Brutus*, and from Plutarch's life. Cf. works listed below, ch. 3, n. 1. On Cicero's education cf. L. Laurand, *De M. Tulli Ciceronis studiis rhetoricis*, Paris, 1907.

[2] Cicero may have studied grammar with the poet Archias, cf. *Pro. Arch.* 6 and M. L. Clarke, "Cicero at School," *G & R* 15 (1968) 18-22.

only the inspiration for the dialogue of Crassus and Antonius in *De oratore*, but many of Cicero's literary and political values go back to this impressionable time of life. Crassus himself had studied with Metrodorus of Scepsis in Asia (*De or.* 3.75) and had heard Academic and Peripatetic philosophers in Athens, especially Charmadas the Academic with whom he read Plato's *Gorgias* (*De or.* 1.47). He could hardly do that without giving some thought to the nature and functions of the orator, and the picture of him and his interests in *De oratore* thus has considerable historical validity.

We do not know the names of any of the teachers (Cicero uses the plural) employed to instruct Cicero and the other young men in Crassus' house. Cicero also frequented, probably about the same time, the house of Aelius Stilo, who was an enthusiastic Stoic and taught grammar and probably rhetoric, as well as writing orations for others (*Brutus* 206-7). Stilo had spent a year in Rhodes when he accompanied Metellus Numidicus into exile in 100 (Suet., *De gramm.* 3.1) and he thus doubtless knew Apollonius Molon and other Rhodian rhetoricians and had met Stoic philosophers like the young Posidonius, all of whom may have influenced his teaching. At Antonius' house Cicero could have heard Antonius' own discussions of rhetoric and he probably met there the Athenian rhetorician Menedemus, who visited Antonius in Rome about 92 B.C. Menedemus may have helped to develop Cicero's enthusiasm for Demosthenes (*De or.* 1.88). Antonius himself had visited Athens and Rhodes some years earlier; at Athens he had heard the Stoic Mnesarchus and, with more approval, the Academic Charmadas (*De. or.* 1.83-93). In Rhodes he listened to the strongly antiphilosophical rhetorician Apollonius *Malakos* (*De or.* 1.126). In addition to the houses where Cicero went, we know one house where he did *not* go, though he wanted to, the house of Plotius Gallus, the first Latin rhetorician.[3]

Cicero's rhetorical studies were partially interrupted by the Social War of 91-88, though he continued to practice exercises of the sort later known as declamation, to attend the one law court which met, and to hear speakers in the assembly (*Brutus* 304-5). Crassus died suddenly in 91; Antonius and other orators were away, some on service, some in exile. It was a time of troubles. In the year 89, after some brief military experience (*Phil.* 12.27), Cicero turned to the study of law and attended the legal consultations of Q. Mucius Scaevola Augur (*Brutus* 306). In 88 the Academic philosopher Philo arrived from Athens, and Cicero claims that he gave himself up wholly to philosophy (*Brutus* 306). The Academy at the time was skeptical in outlook and used rhetoric as a means of attaining probability, as we have seen illustrated in the speeches of Carneades in Rome in 155 B.C. Cicero seems to have found this view congenial (*Tusc.* 2.9; *De or.* 3.110), though before hearing Philo he had been impressed with Phaedrus the Epicurean (*Ad. fam.* 13.1.2). He perhaps continued rhetorical exercises, but despaired of ever using his skill in the law courts (*Brutus* 306). It was possibly in 87, the year of Antonius' death, that Apollonius Molon first came to Rome from Rhodes; more likely he first visited Rome in 81 and Cicero heard his lectures and had the benefit of his criticism then (*Brutus* 307; 312).[4] Although Molon was himself an active orator and wrote much on rhetoric (Quint. 3.1.16), presumably handbooks and

---

[3] Cicero's fellow students included L. Aelius Tubero (*Pro Ligario* 21) and Varro, cf. Casimiro Kumaniecki, "Cicerone e Varrone: storia di una conoscenza," *Athenaeum* 40 (1962) 221-43.

[4] Cf. A. Gudeman, "Ciceros *Brutus* und die antike Buchpublikation," *BPW* 35 (1915) 574-76.

the like, he was also a teacher of declamatory exercises (*Brutus* 316). Both among philosophers and rhetoricians these were apparently now very popular. The greatest orator of the time, Hortensius, practiced (*Brutus* 302), and Cicero, speaking of the period around 84, says that he did too, partly in Latin, more often in Greek, since the best teachers knew only Greek (*Brutus* 310). Among his companions was M. Pupius Piso, slightly older than himself, of Peripatetic sympathies (*De nat. deo.* 1.16), and possibly his teacher in some sense of the word.[5] Meanwhile Cicero had become interested in Stoicism, especially dialectic, and the philosopher Diodotus had come to live in his house (*Brutus* 309). About 82 B.C. he first began to handle legal cases in court (*Brutus* 311).

The rhetorical and philosophical influences upon young Cicero were thus quite varied. Directly or indirectly he came into touch with the best Roman orators and the most famous Greek rhetoricians: Stoics, Academics, Peripatetics, and Epicureans, Asianists and Rhodians, orators who scorned Greek learning and orators who loved it, teachers of philosophical theses, teachers of declamatory exercises. The rhetorical theory of a young man with this background should be rather eclectic, with perhaps the visible stamp of the most recent teacher he had met.

Sometime in these early years Cicero began an ambitious rhetorical treatise, but while writing the second book he began to lose interest, and he never completed anything beyond the two books which survive as *De inventione*.[6] He himself later (*De or.* 1.5) speaks of the

---

[5] Cf. Pseudo-Sallust, *In Cic.* 2; Asconius, *In Pis.* 14; Marx 79-80.

[6] For translation cf. Harry M. Hubbell, *Cicero: De inventione, De optimo genere oratorum, Topica* (Loeb), Cambridge, 1949. Cicero probably intended the title to be *Rhetoricon libri*, cf.

work as inchoate and crude, based on the notebooks (*commentariola*) of his boyhood or adolescence. A Roman boy put on the toga of manhood at the age of fifteen. That would date the rhetorical notebooks on which the work was based to about 91, and would mean that the rhetorical theory contained in the work was derived from the teachers in Crassus' house, or from others whom Cicero knew at the time. Could Cicero have written *De inventione* at the age of fifteen? He was a precocious and ambitious boy, growing up rapidly under pressure of the times. Indeed, Roman orators as a group were precocious: when Cicero defended Caelius in 56 B.C. the principal prosecuting orator, L. Sempronius Atratinus, was only seventeen. Furthermore, industry was more important in the composition of this particular work than original speculation. It may also be a sign of youth that Cicero planned a very large-scale handbook, but lost interest when he had completed discussion of only one of the five parts of his subject.

Of course Cicero could have written the work later and made use of his earlier notebooks, but his own abilities were rapidly developing and he was constantly meeting new rhetoricians, so it seems unlikely that he would revert after more than a year or two to notebooks which must soon have seemed puerile. This gives us a date ranging from about 91 to about 89 or at the most 88 B.C. There is nothing in *De inventione* which Cicero could not have known at this time, no historical reference to any event later than the nineties.[7] Moreover, the reference cited from the beginning of the first book of *De*

Johannes Tolkiehn, "Der Titel der rhetorischen Jugendschrift Ciceros," *BPW* 38 (1918) 1196-1200.

[7] The latest references are the passages involving Crassus, discussed below. The failure to refer to the law of Drusus in 1.92 suggests a date before 91 B.C., cf. Marx 77.

oratore suggests that that work, Cicero's first attempt to treat rhetoric since *De inventione*, is in some sense a replacement for *De inventione*. This view is confirmed by another passage in the same introduction (1.23) where Cicero says that he is not going to discuss the puerile doctrine of his youth, but rather what he learned from the most eloquent and distinguished men he knew; Greek rhetoric is basic for everybody, and easily available, but he has something greater to describe. He then goes on to the scene in Crassus' villa in Tusculum, shortly before the orator's death in 91, and to the characters of his dialogue, Crassus, Antonius, Mucius Scaevola, Cotta, and others. *De oratore* is an offering to their memory, one made all the more necessary in Cicero's mind by the fact that the work he had earlier produced out of his experiences with them now seemed inadequate and lacking in discussion of the really important topics of rhetoric.

A final, and perhaps decisive, evidence of the date of *De inventione* is the reference to Crassus in the work. It is the general custom of ancient rhetoricians, and of many other ancient writers, not to cite living authors as authorities or even name living authors at all. In an analogous situation (*Pro Roscio Amerino* 47) Cicero explains that people might be annoyed at being named. In a letter to Atticus (13.19.3) he says he has, up until that time, avoided representing living people in his dialogues. In the *Brutus* he does not wish to discuss a living orator, but is persuaded to make a special exception in the case of Caesar (244; 248). In the *Orator*, though he is attacking contemporaries, he never mentions a living man except Brutus to whom he writes. Quintilian will not discuss a living author (10.1.104), except for the special case of the poetry of the emperor Domitian. It is probable that neither Dionysius of Halicarnassus nor Seneca the Elder nor Tacitus in the *Dialogus* cite living

men as examples. When in *De inventione* (1.5) Cicero
lists the Roman orators distinguished for both eloquence
and virtue he mentions only Cato, Laelius, the younger
Scipio, and the Gracchi. At the time he wrote *De oratore*
or at any later time in his life he would unhesitatingly
have added both Crassus and Antonius to the list; he
usually thinks of them together. He even mentions them
in his very first speech, the *Pro Quinctio* of 81 B.C. (section 80). The author of the *Rhetorica ad Herennium*
(4.7), drawing on the same tradition as *De inventione*,
has a similar list of great Roman orators including not
only Cato, the Gracchi, Laelius, Scipio, Galba, Porcina,
but also Crassus and Antonius. We may reasonably conclude that they were all dead, the last one to die being
Antonius who was executed by the Marians in 87. Now
in *De inventione* Cicero does mention Crassus once by
name (2.111). It is a rather odd reference: to Crassus'
speech trying to secure for himself a triumph after a
minor engagement in Gaul in 95. He did not get the
triumph, but the attitude in the household may have
been that he made a good speech. Cicero also alludes
(2.122) to the principles involved in the *causa Curiana*
of around 93, but significantly without mentioning Crassus by name. There is no reference at all to Antonius.
A likely conclusion to be drawn is that the teaching on
which *De inventione* is based dates from a time when
Crassus and Antonius were alive. The fact that Crassus
is mentioned once by name is some evidence that he
had died before Cicero completed the text as we have it.
The absence of any reference to Antonius is evidence
that he was still alive, and that the work was therefore
written before 87. Political considerations are not likely
to have influenced Cicero to omit names or he would
not have written the introduction to the first book at all,
which would have been as offensive to Marius as any

109

mention of Antonius. The tone of this introduction belongs entirely to the late 90's.

Perhaps the most probable picture, therefore, is to imagine Cicero studying in the houses of Crassus and Stilo and others and compiling rhetorical notebooks. Then, after the death of Crassus in 91, when the Social War made normal activities difficult, he decided to write up his notes into a treatise. There was probably some market for such works, since the author of the *Rhetorica ad Herennium* (1.1) says that writers on rhetoric are moved by hope of gain.[8] Cicero himself reports (*Brutus* 305) that he spent his time in this period of his life in study, writing, and exercise in speaking. He probably continued working on the treatise until interrupted by military service or by some other studies such as law with Scaevola or even philosophy with Philo. *De inventione* was thus written between 91 and 89 B.C. and is, as Cicero later claimed, a work of boyhood or adolescence.

Cicero had clearly planned (*De inv.* 2.178, cf. 1.9) to discuss all five parts of rhetoric, as the author of *Ad Herennium* does. Of the part he completed, book one deals with the parts of rhetoric and the kinds of oratory, then (1.10-19) with the four *constitutiones* or basic issues of a speech: question of fact, question of law, question of nature of the act, and question of legal procedure. Constitution seems to have been the term in use at the time to translate the Greek *stasis* since it also appears in *Ad Herennium*, but later writers usually speak of *status*, a more literal translation. The rest of book one (20-109) is taken up with discussion of the parts of an oration. The second book is divided into three main parts devoted to the three kinds of oratory: judicial is

---

[8] Cf. Th. Birt, "Verlag und Schriftstellereinnahmen in Altertum," *RhM* 72 (1917-18) 311-16, esp. 313.

given by far the longest section (2.14-154), as was usual, and is subdivided into accounts of the arguments to be used in each kind of *constitutio* and discussion of cases involving interpretation of written evidence. A shorter discussion of arguments in deliberative speeches follows (2.155-176). The last three sections of the work (2.176-78) are apparently intended to dispose of epideictic oratory.

De inventione exercised considerable influence in the Middle Ages and is partly of interest for that reason.[9] Within the history of classical rhetoric its great significance is that it is the first surviving treatise since Aristotle's *Rhetoric* and the *Rhetorica ad Alexandrum,* both written in the fourth century B.C.: it shows us rhetoric in the early first century as it was studied by Cicero and his friends; it gives us a touchstone in estimating the changes which had come into the subject in 250 years and, in the other direction, in estimating the later rhetorical achievements of Cicero. But in discussing these topics it is equally necessary to make use of the other early first century B.C. Latin treatise, the *Rhetorica ad Herennium,* and a few introductory words should be said about it.

The *Rhetorica ad Herennium*[10] was preserved as the *rhetorica secunda* among the works of Cicero, *De inventione* being the *rhetorica prima.* Renaissance Latinists realized that the *secunda* could not be the work of Cicero, and the claims of Cornificius were put forward

[9] Cf. Wilbur Samuel Howell, *The Rhetoric of Alcuin and Charlemagne,* Princeton, 1941, 22-44. We have commentaries on *De inv.* written in late antiquity by Victorinus (Halm 155-304) and Grillius, cf. Josef Martin, *Grillius. Ein Beitrag zur Geschichte der Rhetorik,* Paderborn, 1927.

[10] Cf. Marx; Clarke 23-37; Caplan (introduction, text, translation, and notes); Leeman 25-42; Gualtiero Calboli, *Rhetorica ad Herennium,* Bologna, 1969 (intr., text, and commentary).

111

on the basis of several references to him in Quintilian's discussion of figures. Though there have been objections to the attribution, on chronological grounds, there remains a good possibility that Cornificius was the author.[11] Since, however, we cannot identify Cornificius further, the attribution is not a great help in interpretation. The author was not a rhetorician, but a young man rather like Cicero, writing an account of rhetoric from his notes. He speaks of "our teacher" (1.18) and of his busy private affairs, of his interest in philosophy (1.1), and of his hope of studying other subjects (3.3; 3.28; 4.17). Maybe he was thinking of putting together an encyclopaedia as Cato had done or Celsus was to do. He writes at Herennius' insistence, and in so doing he is the first of a series of authors who fulfill, or pretend to fulfill, the urgent requests of their friends, relations, or publishers.[12] Cicero's *De oratore*, *Brutus*, and *Orator*, the work of the elder Seneca, and Tacitus' *Dialogus* all employ the same conceit. We cannot identify the addressee, C. Heren-

[11] Kroll accepted the attribution, 1100; Caplan rejects it. It has again been accepted by Gualtiero Calboli, "Cornificiana, 2. L'autore e la tendenze politica della *Rhetorica ad Herennium*," *Atti della Accademia di Bologna Classe di science morali. Memorie* 51-52 (1965) and *op.cit.* supra. n. 9, 3-11. Calboli (6-9) thinks it is possible that *Ad Her.* is a youthful work of the grammarian Cornificius known from Macrobius, *Sat.* 1.9.11 and other sources. The evidence against Cornificius is chiefly the chronological order of Quintilian 3.1.19-21: Cato, Antonius, Cicero, Cornificius, Stertinus, Gallio. But Quintilian is here thinking of Cicero as the author of *De inventione*, and *Ad Herennium* is certainly later than that. Quintilian also refers to Cornificius in 5.10.2; 9.2.27; 9.3.71; 9.3.89; 9.3.91; 9.3.98. These passages mostly relate to figures of speech and it is natural enough for Cornificius to be coupled with other well-known writers on that subject, many of whom were Augustans.

[12] Cf. Tore Janson, "Latin Prose Prefaces: Studies in Literary Conventions," *Acta Universitatis Stockholmienesis* 13 (1964) 27-32.

nius, with much greater certainty than the author. There was a tribune of that name who opposed Sulla in 80 B.C., a C. Herennius was convicted of extortion in the early 70's, and a general of that name fought for Sertorius and was killed in Spain in 75. Possibly they were all the same person.[13] The date of *Ad Herennium* must be determined much as the date of *De inventione*, by the references it contains. The latest seems to be the reference (4.68) to Marius' seventh consulship in 86 B.C., which is certain, though dependent on a textual emendation; there is also (4.31) a reference to the death of Sulpicius in 88. The general political interests seem to be those of the early 80's.[14]

The first two and a half books of *Ad Herennium* cover approximately the same ground as *De inventione*, though the organization and many details differ. There follows a brief discussion of arrangement (3.16-18), then the oldest surviving accounts of delivery (3.19-27) and memory (3.28-40). Book four is entirely devoted to style and was written later than the rest of the work (3.1).

The differences between *De inventione* and the *Rhetorica ad Herennium*, and the much-discussed question of their relationship to each other, may be left aside for the moment while we look at what has been added to the content of rhetorical teaching since the fourth century B.C. and try to specify the common characteristics of rhetorical theory in the early first century as seen in the two earliest surviving Latin studies of rhetoric.

[13] Cf. R-E 8.663-64.
[14] A. E. Douglas, "Clausulae in the *Rhetorica ad Herennium* as Evidence of its Date," *CQ* 10 (1960) 65-78, tries to date the treatise later, arguing our ignorance of first century rhetorical treatises, but as seen below we do know something about the sources of *Ad Herennium* and these point to exactly the same time as do the political references.

Hellenistic Additions to Rhetorical Theory

Early Greek rhetorical handbooks consisted primarily of discussion of the parts of a judicial oration: prooemium, narration, proof, and epilogue were the basic parts, but sometimes others were added. Aristotle regarded this as rather trivial, and in composing his *Rhetoric* concerned himself with means of persuasion, which he divided first into artistic techniques and the use of direct evidence. Artistic techniques were, in turn, divided into proof based on logical argument, on ethos, and on pathos. These are found in three kinds of oratory: deliberative, epideictic, judicial. The logical topics of each were discussed, then ethical and pathetical proof. A final book, however, dealt first with style and then with the old subject of arrangement, which brought in the several parts of an oration with remarks on their use in each kind of oratory.[15] The structure of the *Rhetorica ad Alexandrum*, which was influenced both by Aristotle and by sophists, follows a similar order: materials and proofs, then style, then arrangement, but there is no discussion of ethos or pathos, and the account of arrangement instead of proceeding part by part takes up the kinds of orations one by one and the parts appropriate to each. The two treatises differ in many other ways, but this is roughly the relationship of their structure.[16]

Aristotle's *Rhetoric* exercised influence on his immediate successors like Theophrastus, and his concept of the three kinds of oratory became a permanent part of the tradition (Quint. 3.4.1), but ethical and emotional proof were not usually given full recognition and tend to appear only in discussions of the prooemium or peroration.[17] Apparently the *Rhetoric* was little known at first

---

[15] Cf. APG 103-14.   [16] Cf. APG 114-23.
[17] Cf. Karl Barwick, "Die Gliederung der rhetorischen *Technê* und die Horazische *Epistula ad Pisones*," *Hermes* 57 (1922)

hand during the third and second centuries B.C.: possibly the text was even lost until the rediscovery of Aristotle's library about 82 B.C. (Strabo 13.609), but ancient scholars, including rhetoricians, were prone to get their material from their immediate predecessors and not to consult original or basic materials, so that failure to read the *Rhetoric* does not prove it was not available. When he wrote *De inventione* Cicero knew quite a lot about the contents of the *Rhetoric*, but perhaps had not read the text himself.[18] The rhetoricians, furthermore, remained far more interested in the parts of an oration than Aristotle would have wished, and discuss these in connexion with invention, rather than arrangement. This is the case in both *De inventione* and the *Rhetorica ad Herennium*, where the discussion of invention is basically the approach of pre-Aristotelian rhetoricians: the parts of a judicial speech. The three kinds of orations are defined at the outset, then largely forgotten, while the parts of a judicial speech are discussed, then brought in again for consideration in the latter part of the account of invention. This does not leave much to say about arrangement; *Ad Herennium* devotes three sections to it, mostly on the subject of the best order in which to arrange arguments. Finally, the rhetoricians remained more interested in judicial than in any other kind of oratory. The reason for this was partly tradition, partly the belief that the student was more likely to have use for skill in that branch, especially with the decline of the Greek democracies, and partly the fact that judicial cases tended to fall into regular types and it thus seemed easier to reduce the subject to rule than in the case of deliberative ora-

---

1-43; Friedrich Solmsen, "The Aristotelian Tradition in Ancient Rhetoric," *AJPh* 62 (1941) 35-50, 169-90; *APG* 264-68.

[18] Cf. O. Gigon, "Cicero und Aristoteles," *Hermes* 87 (1959) 143-62, who argues that Cicero did not know our text of Aristotle.

tory with its more flexible form and variable subject. The result was that the rhetoricians put judicial oratory first in their discussion and developed categories applicable to it, and this too is seen in *De inventione* and the *Rhetorica ad Herennium.*

De inventione and the *Rhetorica ad Herennium* and the rhetorical theory of Hellenistic times, whatever they may have gained, have lost something in comparison with Aristotelian rhetoric, especially the recognition that ethos and pathos are forms of persuasion parallel to argument. Furthermore, their discussion of argumentation lacks the clear recognition of the basic importance of the enthymeme and example in proof and is concerned largely with the question of how many parts a full argument should have: must each premise be supported by a reason?[19] (*De inv.* 1.57-76; *Ad Her.* 2.27-30). This approach presumably was thought to have educational value in helping students to understand valid argumentation and is part of the academic emphasis of Hellenistic rhetoric. Indeed, practically all of the additions to rhetorical theory made in Hellenistic times stem from the desire to create an academic discipline, a list which could be memorized, or something which applied to classroom exercises. In planning a speech the student can go down a list, checking off the possibility of using various sections and subsections, topics, arguments, tones of voice, gestures, or figures of speech. The best list is the longest, because it provides for the most eventualities. Thus the four basic parts of an oration become six, with the addition of *partitio* or division, which announces the points to be taken up in the following proof, and refutation, which follows proof. Cicero reports (*De inv.* 1.97) that Hermagoras had added a seventh part, digression, for the sake of amplification just before the peroration. This

19 Cf. Michel 174-75.

116

was intended to contribute to the characterization of the participants or to the background of the case and was occasionally used in court for amplification and in declamation or in epideictic; it might be very charming indeed. In any event it could show off the virtuosity of a speaker, like a cadenza added to a sonata.[20] Each of the six parts of the oration has its subdivisions or categories which the student was supposed to understand and be able to illustrate.

By far the biggest addition in Hellenistic rhetoric was the *stasis* theory of Hermagoras,[21] which characteristically applied satisfactorily only to judicial oratory, though Cicero would extend it to deliberative and demonstrative (*De inv.* 2.12; 2.155). The system presented something of a problem in assimilation into a handbook, already carefully organized: where should *stasis* be discussed? In *De inventione* four kinds of *staseis* are explained early in book one (1.6-19), but much of the discussion is postponed to the section on argumentation in book two after the parts of an oration have been discussed. In *Ad Herennium* the discussion comes as part of the account of proof and refutation (1.18-2.46), in other words, in the middle of the parts of an oration. The point of the theory was to get the student to see clearly the central issue in a case; to a practicing lawyer this probably would be self-evident, but rhetoric was taught to boys of fourteen and fifteen and the system provided them with a series of steps or questions to ask which led them to the heart of the matter and at the same time showed them the very considerable number of kinds of cases which

---

[20] Cf. H. V. Canter, "*Digressio* in the Orations of Cicero," *AJPh* 52 (1931) 351-61; Michel 400-403.

[21] Cf. APG 304-13 for an outline. My interpretation there of parts of *stasis* of quality I find to have been anticipated by Robert Philippson, "Ciceroniana I: *De Inventione*," *Neue Jahrbücher für Philologie* 133 (1886) 417-25.

117

might arise. The complexity of the system probably made it seem all the more worth studying. At the time he wrote *De inventione* Cicero did not have all the points quite clear and seems confused about the *quaestio* and the *firmamentum* (*De inv.* 1.18-19), as becomes obvious when one reads the much more logical account in *Ad Herennium* (1.26). On the other hand, Cicero's arrangement is superior to that of *Ad Herennium*, for *stasis* must be determined before the orator begins to speak and influences the nature of the whole speech: it is not some kind of topic of the proof as the arrangement in *Ad Herennium* suggests (1.18).

Discussion of style takes up nearly half of the *Rhetorica ad Herennium*, showing how attention paid by rhetoricians to style had grown since the fourth century. Here it has been taken out of its normal order, which would have put it between arrangement and delivery, and has been made into a separate book at the end of the work. The author divides the subject into two headings: *genera*, or kinds of style, and *res*, literally materials, but perhaps better represented by Caplan's translation "qualities." *Genera* consist of three *figurae*: *gravis*, grand, based on smooth and elaborate construction with imposing words, *mediocris* or middle, based on more ordinary though not vulgar language, and *adtenuata* or plain, which uses everyday language but possesses a purity suggestive of *Latinitas*. We know that such categories were being defined in the fourth century B.C., especially by Theophrastus, and we have seen that they were current in second century Rome. Although here the basis of distinction between the styles is essentially diction, sentence composition (*verborum constructio*) is mentioned in the definition of the grand style, and in a later passage (4.15) this is taken as the essential difference between styles. A writer should use all three styles within a single work for the sake of variety (4.16), an injunction which modern critics of ancient literature sometimes ignore; we are not told when to use which, but the examples given show that the styles are to be adapted to the subject matter, and probably the author regarded that as obvious. These examples he wrote himself, and they repay study by anyone interested in Latin style.

Res are also three in number (4.17): elegance, composition, and dignity. These are an adaptation of Theophrastus' four virtues of style: purity, clarity, propriety, and ornamentation. Indeed, the whole book in a general way may be said to follow the Theophrastan organization of the subject.[22] "Elegance" contains Theophrastus' "purity" and "clarity" (4.17). It is stated that style must be *commoda*, or *adcommodata*, but there is otherwise no discussion of "propriety" as a virtue. "Composition" and "dignity" are two parts of Theophrastus' "ornamentation." The discussion of composition in *Ad Herennium* is inadequate by almost any standard and is really only a list of faults to avoid: frequent hiatus, excessive alliteration or repetition of the same word or homoeoteleuton, and hyperbaton. The composition of periods, which might have been handled here, is discussed later (4.26-27) among figures of speech, nor is anything here said about rhythm in composition. That is not a subject in which the author has much interest, though he mentions it once when he discusses acceptable uses of hyperbaton as a figure of speech (4.44).

Fourth century writers on style were concerned with diction and with qualities or "virtues" of style. The subject of interest to later writers, including the author of the *Rhetorica ad Herennium*, was increasingly the topic of figures of speech. Here sixty-four figures are defined and illustrated. The word *figura* as a translation of Greek

[22] Cf. APG. 273-82.

schemata has not yet come into use, and the term employed is *exornatio*. In the fourth century B.C. the so-called Gorgianic figures, devices of sound and balance, were the best known, but metaphor and other aspects of diction had been discussed, and a distinction between figures of thought and figures of diction was probably recognized in Hellenistic times.[23] *Ad Herennium* divides figures into those of diction and those of thought. Among the former are ten (4.36-45), including metaphor, which are set apart and correspond to tropes, though no special name is used of them.[24] The distinction between figures of diction and figures of thought is based (4.18) on whether the ornamentation is inherent in the polish of the language or whether it gets its dignity from the subject rather than the words, but the author's assignment of a number of figures seems rather arbitrary.[25] Such a list of figures was not very helpful in training an orator to speak persuasively, though it suggested ways that declamations could be artificially elaborated and decorated. The author makes a regular and conscientious attempt to comment on the use of a figure, for example (4.32), homoeoptoton, homoeoteleuton, and paronomasia:

". . . of which the first consists of words with similar case inflexions, the second of words with similar endings, and

[23] Cf. Demetrius, *On Style* 267, very probably written in the third century, cf. G.M.A. Grube, *A Greek Critic. Demetrius On Style*, Toronto, 1961.

[24] On the names of the figures cf. Henri Bornecque, "La façon de désigner les figures de rhétorique dans le *Rhétorique à Herennius* et dans les ouvrages de rhétorique de Cicéron," *RPh* 8 (1934) 141-58. The term trope seems to be first used in Greek in the second century B.C. by Dionysius Thrax (1) and in a Latin work, but as a Greek word, in Cic., *Brutus* 69.

[25] Quint. 9.3.98 criticizes Cornificius for listing five figures of thought as figures of diction, an objection which applies to *Rhet. ad Her.* Rhetorical questions and antitheses seem misclassified, 4.21-2.

the third of words with similarity of sound. They ought to be used very rarely in real speeches, because it does not seem possible for them to be contrived without labor and expense of effort. A striving for this kind of thing seems better suited to entertainment than to real speeches. The result is that persuasion and dignity and seriousness are reduced by these ornaments of style if they are put together in numbers, and not only is the speaker robbed of authority, but actual harm is also done by a speech of this sort because the figures have a trivial charm and spriteliness, not dignity and beauty. The result is that the grand and beautiful continue to please, but the charming and clever quickly satiate the hearing, which is the most discriminating sense. As a result then, if we use this manner of speech frequently we shall seem to take great pleasure in a childish style; at the same time, if only rarely we employ these adornments and scatter them about with some variety, we shall light up the work skillfully with remarkable brightness."

The *Rhetorica ad Herennium* contains discussion of delivery and of memory, and Cicero (*De inv.* 1.9) lists these as subjects which he planned to treat, though of course he wrote only the account of invention. We know that Aristotle suggested and Theophrastus developed a theory of delivery involving voice and gesture as expressions of the emotions of the speaker.[26] The brief account in Cicero's *Orator* (54-60) is probably based on Theophrastus.[27] The version in *Ad Herennium* is much more matter of fact and detailed, but has similar categories. There is first a division into voice and motion of body, or gesture. Voice is treated in terms of magnitude or volume, stability or rhythm, and flexibility or tone, adaptations of Aristotle's suggestion; and tone is then dis-

[26] Cf. APG 282-84   [27] Cf. Kroll 1075.

cussed (3.23-25) as made up of three styles of speaking: *sermo* or conversation, *contentio* or debate, and *amplificatio*, the grand manner of harangue. The three categories largely correspond to the three kinds of style: plain, middle, and grand. The voice must be appropriate (*idonea*) to each of the styles. Aristotle and Theophrastus had, of course, stressed the importance of propriety. Of movement of the body the author says that it must make what is said more probable. Facial expression is apparently the most important, and here a great deal of variety of sentiment is to be sought. Ordinarily the speaker stands in one place, holds his body straight, and uses his right hand to gesture, but in *sermo* it is possible to incline the shoulders forward as though to bring the face closer to the hearer, in excited debate to walk up and down and even stamp the right foot, and in pathetic amplification to reach the extreme of striking the brow or, what was terribly exciting to a Roman audience (Quint. 11.3.123), of slapping the thigh!

The author of *Ad Herennium* claims that many writers had pointed out the importance of delivery; he is perhaps thinking of the anecdote that Demosthenes, when asked what was first, second, and third most important in speaking had replied "delivery" in each case. The second century B.C. rhetorician Athenaeus, among others, had told the story (Philodemus, *Rhet.* 1.193 Sudhaus) and Cicero repeats it in the *Orator* (56). But the author goes on to say that no one had yet written "carefully" on the subject. He is certainly reflecting, perhaps not accurately, his teacher's lectures, but it is clear from his account that interest in delivery had increased greatly as declamation or something like it came into vogue.[28] The whole account of delivery is rather pedantic and

[28] The word *declamatio* is used in *Rhet. ad Her.* (3.20) only of voice exercises.

like some of the other additions to rhetoric bears the stamp of the schoolmaster. Probably "carefully" refers to something like the subdivisions of the various tones (23-24). Declamation encouraged self-expression in delivery since this made the exercises seem more real on the one hand and on the other allowed an experimentation with techniques which might be carried over into the forum. In real oratory the mannerisms of the schoolroom were doubtless more constrained, but viewing the history of oratory at Rome as a whole we can detect a gradual increase in showy delivery. Earlier, scars and wounds had sometimes been used to move pity, and Galba had brought weeping children into court, but these did not figure in the normal view of what constituted good form. C. Gracchus was the first to pace up and down the rostrum, as we saw in the last chapter, and his backstage piper shows an awareness of aspects of voice control. In the *Brutus* Cicero mentions the delivery of some orators: the restrained delivery of Crassus (158), but the lively manner of Antonius (141) where hands, shoulders, side, foot, stance, pace all suited the words and thoughts. The Asianist orators are said to have had a marked singsong manner (Cic., *Orator* 57). Plotius Gallus, the Latin rhetorician, wrote a work on delivery which contained instructions on arranging the toga (Quint. 11.3.143). In addition to the influence of Theophrastus it is possible that professional actors or teachers of singing exercised some influence on the rhetoricians. The author of *Ad Herennium* suggests consulting them (3.20).

When he turns to memory (3.38) he tells us that many Greeks had written on the subject, even listing images corresponding to a thousand words.[29] In a discus-

---

[29] Cf. APG 318. To the ref. there add *Two-fold Speeches* 9 (Diels-Kranz 290, p. 416).

sion in *De oratore* (2.350-60) Cicero lets Crassus attribute the beginnings of memory systems to Simonides of Ceos[30] and mentions as effective practitioners in his own day the Academic philosopher Charmadas and the rhetorician Metrodorus, both known to Cicero's older friends. Diogenes Laertius' description (7.43) of Stoic rhetoric in the third or early second century B.C. includes delivery, but not memory, and it is thus possible that memory did not become a regular part of rhetorical teaching until perhaps the generation before *Ad Herennium*. As in the case of other parts of rhetoric, it is clear that memory as described in *Ad Herennium* is a system to be taught in the classroom and practiced in exercises. For example, the author recommends (3.39) verbatim memorization, despite its admitted difficulty, primarily as an exercise to strengthen the more important memorization of subject matter. The system described by the author involves the use of *loci*, or backgrounds, and *imagines*, or images.[31] A background is a real place with which the speaker is very familiar. In modern life the route followed every day from home to school or work would often be a good background, though the author warns against choosing one with too much traffic to cause confusion to the mind. The background should be mentally divided into separate scenes, about thirty feet apart, each somewhat different from the other; it will not work very well to try to make a separate scene in each intercolumnar space along a perfectly regular portico. It is, however, very important that the background form a continuous series in the mind, since the speaker may want

[30] Cf. Vittorio d'Agostino, "Simonide inventore della mnemotecnica in Cicerone e in Quintiliano," *RSC* 1 (1952-53) 125-27.

[31] Cf. Frances A. Yates, *The Art of Memory*, London, 1966 and Harry Caplan, "Memoria: Treasure-House of Eloquence," *Of Eloquence. Studies in Ancient and Mediaeval Rhetoric*, Ithaca, 1970, 196-246.

to start at any point. Every fifth scene should be numbered by imagining in it something involving the number, for example a gold hand with five fingers for number five.

This series of backgrounds must be studied and reviewed with great care and can be used again and again just as a wax tablet, we would say a blackboard, can be erased and reused. When something is to be memorized, its subject matter must be divided up into scenes and each salient point represented by a physical object. The author gives as a specific example a scene which sums up the prosecutor's presentation of a charge of poisoning motivated by a desire to get an inheritance: we imagine the testator in bed, the defendant at his side, a cup in one hand, the will in the other, and a purse hanging from his finger. This scene must come to the orator's mind at the point in his speech where he is to deliver a refutation and must be put against the background that would come at that point in his speech.

It is possible, but very much more difficult, to use the system to memorize words. Here our images are not the *meaning* of the words so much as something suggested by their *sounds*. The former have the danger of suggesting synonyms, but the latter get the tongue started. Thus, for an English-speaking reciter, *Arma virumque cano* ought not to be memorized as a pile of arms and a man singing, but, perhaps, an arm cut off at the shoulder, lying on a weir, out of which projects a cannon. It seems likely that an orator might use the verbal system occasionally to remember a particular phrase or sentence, especially one he had trouble getting right, or something like the text of a crucial law where it was necessary to be exact. The whole system was doubtless used much more in schools of declamation and perhaps by young men making their first public appearance than by experienced orators. For the latter, thorough knowledge of the subject and careful observation of the effect on the judges or audience soon became far more important than rote memory, and many great orators did not plan ahead the *words* they would use, though they did ordinarily plan the arrangement and arguments. The published text of a speech was usually not a text which an orator had delivered from memory, but one he wrote out after delivery, often with embellishments and improvements on what he had actually said.

The Sources of *De Inventione* and *Ad Herennium*

De inventione and the *Rhetorica ad Herennium* are both part of the same tradition and have many similarities of doctrine, of terminology—a terminology only partially that standardized in Latin—and of examples, even a few instances of word-for-word correspondence. At the same time there are a number of differences between them, and readers have exercised their ingenuity in trying to specify the relationship of the two works.[32] The most probable picture is as follows:

We have already seen that *De inventione* is probably older than *Ad Herennium* and thus cannot be indebted to it. The author of *Ad Herennium* cannot have known

[32] Cf. Marx 111ff. (no direct common source); G. Herbolzheimer, "Ciceros *Rhetorici libri* und die Lehrschrift des Auctor ad Herennium," *Philologus* 81 (1926) 391-426 (a common Latin source but Cicero used Hermagoras too); Caplan xxv-xxxii (no direct common source); Dieter Matthes, "Hermagoras von Termnos," *Lustrum* 3 (1958) 58ff., esp. 81-100 (two different teachers used a common Latin source); Joachim Adamietz, *Ciceros De inventione und die Rhetorik ad Herennium*, Marburg, 1960; Karl Barwick, "Die Vorrede zum zweiten Buch der rhetorischen Jugendschrift Ciceros und zum vierten Buch des Auctor ad Herennium," *Philologus* 105 (1961) 307-14 and "Probleme in den *Rhet. LL.* Ciceros und der *Rhetorik* des sogennanten Auctor ad Herennium," *Philologus* 109 (1965) 57-74; Calboli, *op.cit.* supra n. 9, 25-29.

the text of *De inventione* since he claims (1.16) to be the first to think out (*excogitavimus*) the use of *insinuatio*, or the subtle introduction in three occasions, but the doctrine appears substantially in Cicero (1.23).[33] All the author need be understood to mean is that as far as he knows he is the first to write a full account: his teacher presumably had suggested the idea. Since *De inventione* is incomplete, it probably was not published at the time and was doubtless for years known only to Cicero's brother Quintus (*De or.* 1.5) and a few others. But this particular doctrine is not known otherwise and is therefore evidence that both works are derived from a common source, probably an oral source. Other evidence is the verbal similarity in the definitions of the kinds of oratory (*De inv.* 1.7; *Ad Her.* 1.2) or the parts of rhetoric (*De inv.* 1.9; *Ad Her.* 1.3.), the fact that both writers discuss narrative exercises in their remarks on the *narratio* (*De inv.* 1.27; *Ad Her.* 1.12-13), the use of similar examples from Greek mythology (*De inv.* 1.31; *Ad Her.* 1.17), Greek philosophy (*De inv.* 1.80; *Ad Her.* 2.32), and Roman history (*De inv.* 1.80; *Ad Her.* 2.33), the quotation of the same proverb from Apollonius[34] at the end of the discussion of the peroration, and considerable similarity in the categories of exordium, narration, partition, and peroration. In addition to some important differences in substance and viewpoint, which we will shortly discuss, and differences resulting from the greater

[33] In *Ad Herennium* there are three occasions (*tempora*) for *insinuatio*; in Cicero the hostility it counteracts comes from three causes (*causae*). On the history of the concept cf. E. W. Bower, "Epodos and *insinuatio* in Greek and Latin Rhetoric," *CQ* 52 (1958) 224-30.
[34] Presumably Apollonius *Malakos*. The saying may have originated with Euripides, cf. G. D. Kellogg, "A Study of a Proverb Attributed to the Rhetor Apollonius," *AJPh* 28 (1907) 301-10. Cf. also Karl Aulitzky, "Apsines, περὶ ἐλέου," *WS* 39 (1917) 26-49.

scale but only partial coverage of *De inventione*, there are numerous minor differences in terminology. For example, both authors teach that a speech ordinarily consists of six parts. The parts all correspond and four of the names correspond, but what Cicero calls the *partitio* is known as *divisio* in *Ad Herennium*, and Cicero's *reprehensio* is the other author's *confutatio* (*De inv.* 1.19; *Ad Her.* 1.4). The common source of the two authors was apparently not a treatise, but written notes of the lectures of a teacher, for Cicero speaks of his notebooks (*De or.* 1.5) and the other author says "our teacher thought that . . ." (1.18). Thus, some small differences may come from the inability of the student to record exactly the words of the master, or all that he said, but some word-for-word similarities are possible. Furthermore, there is no reason to think that the two writers studied with their common teacher at the same time; indeed, it is likely that Cicero was some years ahead. The teacher might have added examples from recent events to keep his classes interesting, and he might have changed his mind on some subjects or terms but on other topics delivered verbatim lectures. Cicero recognizes four *constitutiones* along the usual lines of Hermagoras' *staseis*, but the author of *Ad Herennium* specifically says (1.18) that his teacher thought two of the categories could be combined into one. He may only recently have come to that decision, just as Quintilian later changed his views of *status*. Also we cannot rule out, especially in the case of Cicero who clearly had a variety of teachers, the use of a technical term recommended to him by some authority other than the common teacher.

We do not know who this teacher was, but he was probably one of the persons employed by Crassus. He cannot have been Antonius, for one reason because Antonius' three kinds of *staseis* were *factum, non factum*;

ius, iniuria; bonum, malum (Quint. 3.6.45).[35] Cicero, however, has four issues, and *Ad Herennium* (1.24) joins *ius* and *bonum* together into the *constitutio juridicalis*, as Quintilian says writers after Antonius did. The author of *Ad Herennium* is aware of his agreements or disagreements with other sources (1.1; 1.16), but does not claim, as Cicero does, to have drawn on a variety of sources. We may guess that his work, with the exception to be discussed below, represents the doctrines of a single teacher with few modifications. This teacher's source was perhaps one or more Greek handbooks, or the doctrines of *his* teacher. The use of a phrase which Cicero attributes to Apollonius suggests Rhodes, and the example of brevity (4.68) has a Rhodian color to it.[36] Philosophical or political influences on the *Rhetorica ad Herennium*, either directly or through the teacher, have been seen by some critics, but they are not so clear as they have been represented. The author expresses his great interest in philosophy (1.1; 4.69), but he does not indicate to what school he adheres. Compared to Cicero he has very little interest in dialectic, which would seem to rule out Stoicism. Epicurean sentiment has been seen in a few references (2.34; 4.24) and especially in the objections to amphibolies (2.15),[37] but the author is by no means a doctrinaire Epicurean, who would have had little use for rhetoric or would have accepted only an art of epideictic.[38] The political influences are not certain either; a number of examples of technique reflect the

[35] Quintilian's passage does not mean that Antonius had a school or cult of followers, though he certainly influenced Cicero's tastes and point of view. More has been claimed, cf. Rudolf Kroehnert, *De rhetoricis ad Herennium*, Koenigsberg, 1873.
[36] Cf. Caplan 404.
[37] Cf. Marx 83-84; Caplan xxv.
[38] Cf. APG 300-301.

popular side, but there are examples from the senatorial side too.[39]

Of all the passages in *Ad Herennium* which relate to its sources and to contemporary rhetoric, the most interesting is the long introduction to the fourth book, the book on style. This introduction is an attack on what the author calls (4.1) the "Greek" custom of selecting examples from earlier authors rather than coining examples as needed. The author had earlier betrayed antipathy to Greek rhetoricians when he remarked (1.1) that he was passing over some topics which Greek writers included "for the sake of their inane vanity." They are, he claims, fond of showing their learning and of discussing things that have no practical significance but make the subject seem more difficult. It is, of course, a common pose among rhetoricians to claim practicality, and contempt for Greeks was acceptable in many Roman circles, even to Antonius. Throughout the *Rhetorica ad Herennium* no Greek writer, orator or rhetorician, not even Aristotle or Hermagoras, is mentioned by name, though some examples are clearly Greek in origin. In the first three books Roman poets like Plautus, Ennius, Pacuvius, and Accius or orators like Cato, the Gracchi, Crassus, and Antonius are mentioned. In this preface to book four it is admitted that the Greeks have great prestige, but their arguments in favor of selecting rather than coining examples can be refuted (4.4): the Greeks claim that they want to be modest, but it is no more immodest to coin an example than to state a precept (4.4). Examples are not witnesses to the credibility of the rules, which might suggest seeking high authority, but ways of making clear what has been said. Choosing examples may be laborious, but labor is no proof of art, and if it is a sign of artistic ability

[39] Cf. 1.21; 2.17; 4.12; 4.38; 4.45; Caplan xxiv.

to recognize what is artistically written, how much better it is to be able to write artistically (4.7). Choosing examples is furthermore bad pedagogy (4.7); an example ought to be a demonstration of the writer's art (4.9); the coined examples are clearer (4.10), and the author himself welcomes the opportunity for elegant composition which the examples afford.

Probably the author's comments should not be pushed much beyond what he expressly says: he complains (4.5) that if borrowed *examples* are removed, the rhetoricians would have nothing left to claim as their own, but that is not an attack on the view stated, for example, by Cicero in *De inventione* (1.4), that a writer on rhetoric should gather the best *precepts* where he finds them. He implies that the rhetoricians who select examples are incapable of writing their own, but this is not necessarily an attack on Hermagoras,[40] though Cicero describes him (*De inv.* 1.8) as not able to speak in accordance with art. Finally, his criticism of Greek rhetoricians does not necessarily associate him with the school of the *rhetores Latini*, for he is certainly interested in rhetorical theory and philosophical background, and they probably were not. The common teacher of the author and Cicero could hardly be one of these Latin rhetoricians since Cicero was not allowed to associate with them. The attitude toward the Greeks is much that which Crassus or Antonius took in public.

On the other hand, it does seem just to associate the desire to collect rather than coin examples with a stage of classicism, which had gradually been developing since the late fourth century B.C.[41] Classicism is the view that

[40] As claimed by Barwick (1961), *op.cit.* supra n. 32 (1961).
[41] Some signs of it are already evident in Theophrastus, cf. APG 280-81.

literary excellence reached its peak at a certain time in the past and can best be approximated by the imitation of certain approved models. The author approved of imitation (1.3) as constituting, with theory and practice, the common triad of rhetorical education, but he disapproved of anything that might inhibit the student's hopes, especially of any implication that all excellence cannot be attained by one person (4.7-8). Thus he objects especially to choosing examples from a variety of sources. The author's objection to quoted examples is not original with himself; it seems to come from a Greek source since there are references to Greek athletes (4.4), Greek sculptors, and Greek myths (4.9), which is not the author's ordinary style of ornamentation. Almost certainly the theory did not come from the person we have been calling "the teacher," who had used examples borrowed from all kinds of sources. His earlier pupil, Cicero, is slightly apologetic (*De inv.* 2.118) for introducing a coined example, and if the theory came from the teacher we would expect it to be applied throughout the work, not just in the fourth book, which we know the author wrote last and separately. The length of the argument is also a sign that it is a special hobby of the author.

In what immediately follows the author keeps to this theory; he coins rather striking examples of the three characters of style in their good and in their vitiated forms (4.12-16). There are similarities to ideas in other authors, but this is not a major objection. An example of hiatus is apparently coined also (4.18), but then the author announces that nothing prevents him from using examples from others in illustrating *faults*, and he proceeds to quarry Ennius and Coelius Antipater. This is the only qualification he makes, and we should expect the examples through the rest of the book to be his own work. Some discussions of *Ad Herennium* have represented the author as an outright liar,[42] but he keeps to his theory as he understood it. No example of an acceptable adornment of style is cited anywhere in book four which can be proved to be taken verbatim from an earlier writer. On the other hand, the author has to get the subject matter of his examples from somewhere, and it is impossible to expect that they would have no relation to any history or literature. A number of them are translations or adaptations from Greek, especially from Demosthenes' *On the Crown*,[43] without any acknowledgment; the author certainly makes more use of Greek rhetoric than he admits, but Cato, Crassus, and Antonius, sometimes even Cicero, do the same. A few of the Greek examples must have been pretty obviously that to many Romans: *cuius ore sermo melle dulcior profluebat* (4.44) can hardly be anything but Homer's description of the speech of Nestor (*Iliad* 1.249), and "esse oportet ut vivas, non vivere ut edas" (4.39), "One ought to eat to live, not to live to eat," was commonly attributed to Socrates. But the author probably would excuse himself on the ground that the Latin expression of these words is his own, and in fact the versions do not agree word for word with other translations of the same lines.[44] The author has, of course, tried to bring out especially clearly the aspect of an example which illustrates his point. Sometimes he has adopted material from Latin sources,

---

[42] Cf. Marx 112ff.; Caplan xxx-xxxii, is more reasonable.

[43] Among examples pointed out by Caplan are 4.23;34;35; 41;55.

[44] Cicero, for example, says (*De sen.* 3) *etenim ex eius lingua melle dulcior fluebat oratio*. For the other line see Quint. 9.3.85 (also Isidore 2.21.11) and Gellius 19.2.7 (also Macrobius 2.8.16).

but not the exact words; one illustration of repetition (4.19) is based on words of Crassus (Cic., *De or.* 2.226), but considerably outdoes Crassus. Quintilian and other later authors use a few of the examples in *Ad Herennium*, and Quintilian sometimes attributes these to "Cornificius." It is possible to argue that Cornificius is a later writer who got them from a source from which the author of *Ad Herennium* had deliberately stolen them,[45] but this is assuming the author guilty of misrepresentation on highly circumstantial evidence, and a simpler explanation is that the author is himself Cornificius.

Once the probable sources of the *Rhetorica ad Herennium* have been established it is possible to see more clearly the nature of the composition of *De inventione*. Cicero represents himself (2.4) as following in the tradition of Aristotle (2.6) or Hermagoras (1.8) who compiled rhetorical treatises out of a variety of sources. One of these sources was the teacher with whom the author of the *Rhetorica ad Herennium* also studied. Can we identify the source of any of the other material? In a comparison of *De inventione* and those parts of the *Rhetorica ad Herennium* which relate to invention, it becomes evident that there is no considerable part of *Ad Herennium* which lacks a counterpart in *De inventione*, but there are a number of extended passages in *De inventione* which are not found in *Ad Herennium*: the prefaces to books one and two, the discussion of general and special questions (1.8), the account of genus and species in the section on partition, the account of attributes of persons and of action and the discussion of

---

[45] Cf. Douglas, *op.cit.* supra n. 13, who tries to show that the examples do not show the author's usual prose rhythms. But translation and the need to create special effects influence choice and order of words and thus rhythm, which thus represents varying degrees of compromise with the author's own tastes. Some examples are perhaps adaptations of those cited by the "teacher."

induction in the section on proof, the section on the digression, and some parts of the discussion of *stasis*.[46]

In the discussion both of general and special questions and of the digression Cicero expressly disagrees with Hermagoras. These topics might have been discussed by "the teacher" and omitted by the author of *Ad Herennium* as irrelevant and unnecessary and because he does not discuss earlier authorities. In the case of general questions Cicero criticizes Hermagoras for expecting the orator to deal with such philosophical and scientific questions as the shape of the world and the size of the sun, but our other evidence is that Hermagoras in fact had more general, largely ethical and political, topics in mind,[47] and this suggests that Cicero misunderstood Hermagoras or knew him at second hand. In the same section he certainly wants to give the impression that he is familiar with the contents, structure, and style of Hermagoras' writing, but he may have read it only hastily or in parts.

Hermagoras cannot be the major source of the material that does not come from the teacher. Most of that material has one striking characteristic: it is philosophical and chiefly logical or dialectical. Cicero himself twice (1.33; 1.77) specifically points out that he is drawing on philosophical sources to augment rhetorical theory and in a third passage (1.57) seems to mean much the same thing. He does not identify the nature of this philosophy, but there is no reasonable doubt that it is Stoic. In the case of the preface to the first book, which deals with the relation of philosophy and eloquence, the subject was of interest to Academics and Peripatetics as well as Stoics, but Cicero's account goes on to describe the Stoic wise man, who gave the arts to the world and set

---

[46] The two accounts of deduction also differ greatly.
[47] Cf. APG 305.

man upon the course of progress. The Stoic doctrine of the identity of virtues is also present. Posidonius has been suggested as a source for this view,[48] but since Cicero did not meet Posidonius until about 78 B.C., and we know that *De inventione* was written long before that, Cicero could not have gotten the idea from him in person. In fact, the basic view was probably common to most Stoics, for something like it had been taught by Mnesarchus in the late second century and had impressed Antonius (*De or.* 1.83). The Stoics were also more interested in dialectic than were any of the other Hellenistic schools. Cicero says (*Orator* 115) that an orator should emulate either the dialectic of Aristotle or of Chrysippus the Stoic, and his discussions of such topics as genus and species or logical proof can well come from the Stoics. In the latter case it is especially interesting to note that whereas the *Rhetorica ad Herennium* discusses only deduction, Cicero discusses both induction and deduction and describes a truly syllogistic argument of major premise, supporting reason, minor premise, supporting reason, and conclusion, and this may well be Stoic. The author of the *Rhetorica ad Herennium* (2.16) objected strongly to the study of verbal ambiguities or amphibolies, which were especially interesting to Stoics, but Cicero does not betray this animosity (2.116-21).[49] He always retained an interest in dialectic and it may have been encouraged by Antonius (*De or.* 2.111). In the discussion of deliberative oratory, both Cicero (*De inv.* 2.157-76) and the author of *Ad Heren-*

[48] Cf. Alain Michel, "Un type d'argumentation philosophique dans les discours de Cicéron," *REL* 35 (1957) 46-47. In *Rhétorique et philosophie*, 183 and note 115, Michel claims that the theory of hypothetical syllogism in *De inv.* 1.65-66 is also Stoic.

[49] Cf. Dion. Hal., *De comp. verb.* 4; Gellius 11.12; Caplan 86-87.

nium draw on essentially Stoic materials, but Cicero's account is both much longer and more philosophical.[50] Antonius has been mentioned as perhaps encouraging Cicero's interest in dialectic, but it is difficult to imagine Antonius teaching Cicero Stoic philosophy. In the late 80's Cicero studied dialectic with Diodotus, but on the basis of the other evidence that is too late for the composition of *De inventione*. In the late 90's we know of only one person who was an enthusiastic Stoic teacher and whom Cicero claims to have known well. He happens also to have been interested in oratory. This is Aelius Stilo. By process of elimination it thus seems possible that the "philosophic" material in *De inventione* either came directly from Stilo or from books he recommended to Cicero. Cicero's teacher of rhetoric in Crassus' house was apparently not sympathetic to dialectic and impressed that view on the author of *Ad Herennium*, a young man otherwise addicted to philosophy, but his lectures on deliberative oratory did show some influence of Stoic ethics. There was, of course, a great deal of eclecticism, overlap, and interchange of ideas among the various rhetoricians.

When he composed *De inventione* Cicero did not use his knowledge of rhetoric to write about philosophy, but he used his knowledge of philosophy to enlarge and

[50] Cf. W. Kroll, "Rhetorica V: Zur Frage des philosophischen Einfluss," *Philologus* 44 (1935) 206-15 and R-E Suppl. 7.1100-1101. It is sometimes alleged, e.g. Marx and Leeman 92, that *De inv.* shows Peripatetic influences. Contemporary Peripatetic rhetoric had few distinguishing features; similarities to Aristotle and Theophrastus exist, but do not prove Cicero was using a "Peripatetic" source directly, cf. 1.61. In 2.8 he notes the existence of two schools of rhetoric in the 4th cent. B.C., that of Aristotle and that of Isocrates, now fused into one tradition. Cf. Karl Barwick, "Probleme in den *Rhet. LL.* Ciceros und der Rhetorik des sogenannten Auctor ad Herennium," *Philologus* 109 (1965) 57-74.

possibly to deepen his account of rhetoric. This point of view was always congenial to him and reappears especially in *De oratore* where he is able to give it a much more mature expression. It has already been suggested that one of the purposes of *De oratore* was to replace *De inventione*. The composition of *De inventione* and of the *Rhetorica ad Herennium*, both works of considerable labor, is clear indication of the seriousness with which Romans regarded rhetorical theory in the early first century b.c. Education was thoroughly dominated by the discipline of rhetoric: grammar prepared for it, law and philosophy might give it background or a capstone. The position of rhetoric, of course, came from its claim to be practical, to prepare for the forum, especially for the law courts. How closely did an actual speech reflect the rhetorical theory of the time?[51]

As an example, we may consider briefly Cicero's earliest surviving speech, *Pro Quinctio*,[52] said (Gellius 15.28.3) to have been delivered in 81 b.c. The case involved a dispute between a certain Quinctius and Naevius, his late brother's business partner in a ranch in Gaul. Naevius had influential friends and the great orator Hortensius on his side; there were also some political implications involved (69-70),[53] but rhetorically the case is remarkable mostly for the fact that the young advocate for Quinctius happened to become the greatest Roman orator.

[51] Cf. Friedrich Solmsen, "Cicero's First Speeches, A Rhetorical Analysis," *TAPhA* 69 (1938) 542-56; Leeman 91-92. For detailed exposition of the theoretical system of classical rhetoric cf. Volkmann and Lausberg.

[52] Cf. Norden 225ff.

[53] Cf. E. Ciaceri, *Cicerone e i suoi tempi*, Milan, 1926-30, 1.22-23 and Richard V. Desrosiers, "The Reputation and Political Influence of Lucius Cornelius Sulla in The Roman Republic," Dissertation, Univ. of North Carolina, Chapel Hill, 1969, 15-26.

The speech falls into five very clearly marked divisions: first (1-10) an exordium designed primarily to make the judge, C. Aquilius, well disposed. Good will, according to *De inventione* (1.22), is to be had from the person of the speaker, the opponent, the judges, and the case. The theory was Greek and since a Greek litigant ordinarily spoke in his own person, it does not recognize the fact that a Roman advocate could speak both of himself and of his client, one of many ways in which academic rhetoric failed to consider actual court conditions at Rome.[54] Cicero writes academic rhetorical theory, but when he pleads he utilizes every opportunity to win his case. Thus he seeks good will by stressing his own difficulties in speaking, without, so he claims, adequate preparation and faced by the eloquence of Hortensius and the powerful influence of Naevius, and also by presenting his client "affected and afflicted by so many and so great difficulties" (10). The opponent similarly consists of Naevius and his advocates, and Cicero has something to say against the cupidity of the one and the power of the others. Nor does he forget (5) the honesty and responsibility of the judge and his distinguished board of advisers: they will not let influence prevail over truth. There was a kind of necessary etiquette which could not be dropped without dropping also all sign of good breeding. The case itself furnishes a topic for appeal in that Quinctius, who is logically the defendant in the trial, has been forced into a challenge to Naevius' right to seize his property and thus Cicero must speak first (8). Cicero seems to have regarded this exordium as coming under the category of a *causa admirabilis* as described in *De inventione* (1.21), a difficult case, which could yet be handled without *insinuatio*, for there is no question of

[54] Cf. George Kennedy, "The Rhetoric of Advocacy in Greece and Rome," *AJPh* 89 (1968) 428-36.

the case being scandalous or of the judge having been won over by a previous speaker or of being weary. Cicero does not attempt to make the judge attentive or receptive as described in De inventione (1.23); presumably these qualities in him are to be assumed. As required in De inventione (1.25) the language of the exordium may be said to have much seriousness and to aim at dignity rather than brilliance: though these are rather subjective terms, there certainly is nothing either flippant or clever in this part of the speech.

Cicero next promises to make clear the whole case, and the narration begins (11-34). It observes the requirements for brevity, clarity, and credibility (De inv. 1.28-29). Major events emerge in order, but all steps leading to each are not catalogued in painful detail. Credibility was thought to come, among other ways, from the presentation of the characters of the participants: psychological credibility, in other words. Quinctius and Naevius emerge in some depth, antithetical, but possible. In the narrative exercises of the schools Cicero says (De inv. 1.27) that use can be made of conversation, and this is here brought over into the narration of an actual speech, so that we see the polite Quinctius and the arrogant Naevius talking to each other (19).

Next comes the partition (34-36) in which Cicero follows the second of the two types described in De inventione (1.31): a methodical presentation of what the orator intends to discuss. According to the Rhetorica ad Herennium (1.17) there should not be more than three points, and Cicero has three. As a matter of fact, he makes fun of his opponent Hortensius for always having three.

There then follows the proof (37-85) taking up each of the three points one by one. In order to keep the structure clear we will leave aside the techniques of argumentation for the moment. There is no separate part of the speech constituting a refutation, as *De inventione* implies (1.78-90) should regularly be the case, but this is because Cicero is speaking first and has nothing to refute. He does try in the proof to anticipate what Hortensius will say and answer it (63).[55] Nor is there any real digression, but there is a passage (77-80) in which Cicero breaks the continuity of what he is saying to take a new start and revive the judge's interest.

The peroration, according to *De inventione* (1.98-109), should consist first of a recapitulation or summary. This Cicero has in the simplest and most straightforward form (85-90), which *De inventione* warns can become boring, and does. Then there is supposed to be the *indignatio*, or amplification of the emotional topics suitable to the case, designed to rouse hatred against the opponent, and the *conquestio*, or appeal to pity on behalf of the client. Although *De inventione* does not say so, in practice *indignatio* is most appropriate for a plaintiff or prosecutor, *conquestio* for a defendant, and it is only *conquestio* that is employed in the *Pro Quinctio* (91-99). The techniques employed do not well illustrate the fifteen commonplaces listed in *De inventione* (1.106-9). In the speech Cicero's points are his confidence in the judges; the affecting contrast between rustic frugality on the one hand and luxury and license on the other, which has been his theme throughout the speech, between honest simplicity and influential debauchery; the greatness of Quinctius' danger. There is a series of parallel comparisons: "It is wretched to be thrust out of one's own property, it is more wretched to be thrust out unjustly; it is bitter . . . it is more bitter; it is ruinous . . . it is more ruinous. . . ." Then follows description of a touching

[55] Michel 164-69 rather exaggerates the novelty and significance of this.

scene where Quinctius implored Naevius by all that was holy, and a final picture of his misery and appeal to the judge. It is rather obvious stuff when read in cold blood, and the judge, Aquilius, was a hard-headed professional, but the appeal was, of course, expected and would be judged by comparative standards. This was part of the etiquette. Cicero had, further, not only his client to plead for, but his own reputation for eloquence to win; how well the peroration went was in large part a matter of delivery. From his description (*Brutus* 313) of his early manner it seems to have been an unrestrained and unvaried passionate outburst.[56]

It is easy to see why the rhetoricians were so interested in the parts of an oration; that is a specific topic which can be handled clearly. To outline them is the obvious first step in analysis, if perhaps not in composition, and gives one a feeling for the speech as a whole. If we turn now to invention and the substance of the speech, the first question to be asked is what part does the theory of *stasis* or *constitutio* play in the *Pro Quinctio*? The question for the court to decide was whether or not Naevius had taken possession of Quinctius' goods in conformity with the praetor's edict. Cicero's partition claims that he will prove first that Naevius had no grounds to apply to the praetor for a judgment against Quinctius; second, that he could not legally take possession of the goods; third, that he had not taken possession of them (36). Thus Cicero will deal with the *stasis* of quality, of legality, and of fact. Since he complains about the legal form of the proceedings (33; 71), there is also an aspect of the translative *stasis* in the case! The issues are dealt with separately, but at the same time they are all regarded as aspects of the question posed to the court: thus, there

[56] Cicero mentions (77) that the actor Roscius was present in court and advising him.

is no one *constitutio*, and if the theory has helped Cicero it has helped him chiefly in partitioning his argument and enlarging the scope of his defense. One sign of a good as opposed to a mediocre orator is the ability to create a picture of great resources of argument on his side and his intention to deal with fundamental issues rather than with verbal trivialities; it is, for example, the secret of some of the power of Demosthenes. But if Cicero manages to make good use of *stasis* theory it is his own achievement. The theoretical account that appears in *De inventione* (2.53) did not recognize that combinations might arise, though this must frequently have been the case, especially in civil suits. The rhetorical student's chief training, however, was for the great cases of murder, treason, and rape.

In the argumentation of the speech Cicero has woven together matter which is sometimes narrative, sometimes demonstrative. For this kind of composition the handbooks gave no advice, though declamation may have given practice and the teacher of declamatory exercises gave criticism. In Aristotelian terms Cicero makes considerable use of argument from probability, built on the evidence of documents and witnesses who would be introduced after the speech, and of ethos, for the antithesis between the characters of Quinctius and Naevius is one of the most powerful arguments of the speech. Though that possibility would not have emerged from *De inventione*, it was evident to a speaker familiar with the Roman courts. There is also considerable emotionalism in the presentation, and that too was traditional at Rome. The account of argumentation in *De inventione* is more rational and philosophical than this, if rather formalistic. Many of the topics which it includes have, however, some expression in *Pro Quinctio*. Cicero begins his account (*De inv.* 1.34) with discussion of attributes

143

of persons or of actions which are to be used to support arguments. An example of support by attributes of persons might be the description of Alfenus as a wealthy equestrian (*Pro Quinctio* 62) and thus a proper person to have acted as Quinctius' agent in Rome, though Naevius tried not to deal with him. An example of use of attributes of action might be the demonstration (79) that the word to evict Quinctius from his property in Gaul must have been sent by Naevius before he had made application to the praetor for the right to do so, since word could not have covered the 700 miles from Rome to the farm in the less than the three days which intervened.

According to *De inventione* (1.44) arguments are necessary or probable. Necessary arguments are divided into dilemma, enumeration, and simple conclusion. An example of a dilemma might be the claim (73) that Naevius must prove that Alfenus did not succeed in defending Quinctius' property at Rome (and it had been proved that he did) or he must admit that he had not succeeded in taking the property (which would be to throw over the case). A more rhetorical if less necessary dilemma results from Cicero's attempts to suggest why Naevius had taken no legal action against Quinctius for almost two years. The real reason may have been desire to compromise the matter or the very unsettled political situation at the time; Cicero wants the judge to think that it was because Naevius had no case to stand on. "The alternative remains that either gross negligence stood in your way or remarkable generosity. If you say negligence we shall be amazed; if generosity we shall laugh" (41). An enumeration is a form of indirect proof, where possibilities are listed and one by one rejected until one or none are left. Cicero uses this technique (60) in dealing with legal conditions under which Naevius might have taken possession of Quinctius' property in his absence. An inference is a "necessary" one if that is the only inference which can logically be drawn: thus Naevius claimed (57) that Quinctius had given bail on February 5 to appear in court. But Quinctius was not in Rome on February 5. Therefore Naevius has lied.

Probable arguments are of four sorts (*De inv.* 1.47). First, signs. His tearing down of Naevius' placard announcing a sale of Quinctius' property is a sign that Alfenus was acting as Quinctius' legal agent (61). Credibilities are based on the common opinion of mankind. "Who would have been so remiss in business," Cicero asks (38), ". . . as not to claim money from a debtor's heir . . . ?" A judgment is an argument based on religion or on political or judicial decision, for example, the reply of the tribune Brutus announcing his intention to intervene in the case unless Alfenus and Naevius agreed (65) is evidence that Alfenus had taken steps to protect Quinctius' interests. A comparison is an argument based on similarities of character or things, for example, the tie between Alfenus and Brutus (the good praetor?) is paralleled by the tie between Naevius and the unjust praetor Burrienus (69), which proves that Naevius was at no political disadvantage at the time.

It is difficult to find in the speech clear-cut examples of the two formal devices of argument which Cicero recognizes (*De inv.* 1.51-76), *inductio* and *ratiocinatio*. The question of precedents or analogies on which induction is based does not come into the speech, though in a general way Cicero tries to induce a picture of Naevius' worthlessness and cupidity by a series of pictures of his actions. As a more specific illustration of this we may cite Cicero's claim (73-74) that Quinctius' other creditors did not attack him in his absence. What was the reason for this? They weren't scoundrels. Naevius alone attacked him, ergo he is a scoundrel. The argument is amplified by the point that the other creditors were not relatives or friends, whereas Naevius was married to Quinctius' sister, was his partner, knew him well, which according to Cicero made it all the worse. Hortensius would not have had much difficulty in finding possible answers to this argument.

A large number of arguments in the speech could be reduced to syllogistic form, but most are disguised, as is perfectly proper in oratory, for syllogisms are not very easy to listen to. Various parts of the arguments are suppressed or assumed or the parts rearranged. A *ratiocinatio*, as defined by Cicero, is less barren, more interesting. Formally its premises are supported by reasons of some sort, and in manner it is much more expansive, much less stringent. A possible example, in form, is *Pro Quinctio* sections 49-50:

[Major premise] "If fortune has robbed someone of his money, or if the unjust action of another has snatched it away, yet his honesty consoles his want, as long as his reputation is intact. [The latter clause is really a supporting reason; Cicero could have said 'for his reputation. . . .' What follows is an alternative to the major premise which also may be viewed as supporting it by complementing it.] But some men, either disgraced or convicted of crime continue to enjoy their own possessions and do not sit waiting for the aid of others—a thing which is quite wretched—and in their misery they are consoled by this help and solace. [Minor premise] But the man whose goods are sold, who sees not only his valued possessions but also his needed food and dress shamefully set out under the auctioneer's hand, he is not

146

only relegated from the number of the living, but, if such a thing can be, is exiled even below the dead. [Supporting argument] For an honorable death often ennobles even a disgraceful life, but a life so disgraceful as this does not even leave opportunity for an honorable death. [Conclusion] "Therefore (*ergo, hercule!*) he whose goods are possessed under an edict finds all his fame and reputation possessed with them . . ." [and this is amplified and embellished for several lines].

We do not have Cicero's own work on style as a basis of comparison. Most critics have seen in Cicero's earlier speeches strong Asian influences, especially fullness of repetition and verbal amplification, which is evident enough.[57] It is possible to see also (e.g., 44) the influence of Crassus' love of speaking in short *membra*. There are passages which approach the grand style when Cicero deals with the moral issues of the case and the characters of men involved; note for example, the metaphorical passage on the darts of the enemy and the wounds of the defendant in the exordium (8). Some passages of the narration or of the proof could be labeled "plain style," for example, the imaginary dialogue between Cicero and the opposition on the subject of legal procedure (71). Sentences are often long, sometimes because of an attempt at elaborate construction, more often because of amplification, listings, and doubling. In some instances the composition seems very cumbersome,[58] for example: "et is pecuniam, si qua deberetur, non peteret qui, quia, quod debitum nunquam est, id datum non est . . ." (39). There are Gorgianic figures, like the homoeoteleuton in section 11, and rhetorical question and anaphora are prob-

[57] Cf. Norden 225-31; Leeman 97-102.
[58] Cf. L. Laurand, "Sur l'évolution de la langue et du style de Cicéron," *RPh* 7 (1933) 62-72.

147

ably used to excess. Thus the style, like the thought, is not especially subtle. The irony sometimes seems forced (19)[59] and the humor not very funny (29).

The overall conclusion must be that the speech illustrates many aspects of the rhetorical theory Cicero had learned, but that it is more than the theory and that it has been strongly influenced both by Cicero's oratorical predecessors and by practical possibilities which the rhetoricians had not foreseen.

[59] But cf. H. V. Canter, "Irony in the Orations of Cicero," *AJPh* 57 (1936) 457-64 and Auguste Haury, *L'ironie et l'humour chez Cicéron*, Leiden, 1955, 113-14.

CHAPTER THREE

Cicero and His Younger Contemporaries

Not only are the oratory and rhetoric of the Roman republic known to us chiefly through the writings of Cicero,[1] but they are dominated and overwhelmed by his own achievement, for in rhetoric he combined the activities of a Demosthenes with those of an Aristotle. Early Roman speakers and writers seem like prophets preparing the way for him; his eloquent contemporaries take on reality chiefly as his foils; his successors can be understood best in terms of their reaction to him. We have already considered Cicero's early studies, his treatise *De inventione*, and his first extant speech, *Pro Quinctio*. He

[1] For further bibliography cf. L. Laurand, "Notes bibliographiques sur Cicéron," *MB* 18 (1914) 139-56 and 26 (1922) 289-308; Walter Allen, Jr., "A Survey of Selected Ciceronian Bibliography, 1939-1953," *CW* 47 (1953-54) 129-39; R. J. Rowland, "A Survey of Selected Ciceronian Bibliography, 1953-1965," *CW* 60 (1966-67) 51-65, 101-15; S. E. Smethurst, "Cicero's Rhetorical and Philosophical Works: a Bibliographical Survey," *CW* 51 (1957-58) 1-4, 24, 33-41; idem, "Cicero's Rhetorical and Philosophical Works, 1957-1963," *CW* 58 (1964-65) 36-45; idem, "Cicero's Rhetorical and Philosophical Works, 1964-1967," *CW* 61 (1967-68) 125-33; S. F. Bonner, "Roman Oratory: Cicero," *Fifty Years of Classical Scholarship*, ed. M. Platnauer (Oxford, 1954) 340-63 (1968 ed. 421-44). On Cicero and rhetoric cf. V. Cucheval, *Cicéron orateur*, Paris, 1901; A. H. Greenidge, *The Legal Procedure of Cicero's Time*, Oxford, 1901; R. Preiswork, *De inventione orationum Ciceronis*, Basel, 1905; Gaston Boissier, *Cicéron et ses amis*, Paris, 1905; L. Laurand, *De M. Tullii Ciceronis studiis rhetoricis*, Paris, 1907 and "L'histoire dans les discours de Cicéron," *MB* 15 (1911) 5-34; Th. Zielinski, *Cicero im Wandel der Jahrhunderte*, Leipzig and Berlin, 1912; Torsten Petersson, *Cicero: A Biography*, Berkeley, 1920; R. Weidner, *Ciceros Verhältnis zur griechischen und römischen Schulrhetorik seiner Zeit*, Erlangen, 1923; Charles S. Baldwin, *Ancient Rhetoric and Poetic*, New York, 1924,

149

says there (4) that he had handled other cases, but we do not know what they were. It remains now to review chronologically his major creations. Though it is impossible to deal at all fully with the flood of Ciceronian rhetoric, we can perhaps hope to discover some rhetorical features of his chief speeches and the fundamental ideas of his rhetorical treatises. Specifically we must look at whether a speech has a practical and immediate persuasive purpose, or whether its objectives depart from the original conception of rhetoric to something more subjective, more expressionistic, more literary, or even more ironic. We need to consider the relation between Cic-

---

37ff., E. Ciaceri, *Cicerone e suoi tempi*, 2 vols. Milan, 1926-30; L. Laurand, *Études sur le style des discours de Cicéron*, 3 vols. Paris, 1926-28; W.K.A. Drumann and Paul Groebe, *Geschichte Roms*, Band VI "M. Tullius Cicero," Leipzig, 1929. *CAH* 9; L. Laurand, *Cicéron*, 2 vols., Paris, 1933-34; Clarke, pp. 50-84; Walter Allen, Jr., "Cicero's Conceit," *TAPhA* 85 (1954) 121-44; Michael; Leeman, 91-216; Karl Büchner, *Cicero: Bestand und Wandel seiner geistigen Welt*, Heidelberg, 1964; C. Neumeister, *Grundsätze der forensischen Rhetorik gezeigt an Gerichtsreden Ciceros*, Munich, 1964; T. A. Dorey, ed., *Cicero*, London, 1965 (including R.G.M. Nisbet, "The Speeches"); F. Wieacker, *Cicero als Advokat*, Berlin, 1965; A. Thierfelder, "Ueber den Wert der Bemerkungen zur eigenen Person in Ciceros Prozessreden," *Gymnasium* 72 (1965) 385-414; A. E. Douglas, "Cicero," *Greece and Rome, New Surveys in the Classics*, 2 (1968). The *R-E* article (7A. 827-1091) contains Matthias Gelzer, "Cicero als Politiker," 827-1091 and W. Kroll, "Die rhetorischen Schriften," 1091-1103, but no discussion of the orations. The most satisfactory English translations of most of Cicero's works are those in the Loeb Classical Library. There are often introductions and notes, especially to the orations. The Budé series, with extensive introductions, some notes, and French translations, is also very useful. The last complete English commentary on the speeches seems to have been George Long, *M. Tullii Ciceronis Orationes*, 4 vols., London, 1851-58. Commentaries on some individual works are cited below. For lost speeches cf. Julius Puccioni, *Orationum deperditarum fragmenta*, Milan, 1963.

ero's practice and his theory, the generalizing characteristic of one and the philosophical spirit of the other. It will be interesting as well to observe the development of Cicero's own rhetorical personality as defender of the persecuted, threatened, or oppressed, whether it be citizen, provincial, or the Roman state itself. As always in studying this amazingly literate and humane man the clearest result is apt to be the realization of the vast dimensions of his character.

Cicero's Speeches Before His Consulship

The speech which made Cicero famous in the law courts was his brilliant and exciting defense of Sex. Roscius of Ameria on the chilling charge of parricide, probably delivered in 80 b.c.[2] The case occurred during the rule of the dictator Sulla, soon after the notorious proscription which had legalized the murder and confiscation of the property of many of his opponents. According to Cicero the accusation was a plot to dispose of Roscius, concocted by the actual murderer and two others who had shared in the loot. After the murder they put the name of Roscius' father on the list of those proscribed by Sulla, though in fact he was a supporter of Sulla, and in this way made possible the sale of his property. The sale was arranged through the connivance of Sulla's freedman Chrysogonus. Chrysogonus himself bought the property for a fraction of its value, and ejected Roscius from it. No one was apt to run the risk of bidding against Chrysogonus, and it was perhaps equally hoped by the confederates that no one would run the risk of defending Roscius when indicted for parricide. Apparently the

[2] Cf. G. Landgraf, *Kommentar zu Ciceros Rede Pro Sexto Roscio Amerino*, Leipzig, 1914; W. B. Sedgwick, "Cicero's Conduct of the Cause *Pro Roscio Amerino*," CR 48 (1934) 13; Friedrich Solmsen, "Cicero's First Speeches: a Rhetorical Analysis," TAPhA 69 (1938) 542-56; Leeman 97-100.

claim that Roscius' father had been legally killed under the proscription was abandoned once the property was sold.

According to Cicero, none of the better known *patroni* would touch the case, while Roscius himself was apparently a rustic type without much wit for speaking. He had a few good friends, however, and one of them induced Cicero to appear. As a humane and thoughtful young man, Cicero doubtless believed that Roscius was entitled to help, but this was not apt to weigh very heavily if there was no practical possibility of success. The chief attractions to take a chance at defense may have included Cicero's knowledge that public opinion had reacted against the recent reign of terror, the belief that the case would be so well known that underhanded methods would have a reduced chance of success against a defender, the alluring hope that a courageous, just, determined, and eloquent young man who crossed swords with the corrupt, wicked tool of the dictator's favorite would be the hero of the people, and perhaps most important of all a belief on Cicero's part that some of Sulla's more powerful supporters had in fact resolved to eliminate the influence of Chrysogonus.[3] This last possibility creates the real problem in judging the speech. We cannot say with certainty the extent to which the situation was highly dangerous and much as Cicero represents it or conversely whether the trial could in a sense have been a foregone conclusion, deliberately staged by Chrysogonus' opponents. The problem will occur again in Cicero's career. Considering Cicero's general support of Sulla at this time and his ambitious but cautious character, the likelihood prevails that he had some reason to

[3] Cf. Adam Afzelius, "Zwei Episoden aus dem Leben Ciceros," C & M 5 (1942) 209-17.

believe that the speech would not offend Sulla and that he would meet with some support. This does not, however, cancel out the fact that Chrysogonus was dangerous and nasty and could be counted on to put up a good fight if alarmed. The key to success was to avoid the alarm, to take Chrysogonus by surprise. In this Cicero was entirely successful. His intention to defend Roscius and attack Chrysogonus was kept a secret until he rose and spoke (59), and Erucius, the patron of the prosecution, was taken unawares after a rather offhand accusation.

Cicero's defense of Roscius has three parts (35-36): that Roscius did not murder his father, that the murder was in fact the work of Magnus, one of the accusers, and that the whole proceeding was conducted with the help and to the advantage of Chrysogonus. In fixing the guilt (84), Cicero states the famous phrase, which he attributes to Cassius Longinus, *cui bono,* "Who stood to gain?" Chrysogonus is spared not at all, either in the early part of the speech or in the third heading which opens with one of Cicero's celebrated puns (124): "venio nunc ad illud nomen aureum Chrysogonum, sub quo nomine tota societas latuit," "I come now to that golden name of Chrysogonus [in Greek: the golden born], under which name the whole gang hides." Cicero is exceedingly careful to make no criticism of Sulla: Sulla, he asserts, knew nothing of it all, made no money by it, is so taken up by great affairs of state that he cannot possibly know what all his followers do, any more than Jupiter can know all the wickedness of men (131). The late Roscius supported Sulla; Cicero supports Sulla. The tone of this passage is very difficult to judge and heavily dependent on the actual manner in which it was delivered. Cicero may well have hoped for enough ambiguity to satisfy many shades of opinion, and his own views

153

of Sulla were ambivalent: he respected his constitutional achievements but disliked his bloody methods.[4]

Toward the end of the speech there are two interesting features. One is a passage (143) in which Cicero distinguishes between his client's feelings and his own.[5] Roscius has no special ill will against Chrysogonus and company; he is not trying to recover his property; all he wants is acquittal on the charge of perjury. All that has been said against Chrysogonus comes from the heart of Cicero himself, who is unafraid, who cannot keep silent. Cicero's bravery is thus underlined; it is almost made to seem a superabundant expression of his noble indignation. The other point is that with which the speech ends, the conversion of the case from that of Q. Roscius to the universal grounds of law and order at Rome. This is highly characteristic of Cicero and the most conspicuous of the ways in which he may be labeled a philosophic orator: here the generalization was especially effective since it came at a time when men were anxious to reestablish order in society.[6]

Cicero won his case for Roscius and seems not to have suffered for his attack on Chrysogonus. Plutarch (*Cic.* 3) says fear of Sulla was the reason why Cicero chose to go to Greece in 79 B.C., but Cicero himself says that many other cases came to him as a result of success (*Brutus* 312) and that he went to Greece to study rhetoric and especially delivery, since his habit of speaking at the top of his voice and with a tension of his whole body

---

[4] Cf. Richard V. Desrosiers, "The Reputation and Political Influence of L. Cornelius Sulla in the Roman Republic," Dissertation, Univ. of North Carolina, Chapel Hill, 1969.

[5] Cf. George Kennedy, "The Rhetoric of Advocacy in Greece and Rome," *AJPh* 89 (1968) 429-32.

[6] Clarke, p. 78, is quite wrong in denying that Cicero gave attention to the general questions implied in his speeches. Cf. Michel, 201-31.

was ruining his health (*Brutus* 314). It was, after all, not strange for a young Roman with serious rhetorical or philosophical interests to want to study in Greece. Cicero's trip took him first to Athens, where he spent six months studying philosophy with Antiochus the Academic and practicing declamation under the direction of Demetrius the Syrian. Then he continued on to Asia Minor where he names four famous teachers of declamation with whom he studied: Menippus of Stratonicea, Dionysius of Magnesia, Aeschylus of Cnidus, and Xenocles of Adramyttium. Cicero was probably with them during the winter and spring of 78 B.C. He then went to Rhodes and joined the school of Apollonius Molon, from whom he learned how to control his voice and to repress the excess of his style (*Brutus* 315-16), though the restraint was only a comparative one.[7] Rhodes was the seat of the best traditions in Greek rhetoric at this time:[8] practical but thoughtful, imaginative but reasonable, at once artistic and philosophical, and its spirit writ large is what Cicero tried to disseminate at Rome for the rest of his life. Sulla had now died, and Cicero returned from the East to enter political life. He was quaestor in 75 B.C., serving in western Sicily. He also resumed his career in the courts (*Brutus* 319). The style of the speech for Roscius the comic actor suggests that it was delivered at this time, though the internal references may point to a date around 66 B.C.[9] The fragmen-

---

[7] Cf. J. C. Davies, "Molon's Influence on Cicero," *CQ* 18 (1968) 303-14.

[8] Cf. Hatto H. Schmitt, *Rom und Rhodos: Geschichte ihrer politischen Beziehungen seit der ersten Berührung bis zum Aufgehen des Inselstaates im römischen Weltreich*, Munich, 1957 and Felicità Portalupi, *Sulla corrente Rodiese*, Turin, 1957.

[9] Cf. Morris H. Morgan, "On the Date of the Oration *Pro Roscio Comoedo*," *HSPh* 12 (1901) 237-48 and F. Klinger, "Ciceros Rede für den Schauspieler Roscius," *SBA* 1953-54.

tary speech for Tullius may date from 71 B.C.[10] In the following year Cicero's rivalry with Hortensius reached its climax in the trial of Verres.

C. Verres was governor of Sicily in 73 B.C., and because of the slave war in Italy his normal successor was not sent out the following year, nor was he relieved in 71 either. He thus had three years in charge of one of the richest provinces in the Roman empire at a time when responsible Romans had much to occupy their attention elsewhere. Even allowing for some exaggeration on Cicero's part, it seems to be impossible to refute the reputation of Verres as the classic example of the rapacious Roman governor: his basic quality was greed, set as a jewel among the lesser vices of lust, gluttony, cruelty, and cowardice, and polished by a love of art.[11] Verres made rather little pretense of virtue and remarked openly that he would be content with the profits of one year in Sicily; the proceeds of the second year could go

---

There is some discussion of the speech in Wieacker, *op.cit.* supra n. 1.

[10] This is a private case before *recuperatores* about land ownership. Cicero claims that he had expected *stasis* of fact but was met with *stasis* of law and that he is being forced to deal with the defendant's character, but the extant speech does not do so. For discussion cf. Greenidge 551-56 and K. Hubert, "Der Bau der Ciceros Rede *Pro M. Tullio*," *Hermes* 48 (1913) 631-33; Michel 515-17. The speech is not included in the Loeb Library edition, but a translation can be found in the Bohn's Classical Library series, *Cicero's Orations*, trans. by C. D. Yonge, vol. 2, London, 1851.

[11] The punishments inflicted by Verres on Roman citizens perhaps had some justification and no separate charge was brought against Verres on this score, cf. Jérome Carcopino, "Observations sur le *De suppliciis*," *RIDA* 4 (1950) 229-66. Comparison of Verres to Warren Hastings is unfair to Hastings, but Edmund Burke was influenced by Cicero's speeches, cf. H. V. Canter, "The Impeachments of Verres and Hastings: Cicero and Burke," *CJ* 9 (1914) 199-211; Nisbet, *op.cit.* supra n. 1, 57-58.

to his defenders and of the third year to his judges (*Verr.* 1.40). Perhaps the most appalling aspect of the case is the support which Verres' senatorial rank and gold inspired among his fellow senators in Rome and especially from Hortensius, who promised to defend him. Delegations from Sicily had come to Rome soon after Verres' term at last expired, and they sought a prosecutor to initiate action before the standing court concerned with extortion (*quaestio de pecuniis repetundis*). Cicero seems to have been their first choice: he was known to them from his term as quaestor in Sicily. It was doubtless obvious that by successful prosecution he stood to gain as much in reputation as the Sicilians in damages, he was known to be a rival of Hortensius, and as a man without ancestors in public life and with some ties to the popular party, he did not yet feel the necessity of senatorial solidarity against criticism of a fellow senator. These attitudes Cicero somewhat mitigates in presenting to the court. He claims that defense is most congenial to him, which much of his career bears out, and that in prosecuting Verres he is not seeking quick fame in toppling a sensational figure, but is defending oppressed provincials and Roman law; this too was to continue a feature of his career. Moreover, he says that he is by no means weakening the senatorial order, but that the conviction of Verres, already found guilty in popular opinion, is necessary if the senate is to retain any respect and especially if it is to continue to control the juries, as it had done in the decade since Sulla. A bill, ultimately successful, had already been introduced in the assembly to apportion the jurymen between the senate, the equestrian order, and a group called the tribunes of the *aerarium*. It was in the heat of this political controversy that the trial was conducted. The formal charge was that Verres had appropriated forty million sesterces (roughly two million dollars) during his governorship (1.56). This amount was probably chosen as capable of easy demonstration; Cicero presents Verres' real profits as much greater and his crimes as manifold.

The chronology of the case is disputed, but it was spread over about eight months.[12] The charge was probably brought early in January 70 B.C. and was first delayed by the attempt of Q. Caecilius to secure for himself the right to prosecute Verres. This question was settled by a procedure called *divinatio* in which the would-be prosecutors presented their credentials and motives to a jury which decided between them. Caecilius had been Verres' quaestor in Sicily and was thus implicated in his actions. Though he claimed to have quarreled with Verres, he is convincingly shown by Cicero to be Verres' choice for prosecutor, and clearly only token prosecution would have resulted if Caecilius had been chosen.[13] Cicero's speech in this part of the action brings out clearly the political considerations involved in the case and contains (27-47) a very interesting lecture to Caecilius on the qualifications of a prosecutor. Cicero's argument on his own behalf is principally that the most suitable prosecutor is the one most wanted by the plaintiff, here the Sicilians, and least wanted by the defendant, Verres.

After securing the right to prosecute, Cicero demanded and got 110 days to prepare his case, which involved going to Sicily to collect evidence. Even at this early

[12] Cf. F. H. Cowles, "Gaius Verres: an Historical Study," *Cornell Studies in Classical Philology* 20 (1917) and "Cicero's Debut as a Prosecutor," *CJ* 24 (1928-29) 129-49; R.G.C. Levins, *Cicero: Verrine* v, London, 1946, xxvii-xxxvi; L. R. Taylor, *Party Politics in the Age of Caesar*, Berkeley, 1949, 101-18; N. M. Marinone, "Quaestiones Verrinae," *Univ. di Torino, Pubbl. della Fac. di Lett. e Filos.* 2.3 (1950).

[13] But cf. Paolo Fabbri, "Q. Cecilio e la Divinatio," *Historia* 6 (1932) 292-96.

stage it was clear that Hortensius was anxious to prolong the procedure, if possible into the next year when he hoped to be consul himself and when friends of Verres might be in other key positions in the government and courts. Another case was hurriedly brought into court in which a prosecutor demanded 108 days for investigation of charges against a governor of Achaea (2.1.30). This new case thus came into court first and had to be disposed of before the matter of Verres was taken up. As a result it was about three o'clock in the afternoon of August 5th, 70 B.C. before the trial of Verres was begun (1.31).

Throughout the year Cicero showed amazing physical and nervous energy. He managed to gather his evidence in Sicily in fifty days, despite the sudden opposition of Verres' successor as governor, Metellus. He was apparently faced with every kind of attempt to delay the case, to bribe the court or himself, to suppress evidence, and to coerce witnesses. At the same time he was a candidate, and a successful one, for the aedileship, though Hortensius won the consulship. The emotional strain must have been great, but Cicero saw clearly that the prize was worth it, for success against Hortensius would make him the first orator in Rome, and would doubtless also bring him considerable political support.

From the rhetorical point of view the most interesting aspect of the trial is that Cicero's objectives in the case tended to impede each other. The legal problem was to outwit Hortensius' machinations, to convict Verres, and to get some redress for the Sicilians; Cicero wanted also to produce a literary masterpiece which would make his lasting reputation as an artistic orator and would outshine anything Hortensius had ever done. To do so he needed full scope to develop the conventional ingredients of rhetoric and especially brilliant description, vivid characterization, and overwhelming emotion. But as the year progressed it became clear that conviction of Verres was dependent on quick action and the presentation of evidence so clear that no effective answer could be made to it. The grand oratory for which Cicero longed could perhaps be answered in kind by Hortensius, and would certainly take up too much time, since a number of special and regular festivals were scheduled for the fall, thus necessitating adjournments of the court. If the customary long speech for the prosecution, spread out over many days and partly delivered by assistants, were followed by a like effort from Hortensius and by presentation and discussion of evidence and if then the whole procedure was repeated on an even grander scale in a second action, the case could easily be prolonged into the next year when Verres would have a more sympathetic administration (2.1.31). The situation is a significant one for the course of Roman rhetorical history: oratory as a practical device of persuasion is in conflict with oratory as an artistic product or as self-expression of the orator. Cicero solved the problem by dispensing with his opening oration and thus forcing Hortensius to dispense with his too. He introduced his evidence immediately and so effectively that Verres gave up the case and went into exile. He then later published five elaborate orations—to take the place of those which he might have delivered at the second action in the case, required by law if the defense had not been abandoned.[14]

What is called the first action against Verres thus is not a typical opening speech in an extortion trial, which would ordinarily have been very dire and emotional, but

---

[14] The claim of C. Hoeg that the second action was heard is unconvincing, cf. "The Second Pleading of the Verres Trial," *Dragma M. P. Nilsson, Acta Inst. Rom. Regni Sueciae* 2.1 (1939) 264-79.

mysterious in hiding from the defense what evidence would be used and perhaps digressive and purposely irrelevant. Instead it is an introduction to the situation and a presentation of the evidence. It deals primarily with the procedural and political problems involved in the case. Appropriate to the extempore examination of witnesses which it introduced, the tone is conversational (cf., e.g., 1.20-21), and Cicero does not fail to make capital of his own oratorical self-sacrifice (1.32-33). The procedure of moving directly to the introduction of witnesses rather than first covering the whole case in a set speech was not entirely novel, but Cicero thought it wise to introduce his precedents as evidence (1.55). The approach debarred Hortensius from making a reply until after the evidence; he seems to have raised no objections initially, but hoped Cicero would use as much time as possible (1.34). Subsequently he complained that Cicero was convicting a defendant by not speaking against him, a dangerous precedent (2.1.24). It is difficult to determine exactly what action the defense took during the examination of witnesses. Hortensius and Verres were entitled to cross-examine or comment, and this is one way Hortensius could have lengthened the trial. Cicero's second action contains a few references to objections by Hortensius or reaction by Verres at the first action,[15] but the second action is an imaginary procedure and may be no better source of information on the course of the first action than it is on its own existence. On the second day the defense was in despair; on the third day Verres stayed home sick (2.1.20); on the ninth day (2.1.156) Cicero concluded. This was the first time Hortensius could have seized the lead in the case, but he made no reply (*Orator* 129). Since an adjournment had to follow, he may have hoped that time would dilute

---

[15] Cf. 1.71 and 151; 2.24; 3.6 and 41; 4.36, 43, and 46.

the effect of Cicero's attack while Verres worked to influence the jury, but in fact this was judged impractical.
Verres went into voluntary exile and the only further
proceeding was a brief verdict of condemnation and assessment of damages.[16] Verres escaped with a good deal
of his loot, especially his works of art, and lived quietly
and presumably contentedly in exile until put to death
by Antony in the same proscription in which Cicero was
killed, 43 B.C. A man of principle in his way, he had
affronted Antony by refusing him some coveted bronzes,
and according to Lactantius (2.4.37) took pleasure in
knowing that his illustrious accuser had already met his
fate.

Presumably Cicero had made some plans for the second action in case it should occur, and the five speeches
he published under that title thus have some basis in
reality, but he has been freed from inhibiting practical
considerations and allowed free rein in amplification. If
the published orations of Galba, Crassus, and Hortensius
were, as we have seen Cicero complain, paltry reflections
of their actual ability, Cicero need fear no judgment of
his Verrines. They gave him full scope. Amplification is
the most obvious feature of the second action (Tac.,
Dial. 20), not amplification beyond the possible, since
Cicero could have spoken for days if he wished, but
amplification beyond the necessary. Cicero of course
could have written an account of Verres in an historical
monograph, but he found the oratorical form the most

[16] According to Ps.-Asconius (224 and 230 Stangl) the defense
customarily spoke first at the second action. This has usually
been denied, but may be correct, cf. Jules Humbert, *Les plaidoyers écrits et les plaidoiries réelles de Cicéron*, Paris, c. 1925,
199-203. In Quintilian's time (10.1.23) there existed a speech
of Hortensius in defense of Verres. If genuine, it was probably
Hortensius' intended speech for the opening of the trial, cf. *R-E*
16A. 1630.

162

natural, and it was an oratorical reputation which he desired.

The approach is first chronological, then topical. The first speech deals with Verres' quaestorship in Gaul (84 B.C.), his legateship in Cilicia (80-79 B.C.), and his urban praetorship at Rome (74 B.C.). All of this is logically irrelevant to the charge that Verres had extorted money in Sicily, but it was within Roman notions of the appropriate, since it served to establish Verres' character. The subjects had been touched on in the first action also (1.11-12) and evidence had been introduced to support the statements made, for example, about an incident at Lampsacus (2.1.71). Since the opening serves to open both speech and action it is exceedingly serious in tone. There follows a division of the subjects to be covered in all five speeches and then discussion of Verres' career up to his governorship. The last four speeches discuss affairs in Sicily: first (in the second speech) Verres' exaction of money from Sicilian individuals and towns and his relation to the tax farmers, then the grain tithes and purchases, next Verres' theft of works of art,[17] finally Verres' military operations and the punishments inflicted on provincials and even Roman citizens.[18] This too is outside of the indictment except in the cases where Verres extorted money from his victims or their relatives or in so far as Verres could claim that military conditions necessitated certain actions, but the subject allows the fullest scope for Cicero to inflame the jury, as is suitable in a speech which stands as a peroration to the whole case. This last speech concludes with a very elaborate

[17] Cf. E. Thomas, *De signis*, Paris, 1894; Gaston Rabaud, *Cicéron: discours* v, Paris, 1927; i-xxiv; P. Cayrel, "Autour du *De signis*," *MEFR* 50 (1933) 120-55; A. Desmouliez, "L'interprétation du *De signis*," *RU* 58 (1949) 155-66; Michel 323-27.

[18] Cf. E. Thomas, *De suppliciis*, Paris, 1894; Levins, *op.cit.* supra n. 12; Carcopino, *op.cit.* supra n. 11.

appeal to the gods Verres has outraged. The five speeches together thus have an exordium and a peroration, but do not otherwise demonstrate tight oratorical form.

Despite the differing subject matter, all five speeches have many features in common. The narrative and ethical element is prominent throughout with only occasional pieces of argumentation. No opportunity is lost to castigate Verres or to compare him to others who have had some relation to Sicily, including the younger Scipio, Piso Frugi, the great Marcellus (e.g., 2.2.8), and the present governor, Metellus. There are repeated puns on Verres' name, which suggests the Latin word for swine and the verb "to sweep," though Cicero expresses contempt for such things and reports them to show opinion of Verres in Sicily (cf. 2.1.121)! Occasional attempts are made to preserve the illusion of a real speech in court, as when Verres is said to look surprised (2.3.167), and Verres' possible defenses are discussed: the claim that he was a good governor for he sold the right to farm the taxes at a high rate (2.3.40) or defended the province (2.5.1) or that he bought, rather than stole, the works of art which he collected (2.4.8).

The speeches are of extraordinary importance for our knowledge of Roman extortion courts and provincial administration, especially the administration of the grain supply. Cicero, however, intended them to be a great work of art. How do they stand up as an imaginative and creative answer to a rhetorical problem? There is no doubt that Cicero proves his point and that Romans were impressed with his eloquence. There is certainly a skilled arrangement of the material in the interest of variety, easy transitions, and climax. On the other hand many of the rhetorical devices are too patent and there is a lingering impression of purple passages, of vivid writing for its own sake. This helps in making the enormous bulk surprisingly readable: the disgraceful affair at Lampsacus, the house of Verres' mistress in Rome, thronged with clients, the mockery of trials before Verres in Sicily, Verres' journey in a covered litter through the country when first blooms the rose, Verres standing in a purple cloak, his arm around a courtesan, watching his fleet sail off without him to meet the pirates, the crucifixion of a Roman citizen at Messana within sight of the shore of Italy. These are vivid pictures and every reader will have his favorites. The trouble is that they seem wasted or negative effort. Cicero is no longer faced with any real rhetorical problem and he has no goal but to demonstrate his versatility. The speeches are a denunciation of a man defeated and exiled, whose crimes are long since proved, though hardly atoned. The vigor of the picture comes from the sensational and evil. Although the Romans may often have gloried in their vices, they also liked to indulge their national guilt feelings. They have a great deal to say about their own sin and corruption and decadence and they say it with great zest, in oratory and in their historical writing and in the genre called satire. The Greeks were realistic and critical of themselves, but by and large they slept well at night and worked during the day to improve what they disliked. Of the Verrine speeches one must admit that they are splendidly and grossly Roman: vast in size and elaborate in detail, colorful, vivid and sensational, ethical and emotional, guilty and vindictive, unnecessary, but impressive. The development of rhetoric from an art of persuasion to an art of expression is evident.

A contrast with the Verrines is furnished by Cicero's speech *Pro Fonteio*,[19] delivered sometime in the 60's. It

[19] Humbert, *op.cit.* supra n. 16, 215-21 argues that the prosecutor Plaetorius had tried to use against Cicero the same tactic the latter had used against Hortensius, seeking to avoid his open-

is a defense of a governor of Gaul on a charge of extortion and it shows Cicero's ability to rebut the kinds of charges he made against Verres. He uses several topics which might have been used on Verres' behalf: Fonteius has been an effective military commander and supplier (13-14). He is being maligned by provincials, who are at heart enemies of Rome (33) and who think nothing of perjuring themselves (30). The appeal to pro-Roman sentiment and prejudice against the provincials was of course necessitated by the circumstance. Doubtless Cicero regarded the Sicilians as more civilized than the Gauls, but he would have been surprised if asked how the two speeches could come from the same orator. Verres was another case with a different rhetorical problem. Similarly he appeals to equestrian sentiment mindful of the new constitution of the courts. It is possible that Cicero undertook this case partly as a way of ingratiating himself with those senators alienated in his attack on Verres.[20] The speech ends in pure melodrama of a tradition met before at Rome: Do not allow barbarians to snatch Fonteius from the bosom of his mother, from the arms of his sister, a vestal virgin (46-49). The technique of *Pro Fonteio* seems too obvious to a modern ear, and from the vantage point of the centuries it is not a great speech, but Roman audiences did not demand delicacy in pleading and relished seeing all that an orator could do.[21]

A much better speech from about the same time is that

---

ing speech. The extant speech is from the second action (cf. sect. 37). Cf. Pierre Jouanique, "Sur l'interprétation du *Pro Fonteio*, 1.1-2," *REL* 38 (1960) 107-12.

[20] Cf. André Boulanger, *Cicéron: discours* VII, Paris, 1950, 4.

[21] We do not know the outcome of the case, only that Fonteius bought a house in Naples in 67 B.C. (Cic., *Ad Att.* 1.6.1) and that he had some money left. But P. Sulla retired to Naples in 66 after conviction of bribery (*Pro Sulla* 53).

for Aulus Caecina.[22] The case is a private one on the ownership of land, very analogous to the case of Tullius. It was, however, especially suited to Cicero's abilities. Though not a jurisconsult,[23] he always had great interest in the law and was especially proud of his treatment of this complicated case: "I explained involved matters by defining them, I praised the civil law, I distinguished ambiguous words," he said subsequently and chose the speech as the best example of the plain style among his works[24] (*Orator* 102). The rhetorical problem was not only the presentation of complexities, but of a position perhaps rather weak in the law. Cicero's client's rights to possession of the land derived from a will, drawn by a woman who is said to have bought the property through an agent. Both the fact of purchase of the property and the right of Cicero's client to inherit were questioned, as were many other things. Clearly the fact of purchase is fundamental, but this Cicero cannot prove because, he says (17), the evidence is in the hands of his opponent. The litigants both attempted to occupy the property and Cicero's client, after being driven away by an armed band, secured an interdict from the praetor against his opponent. Most of the speech is taken up with discussion of the meaning and application of this interdict, and involves the question of the letter or the

[22] Cf. Boulanger, *op.cit.* supra n. 20, 59-139. Caecina remained a good friend of Cicero and there are extant letters between them, cf. esp. *Ad fam.* 6.7 in which Caecina describes himself as an old client and complains of the censorship under Caesar.

[23] As was claimed by Emilio Costa, *Cicerone giureconsulto*, Bologna, 1927. Cf. Valentin-Al. Georgesco, "*Nihil hoc ad ius, ad Ciceronem*: note sur les relations de Cicéron avec la *iurisprudentia* et la profession de *iuris consultus*," *Mélanges Marouzeau*, Paris, 1948, 189-206 and Harry L. Levy, "Cicero the Lawyer as Seen in his Correspondence," *CW* 52 (1958-59) 147-54.

[24] But cf. Harry M. Hubbell, "Cicero on Styles of Oratory," *YClS* 19 (1966) 171-86.

spirit of the law. Cicero enthusiastically defends the liberal interpretation, though he shows his ability to split hairs when forced (85). His speech is thus in the tradition of Crassus' speech for Curio,[25] as he points out (53ff. and 67ff.). There is also an excellent opportunity for generalization, which is fully exploited. These factors help to make the speech of greater interest and significance than the occasion might have promised. Though we cannot be certain, it seems likely that Cicero was successful. If so, and if injustice was done, which is possible, the fault must be laid to the narrowness of Cicero's opponents who tried to settle the matter in what seemed a quick and easy way, not concentrating on the fundamental issue but on procedure and even there on the wording, rather than the spirit, of the interdict.

Cicero's cleverness in a very complex case is again evident in his defense of Cluentius,[26] which he later chose as an example of a speech employing all varieties of style (*Orator* 103). It is his longest and Pliny (*Ep.* 1.20.4) regarded it as his finest speech. The case had long been a notorious scandal and Cicero himself in an earlier action (*Verr.* 1.38-39; *Pro Caec.* 28) had exploited the same prejudice he now wished to allay.[27]

At the outset the speech involves considerable narrative complexity, stemming from the marriages and mur-

[25] Cf. supra 86-87.
[26] Cf. E. C. Woodley, "Cicero's *Pro Cluentio*: an Ancient Cause Célèbre," *CJ* 42 (1946-47) 415-18; Michel 257-60; 395-401, and 512-15; Gabriele Hoenigswald, "The Murder Charges in Cicero's *Pro Cluentio*," *TAPhA* 93 (1962) 109-23; C. J. Classen, "Cicero *Pro Cluentio* 1-11 im Licht der rhetorischen Theorie und Praxis," *RhM* 108 (1965) 104-41.
[27] Among the more interesting sidelights are why Cicero at an earlier stage in the case had appeared against Cluentius for a doubtful client (49ff.) and the discussion of the legal significance of being black-marked by censors (117ff.).

ders of Cluentius' stepfather, Oppianicus, and from the circumstances of previous trials. There are also legal complexities resulting from the fact that Cluentius was apparently being tried under two different provisions of the *Lex Cornelia* on assassins and poisoners. The more straightforward charge was that he had recently tried to poison Oppianicus; the more complicated, that he had earlier tried to bring about Oppianicus' "judicial" murder by bribing a jury to convict him on false charges of murder and attempted murder. This latter charge was the source of great prejudice in Rome and in the court against Cluentius, and Cicero's primary rhetorical challenge is to try to counteract the prejudice.[28] This he does at such length (cf. Quint. 4.2.16) that not until section 143 does he come to the immediate charges. The charge of judicial murder he wants to dismiss on the ground that it did not apply to knights, but quite cleverly he introduces a dispute between himself and his client in planning the defense, the one seeking to stress the legal technicality, the other insisting on having his reputation cleared and not trying to escape by a technicality (144). This is one of Cicero's many effective uses of contrast and comparison between patron and client. In this same part of the speech he employs another of his favorite and powerful topics, the generalization of the immediate issue into a threat to all law in the state. The discussion of the poisoning charge comes at the end of the speech (160-94) and seems to show that no good evidence had been offered against Cluentius. Cicero's arguments that the allegations are improbable look perfectly adequate, and by this point one is willing to believe that Cluentius' enemies would stoop to anything. The defense is in large part a matter of constructing a satisfactory ethos for the

28 Cf. Classen, *op.cit.* supra n. 26.

major characters: Cicero even manages to make it seem to Cluentius' credit that his most persistent opponent has been his own mother (cf. Quint. 11.1.61-63)!

Cicero won the case and later boasted that he had pulled shades of darkness over the eyes of the jury (Quint. 2.17.21). He perhaps meant specifically in connexion with the bribery accusation,[29] where his argument is a dilemma: either Oppianicus or Cluentius bribed the jury, and since Oppianicus can be shown to have made an attempt, Cluentius must be innocent. Their characters have been developed to make it seem likely that Oppianicus would bribe, unlikely that Cluentius would. The near certainty[30] that both parties had tried bribery is not considered, but Cicero's argument (62) that Cluentius' case was too good to make bribery necessary is hardly convincing, considering the state of the Roman courts. To meet Oppianicus' bribery with bribery may have seemed the only prudent course. The case as a whole, like those of Murena and Ligarius later, is a fine example of what most ancients admired in an orator: not legal knowledge (though Cicero displays a good deal) or logical clarity, but the ability to charm the jury and sweep it off its feet by colorful narrative, vivid characterization, radiant confidence, skillful emphasis and

[29] Cf. Rufianus, p. 42 Halm, where the discussion is of diversionary tactics. Cf. J. Humbert, "Comment Cicéron mystifia les juges de Cluentius," REL 16 (1938) 275-96. Humbert thought the phrase came from a letter to Brutus in which Cicero pointed out how inadequate would have been a speech which regarded proof as the sole function of an orator. In his defense of Munatius Cicero claimed to have "darkened" the case, cf. Plutarch, Cic. 25.1. On Cicero's treatment throughout his career of facts which were against him cf. S. Usher, "Occultatio in Cicero's Speeches," AJPh 86 (1965) 175-92.

[30] In Pro Caec. 29 Cicero indicates that Cluentius used bribes. Cf. Ps.-Asconius 219 Stangl.

deemphasis, and in general the creation of a product of art.

Cicero was praetor in 66 and for the first time addressed the people at an assembly. He says he purposely waited to speak until he was sure of his authority with the people and of his oratorical ability (*De imp. Pomp.* 2).[31] The subject he chose to support was a law proposed by the tribune Manilius under which Pompey, successful beyond all expectation in a special command against the pirates, would now be given command in the long drawn-out war against King Mithridates of Pontus. Julius Caesar also spoke in favor of the law (Dio 36.43.2). Both orators were eager to show themselves friends of the great Pompey and the law was apparently certain of success with equestrian and proletarian voters, who idealized Pompey and were weary of the conduct of the war in the East.[32] Cicero thus spoke as a popular public official addressing an enthusiastic audience on a subject of interest and importance. His speech seems to have been composed with great care, for, given the circumstances, it was his repute as an orator that was mainly in question. The rhetorical problem which he faced was not so much how to convince his audience, as how to avoid antagonizing those in the senatorial party who opposed the law, and especially to avoid criticism of Lucullus, the previous commander against Mithridates. But this was

[31] As praetor he had the right *agere cum populo*, to summon a meeting of the assembly and ask for a vote (Gellius 13.16), but it is not certain that he personally presided over this particular meeting. Manilius could have called it himself. Cicero says at the beginning that his *auctoritas* was increased by the fact that of the various candidates for praetor at the election of 67 he had been the first declared elected.

[32] Cf. Ronald Syme, *Sallust*, Berkeley and Los Angeles, 1964, 87-88. The equestrian class favored Pompey, cf. Tenney Frank, "The Background of the Lex Manilia," *CPh* 9 (1914) 191-93.

not impossible; Lucullus, though unpopular with his troops, was a man of great ability and had had successes in the past which could be openly saluted. Cicero's argument is essentially that Lucullus had been frustrated in his recent efforts and it was time to give a new man a chance, especially since such a man as Pompey was already in the East.

Though the expediency of Pompey's appointment is brought out, as it should be in a deliberative speech, Cicero's oration has similarities to the second action against Verres in that the outcome was not seriously in question. The oration is an expression of oratorical ability, political affiliations and ideals, and an attempt to unify opposing groups. It contains effective expression of Cicero's concept of humane provincial administration and contributes to the picture of his own role in Roman oratory which he had begun developing in *Pro Roscio Amerino* and continued in the Verrines. As usual he has seen possibilities of generalizing and universalizing his theme. He has idealized his portrait of Pompey rather beyond historical recognition into his own ideal of the Roman statesman: not so much what Pompey was, but what Pompey and what every great Roman commander ought to be.[33] In portraying Pompey he may be guilty of flattery and opportunism, but he is also trying to exercise the leadership which he regarded as the duty of the orator. Virtues praised by Pericles in the funeral oration and by Isocrates in the *Panegyricus* are similarly expressions of what those orators would like to see in their subject more than descriptions of what they actually did see. Cicero did not realize that his praise of Pompey in all but divine

[33] Pompey is recommended (27-28) on the basis of his knowledge, courage, authority, and luck. In 29-36 there is discussion of the virtues of a general: effort, fortitude, industry, promptness, policy, plus the more general virtues of morality, temperance, trustworthiness, affability, intelligence, and humanity.

terms probably helped prepare the Roman mind for the absolute rule of the Caesars and even their deification.[34] The idealized nature of the speech is also evident in its great regularity of form.[35] There is exordium, narrative, partition, proof, refutation, and peroration.[36] There is logos, ethos, pathos, but all in moderation. There are all the virtues of style, much variety of adornment—best of all is the comparison of Mithridates to Medea (22)—and great smoothness of composition. Cicero himself regarded the speech as the best example among his works of the middle style (*Orator* 102). All in all, it is an admirable if rather unreal performance.

The Consular Speeches

The high point of Cicero's career came in 63 B.C. With the consulship he acquired a new oratorical weapon, consular prestige. We have nine speeches dating from that year:[37] the three speeches against the grain law proposed by Rullus came at the beginning of the year;[38] then the defense of Rabirius on a charge of treason, and finally in November and December the four speeches against

[34] Cf. M. H. Griffin, "Deification and Cicero's *De lege Manilia*," *CW* 27 (1933-34) 181-82.

[35] Exordium 1-3; narratio 4-5; partition 6; proof 7-50; refutation 51-68; peroration 69-71.

[36] Cf. J. Meusberger, *Quatenus Cicero in oratione de imperio Cn. Pompeii observavit praecepta rhetorica*, Reid (Austria), 1893; Charles E. Little, "The Structure of Cicero's *Oratio pro lege Manilia*," *CW* 5 (1911-12) 82-84.

[37] For a general survey of the speeches of 63 cf. Catherine Saunders, "The Consular Speeches of Cicero," *CW* 10 (1916-17) 153-56. Closely associated with them is the lost *In toga candida* of 64, which can be partially reconstructed, cf. K. Kumaniecki, "De oratione Tulliana in toga candida habita," *Atti del I congresso internazionale di Studi Ciceroniani* 1 (Rome, 1961) 157-66.

[38] Cf. E. J. Jonkers, *Social and Economic Commentary on Cicero's De lege agraria orationes tres*, Leiden, 1963.

Catiline and the speech for Murena, charged with election bribery.

The first speech against the grain law was delivered in the senate and was followed immediately by the second speech on the same subject before the people, so that a comparison between what Cicero regarded as appropriate treatment for each is invited. Although only the end of the first speech is preserved, it is possible to see that the speech before the people followed the same order of topics as that in the senate, but in amplified form (cf. 1.9 with 2.45-46) with many references to the possessions of "the Roman people." Quintilian says (8.3.14) that the senate required a rather lofty manner, the assembly a rather impetuous manner, but this is not borne out in fact.[39] Cicero can be impetuous in the senate, as in the first Catilinarian, or vituperative, as in the speech against Piso. In general his senatorial speeches are less amplified, less ornamented than his speeches to the people and more concerned with clarification of the specific situation,[40] but occasionally he used the senate as a chance for display. In 61 B.C., for example, he wrote to Atticus (1.14.4) a description of an extempore speech in the senate in which he tried to show off before Pompey; all the devices of his rhetorical education and all the commonplaces and catchwords of his other speeches were employed. He thundered so loudly Atticus (who was in Greece) must have heard him there!

All of the speeches of 63 have considerable historical interest. Rhetorically speaking, that for Rabirius, fragmentary though it is, is remarkable as the only extant judicial speech delivered before the assembly, since the

[39] Cf. Clarke 71. The statement is probably derived from *De or.* 2.333-34 and may be influenced by the tradition of demagogic oratory which Cicero discusses in *Brutus* 223-25.

[40] Cf. Dietrich Mack, *Senatsreden und Volkesreden bei Cicero,* Kiel, 1937.

case was brought by an antiquated procedure to the
comitia centuriata. In the *Orator* (102) Cicero takes
Pro Rabirio as the best example of the grand style to
contrast with the simple style of *Pro Caecina* and the
middle style of his speech on the Manilian law. "In it,"
he says, "I blazed forth with every kind of amplification."[41] The speech is characterized by expansion,
doubling, even lists. There are simpler passages which
might qualify as plain (e.g., 20) or middle (e.g., 19)
style, but in general the treatment reflects the very serious
view Cicero took of the case, which is generalized from
a threat to crucify one man to a much more serious threat
to the entire constitution in undermining the right of the
senate to pass a *consultum ultimum* or general decree
of emergency. No speech of Cicero has a more somber
tone, perhaps adopted in part as Cicero's protest at the
almost comic opera proceedings by which Rabirius was
being made a victim.[42]

The *Catilinarians* are doubtless the best known of
all Latin speeches.[43] They make good school texts because they present stirring events of considerable historical significance, also because they are rather short
and not especially difficult Latin. The rhetorical analysis
of the *Catilinarians* is, however, difficult. They do not
conform well to the ordinary requirements of deliberative oratory, though the first and fourth were delivered
in the senate and the other two before the people. Only
the fourth can be said to deliberate about a course of

[41] Cf. Leeman 108-10.
[42] Cf. E. G. Hardy, "Political and Legal Aspects of the Trial
of Rabirius," *JPh* 34 (1915) 12-39 and Josef Langle, "Die
staatsrechtliche Form der Klage gegen C. Rabirius," *Hermes* 68
(1933) 328-40.
[43] Cf. Henri Bornecque, *Les Catilinaires de Cicéron: Étude et
analyse.* Paris, 1936; Henri Bornecque and Edouard Bailly,
Cicéron: discours x (Budé), Paris, 1961; Walter Allen, Jr., "In
Defense of Catiline," *CJ* 34 (1938-39) 70-85.

action, and actually that action is judicial, not political. Furthermore, the parts of the speeches do not necessarily perform their usual functions or relate very clearly to each other. Indeed, it is rather difficult to say what is the principal objective of each speech, with the exception perhaps of the fourth. Usually Cicero seems to have several objectives in mind. This greatly complicates any attempt to define the rhetorical problem which he has posed to himself and the technique by which he has chosen to answer it.

One reason that the *Catilinarians* seem to aim at more than one objective is that Cicero did not publish them until 60 B.C., three years after delivery, when he issued them in an edition with eight other speeches dating from his consulship and compared them to Demosthenes' *Philippics* (*Ad Att.* 2.1.3). Cicero's career was in very serious difficulties during these years, stemming from his actions as consul. As early as the last day of 63 he had been prevented from delivering the customary speech of one going out of office on the ground that he had put to death Roman citizens—the Catilinarian conspirators, though not Catiline himself who was killed in battle—without a trial. Though there were those who disliked Cicero personally, the real issue was senatorial direction of affairs, and the chief legal point in question was the *senatus consultum ultimum,* or general decree of emergency by which the senate authorized the consuls to see "that the state suffered no harm." What a consul could do under this decree was largely a matter of his own prestige and the support which he could get from the senate and public opinion.[44] The senate had passed the decree late in October of 63 and it was the

[44] It is described by Sallust (*Cat.* 29.3) as the power "to get ready an army, wage war, control in all ways allies and citizens, and to have supreme command and jurisdiction at home and at war."

basis of Cicero's actions in putting down the conspiracy, though not apparently of his order to strangle the conspirators, since that had separately and specifically been authorized by the senate. In any event, Cicero was criticized for years, and eventually driven into exile, on the ground that he had exceeded his authority. He naturally replied by trying to make clear his view of the situation in 63 and to glorify his rescue of the constitution. He wrote an account of his consulship in Greek, as well as a poem on it in Latin; moreover, he asked friends to write about it, and seemed to some quite tiresome on the subject (e.g., *De har. resp.* 17).

Under these circumstances it would not be surprising if he had edited his speeches of the year in such a way as to explain more fully his point of view, his justifications for action, and his own good sense. We shall see that he altered other speeches between delivery and publication. In the first *Catilinarian* such passages as those relating to his own fears and justifications (e.g., in 6, 9, 11, and 22) could have been added or revised for later readers. In the fourth *Catilinarian*, and less probably in the first, he may have conflated two different speeches at the same session of the senate into one. But we cannot say with certainty of any passage in the *Catilinarians* that it *must* have been added or revised later.[45]

[45] On the revision of the *Catilinarians*, cf. Constantin John, "Der Tag der ersten Rede gegen Catilina," *Philologus* 46 (1888) 650-65. He argued that the first speech as published is a conflation of two delivered speeches, one an invective against Catiline, the other a report to the senate. Cf. also L. Laurand, *Études sur le style des discours de Cicéron*, 1, Paris, 1928, 8-10; Hans Draheim, "Die ursprüngliche Form der katilinarischen Reden Ciceros," *WKPh* 34 (1917) 1061-71; Albert Rabe, "Die Senatssitzung am 8. November des Jahes 63 v. Chr. und die Entstehung der ersten catilinarischen Rede Ciceros," *Klio* 23 (1929) 74-87; Schanz-Hosius 1.422; Herald Fuchs, "Eine Doppelfassung in Ciceros Catilinarischen Reden," *Hermes* 87 (1959) 463-69.

The assumption that Cicero has later readers at least partly in mind makes the analysis of the *Catilinarians* somewhat more possible. Thus we may say that the first speech, delivered in the senate on November 8th, has several different addressees. First, it was addressed to Catiline and aimed at getting him to leave Rome, without forcing official action against him. Cicero apparently feared such action might fail, and one rhetorical problem was how to conceal his own weakness and induce Catiline to betray himself. Second, the speech was addressed to the senate, as was only proper, and aimed at arousing it to the existing danger and at explaining why Cicero took the course he took, specifically why he did not take more stringent measures. Thirdly, it is also addressed to readers in 60 B.C. and tries to show them why he was justified in taking as stringent measures as he did.

It is likely that Cicero went into the senate not expecting to see Catiline, but intending to report some preparations which he had made. Catiline's presence caused him to alter the form of his speech.[46] The first *Catilinarian* as we have it falls into five parts which correspond to five common parts of a judicial address, almost as though Catiline were indicted before a court.[47] There is first (1-6) an exordium. The opening sections are the work of genius, and break entirely with the tra-

[46] Cf. M. Cary in *CAH* 9.498. Catiline was an effective orator in the demagogic manner. He told Cicero that there were two bodies in the state, one weak with a shaky head, one strong with no head, and to Cato he said that if fire were set to his hopes he would extinguish it not with water but with ruin, cf. Cicero, *Pro Murena* 51. Sallust (*Cat.* 31) summarizes Catiline's reply to the first *Catilinarian*, in which like Antiphon in 411 he argued that it is improbable that he would have acted against the interests of himself and his country and ended with a phrase similar to what Cicero says he addressed to Cato.

[47] Cicero had offered to defend Catiline after the affair of 65 B.C., cf. *Ad Att.* 1.2.1.

ditional form of exordia. Cicero is not playing the role
of the moderate statesman, calm in crisis, and violates
his own injunction (*De or.* 2.213-14) against an emotional beginning. The topics are the present danger, the
historical precedents, the legal weapon of the *senatus
consultum,* Cicero's anxiety, and his plan. These are
really of interest to a variety of audience. The present
danger is for the senators, though it is expressed in indignation to Catiline. The historical precedents and legal
weapon are well known to the senate, but a warning to
Catiline and of interest to future readers. Cicero's anxiety
is a negative factor in dealing with Catiline, but important for his justification in the eyes of posterity. His plan
interests senate and Catiline.

There follows (7-10) a narrative of Cicero's knowledge
of the conspiracy. It has been well observed[48] that great
suspense is created: Catiline presumably does not know
how much Cicero knows, and he is not immediately told.
The allusion is vague in section one, warmer in section
six, but in section eight breaks out in all clarity. The
heart of the speech (11-27) is an argument aimed at
persuading Catiline to leave Rome, but the portrayal of
Catiline's character is more of interest to the senate or
posterity than to Catiline himself. Rhetorically the high
point of the section is the address of the Laws to Catiline,
reminiscent of Plato's *Crito.*[49] This is followed by a short
refutation of Catiline's quite logical demand that Cicero
and the senate vote: possibly some debate had in fact
intervened, possibly Cicero was anticipating a demand

[48] Cf. F. H. Potter, "The Date of Cicero's First Oration
against Catiline," *CJ* 21 (1925-26) 164-76. Whether the date
was Nov. 7 or 8 continues to be debated. Cf. Theodore Crane,
"Times of the Night in Cicero's First *Catilinarian,*" *CJ* 61
(1965-66) 264-67 which contains full bibliography.
[49] Cf. C. C. Coulter, "Plato's *Crito* and Cicero's *In Catilinam*
1," *CB* 33 (1956-57) 1-2.

179

he expected, possibly the section was put into the published speech to answer a demand made after the real speech. Cicero here seems on rather weak ground, and he may have received less support from the senate than he hoped for.[50] The fourth part of the speech is a refutation (27-32), this time addressed to the senate, of complaints that Cicero has not gone far enough. The complaint is put in the mouth of the Fatherland which thus makes a contrast with the earlier address of the Laws to Catiline. Finally (33) comes a brief peroration.

The second *Catilinarian*, delivered next day to the people, does not have so clear a structure, but is similarly composed of explanations of caution and justifications of action,[51] while the third, also to the people, describes on the one hand the capture of the conspirators in Rome, and pleads (27) with the people not to allow Cicero's deeds to injure him. The speech is noteworthy for the introduction of a religious element (18-22). The fourth speech purports to come from the debate in the senate on the punishment appropriate to the prisoners: the *senatus consultum ultimum* is not mentioned and the procedure is represented as a trial by the senate.[52] According to Sallust (*Cat.* 50.3) the senate first judged the conspirators guilty of treason, then debated the appropriate punishment. The republican senate was not a court of law, and such action could only be justified by the claim that the

[50] Cf. M. Cary in *CAH* 9.499 on the basis of *Cat.* 1.20-21 and Diodorus 40. fr. 5a.
[51] Cf. A. Yon, "A propos de la composition chez les anciens: le plan d'un discours de Cicéron (la IIe *Catilinaire*)," *REL* 14 (1936) 310-26.
[52] N.b. *iudicandus* in 18. Cf. Frank C. Abbott, "The Constitutional Argument in the 4th *Catilinarian* oration," *CJ* 2 (1906-1907) 123-25; George W. Botsford, "On the Legality of the Trial and Condemnation of the Catilinarian conspirators," *CW* 6 (1912-13) 130-32; T. Rice Holmes, *The Roman Republic*, ii, Oxford, 1923, 278-83.

conspirators had lost Roman citizenship through making or preparing to make war on the state and that they had been given full warning that action would be taken against them by the issue of the *senatus consultum ultimum*. Sallust, though he praises the first *Catilinarian* (31.6), passes over the other three and in his report of the senatorial trial composed his own version of the speeches of Julius Caesar (51) and Cato (52). There is no particular slur involved: Cicero's speech was published, and the speeches of Caesar and Cato, apparently not published, well represented the contrasting recommendations of imprisonment or execution. They also make a striking political and personal contrast.[53] Cicero himself later admitted (*Ad Att.* 12.21.1) that Cato had summed up the matter in the clearest and fullest way.

To the rhetorician the greater the challenge which the orator successfully meets, the greater his speech. In Cicero's career as we have seen it so far, perhaps the speech for Roscius of Ameria and that for Cluentius most fit this requirement. The first action against Verres qualifies from the point of view of tactics, though the speech itself is not a major achievement. The speech for the Manilian law is a very handsome product, but not of comparable difficulty for the orator. The *Catilinarians* are difficult to assess in this sense. Sallust (*Cat.* 31.6) thought the first was "useful to the country" and we may guess that it did perform an important function in Cicero's control of events. But it is likely that Catiline was planning on leaving Rome even before the first *Catilinarian*, while the second and third do not call for a decision. All of these were probably given to a basically sympathetic

---

[53] Sallust has sometimes been represented as hostile to Cicero, but this was not the case, cf. T.R.S. Broughton, "Was Sallust Fair to Cicero?" *TAPhA* 67 (1936) 34-46 and Syme, *op.cit.* supra n. 32, 105-11.

audience. The fourth speech differs in that a decision was called for and opposition met, but it seems to have been the speech of Cato, not that of Cicero, which carried the day. Of all the speeches of 63 B.C. the greatest purely rhetorical triumph is *Pro Murena*.[54]

The candidates for consul at the election in the summer of 63 were Catiline, Servius Sulpicius, Decimus Silanus, and Lucius Murena. The defeat of Catiline was essential in the eyes of the senatorial party, and bribery was used extensively. This aroused the indignation of Cato the younger, great-grandson of old Cato and an imitator of him as guardian of public morality. Though as anxious as anyone for Catiline's defeat, he threatened prosecution for bribery of anyone who was elected (Plut., *Cato the Younger* 21.2). It turned out to be Silanus and Murena. Silanus, who was Cato's brother-in-law, was left alone, but Murena was prosecuted by a coalition of Cato, the defeated Servius Sulpicius, and two others.[55] Sulpicius may have been motivated by frustrated ambition, Cato apparently by his Stoic philosophy in which all vices were equal and compromise with expediency immoral. The charge of bribery was not unwarranted nor unusual in Roman politics, but was extremely inconvenient for orderly government: Murena's conviction would mean that only one consul was in office at the beginning of 62 when the plots of Catiline might well still hang over Rome, and he or one of his followers might hope for success at a special election. Cicero had campaigned for Servius Sulpicius, but found it possible to support Murena when elected and decided that it was vital to defend him against the charges. The case was heard in

[54] Cf. W. E. Heitland, *Cicero Pro Murena*, Cambridge, Eng., 1903 and André Boulanger, *Cicéron: discours* xi (Budé) Paris, 1957, 9-85.

[55] Cf. Donald M. Ayers, "Cato's Speech against Murena," *CJ* 49 (1953-54) 245-53. On Cato as an orator cf. infra 283.

November, sometime between the second and third *Catilinarian*, after Catiline had withdrawn to his troops in Etruria, but before he had been checked. In Murena's defense there appeared the most prestigious patrons to be found: the silver-tongued Hortensius, the rich and influential Crassus, and the incumbent consul, Cicero. It is likely that Cicero had had collaborators, or at least *subscriptores*, in earlier cases, but we do not know for certain. In his critical works he repeatedly says[56] that when speaking in collaboration he customarily spoke last, delivering as it were a peroration for which his abilities were well suited. *Pro Murena* appears to be an example of this: he says (48) that he must sum up the case, repeating some of the arguments of Hortensius and Crassus, and (54) that Murena has particularly asked him to deal with the third and most specific part of the prosecution, though the others had already answered it. Cicero's particular function, however, seems to have been to destroy the great moral authority of his friends Sulpicius and Cato. This rhetorical problem could not satisfactorily be met by attacking their charge at length, since it apparently was well founded, though Cicero persists for the record in denying it and claiming that it is based on unproved and invalid argument from probability. Nor could it be met by direct attack on the prosecutors and their own characters or careers, like that on the prosecutors of Roscius of Ameria. This would have lost their friendship, which Cicero probably wished to avoid if possible, and even the imaginative Cicero would have been hard put to prove a charge of vice against Cato, or perhaps against Sulpicius.

The answer so effectively tried was to admit the virtue of the prosecutors, but reduce them to the insignificance of well-meaning, unrealistic dabblers in affairs whose

[56] E.g., *Brutus* 190 and *Orator* 130.

183

significance they do not understand. Let them ride their hobbies of the law in one case or Stoicism in the other, good enough in their way, but not of much value in the real world, especially when it is a question of saving the constitution. Sulpicius and Cato are dealt with separately in two different parts of the speech, which has a very clear structure. The exordium (1-10) begins in a solemn and religious tone, not unlike Demosthenes' *On the Crown*. Cicero explains why he has taken the case, though consul, though himself author of a bribery law, though a stern defender of the state, though a friend of Sulpicius and recent supporter of his candidacy. All of this lends weight to the defense of Murena, for there must be an overriding necessity to bring Cicero, despite all of these counterclaims, to Murena's side. Then comes the partition into the three topics of the prosecution (11): *reprehensio vitae* or the criticism of Murena's life —this ought to be the most important, says Cicero, but the opposition had not found much to criticize—the relative claims of Murena and Sulpicius to the consulship (*contentio dignitatis*), and the charge of bribery (*crimen ambitus*). Note that no claim of irrelevance of any of these is advanced; it would not have been admitted at Rome, and Cicero has no desire to concentrate on the bribery charge anyway. Each of the headings is taken up: Murena's life (11-14) and the claims of merit (15-53) follow a chronological order and thus function like a narration. It is in this second part that Sulpicius is destroyed. Murena, whose military exploits were perhaps rather modest, is made into a symbol of the contribution to Roman life of the soldier; Sulpicius, into that of the jurisconsult, and the game is on in a charming antithesis (22). The law is represented at its hairsplitting, literalist worst (25-27);[57] the archaic ritualism of legal formulae

[57] Cf. Michel 455-61.

is irreverently ridiculed (26). A lawyer is nothing in comparison to an orator (24), and Cicero claims he could easily learn all civil law in three days (28). The answer to Cato comes in refutation of the bribery charge (54-85). Cato's fanaticism is vividly outlined (60-66): a man with "a doctrine not moderated or gentle, but, it seems to me, a little too harsh and more austere than the truth or nature allows" (60). All sins are equal: equally wrong, without cause, to wring the neck of a fowl or a father (61). Then follows a spirited imaginary dialogue.

The ridicule, thorough as it is, produced no bitterness or malice. True, Cato went away from the trial remarking, "What a witty consul we have," a contradiction in Roman terms, but he became a friend and close adviser of Murena all the next year (Plut., *Cato the Younger* 21.5-6). More important, he came to modify his views slightly and, in what he regarded as the public interest, condoned bribery in the election of 60 B.C. (Suet., *Jul.* 19.1). To alter the view of a Cato may be fairly labeled a great triumph. It was doubtless widely appreciated that Cicero had elsewhere eulogized the civil law in glowing terms and was personally quite interested in Stoicism; he was not, however, regarded as slippery or insincere, but as witty and quick-witted. The rational argument which moved the jury was the quite real necessity for having two consuls when the year opened: Cicero realized that (*Pro Flacco* 98). What the jury then needed was some excuse, some pretext to reject the complaints of such important accusers and to overlook the immediate issue of bribery. Cicero furnished them with such an excuse. Had they not been carried away by his eloquence? In later sober hours they might, as individuals, admit that justice had not won, though right had. For a few minutes justice and right had seemed identical, and Cato a fuzzy-thinking fanatic. *Pro Murena* makes an interesting contrast with *Pro Rabirio* delivered earlier in the year: in each case the tone is the most important aspect of the speech. Plutarch (*Cic.* 53.3) says that *Pro Murena* was not delivered so well as most of Cicero's speeches because the orator had been up most of the night preparing it. The speech as we have it certainly shows no lack of energy.

We do not know when *Pro Murena* was published, but if Cicero did not have time to publish his other consular speeches until 60 B.C., as important as they were to his political career, it is unlikely that *Pro Murena* was published until later.[58] There is a reference to Cato's opposition to publicans (62) which may have acquired new meaning from Cato's treatment of them in 60 B.C. (Cic., *Ad Att.* 1.18.7). Similarly Cicero's reference (*Pro. Mur.* 6) to his own natural mildness and imposed severity is more significant after his decisive action in December 63 than before it.[59] In section 57 Cicero has omitted his discussion of the charges of Postumius and Servius, inserting simply a heading to show that they came at that point; that he did not work this part of the speech up for publication is a sign that he regarded the treatment of Sulpicius and Cato as the real literary interest of the speech. Pliny (*Ep.* 1.20.7) notes that Cicero has shortened the work.

Critics who do not understand the rhetorical problem of the case have sometimes found Cicero's humor in November 63 B.C. puzzling.[60] How could he be so flip-

---

[58] Cf. André Boulanger, "La publication du *Pro Murena*," *REA* 42 (1940) 382-87 and *Cicéron: discours* XI, Paris, 1957, 17.
[59] Cf. Humbert, *op.cit.* supra n. 16, 137.
[60] E.g., E. Rosenberg, *Studien zur Rede Ciceros für Murena*, Hirschberg, 1902. For a better view cf. Auguste Haury, *L'ironie et l'humour chez Cicéron*, Leiden, 1955, 133-35. Cf. also E. Remy, "Le comique dans le *Pro Murena*," *Nova et vetera* 1 (1912) 1-25, summarized in *WKPh* (1912) 1305-7.

pant with Catiline in Etruria? The answer of course is
that only by flippancy did he think he could keep Catiline from Rome. The peroration (86-90) is much more
serious in tone than the rest and this once suggested the
possibility that the speech was a published conflation of
two delivered speeches, one opening the case, one closing
it.[61] But the explanation does not appreciate the technique of the speech, which is to destroy the influence of
the prosecutors so that the serious political consideration,
indeed no joking matter, can be given its full weight.
There is nothing novel in entertaining an audience and
yet ending on a serious note facing the implication of a
situation in the broadest context. A shrewd psychological
orator may relax his audience only to pull them more
completely into his net.

The years following Cicero's consulship were among
the most difficult in his life as he saw his achievements
and even personal security more and more seriously
threatened until finally he was driven into exile in 58 B.C.
His actions as consul had made him a symbol of senatorial government; he had made enemies among ambitious popular leaders; Pompey, Caesar, and Crassus,
though they first solicited, and solicited unsuccessfully,
his support for their private pact called the first triumvirate, were soon ready to sacrifice him to the insistence
of rabble-rousers like Clodius. We have already seen that
the publication of the orations of 63 was influenced by
these circumstances; it is not surprising that his speeches
during the period take on the quality of defense of himself, whatever the nominal subject. He wrote Atticus in
61 (Ad Att. 1.17.6) that in the past he had taken cases out
of ambition, but now to guard his dignity. He was in
fact called upon to defend a number of his associates
as the opposition hit closer and closer to home: his col-

[61] Cf. Humbert, op.cit. supra n. 16, 119-42.

league in the consulship, Antonius, for whom he had little respect, had to be defended on a charge of treason or violence in 59. Despite Cicero's efforts to defend him, he was convicted.

Of the speeches Cicero delivered in these years we have only three, that for Sulla and for the poet Archias from 62 and from 59 that for Flaccus, who as praetor had arrested the Catilinarians at the Milvian bridge. Sulla was charged with participation in the conspiracy and has generally been thought to have been guilty; Archias' Roman citizenship was attacked, probably as a way of attacking his friends Cicero and Lucullus; Flaccus was accused of extortion while governor of Asia and this charge too has usually been accepted as deserved.[62] Cicero succeeded in winning all three cases. They have in common the fact that he has a good deal to say about himself, regarding the charges as at least partly directed against himself, and that he does not pay much attention to the specific evidence against his clients, but tries to wield his ex-consular prestige while appealing to ethos or pathos in his clients' defense.

In the charming speech for Archias[63] Cicero claims that his client is legally a Roman citizen, though the crucial evidence has been destroyed, but even if he were not, he ought to be made a citizen (4)! In an expansive mood he expatiates on his own debt to Archias and the arts, and he clearly trusts to have his word accepted. His claim that he owes much of his oratorical ability to

[62] Cf. Boulanger, op.cit. supra n. 58 (1957), 92-102 and Syme, op.cit. supra n. 32, 89-90.

[63] Cf. W. Sternkopf, "Die Oekonomie der Rede für den Dichter Archias," Hermes 42 (1907) 337-73; J. H. Taylor, "Political Motives in Cicero's Defense of Archias," AJPh 73 (1952) 62-70 (not entirely convincing); Marcel Orban, "Le Pro Archia et le concept cicéronien de la formation intellectuelle," LEC 25 (1957) 173-91; Paul R. Murphey, "Cicero's Pro Archia and the Periclean Epitaphios," TAPhA 89 (1958) 99-111.

Archias can hardly be allowed considering what we know about his early studies and practical experience.

The defense of Sulla is very much in the grand style, calculated to acquit him on the weight of Cicero's own consular authority: after all, who is better qualified to say whether Sulla was or was not a member of the plot of Catiline than the consul who detected the plot and saved the republic?

The defense of Flaccus is much more varied, with humorous passages almost recalling *Pro Murena*. Both speeches seem to have been defenses of a client whom Cicero knew to be guilty. Why did he take such cases? The defense of Murena we have justified by public expediency; the attack on Flaccus, Cicero's praetor, could be justified as self-defense and the defense of a friend. The most difficult to explain is the defense of Sulla. In theory patrons received no fees, but Cicero at this time was able to borrow a large sum of money from Sulla to buy a new house on the Palatine. That may have had something to do with it (Gellius 12.12.2ff.). Or Cicero may have hoped at this time to conciliate some of the popular faction by not pushing any further against former conspirators.[64] Or he may have hoped for the approval of Pompey, who was Sulla's brother-in-law and whose growing coldness was one of Cicero's most constant worries. Pompey was perhaps hurt not to have had a chance to return from the East and save Rome from Catiline.[65]

In one of his last works, *De officiis*, written in 44 B.C., Cicero discusses the duty of an orator in accepting or rejecting cases offered to him.[66] He may in this philosoph-

[64] Cf. Humbert, *op.cit.* supra n. 16, 142. He compares Cicero's defense of Fonteius.

[65] Cf. Syme, *op.cit.* supra n. 32, 102.

[66] Cf. W. L. Grant, "Cicero on the Moral Character of the Orator," *CJ* 38 (1942-43) 472-78 and Michel 158-59.

ical work be assumed to be free from the immediate pressures which color his statements in orations, though not of course from justifying his own career to himself and to posterity. His position is that it is wrong for an orator to undertake prosecution of a man he believes innocent. Indeed, prosecution is generally to be avoided, but may be justified occasionally by needs of state, or to avenge a wrong, or to protect provincials (*De off.* 2.51). On the other hand, there is not the same objection to defending one who seems to be guilty:

"provided he is not vicious or impious. Popular opinion desires this, custom allows it, common humanity supports it. It is the duty of a judge always to seek out the truth, but of a patron sometimes to defend the appearances of probability (*veri simile*), even if it is less than the absolute truth. I would hesitate to write this, especially in a work on philosophy, were it not that the same doctrine was accepted by Panaetius, the most prestigious of the Stoics. It is in defense that glory and gratitude are most brought to fruition, and to the greater degree if, as sometimes happens, aid is brought to one who seems set upon and oppressed by the machinations of some powerful man. I have often handled such cases, especially that which I undertook as a young man for Sextus Roscius of Ameria against the influence of L. Sulla who was then in power" (*De off.* 2.51, cf. 2.62 and 71).

Elsewhere (*In Vat.* 5) he indicates that his view of prosecution and defense was generally accepted at Rome. Cicero's preference for and pride in his function as defender of the accused is repeatedly stated in the orations, for example in *Pro Archia* 1. That he himself was influenced at times by considerations such as political expediency or financial gain does not affect the sincerity of his belief that defense is, with certain limits, itself a good. If his conscience were satisfied on the basic moral question, other inducements might lend zest to his pleading, but there were limits. He rejects any possibility of defending conspirators other than Sulla (*Pro Sul.* 5-7). It is easy to say that money made the difference in Sulla's case, but we really do not know that to be true. We must not overlook the fact that Cicero was fundamentally a skeptic who thought that probability was all that could be known in most situations. Argument in the manner of the Academics on either side of an issue was congenial to him both in theory and in practice. Finally, it was a deeply rooted belief of antiquity, expressed by both Cicero and Quintilian, that the greatest achievement of the orator came in those cases where the evidence was strongly against the client and where victory had to be obtained by artistic means beyond logical presentation of the evidence. No one was better at this than Cicero. The view is related on the one hand to the intellectual challenge which Isocrates and Greek sophists had felt in rhetoric and on the other to Roman respect for moral authority and emotional intensity as produced by character presentation.

In 60 B.C. Pompey, Crassus, and Julius Caesar joined together in the personal pact known as the first triumvirate. None was very fond of the other, but each saw a hope of attaining certain political goals by joint action (Suet., *Jul.* 19.2). Their common enemy was the senatorial government[67] of which Cicero had made himself the spokesman, not altogether to the satisfaction of some snobbish senators. Cicero was in a sense a friend of each

[67] On the history of the period cf. M. Cary in *CAH* 9.506-36; Frank B. Marsh, "The Gangster in Roman Politics," *CJ* 28 (1932-33) 168-78; Ronald Syme, *The Roman Revolution*, Oxford, 1939, 28-46; Taylor, *op.cit.* supra n. 12, 117-82.

of the triumvirs (*Pro Sest.* 39): he had appeared in court
with Crassus, though he did not like him very well (*Ad
fam.* 1.9.20); he had eulogized Pompey; Caesar had tried
unsuccessfully to win his cooperation in an early stage
of what became the triumvirate (*Ad Att.* 2.3.3). Yet the
extraconstitutional nature of the triumvirate made it a
great threat to Cicero. His most outspoken personal
enemy at this time was P. Clodius, against whom he had
testified in the scandalous affair of the Bona Dea rites
(Plut., *Cic.* 29). Clodius was anxious for political power:
he sought it by becoming a popular leader against the
senatorial oligarchy and by making himself useful to one
or other of the triumvirs, sometimes against the senate,
sometimes against each other. Clodius was tribune in
58 and early in the year brought the crisis in Cicero's
affairs to a head by getting through the assembly a bill
outlawing anyone who had put to death a Roman citizen
without a trial. The triumvirs failed to help Cicero, and
late in March he left Rome for exile in Greece. Subsequently another law specifically declared him an exile.
Cicero remained in Greece, exceedingly depressed, until
August of 57 when he was at last restored by the efforts
of the senate and Pompey, whose relations with Clodius
had become increasingly hostile. The actual legislation
authorizing Cicero's return was an unusual act of the
comitia centuriata.

The *Post Reditum* Speeches

Cicero was received back in Rome on September 4, 57
with great public jubilation and great excitement on his
own part. He delivered first an address of thanks to the
senate, then a similar address to the people. These might
be called epideictic orations, and they are suitably amplified in style. We know that he wrote out the speech to
the senate ahead of time and *read* it "because of the

importance of the contents" (*Pro Planc.* 71), the only time he admits to such a procedure. Cicero is at his most Ciceronian in the opening of his address to the senate; his friends doubtless leaned back with satisfaction and whispered "that's the way to speak," and his enemies groaned with impatience. The address in the senate is not only fulsome in its praise of those who worked for his return, it is forceful in its attack on those Cicero could openly blame for his exile, the consuls of 58, Gabinius and Piso, and the tribune Clodius. Before the people the invective is much less personal (21-23). To the senate Cicero represents his return as in the national interest, to the people as a personal triumph.[68]

For some time after his return Cicero basked in the glory of his reception (*Ad fam.* 1.9.4); he tried to overlook the fact that his return was a favor from Pompey and Caesar and that brother Quintus had promised Cicero would give no trouble (*Ad fam.* 1.9.9); in February 56 he still congratulated himself on his position and popularity (*Ad. Q. fr.* 2.3.7). Little had, however, changed in the facts of political life. The triumvirate still existed. Clodius still hired gangs to intimidate and disrupt. The senate was divided and leaderless. Cicero was able to play at independence until April of 56.

We have from this period seven speeches, including the two speeches of thanks just mentioned. *De domo sua, On his House,* was delivered in the fall of 57 before the college of priests and aimed at the recovery of Cicero's property on the Palatine, overlooking the forum, which Clodius had had confiscated, pulled down, and dedicated as a shrine to Liberty. *De haruspicum responso, On the Reply of the Soothsayers,* was delivered in the senate early in 56 on the subject of the interpretation to be given to certain supernatural noises heard on the outskirts of

[68] Cf. Mack, *op.cit.* supra n. 37, 18-48.

193

Rome. These had become a political issue, for manipulation of the state religion was a regular feature of late republican politics.[69] In the late eighteenth and nineteenth centuries all four of these speeches were commonly regarded as spurious, principally because of their bombastic tendencies, but there is no doubt that Cicero composed them. The bombast is probably best explained by a much greater self-consciousness and insecurity in the period immediately after exile and a resulting striving for effect.[70] Cicero also resumed legal activities on behalf of those he identified with himself or regarded as worthy of help. In this connexion, early in 56, he delivered two of his finest speeches: *Pro Sestio* and *Pro Caelio*.

Two tribunes of 57 who had worked for Cicero's recall were P. Sestius and T. Annius Milo. Both were indicted for violence at the instigation of Clodius. The proceedings against Milo were postponed and then dropped, but Sestius was brought to trial on the tenth of February (*Ad Q. fr.* 2.3.5) and defended by an impressive set of patrons: Hortensius, Crassus, Calvus, of whom more later, and Cicero.[71] Pompey appeared as a witness for the de-

---

[69] Cf. Taylor, *op.cit.* supra n. 12, 76-97.

[70] Cf. N. H. Watts, *Cicero: the Speeches: Pro Archia, etc.*, London, 1923, 46-47; Robert G. Nisbet, *M. Tulli Ciceronis De Domo sua ad pontifices oratio*, Oxford, 1939, xxix-xxxiv; Pierre Wuilleumier, *Cicéron, discours*, XIII, Paris, 1952, 22-28; K. Kumaniecki, "Ciceros Rede *De haruspicum responso*," *Klio* 37 (1959) 135-52. On the circumstances cf. Walter Allen, Jr., "The Location of Cicero's House on the Palatine," *CJ* 35 (1939-40) 134-43; idem, "Nisbet on the Question of Cicero's House," *CJ* 35 (1939-40) 291-95; idem, "Cicero's House and Libertas," *TAPhA* 75 (1944) 1-9.

[71] Cicero refers to Hortensius, *Pro Sest.* 3 and 14. Crassus and Calvus are known from the *Scholia Bob.* 125 Stangl. Caesar is referred to as a friend of Sestius by Cicero (71), but of course was not present. Cf. in general Clemens Korte, *Untersuchungen zu Ciceros Rede für Sestius*, Münster, 1939 and J. Cousin, *Cicéron: discours* XIV (Budé), Paris, 1965.

fense (*Ad fam.* 1.9.7). The trial lasted, perhaps with some adjournments, until March 11th and resulted in the unanimous acquittal of Sestius (*Ad Q. fr.* 2.4.1). Although the opening of the speech reveals Cicero's unhappiness with contemporary political conditions, he saw in the case not only an opportunity to prove his gratitude to Sestius for aid in his recall from exile (3 and *Ad Q. fr.* 2.4.1) but also to preach his own political doctrine of the union of men of good will in the common cause. As usual, he was last to speak of the advocates for the defense (3) and his speech is thus a kind of summation. He announces at the outset that he will concern himself not with separate allegations, but with the whole position of Sestius, including his way of life, his nature, his habits, his love for men of good will, his desire for the safety of the state and for peace. This promise is fulfilled, though not quite in the expected way, for Sestius is repeatedly lost sight of in the shade of Cicero himself who claims indeed (31) that Sestius is being prosecuted for his sake. Sestius' purpose as a tribune was to heal the wounds of the state, and what greater wound was there than the attack on Cicero?

A brief look at the structure of the speech will show the proportions. There is first an exordium (1-5) which explains why Cicero speaks and contains the partition of what he will discuss. Then (6-77) comes a chronological narrative of Sestius' career up into his tribuneship in 57, but there is inserted a long (15-71) account of Cicero's exile and other events of 58 in which Sestius is hardly mentioned. The narration leads imperceptibly into a refutation of the charge of violence (77-95). There follows the most famous part of the speech, a discussion of Cicero's views of the *optimates*: who they are, their goals, their hope of success. This passage was apparently suggested by a remark of the prosecutor (96), but formally it must be called a digression. Finally Cicero returns to Sestius for a brief peroration (144-47). The freedom of form in the speech is typical of Cicero's works at this time, for he is handling cases unprovided for in rhetorical texts.

Pro Sestio contains many splendid passages, among them Cicero's appeal to the Fatherland (45) to testify that for the sake of his fellow citizens he went into exile rather than stayed in Rome to die. The apostrophe recalls Demosthenes' Marathon oath in *On the Crown,* as does the argument that Cicero did the only right thing. The passage continues with an elaboration of the traditional image of the ship of state. Another fine passage is that (120-24) describing the presentation by the tragic actor Aesopus of lines from the Roman tragedian Accius in such a way that they seemed to refer to Cicero.[72]

The long passage on the *optimates,* often praised in the past, has begun to pall on some critics of the mid-twentieth century.[73] Cicero's remarks have the merit of being an attempt at a constructive union of responsible conservative sentiment and of course they help to broaden the significance of the speech in which they appear. It was, moreover, an accepted tradition of ancient oratory that saying so helped make it so: the orator con-

[72] Contemporary significance was often given to passages of drama in this way, cf. Suet., *Galba* 13.

[73] Cf. esp. Nisbet, *op.cit.* supra n. 1, 66. He regards the passage as an addition to the speech for publication. Also cf. the view of J.P.V.D. Balsdon, "Auctoritas, dignitas, otium," *CQ* 10 (1960) 43-50. In reply W. K. Lacey, "Cicero, Pro Sestio 96-143," *CQ* 12 (1962) 67-71. A key slogan is *cum dignitate otium,* also found at the beginning of *De oratore.* On this cf. Charles Wirszubski, "Cicero's *cum dignitate otium:* a Reconsideration," *JRS* 44 (1954) 1-13; R. Gardner, *Cicero: the Speeches Pro Sestio and In Vatinium,* London, 1958, 302-5; M. Fuhrmann, "*Cum dignitate otium:* politische Program und Staatstheorie bei Cicero," *Gymnasium* 67 (1960) 481-500; Michel 556-60. In general, cf. Douglas, *op.cit.* supra n. 1, 15.

fidently states his ideals as existing facts. What Cicero does is to develop the technique of definition, one of the commonest tools of all speakers. Apparently the speech was rhetorically an overwhelming success, for Sestius was unanimously acquitted. It is true that the ideal which Cicero hoped for was not achieved in anything like the form he wanted and that within a few months his program was a failure, but the historical result cannot be blamed on this speech. It derived from the power of the forces against Cicero and the failure of his subsequent tactics. The weakness of the speech, viewed side by side with the great oratory of history, is the fact that it pulls a specious cloak of decency over Roman politics: the result seems unrealistic and, worse, lacking in force. That sharp focus with full recognition of conflict or expediency which characterizes the boldest Greek oratory is lacking here, and the blandness is worsened by the amplification, for example, by the review (106ff.) of the meetings of the Roman people which adds a great deal of verbiage. Cicero can be realistic and incisive, for example, in the speech *On the Consular Provinces* which soon followed, but often he is led to seek other qualities, partly out of search for general significance.

Pro Sestio is not much concerned with its ostensible subject, Sestius; it does not muster its arguments and techniques for a single practical and immediate purpose. Although Cicero's overall objective is to persuade, considerable portions of the speech can easily be viewed as narrative, sometimes even as digressive, in other words, as expressive of Cicero's experience, personality, and thought. He doubtless believed that there was a chance of success for his ideal, but expression was personally important to him, for he had come in his own mind to play a well-defined role in the drama of events, and he was an orator: he could not live without verbalizing.

In the trial of Sestius, Cicero also delivered the speech *In Vatinium.*[74] It was part of the examination of witnesses which followed the *orationes perpetuae* of the patrons. Apparently Vatinius had given evidence for the prosecution in the form of a statement or speech. Among other things he had reproached Cicero with defending Cornelius (5) and thrown his exile in his face (6). Cicero replied to Vatinius next day. He asks him a large number of questions, but most of them are not intended to be answered, except probably for those at the end (40-41) which thus become a cross-examination. The speech is therefore an example of the treatment of witnesses in a trial: Vatinius is very roughly handled.[75]

About a month later Cicero defended M. Caelius Rufus before the same court, though this time the charges were more varied, including not only violence but attempted poisoning.[76] Cicero's colleague was again

[74] Cf. Lewis G. Pocock, *A Commentary on Cicero, In Vatinium,* London, 1926, and Umberto Albini, "L'orazione contro Vatinio," *La parola del passato* 14 (1959) 172-84.

[75] Could Cicero have published a speech composed on the basis of questions and answers at the trial? Cf. Humbert, *op.cit.* supra n. 16. Quintilian (5.7.3-6) says that speeches were sometimes delivered against witnesses and mentions *In Vat.* as an example.

[76] Cf. esp. R. G. Austin, *M. Tulli Ciceronis Pro M. Caelio oratio,* Oxford, 1960. There are numerous historical and rhetorical problems, including the relationship of the spoken and published speech. Cf. Eduard Norden, "Zur Komposition der *Caeliana,*" *SBBerlin* 1913.1, 12-32; Humbert, *op.cit.* supra n. 16, 153-67; Richard Heinze, "Ciceros Rede *Pro Caelio,*" *Hermes* 60 (1925) 193-258; Emma Crownover, "The Clash between Clodia and Cicero," *CJ* 30 (1933-34) 137-47; Felice Lavera, "Quaestioni reguardenti il processo *de vi* di Marco Celio Rufo e l'orazione di Cicerone," *MC* 6 (1936) 167-78; T. A. Dorey, "Cicero, Clodia, and the *Pro Caelio,*" *G & R* 5 (1958) 175-80; Jean Cousin, "Rhétorique dans le *Pro Caelio,*" *Atti del I congresso internazionale di studi Ciconiani,* 2, Rome, 1961, 91-98; Jerzy Linderski, "Ciceros Rede *Pro Caelio* und die Ambitus und

Crassus and he again spoke last, dealing with Caelius' alleged attack on Dio and attempt to poison Clodia, two of the five complaints (23). The speech is another example of Cicero's success in defending a client by cleverness, wit, and style rather than by evidence or proof. He even makes it seem a virtue that he has no witnesses for the defense (22)! As a parade of characters the speech is splendid: there is the young pleader for the prosecution, treated with humiliating condescension by Cicero (6-8);[77] there is Clodia, sister and alleged mistress of Cicero's enemy Clodius, the Medea of the Palatine, not less interesting to posterity as the former love of the poet Catullus; and there is Caelius himself, whose exploits are dismissed as youthful wild oats by the suddenly sophisticated orator. Indeed, Cicero makes considerable effort to present Caelius as potentially a young Cicero who may be expected to develop into a statesman like himself.[78]

The primary rhetorical problem was doubtless the weakness of Cicero's case, and the answer to it is the brilliant color, the entertaining irrelevancies, the vigor and self-assurance of the presentation, and the consular authority shed on Caelius by Cicero himself. The charge that Caelius took gold from Clodia to buy the assassination of Dio is met by a sophistic dilemma reminiscent of that in the *Pro Cluentio*: if Caelius was intimate with Clodia he surely would have told her why he wanted the gold and she would have refused it; if he was not intimate with her she wouldn't have given it to him (53)! The charge of poisoning is met by the claim that Cicero

---

Vereinsgesetzgebung der ausgehenden Republik," *Hermes* 89 (1961) 106-19.

[77] Quintilian, however, thought Cicero was being gentle and fatherly (11.1.68).

[78] Cf. Kennedy, *op.cit.* supra n. 5.

can see no motive (56) and Cicero elaborates into a most improbable comic farce a scene in the baths when the poison is supposed to have been delivered. It was perhaps the greatly admired personification first of Appius Claudius and then of Clodius addressing Clodia (33-36) that won the victory. Cicero's embarrassment is most evident when he tries to play down Caelius' association with Catiline. Caelius had earlier been closely attached to Cicero almost in the way that Cicero had as a young man been attached to Crassus. Then they had become estranged. Cicero probably undertook the defense of Caelius because he had been attacked by their common enemy rather than for great sympathy with his recent actions.

Soon after the victory for Caelius in the spring of 56 Cicero's career, almost always in crisis, reached a turning point. He thought that the triumvirs were drifting apart and he attempted to get the senate to undo some of the actions of Caesar's consulship, expecting that Pompey would not object. He was wrong. The action contributed to the renewal of the triumvirate at Luca and to a great tightening of control by Caesar, Pompey, and Crassus. The alternatives open to Cicero narrowed to cooperation or retirement (*Ad fam.* 1.9.9), and he chose to cooperate. He already had discovered the horrors of exile. Cooperation took the form of supporting in the senate policies of interest to the triumvirs and, worse, undertaking on request the defense of their friends in the law courts. In a long letter to Lentulus written in 54 B.C. (*Ad fam.* 1.9) Cicero discussed his motives, the changed condition of the state, the limited opportunities for public service now open, and the way some of the senatorial party had failed to support him. His basic justification was that he did sincerely respect Pompey and felt a debt of gratitude to him and that Caesar had been his friend in the past and had preserved the appearances of friendship even in recent times. Loss of independence is never an attractive spectacle; Cicero's actions may be regretted without much criticism of himself. His aim had always been a reasonable coalition and it was natural to his character to cooperate when at all possible. Another mitigating factor is the powerful role played by personal relationships and the relatively weak role of ideology or party ties in Roman politics. Finally, though he defended some men he did not like, Cicero did not undertake prosecutions for the triumvirs. We have seen that he attached considerable importance to the right of the accused to a defense and he could feel that he kept faith with this principle. In the rare cases when he spoke for the prosecution he did so of his own free will.

Of Cicero's speeches in the service of the triumvirs three have survived, *De provinciis consularibus* and *Pro Balbo* of 56 B.C. and *Pro Rabirio Postumo* of 54. The first, *On the Consular Provinces,* is an able piece of work.[79] In the normal course of events the consuls of 55 B.C. would be elected in the summer of 56 and would go out to provinces as proconsuls at the beginning of 54. Under the Sempronian law the senate was required to decide before the election of consuls what provinces would be allotted to them to govern two years later as proconsuls. An effort was being made to remove Caesar as governor of Cisalpine Gaul or Transalpine Gaul or both and assign one or both provinces to the new consuls. Cicero opposed this and he was able to do so with considerable enthusiasm since the provinces to be chosen instead were Macedon and Syria, now governed by Piso

[79] Cf. H. E. Butler and M. Cary, M. *Tulli Ciceronis De provinciis consularibus oratio ad senatum*, Oxford, 1924.

and Gabinius, who had been consuls the year he was exiled and whom he had no intention of forgiving. The speech deals in an orderly way with the expediency of removing both Piso and Gabinius and then with the advantage of retaining Caesar in Gaul to complete his conquests, the importance of which are well brought out (32-35). Cicero is candid about his relations with Caesar (40-43): their personal friendship in the past, his opposition to Caesar's measures, the attempts of Caesar to secure his support, and the role of Pompey in bringing them together. And he tries to disarm criticism of his altered political position by pointing out how the senate itself had honored Caesar (38-39).

Cicero's activities in the law courts in the service of the triumvirs were less congenial to him. Although he undertook only defenses, that meant in 54 the defense of Vatinius, whom he had attacked so severely in the extant speech of 56, and then of Gabinius, whom he had so often criticized. As a matter of fact, he prosecuted Gabinius for *maiestas* on his own account and lost the case, then was forced by the triumvirs almost immediately to defend Gabinius on a charge of extortion.[80] The situation was shameful, and Cicero probably was not too disappointed when the defense failed and Gabinius was exiled. Agents of the triumvirs whom he defended included L. Cornelius Balbus in 56 b.c., Rabirius Postumus in 54, and others. The speeches for Balbus and Rabirius (possibly an adopted connexion of Cicero's client of 63) are extant, the former in a case of contested citizenship, the latter on a charge that he received some of the money Gabinius had extorted from provincials.

The most remarkable speech surviving from this period is the invective *Against Piso*, delivered in the senate in

[80] Cf. E. M. Sanford, "The Career of Aulus Gabinius," *TAPhA* 70 (1939) 64-92.

55.[81] Piso, now recalled from Macedon partly through Cicero's efforts in the speech *On the Consular Provinces*, attacked and ridiculed Cicero in the senate. Cicero then replied, though perhaps not at the length and maybe not with the violence of the published version of the speech. Piso also published an attack on Cicero. As Cicero eventually came to realize, Piso was a man of considerable ability and independence. He was certainly not a tool of the triumvirs and thus seemed safe to attack, but Cicero's independence of action was not appreciated and the call to plead for Vatinius and Gabinius came soon afterward. Cicero's extraordinary violence against Piso results largely from his smoldering resentment at his own exile, but it was perhaps worsened by his other frustrations and pent-up emotion. If so, this loss of self-control is the first sign we have met of the effect of loss of freedom of speech on Roman oratory. The speech is purely demonstrative and is not aimed at persuading the senate to any action or decision; it is thus also a document in the development of rhetoric from an art of persuasion to an art of expression. Though, as we have seen, this tendency had been under way for some time, it probably was strengthened by autocracy. The impulse to oratory, deeply engrained in ancient man and fortified by education and tradition, found expression where it could. The most interesting feature of the speech is the attempt to use Piso's interest in Epicureanism to discredit him, just as Cato's Stoicism had been used in *Pro Murena*.

[81] Cf. Philip DeLacey, "Cicero's Invective against Piso," *TAPhA* 72 (1941) 49-58 and R.G.M. Nisbet, *M. Tulli Ciceronis in L. Calpurnium Pisonem oratio*, Oxford, 1961, esp. appendix 6, "The *In Pisonem* as an Invective." Cf. also Wilhelm Süss, *Ethos: Studien zur älteren griechischen Rhetorik*, Leipzig, 1910, 245ff.

In the defense of Scaurus on a charge of extortion in 54 B.C.,[82] a speech which is only fragmentarily preserved, Cicero put heavy reliance on ethos and pathos. Prejudices against the Sardinians are played on unabashedly; every possible influence in Scaurus' behalf is brought to bear by the participation in the case of six distinguished *patroni* and by character testimony from nine ex-consuls, including Pompey. Scaurus himself spoke too, carefully costumed in the untrimmed beard and unkempt clothes of a despairing man, and he cried openly in court. Finally, as the jury filed by to make its verdict, Scaurus with his friends and relations formed two rows of kneeling suppliants. The decision was acquittal, 62 to 8 (cf. Asconius, *In Scaur.* 25).

A final speech belonging to this group is *Pro Plancio*.[83] It is equally emotional, but more personal: Cicero's defense of the man who as quaestor in Macedon had befriended him in exile and who now is being charged with bribery in a successful candidacy for aedile. The ethos is carefully manipulated. At the start (1-17) Cicero seems torn between two friends, one prosecutor, one defendant, but subsequently identifies himself with his client and increasingly talks about himself. It finally emerges (86) that he regards the attack on Plancius as really an attack on himself and the speech is very analogous in its fundamental concern and some of its amplification to *Pro Sestio*. The bribery charge is rather forgotten as the speech unfolds and the rhetorical highlights come in such passages as the *locus* on gratitude (80-81) or the witty refutation of the opponent's points (e.g., 83).

[82] Cf. E. Courtney, "The Prosecution of Scaurus in 54 B.C.," *Philologus* 105 (1961) 151-56.
[83] Cf. W. Kroll, "Ciceros Rede für Plancus," *RhM* 86 (1937) 127-39.

Hortensius was again associated with Cicero in this case (37).

De Oratore

Cicero found another outlet for his rhetorical energy during the course of the year 55. While contemplating his own checked career and the limitations imposed on the orator, he composed a dialogue setting forth his ideal of what the perfect speaker could and should be, the three books *De oratore*.[84] It is one of his most admired works and stands beside or only slightly behind Aristotle's *Rhetoric* and Quintilian's *De institutione oratoria* as a rhetorical classic.

Each of the three books has a prologue of comments by Cicero and a setting of the scene of the ensuing dialogue, which is represented as taking place at various spots on the estate of L. Crassus at Tusculum in September 91 B.C. The characters are Crassus and Antonius and the old augur Scaevola, already discussed in chapter one, also Crassus' younger admirer Sulpicius, Antonius' young friend Aurelius Cotta, from whom Cicero claims he learned of the discussion, and later in the work Lutatius Catulus and Julius Caesar Strabo Vopiscus, uncle of Caesar the dictator. All were distinguished men and able orators, active in the age which Cicero idealized as the high-water mark of effective oratory in Rome. All subsequently found their freedom of speech checked by enemies, while Antonius, Sulpicius, Catulus, and Strabo lost even their lives. In the prologue to the third book Cicero

[84] It was completed by Nov. 55, cf. *Ad Att.* 4.13.2, and probably published by early 54. Cf. Augustus S. Wilkins, *M. Tulli Ciceronis De oratore libri tres*, 3 vols. Oxford, 1888-92; Gwynn, 79-122; Clarke 50-61; G.M.A. Grube, "Educational, Rhetorical, and Literary Theory in Cicero," *Phoenix* 16 (1962) 234-57.

reviews their fate and draws a comparison to his own experience (3.13).

The discussion of the first book[85] takes place in the garden under a plane tree in imitation of the scene of Plato's *Phaedrus*. Crassus and Antonius are the major speakers, but their remarks are interrupted by general discussion from time to time and they are urged on or questioned by others. Crassus' initial praise of oratory (1.30-34) is questioned by Scaevola (1.35-44), who thinks wisdom, not eloquence, is most important in public life. Crassus then (1.45-73) tries to show that the ideal orator will in fact have a wide general knowledge and will be able to state his ideas better than any specialist. Antonius, who then enters the discussion, is less hostile than Scaevola, but he still furnishes the principal conflict of the dialogue. He says (1.80-95) that he agrees in theory with Crassus, but in practice the goal is unattainable. In the second half of the book the two expound their views more fully. Crassus first, with some interruptions, discusses the nature and training of the orator (1.107-203). He puts emphasis on natural ability and does not think there is an art of oratory, since the subject is one of opinion and probability rather than scientific rule, but there is something analogous to an art. He describes the various categories of rhetorical theory and outlines rhetorical exercises, and he concludes with the necessity of studying history and law. Antonius gives an able reply (1.207-62) starting from a restricted definition of the orator not as a man who can speak on any subject, but as one who can use language and argu-

[85] For another outline cf. Edmond Courbaud, *Cicéron: de l'orateur*, 3 vols., Paris, 1922-30, in the introductions to each volume. The structure of the individual books is apparently very carefully worked out in architectural proportions, cf. Mechtilde O'Mara, "The Structure of the De Oratore," Dissertation, Univ. of North Carolina, 1970.

ment effectively in the law courts and in public meetings. The orator ought to acquire knowledge, but it is not his as orator, but as philosopher, or lawyer, or other specialist. In practice not very much philosophy or law is needed. Crassus does not accept this (1.263-65) and accuses Antonius of unduly restricting the orator and making him into an *operarius*, or day laborer, out of desire for debate.

The long second book is largely given over to Antonius, who is made to have moderated his views over the intervening night.[86] He no longer pushes his restricted definition, but as the company strolls about a portico he discusses the orator on the basis of his own experience. His remarks include speculation on the possibility of a rhetorical historiography[87] and in oratory range over the whole area of invention, arrangement, and memory. Most important is the discussion of the three functions of the orator: to win over the audience's sympathy, to prove what is true, and to stir their emotions to the desired action (2.115). This becomes the central concept of Cicero's rhetorical theory and is often called the three *officia oratoris*. In dealing with the emotions the use of humor is mentioned, and an extensive account of that subject is given by Caesar (2.217-90).

The third book takes place in the afternoon of the same day when the company meets in a shady spot. Crassus is the chief speaker and primarily concerns himself with style and delivery, but he is twice led into an *excursus* on the orator's need for a general education and especially knowledge of philosophy. The first of these

[86] Severely criticized by Clarke 52. J. Perret thought Cicero made Antonius modify his views to be in accord with statements in his little work on rhetoric, cf. "A propos du second discours de Crassus (*De oratore* 1.47-73)" *REL* 24 (1946) 169-89, esp. 177.
[87] Cf. infra 292 and note thereto.

(3.52-90) is suggested by the consideration that oratory is something more than correct and clear language. Crassus reviews ancient intellectual history and blames Socrates for separating rhetoric and philosophy (3.60-61). He considers the view of rhetoric of the various Hellenistic philosophical schools (3.62-68) and finds the Academy most satisfactory. A second excursus (3.104-43) is suggested by the importance of amplification in great oratory. To be able to amplify, the orator must have knowledge. The discussion of style is structured around the four virtues of Latinity, clarity, ornamentation, and propriety (3.37), though clarity (3.48-51) and propriety (3.210-12) are only very briefly treated. The extensive account of ornamentation treats diction (3.148-70), including the use of metaphors, and composition (3.171-208), in which appears the first account in Latin of prose rhythm, which Cicero views as a part of the emotional element in oratory. Indeed Cicero's view of style, as his view of ethos and pathos, is essentially a practical one: oratory still aims at persuasion. An interesting passage is the brief discussion (3.180-81) of the beauty of functionalism, taking a sailing ship and the Capitoline temple as examples. The book ends with a tribute to Hortensius (3.228), the rising young orator, which is apparently intended as an imitation of the reference to Isocrates at the end of Plato's *Phaedrus*.

In the letter to Lentulus already quoted (*Ad fam.* 1.9.23) Cicero tells something about the form and contents of *De oratore*:

Since I am dissociating myself from orations and turning to gentler Muses which appeal to me now very greatly, as they have since youth, I have written in the manner of Aristotle, in so far as I wanted to conform to that, three books of discussion and dialogue *On the Orator*, which I think may be helpful to your son Lentulus. They avoid the trite rules and embrace the oratorical theory of all the ancients, both the Aristotelian and Isocratean tradition.

The work is thus connected with the studies which preceded Cicero's public career. By describing the *form* as Aristotelian he probably meant that the various speakers have well-developed viewpoints which they expound at length and that there is not a search for truth by question and answer in the Socratic manner. The extensive use of prologues is also Aristotelian (*Ad Att.* 4.16.2). In another letter (*Ad Att.* 13.19.4) he speaks of the work as the type of dialogue written in the fourth century B.C. by the Academic Heraclides Ponticus in which the speakers are people of a previous generation and the writer plays no part in the discussion. This is perhaps the source of the reservation above about the suitability of calling the dialogue's manner that of Aristotle. We have already noticed reminiscences of Platonic dialogues.[88] Although there is technical rhetorical theory in *De oratore*, the final sentence of the letter quoted is substantiated by the fact that the treatise is primarily not a manual of definition and rule, by the avoidance

[88] On the Aristotelian dialogue cf. Rudolf Hirzel, *Der Dialog*, Leipzig, 1895, 272-308 and Philip Levine, "Cicero and the Literary Dialogue," *CJ* 53 (1957-58) 146-51. Cicero is imitating Plato in introducing old Scaevola only in the first book, like Cephalus in the *Republic* (cf. *Ad Att.* 4.16.3), and in setting the dialogue just before the death of Crassus, who is compared to Socrates in 3.14-15. Cf. Büchner, *op.cit.* supra n. 1, 199. Michel 81-149 stresses wider influences of Plato in Cicero's portrait of the orator as an ideal for imitation. Cf. also his *Le Dialogue des orateurs et la philosophie de Cicéron*, Paris, 1962 and G. Zoll, *Cicero Platonis Aemulus: Untersuchung über die Form von Ciceros Dialogen besonders von De Oratore*, Zürich, 1962.

of technical terms, and by the presence of concepts and teachings found in Isocrates, Aristotle, and their immediate successors like Theophrastus, but neglected or unknown by contemporary rhetoricians. The prologues to the separate books are clearly important in interpreting *De oratore*.[89] In that to the first book (1.1-27) Cicero claims that he had once hoped to have a public career and then to retire, or at least to have a chance to retire if he wished, to a life of leisure and study. Crassus is later said to have had the same hope (2.143), and it was doubtless a common Roman sentiment. He applies to himself the words *otium* and *dignitas* which he had used in a wider sense in *Pro Sestio*. This goal has not proved attainable; since his consulship, he means, his life has been more involved in crisis than ever. He is, however, going to resume his studies in so far as he can. He does not remark that he has been forced, as we know he was, into political eclipse. His brother Quintus Cicero, to whom he dedicates the work, has often asked him to replace *De inventione* with something worthy of his position, something more polished and complete. The book is thus one of the many examples of Roman works represented as being written in reply to the demand of others. It is also a replacement for *De inventione*, a factor of considerable importance. Since Cicero is consciously resuming the studies of his youth, it is not surprising that he looks back to that time, to *De inventione*, and to the influence of Crassus, Antonius, and others whom he had known.

Cicero says (1.4) that he will write *de omni ratione dicendi*, "on the whole theory of speaking," a promise

[89] Cf. M. Ruch, *Le préamble dans les oeuvres philosophiques de Cicéron: essai sur la génèse et l'art du dialogue (Publ. Fac. Lettres Strasbourg* 136) Paris, 1958 and Tore Janson, "Latin Prose Prefaces: Studies in Literary Conventions," *Acta Universitatis Stockholmiensis* 13 (1964) 32-40.

which is borne out by what follows in that the work deals with all five parts of rhetoric as well as with rhetorical education and practice. But it is natural to assume that he will particularly concern himself with the difference in opinion on the capabilities of the orator which he says (1.5) exists between himself and Quintus. This difference is not so clearly stated as it might have been, though the meaning becomes clear as one reads on. Cicero says that he regards "eloquence as comprised within the arts of very learned men, but you [Quintus] think it ought to be separated from the subtleties of theory and attributed to some kind of native ability and practice." We immediately think of the triad nature, practice, art,[90] which Cicero does indeed mention repeatedly (e.g., 1.14), and Quintus' position is certainly to accept two and reject one of these elements, but Cicero's view is not the direct antithesis of Quintus'. As he makes clear later in the introduction (1.19-20), he does not believe that eloquence is derived from knowing the rules of art, though he finds some of those rules interesting; the knowledge he has in mind is *general* knowledge, what we think of as the substance of liberal education. Indeed, no Roman is represented as seriously believing that eloquence is solely the result of studying Greek rhetorical theory. Crassus and Antonius agree that native ability is the most important single consideration (1.113), and with this Cicero and Quintus apparently agree. Crassus and Antonius are represented as disagreeing on the scope of general education needed by the orator, and this is the subject of disagreement between Cicero and his brother also.

There then follows (1.6-16) a passage which is initially rather puzzling. Cicero claims that there have been many

[90] For the Greek antecedents of this commonplace cf. Paul Shorey, "*Physis, melete, episteme,*" *TAPhA* 40 (1909) 185-201.

211

great generals, statesmen, philosophers, but hardly any great orators. Of course what he wants to do is to amplify the orator by stressing the enormous demands put on him. In comparison it is easy to be a general. The inspiration of the passage is doubtless the recorded remark of Antonius (1.94) that he had met many who were *disertos*, capable speakers, but no one who was truly eloquent. But the implication that oratory is some kind of activity separate from statesmanship or philosophy is unfortunate considering the doctrine later to be advanced, and is typical of the lack of precision in the treatise. Moreover, few readers, at least few modern readers, are apt to be convinced that in Rome and Greece there were far fewer good orators than good poets (1.11).

Cicero then gives briefly his own view of the orator (1.16-23). It is this which presumably he expects the dialogue as a whole to confirm in our minds. Rhetoric is a vast subject. Without knowledge of many things it is empty verbiage. Style must be developed and the emotions studied "because all the force and theory of speaking must be applied in calming or exciting the minds of those who constitute the audience" (1.17). There is need for humor, for knowledge of history, for knowledge of law. Delivery must be understood, memory must be sound. Neither rules nor teachers nor exercises can make a man an orator (1.19), but only knowledge of all great subjects and all arts. In practice, however, knowledge of everything is too much to demand, and like others Cicero will concern himself with the knowledge required for judicial and deliberative oratory. This survey brings out not only the center of contention in the dialogue, the question of the scope of the orator's education, but also the specific parts of rhetorical theory which will be given a prominence beyond or different from what they had in ordinary rhetorical treatises of the time.

The dramatic date of 91 of course makes it impossible for any of Cicero's experiences to be mentioned specifically, but it is clear that the elements in rhetoric which Cicero stresses are among the very ones which most distinguished his own practice. From earliest youth he had devoted great care to the development of prose style, studying with the best teachers he could find, practicing declamation, cultivating self-criticism. When he insists in book three (25-36) that there are many good styles and that the orator should be master of all, he is expounding one of his most firmly held theories which was to become his credo in the later quarrel with the Atticists. He had acquired an almost unique emotional power. How many of his speeches owed their success to the emotions he awakened in the audience when perhaps appearances or evidence or influence were against him! Humor had proved a great weapon in cases like *Pro Murena* or *Pro Caelio*. He is always prepared with historical background, especially important for an orator who took his conservative view of Roman political developments. His knowledge of law was famous and put to good use in difficult cases like *Pro Caecina*. His delivery and memory we can only surmise. Cicero's education was certainly more than usually complete, and continued in his adulthood through friendships with poets and philosophers. In speeches, of course, he sometimes deliberately hides his learning, as he claims Crassus and Antonius did, for fear it may prejudice a jury, and he disparages art, philosophy, or law if it meets his purposes, but his study of law, history, literature and philosophy was clearly at a professional level. Nor is this conviction that knowledge is important anything new in his career. It was one of his most deeply held beliefs going back to the first step of his education. The first words of his earliest work, the opening of *De inventione*, are on

213

the subject of the importance of a knowledge of philosophy for an orator, and he regularly recurs to the need for knowledge.[91] It has been claimed that Cicero's view of the orator, specifically of the orator's need for knowledge of philosophy, is derived from the philosophers of the New Academy with whom he had studied, either from Philo or from Antiochus, but the claim has increasingly been abandoned or diluted by recent students of Cicero.[92] Indeed, if Cicero's concept was derived from Philo or Antiochus he has been extraordinarily ungrateful, for he has put exposition of it in the mouth of his other, and earlier, mentor, Crassus, who even speaks rather disparagingly of Philo (3.110)[93] and cannot be expected to have known Antiochus at all. As will be argued below, Crassus' view was influenced by the Academic Charmadas, though his emphasis is different, and it is quite possible that Philo and Antiochus were also influenced

[91] Cf. Marcel Orban, "Rehabilitation de la parole dans le *De oratore* de Cicéron," *AC* 19 (1950) 27-44 and E. Gilson, "Éloquence et sagesse selon Cicéron," *Phoenix* 7 (1953) 1-19.

[92] Cf. Hans von Arnim, *Leben und Werke des Dio von Prusa*, Berlin, 1898, 97-114; Wilhelm Kroll, "Cicero und die Rhetorik," *NJA* 11 (1903) 681-89; ibid., "Studien über Ciceros Schrift *De oratore*," *RhM* 58 (1903) 552-97; ibid., *R-E Suppl.* 7.1086-87; George C. Fiske and Mary A. Grant, "Cicero's *De oratore* and Horace's *Ars poetica*," *Univ. of Wisconsin Studies in Language and Literature* 27 (1929) 11-20. For attempts to counteract these studies cf. Hans K. Schulte, "Orator: Untersuchungen über das Ciceronische Bildungsideal," *Frankfurter Studien zur Religion und Kultur der Antiken* 11 (1935); Michel 81-149; Karl Barwick, "Das rednerische Bildungsideal Ciceros," *Abhandlung der sächsischen Akademie der Wissenschaften zu Leipzig, philolog.-hist. Klasse* 54.3 (1963).

[93] Crassus' words about the Academic school are hard to evaluate: *florente Academia, ut temporibus illis ferebatur* (1.45). Does he mean that the Academy was at its height and so regarded or that it seemed to be at its height, but subsequently improved still more?

by Charmadas. Naturally in the specific exposition Cicero reflects his own studies with Philo or Antiochus and he surely draws on a variety of written sources, but it seems perfectly possible to conclude that the principal arguments of *De oratore* come in a general way from the sources which Cicero himself identifies: the ideas of Crassus and Antonius, their reaction to debates which they heard in Greece, and the teachings or practice of earlier Greeks like Aristotle and Isocrates. The ideal orator who is described is unquestionably a Roman, the clearest evidence being that he is thought of as a *patronus* who will be called on to defend clients in all kinds of cases and to exercise political leadership. It has been rightly observed that "the feeling of pride so palpably permeating the work springs from a conviction that in the political life of the Roman republic oratory has attained a power and a position it had not had with the Greeks since the times of Demosthenes."[94]

Cicero goes out of his way to claim that the dialogue is in accord with the opinions of the speakers, or at least those of Crassus and Antonius.[95] At the end of the intro-

[94] Cf. Friedrich Solmsen, rev. of Schulte, *AJPh* 59 (1938) 108.

[95] The historicity of the dialogue has been doubted, cf. Hirzel, *op.cit.* supra n. 88, 479-93. Some Ciceronian dialogues are quite without foundation, cf. *Ad fam.* 9.8, but they lack the protestations of fidelity found in *De or.* Cf. R. E. Jones, "Cicero's Accuracy of Characterization in his Dialogues," *AJPh* 60 (1939) 307-25; M. Ruch, "Vérité historique, veracité de la tradition, vraisemblance de la mise en scène dans les dialogues de Cicéron," *REL* 26 (1948) 61-63; Levine, *op.cit.* supra n. 88. G. L. Hendrickson, "Literary Sources in Cicero's *Brutus* and the Technique of Citation in Dialogue," *AJPh* 27 (1906) 184-99, argued that "the recognized technique of dialogue impelled him (Cicero) to put his characters in some relation of personal contact with the sources from which he himself drew." In *De or.* Cotta is that link and possibly should be viewed as a tenuous one. But Hendrickson pushed his argument so far that he made a liar of Cicero and suggested that lectures in Athens were not really heard by Crassus or Antonius.

duction to the first book the information is represented as
having been recounted to Cicero by Cotta, who was present (1.26-28), but in the introduction to the second book
Cicero gives an account of his own first-hand acquaintance with Crassus and Antonius, how he lived with
Crassus and heard his discussions and how he questioned
Antonius about his views, of which he had already heard
something from his uncle, Lucius Cicero (2.3). Elsewhere (1.96-98) it is said that Antonius would discuss
the nature of rhetoric but that Crassus had refused to
do so except on this one occasion (cf. also 1.119). Most
pointedly Cicero says that he writes in part to dispel
the notion that Crassus and Antonius were unlearned,
in part to preserve their opinions on eloquence, in part
to rescue from oblivion their fame, for they wrote little
themselves (2.7). This can hardly be a flat lie, and
Cicero points out that if he had chosen Galba or Carbo
as speakers he could have invented what he pleased, but
that there were alive those who had known Crassus and
Antonius as well as he had himself (2.9). Nearly forty
years has elapsed and Cicero doubtless does not remember them exactly as they really were, but they had made a
very strong impression on him and memory was cultivated and more retentive in many ancients than it usually
is today.

Cicero admits, of course, that his information is not
so detailed as he would wish (1.4); perhaps the most
precise description of the situation is that in the introduction to the third book (3.16):

"For I, who was not present at the conversation in
person and to whom C. Cotta reported only the topics[96]
and opinions expressed in this discussion (*tantummodo
locos ac sententias huius disputationis*), have tried to

[96] *Loci* (topics) here must mean *loci argumentorum*, or the
arguments used in support of the opinions expressed.

imitate in his speech the kind of oratory which I had come to know in each orator. But if there is anyone who led by common opinion thinks Antonius to have been a more austere or Crassus a more amplified speaker than I have represented them, he will be either one who did not hear them or one who cannot judge."

That is to say, Cicero knew from Cotta the general position taken by Crassus and Antonius in a discussion and the line of reasoning each followed. Since he was not present he did not know the words used, but he has drawn on his knowledge of each man to imitate his style and to produce a characterization in accord with probability. In the process of writing the dialogue we may assume that Cicero felt free to amplify what was said and to stress what he thought most important; this probably brought into the work a good deal of the technical rhetorical theory. Crassus and Antonius could well have known it, but it seems unlikely that they would have expounded it so systematically, even if nontechnically, on an occasion of this sort. Crassus and Antonius, as we see them in the first book of *De oratore*, are reasonably like their pictures in the *Brutus*, and Antonius' discussion of invention in book two could well be influenced by his own rhetorical handbook. Certainly the accounts of Roman oratory are entirely probable and the discussion of actual speeches of Crassus and Antonius increases the verisimilitude of the dialogue as a whole. To conclude, Cicero's introductions must be taken to mean that the central question of *De oratore*, the extent to which the orator needs a wide general knowledge, was actually discussed by Crassus and Antonius in some way, though not necessarily in the setting here portrayed. They state the subject as they see it, but Cicero is at pains to show that both had had the benefit of hearing Greek discussions of the orator and his training. He confirms the historicity of those occasions by mentioning specific time, place, and people involved and in the case of Antonius by citing Lucius Cicero as a witness (2.3).

Crassus says (1.45) that he listened to Charmadas, Clitomachus, Aeschines, and Metrodorus the Academics, Mnesarchus the Stoic, and Diodorus the Peripatetic in Athens.[97] Metrodorus he had also heard in Asia (2.365). Further, he studied Plato's *Gorgias* in company with Charmadas. All of these philosophers rejected the claims of the orator to greatness and restricted rhetoric to a knack useful in lawcourts and assemblies (1.46). Crassus maintained his independence, however; he says that he disagreed with them then as he still does now (1.47). Even if the sphere of the orator is limited to judicial and deliberative oratory, it demands a knowledge of law, custom, and human nature and of the specific subject on which the orator speaks (1.48). It is thus more than the philosophers have admitted. And conversely, when a philosopher like Democritus or Plato speaks well and other philosophers like Chrysippus do not, it follows that there is such a thing as eloquence apart from philosophy. Scaevola remarks (1.75) that he had heard Apollonius' criticism of philosophy when he visited Rhodes, but he finds Crassus' arguments more responsible and persuasive.

Antonius had heard some of the same philosophers Crassus mentions, including Mnesarchus the Stoic who thought eloquence was one of the attendant virtues of the sage and Charmadas who thought that rhetorical rules amounted to nothing and that the faculty of speak-

[97] Cf. APG 324-25. Cicero's knowledge of these teachers is of course not restricted to what he remembers Crassus and Antonius to have said. He had probably read the works of some of them and knew about them from his other teachers, including Philo and Antiochus.

ing came only to those who learned the discoveries of the philosophers (1.84). He then reports in some detail a dispute between Menedemus, a rhetorician who subsequently visited Rome (1.85), and Charmadas. Menedemus regarded political science as the subject of oratory and cited examples of knowledgeable orators like Demosthenes (1.88). He may be taken as the type of the unimaginative rhetorician and his arguments are not satisfying to anyone. Charmadas' position is much less antioratorical when expounded than it initially seems.[98] He does not think much of rhetoricians' rules, but points out the persuasive force of the orator's own character and the importance of pathos, and he says that knowledge of these subjects is philosophical knowledge (1.88). He admits the eloquence of Demosthenes, but thinks that it came either from native ability or from studying philosophy with Plato (1.89). Antonius claims to have been won over by Charmadas and to have shown his influence in the little handbook of rhetoric which he published (1.93-94).

This is very strange: Antonius in *De oratore* certainly does not expound Charmadas' position, which is philosophy as the basis of eloquence. He does support various subsidiary points: the insignificance of most rhetorical rules, the importance of native ability. Crassus, on the other hand, is really not too far from Charmadas' position. His demands on the orator include the philosophy which Charmadas wants and in much the form in which Charmadas presents it, that is, knowledge of ethos and pathos. He differs principally in applying the name orator to the speaker in all fields and demanding knowledge of subjects not mentioned by Charmadas. And even

---

[98] We are told (1.84) that Charmadas as a sceptical Academic disputed the views of others, and thus he did not necessarily reveal his own.

this he will abandon, for in the third book (3.142) he says that it makes little difference whether the title of orator is applied to a philosopher who has knowledge and eloquence or the title of philosopher to an orator who has the same attributes. This is perhaps the most important single statement for understanding the place of the dialogue in the history of rhetoric. It is also important to notice that of all the philosophical views it is the Academy which Crassus most approves (3.68), and when Cotta says that he has been persuaded by Crassus, he puts it in the words "you have driven me entirely into the Academy" (3.145). Cicero regarded Crassus' position, and thus his own, as somewhat unique in emphasis, but as very close in substance to the views of Charmadas.[99] As has been said, this may also mean they were similar to views of Philo and Antiochus. There clearly was in the early first century B.C. a partial reconciliation of the quarrel between rhetoric and philosophy, and the eloquent philosopher and the philosophical orator almost overlap. To a Hellenistic Greek the centrality of the philosopher was most evident, to a Roman *patronus* and politician the centrality of the orator.

Cicero had written to Lentulus that *De oratore* "embraced the oratorical theory of all the ancients, both the Aristotelian and Isocratean tradition." Specific influence of Isocrates or his followers is difficult to prove, partly because we do not know very much about the details of their teaching. Probably Cicero did not either, though he quotes Isocrates' pupil Naucrates as an authority on one point (3.173), and he may mean the tradition of the professional orators and teachers of rhetoric. Isocrates' conception of the orator is similar to what Cicero

[99] This seems the best answer to the objections of Perret, *op.cit.* supra n. 86.

220

envisages, an eloquent man skilled at advising states, knowledgeable in the workings of the world and especially in history and political theory.[100] Isocrates himself is cited by Crassus in one passage (3.59) as an example of an orator with knowledge, but in another (3.141) he is said to have turned from legal and political oratory to an empty elegance of speech, a not altogether unjustified complaint.

The influence of Aristotle and his successors can be seen more clearly.[101] Specifically, the discussion of invention in book two (2.114-306) is Aristotelian in that it does not deal with the parts of the oration as did the usual rhetorical handbook, *De inventione* for example or the *Rhetorica ad Herennium*; these are left to be mentioned under arrangement (2.307-332). As in Aristotle's *Rhetoric* invention consists of three forms of persuasion: the proof that what we claim is true, the effective presentation of moral character (ethos), and the appeal to the emotions (pathos) (2.115, cf. 121 and 128). The first kind of persuasion is based either on presentation of evidence or on rational argument, and each of these is discussed, as it is in Aristotle. The account of rational argument consists primarily of the list of general topics usable in all cases (2.162-73), the sort of thing Aristotle had discussed in the *Topics* and adapted for the *Rhetoric*. Antonius acknowledges (2.152-53) that the material is Aristotelian and claims to have read both the *Rhetoric* and the *Synagogê technôn* (2.160), but his account is

---

[100] Cf. Harry C. Hubbell, *The Influence of Isocrates on Cicero, Dionysius, and Aristides*, New Haven, 1913; Perret, *op.cit.* supra n. 86, 186-87; Orban, *op.cit.* supra n. 91, 38-45.

[101] Cf. Friedrich Solmsen, "The Aristotelian Tradition in Ancient Rhetoric," *AJPh* 62 (1941) 35-50. On Cicero's knowledge of Aristotle cf. O. Gigon, "Cicero und Aristoteles," *Hermes* 87 (1959) 143-62 and Michel 101.

not directly drawn from any in Aristotle and probably came from some Hellenistic version.[102] It is significant that though the Aristotelian topics are discussed, the real keystone of logical proof in the *Rhetoric*, the theory of enthymeme and example, is totally lacking, which suggests that the *Rhetoric* as we know it can hardly be a major direct influence. A possible explanation is that the version of the *Rhetoric* known in the time of Antonius was one of the earlier stages of its composition and that the version we know was not available until the recovery of Aristotle's library by Sulla (Strabo 13.609). In a letter written about the time of *De oratore* (*Ad Att.* 4.10) Cicero says that he has been studying in the library of Sulla's son and mentions Aristotle by name. This experience may have inspired some of the Aristotelianism of *De oratore*, though Cicero would have wished to avoid the anachronism of attributing knowledge to Antonius which he could not have had.

In the case of ethos, Cicero's insistence on its importance as a form of persuasion on a par with argument and pathos is Aristotelian. His actual treatment is not particularly Aristotelian, for Aristotle had discussed in some detail the appropriate characterization of the young, the old, the mature, the noble, the rich, and the powerful. Cicero's account is brief (2.182) and influenced by the conditions of Roman oratory: both the character of *patronus* and the client are considered. Most striking is the fact that Cicero regards ethos as consisting in presentation of the gentler emotions (2.183). It conciliates and charms the audience and is essentially good natured, a lower level of dramatic intensity than the raging fire of pathos which is the real triumph of the speaker's art. Subsequently (2.212) Cicero speaks of

[102] Cf. Kroll, *RhM*, *op.cit.* supra n. 92, 590 and Solmsen, *op.cit.* supra n. 101, 173.

two styles, one mild, the other vehement, but they are hard to keep separate.

The discussion of pathos (2.185-215) seems to have been adapted to the actual practice of Antonius and Crassus; it contains, for example, the account of Antonius' defense of Norbanus which we looked at in chapter one. Like Aristotle, however, Cicero does discuss how to arouse or allay some specific passions, jealousy, for example (2.209-10).[103]

To the discussion of pathos is appended an extensive account by Caesar of humor in oratory (2.216-89), copiously illustrated with Roman examples.[104] Cicero clearly thought that the subject was important and neglected by students of rhetoric. He mentions a number of ways in which humor is important to the orator (2.236):

"because it secures good will for him by whom it is aroused, or because all admire the sharpness inherent often in a single word, especially in replying to criticism and sometimes in attacking, or because it breaks the adversary or hinders or makes light of or discourages or refutes him, or because it shows that the orator himself is a man of culture, learned, sophisticated, and most of

[103] Cf. E. A. Lusskey, *The Appeal to the Emotions in the Judicial Speeches of Cicero as Compared with the Theories on the Subject in the De oratore*, Minneapolis, 1928; Harry J. Leon, "The Technique of Emotional Appeal in Cicero's Judicial Speeches," *CW* 29 (1935-36) 33-37; Friedrich Solmsen, "Aristotle and Cicero on the Orator's Playing upon the Feelings," *CPh* 33 (1938) 390-404.

[104] Cf. E. Arndt, *De ridiculi doctrina rhetorica*, Kirchain, 1904; Mary A. Grant, "The Ancient Rhetorical Theories of the Laughable: the Greek Rhetoricians and Cicero," *Univ. of Wisconsin Studies in Language and Literature* 21 (1924); George E. Duckworth, *The Nature of Roman Comedy*, Princeton, 1952, 305-14; Haury, *op.cit.* supra n. 60; Michel 271-83; G. Monaco, *Cicerone: il trattato de ridiculis (De oratore II.216-90)*, Palermo, 1964.

all because it softens and relaxes seriousness and tension and by laughter often dissolves troublesome matters which could not easily be disposed of by arguments."

He belittles Greek treatises on humor (2.217), but proceeds to divide up the subject along lines which resemble Greek treatises as we know them. Although the immediate sources cannot be identified, two related traditions seem to have existed. One is that from Aristotle, who has something to say about humor in the *Rhetoric*, the *Ethics*, and the *Poetics* and probably had even more to say in the lost second half of the *Poetics* on comedy, then from Theophrastus' lost work on humor, and probably from a variety of Peripatetic derivatives. The other tradition was an adaptation made by the Stoics to suit their theory of the plain style, known in Rome to Lucilius and other friends of Scipio. In general, two kinds of humor were recognized by ancient theorists, one good natured and pervasive, the other bad natured and intermittent. Cicero calls them *cavillatio* and *dicacitas* respectively (2.218). It was argued that the subject of humor was the unseemly or deformed, but within limits. Great wickedness or great misery was not an appropriate subject (2.236-37). Indeed, the key to the use of humor was propriety, and this is one source of its interest to Peripatetics. A more formal subdivision is that into humor based on words and humor based on a fact, an action, or a thought. This distinction was easy for rhetoricians since it paralleled the differences between figures of diction and figures of thought.

The final part of *De oratore* which shows clear influence of Aristotle's followers is Crassus' discussion of style in book three. If it is compared with the account in the *Rhetorica ad Herennium* and if the fact that Cicero deliberately avoids technical terms is put aside, the most conspicuous difference between the two is the way Cicero's account is built around the four virtues of style: correctness, clarity, ornamentation, and propriety (3.37). In *Ad Herennium* these are mentioned only in an altered form (4.17) and the discussion is almost entirely devoted to figures of speech, which to Aristotle, Theophrastus, and Cicero are only one of the topics of ornamentation. In Cicero the virtues are fundamental, though not treated in equal detail. There can be no doubt that these virtues come from Theophrastus' lost treatise *On Style* of which Cicero and possibly Antonius made direct use.[105] Similarities between Cicero and Aristotle's discussion of style probably come by way of Theophrastus. Among the most conspicuous is the importance attached to metaphor and to prose rhythm. Cicero says that the latter subject was not part of rhetorical studies (3.188) and refers to Aristotle's theories on the subject (3.182-83). There had apparently been little discussion since. Even Cicero does not have much to add at this time, but he continued to be interested in the subject and discusses it in greater detail in the *Orator*.

De oratore is an imposing work partly because of the vivid way it reveals the Roman achievement in oratory, partly because of Cicero's refusal to treat rhetoric in the mechanistic way of the handbooks. In *De inventione* he had made great claims for the orator in the introduction, but the details which followed largely obscured the grand design. In *De oratore* the inadequacy of rules is constantly stressed, almost too much so, perhaps, considering the debt of many portions of the work to rhetorical theory. Cicero was convinced from personal experience of the power and richness of oratory. It was to him a true art form, not art in the ancient sense of a science

---

[105] Cf. Michel 328-39 and APG 273-78. Cicero called Theophrastus his special luxury, cf. Plut., *Cicero* 24.3.

reducible to rule, but in the modern sense of art as a product of the creative imagination, working with defined forms and materials. Cicero had a certain kind of imagination in a very strong form: not an imagination to invent totally new concepts or to break with the past, but an imagination to maximize existing materials and opportunities. It was nurtured by his personal ambition to make as much as possible of his own career, and it made the task of defining and solving rhetorical challenges exceedingly congenial to him. He was a rhetorician in his innermost fiber. Cicero's attitude toward the training of the orator was almost certainly influenced by Crassus, whose objection to the Latin rhetors is represented as essentially similar, a resistance to what he regarded as superficial in not drawing on the full strength of available resources.

It seems necessary to admire the impulse behind *De oratore*. As we shall see, there was apparently some adverse reaction, but Cicero remained satisfied with it, which suggests that some compliments came in as well. He could not work without appreciation. Certainly the work did have a subsequent influence, especially on Quintilian. At the same time, Cicero's basic idea, the broad definition of the orator and the general education which he needs, is not worked out in an entirely satisfactory way. The dialogue form has charm, but covers up some imprecision, for it is entirely too much like a real conversation in which people forget what they have said or change their views for the sake of argument or politeness and in which general agreement does not represent logical necessity, but either weariness or good manners. On the other hand, the dramatic situation and the characterization are not really good enough to make the work stand as a purely literary achievement. One of the most coherent speeches is that of Antonius in book one demonstrating that the orator needs only a rather superficial knowledge of philosophy or law. This is never adequately answered. As though he were an Academic philosopher prepared to argue either side of a case, Antonius is allowed to change his mind overnight so he is no longer troublesome (2.40). Crassus approaches the problem in a different way later on and certainly expounds his views more fully; his insistence on philosophy is in the end dependent on three arguments: historically the orator and philosopher used to be one until Socrates exercised his baneful influence (3.69-73); secondly, his friends insist that he is himself an example of an orator aided by philosophy (3.82 and 90). Thirdly, a philosophical orator clearly has a knowledge beyond that of a nonphilosophical orator, and the greatest orator possible is what is wanted (3.84-85). The last is begging the question; the first two point to the possibility of a philosophical orator rather than prove the necessity of philosophy for the good orator.

A weakness of *De oratore* is Cicero's failure to consider the active and contemplative life as two aspects of the same person, of which the Greek sophists and Cicero himself could be regarded as examples. It is, after all, the total man that needs liberal education, not the orator or philosopher. Cicero by experience came to appreciate this, but he had difficulty in escaping from the rigid categories of the ancient mind in order to express it. He thought of philosophers, orators, generals, and the like, not of men. The work does not allow him opportunity to spell out his ideas on education very fully, but a similar rigidity of factual knowledge and study of technique rather than intellectual training might be feared there. Another area which is left largely untouched is the moral one. The responsibilities of the orator to himself or society and the role of belief in practice is certainly an important question in a comprehensive treatment of the orator. Here Quintilian is considerably better. The primary reason for its absence from *De oratore* is probably Cicero's conception of philosophy. As a rather eclectic Academic he viewed philosophical dogma as only probable and the kinds of problems which Plato saw in the uses of rhetoric do not seem real to him. Decisions have to be made not on the basis of absolute knowledge, but circumstances, probabilities, and expediencies. He takes what may be called the rhetorical view of the world, but he is not very conscious of ignoring all that Plato said nor of what makes the orator a more attractive ideal to him than the philosopher. His view of philosophy would seem to many philosophers to be shallow, and this is probably why no extensive refutation is undertaken of Antonius' claim that the orator needs little philosophy. Antonius has simply overstated what Crassus basically believes. Philosophy does not take much knowledge, he says (3.79); it is not like geometry or music but can be managed by any intelligent person. Perhaps its greatest value for the orator is in furnishing him materials for amplification in his speeches, which in turn of course contributes to his ethos and pathos and thus his victory. Of all the ideas expressed in *De oratore* perhaps the most objectionable is Crassus' claim (3.89) that unless a man can learn a subject quickly he can never learn it at all; it is a doctrine which Cotta and Caesar find immediately attractive (3.145-46) as justifying the belief that anything of value in philosophy can be quickly acquired or ignored, and it belongs in the Roman tradition of deliberate superficiality.

Cicero's view of philosophy in *De oratore*, involving a good deal of lip service but a certain amount of contempt, was his fundamental view. Philosophy always fascinated him, but never satisfied him. His philosophical work always verges on being patronizing. To admit this is not a blanket condemnation: he is doubtless right to some extent. Philosophy has made less "progress" than any other field of human knowledge, though it has certainly contributed a great deal to other disciplines. What is objectionable is not Cicero's position, but his lack of clarity about his position. It is a pity that he had to hedge so much, and that in defining the orator he could not distinguish between knowledge of philosophy and an intellectual vitality which is always curious and always creative and views experience in a philosophical way. It is this which the orator needs. As it is, *De oratore* begins as a work intended to counteract superficiality in rhetoric; it takes a broader view of the subject, but not a very much deeper one.

Cicero's rhetorical career, like his political life, was one of sharp contrasts. *De oratore* is speculative, literary, and expansive; *Partitiones oratoriae*, or *Classifications of oratory*, which followed it is a rhetorical catechism between Cicero and his son, unrelieved by characterization, digression, or adornment. A system of rhetoric is laid out in all its technicality. Although the date is not known for certain, the work was apparently written at a time when the younger Cicero was in the midst of his basic rhetorical education in Rome and the elder Cicero was preparing to leave Rome. Sometime between 54 and his departure to Cilicia in 52 would fit well.[106] Atticism was not yet an issue. Cicero indicates at the beginning that he is trying to give a Latin statement to the rhetoric which his son has studied in Greek and at the end (139) that the work is fundamentally derived from teachings

[106] Cf. Brady B. Gilleland, "The Date of Cicero's *Partitiones oratoriae,*" *CPh* 56 (1961) 29-32.

229

of earlier Academics. It has Academic and Stoic features and is chiefly of interest in reconstruction of rhetorical theory as taught by Hellenistic philosophers.[107]

Pro Milone

During the remaining years of the triumvirate Cicero's most important case was that of Milo.[108] The circumstances are dramatic and involved.[109] Almost complete chaos reigned in Rome in the fall and winter of 53-52 B.C. and the elections for consuls and praetors were repeatedly put off, so that 52 opened with no consuls at all. One candidate was Milo, a friend who had helped to bring Cicero back from exile and the leader of an armed band of thugs. Cicero's enemy Clodius was a candidate for praetor and the leader of another gang. Clodius tried every means of harassing Milo, including discussing his debts in the senate. Cicero countered with a speech on the debt of Milo, now lost, but partly known from a commentary in the *Scholia Bobiensia*. Early in 52 Milo and company met Clodius and company more or less by accident on the Appian Way about ten miles southeast of Rome, a fight took place, and Clodius was killed.

[107] Discussed in greater detail in APG 328-30. Cf. Frank I. Merchant, *De Ciceronis partitionibus oratoriae commentatio*, Berlin, 1910; Paul Sternkopf, *De M. Tullii Ciceronis partitionibus oratoriis*, Monasterii Guestfalorum, 1914; H. Bornecque, *Cicéron: Divisions de l'art oratoire*, Paris, 1924.

[108] Cf. Albert C. Clark, *M. Tulli Ciceronis Pro T. Annio Milone ad iudices oratio*, Oxford, 1895; R. W. Husband, "The Prosecution of Milo: a Case of Homicide with a Plea of Self-defense," *CW* 8 (1914-15) 146-50, 156-59; Marsh, *op.cit.* supra n. 67; Francis P. Donnelly, *Cicero's Milo: a Rhetorical Commentary*, New York, 1934; André Boulanger, *Cicéron: discours* XVII, Paris, 1949.

[109] Information on the trial comes in large part from Asconius' commentary, written a hundred years later. Some of this is translated in the appendix to the Loeb edition, cf. N. H. Watts, *Cicero: the Speeches*, London, 1931, 124-36.

His followers treated him as a fallen martyr and cremated him in and with the senate house. The senate passed a *consultum ultimum* and called upon Pompey to restore order. Pompey had sponsored Clodius in the past and was now standing on the sidelines watching with some satisfaction the collapse of constitutional authority. He quickly accepted the position of sole consul offered him by the senate, an office which was unprecedented and remarkable, almost analogous to that of the emperors. Always before, the principle of the consulship had been collegiality, and election had been by the assembly. Pompey secured the passage of new laws on violence and bribery, designed to set up a special court to deal with the recent lawlessness and especially with Milo's acts. This court was to conduct its business under rules of procedure intended to reduce as much as possible the influence of pathetic oratory as seen, for example, in the acquittal of Scaurus, and to prevent judicial bribery.

As a result, Cicero had to defend Milo under novel and limiting conditions which are known to us partly from Asconius' commentary on the speech. Instead of the usual opening speeches with their opportunity for generality and amplification, the trial began with three days of evidence from witnesses, carefully recorded in the presence of a jury. Then at a perfunctory session on the fourth day a jury of 81 was summoned to meet the next day. The members of this jury had not necessarily heard the evidence (Caesar, *B.C.* 3.1.4), though presumably they had access to it to check statements of the orators. Finally, on the fifth day came the trial itself, all completed in one day. The procedure might be regarded as modeled on that of the Greeks as known to us from the Attic orators, except that at the end, just before the vote, each side was to challenge 15 jurors, leaving a total of 51. The prosecution had two hours in which to speak, the defense three, much less than the usual time in important cases. In order to use the time to the best advantage Cicero was the only speaker for Milo. Not only did he have only a short time to counteract specific sworn testimony, but he had to speak surrounded by armed men and with Pompey anxiously looking down at the forum from the steps of the temple of Saturn, for the initial hearing of witnesses had been so disrupted that L. Domitius Ahenobarbus, Pompey's hand-picked judge, had appealed to him to keep order during the trial. Pompey's intention was probably to see that a legal and orderly trial took place and to protect the jury from intimidation, though he doubtless thought that Milo would be condemned if a proper trial were held. The situation in the city remained tense; Milo expected condemnation; Cicero had more than his usual case of stage fright, and was brought to the forum in an enclosed litter. The supporters of Clodius interrupted him, despite the soldiers. Although he apparently got through his speech, he failed to establish a rapport with the jury and Milo was convicted by a vote of 38 to 13. He went into exile at Marseilles. Among the jurymen was Cato and there was much speculation which way he had voted; no one knew for sure.

A version of the speech which Cicero delivered seems to have been known to Asconius in the next century[110] and was described by a later commentator as "interrupted, unpolished, crude, filled with signs of fear" (*Scholia Bobiensia* 112 Stangl). This version may have been based on notes taken in court. Cicero himself published a revised version which rhetoricians and modern critics have always regarded as almost a perfect speech.

[110] This is, however, questioned by James N. Settle, "The Trial of Milo and the other *Pro Milone*," *TAPhA* 94 (1963) 268-80.

According to an alluring tradition, when he received a copy, Milo remarked with irony that it was just as well Cicero hadn't delivered it or he would never have had a chance to enjoy the mullets of Marseilles (Dio Cassius 40.54.3). The evidence, however, does not indicate that the basic treatment of the two speeches differed and the improvement was presumably chiefly a matter of style.[111]

Pro Milone anticipates some of the conditions of oratory under the empire. The orator speaks in the shadow of a powerful figure whose intentions and interests are not entirely clear. The legal procedure is efficient and limiting: Tacitus (Dial. 38) regarded Pompey's law as permanently affecting the conditions of pleading, but only the time limit became a permanent feature of the law courts, and the old order of speeches and witnesses was eventually resumed (cf. Quint. 5.7.25).

Cicero's published speech for Milo consists of a prooemium (1-6) which starts from the unprecedented conditions under which Cicero must speak. Ethos appears almost immediately in references to the virtues of Pompey and Milo and the madness of Clodius. Then comes a refutation of three charges made by the opposition, all aimed at showing that a trial was hardly necessary in such an open-and-shut case (7-23). One charge was that Milo was an admitted murderer and thus deserved to die (7). Milo had not denied that Clodius was killed by his slave acting under his authority; Cicero will claim that it was done in self-defense against an attack begun by Clodius. The other two charges were that the senate by its resolutions had judged Milo to have acted against the interests of the state (12) and that Pompey had already judged the case by his law and procedures (15). Neither of these is legally valid, since both the

[111] Settle's conclusions, op.cit. supra n. 110, are acceptable to this extent.

senate and Pompey were investigating a situation and dealing with an emergency, not making a judgment of Milo, though Cicero's claim of Pompey's good will toward Milo is not entirely convincing. Next comes a brief narration (24-30). It is needed here since Cicero's picture of the events when Clodius was killed differs somewhat from that given by his opponents. The picture (28) of Milo going home from the senate, changing his clothes, and sitting waiting for his wife, "as happens to us all," has been appreciated by many readers. Then comes Cicero's statement of the crucial question: "Which laid a plot for which?" (30-31) and the proof (32-91) that it was not to Milo's interests to do so and that the circumstances of time and place did not make it probable that he had actually done so. All of this is admirably worked out along the lines taught by the rhetorical schools. The emotional element in the speech becomes increasingly strong, culminating in the peroration (92-105).

Quintilian (6.5.10) did not know what to praise most about *Pro Milone*. He mentions specifically the way refutation is placed before narrative, certainly effective and not what an inferior or more rule-bound orator might have done, also the way Clodius is shown to have been the aggressor, the combination of the plea that Milo did not intend murder with Cicero's approval of Clodius' death, and the substitution of an emotional appeal by Cicero for any demonstration of pathos by Milo himself. The *stasis* of the speech always interested rhetoricians. Cicero could not deny the fact that Clodius was killed by Milo's slave, for which Milo was responsible. He had, however, the choice of two arguments, the legal one, that the action was justifiable homicide in self-defense, or the qualitative one, that the action, even if deliberate, was in the national interest. Brutus, always attracted by grand gestures, favored using the latter and wrote a revision of the speech to show how it should have been done (Quint. 3.6.93). The argument would not have been legally valid; it would have had hope of success only in circumstances in which Cicero could have dominated the court with emotional power, and this in fact he could not expect to do. He makes it clear that he regards Clodius' death as a good thing, but he does not try to save Milo with that argument.

Another feature which should be noticed is Cicero's care in selecting material. He says as little as possible about Pompey's new law against violence under which the case was being tried. It was occasioned by Milo's action and could only prejudice his case. The argument of self-defense is based on the *lex Cornelia* whose provisions are assumed to be applicable as principles of Roman law.[112] It is odd that there was no specific provision for killing in self-defense and that Cicero must deduce it from the right to bear arms in self-defense. There is also a good deal of selecting and coloring in the picture of Milo, whose patriotism and other virtues have not been so evident to historians.

Pompey attempted to follow a course of moderation and restraint consistent with his own ambitions. In subsequent action under his law Cicero and Caelius managed to secure the acquittal, by one vote, of Milo's man Saufeius who had actually struck the blow that killed Clodius (Asconius, *In Mil.* 48), while Clodius' partisan Plancus was convicted (*Ad fam.* 7.2.2). Cicero says (*Brutus* 324) that he was in court every day in proceedings under Pompey's law on violence, as was Hortensius, and that despite the time limitation under the law and the similarity of the cases, they produced good speeches. This was his last period of activity in the law courts, and

[112] Cf. R. Cahen, "Examen de quelques passages du *Pro Milone*," REA 25 (1923) 119-38 and 215-33.

even so it did not take up all his time, for he was completing *De republica* and perhaps *De legibus*. In May 51 he left to be governor of Cilicia for a year.

Cicero did not get back to Italy until November of 50 and since he rather hoped to be given a triumph for a military campaign in his province, he did not come to take his seat in the senate even then. Thus he did not participate in the debates as the crisis between Caesar in Gaul and the senate gradually unfolded into a full-scale Civil War. After spending some time in the vicinity of Rome he went to his villa down the coast at Formiae to watch events as Caesar crossed the Rubicon and Pompey withdrew, first to Brundisium and then to Greece. He kept in touch with both sides and was anxious for a reconciliation, but felt that he was gradually being forced to decide how far he must go in support of the senate and Pompey against Caesar. The unconstitutionality of Caesar's actions clearly constituted the main problems in Cicero's mind, but he was fearful that Pompey might turn out to be another Sulla if given the chance. A letter which he wrote to Atticus (9.4) in March 49 is significant in suggesting the attractions which he and other Romans found in declamation, both as escape or relaxation and as a way of focusing thoughts and defining views:

"In order not to give in entirely to depression, I have taken up certain so-called *theses*, which are both of a political nature and appropriate to the times, that I may keep my mind from complaints and practice myself in the subject proposed. They are of this sort [he gives the list in Greek]: whether you should remain in your country when it is ruled by a tyrant; whether you should by every means bring down a tyranny, even if the state will be generally endangered; whether you should be on guard against letting one (i.e., Pompey) who abolishes tyranny rise too high himself; whether you should try to help the state under a tyrant by the right word at the right time rather than by war; whether retiring somewhere and keeping quiet is politically justifiable under a tyranny or whether you should go through every danger for the sake of liberty; whether war should be waged against a place and siege laid when a tyranny rules it; whether, even if you do not approve of overthrowing tyranny by war you ought yet to enroll yourself among the constitutionalists; whether in politics you should share the danger of benefactors and friends even if their overall policy does not seem right; whether a man who has served his country greatly, but because of this has suffered irremediably and been envied, should face danger willingly for the country or should at some point think of himself and his family and abandon political action against those in power.

"Practicing myself on these propositions and speaking on both sides of the question, now in Greek, now in Latin, I both divert my mind for a bit from my troubles and deliberate about a relevant problem...."[113]

The Caesarians made every effort to win Cicero's good will as a sign of the legitimacy of their regime, and finally on March 28, 49 Caesar himself came to Formiae to see Cicero and ask him personally to return to Rome and take his seat in the senate (*Ad Att.* 9.18). Caesar said Cicero's decision to stay away was a judgment of himself and that other senators would be slow in coming if Cicero did not come. Cicero was unmoved. Finally Caesar said, "Come then and discuss peace." "Accord-

[113] Cf. J. Béranger, "Tyrannus: notes sur la notion de tyrannie chez les Romains, particulièrement à l'époque de César et de Cicéron," *REL* 13 (1935) 85-94; Kroll 1095-96; Michel 588-90.

ing to my own belief?" "Should I dictate to you?" "I shall support a resolution to the effect that the senate disapproves of the expedition to Spain and the sending of an army to Greece and I shall have much to say about the misfortunes of Pompey." "I do not wish those things to be said." "So I thought. That is why I don't wish to be present there, because either I must speak in that way and much more beside which I cannot repress if I am present, or I must not go." Cicero did not go to Rome and regarded his refusal to Caesar as one of the great days of his life. He did eventually join Pompey and the senatorial army in Greece.

After Caesar's victory at Pharsalus Cicero returned to Italy and waited almost a year at Brundisium to make his peace with the victorious dictator when at last he returned in September of 47 after his victories in Asia. The wait had been a long and difficult one for Cicero, but toward the end he was heartened by receipt of a literary epistle *De virtute, On Strength of Mind,* from his young friend Brutus, who though a Pompeian had already been received into friendship by Caesar. When they finally met, Caesar was gracious to Cicero and they resumed their social friendship in so far as Caesar had time for it. A rather tight literary censorship was imposed, to judge from the bitter complaint of Cicero's old client Caecina (*Ad fam.* 6.7). There was, however, only very limited opportunity for deliberative and judicial oratory and no opportunity for real political influence. As he had done under the triumvirate Cicero turned to literary and philosophical studies with the idea of making them serviceable to Romans. It has been generally agreed that one of his greatest achievements was his contribution to the Latin language, which he made into a vehicle of critical and philosophical thought adequate for the next fifteen hundred years. Two of Cicero's works from this period are among the major discussions of rhetoric surviving from antiquity, the dialogue called the *Brutus* and the treatise entitled *Orator*.

Brutus

It is ironic but not entirely surprising that the first major treatises on Roman rhetoric, *De oratore*, *Brutus*, and *Orator*, were produced at a time when Roman rhetoric in its traditional forms was being checked. We have seen a keen interest in rhetoric among Romans for over a hundred years, but a persistent distrust of rhetorical learning. In the 50's and 40's, however, there was enforced leisure among orators of training and experience and at the same time a pressing concern about the practical role of the orator and a frustration or anxiety which added fuel to literary dispute. The history of rhetoric in Hellenistic Greece and imperial Rome show similar influences.

Cicero's *De oratore* was, as far as we know, unprecedented in published Latin literature in subject and scope, though influenced by the ideas of Romans when Cicero was a boy. Reaction to it might be expected. The kind of oratory which Cicero approved and practiced, amplified in subject, rich in style, belonged to a distinct tradition with which Crassus, Hortensius, and others may be associated, but it was hardly the only view of oratory at Rome. The preference for a plainer style with a high value assigned to purity of diction and avoidance of amplification was an equally persistent tradition. No particular reason need be sought for its strength in the early 40's: fashions change, but the war may have accelerated change in fashion, and for some, though hardly for Brutus, Caesar's taste may have seemed a more powerful influence than Cicero's. In earlier times the plain style had been uncompromising morality and blunt

239

straightforwardness, and as such was nurtured by the Stoics. But Stoic study of language helped make exactness of diction the fundamental virtue of style and this in turn produced an elegant sensitivity in the choice of words and made possible in poetry, in Catullus for example, a personal expression which is intensely emotional. We must not regard the orator in the plain style as unemotional, but his emotion is that of a sharp sword or intense and sudden piercing flame, not of a massed army or a wall of fire, and he expresses his emotion by the choice of words and by their delivery, not by the number of words, the piling up of clauses, the multiplication of examples, or other kinds of amplification. The plain orator thinks that verbosity dilutes rather than intensifies sincere emotion; the orator in the grand style thinks emotion must be fed a rich and ample diet to develop its strength to the full.

We have associated preference for the plain style with the *Latinitas* movement, interest in pure diction. In the mid-first century, as perhaps earlier as well, it was also associated with the grammatical movement called analogy.[114] Analogy was basically a doctrine aiming at simplicity and purity of grammatical inflexion. It seems likely that Julius Caesar's treatise *De analogia* was a reaction to the picture of the orator in *De oratore*, perhaps specifically to the somewhat slighting treatment of purity and clarity of style in book three (48-49).[115] We do not know the exact time of composition, but Caesar wrote it during his passage over the Alps on

114 On the relationship between the two cf. Albrecht Dihle, "Analogie und Attizismus," *Hermes* 85 (1957) 170-205.

115 Cf. G. L. Hendrickson, "The *De analogia* of Julius Caesar: its Occasion, Nature, and Date with Additional Fragments," *CPh* 1 (1906) 97-120. In practice Cicero's standards of diction were high, cf. Laurand, *Études, cit.* supra n. 1, 1.25-30.

return to Transalpine Gaul from a judicial circuit of northern Italy (Suet., *Julius* 56.5). It was a kind of pamphlet, thought out as he rode, written down during rest stops, and dedicated to Cicero. Caesar dealt with a broader subject than the title indicated, with the "principle of speaking Latin most accurately," calling choice of word the origin of eloquence; and he said to Cicero in the introduction, "If some men have labored with study and practice to be able to express their thoughts with distinction—and here we must recognize your contribution to the fame and dignity of the Roman people as a kind of leader and inventory of richness—must we as a result regard knowledge of simple and familiar language as something to be left aside?" (*Brutus* 253). The exact and clear style which Caesar favored is well illustrated in his commentaries on the Gallic and Civil war, and appeared also in his oratory (Cic., *Brutus* 252).[116]

Another movement with which *Latinity* became involved is Atticism, the pursuit of allegedly Attic standards of purity and grace. We know Greek Atticism first from Dionysius of Halicarnassus, whose rhetorical works were written during the last third of the first century B.C. in the generation after Cicero's death, but Dionysius, in the introduction to his study *On the Ancient Orators*, represents the reform in style, and especially diction, as having begun somewhat earlier and by his own time almost victorious.[117] He attributes this reform to Roman influence. Modern attempts to identify a Greek source for Atticism in the second or earlier first century have proved unsuccessful, though the ultimate development of literary Atticism may have been reinforced by a reaction evident in Greek sculpture and by the grammatical

[116] Cf. infra 283-92.
[117] Cf. APG 337-40 for a translation.

241

studies at Pergamum or elsewhere.[118] Cicero had not heard of Atticism when he wrote *De oratore* in 55 and he never alludes to any Greek source for the movement. Thus it seems best to regard Atticism as something developed in Rome in the period around 50 B.C. Just as the neoteric poets of that age found models in earlier Greek sources, so orators with a strong literary bent, including some like Calvus who were also poets, sought analogous Greek prose models. It is not surprising that the oratory of a Lysias or a Hyperides would have appealed to a literary enthusiast like Calvus. This movement, once begun, persisted in Latin for a few generations and became one of the very few features of Roman literary history to influence Greeks. The term neo-Atticism is perhaps better used than Atticism as a way of stressing that we seem to have to do with a rather specific, artificial, and Roman stylistic fad rather than a continuous Greek tradition.

The most interesting aspect of neo-Atticism is a tendency toward classicism. *Latinitas* had not seen models of Latin style in early Latin authors, though it might revive old words occasionally to fill a need, and its effect on language was not to freeze it, but to clarify it and make it vigorous. Neo-Atticism on the other hand

[118] Cf. U. von Wilamowitz-Moellendorff, "Asianismus und Attizismus," *Hermes* 35 (1900) 1-52. He suggested (46-47) Apollodorus of Pergamum cf. infra 338-39. Other discussions are those of Norden 149-50; Ludwig Radermacher, "Ueber die Anfänge der Atticismus," *RhM* 54 (1899) 351-74; Franz Nassal, *Aesthetisch-rhetorische Beziehungen zwischen Dionysius von Halicarnass und Cicero*, Tübingen, 1910, 9-10; H. Heck, *Ueber die Entstehung des literarischen Attizismus*, Munich, 1917, 5-15; D'Alton 215. On Atticism and sculpture, A. Desmouliez, "Sur la polémique de Cicéron et des Atticistes," *REL* 30 (1952) 168-85. For an attempt to counteract the search for a Greek source cf. A. E. Douglas, "M. Calidius and the Atticists," *CQ* 5 (1955) 241-47 and Pasquale Giuffrida, "Significati e limite del neoatticismo," *Maia* 7 (1955) 83-124.

was fundamentally classicism:[119] it rejected two hundred years of history of language and literature and saw the standard of language, composition, form, and rhetorical technique and the summit of literary achievement as something in the rather remote past, to be imperfectly approximated by study and imitation. It preferred external and learned rules of purity to audience reactions as a standard of judging. It was an acceptance of the fact that the history of creative Greek literature and of practical persuasion in oratory was at an end. This point of view recommended itself to Romans at a time when oratorical achievement in Latin seemed less likely and when there was some danger of artificiality and empty pomposity in overdoing the manner which Cicero typified at its best. Fortunately for the continued development of Latin literature the situation in Latin was not quite analogous to that in Greek. The imitation of Greek models in Latin was a far more creative process than the imitation of Greek models in Greek. Virgil, Horace, Propertius, and others all imitate, but the result is a new achievement. When Latin literature is itself classic enough to be imitated, the process had equally dreary results. Cicero valued the Greek classics as highly as anyone in Rome and thought imitation was a valuable literary exercise, but he opposed anything that seemed to limit the matter or manner of literature. He had a strong feeling for the power of creation and invention which required scope for expression, and he saw little attraction in the polishing of tiny jewels; thus his remark that even if he had another lifetime to spend he would not have time for lyric poetry.[120]

[119] Giuffrida, *op.cit.* supra n. 118, makes an interesting but unsuccessful attempt to deny this.
[120] Cf. Tenney Frank, "Cicero and the *poetae novi*," *AJPh* 40 (1919) 396-415.

Cicero's principal literary antagonists, in addition to Caesar, were Calvus, Brutus, and Asinius Pollio. He carried on a correspondence, now lost, with Calvus and Brutus on the subject of style.[121] Tacitus (*Dial.* 18) sums it up as showing that to Cicero Calvus seemed *exsanguem et aridum*, "bloodless and dry," Brutus *otiosum atque diiunctum*, "tedious and disjointed," while Calvus called Cicero *solutum et enervem*, "formless and flabby," and Brutus found him *fractum atque elumbem*, "pulpy and out of joint." The terms of literary criticism in Latin, largely physiological metaphors, are never easy to translate and often seem rather vague.[122]

Since we have only a few words from the twenty-one books of short speeches (Tac., *Dial.* 21.1) which Calvus published before his early death, apparently in 47 B.C., it is hardly possible to get a very satisfactory idea of his oratory.[123] His most famous speeches were the series against Vatinius, the man whom Cicero had attacked in 56 and defended in 54 B.C. The fullest description of Calvus' oratory is in the *Brutus* (283-84) but is probably somewhat colored by Cicero's prejudices. According to Cicero, Calvus was well read; his style was carefully worked; he spoke with elegance, but he was excessively self-critical and meticulous and the result seemed a loss of vitality. His speech was appreciated by the learned, but was swallowed up (*devorabatur*) in the forum, that is to say, its finish was wasted. In the dialogue Brutus is here made to say that Calvus liked to be called Attic and

---

[121] Cf. G. L. Hendrickson, "Cicero's Correspondence with Brutus and Calvus on Oratorical Style," *AJPh* 47 (1926) 234-58. On the nonliterary side of the relationship cf. Eric S. Gruen, "Cicero and Licinius Calvus," *HSPh* 71 (1966) 215-33.

[122] Cf. Charles Causeret, *Études sur la langue de la rhétorique et de la critique littéraire dans Cicéron*, Paris, 1886 and D. Pazzini, "La critica letteraria nel *Brutus* di Cicerone," *Aevum* 36 (1962) 355-69.

[123] Cf. ORF pp. 492-500 and Leeman 138-42.

that was why he purposely aimed at this thin or meager style. The remark rather suggests that Brutus would not call himself an Atticist, but elsewhere (*Ad Att.* 15.1a.2) Cicero treats Brutus as a neo-Atticist. Here he goes on to present Calvus as one misled by his own theories who does not realize the variety of the Attic orators: it is all right to be neo-Atticist if you define that in an adequately broad way. In a letter to Trebonius (*Ad fam.* 15.21.4) Cicero's estimate of Calvus is more favorable, but the criticism is similar in kind: Calvus lacks force. This might suggest to a modern reader that Calvus was austere and unemotional, but that would be wrong. If anything Calvus was rather too violent in delivery and while carried on by emotion would rush across the court to face his adversaries. "Nothing was placid, nothing smooth, everything excited and in motion," says the elder Seneca (*Contr.* 7.4.8), and Quintilian agrees (10.1.115) that Calvus was often vehement. The lack of force which Cicero felt was not, therefore, a lack of passion: from Cicero's point of view his speech was thin; it lacked the amplification characteristic of Cicero: the doubling and tripling of words, the addition of elaborating clauses, the fullness of idea and expression which sweeps the audience on or crushes the opponent beneath its weight.[124] Catullus would have seemed equally lacking in force to Cicero: his poems are too short, too unsubstantial. Cicero preferred the ponderous lines of Ennius which had something to them, and he would probably have shared some of the literary opinions of Aeschylus in Aristophanes' *Frogs.* To Cicero the key to force was in the massing and

[124] The lack was comparative, not absolute, cf. the fragment of Calvus quoted by Quintilian in his discussion of climax (9.3.56): "As a result of this not only trials for extortion, but for treason, not only trials for treason but trials under the Plautian law, not only trials under the Plautian law but trials for bribery, not only trials for bribery, but all trials will be abolished."

grouping of words, including their rhythmical composition, and in his writings to Calvus and Brutus he thus emphasized composition. One fragment of a letter to Calvus (Nonius 469) contains a paraphrase of Aristotle's explanation of the attraction of the periodic sentence. It is possible that Brutus' composition of a defense for Milo was part of the controversy between himself and Cicero, though nothing is said about the style of that speech. Most of the discussion was later in date, however, perhaps brought about by evaluation of Calvus after his death. We know that composition was a subject of dispute since Brutus objected to the clausula of cretic and spondee, which Cicero so favored, and tended himself to write in a kind of artless iambic rhythm (Quint. 9.4.63 and 76). This explains also why composition is such an important topic in the *Orator*. Brutus was a better philosopher than orator (Quint. 10.1.123; Tac., *Dial.* 21.5) and is made to say in the *Brutus* (23) that his interest in rhetoric is more in study than in practice. Ancient references to his oratory stress its dullness.[125] Cicero's interest in Brutus, to whom he dedicated at least six works, seems at heart a personal affection which Brutus may not have entirely reciprocated. They shared an interest in philosophy and many political opinions, but Cicero never converted Brutus to his literary attitudes.

The *Brutus*[126] opens with a prologue in memory of

[125] E.g., *Ad Att.* 15.1a.2, cf. Norden 220. Cf. E. J. Filbey, "Concerning the Oratory of Brutus," *CPh* 6 (1911) 325-33 and C. Morawski, "De M. Junii Bruti genere dicendi," *Eos* 17 (1911) 1-6.

[126] Cf. Martin Kellog, M. *Tulli Ciceronis Brutus de claris oratoribus*, Boston, 1889; O. Jahn and W. Kroll, *Ciceros Brutus*, Berlin, 1908; G. L. Hendrickson, *Cicero: Brutus*, London, 1939; Edward A. Robinson, "The Date of Cicero's *Brutus*," *HSPh* 60 (1951) 137-46; K. Kumaniecki, "Tradition et rapport personnel

Hortensius, who had died in 50 B.C. Hortensius was doubtless chosen primarily as a symbol of the style of oratory Cicero approves, to be thought of in contrast to the neo-Attic orators. In the introduction, however, it is not Hortensius' eloquence that is stressed, but his good fortune in dying when he did, for he might have lived on, as Cicero did, to see "the forum of the Roman people, which had been a kind of theatre of his ability, robbed and deprived of his trained voice which was worthy of Roman and Greek ears" (6). Hortensius is thus also a political symbol to be associated with Cicero himself. The note of political despair recurs throughout the *Brutus*.[127] Although the topic of oratory is chosen as a diversion from political worries (9-11) and might thus be compared to the interest in declamation and rhetoric under the empire, the result is to throw the existing situation into darker relief. It has even been plausibly suggested that one of Cicero's objectives was to incite Brutus to rid Rome of Caesar.[128] Hortensius is repeatedly referred to in the dialogue and his oratory is discussed in some detail at the end, balancing the discussion of his political fortune at the beginning. Thus he becomes a unifying literary and political figure for the entire work.

After the introduction there comes (10-24) a description of the circumstances of the dialogue, a conversation between Cicero, Brutus, and Atticus while waiting for news about Caesar's war in Africa sometime early in 46 B.C. The dramatic date can be gathered from the fact that Cato is spoken of (118) as still alive, and he committed

---

dans l'oeuvre de Cicéron," *REL* 37 (1959) 171-85; A. E. Douglas, *M. Tulli Ciceronis Brutus*, Oxford, 1966.
[127] Cf. Matthias Gelzer, "Ciceros *Brutus* als politische Kundgebung," *Philologus* 93 (1938) 128-31.
[128] Cf. J.P.V.D. Balsdon, "The Ides of March," *Historia* 7 (1958) 91 and Douglas, *op.cit.* supra n. 126, 233.

suicide after the battle of Thapsus in April, but the fact of reference to Cato is perhaps some evidence that the work was composed or revised after his death. Cicero here records his thanks for writings sent him by Brutus and Atticus during the last difficult year. The *Brutus* is specifically dedicated to Brutus in return for his letter *De virtute* to Cicero;[129] a later dedication to Atticus is promised in return for the treatise on chronology, originally inspired in turn by Cicero's *De re publica* (19). It was Atticus' treatise that suggested and facilitated Cicero's study of the history of Roman oratory.

On first reading, *Brutus* seems a rambling, generally chronological survey of the history of Roman oratory. But like *De oratore* it is rather carefully structured. The three main parts are the introduction, the brief review of the history of Greek oratory (25-52), rather like a narration in a speech, and then the main body of the work which proceeds by oratorical generations, discussing consular orators first, then the lesser figures.[130] This main section is varied by carefully placed "digressions," all relating to the neo-Atticism controversy which gives coloring to the entire work. One of these digressions is placed just half way through the discussion (183-200) and deals with the central issue of how oratory should be judged, by esoteric literary standards as the neo-Atticist were doing or by popular judgment and effectiveness as Cicero reasonably demands. The three functions of the orator are taken over from *De oratore* in support of Cicero's position (185) as are the speeches of Crassus and Scaevola in the *Causa Curiana*. Two other digressions are closely

---

[129] Cf. G. L. Hendrickson, "Brutus *De virtute*," *AJPh* 60 (1939) 401-13.

[130] Cf. A. E. Douglas, "*Oratorum aetates*," *AJPh* 87 (1966) 290-306.

connected and balanced. The first (70-76) comes early in the account of Roman oratory and after its first great practitioner, Cato. Cicero here develops an analogy— something of a rhetorical commonplace—[131] between the history of oratory on the one hand and the history of sculpture and painting and also Latin poetry on the other. The objective of this digression is to reinforce the assertion Cicero has just made (66-67) that Cato could be viewed as a Roman equivalent to Lysias both in terms of the stages of oratorical development and in terms of style, though the neo-Atticists illogically ignore him. Balancing this digression is one (292-300) which comes just before the last part of the account in which Atticus takes up and ridicules Cicero's glorification of early Roman oratory, including the assertion that Cato was a Roman Lysias (293). Cicero sticks to his guns, but the digression adds liveliness to the dialogue and shows that he did not mean his claim to be taken too literally. Some Roman neo-Atticists did develop an interest in archaic Latin; thus we find Thucydideanism combined with imitation of Cato in the historical monographs of Sallust.

In addition to these three symmetrically placed digressions, the passage on the oratory of Marcellus and Caesar (248-62) also creates a break in the sequence of the thought and the ostensible plan of the work. Although he would like to avoid invidious remarks about living orators, Cicero yields to the temptation of commenting on his two greatest living oratorical contemporaries by making Brutus describe the one and Atticus the other. Although the neo-Atticism movement is not specifically mentioned, it is clear that Marcellus, the senatorial orator, belongs both politically and stylistically with Hor-

[131] Cf. R. G. Austin, "Quintilian on Painting and Statuary," *CQ* 38 (1944) 17-26.

tensius and Cicero, while the radical Caesar is an exponent of *Latinitas* and the plain style and close in spirit to neo-Atticism.

Cicero's review of the history of Greek oratory deals with the subject first from a practical or oratorical viewpoint (25-38), then from a theoretical or rhetorical viewpoint (39-51). Some of the points stressed have their counterpart in the ensuing discussion of rhetoric at Rome, though the analogy is not so carefully worked out as might be expected. Eloquence is said to have reached full development in Greece later than the other arts (26). Second, its history is marked by various stages of development: Pericles was the first really great orator and the earliest to have been influenced by theory, for which relative peace was necessary (44-45). The high point of Greek oratory came in the fourth century with Isocrates, who was the first to pay attention to rhythm (32-34), and especially with Demosthenes (35). Third, oratory flourished only at Athens, until it sailed to Asia, where its diction was corrupted, and to Rhodes (51). Cicero remarks on the academic quality of the oratory of Demetrius of Phaleron (37-38) and deplores the tastes of Asianist orators, but does not particularly stress the decay of Greek oratory nor does he give any reasons, political or cultural, for changes in the fourth century or later.

The account of Roman orators is an important contribution to Roman artistic self-consciousness. The discussion is so varied that the danger of falling into a dull listing of names is largely avoided. Various stages of development are remarked, as in Greece. The first Roman definitely known to have been eloquent was M. Cornelius Cethegus (57), consul in 204 B.C. Thus oratory at Rome was also late in developing. The first orator whose speeches are worth reading is Cato, but he is not yet sufficiently polished (69). A richer style of speaking begins in the time of C. Sulpicius Gallus (78), but the first Roman to wield the legitimate tools of the orator, to digress, to delight, to move, to amplify, to employ pathos and commonplaces, was Galba (82). A new high point came with Gaius Gracchus, outstanding for native ability, dedication, and learning (125). At last, in Antonius and Crassus, Latin oratory attained the level of Demosthenes and Hyperides (138). Though implicit in the praise of Galba and others, Cicero's differences with the neo-Atticists become clearer in the discussion of Antonius, for he notes (140) that Antonius was not particularly distinguished by purity of diction, a negative virtue at best. "It is not," says Cicero, "such a wonderful thing to know good Latin as it is shameful not to know it." Later on (213-14) Curio is cited as an orator with pure diction because of his family background, but completely uneducated in any other respect. Orators who do not come from Rome lack a certain something, just as do non-Attic Greeks (170-72).[132] Cicero admits that there are two kinds of good orators, *unum attenuate presseque, alterum sublate ampleque dicentium,* "those speaking simply and succinctly, and those grandly and amply," "although that is better which is more splendid and magnificent" (201). Both can be overdone. He always pleads for variety: "Those can both be very great who are unlike each other," he says (204). Cicero's approach is never to condemn neo-Atticism by name. Its ordinary characteristics he criticizes; the term itself he always redefines to mean all that was good about the great Greek orators: "All who speak well speak in the Attic style" (291). Not all Attic excellences are to be found in Lysias or Thucydides, but if only one model is

---

[132] Cf. E. S. Ramage, "Cicero on Extra-Roman Speech," *TAPhA* 92 (1961) 481-94.

taken he ought to be the greatest and most varied, Demosthenes (289).

As we have said, the final orator to be discussed by Cicero is Hortensius (301-28), with whom Cicero compares and contrasts his own career. He labels Hortensius an Asianist (325) and gives the explanation of that term which we examined toward the end of chapter one; he does not treat it as the opposite of neo-Atticism, but its characteristics are un-Attic. Presumably he is trying to counteract those who labeled himself Asianist. The dialogue concludes (329-32) with Cicero's words of regret at the present state of eloquence in Rome and the resulting lack of opportunity for Brutus. The very end of the work is lost.

The *Brutus* has about it a studied informality. The flow of a discourse along a generally chronological but digressive course is maintained throughout. There is no careful working out of the analogy between the history of rhetoric in Greece and in Rome, only certain points of contact. The importance of rhythm in the greatest oratory is stressed in connexion with Isocrates, but only casually observed in the later Roman orators and is largely left to the *Orator* for elucidation. On the other hand, as though to conciliate the neo-Atticists, the diction of an orator is almost always noticed. Cicero's own style throughout the work is remarkably elegant, as pure as the neo-Atticists', though not so plain. The controversy over neo-Atticism is certainly often evident, but no debate between Cicero and Brutus is set forth and one almost gets the impression that Brutus agrees with Cicero on the subject of style. Of all the rhetorical works of Cicero there is least need to ask about the sources of the *Brutus*. The critical categories mentioned are drawn from the traditional system of rhetoric; the opinions expressed are those of Cicero himself based on his study and reading and the orators he had heard and are advanced as his own views. He doubtless expounded them when he could, though there is no need to insist on the historicity of a single conversation on Greek and Roman oratory at the time and place indicated in the *Brutus*. Cicero claims that Brutus continually urged him to literary composition. One result of this was the panegyric of Cato the younger which Cicero wrote with some nervousness after Cato's death in April 46. He hoped Brutus would take some of the responsibility for it (*Orator* 35). Though now Caesar's governor in Cisalpine Gaul, Brutus made no secret of his love for the old government, and himself published a eulogy of Cato in which, incidentally, the description of Cato's role in punishing the Catilinarian conspirators did not altogether please Cicero (*Ad Att.* 12.21.1). There was also a eulogy by Cicero's friend Fadius Gallus (*Ad fam.* 7.24.2). In the following year Hirtius and Caesar each replied with an *Anticato* (*Ad Att.* 12.40.1 and 13.50.1). The impossibility of a public funeral and a traditional funeral oration perhaps started this literary contest;[133] its effect was to create a myth around the figure of Cato which made him a favorite subject for writers and declaimers of the empire.

Orator

Another work which Cicero claims was produced at the insistence of Brutus is his last rhetorical treatise, *Orator*.[134] Brutus' insistence is perhaps more than a lit-

[133] Cf. Fridericus Vollmer, "Laudationum funebrium Romanarum historia et reliquiarum editio," *JKPh Suppl.* 18 (1891) 469.
[134] Cf. J. E. Sandys, *M. Tulli Ciceronis ad Brutum Orator*, Cambridge, Eng., 1885; Wilhelm Kroll, *M. Tulli Ciceronis Orator*, Berlin, 1913, reprinted 1961; Otto Seel, *Orator*, Heidelberg, 1952; Mary A. Grant and George C. Fiske, "Cicero's

erary convention since it is not only mentioned several times in the work itself (1;3;52; and 174), but is referred to in a letter to Atticus (14.20.3). As a result of this the *Orator* has an especially personal tone, and Cicero's desire to combat Brutus' sympathy with the neo-Atticists and defend his own style of oratory is unusually evident.[135] It is even possible that portions of the *Orator* were drawn from Cicero's letters to Brutus and then put together for publication in the present work, whose structure has been criticized as repetitive and disorganized.[136]

Repetitions there certainly are, but an overall plan is easily recognizable. There is first (1-36) an introductory discussion which deals with the heart of Cicero's concerns: he seeks to describe an ideal orator beyond any who has ever lived and uses the Platonic forms to help explain what he has in mind. This is quite appropriate to Brutus' interests in philosophy in general and Plato in particular. Then Cicero expounds the doctrine that there are three styles, not one. The perfect orator must master all (20); no Roman has done so, and among the Greeks only Demosthenes comes close (23). Apparently Brutus had expressed an admiration for Demosthenes (105) which Cicero appeals to in his argument against preference for the simple style. Finally, the errors of the neo-Atticists are openly revealed (28-32). Their definition of Attic is too narrow, and those who adopt Thucydides or Xenophon as models do not even imitate orators. This

---

Orator and Horace's *Ars poetica*," *HSPh* 35 (1924) 1-75; H. M. Hubbell, *Cicero: Orator*, London, 1939; Michel 143-45; Leeman 145-55.

[135] Cf. Sebastian Schlittenbauer, "Die Tendenz von Ciceros *Orator*," *JKPh Suppl.* 28 (1903) 181-248.

[136] Cf. Remigio Sabbadini, "La composizione dell' *Orator* Ciceroniano," *RFIC* 44 (1916) 1-22 and A. Yon, "Sur la composition de l'*Orator* de Cicéron," *BAGB Lettres d'Humanité* 17 (1958) 70-84.

introductory section then returns to Brutus' request (33-35) and the Platonic ideal (36).

The second part of the work (37-139) is a rather uneven survey of rhetorical theory, not unlike that given by Antonius and Crassus in the second and third books of *De oratore*. The usual topics and categories are there: kinds of oratory, parts of rhetoric with some discussion of each, but Cicero elaborates only what is relevant for the picture of the orator he wishes to stress, defined (69) as "one who can speak in the forum—i.e., in law courts—or on public questions in such a way that he proves, delights, and stirs his audience." We see here again the three functions of the orator from *De oratore*. In the picture of this man it is style that is most fully discussed. Propriety will determine what style to use (70-74): the plain style (75-90) avoids rhythm and periodicity and has no objection to hiatus. Its ornamentation must not be noticeable. A distinctive feature should be its use of wit, an ingredient on which Cicero prided himself. Calvus shows signs of wit, but Brutus does not. The middle style described (91-96) is really that of Isocrates, though he is not named and Demetrius of Phaleron is made the example. It has little vigor, much smoothness and ornament. The grand style (97-99) is full, rich, stately, elaborate, powerful, but it needs to be varied with the other styles, and unless skillfully managed it can fall flat. Though Cicero insists on the necessity of combining styles (74), he confusingly persists in speaking of the middle or grand orator (e.g., 98-99). He cites examples of each style and of varied styles from his own speeches (102-8).[137] Then, as in *De oratore*, the knowledge needed

---

[137] Cf. Laurand, *op.cit.* supra n. 1, 3.284-306; P. Gotzes, *De Ciceronis tribus generibus dicendi in orationibus pro A. Caecina, de imp. Cn. Pompeii, pro C. Rabirio perd. reo adhibitis*, Rostock, 1914; Hubbell, *op.cit.* supra n. 22.

by the orator is discussed (113-20), including logic and other parts of philosophy, law, and history.[188] Here is inserted (121-39) a dry summary of rhetorical rules for invention, partition, and style which goes over some of the ground already covered.

The first two parts of the *Orator* are preparatory and even introductory. Cicero repeatedly indicates that what is most important and most difficult is still to come (e.g., 51, 61, 75, 100, 134). The third part of the *Orator* (140-238) is a very full discussion of the aspect of style most neglected by the neo-Atticists, composition. This is introduced by an apology aimed at counteracting the common ancient contempt for teaching (140-48): "Why is it shameful to learn what it is honorable to understand, or why is it not glorious to teach what is most becoming to know?" (142). The basis of what Cicero says is derived from Isocrates, Aristotle, and Theophrastus, but he has applied the Greek theories to Latin and he has much more to say about rhythm than any earlier author (174). Into the discussion of the collocation of words is inserted an attack on the analogists (155-62), perhaps the best proof that analogy and neo-Atticism were linked. The account of the periodic sentence recognizes two forms, that in which the grammatical structure gives the balanced rounding or completeness, for example an antithesis, and that in which, quite apart from the meaning, the rhythm of the words achieves a form which is complete because satisfying to the ear. The discussion of rhythm (168-236) is the most detailed part of the work. It begins with an introduction (168-73), followed by a partition (174). The origin, cause, nature, and use of rhythm are successively handled and examples of the effect of rearranging words and thus breaking up the rhythms are given (232-33). There should not be com-

[188] Cf. infra 292 and note thereto.

plete lines of verse nor usually a succession of similar feet, but combinations of different feet. Cicero praises combinations of cretic, paeon, and spondee with iamb, tribrach, and dactyl, but some of these are not the commonest features of his own style and he probably is approaching the subject from a theoretical viewpoint rather than analyzing actual speeches.[139] A discussion of the utility of rhythm is then added (227-36) which is rather general and balances the introduction of 168-73. At the end of the work Cicero does not seem particularly optimistic about his success in convincing Brutus of the superiority of his conception of style, and we know from a letter to Atticus (14.20.3) that he did not.

The *Orator* invites comparison with *De oratore*, written nearly ten years before. There is no fundamental change of view, but the point at issue is different. In *De oratore* it was the education needed by the orator, especially the need for philosophy and law, that was under discussion; Cicero's conception of style is set forth, but is unquestioned. In the *Orator* the importance of philosophy is mentioned, but unchallenged. Brutus and Cicero were largely in agreement about that. It is the Ciceronian style which has been called in question and is being defended. From a purely literary point of view *De oratore* is the greater work. The introductions and the dialogue form with its characterizations add much. *Orator* is repetitive, digressive, perhaps hastily put together, uneven in structure because of Cicero's desire to stress particular points. Some parts have charm, others are either difficult

---

[139] Cf. W. Schmid, *Ueber die klassische Theorie und Praxis des antiken Prosa-rhythmus* (*Hermes Einzelschriften* 12), Wiesbaden, 1959; L. P. Wilkinson, *Golden Latin Artistry*, Cambridge, Eng., 1963, 135-64; Adolf Primmer, "Cicero Numerosus: Studien zum antiken Prosarhythmus," *SAWW* 257 (1968), Ancient testimonia on prose rhythm are collected by A. C. Clark, *Fontes prosae numerosae*, Oxford, 1909.

or dry or even boring. But for all its artistic faults, it has a logical coherence which *De oratore* lacks. Cicero failed to convince Brutus because of Brutus' own personal tastes and commitments, not because he failed to make a good case. Surely Lysias, Thucydides, and Xenophon were not the best stylistic models for imitation at the Roman bar, if models had to be found. Surely the best orator must be the master of all styles and know when and how to employ each. The neo-Atticists were abandoning practical persuasion for arbitrary critical perfection. In stating his case Cicero has neatly, and apparently with originality,[140] combined the traditional doctrine of the three kinds of style with the three functions of the orator which he had discussed in *De oratore*. His teaching has theoretical simplicity and it has the cogent examples of the achievements of Demosthenes and himself. Political circumstances and changes of taste made Cicero's major activity at this time a defense of his prose style. There are no ancient and few modern examples of more knowledgeable criticism by a first-rate author of the genre in which he himself worked.

In addition to those we have discussed, there are two other less important works by Cicero relating to aspects of rhetoric. *De optimo genere oratorum, On the Best Kind of Orators,* is an introduction to a projected but apparently never completed, translation of Aeschines' and Demosthenes' *On the Crown.* The project was probably part of Cicero's answer to the neo-Atticism movement and can be dated about the time of *Orator.*[141]

[140] Cf. Kroll 1101 and A. E. Douglas, "A Ciceronian Contribution to Rhetorical Theory," *Eranos* 55 (1957) 18-26; Michel 155-56.
[141] Cf. G. L. Hendrickson, "Cicero *De optimo genere oratorum," AJPh* 47 (1926) 109-23. Unconvincing is the recent attempt to prove the work spurious, cf. Albrecht Dihle, "Ein Spurium unter den rhetorischen Werken Ciceros," *Hermes* 83

Topica,[142] written in the summer of 44 B.C., is an exposition of the topics of arguments (genus, species, similarity, difference, and so forth) to which are added some notes on *stasis* theory or other aspects of rhetorical invention. Aristotle's *Topics* had inspired the original question from Trebatius to Cicero about the subject, but Cicero wrote his account from memory and seems to have drawn on Peripatetic and Stoic sources in a presentation of the general subject as he understood it (*Ad fam.* 7.19).

The Caesarian Speeches

After returning to Rome in 47, Cicero had resumed attendance at meetings of the senate, which became more of a club than a deliberative body, but he did not enter into any debate until September 46 when Piso, Caesar's father-in-law and Cicero's old enemy with whom he gradually became reconciled, brought up the case of Cicero's friend Marcellus, whom we have met in the *Brutus*. The old aristocrat had stubbornly resisted Caesar and was in exile on Lesbos. Marcellus' cousin flung himself at Caesar's feet and the senators, by predetermined arrangement, crowded round begging mercy for Marcellus. It was Caesar's announced policy to forget the past and try to find support for the future, and he rather reluctantly agreed to forgive Marcellus. At this, various tributes poured forth and Cicero, enheartened at the possibility of reestablishing some semblance of constitu-

---

(1955) 303-14 and E. Bickel, "Die Echtheit von Cicero, *De opt. gen. or.*," *RhM* 98 (1955) 288.

[142] Cf. Benedetto Riposati, *Studi sui Topica di Cicerone*, Milan, 1947 and, "Quomodo *Partitiones oratoriae* cum *Topicis* cohaereant," *Att. del I Congresso internazionale di studi ciceroniani*, Rome, 1961, 253-63. For a translation of *De opt. gen.* and *Topica* cf. H. M. Hubbell's Loeb Library vol. of Cicero's *De inventione*, Cambridge, 1960.

tionalism, could not resist rising to his feet to thank Caesar in the extant *Pro Marcello*. The speech is thus not a defense of Marcellus but a panegyric of Caesar and like good panegyrics it tries to influence the future by selected praise of the past. Caesar must give the state stability, which of course requires some constitutional basis. Among the most striking passages is that (29) in which Cicero calls on Caesar to consider the verdict of history.

Pro Marcello is one of the so-called Caesarian speeches. The other two are judicial and were delivered before Caesar, who as dictator assumed judicial powers. The first, *Pro Ligario*, is one of Cicero's two or three cleverest speeches, but the circumstances under which it was delivered and thus its evaluation are complex. The traditional view has been somewhat as follows: Ligarius was one of many adherents of the senatorial party, like Marcellus, left in exile in 46 B.C. His friends at Rome worked for his recall, and Cicero, who was among them, wrote him two extant letters describing the difficulties of getting in to see Caesar, but confidently predicting his pardon. Then a cloud appeared. As legate in Africa at the outset of the Civil War Ligarius had affronted the two Tuberos: indeed he had refused to let them come ashore, though the elder was the duly constituted senatorial governor for 49. The Tuberos thereupon went on to Greece, joined Pompey, and fought at Philippi, but asked pardon afterward and were quickly forgiven by Caesar. When the pardon of Ligarius seemed likely, the younger Tubero, still rankling at the old affront, tried to prevent it by bringing a criminal charge before Caesar, who heard it publicly (*Pro Lig.* 6) at the end of September 46. Cicero ironically treats the charge as solely the "crime" of being in Africa. Quintilian (11.1.80) says that Tubero charged Ligarius with supporting King Juba of Numidia and the Africans against Rome, in other words with *perduellio*. In Plutarch's life of Cicero (39) there is a memorable description of the trial in which Caesar asks his friends, "What harm in hearing Cicero speak after so long a time, since the accused has long ago been judged a wicked man and an enemy?" But Caesar was in for a surprise and thoroughly moved by the speech, turning pale, shaking at mention of Pharsalus, dropped his papers. At the end, "He was forced to acquit the man of the charge." The speech thus becomes one of the most signal triumphs of pure eloquence known.

There are, however, several objections to Plutarch's story.[143] It was *not* a very long time since Caesar had heard Cicero, for the speech for Marcellus had been delivered the same month. Nor from Cicero's letters does it appear that Ligarius had in fact "long ago" been condemned in Caesar's mind, rather the opposite. Further, Plutarch fails to mention that Cicero was the second of two advocates for Ligarius, as appears from the beginning of his speech. C. Pansa had already spoken on Ligarius' behalf. Now Pansa was a great favorite with Caesar, as well as an oratorical protégé of Cicero, and it is unlikely Pansa would have wanted or been allowed to defend in public a man whom Caesar had determined to convict. The matter would have been handled behind the scenes. Plutarch's picture of the situation must be wrong, and if Caesar said anything like what is reported he must have said it tongue in cheek, but been taken seriously by some unenlightened bystander. Possibly the whole thing was staged. Caesar apparently made much of the trial for the sake of the favorable publicity it

---

[143] The interpretation of the speech given here is basically that of Gerhard Walser, "Der Prozess gegen Q. Ligarius im Jahr 46 v. Chr.," *Historia* 8 (1959) 90-96. Cf. also Kazimierz Kumaniecki, "Der Prozess des Ligarius," *Hermes* 95 (1967) 434-57.

would give him and perhaps in the hope that it would encourage others guilty of the "crime" of being in Africa (Varus and Labienus, for example, still holding out in Spain), to stop their resistance and seek for mercy. Young Tubero, thoroughly piqued at Ligarius, may not have realized the circumstances which had been set up; the elder Tubero took little part in the trial and seems to have been annoyed after it was over (*Ad Att.* 13.20.2).

What was Cicero's position in the situation? Old Tubero had been his close friend, whereas we know of no special reason for him to be interested in Ligarius. He had consistently favored reconciliation and disapproved of bickering among the senatorial party, and once he had spoken for Marcellus he thought he might as well go on cooperating with Caesar. It is significant that he does not deal seriously with the charge: he does not stress the fact that Ligarius was acting under orders of a superior—this would tend to make Caesar's clemency less remarkable—nor does he have anything to say about Ligarius' relations with King Juba, though Juba's hostility to Caesar is frankly mentioned (24). Cicero pleads, as he points out (30), not with the arguments appropriate for a jury, but those for a parent: forgive him, he erred, he made a mistake, he didn't think, never again! The speech throughout is ironic: the charge is the "novel" crime of having been in Africa (1). The accuser is in a worse situation than the accused, since he had *wanted* to be in Africa and then had gone on to Pharsalia and drawn his sword against Caesar (9-10). Ligarius, on the other hand, really didn't want to be in Africa at all, according to Cicero, but home with his brothers. Thus the accuser is himself guilty of the charge, and, furthermore, the orator for the defense cannot speak on behalf of his client without convicting himself (6-7), since he had chosen the other side in the war. All of this is hardly designed for the hard-headed Caesar, one of the least emotional of men, but for the general public and the mills of Caesarian propaganda. When Cicero speaks for Caesar's ear, as he does in *Pro rege Deiotaro*, there is less emotionalism.

Pro Ligario is exceedingly clever. Nothing could more clearly bring out Caesar's clemency. Here, for example, is Cicero's description of the Civil War (19):

"You, Caesar, at the beginning thought it a secession, not a war, not an example of the hatred of enemies, but of civil dissension in which both sides desired the safety of the state, but partly by design, partly by passion strayed from the common good. The rank of the leaders was nearly on a par; not equal perhaps the rank of the followers. The cause was a doubtful one, since there was something to approve on either side. Now that side which the gods aided must be judged the better,[144] and in truth, since your clemency is known, who will not approve a victory in which no one died unless he had taken up arms?"

Like much of Cicero's oratory the passage should not be read with too critical an eye to its logic or its consistency with other remarks of the author. It is enough that Cicero had felt some doubts at Formiae.

The speech was soon published[145] and much approved by Caesar's supporters. The dictator himself was sent a

144 A *sententia* which may have suggested Lucan's more celebrated *victrix causa deis placuit, sed victa Catoni, De bello civili* 1.128.

145 Cicero tried unsuccessfully to eliminate the reference to Corfidius from the published version when he discovered it was anachronistic, *Ad Att.* 13.44. He rejected a suggestion to insert reference to Tubero's wife and stepdaughter on the ground that copies were too widely distributed and that it would annoy old Tubero, *Ad Att.* 13.20.

complimentary copy (*Ad Att.* 13.19.2). As for the pardoned Ligarius of whom Cicero had said "never again," he bided his time, and Caesar could have caught a glimpse of his face on the Ides of March of 44.

The third Caesarian speech is that given in 45 for King Deiotarus of Galatia. The case is analogous in that a private enemy, the king's grandson, tried to arouse Caesar's hostility for his own ends. It was tried in Caesar's own house (5), a custom which many emperors would follow to the disadvantage of orators. Apparently Caesar never got around to making any decision in the case before his death.

Cicero's Philosophical Works

The years 45 and 44 are those in which Cicero produced the great series of philosophical works which transmitted knowledge of Hellenistic philosophy to later times and enriched the Latin language. He had of course long studied philosophy, but the death of his daughter Tullia in February 45 and the political retirement into which he had been forced caused him more than ever to turn his attention in that direction. He was anxious to keep busy and, if possible, usefully busy. In most of these works he keeps himself in the background and employs a dialogue form, set in the second century in the case of *De senectute* and *De amicitia,* more often in his own age and peopled with his friends. On abstruse subjects he likes to follow the Academic custom of letting others expound different sides of a question and avoiding much expression of his own views. In *De finibus* he plays the role of critic throughout; in *De natura deorum,* at the very end, he judges one argument "closer to the semblance of the truth." In *De divinatione* he plays a larger, but negative role, refuting the claims of superstition. A number of the works cut close to his own heart, for example, the now lost treatise on consolation written after his daughter's death and the *Tusculan Disputations*,[146] the first book of which denies the need to fear death and the last of which considers the sufficiency of virtue for happiness.

Cicero is no less a rhetorician when he is a philosopher, and behind his pose of suspending judgment there burns a desire to persuade, especially to persuade himself. Some of the works relate to rhetoric in additional ways. The *Tusculans*, for example, are cast in a rather obvious rhetorical form (cf., e.g., 1.112), and the introduction to the second book touches on a topic discussed in the *Brutus*, the popular nature of oratory and the inappropriateness of the meager Attic style, contrasted with the more select audience for philosophy.

Of all the philosophical works of the period the one most closely related to rhetoric is probably the last, *De officiis*, a treatise on moral duties, not written as a dialogue, but as a systematic exposition by Cicero himself addressed to his son.[147] The categories and classifications are based (1.7-10; 3.7) on a work by the Greek Stoic philosopher Panaetius, whom we met in the Scipionic circle. The first book discusses the cardinal virtues of wisdom, justice, fortitude, and temperance. In examining justice Cicero has in mind both relations between individuals and between states and he considers briefly the principles of human society. Reason and speech are its distinguishing features (1.50). The claims of country

---

146 Cf. Alain Michel, "Rhétorique et philosophie dans les *Tusculanes*," *REL* 39 (1961) 158-71.

147 Cf. Milton Valente, *L'éthique stoïcienne chez Cicéron*, Paris, 1956; Ronald Syme, *The Roman Revolution*, Oxford, 1939, 145; H. A. K. Hunt, *The Humanism of Cicero*, Melbourne, 1954, 159-87; L. Ramaglia, "Le esemplificazioni nel *De officiis*," *RSC* 3 (1955) 193-202; S. E. Smethurst, "Politics and Morality in Cicero," *Phoenix* 9 (1955) 111-21.

override all other duties (1.57). Fortitude is shown by an indifference to externals and a willingness for great, useful, difficult, or dangerous undertakings (1.66). A man should engage in public life if he can do so without forfeiting his independence (1.73).[148] In public life a man must serve the common interest, not his own or that of a party (1.85). Personal enemies should be treated mildly and with courtesy (1.88-89). Temperance is a matter of propriety (1.93). Oratory and conversation are contrasted (1.132), and it is said that voice and style must suit the subject (1.133-34). If two duties come into conflict, an active duty must be preferred to a contemplative duty (1.153). To speak eloquently and wisely is a better thing than to think shrewdly without eloquent expression, for thought involves only the thinker, while eloquence embraces those with whom we are bound in society (1.156).

The second book opens with consideration of dogmatic rules of duty: Cicero regards them as probabilities, not certainties. He then proceeds to discussion of *utile*, the expedient, though it cannot be separated from *honestum*, the honorable (2.9-10). For men to be of maximum advantage to others they must know how to move men's minds and draw them to their objectives, which is done by wisdom and virtue. Since the latter includes control of the passions, we have a philosophical counterpart to rhetoric, which is of course a matter of logic, pathos, and ethos. Cicero examines (2.21) the motives for action to which appeal can be made: good will, honor, confidence, fear, hope of reward, profit to those involved. During the discussion of these, Cicero speaks of the contribution of eloquence to a man's glory (2.48) and there occurs the passage quoted earlier on the duties of the

[148] Cf. E. de Saint Denis, "La théorie Cicéronienne de la participation aux affaires publiques," *RPh* 12 (1938) 195-215.

advocate to prefer defense over accusation (2.49-50).[149]

The third book deals with apparent conflicts between what is morally right and what is expedient. These are only apparent, since what is wrong is never expedient, but judgment is often difficult. Cicero examines expediency in conflict with each of the four cardinal virtues in turn, using examples drawn from law and history. General duty and the expediency of society or the state must have precedence over individual duty and expediency, we are told (3.21-23). Devotion to a friend must not prevent duty to the state (3.43). A conclusion would be the rightness of Caesar's death at the hands of his friends or of Cicero's attack on Antony, who had to some extent been a friend. It is always right to kill a tyrant, and power unjustly obtained brings suffering to the holder, so it is not desirable (3.84). "Whose life can be expedient to him when the condition of that life is such that one who takes it will be met with the greatest thanks and glory?" (3.85).

The last point suggests the underlying subjectivity of moral judgments. What seems to one person done out of lust for glory or power may to another seem done out of self-sacrificing patriotism. There was no time in Cicero's life when the questions examined in De officiis were not significant, but they must have been especially pressing in the autumn of 44 B.C. when the work was composed, and the choice of subject certainly supports his own concern. He takes a rather hard and superior line in De officiis: there is to be no compromise with virtue, and his political actions at the time show a similar assurance. As he advises, he accepts in practice duty to the state as his fundamental goal. Given his past career there could be very little doubt of his definition of this: it is preservation of the republic along the lines he had

149 Cf. supra, 190.

known it with the senate at the head and at the head of the senate the wisest and most experienced of the consulars, especially himself. It has seemed to some historians[150] that he was blinded by his own ambition and glory, albeit defined as patriotism, when the true expediency for the state was compromise and concord between the factions of Antony, Octavian, and the senate. The reality of the duties described in *De officiis* may be acknowledged, but their definition remains writ in water.

The *Philippics*

For considerable periods of time in the year after the assassination of Julius Caesar, Cicero was presented with the opportunity for political action and his oratory once again became a factor in history. Though he rejoiced in Caesar's fall, he had not been among the conspirators. In the immediate aftermath of the Ides of March he played a conciliatory role between the tyrannicides and the heirs of Caesar's power, especially Antony who was consul and thus head of state. Cicero's major achievement at this time was a general amnesty reminiscent of that in Athens after the overthrow of the Thirty Tyrants. Brutus and Cassius had made no political plans and though both in office as praetors, they were eventually forced to withdraw from the city. Antony was initially shaken and disposed to be cooperative; thus some semblance of constitutional government was possible. This was aided by the confirming of Caesar's acts and appointments. On the first of June, however, Antony as consul summoned the senate and tried to make changes in the assignment of provinces in order to secure further his own position. Specifically he wanted command of Cisalpine Gaul as proconsul. Cicero and some others failed to attend the meeting (*Phil.* 2.108), but the senate as a whole

[150] Cf. Syme, *op.cit.* supra n. 147, 144-46.

was not intimidated and refused Antony's request. Antony then ignored the senate and got what he wanted from the assembly.

This action in Cicero's view destroyed any immediate hope for constitutional government, and he decided that nothing could be done so long as Antony was in office as consul. He would himself go away until the end of the year, and he set out for Pompeii and Syracuse with the intention of visiting Greece. Possibly it is true that in the summer "the cause of ordered government was still not beyond hope,"[151] whereas in autumn it was. Certainly some independence was still possible, for on the first of August a meeting of the senate was held by Antony at the request of Brutus and Cassius to make legal their continued absence from the city, where mob action was always a danger. At this meeting Cicero's old opponent L. Piso spoke his mind against Antony but was given no support by other senators. It would have been a fitting time for Cicero to have been there.

Hearing encouraging news from Rome, Cicero abandoned his plans to go to Greece in August and started back, intending to attend the meeting of the senate called for the first of September. Though there in time, he did not attend the senate. Antony came, delivered a speech against Cicero, and proposed offerings to the now deified Caesar. The next day, while Antony went to Tibur, Cicero came to the senate to give the *First Philippic*. Though it criticized Antony, personal invective was avoided and the tone was moderate throughout. Cicero defended his absence from Rome, which had clearly been resented by some. No specific action is called for in the speech; Cicero ends with the statement that his life has been long enough in years and glory: "If something be added to it, it will accrue not so much

151 Cf. Syme, *op.cit.* supra n. 147, 139.

to me as to you and the republic." By now Cicero had nerved himself to play the role he regarded as right, and from this he did not subsequently waver.

The term "Philippic" was applied by Cicero himself, perhaps not very formally, to his attacks on Antony (*Ep. ad Brut.* 2.4); he had earlier used it of his attacks on Catiline. To a limited extent (e.g., *Phil.* 3.34-36) he had in mind an awakening of Roman apathy, as Demosthenes aroused the Athenians to an awareness of their danger, but the real point of the title is to compare the violent invective of Demosthenes against Philip to that against Antony. The first two speeches differ from the other fourteen, the first because of its tone and the fact that it is separated in time, the second because it was not a speech at all, but a pamphlet composed during October 44 as a reply to a speech of Antony, in the senate on the 19th of September, which Cicero, though summoned by Antony, had avoided in the interests of peace. Antony delivered a furious attack on Cicero (*Ad fam.* 12.2.1). In revising and perfecting the text of his reply Cicero consulted his friends (*Ad Att.* 16.11). The result was published late in November, about the same time as *De officiis*. By then Antony had gone to Gaul, and his absence made possible free debate in the senate from November until sometime late in the spring of 43, thus giving Cicero scope for the remaining *Philippics*, which were actually delivered.[152]

The object of the *Second Philippic* is first to defend

[152] Cf. E. Remy, "La VIIIe *Philippique* de Cicéron," *LEC* 7 (1938) 30-40; J. C. Plumpe, "Roman Elements in Cicero's Panegyric on the *Legio Martia*," *CJ* 36 (1940-41) 275-89 (re *Phil.* 14); Hartvig Frisch, *Cicero's Fight for the Republic: the Historical Background of Cicero's Philippics*, Copenhagen, 1946; *CAH* 10.1-25; M. Delaunois, "Statistiques des idées dans le cadre du plan oratoire des *Philippiques* de Cicéron," *LEC* 34 (1966) 3-34.

Cicero against Antony's attack (2.1-43) and second, and more important, to discredit Antony thoroughly both as a politician and as a person. The speech owes its fame to the malice with which the attack is worked out; there is a kind of perfection of detail as in Cicero's other undelivered orations, the second action against Verres. In tone the speech most resembles attacks on Piso, Gabinius, or Clodius.

For all its art the *Second Philippic* can hardly be judged a success; it hardened opposition between the senatorial and Caesarian parties to the point of making compromise very difficult, and especially it hardened antipathy between Cicero and Antony, once relatively good friends, to the extent that Cicero's death was the first demand of Antony in the proscriptions of the following year. The speech won no supporters to the senate, no admirers to Cicero save in the lurid-minded rhetorical schools of the empire. On the other hand it did Antony little political, not to say military, harm. The discrediting of Antony with Romans had to await the subtler techniques of Octavian ten years later.

What the *Second Philippic* best illustrates is the unattractive side of ancient oratory: unbridled use of attack on family and personal life as a means of discrediting the character of the opponent and a general willingness to use lies and deceit and sophistry on behalf of a cause regarded by the orator as good. The first of these, personal slander, may be labeled traditional, but the fact tended to make it unpersuasive. In order to give the personal attack any force at all its violence had to seem unprecedented, and this was virtually impossible. The sexual perversions of Antony's youth are pretty usual stuff in ancient political attack; the tasteless description of Antony's vomiting is Cicero's own inspiration. Among the misleading statements are the claim that Antony had

271

previously arranged to save himself when Caesar was assassinated (2.34), or that he alone had bid on Pompey's property when auctioned off after Pompey's defeat (2.64), or that after being personally responsible for the Civil War he was too much a coward, or voluptuary, to fight in it (2.70-71). It does not seem very likely that Antony stole 700,000,000 sesterces from the temple of Ops (2.93), though he may have gotten his hands on some of Caesar's money; Antony had not lost the province of Crete (2.97); and so on. Cicero's horror of the political use of augury (2.83) is a comparatively minor example of an insincerity. The moral superiority of the orator is offensive throughout, perhaps especially at the end where Cicero contrasts Caesar and Antony to the former's advantage. Antony emerges as a kind of sick but dangerous child, playing at being Caesar, not a very convincing picture of a man who dominated world history for thirteen years.

Cicero's *Philippics* may be taken to represent the old oratory of the republic with ethos and pathos as predominant qualities, an oratory which nominally aimed at persuasion, which had, however, now become unpersuasive and expressed the antagonism of the orator rather than effected his purpose. In a more limited sense the technique for winning control used by Antony was also obsolete: it consisted in the figure of a popular general supported by a good army. The utility of an army should not be maligned, but Antony could not succeed at Rome by being a latter-day Marius or Caesar, certainly not as an Alexander. Something new, and as it turned out permanently triumphant appeared in Roman history in the spring of 44 B.C., a man who was neither a great general nor a great orator, but yet used force and persuasion to conquer the world, win men's loyalty and even enthusiasm, and found the Roman empire. Neither Antony nor Cicero took very seriously the young Octavian who at the age of eighteen arrived in Italy, advertising himself as the heir and avenger of Julius Caesar. Cicero found him at first a charming boy who, beyond his years, seemed to appreciate Cicero's greatness (*Ad Att.* 14.11.2), then a tool who could be used by the senatorial party, a young man "to be praised, honored, and tossed aside" (*Ad fam.* 11.20.1), subsequently perhaps a potential ruler who might be led by an elder statesman, finally his murderer. The young Caesar brought with him a new art of persuasion, propaganda. Not indeed wholly new: slogans and statues, games and festivals, poetry and religion had all been used for political purposes before, but never to the extent or with the subtlety that Octavian developed.[153] His modesty, his piety to the memory of Caesar, his respect for Cicero and the senate, his eagerness to pay the bequests of Caesar's will, his veneration of the painful relics of Caesar's reign: the crown that had been thrice refused, the bloody cloak of the Ides of March; all this was part of a role played by the world's greatest actor for the next fifty-seven years. It is hardly surprising that an old senator fond of hearing himself talk was taken in and accorded the youngster some praise in the *Third Philippic.* Cicero made a fatal error, but it is unhistorical and unrealistic to blame him. In the one good as he saw it, victory of the senate over Antony, every expediency was honorable. He could hardly see a threat in a boy of eighteen with a good education and a weak constitution, and after republican government had survived for five hundred years he can hardly have foreseen the principate. Recent threats had all taken the form of successful generals who had then made them-

[153] Cf. Syme, *op.cit.* supra n. 142, 149-61 and Paul Jal, *La guerre civile à Rome: étude littéraire et morale,* Paris, 1963, 82-230.

selves temporary dictators, as Cicero felt sure Antony was trying to do.

Cicero published twelve *Philippics* based on speeches delivered between December 20, 44 and April 21, 43. One or two additional speeches of the same sort were delivered, but not preserved. The fourth and sixth were addressed to the people at meetings called by a magistrate to give Cicero a chance to explain decisions of the senate. The rest were given in the senate itself and conform to the procedures of that body where a magistrate asked specific senators for their views on the matter at hand. The senator replied, but not necessarily on the subject proposed; he ended with a specific proposal or with approval, revision, or amendment of a previous opinion. Cicero's policy throughout these speeches is to prevent any appeasement or even negotiation with Antony and if possible to get him declared a public enemy. He was successful in preventing conciliation, which the consuls of 43, his young protégés Hirtius and Pansa, would have accomplished, but he could not block negotiations, and Antony was not at this time declared a public enemy. The last *Philippic* was spoken on the question of a public thanksgiving for the first of the two victories in the war of Mutina, but not long after the second victory it became clear how little that victory meant. Cicero remained active in Rome while Antony and Lepidus joined forces in Gaul, and he attempted unsuccessfully to get Marcus Brutus to invade Italy with the forces he commanded in Macedon and Greece. The last of Cicero's letters was written in mid-summer of 43. In August Octavian marched on Rome and was elected consul. Nothing is known of Cicero's life during the fall. In November, Octavian joined with Antony and Lepidus to rule the world in the second triumvirate and

274

to dispose of their enemies by gentle means of proscription. According to Plutarch, Octavian held out for two days, but finally gave in to Antony's demand for Cicero's blood (*Cicero* 46). Unfriendly declaimers later liked to imagine Cicero debating whether to seek mercy from Antony by burning the *Philippics* (Seneca, *Suas.* 7), but there was no question of that.[154] Cicero fled without panic from Tusculum to his villa at Formiae, and planned to take a boat into exile. But a tool of the triumvirs caught him in his litter on the 7th of December, 43, and he was killed, according to unreliable tradition, by a former client.[155] His head and hands, which spoke and wrote the *Philippics*, were cut off and nailed over the rostrum at Rome. He might be thought to have prophesied his fate when, eleven years before, he wrote the preface to the third book of *De oratore* and described the deaths of his early heroes, Crassus, Antonius, and Caesar.

Cicero's position as the greatest Roman orator can hardly be questioned. It is assured by the quality and quantity of his speeches and by his own rhetorical criticism and theory. He was almost equally adept at argument, at presentation and destruction of character, and at emotional appeal. Although we have seen in his works signs of the growing separation of rhetoric and persuasion, his oratorical triumphs, especially in his earlier and mid-career, were practical ones, for example, the conviction of Verres, the intimidation of Catiline, and the acquittal of Roscius or Murena or Caelius. It has been estimated that his speeches were successful about 82

---

[154] Cf. Helene Homeyer, *Die antiken Berichte über den Tod Ciceros und ihre Quellen*, Baden-Baden, 1964.

[155] The chief accounts are those in the elder Seneca (*Suas.* 6-7), which quotes Livy's lost description (6.17), and in Plut., *Cic.* 47-49.

percent of the time.[156] As became clear in his dispute with the neo-Atticists, he always regarded rhetoric as a practical art to be judged by its effectiveness with the audience.

At the same time, he valued his speeches as works of Latin literature, and after delivery he carefully worked up many for publication. In this he was motivated by three factors, at least: first, some of the speeches, and especially those of his consulship, were published as defense and explanation of his political actions. Secondly, he was never without desire for fame, glory, and influence, not only among contemporaries, but in the minds of posterity. Thirdly, he conceived a responsibility for the artistic development of Latin oratory, whose history he traced in the *Brutus*, and offered the published speeches as literary and educational models for imitation.[157]

The extent to which the published version of his speeches differed from the spoken has been much debated and is touched upon in connexion with several speeches discussed above.[158] *Pro Milone* is apparently one extreme of a work differing considerably in style, though not in argument, from the oration actually delivered; the speech of thanks to the senate on his return from exile is the opposite extreme, a speech read verbatim. Cornelius Nepos is quoted by Jerome (23.365 Migne) as having said that the published version of the peroration of Cicero's speech for Cornelius was identical to what was delivered. According to Quintilian (10.7.30)

---

[156] Cf. J. E. Granrud, "Was Cicero Successful in the Art Oratorical?" *CJ* 8 (1912-13) 234-43.

[157] Cf. e.g., *Ad Att.* 2.1.3; 4.2.2.; *Brutus* 123.

[158] Cf. Laurand, *Études, cit.* supra n. 1, 1-23 and James N. Settle, "The Publication of Cicero's Orations," Dissertation, Univ. of North Carolina, 1962.

Cicero and other orators often wrote out the exordium
of a speech before delivery, but only outlined the rest
of the argument. He says Cicero's notes survived and
were collected by Tiro. In his revisions Cicero thus often
had notes to go on. He had planned his speeches carefully, he had a highly trained memory, and he doubtless
could have reproduced a speech nearly word for word
if he wanted to. If he changed something, he changed
it deliberately, either to incorporate what he wished he
had said or to help the speech serve a new purpose. Many
of the speeches are doubtless almost as delivered, but
between the extremes represented by *Pro Milone* and
Post reditum in senatu there was doubtless variation
in the degree of revision. Thus the *Catilinarians*, which
became crucial political documents, show signs of altera-
tion. It has been suggested that the judicial speeches
might be conflations of two speeches, further revised to
include material from the *altercatio*, but this view is
based on little solid evidence and has not been widely
accepted.[159]

Cicero's oratorical career was spread over about forty
years, and some change or development is naturally to
be expected in this period of time and with such great
experience. We have already seen the extent to which
development occurs in his rhetorical theory: the very
early *De inventione* is purely a work of school learning,
somewhat imperfectly digested. It was supplanted by
De oratore, the thoughtful outgrowth of his own experience and wider study. Changes from *De oratore* to *Brutus*
and *Orator* are not fundamental ones, despite the passage
of nearly ten years. Rather, the two later works elaborate
and develop Cicero's views on the history of oratory,
on the duties of the orator, and especially on prose style,

[159] Cf. Humbert, *op.cit.* supra n. 16.

including rhythm; some of the statements are colored by specific contentions of the time. Cicero never fundamentally changed his view of the orator; his interest in styles, however, seems to increase as his opportunities for persuasion were curtailed. In this he anticipates developments of the next generation.

The orations represent slightly less straightforward development, because the influences upon them are more immediate and varied: changes in attitudes of audience and judges, changes in historical circumstances, changes in procedure. In terms of technique Cicero is already mature in *Pro Roscio Amerino*, but a number of speeches of his later period show greater freedom in structure and his own role in the speeches changes from the appeal of sympathetic interest in a courageous young man to the easy authority of the consular statesman. Stylistically there is a quite evident difference between the earliest speeches, like *Pro Quinctio* and *Pro Roscio Amerino*, and speeches of the consulship and later. Probably it is not too much to say that the earliest speeches show signs of Asianism, perhaps encouraged by a desire to equal Hortensius. There is excessive use of Gorgianic figures and of the Asian dichoree and there is a rather academic observance of partition. The *Verrines* already show considerably greater control over the material. One of the best signs of Cicero's development is his increasing ability to employ irony, of which there are signs in the *Verrines*, but which reaches fruition in *Pro Murena*, *Pro Caelio*, and *Pro Ligario*. If it is possible to distinguish an early period and to regard the *Verrines* as a transition to the mature period, it is not so easy to see a general difference between middle and late speeches. The prose of the *Philippics* is substantially that of the speeches which precede them. Indeed, there is far greater differ-

ence in style between orations and letters than between
early and later orations of the same type.[160]
Many persons hold in mind some kind of picture of
the oratorical style of Cicero and might easily agree that
it is characterized most by fullness, resulting from persistent amplification and the use of rhetorical figures, by
periodic rhythmical sentence structure, and by dignity
approaching pomposity. These qualities can all be illustrated from many works of Cicero and are perhaps a
predominant feature of *De Imperio Pompeii* or *Pro
Sestio*, but every true student of Cicero must protest that
they are not in fact the predominant characteristics of
his work as a whole. Cicero is not a Latin Isocrates. At
least as evident are variety, wit and self-criticism. Cicero
claims that a great orator must equally be the master
of the grand, the middle, and the plain style, and he
illustrates these (*Orator* 102-3) from the *Pro Rabirio*,
the *De Imperio Pompeii*, and the *Pro Caecina*, respectively, but he claims that all styles can be found in the
Verrines, and *Pro Cluentio*, and this is generally the case.
Few authors exhibit anything like Cicero's stylistic variety, ordinarily beautifully adapted to the requirements of
the case. Cicero's wit has often been remarked in these
pages and is similarly a technique of persuasion, not a

---

[160] On the development of Cicero's style, cf. Norden 226-31;
P. Parzinger, *Beiträge zur Kenntnis der Entwicklung des cicero-
nischen Stiles*, Erlangen, 1910-12; Grant Showerman, "Cicero
the Stylist: An Appreciation," *CJ* 8 (1912-13) 180-92; Laurand,
opera cit. supra n. 1, esp. *Études sur le style*; idem, "Sur l'évolution de la langue et du style de Cicéron," *RPh* 7 (1933) 62-72;
S. E. Sprott, "Cicero's Theory of Prose Style," *PhQ* 34 (1955)
1-17; Leeman 91-167. On prose rhythms cf. Theodor Zielinski,
"Das Clauselgesetz in Ciceros Reden: Grundzüge einer orator-
ischen Rhythmik," *Philologus Suppl.* 9 (1904) 589-875; idem,
Der constructive Rhythmus in Ciceros Reden, Leipzig, 1914; also
Primmer and other works cited supra, n. 139.

form of self-indulgence. By self-criticism is meant not only the fact that Cicero is both orator and rhetorician and that he fairly considers his own successes and failures, but also the fact that he is a persistent and deliberate seeker after purity of diction. Though he added many words to the Latin language, he exercised much greater discrimination than many of his contemporaries in the words which he would use.

Cicero's variety, wit, and self-criticism are underlined by comparison with Demosthenes, the greatest of the Greek orators known to us, for unfortunately the oratory of Pericles we cannot really know. Comparisons of Cicero and Demosthenes are commonplace among the later rhetoricians.[161] For all the greatness of Demosthenes, the overall eminence of Cicero is not difficult to maintain. He was not only a statesman and orator, but a philosopher and a poet. He had not only power and determination, but wit and charm. His influence on subsequent intellectual history has been infinitely greater. As a man he escaped the charges of venality made against Demosthenes, and as a thinker and statesman he showed somewhat greater imagination and flexibility.

If it be asked which of Cicero's published speeches is the finest, the answer is clear: that for Milo. Both in argumentation and in style it is superb and has been so regarded by all rhetoricians. It both fulfills the traditional rules of rhetoric and demonstrates the originality of its author. It contains all his virtues and few of his incipient vices. Further, the subject was a difficult and significant one. But Cicero's actual defense of Milo was not itself a

---

[161] Cf. "Longinus" 12.4; Quintilian 10.1.106; Plutarch's comparison abstains from literary judgment. Cf. also Eric Laughton, "Cicero and the Greek Orators," *AJPh* 82 (1961) 27-49; H. Rahn, "Demosthenes und Cicero. Zur Frage der geistigen Einheit der Antike," *Atti del I Congresso internazionale di Studi Ciceroniani*, Rome, 1961, 265-82; Nisbet, *op.cit.* supra n. 1, 76.

triumph. Indeed, it was a failure, and the great speech which we read never had a fair expression. If we ask then what was Cicero's greatest *speech*, the question becomes more difficult. The second action against Verres and the second *Philippic* are ruled out of the discussion as never delivered. In the judgments of later Romans like Pliny and Quintilian the palm probably went to *Pro Cluentio*, where the purely rhetorical triumph was the greatest, victory for a questionable client under very difficult conditions. On the other hand, the subject was not one of great significance. The other speeches of greatest rhetorical achievement in major cases are *Pro Roscio Amerino*, the first speech against Verres, *Pro Caelio*, and *Pro Murena*. The first, however, lacks Cicero's finished style. The second is superior in tactics, but not in a literary sense, and is not typical enough to stand as the pinnacle of Cicero's achievement. Both *Pro Caelio* and *Pro Murena* show Cicero's style and technique at its highest development; both are typical of his manner and personality at its best. Both are difficult and significant cases, but the issue in the second was a matter of national importance and if we were to choose one speech in which the orator used all his knowledge and all his wit for what he believed to be a worthy national purpose, it would be the speech for Murena. Its achievement is even greater when we remember that it came in the midst of the Catilinarian conspiracy and after a night of toil. There are, of course, other good speeches: in the Manilian law the rhetorical problem was perhaps not too great, in the treatment of Catiline the achievement is more one of leadership and nerve than of oratorical powers. *Pro Sestio* is able, but slightly too pompous, and it is not clear that the speech was entirely effective. The cleverness of *Pro Ligario* is called in question by the possibility that the situation was somewhat staged. The *Philippics* were self-

281

defeating. But others will prefer other speeches—Cicero himself seems to have thought very well of *Pro Rabirio*—and after all there is enough variety for every taste.

Cicero's Contemporaries

Cicero was the greatest rhetorical figure of his age, indeed of Roman history. But to some of his contemporaries and successors this was not self-evident; his own protégés were soon eliminated and the circumstances of oratory changed to the extent that his like was impossible.[162] Temporarily it may even have seemed that he was out of touch with the influences and movements of the second half of the first century B.C. In fact, from the perspective of centuries, we can see that Cicero was aware of most of what was going on, encouraging some things, resisting others.

In Cicero's youth and for much of his maturity his principal oratorical rival was Hortensius, whose oratory was regarded by many as Asianistic. In addition to Calvus and Brutus, whom we have already considered, other famous orators of the second quarter of the century were M. Crassus, the triumvir, whom Cicero found colorless (*Brutus* 233), C. Calpurnius Piso, whose style was full and whose delivery lively (*Brutus* 239), and Pompey, whose speaking ability was overshadowed by his deeds, but was apparently adequate (Seneca, *Ep.* 1.11.4; Tac., *Dial.* 37.3). Cicero praises especially his voice and delivery (*Brutus* 239). Of the orators in the grand style in the mid-century Cicero most praises M. Claudius Marcellus, balancing him off as we have seen against Caesar both politically and rhetorically (*Brutus* 248).

---

[162] Cf. G. R. Throop, "Ancient Literary Detractors of Cicero," *Washington Univ. Studies* 1.2.1 (1913) 19-41 and Leeman 136-38.

As for the younger Cato, on one occasion (*Ad Att.* 2.1.8) Cicero complained that he spoke as though he were living in Plato's republic and not among the dregs of Romulus, but considering his career as a whole Cicero allows that for a Stoic he was remarkably effective, especially at discussing philosophical topics in oratorical forms (*Brutus* 118-19; *Paradox. Stoic.* 1) and at exhorting and informing the senate (*De legibus* 3.40).[163] He had a great deal to say and was the champion Roman filibusterer. Though few fragments survive, the speech attributed to him in Sallust's *Catiline* perhaps captures some of the moral effect of his oratory. Sallust seems to model his younger Cato on the memory of the elder.[164]

Cato is not associated with neo-Atticism. Perhaps it was too new or too Greek a thing to suit him. As for M. Calidius, once regarded as part of the movement, he must be disqualified since his style was rhythmical and figured (*Brutus* 274-76) and Cicero discusses him before turning to neo-Atticism as such.[165] A more important orator with neo-Atticist leanings was Julius Caesar.

C. Julius Caesar

For the study of Caesar's oratory we have only limited information: there are brief descriptions in Cicero and other writers, a few references to the occasion or content of speeches, some reports in the *Commentaries* on the Gallic and Civil Wars, a very few fragments. For Cae-

[163] Cf. Plut., *Cato the Younger*, passim; R-E 22.168-211; for the fragments ORF; pp. 404-15. Cf. Haviland Nelson, "Cato the Younger as a Stoic Orator," *CW* 44 (1950-51) 65-69 and Ayers, *op.cit.* supra n. 55.
[164] Cf. D. C. Earl, *The Political Thought of Sallust*, Cambridge, Eng., 1961, 101.
[165] Cf. A. E. Douglas, "M. Calidius and the Atticists," *CQ* 5 (1955) 241-47.

sar's general rhetorical methods we have the broader base of his writings and the picture of his public relations given in historical sources.[166] To Cicero the most characteristic feature of Caesar's oratory was the elegance of his diction, which seemed to be an inheritance from a Roman household of speakers of pure Latin, further refined by extensive and careful literary study (*Brutus* 252). The few fragments of Caesar's speeches are simple in both diction and composition, but Cicero says that Caesar added ornaments, so his style was not always plain. Indeed, the effect was one of splendor, augmented by effective delivery and sincerity (*Brutus* 261). Cicero, of course, had often heard Caesar speak, but a number of published speeches were available when the *Brutus* was written and a few more of doubtful authority were known later (Suet., *Julius* 55.3). Quintilian (10.1.114 and 10.2.25) notes Caesar's elegance, but is more impressed by his force: Caesar spoke as he fought. His style was doubtless influenced by the theory of analogy which led him to write the grammatical treatise mentioned above.

Caesar's oratorical career began with prosecution of Dolabella for extortion in 77 B.C. As in the case of Cicero's subsequent prosecution of Verres, Caesar had first to win a *divinatio* in which he seems to have modeled himself on a speech by Caesar Strabo, the character in *De oratore* (Suet., *Julius* 55.2). The actual prosecution, which pitted Caesar against Cotta and Hortensius (*Bru-*

---

[166] Cf. Norden 209-12; L. Holtz, C. *Julius Caesar quo usus sit in orationibus dicendi genere*, Jena, 1913; K. Deichgraeber, "Elegantia Caesaris: zu Cäsars Reden und Commentarii," *Gymnasium* 57 (1950) 112-23; Frank E. Adcock, *Caesar as Man of Letters*, Cambridge, Eng., 1956; W. T. Avery, "Caesar, the Man of Letters," *CW* 50 (1956-57) 26-28; P. T. Eden, "Caesar's Style: Inheritance versus Intelligence," *Glotta* 40 (1962) 74-117. For fragments and testimonia cf. *ORF* pp. 383-97. Suetonius, *Julius* is a major source on Caesar's speeches.

tus 317), was a failure, but Caesar nevertheless won a reputation among the patrons of the day and his speeches long continued to be read. He then went off to Rhodes to study with Apollonius Molon from whom Cicero had recently returned, but the next year he was back, prosecuting C. Antonius Hybrida. His political career for the next fifteen years was not particularly distinguished, and apparently he only rarely appeared in the law courts.[167] Occasionally he spoke in the assembly, and he delivered a famous funeral laudation of his aunt Julia, the widow of Marius. Suetonius quotes (*Julius* 6) a bit of the speech which shows that it followed the ordinary pattern of tracing the ancestry of the deceased: The Julian house is claimed to derive from Venus, a point which was to have considerable significance in the symbolism and propaganda of the family later on. The audacious claim is advanced by Caesar in simple and graceful Latin. All in all, unlike some funeral orations this seems to have been a distinctly artistic work.

Of Caesar's earlier orations the most interesting, if only we had it, would probably be that in the senate on the question of the punishment of the Catilinarian conspirators.[168] Cicero reports Caesar's speech in the fourth *Catilinarian* (7-10), indicating that it was based on the argument that death is not a punishment but a fact of nature, a relief from toil and suffering, often welcomed

[167] About 73 B.C. he probably prosecuted M. Juncus for extortion, cf. Hallfried Dahlmann, "Caesars Rede für die Bithynier," *Hermes* 73 (1938) 341-46. Dahlmann thought the fragments show the influence of analogy and *sermo cotidianus*. A speech for Decidius the Samnite (Tac., *Dial*. 21) may belong about the same time.

[168] Cf. Holmes, *op.cit*. supra n. 52, 1.467; E. G. Hardy, *Some Problems in Roman History*, Oxford, 1924, 40; F. Lämmli, "Sallusts Stellung zu Cato, Caesar, Cicero," *MH* 3 (1946) 94-117. Earl, *op.cit*. supra n. 164, 95-103; Syme, *op.cit*. supra n. 32, 103-20.

by the wise. A more suitable punishment for the conspirators would be lasting imprisonment in the cities of Italy with no hope of alleviation and with all possible legal guards against escape or pardon, the cities being made responsible for the safekeeping of the conspirators. Cicero's words seem to suggest an unusually intellectual tone for a Roman speech, but he was trying to counteract Caesar's impression and sought to imply a bloodless indifference to the national crisis. We have already seen that the fourth *Catilinarian* is not an entirely reliable document of what was said at the time. According to Plutarch (*Caesar* 7.5), Caesar argued that putting the conspirators to death was neither in accord with tradition nor just and also recommended imprisonment until the crisis was over and then legal trial. The version in Sallust (*Cat.* 51) is more Sallust than Caesar as the style shows. It omits the point of making the cities of Italy responsibile for the conspirators' imprisonment and it is vague as to whether the imprisonment is to be permanent or temporary. Furthermore, one rather hopes that Caesar's knowledge of Roman history was more accurate than what Sallust, who did not have to expect rebuttal, gives him. But even if neither style nor substance is quite that of Caesar, Sallust certainly hoped to convey an impression of Caesar's ethos primarily through contrast between him and Cato. The impression is one of reason and restraint. Caesar begins by calling for cool heads; Cato says that Caesar has spoken *composite*, an ambiguous word which renders lip service to the speech of his opponent, but implies a lack of fire. The patience and humanity which are the fabric of Caesar's speech are the qualities he sought to use in dealing with the senatorial opposition during and after the Civil War and possibly more evident in hindsight than they were in 63. One clever feature of Caesar's speech in Sallust is the citation of the elder Cato in support of Caesar against the younger Cato.

Caesar's consulship in 59 B.C. was famous for the persistent attempt of his colleague Bibulus to forestall action by declaring unfavorable omens and Caesar's equal persistence in ignoring the omens. At the end of the year, on the eve of his departure for Gaul, he was forced to justify himself in the senate. He published the speeches (*Scholia Bobiensia* 130 Stangl), doubtless in hopes that they would be read in his absence. Nine years was an unusually extended absence from the city for a Roman statesman. Caesar usually spent the winters in northern Italy, which facilitated contact with the political situation at home, but to the inhabitants of Rome he became something of a myth. Brutus, in Cicero's dialogue (249), could justly claim that he was unfamiliar with Caesar the orator, and Cicero's own memory was somewhat out of date.

We have some evidence of Caesar's rhetoric during this period in his *Commentaries. Commentarius* is a word we have met before as meaning the notes an orator composed in preparing a speech. Subsequently he might use them to produce a polished literary version for publication. In the case of historical writing a *commentarius* is a notebook of recent or contemporary events, usually by an actor in them.[169] It sets down facts or impressions which can then be utilized, ordinarily by another, in writing a proper history, which to the Romans was a literary genre close to poetry, not a scientific or social study (Quint. 10.1.31). The commonly cited example is Cicero's "commentary" on his consulship which he promised to send to Lucceius if the latter would write a history

[169] Cf. Friedrich Bömer, "Der *Commentarius*: zur Vorgeschichte und literarischen Form der Schriften Caesars," *Hermes* 81 (1953) 210-50.

starring himself as hero (*Ad fam.* 5.12.10). He also sent a set of Greek notes (*hypomnema*) to Posidonius for the same purpose, but the latter diplomatically replied that it was too fine a job already to admit of adornment (*Ad Att.* 2.1.2). Cicero says something similar of Caesar's *Commentaries* (*Brutus* 262):

"They are naked, straight standing and handsome, devoid of all adornment of speech, like undraped statues. But while he desired to offer a source book to others who want to write history, he has perhaps pleased second-raters who want to singe them with curling irons and has deterred intelligent men from writing, for there is nothing sweeter in historical writing than pure and lustrous brevity."

The commentary form accounts for the fact that the speeches in the *Gallic* and the *Civil Wars* are ordinarily short and in indirect discourse, though in the course of the work there seems to be some tendency away from a strict commentary in the direction of historical composition involving more dramatic presentation.[170] Most of the speeches are, of course, by or to officers, troops, or barbarians. The *Civil War*, however, reports (1.32) Caesar's first speech to the remnants of the senate after his invasion of Italy. Its purpose seems to have been twofold, to justify the speaker to a legitimate constitutional body and to get the senate to send messengers to Pompey seeking peace. Through Caesar's brief report it is possible to see some of the rhetorical features of the speech. It began with a narration of the wrongs done by his opponents and expounded his own avowed goal: a consulship, not some special office. The motion that he be allowed

---

[170] Cf. D. Rasmussen, *Caesars Commentarii: Stil und Stilwandel am Beispiel der direkten Rede*, Göttingen, 1963.

to stand for the consulship *in absentia* was, he claimed, properly presented by the tribunes, but improperly delayed by Cato's filibuster and dishonestly impeded by Pompey, who would neither oppose it openly nor tolerate its implementation. A contrast was built up between Caesar's own long-suffering and the bitterness of the opposition. The rationalism of his speech in the Catilinarian debate was thus again evident. Once the groundwork was laid, he called on the senate to face its responsibility and join with him in administering the state; if they failed he would do it alone. He is without fear. Then he called for envoys to be sent to Pompey and concluded with a pledge to triumph through justice and right. The speech was apparently characterized by a logical tone and a strong ethical element, brought out in part through contrast of himself and his opponents. It implies room for emotion on the part of a man less controlled than Caesar, but does not openly indulge it. The style cannot adequately be judged from the summary, but was doubtless vigorous and straightforward. Certainly the diction is pure. Perhaps the delivered speech was subtler than the report, which sums up the intent of a whole passage in the words *patientiam proponit suam*, "[Caesar] expounded his patience." The picture of Caesar here is basically the picture which emerges from the *Commentaries* as a whole and was clearly one reason for their publication, but we should not overstress this as a dominating influence of political propaganda. At the time of publication Caesar seems to have had little to gain, while the enhancement of his own glory was a perfectly natural Roman impulse. The rhetoric of the *Commentaries* as a whole is thus primarily a persuasive presentation of Caesar's ethos: the magnitude of his military achievements, the justification of his movements, the fairness and determination of his decisions. Centurions and soldiers are praised, but the officers on his staff are rarely allowed to share the stage with the author.

Ancient historians like to compose addresses for generals on the eve of battle. In fact, military oratory was likely to have been direct and even earthy rather than crafty rhetorical appeal. Caesar was particularly good at winning the confidence of his troops. We have a fragment of a speech to his nervous troops during the African campaign of 46 B.C. According to Suetonius (*Julius* 66) he cried:

"Know that in a very few days a king will meet us with ten legions, thirty thousand horsemen, a hundred thousand lightly armed men, and three hundred elephants. Everyone should stop thinking and worrying beyond that point and should believe me, since I know well what I am doing. Either that or I'll order him put aboard the oldest ship we've got and sent wherever the wind may blow him."

These effective words show Caesar at his best. There is wit, humor in the climactic list of the enemy and in the punishment indicated, but there are authority and realism too. This is not a threat by a nervous or uncertain commander but a glimpse of a man who understands but savors the dangers of command. At a time of great emotional tension its directness had far greater appeal than a more elaborate oration such as the historians sometimes supply.

The speeches in Caesar's *Commentaries* are in indirect discourse except that in the seventh book of the *Gallic War* there are two speeches in direct discourse (7.50 and 77) and in the *Civil War* there is a directly reported speech of Curio (2.32) as well as a number of short direct quotations. It seems to be significant that Caesar did not personally hear the speeches he gives in direct form; thus his function in these cases becomes more that of a literary historian than that of the author of a *commentarius*. Rhetorically the most interesting of the direct speeches is that of Critognatus to the other Gauls besieged at Alesia (7.77). Caesar says that he includes it "because of its singular and abominable cruelty." He means the recommendation, inconceivable to a Roman, that the besieged feed on the flesh of those too young or too old to fight. There is thus a rhetorical challenge in the presentation of a barbarian chief to a Roman audience in such a way as to chill the blood, but retain plausibility. Presumably Caesar felt entirely free in the composition and style of the surrounding argument. His approach is to make Critognatus reason like an old Roman, but carry his application of principle beyond the limit which religion and civilization would impose. Thus the speaker begins rather in the spirit of Appius Claudius denouncing the peace with Pyrrhus, but pushes to the conclusion that the garrison must hold out even by cannibalism. The speech ends with a barbarian view of Rome, driven by envy of the Gauls to subdue and enslave them. Critognatus does not recognize his own need to be civilized.[171]

As dictator, Caesar does not seem to have made any special use of oratory, and though he was conscious of the persuasive effects of propaganda and fostered the myth of his *clementia*, his attempts in that direction are relatively slight when compared with what Augustus was to do. Caesar's rhetorical, like his political and military, career seems to suggest an increasing impatience with delay and artificiality. The principal exception was perhaps the *Anticato*, a reply to Cicero's encomium of

[171] It is interesting to compare this speech with that of Calgacus in Tacitus' *Agricola* 30-32. Tacitus' barbarian is not "barbaric" and the superiority of Rome is no longer so evident.

the dead Cato.[172] Caesar apparently took a serious view of the developing myth of Cato, which Brutus joined in encouraging and Hirtius in counteracting. The work won Cicero's literary approval (*Ad Att.* 13.50.1). Cicero (*Topica* 94) says that Caesar employed all three kinds of *stasis* in his attack: he denied the fact of the deeds attributed to Cato, the words used to describe them, and the rightness and legality of the actions.

Sallust

Cicero (*De leg.* 1.5) called history an *opus . . . oratorium maxime* and in *De oratore* (2.62-66) outlined an art of historiography, which is modeled on a normal rhetorical treatise. All the Roman historians are a part of the rhetorical traditions of Rome and though detailed analysis of them would be out of proportion here, an understanding of the history of rhetoric at Rome requires a glance at the chief rhetorical features of the major writers as we come to the period in which each lived.[173]

C. Sallustius Crispus is the earliest Roman historian whose works are preserved.[174] He seems (cf. Suet., *De gramma.* 10) to have been a student of L. Ateius Philol-

---

[172] Cf. A. Dyroff, "Zu den Anticatonen des Caesar," *RhM* 50 (1895) 481; A. Klotz, *Caesarstudien*, Leipzig, 1910, 152-59; R-E 10.264-66.

[173] Cf. Hermann Peter, *Die geschichtliche Literatur über die Römische Kaiserzeit bis Theodosius I und ihre Quellen*, 2 vols., Leipzig, 1897, esp. 1.3-53 and 2.280-326; Norden 81-91; F. H. Colson, "Some Considerations as to the Influence of Rhetoric on History," *PCA* 14 (1917) 149-73; Wilhelm Kroll, *Studien zum Verständnis der Römischen Literatur*, Stuttgart, 1924, 87-116 and 331-84; D'Alton 491-524; B. L. Ullman, "History and Tragedy," *TAPhA* 73 (1942) 25-53; Michel Rambaud, *Cicéron et l'histoire*, Paris, 1953; Leeman, 67-88 and 168-97.

[174] Cf. A. D. Leeman, *A Systematical Bibliography of Sallust* (1879-1964) Leiden, 1964; Earl, *op.cit.* supra n. 164 and Syme, *op.cit.* supra n. 32.

ogus, "a rhetorician among the grammarians and a grammarian among the rhetoricians," and the friendship continued into later life. Asinius Pollio, who also knew Ateius, attributed Sallust's fondness for archaism to him. A brief and undistinguished political career culminated in Sallust's expulsion from the senate in 50 B.C. (Dio Cassius 40.63.4). Subsequently, he began over again as an adherent of Caesar, was quaestor and praetor (and thus, of course, again a senator) and held military command, but with Caesar's death he retired from politics to enjoy his wealth, some of it probably acquired as governor of Numidia and Africa in 45, to contemplate the decadence of his fellow countrymen, and to write history until his own death about ten years later. We have the mongraphs on the Catilinarian conspiracy and on the Jugurthine war and fragments of an annalistic *History* which began with the death of Sulla.

Sallust's greatest and most obvious significance in the history of rhetoric is stylistic.[175] Though a short generation younger than Cicero, he is totally un-Ciceronian. His "immortal rapidity" (Quint. 10.1.102) probably should be viewed as a variation of neo-Atticism; it is simple and brief, but has two distinguishing features, deliberate archaism (most conspicuously imitation of the language of Cato and other second century writers) and imitation of Thucydides. Sallust's archaism is partly moral in origin; that is, he wants to return if possible to the way of thought of Romans in the great period before the fall of Carthage. But it is also strongly aesthetic. We have already seen Cicero urging imitation of Cato upon the neo-Atticists and he also had remarked (*Orator* 30) but did not name "a new and unheard of group of ignoramuses" who, not content with Lysias, took the

---

[175] Cf. Norden 200-209; W. Kroll, "Die Sprache des Sallusts," *Glotta* 15 (1927) 280-305; Leeman 179-87.

historian Thucydides as their Attic model, even in judicial and deliberative oratory. Cicero's objections to Thucydideanism in historical composition would have been less. We do not know what Sallust's own oratory was like. The only orator named as an imitator of Thucydides is T. Annius Cimber, praetor in 44 B.C., whose bizarre style is attacked in the second *Catalepton* attributed to Virgil.[176]

When it is said that an historian like Sallust is "rhetorical" the meaning commonly is that he has regarded his task as a rhetorical challenge, the presentation of events of varying interest in striking literary dress including speeches composed for the characters. Or more superficially, that he uses techniques of argument or more often of style learned in the rhetorical schools. Sallust, and Livy and Tacitus, too, are rhetorical in both these senses. But they also show signs of being rhetorical in a more fundamental way: in exploiting the art of persuasion to plead a cause.[177] This is one of the chief ways in which Roman historians differ from Herodotus, Thucydides, and Xenophon, though the development had begun in Greece with the followers of Isocrates and the historians of Alexander. Both of Sallust's historical monographs are given an artistic unity by the author's desire to demonstrate the moral collapse of the Roman republic, and especially the senatorial class, in the period after the victory over Carthage. Avarice figures as the key vice. The theory in each case is expounded in a preface and

[176] Cf. Quint. 8.3.26-29 who identified the subject as Cimber and regarded the poem as a genuine work of Virgil. Cf. Henry R. Fairclough, "On the Virgilian Catalepton II," *TAPhA* 47 (1916) 43-50; H. G. Strebel, *Wertung und Wirkung des thukydidischen Geschichtswerkes in der griechisch-römischen Literatur*, Munich, 1935.

[177] Cf. Colson, *op.cit.* supra n. 173.

taken up later in the work in a digression.[178] It is further illustrated by the characters of the chief participants, partly seen through speeches, and to a lesser extent by the historical narrative. Sallust thus has a generalized idea to convey, but in each case he regarded the specific historical incident he is discussing as a crucial incident in the collapse. The Jugurthine war was "the first opposition to the insolence of nobility" (*Jug.* 5.1). The Catilinarian conspiracy showed how a single corrupt individual, summing up all the vices of the nobility in himself, could shipwreck the entire state (*Cat.* 4). Both monographs seem to suggest (*Cat.* 4; *Jug.* 4) that Sallust has a personal purpose as well: to counteract the memory of his own rather unprepossessing career by disassociating himself from the more vicious tendencies of his age and constructing a permanent literary monument to virtue. The monographs should not be read primarily as political documents commenting on the triumviral period in which they were written, though there may be an occasional allusion to contemporary leaders.[179]

Sallust's historical monographs are carefully constructed and on similar principles. The *Jugurtha* was, however, written second and is longer and more fully developed. In both cases there is a preface or exordium stating Sallust's moral views and the importance of his subject. Next, like Thucydides in the *Pentekontaetia*, he inserts a *narratio* dealing with the background material which he regards as necessary for the understanding of his subject (*Cat.* 5-16; *Jug.* 5.3-19). Then comes the body of the work: the historical narrative is divided into

[178] Cf. A. D. Leeman, "Sallusts Prologe und seine Auffassung von der Historiographie," *Mnemosyne* 7 (1954) 323-39 and 8 (1955) 38-48.
[179] Cf. Syme, *op.cit.* supra n. 32, 122.

parts by digressions and by the insertion of speeches. In the *Jugurtha*, for example, the account of the first phase of the war ends with the digression on faction (41-42), which could be labeled a rhetorical commonplace. The second phase of the war ends with the digression on the *Philaeni* (79), which is a fable such as boys learned to compose in the rhetorical schools. There are also character descriptions of Jugurtha, Marius, and Sulla, and an ecphrasis, or description of Africa (17-19). The *Jugurtha* has six main speeches, composed according to rhetorical rules[180] and analogous to the *suasoriae* practiced in rhetorical schools. The *Catiline* has the striking debate between Caesar and Cato, followed by a comparison of the two speakers. There are two speeches by Catiline, one near the beginning, one near the end. The structure of both monographs can be worked out in greater detail, but the basic building materials are obvious to one familiar with the system of rhetoric taught in Sallust's youth as known from *De inventione* or *Ad Herennium* and the rhetorical exercises of the period as listed by Suetonius (*De rhet.* 25.5).

Sallust's *Histories* undoubtedly contained similar rhetorical materials. The speeches and letters have been preserved in a manuscript which also contains the speeches and letters of the *Catiline* and *Jugurtha*, a clear indication of the interest with which later antiquity read the products of the rhetorical art of the historian.

Pamphlet literature, as exemplified by the *Anticato* of Caesar, had some currency in Rome, and it is tempting to see it also in four small works preserved with the writings of Sallust: a speech and letter addressed to the aging Caesar and a speech against Cicero, all three attrib-

---

[180] But the artificial structure which R. Ullmann tried to see in the speeches is entirely imaginary, cf. *La technique des discours dans Salluste, Tite-Live, et Tacite*, Oslo, 1927.

uted to Sallust, and a speech against Sallust which pretends to be a work of Cicero. The first two are rather convincing and an enormous amount of scholarship has been expended on all, far out of proportion to their real value.[181] Despite some authoritative supporters it seems unlikely that any of these is what it purports to be. The first two would have to be products of about 46 and 50 B.C. respectively and yet they seem to imitate the style and thought of Sallust's historical monographs written some years later. All these documents are probably declamations or exercises of rhetorical schools, most likely written in the Augustan period when taste for the Ciceronian was at a low point. The picture of moral regeneration urged is rather like the program followed by Augustus. This interpretation does not destroy the historical significance of the works, but makes their evaluation considerably more difficult.

Mark Antony

Antony hardly rivaled his grandfather as an orator (Cic., *Phil.* 2.42), but on at least three occasions in his career his speeches were of great historical significance.[182] Though he had been one of the prosecutors of Milo in 52 (Asconius, *In Mil.* 36), his first major rhetorical performance came during his tribunate when, in the closing days of the year 50 B.C., he tried to defend Caesar's interests before the senate. Cicero, who was not in Rome, received a text of a speech in which Antony inveighed against Pompey's entire career, complained about those who had been condemned, and threatened war (*Ad Att.* 7.8.5).

To posterity Antony's most famous speech will always

---

[181] Cf. "Appendix II, The False Sallust," in Syme, *op.cit.* supra n. 32, 314-51.
[182] Cf. ORF 468-76.

be the funeral oration for Julius Caesar, of which there are versions in Appian (*Civil Wars*, 2.144-6) and Dio Cassius (44.36-49), a description in Suetonius (*Julius* 84), and mention in Quintilian, Plutarch, and other writers. Suetonius' account has usually been taken as the most reliable,[183] but the references in Cicero (*Ad Att.* 14.10.1; *Phil.* 1.32 and 2.90-91) provide the firmest basis for reconstruction. In the latter passage Cicero seems to indicate that Antony's speech had three distinct parts, a *laudatio*, a *miseratio*, and a *cohortatio*. Appian's version is likely to be derived from Asinius Pollio's contemporary account and seems closest to fulfilling the outline of Cicero. Apparently a funeral procession of more or less the usual sort came into the forum where Antony delivered his speech. First he read, or had a herald read, decrees of the senate granting honors to Caesar, and he commented briefly after each. Then the oath of the senators to defend Caesar was read. This much is what Cicero called the *laudatio*. When Antony had the crowd's sympathy he continued with a *miseratio* which referred to Caesar's favors to those who subsequently killed him. The speech became increasingly dramatic with some elements of staging. A voice or voices was heard to cry out from Caesar's corpse, a wax image of his wounded body may have been revealed, and as a climax Antony exhibited the very clothes in which Caesar died, still matted with his blood. This last portion is what Cicero called the *cohortatio*, and its effect was to incite a general riot. Roman funerals had always been colorful, with mourners wearing masks of the ancestors of the deceased, but on this occasion the tendency was carried to a remarkable extreme.[184]

[183] Cf. Monroe E. Deutsch, "Antony's Funeral speech," *Univ. of California Publ. in Classical Philology* 9 (1926-29) 127-48.
[184] For a more detailed presentation of the evidence see George

The third occasion on which Antony figured as an orator was the duel with Cicero in the second half of 44 B.C. His most important attack on Cicero was that of September 19th to which the second *Philippic* is a reply. Cicero stresses the violence of Antony's invective (*Ad fam.* 12.2 and 25.4), its incoherence and inconsistency (*Phil.* 2.18), its clumsy wit (*Phil.* 2.20). Antony is represented as having practiced declamation in preparation for his speech and as vainly lavishing vast sums on his teacher of rhetoric, Sextus Clodius (*Phil.* 2.43). The earlier part of Cicero's reply (3-43) claims to answer specific charges which Antony has made against Cicero, going back at least to the time of the latter's consulship (*Phil.* 2.12).

Although, as said before, we must assume exaggerations and coloring in Cicero's answer, the picture of Antony's oratory as vigorous in the extreme and extempore in manner is consistent with other sources. Plutarch calls Antony an Asianist (2.4) and draws a comparison between Antony's style and his flamboyant way of life. But we should not regard the label Asianist here as resulting from any particular aesthetic judgment. Suetonius (*Aug.* 86. 2-3) quotes Augustus' criticism of Antony's style as "insane," aiming more at creating amazement than conveying ideas, and alternating wildly between imitation of Annius Cimber, the Thucydidean, the archaic diction of Sallust, and the empty but verbose *sententiae* of the Asianists.

To conclude, there were a number of effective orators among Cicero's later contemporaries, speakers who made good use of their skills for practical persuasion. They may be associated in varying degrees with the At-

---

Kennedy, "Antony's Speech at Caesar's funeral," *QJS* 54 (1968) 99-106.

ticist and Asianist movements. Some, like Caesar, had an interest in literary theory. Others, like Antony, show little concern with such matters. Declamation was practiced, but as a training exercise. There is no sharp break with the traditions of Roman oratory as developed in the second and earlier first century; the dictatorship of Caesar was not long enough continued to undermine or materially affect Roman rhetoric, and though from 60 B.C. onward armed force was the ultimate arbiter of Roman affairs, the deliberations of the senate and sometimes the meetings of the assembly were still endowed with real meaning. Disruption of the law courts occurred, but was temporary. In artistic achievement and in variety of style none of his contemporaries approached Cicero, which is probably the original reason why none of their speeches are preserved.

CHAPTER FOUR

Oratory and Rhetorical Criticism in Augustan Rome

The victory of Caesar's heir, Octavian, over Antony at the battle of Actium in September of 31 B.C. marks the end of the moribund Roman republic. In the following years Octavian, with the help of Agrippa, Maecenas, and other lieutenants, created a new government which endured for centuries: the Roman empire or, more accurately, the principate. A variety of constitutional traditions and religious forms were used to mask the reality of the emperor's power, the restoration of the republic was proclaimed, and the spirit of the age was summed up in 27 B.C. when Octavian assumed the name Augustus, charismatic but vague. Until his peaceful death in A.D. 14 he ruled Rome with a firm, paternal hand. Italy and the provinces alike found relief from decades of civil war. Frontiers were more solidly defined, urban and provincial administration reformed, cities rebuilt and beautified, and every possible encouragement given to the arts as expressions of Roman destiny and of the loyally constructive force of Roman creative genius. Especially during the first decade of the principate a new Golden Age, the Age of Augustus, seemed to bloom, and though the later blossoms were somewhat pale, the aroma lingered.[1]

Rhetoric played an important part in the intellectual and aesthetic life of the Augustan Age: it maintained its

---

[1] For the history of the period cf. *CAH* 10; Ronald Syme, *The Roman Revolution*, Oxford, 1939; Donald Earl, *The Age of Augustus*, New York, 1968. On changes in legal procedure cf. A.H.M. Jones, "Imperial and Senatorial Jurisdiction in the Early Principate," *Historia* 3 (1955) 464-88.

dominant position in the educational system, it continued to be the disciplinary core of literary criticism, it influenced the techniques and qualities of poetry and literary prose. Judicial oratory flourished under only slightly altered conditions; political oratory, however, lost ground while new forms of persuasion, a new rhetoric in the verbal and visual arts, arose to influence public opinion. Developments can perhaps be best made clear if we begin with a consideration of the traditional forms of oratory, then move on to the fashion of declamation in the schools and to rhetorical theory and criticism as it was taught. In the next chapter we shall turn back to look at the new rhetoric of empire as developed by Augustus and his associates.

Augustan Oratory

Freedom of expression in Rome was a relative matter. It was not something to which every citizen was entitled, but something he might derive from noble birth or wealth or might achieve by successful public service and personal merit. The freedom of an individual was limited by that of his peers and superiors; when Augustus excelled all men in authority their rights of expression shrank in proportion. The late republic had been characterized by an almost complete breakdown in public responsibility among the ruling classes; this Augustus tried to counteract in every possible way. His theoretical goal was a loyal and constructive aristocracy which would cooperate with him in the preservation of order and public administration. Discussion of policies and needs in the senate was a part of his concept of how this should be brought about, but some reform of the senate seemed a necessary preliminary. He first considerably reduced the number and revised the list of members (Suet., *Aug.* 35). It could be called a purge. To show the importance he

302

gave to the senate he regularly attended and consulted it. His interest could be felt as intimidation, and through the tribunate he had veto of any action. Thus it proved difficult to attain the kind of responsible reaction he wanted.[2] Sometimes the senate would veer wildly into abject flattery and at other times rather arbitrarily oppose him. Once he ran out of the chamber in anger at opposition and was followed by cries that senators should be allowed to say what they liked about the state (Suet., *Aug.* 54). Constrained as it was, the senate was the only possible scene of political oratory, for the function of the assemblies became purely formal. Under Augustus they met to elect magistrates, though he usually indicated what candidates he preferred. His successor transferred these elections to the senate. No forum was left for a fiery demagogue. Orderly and efficient operation was also the watchword in the law courts, where the emperor also took a personal interest, sometimes presiding all day (Suet., *Aug.* 32-33). From the point of view of ordinary litigants conditions were much improved, but the great political trials of the late republic disappeared. There was still an occasional opportunity for a patron to speak in a colorful criminal case and under Augustus' successors treason trials attracted enormous interest.

In sum, although Augustus did not set out to limit freedom of speech or suppress oratory, his enormous personal power was inhibiting and could not help but affect the conditions of oratory. Three general effects can be observed. The already existing tendency of Roman nobles to withdraw from public life was encouraged. A sense of anxiety or frustration was instilled in some of those who tried to participate. And thirdly, since eloquence continued to be regarded as a virtue, increased rhetorical

---

[2] Cf. Chester G. Starr, *Civilization and the Caesars: the Intellectual Revolution in the Roman Empire*, Ithaca, 1954, 63-88.

importance was given to less controversial oratorical forms including minor judicial cases and the art of declamation in schools and at home.

The man who deserves the title of the greatest Roman orator in the decades after the death of Cicero is almost certainly C. Asinius Pollio, soldier, statesman, poet, historian, orator, critic, and patron at the bar, whose varied interests and long life (76 B.C.-A.D. 4) brought him into contact with every major figure of the Golden Age.[3] Pollio began his career in 56 B.C. when, with considerable independence and probably equal ambition, he opposed the recall of Lentulus Spinther, thus antagonizing Pompey, who was anxious to secure Spinther's command for himself. Like Cicero and Caesar and others before him he followed this political debut with an educational trip to Greece, and like them he returned to seek fame through prosecution, in this instance prosecution of Cato for his intercession against the election of 55. The action was a political affront to Pompey and Crassus, whose election had resulted. Perhaps Pollio would have opposed Caesar with equal determination, but he became an intimate of Caesar's friend and representative Curio, so that when the die of the Rubicon was cast Pollio had already joined his fate with Caesar's. Caesar found him a valued lieutenant, especially in Africa and Spain, and on Caesar's death he was in office as propraetor of Further Spain. Thus, what began as a promising republican career in which the oratory of the senate and assembly might have been a major factor was, by Caesar's victory, converted into an administrative trust. Pollio held to his position in the uncertain months which

---

[3] Cf. J. André, *La vie et l'oeuvre d'Asinius Pollio*, Paris, 1949. For fragments and testimonia cf. *ORF* pp. 516-26. A characteristic story about Pollio is his friendship with the historian Timogenes to spite Augustus, cf. Seneca, *De ira* 3.23.

followed. When at last he again committed himself, it was to Antony, on terms which included the consulship of 40 B.C. To Antony he was remarkably loyal; put in charge of Cisalpine Gaul he held an Antonian army against Octavian's back for over two years and on behalf of Antony he negotiated the treaty of Brundisium and assumed briefly the promised consulship. His public career was then crowned with the proconsulship of Dalmatia, whence he returned home for a triumph—and retirement before he was forty. There was, in fact, little to which he could aspire in the Augustan state. Rather remarkably he carved for himself a new position as an advocate and a man of letters and preserved his dignity and his independence of Augustus for nearly forty years. This splendid achievement he owed above all to his intellect: his manifest hatred and regret for civil war won him sympathy, and his willingness to shoulder duty and make responsible decisions when necessary won him respect. He was one of the first to recognize the abilities of Virgil and he long enjoyed the friendship of Horace. The disappearance of his poetry and more especially the loss of his vigorous history of the Civil War is one of the major tragedies in the history of Latin literature.

Pollio was both the last relict of the republican and the first example of the imperial orator. Unfortunately, only the most meager fragments survive from his speeches. His prosecution of Cato was doubtless not unlike other such attacks of that period, but the independence of spirit which he retained under Augustus was occasionally demonstrated in his speeches: for example, when speaking for Aemilius Scaurus he pointedly warned the court against influence from high places prejudicial to his client (Quint. 9.2.24), and he openly protested to the senate against the danger of the *lusus Troiae* (Suet., *Aug.* 43.2), Augustus' pet military exercise for young aristocrats. On the other hand, his primary oratorical activity under the principate was not public debate, but the kind of judicial action which had been too minor for the attention of Cicero or others earlier. Tacitus (*Dial.* 38.2) names him as the author of the earliest well-known speech delivered before the centumviral court, a body which was to become an important scene of imperial oratory. This case, which was for the heirs of Urbinia, as well as his defense of Nonius Asprenas, has a sensationalism about it suggestive of the schools of declamation (Quint. 7.2.26; Pliny, *Nat. hist.* 35.164). Pollio was interested in declamation, but in the republican tradition that did not engage in it publicly. Indeed, he seems to have regarded it for what it was, a form of practice for the law courts and not a game to be played for itself.[4] At the same time, Pollio appears as the inventor of recitation, the custom whereby a Roman author presented his new compositions orally to invited guests and the public at large (Seneca, *Contr.* 4. *pr.* 2). Everything that we know about ancient literature, both poetry and artistic prose, suggests that it was intended to be read aloud, but often by a person to himself or by a slave to a single reader.[5] Recitations had taken place in Athens in the fifth and fourth centuries, but in Rome had been restricted to private groups (e.g., Cic., *Ad Att.* 16.2.6).[6] The object of public, or at least semipublic, recitation was perhaps to encourage a wide interest in literature; the effect was to increase or emphasize the oratorical aspect of literature and this in turn tended to

---

[4] Cf. André, *op.cit.* supra n. 1, 78.

[5] Cf. Josef Balogh, "Voces paginarum," *Philologus* 82 (1927) 84-109 and 202-40 and Bernard M. W. Knox, "Silent Reading in Antiquity," *GRBS* 9 (1968) 421-35.

[6] Cf. André, *op.cit.* supra n. 1,117 and A. C. Dalzell, "Asinius Pollio and the Early History of Public Recitation at Rome," *Hermathena* 86 (1955) 20-28.

increase its rhetorical qualities. Recitation, like declamation, helped to fill some of the void left by the disappearance of political oratory in a culture taught to regard speech as the noblest human art. The descriptions of Pollio's speeches indicate that his primary concern was with argument and persuasion. "By pleading rightly," Pliny reports him as having said (*Ep.* 6.29.5), "it results that I often conduct a case, by often conducting a case that I do so less rightly." Quintilian (10.1.113 and 10.2.25), seeking a single word to describe Pollio, settles on *diligentia*; his style is universally described as harsh, that of an age before Cicero, though occasionally a clausula was admitted.[7] Pollio's style was certainly plain and probably to be associated at least loosely with the neo-Atticist movement. His famous criticism of Livy for *Patavinitas* (Quint. 8.1.3) suggests an opposing value for *Latinitas*.[8] The theory that he should be regarded as Thucydidean is not specifically suggested by the comment of any ancient critic, though several modern scholars have advanced it.[9] That he was influenced by Thucydides is perhaps not improbable; that Cicero had him in mind when rebuking Roman Thucydideans seems to go well beyond the evidence. If Pollio became, as the elder Seneca calls him, *infestissimus famae Ciceronis* (*Suas.* 6.14), this is likely enough from a loyal and true friend of Antony.[10]

[7] According to Seneca (*Ep.* 100.7) it was ordinarily the same one, which André, *op.cit.* supra n. 1, 112 interprets as the dichoree. Quint. 9.4.132 may suggest a fondness for long syllables rather than for a specific single foot.

[8] Cf. Kurt Latte, "Livy's *Patavinitas*," *CPh* 35 (1940) 56-60; L. A. MacKay, "On Patavinity," *CPh* 38 (1943) 44-45; Joshua Whatmough, "A Last Word on *patavinitas*," *CPh* 38 (1943) 205; W. H. Alexander, "*Patavinitas*," *CW* 43 (1949-50) 245.

[9] Cf. André, *op.cit.* supra n. 1, 108-9 and Leeman 162-63.

[10] In the published version of his speech for Lamia (Seneca, *Suas.* 6.15) Pollio claimed that Cicero was eager to disown the

An orator whose career is partially analogous to that of Pollio is M. Valerius Messalla Corvinus.[11] Born in 64 B.C., he was too young to share Pollio's opportunity of being a republican orator, but he played a role in the Civil War, first with Brutus and Cassius, then with Octavian, in whose cause he fought Antony. In later life he ceased to hold public posts and, like Pollio, devoted himself to literature, but, again like Pollio, he sometimes appeared at the bar and in the senate, where in 2 B.C. he was given the great honor of conferring the previously refused title of "father of his country" on the emperor (Suet., *Aug.* 58). Though Messalla was clearly regarded as one of the most eloquent men of the Augustan age, his speeches have not left enough traces to be appreciated. Seneca (*Contr.* 2.4.8) calls him a man who demanded precision in all parts of study and a very careful critic of the Latin language. Quintilian (4.1.8) and Tacitus (*Dial.* 20.1) both mention his apologetic tendency in introductions to dwell on his poor health or other disadvantages. The latter perhaps suggest a rather rigid adherence to convention and the former a pure simple style. As we shall see, the rhetorical theory of the period as taught in the Apollodorean and Theodorean schools tended to encourage rigidity. Perhaps Messalla saw some of the qualities he admired in the poet Tibullus, whom he patronized. Subsequently the emperor Tiberius is said (Suet., *Tib.* 70) to have modeled his Latin oratory on that of Messalla.

In the case of Pollio there was some hint of resentment that his freedom of expression was inhibited by the new political circumstances in Rome; this quality is even

---

Philippics. This conceit was surely designed to strengthen Pollio's own case and is not much of a condemnation of Cicero considering Pollio's sympathy with Antony.

[11] Cf. ORF pp. 529-34.

more evident in two other orators of the day, Titus Labienus and Cassius Severus. Both were driven to extremes of irritability and even psychopathic irresponsibility by a sense of frustration and helplessness. Labienus is primarily known from the description of him given by the elder Seneca (*Contr.* 10. *pr.* 4-8). Despite many handicaps and considerable opposition he had become a remarkable orator, primarily because of a natural genius for forceful expression. The moral tone of his speech was old fashioned, but he used the new, vigorous post-Ciceronian style. Most conspicuous was his *libertas*, a ferocity in attacking all ranks of men, which earned him the nickname "Rabid," and a freedom of speech about recent history. "In an age of extraordinary peace," Seneca says (*Contr.* 10. *pr.* 5), "he had not yet laid down the passions of the age of Pompey." He carried a chip on his shoulder which was an invitation to disaster, and he had the distinction of becoming the first Roman whose works were ordered burned by the senate.[12] The decree, which is to be dated around A.D. 12, doubtless resulted as much from the personal hostility of the senators as from a desire to please the emperor, who seems to have kept out of the matter. Seneca says that the man who introduced the decree subsequently suffered a similar censorship: though he names no names, Aemilius Scaurus is a good possibility. Labienus dramatically refused to outlive his work, had himself carried to his tomb, and there committed suicide. Copies of his writings were saved and republished in the reign of Caligula (Suet., *Calig.* 16).

For all his evident paranoia, it would be interesting to know more about Labienus' historical works and speeches. We know that he spoke for Bathyllus, a freed man of Maecenas (Seneca, *Contr.* 10 *pr.* 8), and against

[12] Cf. Clarence A. Forbes, "Books for the Burning," *TAPhA* 67 (1936) 114-25.

Pollio in the celebrated case of the heirs of Urbinia (Quint. 4.1.11), where Pollio claimed that the very fact Labienus appeared was proof of the badness of the case! Seneca cites a number of his private declamations, of which the most interesting (*Contr.* 10.4.17-18) was a defense of a man who deliberately crippled some abandoned children and forced them to earn money for him by begging:

"It is strange that men should bother to care what a beggar does among beggars. The first men of the state use their wealth in violation of nature. They have flocks of eunuchs; they mutilate grown men in order to make them fit no longer for indulgence of lust, and because they are shamed of their own manhood they try to see that there exist as few real men as possible. Nobody runs to the defense of these dainty and beautiful victims; what exercises your minds is a man who rescues from loneliness infants who would have died if he hadn't rescued them; you don't care that men of fortune amuse their loneliness with prisons full of free-born youths; you don't care that they take advantage of the simplicity of wretched boys and trap in their gladiator schools all of the handsomest and most suited candidates for the national service."

The quotation suggests some of Labienus' bitter force and why he did not endear himself to influential Romans. To judge from this passage, which seems typical of Labienus as described, he was strongest in attack, and found it the best defense. His rhetoric was diversionary; we are set against the wealthy degenerates, but hardly persuaded of the innocence of the master of the beggars. Argument plays no role; emotion and style as seen in voice, choice of words, and antithesis are everything.

Another orator who shows signs of bitterness is C.

Cassius Severus. When Quintilian wants a single word to describe him, he chooses *acerbitas* (12.10.11), and in the survey of the history of oratory, where he praises his native ability, urbanity, and style, he adds *acerbitas* as well and grants Severus "more bile than brain" (10.1.116-17). There are a number of anecdotes of his puncturing the rhetorical pretensions of others (e.g., Seneca, *Contr.* 3. *pr.* 16-18; Quint. 6.1.43; 8.2.2; 11.3.133). He caused Augustus considerable embarrassment by his prosecution of the emperor's friend Asprenas for poisoning (Suet., *Aug.* 56.3); Quintilian quotes (11.1.57) what are probably the taunting opening words: "The gods are good; I live, and what gives me delight in life is that I see Asprenas a defendant!" Cassius was often in court in his own defense (Seneca, *Contr.* 3. *pr.* 5), but one suspects that unlike Cicero he delighted in the prosecution of others. As time went on he became more and more a thorn in the side of the regime and Augustus was eventually led to apply the *maiestas* or treason law against his satiric writing, the first time it had been so used (Tac., *Annals* 1.72). Exiled to Crete by decree of the senate about A.D. 8, he still would not keep silent and was tried again and further degraded in A.D. 24 (Tac., *Annals* 4.21). He finally died in utter destitution on Seriphos around A.D. 33 (Jerome, *Chron.* s.v.).

The elder Seneca knew Cassius well and devotes to him the preface to book three of the *Controversiae*. Seneca begins by stressing his true persuasive force: every word counted, the audience was entirely in his control. Though he made rather full use of notes, he was infinitely better when speaking extemporaneously than when prepared. His power came from native ability, not from study. Since his presence and delivery were an important element in his effectiveness, his published speeches did not do him justice. Cassius sometimes practiced declamation, but with indifferent success, and part of Seneca's preface is a report of an interview with him on the reason for this. First, Cassius claims that different people are good at different things, but eventually his scorn for declamation comes out: "In declamation what is not superfluous when the whole thing is superfluous?" (*Contr.* 3. *pr.* 12). What he wants is the real life and the dust of the forum. Seneca does not stress the bitterness of Cassius, and probably knew him chiefly in his earlier years.

To rhetoricians of the empire Cassius Severus seemed the real beginning of their own age. Aper, the modernist in Tacitus' *Dialogus* (19), praises him for abandoning the tiresome introductions, long narratives, many divisions, and the like of older orators. Messalla (26) is less complimentary: Cassius showed "more bile than blood. He was the first orator to hold logical order in contempt, to set aside modesty and taste in language: ill trained in the very arms he uses and often falling on his face in his zeal to strike, he does not fight but brawls."[13] Whatever qualitative judgment of Cassius is made there is no doubt that we have left behind the age of Cicero.

Declamation

The most important new manifestation of speech in Augustan rhetoric is the greatly increased popularity of declamation.[14] In chapter one we considered the evidence

[13] Cf. Quint. 10.1.117 cited supra.

[14] The best discussions of declamation are Henri Bornecque, *Les déclamations et les déclamateurs d'après Sénèque le père*, Lille, 1902 and S. F. Bonner, *Roman Declamation in the Late Republic and Early Empire*, Liverpool, 1949. Cf. in addition Victor Cucheval, *Histoire de l'éloquence romaine*, I, Paris, 1893, 217-93; A. S. Wilkins, *Roman Education*, Cambridge, Eng., 1905; Gaston Boissier, "The Schools of Declamation at Rome," *Tacitus and Other Roman Studies*, London, 1906, 163-94 and also his article "*declamatio*" in Daremberg-Saglio, *Dictionnaire des antiquités grecques et romaines* II, Paris, 1892, 34-36; Nor-

for oratorical practice exercises in the late second and early first century B.C. Subsequently these became commoner. Suetonius reports (*De gramm. et rhet.* 25.3) that Cicero continued to declaim in Greek until he was praetor and in Latin until old age and mentions as his companions the ill-fated consuls of 43 B.C., Hirtius and Pansa, whom Cicero labeled his *discipulos et grandis praetextatos*, or "overgrown schoolboys."

The implication seems to be that rhetorical exercises by adult orators were unusual, but Cicero lent the practice respectability. Cicero's adult exercises in declamation were a form of recreation or of solace. In the earlier years he would go to the school of the grammarian-rhetorician Gnipho "after the labor of the forum" (Macrobius 3.12.8), and toward the end of his life in times of trouble he turned to speaking on philosophical themes (*Tusc. disp.* 1.7; 2.26; 3.81; *Ad Att.* 9.4). Pompey (Suet., *De gramm. et rhet.* 25.3) resumed declamation as practice for a speech against Curio. When Antony and Octavian declaimed during the war at Mutina, they may have thought it contributed to their verbal agility, and they probably found that it freed their minds from the pres-

---

den 273-300; R. Kohl, *De scholasticarum declamationum argumentis ex historia petitis*, Paderborn, 1915; M. Schamberger, *De declamationum Romanorum argumentis*, Halle, 1917; Aubrey Gwynn, *Roman Education from Cicero to Quintilian*, Oxford, 1926; William A. Edward, *The Suasoriae of Seneca the Elder*, Cambridge, Eng., 1928; Werner Hofrichter, *Studien zur Entwickelungsgeschichte der Deklamation von der griechischen Sophistik zur römischen Kaiserzeit*, Ohlau, 1935; Kroll 1119-24; A. Fred Sochatoff, "Basic Rhetorical Theories of the Elder Seneca," *CJ* 34 (1938-39) 345-54; E. Patrick Parks, "The Roman Rhetorical Schools as a Preparation for the Courts under the Early Empire," *Johns Hopkins Univ. Studies in Historical and Political Science* 63.2 (1945); D. L. Clark, "Some Values of Roman *declamatio*," *QJS* 35 (1949) 280-83; Clarke 85-99; Marrou 284-91; Leeman 219-37.

sures of public affairs. Octavian was only nineteen years old and fresh from rhetorical studies in Apollonia (Suet., *Aug.* 89). Thus it probably seemed very natural to him to continue exercises when he had the time. One of the reasons for the popularity of declamation may be that the future emperor first came to power and began to influence fashion at a time when he was hardly beyond the status of a student. In any event, the example of distinguished practitioners from every political camp was almost certain to encourage imitation.

The picture of the development of declamation is slightly confused by the historical comments of the elder Seneca (*Contr.* 1. *pr.* 12):

"Cicero did not declaim what we now call *controversiae* nor the kind of exercises which were spoken before Cicero's time, called *theses*. This particular kind of exercise which we practice is so new that its name also is new. We speak of *controversiae*, Cicero called them *causae*, or legal cases. The term *scholastica*, itself Greek, but so completely taken over into Latin that it is used as though it were Latin, is even more recent than *controversiae*. Similarly, *declamatio* is not to be found in any author earlier than Cicero and Calvus, who distinguished declamation from *dictio*, or speaking. Calvus said that he declaimed not too badly and that he spoke well. To declaim he thinks to be a form of practice at home, to speak to be a matter of real pleading. The name has only recently come to be applied, for the enthusiasm itself is recent. There is no difficulty in my having known from the cradle a thing born since I was."

To Seneca looking back it seemed as though there had been quite a radical change which we may divide into two steps. The difference was in part one of terminology, but the first step involved change in the materials of declamation from those of a *thesis*, which should be concerned with general and rather philosophical questions (Should a man marry?) to those of a *causa*, which would seem to be a more concrete judicial case like that to which Antonius had objected. Seneca ignores the well-documented existence of *hypotheses* before the time of Cicero, and he seems to exaggerate the role of *theses* as rhetorical exercises. It was chiefly found in the philosophical schools. His first change is, therefore, not entirely historical.[15] References to themes for declamation in *Rhetorica ad Herennium* also suggest that there had not been a vast change, though subjects involving piracy, rape, and adultery had not yet appeared in the early first century B.C., and declaimers had a much less free hand in rewriting history to suit their convenience or to provide rhetorical challenges. Suetonius reports that the older *controversiae* were either drawn from history or from some recent real happening and that old published collections even included reference to a specific scene or events. Some *controversiae* in Seneca's collection contain specific names and chronological references (4.2; 6.5; 7.2; 8.2; 9.1-2), but the cases are almost certainly imaginary and the specific references produce a lurid sensationalism rather than verisimilitude, as when the Athenians demand 100 talents retribution from Elis whose citizens are imagined to have cut off both hands of the sculptor Phidias (*Contr.* 8.2). Seneca also points out (*Contr.* 7.2.8) that it was a conceit of the declaimers with little or no historical evidence that the man who killed Cicero had earlier been defended by him on a charge of parricide. The second step in Seneca's account, though not

---

[15] On the *thesis* cf. von Arnim 82ff.; H. Throm, *Die Thesis: ein Beitrag zu ihrer Entstehung und Geschichte*, Paderborn, 1932; Hofrichter, *op.cit.* supra n. 14, 4ff.; M. L. Clarke, "The *Thesis* in the Roman Rhetorical Schools of the Republic," *CQ* 1 (1951) 159-66.

clearly described, is more historical. Through the age of Cicero exercises of declamation were carried on by youths in school or by adults privately in the homes of the speakers; declamation by adults was so rare as to cause comment. In the Augustan period declamation became a public activity and was common and fashionable for adults. Although psychological and political causes may be involved in the continued appeal of declamation, certainly the example of the emperor, who did not need to declaim to find an opportunity for oratory, contributed greatly in setting the fashion, as did the tastes of an age which appreciated style, technique, and artistic effects as virtues in themselves. Seneca apparently intends us to understand that the artistic qualities of declamation as he knew it, and especially the sententious style which his examples illustrate, were a development of his own lifetime.

Declamation (Greek *meletê* or *scholastica,* Latin *declamatio*)[16] provided exercise in both deliberative and judicial oratory. The deliberative exercise was regarded as easier (Tac., *Dial.* 35) and by the Augustan age was undertaken by students as soon as they had finished the program in composition (*progymnasmata*) which was a standard part of the curriculum of the grammar schools. In a deliberative declamation the speaker composed what was called a *suasoria,* a speech dealing with a dilemma confronting some historical or mythological person or persons. It was possible to speak a *prosopopoeia* (Quint. 3.8.49), a speech in the first person, for example, Seneca's third *suasoria* where Agamemnon deliberates with himself whether to sacrifice Iphigenia, or to address someone in the second person, for example, Seneca's first *suasoria* where the student is asked to give advice to Alexander

[16] On the terminology cf. Hofrichter, *op.cit.* supra n. 14, 11ff. and Bonner 20ff.

the Great on the question of whether or not to cross the ocean after having conquered everything else. The historicity of a *suasoria* was not a major consideration; among those described by Seneca two of the most interesting involve some distortion of relatively recent history: number six, in which Cicero deliberates whether to beg forgiveness of Antony, and to a greater extent number seven, in which the same orator deliberates whether to burn his writings when he is told he can thereby save his life. There is no likelihood that Cicero was ever given such a choice. Subjects from the history of the empire were not regarded as suitable, for they might detract from the imperial dignity (Suet., *Aug.* 89.3) or suggest lack of enthusiastic unanimity.

The more difficult judicial declamation was the *controversia* in which one or more laws, Greek, Roman, or imaginary,[17] were stated, for example (Seneca, *Contr.* 1.1), "Children should support their parents or be imprisoned." Then some unusual circumstances were imagined, for example:

"Two brothers are on bad terms; one has a son, the other falls into poverty. Despite the orders of his father the young man provides support for his uncle. As a result he is disowned. The uncle adopts him and subsequently becomes rich through an inheritance. At the same time the young man's natural father begins to be in want. Against the order of his adoptive father he aids his natural father. He is again disowned, this time by the adoptive father."[18]

[17] The historicity of the laws cited in declamations has been much discussed, cf. esp. Bonner 84-132, who concludes that most were Roman laws, praetors' edicts, or custom. Some may have been obsolete, a minority Greek, a few fictitious.

[18] Parks, *op.cit.* supra n. 14, 69-73 translates some treatments of this theme. The situation was not totally impossible, cf. Pliny, *Ep.* 8.18.4.

The orator may speak in the person of the young man or of the adoptive father or as an advocate for either side.[19] He may imagine almost any mitigation, complication, or explanation of conduct which he wishes; he is not bound by any law other than that specified or by any rule of legal procedure or evidence. For example, in one case (Seneca, *Contr.* 7.3) a young man who has been thrice disinherited and thrice reinstated by his father is found preparing a drug under suspicious circumstances. Is it a poison destined for the father or for the young man himself? Is it perhaps only a sleeping potion? The declaimer may choose whatever suits him for prosecution or defense or he may invent any other explanation. A declaimer was not ordinarily expected to speak on more than one side of a case on any one occasion.

Declamation in the Roman empire was principally carried on by teachers, students, and adult guests in rhetorical schools, which provided the only extensive form of secondary education,[20] just as grammar schools provided the only primary education. All schools were privately operated, for the government did not support education. Formal schooling for most Roman boys was restricted to the arts of reading, writing, and speaking. Girls learned whatever rhetoric they learned at home and had neither training nor opportunity for declamation, though a few exceptional women whose life brought them into public affairs did occasionally acquire facility at speaking.[21] The

[19] If the litigant is a woman, a slave, or often if the suit is between relatives the role of advocate is preferred; otherwise, the person of the litigant is preferred. This may reflect the influence of Greek courts, but is also more vivid. Cf. Quint. 3.8.51 and *Decl. min.* 260, *sermo*; Bonner 52f.; Clarke 92f.

[20] But cf. S. L. Mohler, "The *iuvenes* and Roman Education," *TAPhA* 68 (1937) 442-79 who examines the role of the *collegia iuvenum*.

[21] For example, Cornelia, Laelia, and Hortensia, cf. Quint. 1.1.6.

number of schools of rhetoric in Rome cannot be estimated very exactly. Each school was the operation of a single rhetorician and rhetoricians naturally came and went. Of about 110 declaimers mentioned by the elder Seneca in his discussion of a period roughly corresponding to the age of Augustus, some were pupils in the schools, a few were nonacademic adults, some were teachers from abroad who visited Rome only briefly. There were doubtless declaimers and schools not mentioned by Seneca. Speaking of the period around 100 B.C. Suetonius (*De gramm. et rhet.* 3.3) says that there were then over twenty large *grammar* schools in Rome at one time. A hundred years later the number surely would have been greater and Horace speaks (*Epist.* 1.19.40) of "tribes" of grammarians. Perhaps there was an approximately corresponding number of rhetorical schools. The line between grammar and rhetoric was not very hard and fast, and most grammatical exercises could be thought of as parts of potential declamations. Suetonius says that some of the early grammarians taught rhetoric, and Quintilian (2.1.1-6) complains of their tendency in his time to overreach their subject and prevent boys from graduating to the rhetorical school as soon as possible, though he admits that a few grammarians may have been competent rhetoricians. He wants a boy to begin with a rhetorician while still studying with a grammarian (2.1.13) and outlines (2.4.5) an introductory curriculum to be used by a rhetorician which is similar to the one which some grammarians followed. Ordinarily the rhetoricians restricted themselves to lectures on rhetorical theory and criticism of *suasoriae* and *controversiae*. Practice in writing commonplaces, descriptions, comparisons, and the like came chiefly in the grammar schools except in so far as these were incorporated into declamations.

Modern writers have reconstructed out of the piecemeal evidence a rather vivid picture of a rhetorical school in the early empire.[22] The age for beginning rhetorical exercises varied somewhat, but perhaps around fourteen was common in the age of Augustus.[23] The classes were often large (Quint. 10.5.21). The boys sat on some kind of benches facing the teacher (Quint. 2.2.9-12), who himself sat in a large *cathedra*.[24] Quintilian gave graded lectures on rhetorical theory (1. *pr.* 7) and other rhetoricians certainly did likewise. The last four chapters of the rhetorical handbook falsely attributed to Dionysius of Halicarnassus are perhaps notes on texts of such lectures dating from the second century A.D. or later. Chapter ten, one of the better parts, discusses possible mistakes of declaimers in characterization, presentation, style, and in each of the four parts of speech. Ordinarily, when a teacher assigned a subject for declamation he made some comment (*sermo*) on the possible treatment (Quint. 2.5.1). The collection of excerpts known as the *Minor Declamations* of Quintilian preserves a considerable number of brief *sermones* of this sort. The teacher might also declaim on the subject himself (Quint. 2.2.8). The boys *wrote* their speeches and the teacher then heard and corrected them.[25] When an approved version was achieved the boy set to work to memorize it in preparation for a public delivery before his fellow students, relatives, and guests (Quint. 2.7.1). Thus memory and delivery were exercised as well as the other three parts of classical rhetoric, invention, arrangement, and most of all, style. The poet Persius (3.44-47) mentions how much

[22] Cf. the works cited in n. 14 supra, esp. Bornecque 55ff.; Edward xxif.; Parks 61-67; Bonner 51ff. Also Marrou 286.

[23] Relevant passages include Seneca, *Contr.* 3. *pr.* 15; Quint. 2.1 and 2.2.14; Tac., *Dial.* 35.

[24] Cf. illustrations in Boissier, "*Declamatio*," cit. supra n. 14.

[25] Cf. Seneca, *Contr.* 9. *pr.* 1 (*scribit*); Quint. 2.6.2: 10.6; Juv. 7.152.

he hated these public exhibitions which became common in the Augustan age, but for some time were not held by all teachers (Seneca, *Contr.* 10. *pr.* 4). It seems possible that other teachers welcomed visitors at almost any time. On those days when his doors were open to the public the teacher himself probably declaimed on the same subject as his students. Anyone might come (Seneca, *Contr.* 3. *pr.* 16), and the guests had an opportunity to speak *extempore* on the themes proposed, though they ran the risk of facing the teacher's often stern comments (Seneca, *Contr.* 1.3.11; 7. *pr.* 9). The students kept notebooks in which they collected passages from declamations praised by the teacher (Quint. 2.11.7). One reference (Seneca, *Contr.* 3. *pr.* 10) suggests that the guests sometimes wandered in and out to avoid the duller parts of the program. Declamation in Greek often followed declamation in Latin, one in the toga, the other in the pallium (Seneca, *Contr.* 9.3.13). Public exhibitions of this sort might last two or more days (Seneca, *Contr.* 1.3.11; 1.7.13; 2.1.25) and were widely attended, even by distinguished and presumably busy people like the emperor or his minister Agrippa who seems to have visited the school of young Lucius and Gaius Caesar (Seneca, *Contr.* 2.4.12). Declamation also continued in private homes in somewhat the manner of Cicero's time (Seneca, *Contr.* 4. *pr.* 2; 10. *pr.* 4; perhaps 3. *pr.* 1) and later there were exhibitions in connexion with visits of traveling sophists or at some of the public games which included oratory.[26] Declamation should be distinguished from public and private recitation of works of literature, a custom begun as we have said by Asinius Pollio.

The only Latin declamations surviving in complete form are 19 attributed to Quintilian, possibly the work

[26] Cf. Suet., *Nero* 12.3 and *Dom.* 4.4.

of some of his followers, but there is a collection of excerpts from 145 declamations also attributed to Quintilian and another collection of excerpts bearing the name of the second century A.D. author Calpurnius Flaccus. In Greek we shall find a number of declamations among the works of the sophists to be discussed in chapter eight. Quintilian discusses the theory and technique of declamation repeatedly in the *Institutio* (esp. books two and the fifth chapter of book ten) and many later Greek and Latin rhetorical treatises offered preparation for declamation, but the most important source of information is the fragmentary and rambling, but beguiling, work of the elder Seneca. Although not actually written until the third or fourth decade of the first century A.D., it describes declamation in the Augustan age, and its venerable author must have seemed to many a relict of another era. It will not, therefore, be great violence to chronology if we consider him at this point.

Seneca the Elder

Lucius Annaeus Seneca was born in Cordoba in Further Spain some time in the 50's B.C.[27] He was, he says (*Contr.* 1. *pr.* 11), old enough to have heard Cicero in 43 B.C., but was prevented from coming to Rome by the Civil War. Eventually, however, he studied rhetoric at Rome with Marullus (*Contr.* 1. *pr.* 22). Since he appar-

[27] Cf. works cited supra n. 14; R-E-1.2237-40; H. Bardon, *Le vocabulaire de la critique littéraire chez Sénèque le rhéteur*, Paris, 1940. For translations cf. Edward, *op.cit.* supra n. 14 (*Suasoriae*) and Henri Bornecque, *Sénèque le Rheteur: Controverses et Suasores*, 2 vols., Paris, 1932. There is no English translation of the entire *Controversiae*, though a Loeb volume is planned. Parks, *op.cit.* supra n. 14, 69-78 translates 1.1.1-12 and 1.2.1-12, Leeman (in notes on 219-44) translates several passages, and all the prefaces have now been translated by Lewis A. Sussman, "Early Imperial Declamation: a Translation of the Elder Seneca's Prefaces," *SM* 37 (1970) 135-51.

ently never taught rhetoric himself, the name Seneca
Rhetor, sometimes given him, is a misnomer. His extant
works give the impression of a man on the fringe of intellectual circles, fond of listening to declamations, but
probably busily engaged for most of his life in commercial, legal, or civic enterprises, most likely the administration of estates in Spain or some other investments
suitable to a wealthy equestrian family.[28] His memory was
extraordinary (*Contr.* 1. *pr.* 2) and in the semiretirement
of old age he put it to use[29] in the composition of two
works describing the period through which he lived, one,
now lost, on recent Roman history and the other, the
extant work, on declamation and declaimers in Augustan
Rome, dedicated to his three sons. Of these, one, Nova-
tus, was adopted by his father's friend Gallio and is
known to history as proconsul of Achaea at the time of
St. Paul's ministry to Corinth (Acts 18:12), a second
was the philosopher-dramatist-statesman bearing his
father's identical name, Lucius Annaeus Seneca, and a
third was Mela, father of the epic poet Lucan. The elder
Seneca probably died around A.D. 39; in any event he did
not live to see his son the philosopher exiled in 41.[30] He
was a republican at heart, a native of a Pompeian city, a
hater of political bookburning (*Contr.* 10. *pr.* 5ff.), a
suitable grandfather for Lucan. Significantly, his work on

[28] On the Spanish connexions cf. *Contr.* 9. *pr.* 3; Seneca the
Younger, *Ad Helviam* 19.2; Martial 1.61.7-8; Tac., *Ann.* 14.53.
Cordoba was a cultural center in the first cent. B.C., cf. Cic.,
Pro Arch. 26. *Contr.* 4. *pr.* 3 implies at least two periods of resi-
dence at Rome.

[29] The latest event mentioned seems to be the death of Scaurus
in A.D. 34, *Suas.* 2.22. O. Immisch, "Wirklichkeit und Literatur-
form," *RhM* 78 (1929) 114-16, objected to Seneca's claim to
verbatim memory, but it is insisted on in *Contr.* 1. *pr.* 2. Possibly he had some student notebooks, cf. Quint. 2.11.17.

[30] His historical work may have described Tiberius' death in
37, cf. Suet., *Tib.* 73.2.

declamation and his history were both apparently deliberately held back for posthumous publication.[31] Knowledge of the former by later Roman authors is difficult to demonstrate, but some passages in Quintilian may come from it (9.2.42, 91, 95, 98) and it may have been known to others interested in declamation.[32]

The full title of Seneca's work is *The Orators' and Rhetors' Sententiae, Divisions, and Colors*. It consisted originally of ten books on *controversiae* and two or more[33] books on *suasoriae*. Books three, four, five, six, and eight of *controversiae* and all but the first book of the *suasoriae* have been lost, but we have a series of extracts of all books of the *controversiae*, both lost and extant, made in late antiquity. When complete, each book seems to have consisted of a preface (we have those to books one, two, four, seven, nine in part, and ten of the *controversiae*, but none for the *suasoriae*), followed by chapters on a number of declamations, more or less at random. The discussion of each theme of declamation is divided into parts. The first reports the *sententiae*: striking, brilliant, witty, elegant, pointed, or unusual remarks of the declaimers. Although some *sententiae* sound like maxims, capable of use in many contexts, "what e're was thought, but ne'er so well expressed," most have a direct relevance to the subject. The different categories are discussed by Quintilian (8.5). Typical is that of Porcius Latro, Seneca's friend and favorite declaimer, "I have no fear that judges may bind hands which pirates have loosed"

[31] This seems clear from the fragment of the younger Seneca's essay *On the Life of his Father*, cf. *Breslauer philologische Abhandlung* 2.3 (1888) xxii: "If I had given into the hands of the public whatever my father composed and wished published, he would himself have adequately provided for the distinction of his name. . . ."

[32] Cf. Schanz-Hosius 2.341.

[33] Some MSS read at the end "Liber primus explicit, incipit liber secundus," cf. Edward, *op.cit.* supra n. 14, p. xxx.

(*Contr.* 1.7.1). Here the "point" is the emotional argument *a fortiori*, one of the commonest bases of *sententiae*, built on the probable contrast between the humanity of pirates and judges, emphasized by the antithesis between binding and loosing: "If the pirates were so merciful as to let me go, surely I have nothing to fear from a court of law!" The self-assurance of the remark is part of the ethos of the speaker. Fondness for *sententiae* in prose was certainly fostered by poetry in the first instance, especially tragedy, comedy, and epigram.[34] One type of *sententiae* involving an extreme metaphor, for example, "He washed out his disinheritance with poison," seems to have come into declamation from the mime, another from the Atellan farce (cf. *Contr.* 7.3.8-9 and 7.4.8). Some declamations consisted of a series of epigrams strung together with little connexion. It must be remembered that Seneca deliberately chooses striking *sententiae*, purple passages of declamation as it were, and his quotations, though extensive, may thus not be entirely fair samples of declamation as a whole.

The second part of each of Seneca's discussions is devoted to the divisions given the topic by the declaimers, who, it will be remembered, had considerable latitude. "Division" does not refer to arrangement of the speech, but to the logical divisions of the subject into its principal issues, usually along the lines of the theory of *stasis* originally developed by Hermagoras. Hermagoras made an overall division into questions of law and questions of fact or justice. This commonly appears in Seneca as a division between law and equity. The divisions of Porcius Latro almost always involved the question *an liceat*, "Is it permitted?" and *an debeat*, "Is it right?"

[34] *Sententiae* in epigram seems to have been studied by the Augustan poet Domitius Marsus, cf. Edwin S. Ramage, "The *De urbanitate* of Domitius Marsus," *CPh* 54 (1959) 250-55.

(cf., e.g., *Contr.* 1.1.13; 7.1.16-17). If there is no doubt about the law, the question then becomes one of fact, definition, or quality (cf., e.g., *Contr.* 2.5.10). Seneca occasionally uses the technical term for *stasis* of fact, *coniecturalis* (cf. *Contr.* 7.3.6; 7.7.10; 9.6.10), but he is not very rigid in his classification. Sometimes rather considerable subdivision of the question or involved argumentation is found (e.g., *Contr.* 9. *pr.* 1), though declaimers often neglected argumentation (cf. *Contr.* 9. *pr.* 1) and relied on ethos, pathos, and general hyperbole for proof. They were much given to arguing along *a fortiori* lines from an unwarranted assumption to a foregone conclusion, for example (*Contr.* 1.6.1), "I deny my house to one who should be denied the earth."

A third section occurs in Seneca's discussions of the *controversiae* but not of the *suasoriae*: it discusses the *color* given the case by a variety of declaimers, which means the particular interpretation of events or motivation which they adopted as the basis of prosecution or defense.[35] A defense against a murder charge might, for example, be the color of insanity. The first *controversia* of the seventh book is a complicated one involving a father, a stepmother, two sons, a charge of parricide, and adventures with pirates. Should the declaimer speaking for the son employ the *color* of attacking the stepmother, a traditional virago, and to what extent? Seneca praises Latro (7.1.20) for the subtle and incidental way he brings a disparaging reference to the stepmother into a narrative where the principal *color* is the son's plea that he could never have brought himself to kill his father, a *color* based on the ethos of the speaker.

[35] Cf. *Webster's New International Dictionary of the English Language*, 2d ed., s.v. "color, 10": "an appearance or pretense taken as justification; pretext; show or reason; also, formerly, excuse, disguise. 'Which . . . afforded a color for detaining the troops.' J. S. Mill."

The discussions of declamation on different themes are drawn from different exhibitions over a sixty-year period ranging from the second triumvirate to the reign of Tiberius as Seneca happens to recall them; the speakers quoted include professional teachers of rhetoric like Marullus or Cestius or the Greek declaimers mentioned at the end of each chapter.[36] Cicero had thought the Greeks were the best teachers, but the situation had changed by Seneca's day and he is rather contemptuous of them.[37] Included also are precocious pupils of the teachers of declamation, for example, Cestius' star pupil Alfius Rufus (*Contr.* 1.1.22) or the poet Ovid in his student days (*Contr.* 2.2.8-12), and a few nonacademic declaimers like Aemilius Scaurus (*Contr.* 10. *pr.* 3) and Asinius Pollio (*Contr.* 4. *pr.* 2), both of whom must be included in the class of *oratorum* rather than *rhetorum* in the title of the work. It is possible to divide the declaimers roughly into types: some, like Cassius Severus, were effective speakers in practice, but rather poor in the schools (*Contr.* 3. *pr.* 1ff.); others, like Albucius Silus, were brilliant declaimers, but more or less unsuccessful in court (*Contr.* 7. *pr.* 6; 9.1.1), and a considerable number, the so-called *scholastici*,[38] probably never appeared in court at all. Some speakers adhered to the rules of Apollodorus (*Contr.* 10. *pr.* 15); others were followers

---

[36] Bornecque, *op.cit.* supra n. 14, 139 lists the following as teachers: Gorgias of Athens, Lesbocles and Potamon of Mitylene, Aeschines, Plution, Volcarius Moschus of Marseilles, Porcius Latro, Albucius Silus, Arellius Fuscus, Cestius Pius, Corvus, Marullus, Fulvius Sparsus, Buteo, Gargonius, Rugellius Blandus, Hermagoras, and Nicetes.

[37] Cf. "Greek insolence" in *Contr.* 1. *pr.* 6 and 10.4.23.

[38] Cf., e.g., *Contr.* 1.7.15; *Suas.* 6.14; Tac., *Dial.* 26.8. Bonner 63 says that *scholastici* were "purists and preferred the Attic correctness of language," but the passage he cites (*Contr.* 4. *pr.* 9) suggests euphemism and affectation rather than purity, cf. also 7. *pr.* 4.

327

of Theodorus (*Contr.* 2.1.36; *Suas.* 3.7). The literary style of the declamations quoted by Seneca shows some, but not great, variation. Although a few declaimers were professed Asianists (*Contr.* 10.5.21), it would be a mistake to connect the "new style," as it is generally called, with any stylistic movement of earlier generations. It is a new phenomenon developed for the circumstances. Sentences are much shorter than in Ciceronian Latin. There is a staccato effect from constant asyndeton, from the fondness for anaphora, from the tendency to seek alliteration and Gorgianic figures, and above all from the repeated occurrences of rhetorical questions and *sententiae*. The diction is quite pure and the prose rhythm often Ciceronian.[39]

Feelings among the declaimers were often intense and the discussions at public declamations sometimes acrimonius. Cassius Severus especially distrusted the affectation of the schools. Seneca quotes his description of a dispute with Cestius Pius thus (*Contr.* 3. *pr.* 16-17):

"I remember going to his school when he was about to recite his version of a speech against Milo. As was his wont, Cestius spoke admiringly of himself: 'If I were a Thracian gladiator I would be the Great Eusius; if I were an actor I would be the great Bathyllus; if a horse, Milissio.' I couldn't contain my anger and cried out, 'If you were a sewer, you'd be the Cloaca Maxima [the great sewer of Rome].' Everybody laughed loudly and the students all turned around to see who had such thick-necked insolence. Although Cestius had been going to improve on Cicero, he couldn't think of anything to say to me and refused to continue unless I left the house. I said that I wouldn't leave a public bath unless I had been washed! Subsequently I decided to get satisfaction for

[39] Cf. Norden 270-300 and Leeman 224-37.

Cicero from Cestius in the forum. As soon as I met him I summoned him to court before the praetor, and after I had poured forth as much as I wanted of our jokes and insults, I demanded that the praetor indict him under the law against undefined offense. Cestius was so upset he hired a lawyer. I then brought him before another praetor and demanded an indictment for ingratitude. Next, before the urban praetor I demanded that a guardian be appointed for him. When his friends came running to this scene and making complaints, I said that I would cease to be troublesome if he would swear that Cicero was more eloquent then he, but neither in jest nor in earnest was it possible to get him to do this."[40]

This passage is taken from one of the seven surviving prefaces to individual books of the *Controversiae* and is fairly typical of their style. They contain vivid sketches of individual declaimers, as well as a certain amount of literary criticism and comment on the state of eloquence in Seneca's time,[41] and they are written in an unpretentious Latin unlike the efforts of the declaimers.

Seneca the Elder emerges from his work as an amiable old admirer of time past, once an habitué of the schools of rhetoric and pleased to relive the good old days by putting down his memories for the information of his three sons. He is a believer in imitation of writers and speakers of an earlier, more classic age as the basis of

[40] Cestius Pius was a leading rhetorician and earned for himself a chapter in the lost part of Suet., *De rhet.* Cf. *R-E* 3.2008-11. He came from Smyrna, but taught in Latin. Here he has composed a speech intended to improve on Cicero. Undefined offense is not a real charge. Ingratitude was a favorite charge among the Romans, but not a crime, cf. Seneca the Younger, *De ben.* 3.6-8. The appointment of a guardian would suggest insanity.

[41] Cf. Lewis A. Sussman, *The Prefaces and Literary Criticism of the Elder Seneca*, Dissertation, Univ. of North Carolina, 1969.

excellence (cf. *Contr.* 1. *pr.* 6). He represents his sons as anxious to learn from him and addresses Mela in particular as interested in declamation (*Contr.* 2. *pr.* 4), but most of the impulse for writing the book probably came from himself. The younger Seneca occasionally shows his father's specific influence,[42] for example in his 114th *Epistle*, but in the 97th *Epistle* he appears to disagree with his father. He probably resented the old man's aversion to philosophy (*Ep.* 108.22) and he certainly disapproved of those who listened to philosophical lectures with an ear to the rhetoric (*Ep.* 108.5-8), though, of course, he himself made an abundant use of rhetoric in all his writings.

There is no better witness than the elder Seneca to the importance which educated Romans of the early empire attached to rhetoric. He is not himself an orator seeking fame or a teacher seeking students. As a hard-headed man of property, conservative, disdainful of philosophy, he might be expected to view with suspicion or impatience those very ornaments of style or wit which he admires. Yet to Mela, whose avoidance of a public career he rather approved, he says: "Devote yourself to eloquence. The passage from it to all the other arts is an easy one; it provides a useful tool even to those whom it does not train to be professional speakers" (*Contr.* 2. *pr.* 3). Oratory may be one of the necessities and certainly is one of the graces of life.

Criticism of Declamation

Seneca was not unaware of some of the weaknesses of declamation: all the amenities of life can naturally be carried to the point of tastelessness. He generally puts

[42] Cf. E. Rollard, *De l'influence de Sénèque le père et des rhéteurs sur Sénèque le philosophe*, Ghent, 1906; C. Preisendanz, "De Senecae rhetoris apud philosophum filium auctoritate," *Philologus* 67 (1908) 68-112; Leeman 266 and 270.

criticism of declamation into the mouths of others; the furthest he goes himself is the remark in the preface to the tenth book where somewhat conventionally he is confessing weariness with the work: "Studies of the *scholastici* have this quality: touched upon lightly they delight, dwelt upon and brought under closer scrutiny they become tiresome." The criticisms which he quotes from others chiefly involve the remoteness of the conditions of declamation from the actual speaking conditions in the forum for which they were nominally a training. Habits learned in schools could be disastrous in the forum, as Albucius discovered (*Contr.* 7. *pr.* 7-8) when he tried a fancy figure of speech and cried out to his opponent in court:

"Swear, but I shall dictate the oath: swear by the ashes of your father which are unburied; swear by the memory of your father; swear . . . and all the rest of the commonplace. When he had finished Lucius Arruntius [patron for the opponent] arose and said, 'We accept the condition; my client will swear.' 'I wasn't offering a condition,' protested Albucius, 'I was employing a figure.' Arruntius persevered. The board of judges was eager to put the finishing touches on a case all but concluded. Albucius shrieked, 'If you get away with this it is the end of figures of speech!' Arruntius replied, 'Let it be the end; we can live without them.' Arruntius won, and Albucius never accepted another brief. He told his friends, 'Why should I speak in the forum when more people hear me at home than hear anyone in the forum? I speak when I want to; I speak as long as I like; I speak for whichever side I wish.' "[43]

[43] For other criticisms of declamation cf. *Contr.* 3. *pr.* 12; 9.5.15; later the opening chapters of Petronius; Martial 6.19; modern works listed in n. 14 supra.

To some orators the schools, for all their academic disputes, seemed orderly and friendly, but the forum was frightening and perhaps rather vulgar. Even the able Porcius Latro suffered from stage fright when he undertook to plead in an open-air law court. An exercise, Votienus says (*Contr.* 9. *pr.* 4), ought to be more demanding than a true contest. In so far as declamation was an exercise it was losing touch with reality; many of its devotees, however, regarded it as a joy in itself.

In evaluating declamation it is appropriate to distinguish its role as a school exercise for the young and its function for adults. To the young it taught poise, self-assurance, and verbal agility. It was never intended to teach law or legal procedure, any more than the rhetoricians of republican Rome or Hellenistic Greece were regarded as teachers of law, for the advocate was expected to get legal technicalities from a jurisconsult.[44] Declamation, like liberal education, was supposed to develop the mind and sensitivities and to teach an approach to practical problems more than to impart vocational information. The declaimers do not operate under strictly Roman laws, though it has been shown that the laws which are posited are in fact often similar to Roman law, and there is no reason why a sensible student trained by a responsible rhetorician should not have been able to make an adjustment to the courts of law. Declamation did rather incidentally provide a student with familiarity with some technical legal terms. Though charges like parricide or tyrannicide, which appear in declamations, would occur rarely, and procedures like ingratitude would never be met at all, a considerable number of declamations involve cases of disinheritance; one of the most active legal areas in the early empire were the inheritance cases be-

[44] There were separate schools of law, cf. Bonner 45 and A.M. Honoré, *Gaius*, Oxford, 1962, 18-45.

fore the centumviral court. The problems of conflicting law or definition or motivation and the rest which are met in declamation all occurred, though perhaps in a more pedestrian manner, in legal practice.[45] At its best, declamation is an exercise of imagination. The student is confronted with a challenging case and asked to make the most of it, to imagine the possibilities in proof, exposition, and presentation (cf. Quint. 10.4.11).[46] A considerable amount of emphasis was put by some of the teachers on imaginative psychological presentation of the character who speaks. Imagination had some carry-over into literature, but only in a limited sense. Roman students developed an extraordinary eye for conceits and verbal effects. They applied imagination to the choice of situations involving rhetorical challenges —"What could one say about or in such and such a circumstance?"—or to the choice and combination of words, or to things like the invention of motive, but not to the more profound aspects of literature or intellectual endeavor. Declamation did not encourage careful observation of the world and an imaginative recreation or presentation or analysis of it. It did not give the student any challenge in searching out materials for rhetoric or demand of him any profound background knowledge.[47] Modern education tries to do most of these things and is infinitely more varied, though ordinarily less verbally sensitive. The result of the Roman system was an art form with a great deal of imagination, extraordinarily limited.

[45] Cf. supra n. 17. Also Charles S. Rayment, "Three Notes on the Roman Declamation," *CW* 45 (1951-52) 225-28.

[46] Leeman 233 notes that the repetition of the subjects of declamation increased the difficulty for a speaker who wanted to be original.

[47] Some of the better declaimers had good general knowledge, e.g., Porcius Latro of history (cf. *Contr.* 1. *pr.* 18) and Fabianus of philosophy (*Contr.* 2. *pr.* 1ff.)

The subjects were not solely ravished maidens, pirates, parricides, and poisoners as is sometimes thought,[48] though these existed in considerable numbers. The declamation by the poor bee-owner whose wealthy neighbor spread poison on the flowers (Quint., *Decl. mai.* 13) is not typical, but shows some of the possible variation. Most of the subjects of declamation were, of course, designed to be exciting and to interest the young. Many of them are built around problems of adolescence and young manhood. The best example is the recurring question of the relationship of children to parents. This is the great problem which every adolescent is facing or avoiding; today we favor school texts which relate to the problem in some way: versions of the Orestes or Electra or Oedipus story, *Hamlet, David Copperfield, Tom Sawyer, Sons and Lovers, Portrait of the Artist, Catcher in the Rye.* Roman educators invited youths to consider the question of child-parent relationships under various extreme conditions and to speak about it. Ancient students had, of course, already read the *Odyssey* and probably much of Greek drama. Declamation suggested the universality of the situation, and perhaps had an advantage for some in that the student wrote and spoke in the first person and any catharsis was thus more direct.

The stance taken by a declaimer is always moral; the sophistic argument that might makes right is never acceptable. What the boys learned and what society wanted them to learn was how to preserve moral appearances. This was particularly acceptable to Augustus, who sought

[48] When declamation was being developed in late Hellenistic times piracy was a major problem. Pompey's command helped a great deal, but did not totally abolish piracy, cf. Henry A. Ormerod, *Piracy in the Ancient World*, Liverpool and London, 1924, 248ff. Cf. also D. B. Kaufman, "Poisons and Poisoning among the Romans," *CPh* 27 (1932) 156-67.

a return to old-fashioned conventions and morality, at least in appearances.

The very first declamation discussed by Seneca, for example, ends (1.1.3) with commonplaces, each made memorable as *sententiae*, the kind of facts of life which Greeks learned from the drama and which must be said and seen many times before they are in fact comprehended: "All happiness is unstable and uncertain. Who would believe that Marius, as he lay among the ruins of Carthage, had once been consul or would be again? Moreover, why do I cite such remote examples as though there were none in my own household? He who sees my father and my uncle learns what the fortunate must fear and of what the unfortunate must not despair." A good example of a speech not lacking in educational and humanitarian sentiment is that of Julius Bassus in the sixth declamation of Seneca's first book. In faithful love for the daughter of a pirate king a young man pleads his duty to his oath, the unimportance of rank, and the servility of a poor husband when forced to marry a wealthy wife. It is interesting that the second argument was acceptable; it shows the idealism of the schools. The whole is maudlin, superficial perhaps, but perhaps moral and educational, too. The declamations are probably too restricted in subject and in the demands of preparation and thoughtfulness made on the speaker to be first-rate education. The student acquired the basic moral concepts, nevertheless. He saw to some extent the relativity of these concepts and the way they could be applied to different courses of action.

After their formal schooling was over, some adults chose to continue to practice declamation. Why? The custom was, of course, limited to a group of intellectuals with literary interest, chiefly at Rome, but also in some of the more Romanized towns of Spain and Gaul and in the East. The first and most important reason was the influence of Cicero and his friends and then of Augustus and his. It was something innocuous to do in the good company of elegant friends (cf. Pliny, *Ep.* 2.3.). It exercised the artistic abilities and the wits. Even the irascible Juvenal, whose opinion of declaimers seems low, himself declaimed, as the ancient *Vita* (1) claims, "for the sake of his mind rather than to prepare himself for school or forum." Quintilian (10.5.14) thought that adult declamation was valuable in nourishing the orator with its rich food (*pabulo laetiore*—he means its imaginative opportunities) and in refreshing him when tired in the forum. Declamation for many Romans was fun. It had, too, a number of psychological attractions for them. Since most Greeks and Romans were educated to believe that speech was the highest and most characteristically human act, declamation made it possible for them to speak when other opportunities might be lacking and to speak in a colorful or powerful way when other opportunities might be humdrum. As for students, so for adults there was a catharsis: the declaimer, as Cicero had found (*Ad Att.* 9.4), could discuss political themes which might not otherwise be entirely safe; thus cases involving tyrannicide became favorites. He could give free rein to his emotions, put himself entirely into the case, and release his inner tensions in an act of creation (cf., e.g., Seneca, *Contr.* 4. *pr.* 6). The writing of poetry, for example Lucan's epic and Seneca's tragedies, and of philosophy performed similar cathartic functions, though they implied a withdrawal from active life, while declamation had the virtue of pretending to be practical. Acting, of course, was very much a part of declamation, which thus performed some of the function of athletics, in which the Romans did not much indulge. The total artistic achievement of adult declamation seems not to have been much greater than that of student declamation. The creations were witty and verbal; they did not stimulate the thinking of contemporaries, nor challenge views, nor offer intellectual leadership, none of which was possible. Declamation did satisfy the personal needs of declaimers.

Declamation is thus a typical institution of the Roman empire. It took much practice and training to be performed well. There were rules to the game and a high standard of achievement was expected within the rules. It is important to realize that the declaimer was not essentially aiming at persuasion, but at expression, of himself and of his art. The material which is expressed is well worn and would continue to be so until society was completely shaken up by Christians and barbarians. There is no intellectual experimentation, but an intricately varied surface detail; art is valued for itself.

Greek Rhetoricians in Augustan Rome

Augustan Rome was thronged with Greek rhetoricians. According to Horace (*Serm.* 1.5.2-3) the rhetorician Heliodorus was by far the most learned of the Greeks; no other writer thought him worth mentioning. Seneca the Elder quotes from Greek declaimers occasionally at the end of a chapter, most of whom were probably teachers of rhetoric. We hear about Timagenes, for example, who fell out with Augustus but enjoyed the friendship of Asinius Pollio (Seneca, *De ira* 3.23). There were, of course, teachers of rhetoric in other parts of the world, some of whom occasionally visited Rome. Gorgias of Athens had some fame. He had briefly been the teacher of Cicero's son and was the author of a short

337

work on figures of speech which P. Rutilius Lupus adapted into Latin. It is of interest as representing Asianist tastes.[49]

The most venerable of the Greek rhetoricians of the age was probably Apollodorus of Pergamum, founder of the Apollodorean school, which persisted for generations.[50] We do not know when he came to Rome or why, but he was already regarded as a senior scholar there in 45 B.C. when Julius Caesar arranged for him to take charge of the education of young C. Octavius, the future Augustus, and accompany him to Apollonia on the east shore of the Adriatic (Suet., *Aug.* 89), where the news of Caesar's assassination reached them. To have been chosen by Caesar is a sign of Apollodorus' reputation and probably also a qualitative judgment. Caesar was too interested in oratory to entrust his heir to a teacher whose ideas he disapproved.

It was once thought that Apollodorus was a leading figure in the neo-Atticism movement and possibly even responsible for its appearance in Rome.[51] He could make a convenient link between the Stoic grammarians of Pergamum and the orators of mid-first century Rome. But this hypothesis is built on questionable assumptions and is chronologically difficult. Against it the argument from silence is powerful: we have enough references to Apollodorus in later writers to reconstruct the outlines of his thought. These references never connect him with Atticism and indicate instead that the area of rhetoric

---

[49] Cf. Halm 3-21 and Edward Brooks, Jr., *P. Rutilii Lupi De Figuris Sententiarum et Elocutionis*, Leiden, 1970. Rutilius refers to Gorgias in 2.12. Cf. also Quint. 9.2.102 and 9.3.89.

[50] Cf. M. Schanz, "Die Apollodoreer und die Theodoreer," *Hermes* 25 (1890) 36-54; R-E 1.2886-94; G.M.A. Grube, "Theodorus of Gadara," *AJPh* 80 (1959) 337-65; APG 335.

[51] Cf. U. von Wilamowitz-Moellendorff, "Asianismus und Attizismus," *Hermes* 35 (1900) 46-47.

of interest to him was primarily invention, including *stasis* theory and arrangement. He thus seems to be closer in spirit to Hermagoras and earlier generations than to Dionysius and the Greek Atticists who follow. Caesar could well have respected Apollodorus' concentration on the essentials of persuasion, but it is likely that Apollodorus did prefer a rather simple style. The only fragment which deals with style is preserved by Quintilian (9.1.12) who says that if we are content with the earlier and general meaning of "figure" which made everything figured, then it is "not surprising that Apollodorus, according to Caecilius' report, thought that rules about figures were *incomprehensibilia*."[52] That is, figures would be so numerous as to defy definition. Quintilian elsewhere (3.1.18) says that Apollodorus' views can be best learned from his pupils and seems to know of only two published works, a handbook of rhetoric addressed to Matius and a letter to Domitius.

According to Jerome's *Chronicles* Apollodorus flourished about 64 B.C., a likely date, and was the teacher of Calidius and Augustus. His interests seem to have been restricted to judicial oratory (cf. Quint. 3.1.17), where his rules of *stasis* and division could best be applied. Of these rules the best known and most certainly genuine were those requiring every speech to contain the four divisions: prooemium, narration, proof, and epilogue in that order and only that order.[53] Narrative and proof, according to Apollodorus, must precede pathos (cf.

[52] I have not seen G. Ballaira, "La dottrina delle figure retoriche in Apollodoro di Pergamo," *Quaderni Urbinati di Cultura classica*, no. 5 (1968) 37-91. From the abstract in *L'Année Philologique* the author appears to present evidence that Apollodorus made an exhaustive study of figures of speech and of thought, which has seemed unlikely to other scholars.

[53] This follows from Sen., *Contr.* 2.1.36 and the treatment in *Anonymus Seguerianus*, esp. 26-29 (357-58 Spengel-Hammer).

Quint. 5.13.59). His definition of the object of oratory
was strictly utilitarian, "to persuade the judge and lead
his decision to that which the orator wishes" (Quint.
2.15.12). The overall impression is one of a logically
coherent, but inflexible theory. Perhaps its very inflexi-
bility was a sign of Stoic influence. A later writer criticized the Apollodoreans for not realizing that they were
treating the art of rhetoric as though it were a science
with infallible rules.[54] Even in declamation the Apollodoreans imposed more rules than did other rhetoricians,
limiting the speaker's freedom in treating his case (Seneca, *Contr.* 1.2.14).

Slightly younger than Apollodorus, but as eminent,
was Theodorus of Gadara. He left a larger collection of
writings (Quint. 3.1.18) and in some matters seems to
have been more reasonable than Apollodorus, but in
other details was apparently quite pedantic.[55] Quintilian
(5.13.59) condemns Theodorus along with Apollodorus
as one who did not himself speak in the forum, but tried
to make up impractical rules about how it should be
done. His followers, the Theodoreans, were regarded as
rivals of Apollodoreans, and much of what we know
about Theodorus involves the contrast between his
theories and those of Apollodorus. For example, the
Theodoreans were less dogmatic about the necessity for
the standard four parts of an oration, but Theodorus was
quite rigid in insisting that the judge must always be
prepared in the prooemium for the points to follow (cf.

---

[54] Cf. Alexander, son of Numenius, in *Anonymus Seguerianus*
30-31 (358-59 Spengel-Hammer).

[55] Grube, *op.cit.* supra n. 50, has demolished the attempt of
Mutschmann and Rostagni to attribute a far-reading literary
theory to Theodorus. Cf. H. Mutschmann, *Tendenz, Aufbau,
und Quellen der Schrift vom Erhabenen*, Berlin, 1913, 46-70
and A. Rostagni, *Anonimo del Sublime*, Milan, 1947, xiii-xviii.

Quint. 4.1.24). Quintilian (2.15.21)[56] preserves Theodorus' definition of rhetoric as "an art of invention, judgment, and expression, with suitable ornament, on a scale which can embrace whatever is persuasive in each case on a matter involving a citizen (*in materia civili*)." This clearly embraces more than judicial oratory and demonstrates interest in style. The latter is confirmed by the appearance in the treatise *On Sublimity* (3.5) of a term *parenthyrson*, "thyrsus waving," which the author says is what Theodorus "used to call" the fault of meaningless emotion. The form of the verb has often been taken to mean that the author had known or studied with Theodorus.[57] Theodorus' most famous pupil was the future emperor Tiberius, whom he taught in boyhood (Suet., *Tib.*, 57), presumably in Rome around 30 B.C. Later he settled in Rhodes, where Tiberius in self-imposed exile attended his lectures (Quint. 3.1.17). Among rhetoricians his influence long persisted. Theodorus' pupil Hermagoras lived through much of the first century (Quint. 3.1.18), and the school's teachings play an important role in the work of Alexander, son of Numenius, in the second century, whose views are imbedded in a later treatise known as the *Anonymus Seguerianus*. Theodorean influence can also be seen in the last chapters of the *Technê* falsely attributed to Dionysius of Halicarnassus.[58]

Apollodorus and Theodorus have close ties with earlier and later rhetorical theory. Despite personal relationships to Augustus and Tiberius there is, however, little to asso-

[56] The definition in Quint. 2.15.16 is probably a briefer summary of the same.
[57] Cf. Mutschmann, *op.cit.* supra n. 55, 51 and Rostagni, *op.cit.* supra n. 55, x, answered by Grube, *op.cit.* supra n. 50, 360n.
[58] Cf. Georg Thiele, rev. of Usener, GGA 159 (1897) 243-47.

ciate them specifically with the intellectual history of the Augustan period. Of the latter, Dionysius of Halicarnassus and Caecilius of Calacte may be taken as more characteristic.

Dionysius of Halicarnassus

The Augustan rhetorician best known to us, the only one with extant works, and indeed the first Greek writer on rhetoric for three centuries whose works survive, is Dionysius of Halicarnassus.[59] About the man little is known. In the introduction to his historical work he says (*Rom. Ant.* 1.7.2-4) that he came to Rome in 30 B.C. and had lived there for the next twenty-two years, that he learned Latin, and knew many of the learned men of the time. This is consistent with the names he mentions and the few references to him in later writers such as that in Quintilian, who puts him with other Augustan authors (3.1.16).[60] It is likely that he was a private tutor of grammar and rhetoric to the sons of various Roman

[59] Cf. Max. Egger, *Denys d'Halicarnasse: Essai sur la critique littéraire et la rhétorique chez les Grecs au siècle d'Auguste*, Paris, 1902; R-E 5.934-91; Charles S. Baldwin, *Ancient Rhetoric and Poetic*, New York, 1924, 103-22; S. F. Bonner, *The Literary Treatises of Dionysius of Halicarnassus: a Study in the Development of Critical Method*, Cambridge, Eng., 1939. The standard Greek text is that of Hermann Usener and Ludwig Radermacher, *Dionysii Halicarnassei quae exstant*, vols. v-vi: *Opuscula*, Leipzig, 1899, reprinted Stuttgart, 1965. There is no complete translation or commentary, but cf. A. M. Desrousseaux and Max. Egger, *Denys d'Halicarnasse: jugement sur Lysias*, Paris, 1890 and W. Rhys Roberts, *Dionysius of Halicarnassus: the Three Literary Letters*, Cambridge, Eng., 1901 and *On Literary Composition*, London, 1910.
[60] Cf. W. Rhys Roberts, "The Literary Circle of Dionysius of Halicarnassus," CR 14 (1900) 439-42; Johannes Tolkiehn, "Dionysius von Halicarnassus und Caecilius von Calacte," WKPh 25 (1908) 84-86; G. P. Goold, "A Greek Professional Circle at Rome," TAPhA 92 (1961) 168-92; G. W. Bowersock, *Augustus and the Greek World*, Oxford, 1965, 130-32.

aristocrats; his treatise *On Literary Composition* was dedicated to a young man named Metilius Rufus as a birthday tribute and refers to their "daily exercises" together (20 p.94, U.-R.). Indeed, all of his critical and rhetorical writings can be associated with this kind of teaching. His *Roman Antiquities*, on the other hand, "the monument of his soul" as he calls it (1.1.2), must be viewed as the love of his leisure hours, intended to be his literary masterpiece. It is addressed to no patron or pupil, but to the Greeks of all time.

Although Dionysius clearly knew the rhetorical system as a whole, and in the essays on the orators touches on traditional theories of invention and arrangement, his enthusiasm for rhetoric was limited to its aesthetic and artistic side. His rhetorical theory is thus a much more limited thing than was that of Aristotle or Hermogenes, and Cornificius or Cicero. Dionysius has little interest in the art of persuasion. When he refers to contemporary works, for example in the introduction to *On the Ancient Orators*, it is mostly to historical, philosophical, and literary compositions that he is looking, and his critical system is only directly connected with oratory in that, to his mind, the best examples of Greek prose styles for imitation are the works of the Attic orators. In analyzing these works he is not unaware that they were intended for practical ends, and he regularly devotes a part of the discussion to the author's treatment of the subject matter, but he most extensively subjects to scrutiny the choice of words, the way these are combined into units, sometimes the rhythm and figures, always the overall quality or category of the style, and usually how to distinguish the style of one author from another's. Such a point of view is directly analogous to the development of oratory into declamation, which we have just witnessed. There is no discussion of declamation in the general works of Dionysius, but it was, of course, a leading part of the "daily exercise" of boys like Metilius Rufus, and Dionysius may be assumed to have declaimed in Greek himself.

Dionysius' work is of considerable significance in the history of criticism, particularly because of his development of a comparative method, his experiments with rewriting of passages to illustrate the effects of composition, and his evaluations of authenticity. This has, however, been adequately discussed by others.[61] What we most need to examine here is Dionysius' relation to the traditional theories of rhetoric and his own contribution to them.

Most of Dionysius' critical works contain cross-references of some sort which make it possible to arrange and study them in a chronological sequence. No absolute dates are known, but the period between 30 and 10 B.C. is certainly the general time. After a careful study Bonner concluded that the order of composition of the extant works was as follows:[62] *On Imitation*, the first half of *On the Ancient Orators* (*Lysias, Isocrates,* and *Isaeus*), the first *Epistle to Ammaeus*, the first thirty-three sections of the essay *On Demosthenes* (also a part of *On the Ancient Orators*), the treatise *On Literary Composition*, the rest of the essay *On Demosthenes*, the *Epistle to Pompeius*, the essay *On Thucydides*, the second *Epistle to Ammaeus*, and the essay *On Dinachus*. The most debated parts of the chronology of Dionysius' extant works involve the place of the first *Epistle to Ammaeus*, which

[61] Cf. H. P. Breitenback, "The *De compositione verborum* of Dionysius of Halicarnassus Considered with Reference to the Rhetoric of Aristotle," *CPh* 6 (1911) 163-79; Bonner, *op.cit.* supra n. 59; G.M.A. Grube, *The Greek and Roman Critics,* Toronto, 1965, 207-30. On study of authenticity cf. M. Untersteiner, "Dionisio di Alicarnasso, fondatore della critica pseudepigraphica," *AFC* 7 (1959) 72-93.
[62] Cf. Bonner, *op.cit.* supra n. 59, 38.

some scholars regarded as an early work because of its lack of specific reference to other writings of Dionysius, and the relation of *On Literary Composition* to the essay *On Demosthenes*. We hear of a number of works which have not survived, including a polemical treatise *On Political Philosophy* (*On Thuc.* 2) and a work on figures (Quint. 9.3.89). On the other hand, the rhetorical handbook and some short essays attributed to Dionysius are not genuine.[63]

Bonner thought it likely that the *Epistle to Ammaeus* postdated Dionysius' discussion of Isaeus' influence on Demosthenes in *On Isaeus*, but it is impossible to be certain of this, and since the essay relates to literary history and not style it is difficult to compare it to Dionysius' developing technique. In fact, the *Epistle* could have been written at almost any time; it is a refutation of an unnamed Peripatetic philosopher[64] who sought to prove that Demosthenes had learned his knowledge of rhetoric from Aristotle. It is interesting to see a literary dispute of the Augustan age, even though the argument falls into the commonplace of trying to associate two famous men as master and pupil: Demosthenes was more often called a pupil of Plato.[65] It is also interesting to see that the Peripatetics seem to be adhering to Aristotle's own views of rhetoric, well known at this time from the republication of his works, whereas other schools like the Academics and Stoics had changed their point of view a good deal in the Hellenistic period. Dionysius attempts to refute the argument on chronological grounds, showing that Demos-

---

[63] For discussion of these cf. infra 634-36.

[64] The origin of the view is attributed to Critolaus by A. H. Chroust, "The *Vita Aristotelis* of Dionysius of Halicarnassus (1 *Ep. ad Amm.* 5)," AAntHung 13, (1965) 369-77.

[65] E.g., Cic., *De or.* 1.89; *Brutus* 121; *De off.* 1.4. The view was based on a spurious epistle of Demosthenes, cf. Cic., *Orator* 15.

thenes and Aristotle were contemporaries, and that the *Rhetoric* was composed after most of Demosthenes's speeches. Unlike many earlier rhetoricians, Dionysius was well informed about Aristotle and directly influenced by him. He may indeed have started his studies with the Peripatetics.[66] What he proves, however, is not that Demosthenes could not have learned rhetoric from Aristotle, but that he did not use the *Rhetoric*, which is not quite the same thing, since we know that the *Rhetoric* was developed over a considerable period of time while Aristotle was lecturing on rhetoric.[67] On the other hand, the argument that Demosthenes had learned from Aristotle was presumably based on an attempt to show the orator's application of Aristotelian theory set forth in the *Rhetoric*, so that at the very least Dionysius shows that the argument is not necessarily valid and, in fact, it is doubtless invalid.

Of Dionysius' critical works the two most important in the history of rhetoric are the treatise *On Imitation* and the series of studies *On the Ancient Orators*. *On Imitation* is apparently the earlier.[68] Its contents are summarized by Dionysius himself in the *Epistle to Pompeius* (3): "The first book of the work embraces the whole examination of imitation, the second deals with the men who should be imitated; poets and philosophers, historiographers and orators, and the third, still incomplete, with the manner in which imitation should be carried out." A long quotation from book two follows, dealing

---

[66] Cf. S. F. Bonner, "Dionysius of Halicarnassus and the Peripatetic Mean of Style," *CPh* 33 (1938) 257-66.

[67] Cf. *APG* 84, n. 73.

[68] Cf. Bonner, *op.cit.* supra n. 59, 37, who points out that Dionysius had not yet come to recognize the historical importance of Isaeus as a forerunner of Demosthenes, but, cf. infra n. 81.

with the comparative merits of Herodotus and Thucydides. We do not know whether or not the work was ever completed; the fragments, in addition to this, are a few quotations from book one and an epitome of book two preserved in manuscript.

Imitation (*mimêsis*) is a distinguished concept with a long and varied history, central to Platonic philosophy and other thought derived therefrom. As a critical term it is most frequently used to mean the artistic representation of reality, a sense found, for example, in Aristotle's *Poetics*.[69] More common, however, in late Hellenistic and imperial times is the concept of imitation as a technique of literary creativity by which a writer or student deliberately imitates the form or thought or especially the style of a great literary model who thus becomes a touchstone of taste. Imitation in this sense is a feature of the classroom and often reflects a pedagogic point of view: the teacher has presented a student with a classical model to imitate, copy, or emulate.

The first book of Dionysius' *On Imitation* may have included a definition of rhetoric as "the artistic faculty of persuasive speech in political matters, having the goal of speaking well" (fr. 1).[70] The definition itself is a development of Aristotle's in the *Rhetoric*, intended to answer the Hellenistic objection that rhetoric does not

[69] Cf. Richard McKeon, "Literary Criticism and the Concept of Imitation in Antiquity," *Modern Philology* 34 (1936) 1-35, reprinted *Critics and Criticism: Ancient and Modern*, Chicago, 1952, 160-68; Erich Auerbach, *Mimesis: the Representation of Reality in Western Literature*, Princeton, 1953; Hermann Koller, *Die Mimesis in der Antike*, Berne, 1954; W. J. Verdenius, *Mimesis: Plato's Doctrine of Artistic Imitation and its Meaning to Us*, Leiden, 1962.

[70] For the fragments cf. Usener-Radermacher, *op.cit.* supra n. 59, 6.197-217. Fr. 1 is cited by several late Greek rhetoricians, cf. 6.17; 7.15 etc. Walz.

deal with all subjects; if it really comes from *On Imitation*,[71] its presence served to orient the whole work firmly to rhetorical composition. "Speaking well" as the goal of rhetoric would be another indication of the turn from emphasis on the practical purpose of rhetoric to emphasis on style. Artistic, not logical, integrity is what matters. Quintilian, who is especially close to the point of view of this work of Dionysius, accepts the art of speaking well as an adequate definition of rhetoric. Another fragment (3) defines imitation (*mimêsis*) as "an activity receiving the impression of a model by inspection of it," while emulation (*zêlos*) is called an "activity of the soul impelled toward admiration of what seems to be fine." Emulation thus logically comes first; it is a psychological activity which produces literary activity. The remaining fragments of book one and the epitome of book two make clear, what Quintilian (10.2) also teaches about imitation, that it is not a matter of copying the mannerisms of an author, but of understanding an author's strengths and producing a counterpart to them, and that exclusive imitation of a single author, however great, is not adequate. The student must come to understand the characteristic qualities of many models and try to combine these creatively in his own work. Thus, instead of restricting himself to the virtues of Lysias, or even Demosthenes, as a previous generation of critics had suggested, Dionysius considers the whole range of classical Greek literature as appropriate models for style. His survey presupposes the existence of lists of authors of various genres, perhaps drawn up originally by grammarians. Quintilian (10.1.54) mentions Aristarchus and Aristophanes as a source of one list. The famous canon of the

[71] This is supported by fr. 5 in Usener-Radermacher which takes up "faculty" again and by the lack of any other work of Dion. Hal. to which it can conveniently be attributed.

ten Attic orators is not here used by Dionysius; he mentions only Lysias, Isocrates, Lycurgus, Demosthenes, Aeschines, and Hyperides; subsequently he devoted *On the Ancient Orators* to a different combination. Different critics and even a single critic at different times apparently had different lists. The existence of other discussions of Greek writers, doubtless known to Dionysius, seems implicit in a passage in Cicero (*De or.* 2.90-96), and they are of course imitated later by Quintilian (10.1.46-84) and Dio Chrysostom.

Dionysius speaks of those qualities of which he approves as *aretai*, "virtues," and his critical system is in origin a variation of the virtues of style of Aristotle and Theophrastus. In the system as expounded in *On Imitation* (3), and also later in the essay *On Thucydides* (22), there are three "necessary" virtues in all styles: correctness and clarity, which are from the Theophrastan tradition, and brevity, which the Stoics had added (Diogenes Laertius 7.59). Ornamentation, the third of the Theophrastan virtues, is broken down into various "additional" virtues. This second list, almost by definition, varied from time to time, but at least some of the possible qualities are to be expected in any good style. In the comparison of Herodotus and Thucydides (3.16ff.) those qualities mentioned are vividness, imitation of ethos and pathos, a group of qualities involving force, and another group involving charm. Finally there is "the most important" virtue, propriety, which was also the last in the traditional system and which Dionysius perhaps regarded as more in the category of a necessary than an "additional" virtue. We will eventually see this system given further development in the *Aristides Rhetoric* and in Hermogenes' *On Forms*.

Study of models of imitation invites the critic to make comparisons, and comparison thus becomes a major device of literary analysis in the Augustan and imperial period. Dionysius' comparison of Herodotus and Thucydides from *On Imitation* is quoted in its entirety in the *Epistle to Pompeius*. Both subject and style are considered, the latter in terms of the virtues just discussed and in an adequate, if rather routine, way. But the comparison of subject matter is one of the most horrendous literary judgments ever written: that Herodotus is much superior to Thucydides since the latter wrote on an unsuitable subject, began at the wrong place, and treated it in the wrong way. Bonner concluded that Dionysius' *On Imitation* is a good example of the mechanical method of criticism in which a set of categories are laid down and rigid application followed,[72] but it is possible to see also a reflection of the values of Augustan Rome in such a view. Augustus was not enamored of Thucydides or his imitators.

On the Ancient Orators, the second book inviting special attention, begins with an introduction providing our best information on Dionysius' attitude to the stylistic influences of his own age.[73] It was his belief that, beginning with the death of Alexander the Great (323 B.C.), "the ancient and philosophical rhetoric" was "scorned and subjected to insult." It was replaced by something else which is described as theatrical and ignorant, and a metaphor of the rejection of an Attic wife or an Asian mistress is developed. Starting with Dionysius' own age, however, reaction has set in; possibly this is an act of God, he says, possibly the operation of a natural cycle, possibly it comes from an intelligent human impulse. Men are again "conscious of philosophy," and only in Asia does the tasteless style linger on in popularity. Dionysius goes

[72] Bonner, *op.cit.* supra n. 59, 41.
[73] Translated in the Appendix to *APG* 337-40.

on to give primary responsibility for this Atticist reaction to the virtuous and responsible rulers of Rome, men of education and judgment, whose "commendation has encouraged the intellectual element in every city and has forced the ignorant to learn sense." The result has been the publication of worthwhile histories, charming discourses, and admirable philosophical treatises. In the final part of the introduction Dionysius states his own purpose, which is to strengthen the new eloquence with an evaluation of the ancient orators and historians and their characteristics, something which he thinks will be useful to "persons practicing political philosophy," and something which as far as he knows has not been done. He proposes to discuss the orators chronologically and take up the historians sometime in the future. There will be a comparative account of the three older orators, Lysias, Isocrates, and Isaeus, and then of a later generation, Demosthenes, Hyperides, and Aeschines. These six he regards as better than the others. In the beginning of the later essay *On Dinarchus* he labels the first three "inventors" and the other three "perfecters" of style. This passage provides much food for thought.

Our knowledge of Hellenistic rhetorical theory and oratorical style is limited. It certainly seems to have been the case that philosophical rejection of rhetoric led to rejection of philosophy on the part of rhetoricians in the Hellenistic period. Dionysius implies that this quarrel was the reason for the corruption of prose style, something of an oversimplification on chronological grounds; it is, however, clear that Stoics with interest in diction and simplicity, and probably the reasonable Academics and Peripatetics as well, exercised a check on stylistic excesses in their schools, a check which was lacking in the schools of nonphilosophical rhetoricians, especially in

Asia.[74] A great deal of Hellenistic Greek was neither Asian nor antiphilosophical but simply undistinguished, the kind of writing which develops in bureaucracies and commercial establishments. Historically this style developed into what is called *koinê*, seen in the Greek writings of the early Christians.

More interesting, and quite clear, is that Dionysius knows nothing of an Atticist reaction among Greek writers before his own time. That is to say, in the opinion of the most widely traveled and well-informed Greek rhetorician of the age of Augustus, Greek criticism afforded no original impulse for neo-Atticism in Latin. We have already seen that the originality of Latin neo-Atticism is consistent with Cicero's description of it.[75] Dionysius credits the beginning of the Attic reaction among Greek writers to the influence of the virtuous rulers of Rome. This we might more freely state as an observation that Romans interested in rhetoric refused to put up with many of the affectations of the Asianists. They wanted to speak or write a Greek analogous to the simpler manner of their own pure Latin and in the tradition of the Attic orators. It is perhaps also likely that there were moral implications in this preference, as we have suggested there were in Sallust's choice of style. What Romans Dionysius has in mind is not certain, but Augustus and his ministers would seem to be a good possibility.[76] We have already seen that Augustus' influence contributed to the popularity of declamation. An element of flattery in

[74] Cf. Friederich Blass, *Die Griechische Beredsamkeit in dem Zeitraum von Alexander bis auf Augustus*, Berlin, 1865.

[75] Cf. supra 241-42.

[76] Egger, *op.cit.* supra n. 59, thought Dionysius meant Cicero. Harry M. Hubbell, *The Influence of Isocrates on Cicero, Dionysius, and Aristides*, New Haven, 1913, 46, suggested Messalla. Octavian and his collaborators is the opinion of Americo De-Propris, "Cicerone e Dionisio," *Paideia* 2 (1947) 227-34.

giving the emperor credit for a literary movement already underway cannot be entirely ruled out, but the whole spirit of the Augustan age was a return to the chaste and classic models of the past. To come from the Asia of Halicarnassus to the neo-Atticism of Rome after Actium must indeed have seemed a dramatic change, and with the mercurial Antony eliminated, the future of literary composition seemed clear. Augustanism was a very Roman thing, and thus at its roots Latin. Dionysius' words add strength to the belief that in the last decades of the first century there was for the first time an influence of Latin letters upon Greek. A further indication of this influence may be seen in the fact that in this period for the first time a Greek writer, Caecilius, dared to discuss Latin style in a celebrated comparison of Cicero and Demosthenes, soon repeated by "Longinus." We know that Dionysius acquired a good knowledge of Latin (*Rom. Ant.* 1.7.2); his thought is often close to that of Cicero and the possibility cannot be ruled out that he had read *De oratore* and *Brutus*, and *Orator*.[77] At very least he had talked to Romans who had read them and were interested in the topics they discuss.

In this introduction Dionysius describes the restored eloquence as philosophical and intellectual; out of context the remarks could be taken to be the work of a philosopher, which Dionysius certainly was not. What he means may partly be guessed from what he subsequently says about the moral and intellectual virtues acquired by reading Isocrates. Philosophical thus means cultural and serious and is not to be associated directly with the schools, nor does it appear to be directly connected with

[77] Cf. DePropris, *op.cit.* supra n. 76. F. Nassal, *Aesthetisch-rhetorisches Beziehungen zwischen Dionysius von Halicarnassus und Cicero*, Tübingen, 1910, 9-10, saw the similarity between Cicero and Dionysius, but attributed it to a common source which he rashly identified as Caecilius of Calacte.

subject matter. The philosophical and intellectual qualities emerge in the style and the tone, not in the thought and meaning, and when at the end Dionysius proclaims his desire to be useful to political philosophers he means a desire to perfect a mode of dignified discourse for writers on serious subjects in Greek.

In Dionysius' plans to encourage the further development of the Attic style the dominant feature is classicism, the study and imitation of the classical Greek writers and most of all the Attic orators. Individual Greek writers like Isocrates or Demosthenes had always exercised an influence, but until Dionysius' age this influence was that of a general stream or tradition rather than a deliberate and conscious imitation of qualities learned by historically sophisticated study. Dionysius specifically says that as far as he knows the kind of study he is attempting has not been undertaken before. For it, that is, for a conscious harking back to the standards of another age, there were few precedents in Greek intellectual history. A possible instance is the study of Aristotle by first century B.C. Peripatetics, of which we have seen that Dionysius was aware. Another possible antecedent is Roman imitation of Greek originals, and Dionysius' reference in the introduction to Roman influence would seem to give this the greater significance. A generation before Dionysius, at a time when nothing of the sort, so far as we can see, had begun in Greece, Cicero was turning to Demosthenes and Plato and other writers as sources of techniques, style, ideas, and imitation.

The introduction concludes with the claim that Dionysius will discuss six orators, three older ones: Lysias, Isocrates, and Isaeus, and three later: Demosthenes, Hypereides, and Aeschines. The last two essays are lost and that on Demosthenes seems to have been revised or written on an altered plan. We can, therefore, only look at the first three as a unit. The essay on Lysias is divided into four main parts: (1) Lysias' life (ch.1); (2) the "virtues" of Lysias' style (2-14); (3) Lysias' virtues in treatment of the subject matter, including consideration of the genre in which he worked and his partition (15-19); (4) consideration of examples of Lysias' work and some discussion thereof. The essay on Isocrates was apparently intended to follow a similar scheme, but the proportions are different since style is briefly described and subject matter is discussed at length, primarily in terms of Isocrates' moral and philosophic models for imitation, and a section is inserted on criticisms of Isocrates. In the case of the essay on Isaeus the same basic plan is evident, but this time disarranged by the large amount of comparison between Isaeus and Lysias which is inserted. In all the essays, the discussion of the orators' lives is inadequate, and in all the discussion of style is cast in terms of the "virtues." These are fundamentally the virtues Dionysius set forth in *On Imitation*, but not exactly so. In this as in the structure of the essays, Dionysius seems to have moved away from rigid categories toward a greater freedom to present the characteristics of the authors as he felt them. The terms "necessary" and "additional" virtues are not used; the first three virtues of Lysias and Isocrates are purity, use of proper diction, and clarity; brevity is pushed further down the list in the case of Lysias and since it is not a characteristic of Isocrates at all, it does not any longer seem to be "necessary."

In considering the subject matter of Lysias, Dionysius principally cites the requirements set forth by writers of rhetorical handbooks and shows how Lysias conforms to these. The discussion of the subject matter of Isocrates is, however, considerably more significant and furnishes a connecting link between the Academics and Cicero on the one hand and the second sophistic and Quintilian on

355

the other. According to Dionysius Isocrates can instill philosophical eloquence and those who give their attention to him can become not only clever speakers, but noble in character and useful to their family, their city, and all of Greece. Thus, Dionysius declares that those who seek to attain not merely some part of political power, but its entirety should keep Isocrates' works in hand. He will teach them "true" philosophy, that is not only theoretical but practical philosophy, not what makes life untroubled but what benefits mankind (*Isoc.* 4). The discussion continues with a list of qualities which are developed in an individual by study of particular passages of Isocrates: patriotism, nobility, justice, reverence, eloquence, persuasive power, and the like. Although Dionysius says a good deal about Isocrates and appears to have a practical intention here in the training of orators in his own day, he does not spell out as Cicero did earlier and Quintilian was to do a concept of the ideal orator, and the contemporary implications remain quite vague. Presumably he means that Romans destined for authority should look beyond the art of public speaking described in the handbooks to something more philosophical or humanistic, and this is certainly in the spirit of the Augustan age.[78]

The short essay *On Isaeus* which follows is chiefly interesting for the development of critical method which it illustrates.[79] The basic problem which Dionysius found was to distinguish the style of Isaeus from the rather similar style of Lysias, and this he does by taking up specific qualities common to both writers, illustrating and distinguishing them by quoting from similar contexts. The essential difference between the two is the greater arti-

[78] Cf. Hubbell, *op.cit.* supra n. 76, 41-53, and Bonner, *op.cit.* supra n. 59, 12-14.
[79] Cf. Bonner, *op.cit.* supra n. 59, 52-77.

ficiality of Isaeus' style and thought. Usually Dionysius
assumes that his feeling for the passages will be shared
immediately by readers, but twice (7 and 11) he takes
the additional step of rewriting sentences to illustrate the
effect of structure. This procedure, sometimes called *metathesis*, he pursues further in the treatise *On Literary
Composition*.[80] On Isaeus ends (19-20) with a note on why Dionysius
has omitted discussion of other orators. He has taken
Isocrates as the best example of poetic adornment and
what is elevated and impressive and has thus omitted
both Isocrates' predecessors Gorgias, Alcidamas, and
Theodorus, and his contemporaries or successors: Anaximenes, Theodectes, Theopompus, Naucrates, Ephorus,
Philiscus, and Cephisodoros. Similarly, Lysias is superior
to Antiphon, Thrasymachus, Polycrates, Critias, and Zoi-
lus among those who aim at exactness of word and practical oratory. In the next essay Dionysius groups the style
of some of these writers in a different way. What he
means here is that Isocrates is the best of the epideictic
or sophistic orators, Lysias the best of the practicing deliberative or judicial orators. Isaeus falls into this second
group, but special treatment has been accorded him,
Dionysius says, because he is "the seed and source" of
deinotês, that power of speech most evident in Demosthenes. This judgment was probably a common one in
the Hellenistic period.[81] Dionysius is now ready to turn
to the "perfected rhetoric and strength of practical
speech" which he finds in Demosthenes, Hyperides, and
Aeschines.

The essay *On Demosthenes*, as preserved in the manuscripts, begins abruptly in the course of a long quotation

[80] Cf. Nathan A. Greenberg, "Metathesis as an Instrument
in the Criticism of Poetry," *TAPhA* 89 (1958) 262-70.

[81] Dionysius refers (*Isaeus* 1) to this as a view held by Hermip-
pus and (*ibid.* 4) Pytheas.

357

from the third book of Thucydides. At the end of the quotation Dionysius says that Thucydides is the "standard and canon" of a style which is elaborate, extravagant, ornate, replete with all additional adornment. A few lines later Gorgias is mentioned side by side with Thucydides as though he had earlier been discussed. Syrianus (RG 5.548 Walz) preserves some remarks on Gorgias, with a considerable piece of Gorgias' *Funeral Oration* as taken from "Dionysius the elder in the second book of his work *On Characters,*" which could well be a description of the second part of *On the Ancient Orators.* It thus seems likely that the essay *On Demosthenes* began with an introduction on kinds of style and took up the grand style with Gorgias and Thucydides as examples. Reference to Thucydides, and not even to a speech in Thucydides, but to the civil war at Corcyra, is unexpected in terms of the scope of the earlier portions of this work and indicates that Dionysius' critical horizons have continued to enlarge. Possibly some time intervened between the writing of the separate essays. Over against the Thucydidean character of style is set the smooth and plain, of which Lysias, who is called a contemporary of Gorgias and Thucydides, is taken as the model. According to Dionysius the various writers are like the harmony of a scale, with Thucydides and Lysias at opposite ends. The one astonishes, the other charms; the one stretches and strains the mind, the other relaxes and softens it. One aims at pathos, the other at ethos; this antithesis is then further developed.

These are, in Dionysius' view, the only two separate kinds of style. The third style to which he next turns (3) is a mixture and harmony of the other two. Theophrastus had made Thrasymachus the example of it; to Dionysius, Isocrates among the orators and Plato among the philosophers are better examples, and he proceeds with a discussion of all three. This is again a widening of the critical horizons beyond what might have been expected. It is somewhat surprising to encounter Isocrates here as an example of mixed style after meeting him earlier as the foremost example of the artificial epideictic orator, but as we have said, that is a somewhat different category. Dionysius has little difficulty in showing that in diction, in composition, and in use of pathos and ethos Isocrates draws together elements seen in both Thucydides and Lysias. A second example of the mixed style is Plato, good when he is simple and plain, but often tasteless and excessive in his use of adornment. Finally (8), we reach Demosthenes, who combines the best features of the style of all previous writers. Demosthenes is then compared first with Thucydides (9-10), next with Lysias (11), and later with Isocrates (18-22) and Plato (23-32).

At about this point in the essay Dionysius apparently set it aside to write his treatise *On Literary Composition* (to which he refers specifically in chapter 49). That work outlines a theory of three styles of harmony or composition, the rugged, the smooth, and the blended, and when Dionysius resumed work on the essay on Demosthenes he brought these in. The exact point of break between the two parts is somewhat difficult to specify, but probably comes at the end of chapter thirty-three.[82] Dionysius does not attempt to relate the three styles which he had earlier discussed to these three harmonies or styles of composition nor to the concept of styles of epideictic and forensic genre. Isocrates is a writer of the mixed style, smooth harmony, and epideictic genre; Thucydides is grand style, rugged harmony, and epideictic genre; Demosthenes is mixed style, blended harmony, and all genres. The first

[82] Cf. Ernst Kalinka, "Die Arbeitsweise des Rhetors Dionys," WS 43 (1922-23) 157-68 and 44 (1924-25) 48-68; Bonner, *op.cit.* supra n. 59, 32.

concept, the traditional styles or characters, is the widest and most general: it includes diction, the use of figures, and the tone of a work. Composition, or harmony, is a much more specific matter of the juxtaposition of words and their combination into phrases and clauses. As discussed in *On Demosthenes*, Aeschylus, Pindar, and Thucydides are taken as examples of the rugged style (38-39); Hesiod, Sappho, Anacreon, and Isocrates of the florid or smooth (40); Homer, Herodotus, Plato, and, of course, Demosthenes of the blended (41). There is a short but interesting discussion (36) of why different authors use different harmonies. The reasons given are first, natural predisposition; second, acquired principles of taste, third, contemporary fashion; and fourth, imitation of a model, and actually there are many variants or combinations among the three chief styles (37). After outlining the theory Dionysius considers the style of Demosthenes, including his rhythm (47-48) and delivery (53), how to recognize his genuine speeches (50), and Aeschines' criticism of Demosthenes' style. The essay is thus ultimately a fairly complete treatment of Demosthenes' literary qualities, though considerable portions of it are devoted to writers other than Demosthenes. Comparative criticism is repeatedly evident and there is some rewriting of passages to illustrate discussion of qualities (e.g., 20).

In addition to these works, several of Dionysius' other treatises have some rhetorical interest. His major critical treatise is *On Literary Composition*, to which we have just referred. In this after an introduction (1-5), he considers first (6-9) the grouping, shaping, and tailoring of clauses, then (10-20) the sources of the two qualities which he most desires in composition: *hêdonê* or charm, and *to kalon*, or beauty. The sources turn out to be the same four factors in each case: melody (*melos*), rhythm, (*rhythmos*), variety (*metabolê*), and propriety (*to pre-*

pon). The critical procedure is analogous to the distinction of virtues of style, and the qualities correspond to some extent, but there is no intent that one set directly imitate the other. Next (21-24) comes the discussion of the three kinds of composition which we have just considered: the rugged, of which Pindar and Thucydides are given as example, the smooth, of which the best instances are Sappho and Isocrates, and the blended, a kind of mean or fusion of the other two, of which Homer and Demosthenes are the best examples. Dionysius makes it clear in this section that he is developing an idea of his own and that no technical rhetorical terms exist for these categories. In order to describe composition he has made use of a critical procedure analogous to the description of style as a whole (the three characters), much as the sources of charm and beauty are influenced by the concept of the virtues, but it is not possible to identify any specific connection between the harmonies and the styles, since the latter include many more factors. The influence of the concept of the harmonies has not been very great, but it shows how strongly Dionysius himself was influenced by standard rhetorical theory and yet how his personal taste and judgment were able to make themselves felt as he developed in experience and assurance.

Dionysius presents his harmonies as original with himself. In the introduction he also stresses that the whole matter of composition had few antecedent studies "among the ancients." He doubtless means that a few relevant passages existed in the third book of Aristotle's *Rhetoric* (cf. his references to it in 25) and in Theophrastus' *On Style*, but that little had been written on the subject since then. Cicero had, of course, similarly stressed the paucity of discussion of rhythm, which is an important part of composition, and Dionysius, as we have seen, was under strong Roman influence. As elsewhere, Dionysius presents the history of Greek prose style from the end of the fourth century to his own age as a barren wasteland. Stoic discussions seemed to him both turgid and irrelevant. He never praises the literary style of any writer of the third, second, or first century, thus confirming our belief that neo-Atticism was a phenomenon of his own time, and he lists quite a number, including the great Polybius, as writers whom no one has the patience to read.

To conclude with the treatise *On Literary Composition*, we must return briefly to its introductory chapter. We are told here that the subject is a necessary one for all who would practice political speech. But not a single word in what follows relates composition to persuasion. Dionysius' concerns are solely with style and the production of a speech (for whatever purpose) endowed with charm and beauty. Secondly, we are told that the study of ideas and subject matter is impossibly difficult for the young; it requires matured understanding and experience. What fascinates the young, what they can be led to understand, and what they should be most trained in, are style and the beauty of language. This is not totally illogical, but it is significant here as indicative of the point of view which made declamation the primary feature of rhetorical instruction, subordinating argumentation to adornment.

Dionysius planned to continue his study of Demosthenes, so far limited to the orator's style, into an examination of subject, as he did in the case of the earlier orators. He interrupted the plan, however, at the request, he says (*On Thucydides* 1), of Q. Aelius Tubero[83] to discuss in greater detail his views on Thucydides as an object of

---

[83] Cicero's opponent in *Pro Ligario*, jurisconsult and historian. Apparently he admired and imitated Thucydides, cf. *On Thuc.* 25; Bowersock, *op.cit.* supra n. 60, 130.

imitation. Apparently work on Demosthenes was not resumed. The essay *On Thucydides* makes much use of rhetorical categories, especially in the first half, but as he gets deeper into the analysis of Thucydides' style Dionysius shows his independent judgment and often brings out his points by the characteristic device of rewriting passages of the historian. We have already noted the role Thucydides had come to play as model of an extreme version of Atticism: archaic, disjointed, brief, sometimes obscure. Dionysius attempts to be fair, as he does in discussing Plato, though in both cases with less than perfect success. He admits some virtues in Thucydides' treatment of his subject (5-20), though even there the arrangement is criticized, and the treatment regarded as sometimes inappropriate, but in terms of style Dionysius declares himself strongly opposed to those "who propose that man as the canon of historical study and the standard of power (*deinotês*) in public speech" (*On Thuc.* 2, cf. 35 and 55).

The final essay of Dionysius on an orator is *On Dinarchus*. It is primarily of interest as a source of information about Dinarchus and his works and especially the judgment of what was genuine and what spurious, which Dionysius felt was inaccurately dealt with by Callimachus in the Alexandria library and by the scholars in Pergamum as well.

Dionysius of Halicarnassus is a significant figure in the history of Roman rhetoric. In his career and works we can see the chief influences of the age: Rome replaces the cities of Greece as the center of rhetorical study; Roman statesmen exercise influence on taste; the influence of Latin writers on Greek is detectable for the first time; style has become the primary topic of rhetorical interest, and classicism and imitation are the foundation of literary theory. Rhetoric has ceased to be concerned primarily with persuasion and reveals itself as an art of expression.

Caecilius of Calacte

What we know of the life of Caecilius comes chiefly from references in late Greek anthologists and encyclopaedists.[84] Some of the information may not be very reliable. It is said that he was born a slave, this his name was originally Archagathos, and that he was a Jew. That he was a Greek speaking Sicilian who bore the name of a Roman family with many clients in that island seems certain. Dates are difficult to determine: the sources associate him with the Augustan age, which is confirmed by Dionysius' reference (*Ep. to Pomp.* 3) to him as a contemporary and friend. Their friendship need not be elaborated into a close professional association any more than certain differences in viewpoint should be made the basis of an hypothesis that they were bitter rivals.[85] Since Dionysius does not seem to refer to Caecilius' published works, these may well be later than Dionysius' own writings.[86] Caecilius knew Apollodorus (Quint. 9.1.12) and probably Theodorus as well, but there is no evidence to make him the pupil of either, and his interests were quite

[84] Cf. Athenaeus 6.272f.; 11.466a; *Souda* s.v. "Caecilius," "Hermagoras," and "Timagenes." Modern discussions of Caecilius include Kasimir von Morawski, "De Dionysii et Caecilii studiis rhetoricis," *RhM* 34 (1879) 370-76; Maximilian Rothstein, "Caecilius von Kalakte und die Schrift vom Erhabenen," *Hermes* 23 (1888) 1-20; Richard Weise, *Quaestiones Caecilianae*, Berlin, 1888; *R-E* 3.1174-88: W. Rhys Roberts, "Caecilius of Calacte: a Contribution to the History of Greek Literary Criticism," *AJPh* 18 (1897) 302-12; Atkins 2.106-8. For the fragments cf. Ernestus Ofenloch, *Caecilii Calactini fragmenta*, Leipzig, 1907, reprinted Stuttgart, 1967, but Ofenloch included both undoubted fragments and also a great deal of questionable material which he thought showed Caecilius' influence.

[85] Cf. Blass, *op.sit.* supra n. 74, 169-221; Roberts, *op.cit.* supra n. 60; Tolkiehn, *op.cit.* supra n. 60.

[86] The introduction (esp. 4) to *On the Attic Orators* could hardly have been written if Caecilius had already published his work *On the Character of the Ten Orators*, discussed below.

different from theirs. Although Caecilius, like most rhetoricians, composed an *Art of Rhetoric*,[87] his most famous and influential works were devoted to the study of figures of speech and to the Atticism movement. Quintilian says (9.3.89) that figures of speech were treated in greatest detail by those who had devoted separate works to the subject, as opposed to those who included discussion in more general works on rhetoric. Caecilius is the first person he names, and on five occasions he quotes Caecilius' views about figures, primarily to disagree with them. In many passages he may follow Caecilius without mentioning him. Since there are also references in a number of later Greek rhetoricians we can be certain that Caecilius' work was influential. The epitome of Phoebammon quotes (*RG* 3.44 Spengel) his definition of a figure as "a turning (*tropê*) to a form of thought (*dianoia*) and diction (*lexis*) which is not in accordance with nature." From this we may deduce that he did not distinguish between tropes and figures, but did discuss the two usual kinds of figures. All the surviving fragments refer to figures of diction, and much of Caecilius' effort probably went into classifying, naming, and illustrating these. *Schêma*, or figure, was sometimes used in a more general way to mean a configuration of thought or language and it could thus be argued that all language is figured. Quintilian (9.1.10-13) says that there was no small argument on the subject among rhetoricians. Dionysius (*On Lit. Comp.* 8) speaks of figures as "unlimited" and what is labeled chapter nine in the rhetorical handbook falsely attributed to Dionysius says at the beginning that there is no language which is not

---

[87] Ofenloch, *op.cit.* supra n. 84, thought it showed strong Aristotelian influence. Caecilius distinguished three kinds of *stasis*, Quint. 3.6.48, and used the term *apodeixis* for enthymeme, Quint. 5.10.7.

figured.[88] We have already seen that Apollodorus thought discussion of figures was in such circumstances meaningless. To judge from Caecilius' definition just quoted, his position was that direct unfigured language could exist and that any departure from it should be thought a figure. The phrase "not in accordance with nature" was, however, an unfortunate way to put it. Quintilian follows the basic meaning, but avoids labeling figures unnatural. The definition also fails to say, what Caecilius surely assumed, that the departure from natural expression must be done for a reason and that it is a deliberate form of emphasis or adornment. Quotations or passages presumed to have been influenced by Caecilius do not show much concern with the psychology of figures, that is, with the different literary effect of different figures, and Caecilius' contribution to the subject was mostly the number of figures he defined and the careful distinctions he made between similar figures. The fragments draw illustrations primarily from Demosthenes, but also from Herodotus, Thucydides, and the poets: Homer, Sophocles, Euripides, Eupolis. Since the Atticists' favorite model Lysias is not a very good source for figures his absence is not strange, but the absence of Plato is intentional. Caecilius, as we shall see, did not admire his style.

The works of Caecilius listed in the encyclopaedia known as the *Souda* are not those mentioned so far, but chiefly relate to Atticism. *How the Attic Style Differs from the Asian* and the *Comparison of Demosthenes and Aeschines* are known only from the titles, though the second of course suggests Cicero's *De optimo genere oratorum*. The *Essay on Lysias* tried to show the superiority of that orator over Plato and was too prejudiced or contentious to be successful (cf. *On Sublimity* 32). *On the Character of the Ten Orators* was a major work and

[88] Cf. also Alexander in *RG* 3.12.15 Spengel.

perhaps responsible for the formation of the canon of ten Attic orators.[89] Certainly there is no evidence that the canon existed earlier nor any particular need for an exclusively Attic canon, omitting Gorgias and Demetrius of Phaleron, for example, except as models for the Atticists. "Character" commonly meant stylistic character and the work probably somewhat resembled Dionysius' *On the Ancient Orators*. Both contained a discussion of lives of the orators, but a feature of Caecilius' work was quotation of decrees relating to them. Both rhetoricians were also concerned with the question of genuine and spurious speeches; in the important case of Lysias they agreed as to the number genuine (Ps. Plutarch, *On the Lives of the Ten Orators* 836), whereas in the case of Isocrates (*ibid.* 838) Dionysius accepted twenty-five and Caecilius twenty-eight. Dionysius' method is rather circular in that he seeks to define the character of a particular orator out of surviving speeches and then uses that character to determine which speeches are genuine, but this is slightly less dangerous than it sounds since certain speeches were usually above suspicion. Caecilius' method may have been similar. Our best source of information about Caecilius' work seems to be the collection called *Lives of the Ten Orators*, preserved in the writings of Plutarch, but compiled by some unknown rhetorician of the second century A.D.

The text of the *Souda* is corrupt in the middle of the list of Caecilius' works. It appears to speak of a lexicon called *Against the Phrygians* (i.e., Asianists) in two books and a work in an unknown number of books called *Callirhêmosynê*, or elegance of language, unless

---

[89] Cf. J. Brzoska, *De canone decem oratorum Atticorum quaestiones*, Breslau, 1883; P. Hartman, *De canone decem oratorum*, Göttingen, 1891; more negative, A. E. Douglas, "Cicero, Quintilian, and the Canon of the Ten Attic orators," *Mnemosyne* 9 (1956) 30-40.

they are the same work. In any event we can be reasonably certain that Caecilius compiled at least one lexicon of Atticism, alphabetically arranged. A considerable number of definitions and discussions of words in the *Souda*, Gregory of Corinth, and late lexicographers are thought to have been derived from Caecilius' work.[90] The extant lexicon of the Attic orators by Harpocration, written perhaps in the first century A.D., is predominantly historical and legal rather than stylistic.

Two other works on style by Caecilius are of special interest. One is a *Comparison of Demosthenes and Cicero*. The title is given in the *Souda*, but Plutarch (*Demos.* 3) criticizes the presumption of Caecilius, "a man who never knew when to stop," in trying to deal with Latin style, like "a dolphin on dry land." Plutarch himself will not try to say which orator was more ornate (*hêdion*) nor which more vigorous (*deinoteros*), but it is easy to guess that Cicero is the first and Demosthenes the second. Caecilius' comparison probably suggested the comparison in *On Sublimity* (12) and possibly was a part of his own essay *On Sublimity* to which the extant treatise, often attributed to a "Longinus," is a reply. "Longinus'" criticisms make it possible to characterize Caecilius' essay briefly. It is said at the outset that Caecilius' treatment was unworthy of its exalted subject, unimaginative, and of little practical help to a writer. Caecilius had written as though no one had ever heard of sublimity and tried to demonstrate what it was by collecting many examples, but he ignored the question of how a writer can develop his own powers and attain sublimity in his work. Such a criticism could be applied to much Augustan rhetoric as it abandoned its goal of teaching

[90] Cf. Karl Boysen, *De Harpocrationis lexici fontibus quaestiones selectae*, Kiel, 1876 and Ofenloch, *op.cit.* supra n. 84, xxxix-xl and 138-93.

persuasion. Apparently Caecilius illustrated faults of
style as well, since subsequently (4) "Longinus" mentions that many examples were cited of the frigidity of
Timaeus, a Hellenistic historian who wrote in an Asian
style. Caecilius also criticized Theopompus (31). The
extant treatise lists (8) five sources of sublimity. Two
of these, powerful thought and pathos, are largely innate. Three others are matters of art: figures, diction,
and word arrangement. Caecilius is said to have omitted
"some" of these, but only pathos is explicitly mentioned
as omitted. We can be certain that figures were discussed, not only because of Caecilius' interest in the subject, but because "Longinus" refers to his discussion of
metaphor (31-32), in which he limited the number to
two or at most three in a passage. Apparently Caecilius
was the first critic to try to define the form of literary
elevation which the Greeks called *hypsos*, or sublimity.
In doing so he collected numerous examples of passages
which succeeded and passages which failed. Among the
writers rebuked were not only Theopompus and Timaeus, but almost certainly Plato; some of the defense
of Plato in *On Sublimity* is directed against Caecilius.
Caecilius, we may suspect, tended to see the source of
the quality he was seeking not so much in imagination,
certainly not in emotion, but in somewhat more technical matters of technique. His was a restrained, Atticist
conception of the sublime.

"Longinus"

Discussion of Caecilius leads easily into a consideration of the extant treatise *On Sublimity*, the most sensitive piece of literary criticism surviving from antiquity.[91]

[91] Cf. esp. the editions of W. Rhys Roberts, *Longinus On the
Sublime*, Cambridge, Eng., 1899 and D. A. Russell, *"Longinus"
On the Sublime*, Oxford, 1964. Also E. G. Sihler, "The Treatise

The scribes who copied the manuscripts did not know the name of the author and attributed the work to either Longinus, meaning Cassius Longinus of Palmyra, a famous rhetorician of the third century A.D., or to Dionysius, who was certainly interested in many of the topics discussed in the treatise. But the author's attitude toward Plato seems inconsistent with Dionysius' views, and the contents are remote from the interests of the third century. Possibly some other Longinus was the author. Modern suggestions have included the Pompeius to whom one of Dionysius' letters is addressed, a Dionysius Longinus, and Theon the writer of *Progymnasmata*, but these are no more than guesses.[92] The addressee is a certain Postumius Terentianus, presumably a Roman patron or the son of a Roman patron, but he cannot be identified either.

The date of composition is less uncertain. First, the author writes in answer to the treatise of Caecilius. Since

peri hysous, a Rhetorical and Didactic Treatise," *TAPhA* 30 (1899) xiv; H. Mutschmann, *Aufbau, Tendenz, und Quellen der Schrift vom Erhabenen*, Berlin, 1913; W. Rhys Roberts, "Longinus *On the Sublime*: some Historical and Literary Problems," *PhQ* 7 (1928) 209-19; F.R.B. Godolphin, "The Basic Critical Doctrine of Longinus, *On the Sublime*," *TAPhA* 68 (1937) 172-83; Walter Allen, Jr., "The Terentianus of the *peri hypsous*," *AJPh* 62 (1941) 51-64; E. Olsen, "The Argument of Longinus' *On the Sublime*," *MPh* 39 (1942) 225-58; G.M.A. Grube "Notes on the *peri hypsous*," *AJPh* 78 (1957) 355-74; idem, *On Great Writing* (intro. and trans.) New York, 1957; Winfried Bühler, *Beiträge zur Erklarung der Schrift vom Erhabenen*, Göttingen, 1964; Grube 340-53.

[92] For Pompeius cf. G. C. Richards, "The Authorship of the *peri hypsous*," *CQ* 32 (1938) 133-34 and G. P. Goold, "A Greek Professorial Circle at Rome," *TAPhA* 92 (1961) 168-92. For Dionysius Longinus, M. J. Boyd, "Longinus, the *Philological Discourses*, and the Essay *On the Sublime*," *CQ* 7 (1957) 39-46. For Theon, Italo Lana, "Quintiliano, il Sublime, a gli *Esercizi preparatori* di Elio Teone," *Pubbl. della Fac. di Lett. e Filos. della Univ. di Torino*, 3.4 (1951).

the latter's treatise *On Sublimity* does not seem to have
become a classic in any sense it is likely that its publication was relatively recent. There is a reference to
Theodorus (3.5), who could well be Theodorus of
Gadara whom we have just considered,[93] and there is no
reference to anyone who is known to have lived later
than the Augustan age. The author is a Greek, possibly
from Alexandria: his language is closer to that of Philo
of Alexandria than of anyone else and there are a few
similarities to Philo's thought.[94] On the other hand, the
cultural environment is definitely Roman, for Cicero is
discussed and of course Caecilius worked in Rome. The
most likely time for a Greek rhetorician or critic to have
come to Rome and to show serious interest in Latin was
the Augustan period which attracted Dionysius, Caecilius, and others. Like them, the author's real interest
is in literary style. On the other hand, the remarkable
and favorable reference to the "Jewish lawgiver" in the
treatise (9.8) is not likely to have been written in the
years immediately after A.D. 19 when the Jews came into
great disrepute in Rome and were expelled.[95] At the end
of the treatise there is a discussion of the decline of eloquence, a commonplace throughout the first century
B.C., but the similarity is closest to the discussion in the
elder Seneca. The benefits of peace seem recognized, the
political explanation of decline is not stressed, and the
moral faults of avarice and idleness are. The defense of
Plato as a stylist would be an anachronism in the later

[93] It is not, however, possible to conclude that "Longinus"
must have been a student of Theodorus. Cf. Grube, *op.cit.* supra
n. 50.
[94] Cf. Eduard Norden, "Das Genesiszitat in der Schrift vom
Erhabenen," *ADAW* 1954.1 and Russell, *op.cit.* supra n. 91,
xxix-xxx and xl-xli.
[95] Cf. Josephus, *Ant.* 18.3.5; Tac., *Ann.* 2.85.5; Suet., *Tib.* 36;
Dio 57.18.5a.

first century A.D. or subsequently, but was a real issue in the Augustan period.[96] All in all these considerations point to composition during the later years of Augustus or the earliest years of Tiberius, up to A.D. 19. This date is consistent with the contents and theories of the author, which are indeed similar to those of Dionysius or Caecilius and relatively unconnected with those of later writers like Quintilian or Hermogenes.

To modern readers the interest of *On Sublimity* has largely been as a work of sensitive criticism. Its critical excellence comes primarily from the success with which the author is able to take pieces of Greek literature which have a powerful effect upon himself and isolate the features of the passage which produce the effect.[97] The principal authors discussed are Homer, Plato, and Demosthenes, but there are many other references including a discussion of a poem of Sappho and a comparison of the style of Demosthenes and Cicero. But literary judgment was not the author's chief interest. He criticizes Caecilius for quoting many examples, but never saying how sublimity is produced. His own goal is more practical. He thinks of his readers as would-be writers or even more specifically as men in public life, in other words, orators (1.2). Their literary creations will aim at persuasion, but if they are great they may go beyond that to something much more thorough and convincing, the creation of an ecstasy in reader or audience (1.4). Some of what goes to make up excellence can hardly be taught, though genius needs art as a control and a basis of judgment (2), and

---

[96] Cf., e.g., Quint. 10.1.81; Tac., *Dial.* 31.9; Friedrich Walsdorff, *Die antiken Urteile über Platons Stil*, Bonn, 1927.

[97] The best examples are perhaps those in chs. 9 and 16. Russell, *op.cit.* supra n. 91, 89 on ch. 9 quotes Gibbon's *Journal* of 3 Sept. 1762; "The ninth chapter is one of the finest monuments of antiquity . . . he tells me his own feelings upon reading . . . and tells them with such energy that he communicates them."

to some extent quality can be attained by understanding and especially by imitation (13.2-4), not a servile imitation, but one which captures the creative spirit of the masters.[98] "Longinus" assumes and utilizes the traditional rhetorical system, but his rhetoric is a highly philosophical one, and his unembarrassed objective is not technical excellence, but genuine greatness. No ancient critic is so clear about the difference between what is great and what inferior.

"Longinus" is the first of several authors who might be said to offer a kind of program to reinvigorate literature, or better in his case, to utilize and bring to full expression the genius which exists, but that program is not one of simple techniques or new educational methods or even political change. It requires the individual soul of the writer to free itself from everything material and temporary, and to give expression to the ages of his own greatness.[99] The program was clearly not one for mass implementation, but it had a certain validity. Partly through Stoicism a few imperial writers, the younger Seneca and Persius, for example, or the emperor Marcus Aurelius, did by conscious effort achieve a relatively universal vision and thus greatness.

"Longinus" defines sublimity, *hypsos*, only as a summit and excellence of literature (1.3), but he appears to mean by it those flashes of greatness which make a passage immortal.[100] *Hypsos*, his examples show, occurs in short inspired bits. It is not a style or quality of an entire work, even of the greatest, and is certainly not to be

[98] Cf. Atkins 2.223.
[99] Cf. Charles P. Segal, "*Hypsos* and the Problem of Cultural Decline in the *De sublimitate*," *HSPh* 64 (1959) 121-46.
[100] Cf. Grube's article, *op.cit.* supra n. 91. The term sublimity was a happy thought of D. A. Russell in his translation "*Longinus*" *On Sublimity*, Oxford 1965, avoiding the sentimental religiosity of "the sublime."

identified with the grand style. Any style may have moments of sublimity; the effect is one of irresistible ecstasy (1.4). There are, "Longinus" says (8), five sources of this great quality:

"First and most important is a power of forming great thoughts, as I set forth also in my work on Xenophon. Second is frequent and overpowering emotion. These two sources of *hypsos* are for the most part inborn faculties, the others are produced through art: the molding of figures in a particular way (and figures are of course of two sorts, those of thought and those of speech), and in addition noble diction, of which the parts are choice of words and their metaphorical and artificial usage. The fifth source of greatness, and something which links together everything before it, is distinguished and exalted composition."

Since "Longinus" had insisted on the importance of the first quality in another work, it was probably a favorite point with him. He quotes his own earlier statement that *"hypsos* is the echo of a great soul"* (9.1). He does not mean philosophical or political thought or some special brilliance in reasoning, but a quality best seen in poetry or descriptive prose where the author's own *imagination* makes it possible for him to look at something in a much grander way than another might. Homer's description of the noble silence, rather than bickering, with which Ajax meets Odysseus in the underworld is an example, or the utterances of Alexander the Great (9.2), or the serene picture of the advance of Poseidon in the *Iliad* (9.8). It is here that "Longinus" makes a remarkable reference to Moses and the *hypsos* he feels in the biblical description of the creation of light. There is some similarity in kind if not in quality between this imaginative insight and the conceits and hyperboles of the de-

374

claimers, but the latter often involve too great a striving for novelty (3.3-5). "Longinus" gives a number of examples of failures in conception by earlier authors. Although the specific problem of literary decadence in contemporary times is reserved for the last chapter of the work, where it is discussed almost as an appendix, the whole treatise begs the question of whether the *hypsos* which "Longinus" finds in classical authors can in fact be produced at all any longer. "Longinus' " answer to this appears to be yes, it can, because the necessary greatness of soul can occur at any time.[101] The writer must write for the ages, not for the moment. He should imagine Homer or Demosthenes listening to his words and try to satisfy their judgment (14).

Pathos, or emotion, is the second ingredient of *hypsos*. It was a quality not always successfully managed by writers after the Augustan poets, and the primary reasons were probably the attempt to outdo other descriptions and lack of understanding of the emotions which the writer tried to describe or awake (15.8). Caecilius, according to "Longinus" (8.1-2), had omitted pathos entirely from his description of emotion, perhaps on Atticist principles. Many good writers thought that no emotion was better than false emotion, and even "Longinus" does not insist that it is an essential ingredient of all *hypsos*; indeed, some forms of pathos such as pity, grief, and fear are unsuitable (8.2). Much of Greek tragedy is thus removed from the possibility of attaining *hypsos*. What "*Longinus*" most admires is the pathos of enthusiasm or indignation as seen in Homer or Demosthenes. Despite the outline of chapter eight, specific discussion of pathos is lacking from *On Sublimity*, and at the end it is reserved for treatment in a separate treatise. There may have been some explanation of the reason for this in the

[101] Cf. Segal, *op.cit.* supra n. 99, 136.

lacuna[102] in chapter nine, and actually some of what is said in that part of the treatise relates to pathos, for example, the discussion of the transition from the strong emotions of the *Iliad* to the lesser emotions and emphasis on character of the *Odyssey*, which "Longinus" regards as a work of the poet's old age (9.11-15). We might justly conclude that even genius cannot indefinitely maintain pathos.

The first two sources of *hypsos* are often regarded as parts of invention, the first general heading of most rhetorical treatises, the other three as parts of style. In discussion of the latter, "Longinus" keeps much closer to conventional rhetorical theory. Although he avoids the interminable lists of figures which had become usual, figures are to him a vital part of good writing and he tries to explain their function and psychological bases.[103] He is, of course, an ancient critic trained in ancient rhetorical education, and he assumes that a process of ornamentation is part of good writing. What is appropriate in poetry is not necessarily appropriate in prose. His most valuable point is probably that figures and tropes, even though artificial, can seem natural in a context which is striking in thought or emotion (17; 32).

The discussion of diction contains two interesting points. One is the admission of vigorous colloquial words into literary vocabulary provided they are expressive (31), though subsequently undignified words are objected to in a passage which seems out of its logical place (43). Apparently the crucial distinction is the suitability and meaningfulness of the word in the particular context. The other point is a famous digression

---

[102] All extant manuscripts appear to be copies of *Parisinus* 2036 which has lost folia in six places. About a third of the treatise is probably missing.
[103] Cf. Atkins 2.229.

which extends from chapter thirty-three through thirty-six on the inferiority of flawless mediocrity—as seen, for example, in Apollonius of Rhodes, Lysias, or Hyperides —to true greatness, even with an occasional failure in noble effort—as seen in Homer, Plato, or Demosthenes. Though certainly a classicist, "Longinus" is by no means a strict Atticist, either in theory or practice of vocabulary or in models for imitation. He briefly considers (39-42) the fifth source of *hypsos*, composition, and tries (39) the critical device which Dionysius of Halicarnassus had developed of rewriting a passage to show how important its rhythm is. The treatise ends with a brief discussion of the decline of eloquence, to which we shall return in chapter six.

"Longinus" excels other ancient critics in his vision and imagination and at the same time in the practicality which he demonstrates. These qualities at Rome are found otherwise only in the greatest of the Augustan writers, especially in Virgil and in Horace, while "Longinus' " hopes for literature are best paralleled in the hopes of Augustus for the Roman state under his new program. That program made use of some of the traditional techniques of rhetoric, but also developed a new rhetoric of its own. Before continuing with the history of oratory and rhetorical theory, it will be of interest to consider the wider role of rhetoric in Augustan Rome.

CHAPTER FIVE

Augustan Rhetoric and
Augustan Literature

In addition to the oratory and criticism which we have considered, other artistic products of the Augustan age contain manifestations of rhetoric. This chapter is a brief excursus, intended only to suggest some ways in which the work of Augustus himself or the writings of Virgil, Horace, Ovid, and Livy relate to rhetoric. In none of these cases should rhetoric be regarded as a satisfactory basis for evaluating the total achievement of the man, though there is a noticeable increase in the influence of school rhetoric on Livy and Ovid, the younger of the writers, contrasted with Virgil and Horace. The situation of Augustus is unique.

Augustus

As a practitioner of the art of persuasion the greatest rhetorician of antiquity was the man born C. Octavius, who after adoption by Julius Caesar in 44 B.C. is known as Octavian and in 27 became the emperor Augustus. He succeeded, where Isocrates and Alexander, Cicero and Caesar had failed, in adapting old traditions to new needs so as to create a political institution which embraced the entire world of western civilization and proved stable enough to endure for centuries.

Augustus was the grandnephew and designated heir of Julius Caesar.[1] At the time of Caesar's assassination he

[1] The basic ancient sources are Cicero's letters from 44 and 43; Augustus' own account of his deeds, *Res gestae divi Augusti* (translated by Frederick W. Shipley in the Loeb Library edition of Velleius Paterculus, London, 1924); Velleius Paterculus 2.58.123; Suet., *Aug.*; Appian, *Civil Wars* 2-5; Dio Cassius 44-56.

was eighteen years old and studying rhetoric with Apollodorus at Apollonia. With remarkable resolution he returned to Rome to claim his inheritance and to plunge into the dangerous game of politics in competition with Antony, Lepidus, the tyrannicides, and the senatorial leaders, including Cicero, for control of the reins of state. His call of vengeance for Caesar brought him support from many of Caesar's followers, and the failure of his leading opponents to realize his ambition, his ability, and his ruthlessness gave him an advantage in outwitting them. He showed a remarkable cleverness at manipulating political and military forces, joining first with the senate against Antony, then with Antony against the senate. Antony won the battle of Philippi for him against Brutus and Cassius in 42, and Agrippa won the battle of Actium for him against Antony in 31. Unlike Caesar, he lacked military genius, but his instinct to use others secured him military victory, and by manipulating public opinion, by giving new meaning to old words, and by inspiring enthusiasm for a national cause he was able to convert what otherwise might have been a temporary despotism into a political system which disguised military autocracy in the venerable dress of republican institutions. He was, of course, aided by a general weariness with civil war and by the fact that his policies offered solid benefits to all orders of society; as time passed he seemed more the responsible statesman than the ambitious opportunist and in the end the patriotism of his lasting achievements outshone the cruelty of his early methods. The greatest blot on his memory were the pro-

---

Important modern works include T. Rice E. Holmes, *The Architect of the Roman Empire*, 2 vols., Oxford, 1928-31; Mason Hammond, *The Augustan Principate*, Cambridge, 1933; *CAH* 10; Ronald Syme, *The Roman Revolution*, Oxford, 1939; Donald Earl, *The Age of Augustus*, New York, 1968.

scriptions in which, however reluctantly, he joined with Antony and Lepidus in 43 and which encompassed the murder of Cicero. Lepidus was early eclipsed, but for twelve years Antony remained a potent threat. Caesar had not been a master of controlling men's minds: he was too straightforward and too impatient. Antony was subtler and less scrupulous and provided a worthy opponent on whom Octavian sharpened the blade of his art of propaganda.[2] Antony's appeal was imaginative, romantic, and personal. He could easily be made to seem adventurous, radical, dangerous, and even foreign. Octavian was in effect perhaps more radical still, but able to draw to himself all the weight of Roman tradition: social, political, and intellectual. He was on the side of the Roman state, the Roman family, and the Roman gods, and at Actium in 31 B.C. these combined to put to flight Antony, Cleopatra, and the barbarians of the East.

With Antony removed, Octavian stood alone and proceeded to rebuild the state and to engender out of cold blood a new age of living gold. The position he created for himself in stages was summed up in the honorific title Augustus, taken in 27 B.C. He excelled others in the substance of military power, in the number of titles he

[2] Cf. Alfred Sturminger, *Politische Propaganda in der Weltgeschichte*, Salzburg, 1938, 42-59; Syme, *op.cit.* supra n. 1, 459-75; M. P. Charlesworth, "*Pietas* and *victoria*: the Emperor and the Citizen," *JRS* 33 (1943) 1-10; Jean Béranger, *Recherches sur l'aspect idéologique du principat*, Basel, 1953; Hans Volkmann, *Cleopatra: a Study in Politics and Propaganda*, London, 1958; Chester G. Starr, *Civilization and the Caesars: the Intellectual Revolution in the Roman Empire*, Ithaca, 1954, 33-62; Charles Wirszubski, *Libertas as a Political Ideal at Rome during the Late Republic and Early Empire*, Cambridge, Eng., 1950; Harold Mattingly, *Roman Imperial Civilization*, London, 1957, esp. 47; J. K. Newman, *Augustus and the New Poetry*, Brussels, 1967, 9-30.

held, and in the prestige of authority, but not in the power of any one office. In theory his power was based on his position as a patron with clients throughout the world, on the proconsular imperium, which made him governor of several key provinces, but with the right to delegate power to grateful lieutenants, and on the tribunician power which in the city of Rome gave him the popular appeal of a defender of the people and solid right to convene the senate and veto its will. No crass kingship, no nervous break with republican offices, no dictatorship, not even a censorship was permitted or needed. Augustus never sought, but was always prevailed upon to assume, his sacred trusts when the state needed him. The need continued until the day of his death in A.D. 14. On his deathbed he asked if he had not played well in the comedy of life (Suet., *Aug.* 99).

Augustus studied rhetoric with Apollodorus (Suet., *Aug.* 89) and continued to practice declamation during the early part of his public career (*ibid.* 84). All the sources indicate that he was the master of traditional rhetoric and an able speaker. He had little sympathy with anything except the simple style, but demanded that it be elegant and tasteful. He hated epigram, artificial word order, or anything which detracted from clarity (*ibid.* 86). We may assume that his standards were not unlike those of Julius Caesar and his style may be generally associated with the neo-Atticist movement. It is likely that his stylistic tastes and early interest in declamation were imitated by many of his contemporaries.

For all his training and ability, Augustus apparently never made a major speech. We have references to his delivery of funeral orations, though none had any special effect, and he addressed the troops and citizens from time to time and the senate frequently, but primarily he used oratory to present his decisions rather than to impel others to action.[3] As a result, his utterances became exceedingly deliberate. Suetonius reports (*ibid.* 84) that to avoid the danger of forgetting anything and to avoid wasting time memorizing what he wanted to say, he adopted the technique of reading everything. This applied not only to his formal oratory, but in conversations with individuals and even with his wife he read from notes prepared ahead of time, "lest he say too much or too little!"

To win men's minds without opening the door to the dangers of public debate Augustus developed new techniques of verbal and visual persuasion which took over some of the functions and adapted some of the methods of traditional oratory. The orator becomes a standard form in imperial sculpture and the iconography borrows from the rules of gesture and delivery.[4] Coins, monuments, and buildings employ devices analogous to rhetorical commonplaces, as when Augustus adorned the doorway of his ostentatiously simple house, and sometimes his coins as well, with the laurel of the victor and civic crown of one who had saved the life of a Roman citizen. Something rather close to methods of rhetorical proof is inherent in the repetition of key ideas on coins or inscriptions, such as the claim that Augustus had reestablished the republic. There was appeal to ethos when the emperor was shown on a frieze with shining honest

[3] References in Henrica Malcovati, *Caesaris Augusti operum fragmenta*, Turin, 1928. For a fragment of Augustus' funeral speech for Agrippa cf. L. Koenen, "Die *laudatio funebris* des Augustus für Agrippa auf einem neuen Papyrus," ZPE 5 (1970) 217-83.

[4] Cf. Richard Brilliant, "Gesture and Rank in Roman Art: the Use of Gesture to Denote Status in Roman Sculpture and Coinage," *Memoirs of the Connecticut Academy of Arts and Sciences* 14 (1963).

face performing some good or pious task, and to pathos when the horrors of barbarian invasion are represented as repelled.

One of the most interesting features of the new Augustan "rhetoric" is its use of imitation. Although we cannot claim that this imitation is a deliberate counterpart of the imitation taught by classicizing rhetoricians such as the neo-Atticists, a similar philosophy lies behind the technique: excellence can be imparted to the contemporary by a careful study of the noble quality of the past. Instead of taking classical Greek writers as models for literary imitation, the new Augustan "rhetoric" inculcated a moral imitation of the creed of heroes of the past, especially the half-legendary heroes of earlier Rome. The goal was a style of life: patriotic, serious, self-sacrificing. The poetry of Horace and Virgil and the history of Livy set forth these models in the grandest terms, and Augustus lost no opportunity to present them visually to the Romans. The best illustration is the new forum which he constructed and which is called after him. In the center stood the temple of Mars the Avenger, the god of his victory over the assassins of his father, and around it in a semicircle a Roman hall of fame, with statues of the approved models of the past in triumphal dress, while to the side, greater than life size, rose a statue of the emperor himself.[5] In the dedicatory edict the emperor claimed that his object had been "that he himself, while he lived, and the rulers of future ages, might be required by the citizens to turn their attention to the lives of these men as exemplars of their own lives" (Suet., *Aug.* 31.5). A more exquisite, and better preserved example of Augustan rhetoric at its best is the *ara pacis Augustae*

[5] Cf. Henry T. Rowell, "Vergil and the Forum of Augustus," *AJPh* 62 (1941) 261-76 and Paul MacKendrick, *The Mute Stones Speak*, New York, 1960, 145-50.

in the *campus Martius,* the altar of Augustan peace which blends the human pageantry and achievements of contemporary Rome with the world of nature and the legends of Rome's foundation.[6] This is not oratory, but a manifestation of epideictic rhetoric, an eloquent encomium of Rome and Augustus with its own invention, arrangement, style, and delivery.

Augustus' new rhetoric was reasonably successful. It united and stabilized the Roman world and created ideals and symbols which were long influential. Most of his successors imitated Augustus' techniques, though none with his subtlety. He was aided by a remarkable group of writers who had the patriotism to look beyond personal resentments and reservations to the ideals implicit in the new policies and who gave eloquent expression to the *pax Augusta.* Maecenas and Messalla were often a vital link between the emperor and contemporary writers, and one suspects that they channeled communications in both directions: not only the emperor's wishes, but the objections and suggestions of the poets, for there never was a real possibility that writers of the genius of Virgil or Horace would be content to sing as directed. The result was a golden age of literature which combined traditional rhetorical techniques and the new persuasive symbols of Augustus into a permanent expression of Roman ideals.

Rhetoric and Poetry

Latin poetry, and especially the poetry of the empire, is regularly said to be rhetorical.[7] Chiefly what is meant

[6] Cf. MacKendrick, *op.cit.* supra n. 6, 152-66; Earl, *op.cit.* supra n. 1, 113-16.

[7] Cf. Norden 883-93; Kenneth Burke, *Counter-Statement,* New York, 1931; W. S. Howell, "Rhetoric and Poetics: a Plea for the Recognition of the Two Literatures," *The Classical Tra-*

is that poetry exhibits techniques learned in the rhetorical schools, but the relationship between rhetoric and poetry can become rather complex. Poetry is fundamentally a significant imitation of reality. The poet presents a world in which certain qualities of interest to him are defined or shaped more clearly than they often seem in the world of nature. His objective is more often understanding than change, and to that extent poetry is closer to philosophy and to history than to oratory. In most of Greek poetry the qualities in which poets are interested are moral ones. A recurrent theme, for example, is justice and injustice. From contemplation of the experience of Achilles or Prometheus or Electra or Hippolytus the audience may go back to everyday life with increased understanding, but not necessarily stirred to action against injustice, which was often viewed in antiquity as a permanent quality of life.

Rhetoric is basically the art of persuasion and thus directed at change: at the correction or prevention of injustice, at the taking of expedient public action, at attitude change about people or things. In pursuit of persuasion, Greek rhetoricians constructed an elaborate system of techniques of argument, arrangement, style, and the like. The presence of these secondary characteristics in literature is often taken to be proof of the presence of rhetoric itself; in a similar way oratory is sometimes said to be poetic if it contains the secondary characteristics of poetry, such as rhythmical and acoustical effects. One factor which complicates the situation is the development of what may be labeled a rhetorical philosophy. In its simplest form this is a confidence in debate: rhetorical exposition is necessary for the choice of action

dition: *Literary and Historical Studies in Honor of Harry Caplan*, Ithaca, 1966, 374-90.

because the society in which we live is so complicated
that reliable decision can be made only on the basis of
full exposition. To many people or in many circumstances, however, the basis of these choices remains indefinitely uncertain. The rhetorician's response to this
is not to abandon his rhetoric, but to dismiss the importance of the choice. He turns his attention to technique and invites the judge to choose, not on the basis
of substance or principle, but on the basis of aesthetic
or emotional preference. The employment of rhetorical
technique for itself is far more persistent than confidence in debate and becomes an accepted value when
debate is not possible. At Rome the phenomenon is best
seen in declamation. In a sense this is a turn by oratory
in the direction of poetry, but it lacks the significance
of poetry and is an imitation not of reality but of art.

Of course, poetry can be rhetorical in the true sense
of the word: it can aim at action or attitude change,
and its rhetoric can occur on two levels. In dramatic or
narrative poetry a character can employ rhetoric to persuade another, and in any poetic form the poet can employ rhetoric to influence the attitude of his reader. The
first of these levels is common enough in Greek literature
from Homer on, where there is often poetic oratory and
sometimes even formal debate by characters. The second
occurred in a rudimentary form when Greek philosophers like Empedocles versified their works, but as a
high artistic product it is mostly a creation of the
Romans who seem to have expected a practical seriousness from their poets. Latin epic and tragic poetry from
the time of Naevius and Ennius and later lyric poetry as
well included a strong persuasive element, such as the
call to national destiny or to a better life, and the only
original Roman poetic form, satire, always contained the
lurking hope that man could be improved if he saw the

386

folly of his ways. It was not difficult for Roman poets to add the new Augustan rhetoric or propaganda to their armory of techniques and materials.[8]

With the arrival of the empire the opportunities for persuasion in oratory decreased. We have already seen the process in the case of Augustan orators. The persuasive qualities of poetry were less inhibited. Under Augustus they reach their highest achievement, while several later emperors went out of their way to encourage poets. Poetry can criticize without exacerbating. It can present the evils of tyranny to a tyrant or the virtues of freedom to a despot as long as it gives the impression of aiming primarily at literary distinction and preserves its innate ambiguity and universality. There are limits which could roughly be defined from the experience of Ovid or Lucan or Juvenal. But at a time when political oratory grew silent, the poets continued to teach, to charm, and to move with the techniques of both the old and the new rhetoric. All of the various rhetorical qualities of poetry are evident in Virgil's work, though he shows at the same time an aversion to rhetoric in its more academic manifestations.

Virgil

P. Vergilius Maro apparently had a more or less ordinary rhetorical education, begun at Milan near his home, but completed at Rome possibly with Epidius, with whom Antony and Octavian also studied at one time.[9]

***

[8] Cf. Gordon Williams, *Tradition and Originality in Roman Poetry*, Oxford, 1968, esp. chs. 6 and 9.

[9] Virgil was born in 70 B.C. and thus seven years before Augustus. From the ancient biographies it would appear that his education at Cremona, Milan, and Rome fell in the period 55-50. The *Eclogues* were written in the years just before and just after 40, the *Georgics* between 37 and 29, the *Aeneid* between 29 and Virgil's death in 19. The reference to Epidius comes from

According to the Suetonian-Donatan biography (15-16), he pleaded one case before a panel of judges, but only one, for he was very slow and ineffective in speech, though later in life he became excellent at recitation (*ibid.* 29). Possibly the case was his own, connected in some way with the loss and recovery of the farm to which he later refers in *Eclogues* one and nine. Ovid too had a brief experience in public life, and it is probable enough that many young men experimented to see what success they would have in using their rhetorical training before turning to other activities. Virgil went from rhetoric to philosophy and to that philosophy in particular which most scorned rhetoric, Epicureanism. We have a collection of fifteen poems called the *Catalepton*, at least some of which are probably by Virgil, written early in life.[10] The fifth could date from the time when Virgil decided to study with the famous Epicurean philosopher Siro:

> Get away from me, you rhetoricians' jars swollen,
>   but empty,
> Words bursting with un-Greek hot air.[11]
> And you too, Selius and Tarquitius and Varro,
>   You breed of pedants dripping with fat.
> Get away, empty cymbal of youth.
>   And you, O Sextus Sabinus, care of my cares,
> Farewell; farewell now, my handsome friends.

---

a biography in the Berne manuscript; cf. Jacob Brummer, *Vitae Virgilianae*, Leipzig, 1933. Epidius is known from Suet., *De gram. et rhet.* 28.

[10] Cf. Norman W. DeWitt, *Virgil's Biographia Litteraria*, Toronto, 1923, 33-35 and R.E.H. Westendorp Boerma, *P. Vergili Maronis Catalepton*, Assen, 1949.

[11] Accepting Münscher's emendation of the text, cf. L. P. Wilkinson, "Virgil, *Catalepton* v, 1-2," *CQ* 43 (1949) 140.

I set sail for happy havens,
   Seeking the learned discourse of the great Siro.
And I will free my life from every care.
Get away, Latin Muses, you too get away, I
   mean it,
   Sweet Latin Muses, for I will confess what
   is true,
You have been sweet. And yet, come see again
   My pages, but do it from time and time and
   modestly.

Virgil here objects to the faults of declamation in an iambic verse form traditionally used for invective. The poem, with its abrupt changes of mood, reflects his dislike of rhetoric and his inability to escape his own literary impulses.

This aversion to rhetoric in its academic form continued with Virgil: contempt for the life of the forum is a feature of the panegyric of country life which ends the second *Georgic* (502; 508-10) and oratory, with sculpture, is dismissed as an art for Greeks in the climactic lines of the sixth *Aeneid* (849). Yet there is some modification. The early *Bucolics* or *Eclogues* are Virgil's least rhetorical works. The *Georgics* already have a cause to plead, the virtues of the agricultural life, and begin to draw on some of the themes of the new Augustan rhetoric. An example is the end of the first *Georgic* (466-514). Under different circumstances or in the hands of another author, the substance might have taken the form of an oration in the senate or to the people; as it is, highly emotional verse finds a peroration for the poem in presenting the evil condition of Rome and looking to Octavian as the only hope of salvation. The first point is proved by examples of portents. Example of course is one of the basic devices of rhetorical argument. There are a variety of rhetorical figures including rhetorical question and personification. Details make the brief pictures vivid, what the rhetoricians would call *enargeia* (cf., e.g., *Ad Her.* 4.68-69). There is hyperbole, hyperbaton, epithet, metaphor, litotes, metonymy. The second point is made by prayer to the gods, by apostrophe to Octavian, by another listing of examples, this time of the evils he should correct, and finally by a simile. What we mean in speaking of various levels of rhetoric can be seen in this passage. First there are the techniques taught in rhetorical schools, though of course long shared with poetry. Secondly, there is persuasive intent: the passage was apparently written before the battle of Actium and Virgil is making a real appeal to Octavian to save Rome and restore lasting peace. Thirdly, the passage is a part of the new Augustan rhetoric as well. Though written before Actium, it was published after the victory and has become a part of the program of Augustus, Maecenas, and Virgil to win men's minds. The horrors depicted are to be contrasted by the reader with the peace secured; the greatness of the empire is implicit in the geographical list: Rome, Sicily, Germany, the Alps, the Po, Greece, the East to the Euphrates. The gods have shown their love. Octavian has risen to his duty. He succeeds where Caesar failed. And the tragic simile at the end is only a haunting "it might have been."

All of these features can be found in the *Aeneid* on a much vaster scale. At the level of rhetorical technique Virgil's diction is less remarkable than his composition: he avoids all fads and aims at a pure but flexible Latinity. A slight flavor of archaism is often imparted to the language of the gods.[12] In composition Virgil's greatest achievement has been thought to be his adaptation of

[12] Cf. L. R. Palmer, *The Latin Language*, London, 1954, 111-14.

the periodic style to the hexameter, something not far advanced in earlier poetry.[13] This is accomplished with high emotional effect by means of parataxis and such figures as rhetorical question, antithesis, anaphora, and isocolon.[14] Figures of speech certainly abound, but again it must be remembered that many of these were traditional poetic devices and perhaps only the commonest and most obvious, such as rhetorical question or paraleipsis, should be labeled clearly rhetorical. It has been rightly pointed out that the rhetorical quality of passages in Virgil often comes not so much from the use of figures as from their frequency.[15] The unique subjective style which Virgil developed is partly dependent on these devices; whether or not the conception of that style was influenced by rhetoric is difficult to determine. In a sense Virgil is like an advocate, identifying himself at will with his client, in this case his characters. But Greek tragedy and subjective poetry as written by Catullus also contributed to this achievement and it is furthermore a very personal development of his own genius.[16] In the Homeric poems the greatness is generally in the conception, as "Longinus" stresses. In the *Aeneid*, though there is imaginative grasp and nobility of conception, most readers have found the excellence highest in the style and expression. In almost every line of Virgil there is some felicitous combination of thought with words or

[13] Cf. W. F. Jackson Knight, *Roman Vergil*, London, 1944, 180-281; Palmer, *op.cit.* supra n. 12, 115; L. P. Wilkinson, *Golden Latin Artistry*, Cambridge, Eng., 1963, 189-212. Periodicity is played down by Kenneth Quinn, *Virgil's Aeneid: a Critical Description*, London, 1968, 414-40.

[14] Cf. Wilhelm Kroll, "Die originalität Vergil's," *NJA* 21 (1908) 513-31, esp. 524ff.

[15] Cf. M. L. Clarke, "Rhetorical Influences in the *Aeneid*," *G & R* 18 (1949) 25.

[16] Cf. Brooks Otis, *Virgil: a Study in Civilized Poetry*, Oxford, 1963, 41-96 and 385.

sounds or rhythms which have echoed ever since in the ears of humanity. Virgil's genius contributed to Roman taste for *sententiae*, but set a standard of profundity and poignancy of which the declaimers despaired. The *Aeneid* became a classic and a textbook on its publication. It canonized the standards of poetic language in Latin, furnished a vast source of quotations, and was quarried more frequently and more consistently by the rhetoricians than was any other Latin poem.[17]

The *Aeneid*, in conformity to the epic tradition, makes considerable use of oratory; there is a smaller percentage of total speech than in Homer,[18] but Virgil's speeches are usually more formal, less conversational. Some of them approximate the conditions of real oratory,[19] and it is natural that these conform most closely to rhetorical rules. Rhetorical analysis of speeches in Virgil has been practiced since antiquity, for example by Macrobius at the end of the fourth century and Eduard Norden at the end of the nineteenth.[20] The longest speeches are Aeneas' extended narrative of his wanderings which consumes books two and three and Anchises' remarks to Aeneas which take up the second half of book six. Both

---

[17] Quintilian, for example, refers to specific passages in Virgil about 150 times, primarily in his discussion of style in books 8 and 9.

[18] There are said to be 331 speeches in the *Aeneid* making up about 38% whereas speeches make up about 50% of the Homeric poems, cf. H. C. Lipscomb, "Aspects of the Speech in Vergil and the later Roman epic," CW 2 (1908-1909) 114-17.

[19] Cf. Clarke, *op.cit.* supra n. 15, 14-27, esp. 20ff.

[20] Cf. Macrobius, *Saturnalia* 4 and 5.1; Eduard Norden, "Ein Panegyricus auf Augustus in Vergils Aeneis VI. 791-805," *RhM* 54 (1899) 466-82; K. Billmayer, *Rhetorische Studien zu den Reden in Vergils Aeneis*, Würzburg, 1932; Roger Allain, "Éloquence et poésie chez Virgile (d'après deux discours d'Énée)," *Revue universitaire* 56 (1947) 219-25. In reply to Norden cf. Franz De Ruyt, "L'élégie di Marcellus dans l'Énéide: rhétorique ou lyrisme?" *LEC* 2 (1933) 138-44.

of these are beyond the scope of ordinary oratory, though Norden analyzed the latter as a panegyric of Rome. Closer to the circumstances of ordinary oratory and to the materials taught in the schools is the appeal of the Greek Sinon to the Trojans in book two (69ff.). It can be analyzed as a rhetorical *suasoria*.[21] What is most remarkable is the effective ethos by which Sinon makes his situation seem a result of his own friendship for Palamedes and the wickedness of Ulysses.

The scenes between Dido and Aeneas in book four, especially when Aeneas prepares to depart (296ff.), are excellent examples of the rhetoric of pathos, as used also by dramatists like Euripides. Dido reminds Aeneas of their love, his oaths, the unsuitability of the season for navigation, the fact that he is sailing to an unknown destination, then pleads with him by the hand of friendship, their abortive marriage, the unpopularity she has earned because of him, her own danger, her desolation. All of this is rhetorical in the primary sense of the word; it aims at persuasion. The greatest literary achievement of the book, however, is Dido's final scene on the funeral pyre, and especially the imagery of light and dark, day and night, life and death woven into it with the funeral pyre beneath and the Sun above. To the latter she addresses her emotional plea for vengeance, eternal enmity between Carthage and Rome, and a future avenger who is of course Hannibal. Is this rhetorical? Some persuasion is intended and the technique is a magnificently full development of the possibilities inherent in the situation, which had become the field of rhetoric. Both the style and the imagined delivery are within the scope of formal

21 Cf. Richard Heinze, *Virgils epische Technik*, Leipzig and Berlin, 1928, 8-12 and Henry W. Prescott, *The Development of Virgil's Art*, Chicago, 1927, 306-10. Heinze 431-35 discusses Rhetorik in Virgil with a warning against over-attributing poetic qualities to rhetoric.

rhetorical teaching. Much of the *Aeneid* is obviously
Homeric in inspiration.[22] What is un-Homeric about
this passage is not so much that it lacks a direct Homeric
model as the care with which it is worked out, a habit
encouraged by the rhetorical schools. Inspiration is not
lacking, but it finds its expression through conscious use
of art. The extremely developed use of a set of symbols
as employed here is certainly not part of the rhetorical
tradition and hardly occurs in oratory; it is essentially
poetic and its principal antecedent is in the work of the
tragic poets.

The passage of the *Aeneid* which most accurately reflects the conditions of political debate is the scene between Drances and Turnus in book eleven. Drances is
first sent by King Latinus to the Trojans to arrange a
truce for the burial of the dead. He is resentful of Turnus
and seizes the occasion for a brief tribute to Aeneas, begun with a series of rhetorical questions (11.124ff.). He
then returns among the Latins and fans popular ill will
against the war and Turnus. He thus seems a factionalist
in the tradition of the late first century B.C. Though in
the long run he is on the side of destiny and the right,
his emotions are represented primarily as cowardice and
hatred of Turnus. Commentators[23] have sometimes
thought that Drances was Virgil's picture of Cicero,
while Turnus might possibly be thought of as influenced
by Antony; Demosthenes, Cicero, and the typical orator
was thought to cut a poor figure on the battlefield, and

[22] Cf. Macrobius 5.2-10 and G. N. Knauer, *Die Aeneis und
Homer: Studien zur poetischen Technik Virgils mit Listen der
Homerzitate in der Aeneis*, Göttingen, 1964.

[23] Cf. John Connington, *The Works of Virgil with a Commentary III*, London, 1883, on 11.336; Th. Zielinski, *Cicero im
Wandel der Jahrhunderte*, Leipzig and Berlin, 1912, 11 and 279-
80.

Cicero had of course been torn between Pompey and Caesar, then became the implacable foe of Antony. After envoys return to the Latins from Diomedes reporting that he has refused them his help, Latinus calls a council. He proposes giving up land to the invading Trojans or else building them a fleet in which to sail away. Drances then steps forward and is briefly described (11.336ff.). He is goaded on by the glory of Turnus, and of course ambition and competition were very strong influences upon Roman orators. He is described as eloquent, but cold in war, not too bad in council, powerful in sedition. His mother is noble, but his father is low-born. He is thus the *novus homo*, like Cicero, anxious to rise. His speech could be divided into something like the usual oratorical parts. Primarily it attacks Turnus and accuses him of pride, for Virgil is trying to build up a picture of Turnus as a tragic hero and thus a worthy opponent to Aeneas. There is irony in the speech which ends by taunting Turnus with cowardice, a dangerous argument, for cowardice is Drances' own weakness. In his reply Turnus exploits the situation fully and draws out all the rhetorical vigor available to the determined patriot. Yet Drances' words continue to rankle him in the next book (12.644).

The picture of the traditional orator in the *Aeneid* is thus somewhat unflattering, but Virgil acknowledges the power of speech on the part of those who have a cause to plead. This includes gods like Venus and Juno, whose debate at the beginning of book ten contains some of the most spirited rhetorical fireworks in the poem. Aeneas, like Augustus, makes rather little use of rhetoric, though he can effectively encourage his men (as 1.198-207) or successfully appeal to Evander for an alliance (8.127-51). The passage in which the orator is most

favorably presented is a celebrated simile in book one
(148-56) where Neptune calms the storm roused against
Aeneas by the intrigue of Juno:

> Just as among a great people, when as often
> happens there rises
> Sedition, and the common mob seethes with
> unrest;
> Firebrands and stones begin to fly; anger
> furnishes arms;
> Then if by chance they see some great man,
> distinguished
> By his sense of duty and his deeds, they grow
> silent and await him
> With pricked up ears. He controls their minds
> with words and calms their breasts.
> Thus all the crash of the deep fell silent, when
> its sire
> Looking out over the sea, borne on under a
> cleared sky, steered
> his horses and as the chariot flew on behind
> He gave them full rein.

The specific source of the simile is perhaps an incident
involving the younger Cato,[24] but the figure is that of the
idealized *bonus orator* whom Cicero sought. The lines
are in fact quoted by Quintilian (12.1.27) in the chapter
in which he completes his picture of the perfect orator.
It is difficult to believe that Virgil really means us to
think of a traditional republican orator; the *Georgics*
had disposed of that concept. The only real possibility
for an authoritative peacemaker is the person of Augus-

[24] Cf. Plutarch, *Cato the Younger* 44.4 and Viktor Pöschl,
The Art of Vergil: Image and Symbol in the Aeneid, Ann Arbor,
1962, 20-21.

tus just as Quintilian's perfect orator could hardly be achieved except in the person of the emperor.

This brings us to the final level of rhetoric in the *Aeneid*, the level of the persuasive exposition of the Augustan ideal. Rhetoric in this sense is not limited to speeches: the poem as a whole is a statement of Roman destiny and of Roman virtue, but certain passages make more specific use of devices of Augustan rhetoric. Contemporary times are associated with heroic myth; the end of war and a golden age of peace are prophesied; gods and men are united; in a few passages Augustus and his work are specifically mentioned. The major contexts are the great speech of Jupiter in book one, the pageantry of future Roman history in the underworld in book six, and the designs on the shield of Aeneas in book eight. Comparisons with features of the forum of Augustus or the *ara pacis Augustae* are easily drawn. The addressee of this rhetoric is the Roman world in general and perhaps the Italian upper classes in particular—Virgil emphasizes the union of Roman and Italian and he is no democrat. At the midpoint of the poem he addresses this audience: "You, O Roman, remember to spare the conquered and cast down the proud," which in a way is the moral of the poem and exactly what Aeneas does. It is, however, possible that occasionally Virgil has in mind another recipient, the emperor himself, whom he would exhort to humanity and perhaps occasionally urge to specific action such as recovery of the standards lost to Parthia.[25]

[25] On the last point cf. *Aeneid* 7.606. On the general topic of Virgil and Augustus cf. further F. Bömer, "Vergil und Augustus," *Gymnasium* 58 (1951) 26-55 and C. G. Starr, "Virgil's Acceptance of Octavian," *AJPh* 76 (1955) 34-46. There has been little discussion of the *Aeneid* as addressed to Augustus, but the idea seems implicit in statements such as that of Quinn,

Horace

Q. Horatius Flaccus, the second great poet of the Augustan age, had even less sympathy for traditional rhetoric than did Virgil, though of all the Augustan poets he is the one who has the most to say about literature, criticism, and technique.[26] Somehow he may even have escaped the rhetorical schools, as unlikely as that seems: we hear about his studies with grammarians in Rome and with philosophers in Athens, but nothing in between (*Epist.* 2.2.41-45). More probably he had some rhetorical training, but neglected to mention it since it was not an important experience to him. His opinion of the rhetorical schools can be pretty clearly deduced from the only occurrence of *declamare* in his works, *Epistles* 1.2.2, where he says that while Lollius, the addressee, has been declaiming at Rome, he himself has been reading Homer at Praeneste, "a worthwhile occupation from which one can learn more philosophy than from the professional philosophers."[27] Declamation is

---

op.cit. supra n. 13, 54, "The *Aeneid* is a poem about a leader who has to learn to lead, who makes the mistakes that leaders make."

[26] Horace lived from 65 to 8 B.C. He published *Sermones* I about 35, II in 30, *Epodes* in 30, *Odes* I-III in 23, *Epistles* I in 20, *Carmen saeculare* in 17, *Odes* IV in 13. *Epistles* II was written at different times: 1 about 13, 2 about 19, and 3 (*Ars poetica*) between 12 and 8, cf. George E. Duckworth, "Horace's Hexameters and the Date of the *Ars Poetica*," *TAPhA* 96 (1965) 73-95. On rhetoric in Horace cf. R. K. Hack, "The Doctrine of Literary Form," *HSPh* 27 (1916) 1-65; G. L. Hendrickson, "Horace and Valerius Cato," *CPh* 11 (1916) 249-69 and 12 (1917) 77-92; 329-50; J.F.D'Alton 353-437; Rudolf Helm, "Reden in den *Oden* des Horaz," *Philologus* 90 (1935) 352-71; additional works cited in the following notes.

[27] This epistle is a *protrepticus* or exhortation, often to philosophy but in this case to literature. There is much rhetorical coloring for the sake of the addressee, cf. Max Siebourg, "Horaz und die Rhetorik," *NJA* 25 (1910) 267-78, esp. 275ff.

otherwise apparently beneath Horace's notice, and he
is not very fond of recitation either (*Serm.* 1.4.73). The
reader gets an occasional glimpse in Horace's works of
the busy legal life of the ancient world (e.g., *Serm.* 1.7
and 1.9), and some of the *Epodes* have themes or references which slightly resemble those of declamation.
There is also a great deal of use of devices of style, for
example, the figure praeteritio,[28] or techniques of proof,
like the use of examples. Much of this comes from the
poetic tradition rather than from formal rhetoric. Some
of the literary influences and critical movements which
appear in rhetoricians like Dionysius of Halicarnassus
have counterparts in Horace's works, and similarities
have been traced between his writings and the rhetorical
and philosophical works of Cicero,[29] but the significance
of these similarities can be exaggerated. Horace made
use of literary theories which in turn had been influenced
at some time in the past by rhetorical studies. There
was not much influence of rhetorical theory directly
upon him. His literary preferences are for lyric poetry
and for those humble forms of verse which he calls
epistles and satires or conversation pieces (*sermones*).
He never glorifies the orator; when he admired a speech
it was admiration of the substance or speaker rather than
the treatment, as seen, for example, in his description of
Regulus (*Odes* 3.5). It is significant that he thought
mediocrity tolerable in law or in oratory, whereas it was
not in poetry (*Epist.* 2.3.369-73).

Despite his personal avoidance of the active life,
Horace, like Virgil, took seriously Augustus' attempt to

[28] Cf. Steele Commager, *The Odes of Horace,* New Haven,
1962, 112.
[29] Cf. Mary A. Grant and George C. Fiske, "Cicero's *Orator*
and Horace's *Ars poetica,*" *HSPh* 35 (1924) 1-75 and George
C. Fiske, "Cicero's *De oratore* and Horace's *Ars poetica,*" *Univ.
of Wisconsin Studies* 28 (1929).

give a renewed coherence, meaning, and order to Roman life.[30] His *Satires* contribute to a moral reawakening as do many of the *Odes*, especially the six at the beginning of the third book known as the *Roman Odes* where appear many of the symbols associated with the new Augustan rhetoric.

The work of Horace most obviously connected with rhetoric is his *Ars poetica*, or *Art of Poetry* (*Epist.* 2.3). This is a long and difficult poem in which Horace discusses not his own art of lyric poetry, which would greatly interest modern readers, but the art of dramatic and epic poetry, which he apparently wanted his contemporaries to understand. The work is thus apparently to be associated with Augustus' desire to produce a major literature for a new golden age. It is directed, as are *Satires* 1.4 and 10, against the new generation of poets who followed the tradition of Catullus, many of them politically as well as aesthetically opposed to the new regime, who saw art only in small and highly polished works, written in the spirit of Alexandrianism.[31] Horace thought (what Virgil proved) that polish could be attained in large scale works. The critical issue thus is a Roman counterpart of that in third century Alexandria between Apollonius of Rhodes, who believed in the possibility of successful modern epic, and Callimachus, who did not.

In his discussion of serious art forms Horace has drawn on a Hellenistic critic named Neoptolemus of Parium, who apparently wrote a rather systematic treatise on poetics.[32] Horace has been to some pains to weave to-

[30] Cf. E. Doblhofer, *Die Augustuspanegyrik des Horaz in formalhistorischer Sicht*, Heidelberg, 1966.

[31] Cf. Brooks Otis, "Horace and the Elegists," *TAPhA* 76 (1945) 177-90 and C. O. Brink, *Horace on Poetry: Prolegomena to the Literary Epistles*, Cambridge, Eng., 1963, 219-26.

[32] Cf. Christian Jensen, "Neoptolemos und Horaz," *APA* 14

gether the materials in a way more poetic than systematic and thus has provoked a great deal of analysis by modern scholars, each using a somewhat different system drawn from Hellenistic poetics or rhetoric.[33] Norden,[34] for example, regarded the Ars poetica as basically following the organization of a rhetorical handbook, with discussion in turn of invention, arrangement, and style, but this system can be imposed only with considerable strain and its deliberate presence would actually be quite surprising considering Horace's general lack of interest in rhetoric.[35] What traces there are of the system come not from Horace's own intentional use of it, but from the fact that Greek treatises on poetics had discussed topics of invention, arrangement, and style. It is impossible to define the exact relationship between the development of poetic theory and the development of rhetorical theory, though the latter began first, was doubtless more widely studied, and since it had practical claims probably led the way. Even in Aristotle it is clear that the relationship between rhetoric and poetics was a reciprocal one, as seen, for example, in his gradual construction of a theory of metaphor. All ancient criticism, both poetic and rhetorical, makes a division between subject and style, or res and verba, and this is a conspicuous feature of the Ars poetica. In practice, especially in the Odes, Horace can rarely be said to decide what he wants to say and then to choose words and ornaments by which to say it, as theory implies he should; the total poem is, in fact, a much closer synthesis of the two in which idea

---

(1919) and Philodemos über die Gedichte, Fünftes Buch, Berlin, 1923; Atkins 2.47-103.

[33] For a summary cf. Brink, op.cit. supra n. 31, 3ff.

[34] Cf. Eduard Norden, "Die Composition und Litteraturgattung der Horazischen Epistula ad Pisones," Hermes 40 (1905) 481-528.

[35] Cf. Brink, op.cit. supra n. 31, 175f.

leads to words and words back in turn to possible development of idea. But like other ancient critics Horace looks to traditional theory rather than to a description of his practice. Virgil's methods of composition as described in the Suetonian-Donatan life (23) seem to have resembled a rather straightforward composition of the subject in prose and then a conversion of this into verse, but again it is very difficult to believe that there was not a great deal of creative interaction. Obviously both poetic critics and rhetoricians are interested in problems of diction, and Horace's discussion of this topic brings him close to the neo-Atticism movement. He has indeed been called a neo-Atticist,[36] but if so he was a very moderate one who was perfectly willing to allow word coinage (*Epist.* 2.3.46-59), and it is unlikely that he cared to think of his discussions with other poets as on quite the same level as the disputes among the rhetoricians and orators.

The aspects of Horace's criticism which are of the widest significance and most relate to the history of rhetorical theory are those involved in two other aspects of the creative process. He appears to believe in imitation of literary models as a source of excellence, especially in the case of epic and drama.[37] He does not apply it to oratory, which is a sign that he does not regard oratory as a serious literary form. He rejects, especially in the *Epistle to Augustus* (*Ep.* 2.1), the notion held by some of his contemporaries which Cicero had tried to encourage in the *Brutus*, that there were Roman classics from the second century B.C. to which a Roman writer could look. The sole worthy models of imitation as far

---

[36] Cf. M. B. Ogle, "Horace an Atticist," *CPh* 11 (1916) 156-68.

[37] Craig LaDrière, "Horace and the Theory of Imitation," *AJPh* 60 (1939) 288-300.

as Horace is concerned are Greek. Even more important to him than imitation, however, is the theory advanced in the *Ars poetica* (291) of the *labor limae*, the work of the file, by which a writer, starting perhaps with an idea, then imitating a model in the choice of means of expression, gradually perfects his work by a continued revision and polishing. A poet is even advised (388) to set aside a provisionally complete poem until after the ninth year and then to revise it again. Horace's predecessor in satire, the second century B.C. poet Lucilius, had glorified in improvisation: Horace claims Lucilius could dictate two hundred muddy verses an hour standing on one foot (*Serm.* 1.4.9-10). It is clear that the poets of the early empire were more painstaking: Virgil described his own revisions as "like a mother bear licking her cubs" (Suetonian-Donatan *Life* 22). The teachers of rhetoric in the schools encouraged the same approach, for the school boy was not taught to think and speak quickly on his feet, but to write and rewrite his declamations until they satisfied himself and his master and could be memorized.

The idea of achieving excellence by constant rewriting becomes a permanent part of rhetorical teaching as well as of poetic criticism (cf., e.g., Quint. 10.4). With the great literature of Greece and Rome as background, the empire had very high standards of literary excellence. The general failure throughout the world of intellectual invention did not destroy this sense of quality, and the author who was bent on excellence felt he had no choice but hard work and a constant polish. If he was unable to work hard, of course, quality would decline, which is what the elder Seneca felt had happened in declamation during his lifetime. The younger generation of declaimers found life too easy, too comfortable, too unchallenging. One of the many things meant by saying that the poetry of the empire becomes highly rhetorical is this, that technique has to replace invention and inspiration, and literary decline comes when technique becomes too tiresome or too difficult.

Commager[38] has pointed out how the process is already evident in the fourth book of Horace's *Odes*. These were apparently written at the urging or even the insistence of Augustus when Horace personally would have preferred to abandon the form. They include celebrations of victories by members of the imperial household and a number of other official themes.[39] They exhibit very careful arrangement among themselves, internal structure, choice of word, composition of line. They have all the virtues resulting from *labor limae*. But they have almost universally been judged to lack inspiration.[40] The security of Augustan rule no longer made the pleading of its cause so important or so stimulating. Horace was only gradually won over by the regime, but in time he became bored by it. He is unable totally to disguise the fact that the persuasion of the fourth book of *Odes* comes from deliberately marshalling examples, from choosing words which are believed to have ethical and pathetical qualities, and from making an intellectual response to an aesthetic challenge. This is not to rebuke Horace. Augustanism was probably worth the effort, and Horace had indeed the duty of a patriot and friend of Augustus. There is considerable achievement in responding successfully to rhetorical challenge. This point of view was not, however, entirely congenial to Horace. The early poems,

[38] Cf. *op.cit.* supra n. 28, 231ff.

[39] Cf. Janice M. Benario, "Book 4 of Horace's *Odes*: Augustan Propaganda," *TAPhA* 91 (1960) 339-52.

[40] Cf. Benario, *op.cit.* supra n. 39, 339 and works listed there; Commager, *op.cit.* supra n. 28, 226-34. A partial exception is Gordon Williams, *Tradition and Originality in Roman Poetry*, Oxford, 1968, 88.

where he is more himself, do not show a fondness for setting up a challenge and seeing what can be done. They are personal expressions of emotions or experiences. If they show a tendency to view two sides to some questions[41] this probably should not be referred so much to a rhetorical origin or a sophistic viewpoint as to Horace's own philosophy of disengagement and his personal experience. The closest thing to a rhetorical challenge in the early Horace is his fondness for parody which occasionally leads him into the elaboration of a conceit.[42]

Virgil made an effective use of rhetoric as part of his high seriousness of purpose. Horace turned to rhetoric unenthusiastically to fulfill his duty. Both were interested in persuading an audience to share their viewpoints. Ovid and Livy are much more thoroughly imbued with a rhetorical view of life and art, but for them persuasion is relatively unimportant as a goal. For both, however, there was some souring in the satisfaction of art. Ovid's misfortune was that he was given a cause to plead, Livy's, that art could not give him total escape from contemporary reality.

Ovid

Around 30 B.C. P. Ovidius Naso was sent from his native Sulmo in central Italy to study rhetoric at Rome in preparation for a career in public life.[43] His father

[41] Cf. Commager, op.cit. supra n. 28, 104-20.
[42] Cf. Commager, op.cit. supra n. 28, 130-36.
[43] Cf. A. L. Wheeler, "Topics from the Life of Ovid," AJPh 46 (1925) 1-28. Ovid was born in 43 B.C. The Amores and Heroides were probably first published around 16 B.C., the Ars amatoria around 1 B.C. Ovid was working on the Metamorphoses and Fasti when exiled in A.D. 8. The Tristia were complete by A.D. 12. Epistulae ex Ponto were written between 12 and 16, soon after which Ovid presumably died. For general discussions of Ovid cf. L. P. Wilkinson, Ovid Recalled, Cambridge, Eng., 1955 and Brooks Otis, Ovid as an Epic Poet, Cambridge, Eng., 1966.

thought that poetry, Ovid's great joy even in early youth, was unprofitable and liked to point out that Homer left no wealth (*Tristia* 4.10.22)! Ovid escaped from his father's designs after a short career in minor offices (*Tristia* 2.93-96; 4.10.33-35) and had no regrets that he was not an advocate (*Amores* 1.15). We have, however, a picture of Ovid in the rhetorical schools as the elder Seneca remembered him about sixty years later. It comes as part of Seneca's discussion of a case in which "a husband and wife swore that if anything happened to one, the other would die. The husband, while traveling abroad, sent back a messenger to his wife to say that her husband had 'passed on.' The wife leaped from a high place. She survived and is ordered by her father to leave her husband. She refuses. She is disinherited." Seneca says (*Contr.* 2.2.8-12):

"I remember that this *controversia* was declaimed by Ovidius Naso as a boy before the rhetorician Arellius Fuscus, whose pupil he was. Ovid was an admirer of Latro [Seneca's own friend and idol], although he cultivated a different kind of speaking. He had a talent which was elegant, appropriate, and appealing. Even then his speech seemed more than anything else like a poem in prose. So zealously did he listen to Latro, that he took over in his verses many of the latter's *sententiae*. On the theme of the judgment of the arms [of Achilles between Ajax and Odysseus] Latro had said, 'Let us cast the arms into the midst of the enemy, and seek them there.' Ovid said (on the same subject: *Meta.* 13.121-22):

Let the brave hero's arms be cast in the midst of the
   foe;
Then order them recovered.

"He borrowed still another idea as well from Latro's treatment of the *suasoria*. I recall that Latro said in one of his *prooemia* something that the *scholastici*[44] memorized verbatim, 'See you not how an unmoved torch smolders, but how when shaken it reveals its fire. Leisure softens men; an unused sword rusts: idleness stupefies.' Ovid said (*Amores* 1.2.11-2):

I have seen leaping flames wax strong as a torch is tossed,
And again die down when no one waves the brand.[45]

"(9) At the time when he was studying, Ovid was considered a good declaimer. The following *controversia* at least he declaimed before Arellius Fuscus with much greater ability than the others present, in my opinion, though he hastened through the topics in no particular order. I remember this passage from his speech (the husband addressing the father):

" 'My principal task is this, to induce you to grant that love may exist in a husband for a wife, in a wife for a husband. If you permit them to love, then it follows that you permit them to take oaths to their love. What do you think was the oath which bound us? Your own sacred name. If she should violate her oath, she invoked upon herself the anger of her father, I the anger of my father-in-law. Spare us, father. We have not broken our oath. [To the audience] See with what unbridled love our accuser is over powered! He complains because anyone except himself is dear to his daughter. Why should he divert her from her inclination? Good gods, what love did *he* have for *his* wife? (10) He loves his daughter and he disinherits her; he is distressed that she has been endangered, and he takes her from the man without whom she

---

[44] Cf. supra 327.
[45] The reminiscence of Latro here is an expression of the basic theme of the poem and not an incidental ornamentation. The idea becomes a commonplace, cf. Tac., *Dial.* 36; Pliny, *Ep.* 4.9.

says she cannot live. He passionately laments the peril of a daughter whom he almost lost, while giving advice to others that they should love with moderation. In love it is easier to reach an end than to reach a mean. [To the father again] What do you want? That lovers keep to the limits which you approve? That they do nothing without forethought? That they commit themselves to nothing that they are not ready to swear to in court? That they weigh every word with reason and responsibility? That is how old men love. You know little of our quarrels: we have sometimes argued and sometimes relented and what perhaps you do not believe, we have sometimes broken our word. What business is it of a parent what lovers swear to each other? If you will believe it, it is not even the business of the gods. (11) Do not, my wife, feel pride that you are the first to have sinned. Other wives have perished with their husbands. Other wives have perished *for* their husbands. Every age will honor them. Every artist will celebrate them. Come, father, bear up under your good fortune. What a great exemplar you have at how little cost! For the future, as you request, we have been made more careful. We confess our error. We who took the oath forgot that there was a third one who loves us more. O gods, may it always be so. Do you persist, father? Receive back your daughter. I who have sinned am the one who deserves punishment. Why should I be the cause of disgrace to my wife and of childlessness to my father-in-law? I shall leave the state. I shall flee. I shall become an exile. As well as I can, I shall bear my loss with wretched and painful endurance. I would die, but that would not mean death for me alone.'

"(12) Despite this example, Ovid rarely declaimed *controversiae* and only those in which there were possibilities of developing *ethos*. He enjoyed *suasoriae* more. All

408

argumentation was an annoyance to him. He used words with great restraint, except in his poems, where he was not blind to his faults, but loved them. There is clear proof of this, for once when he was asked by his friends to expunge three verses, he demanded in turn that he might choose out three against which they were to say nothing. The condition seemed equitable. His friends privately wrote down those they wished abolished, he those he wished saved. In both lists the verses were the same. According to Albinovanus Pedo, who was one of the judges, the first was:

semibovemque virum semivirumque bovem (*Ars amatoria* 2.24)
a semi-bovine human and a semi-human bull (of the Minotaur).

The second was:

et gelidum Borean egelidumque Notum (*Amores* 2.11.10)
both icing Boreas and de-icing Notus (North and South winds respectively).

The third [is lacking].

From this it appears that this man of the greatest genius did not lack judgment for curbing the license of his poetry, but lacked the will. He used to say sometimes that a face was more becoming in which there was some blemish."[46]

This passage is typical of declamation and of Ovid and shows well the connexion between the two.[47] In part

[46] On the last point cf. Maurice P. Cunningham, "Ovid's Poetics," *CJ* 53 (1957-58) 253-59.
[47] Seneca's version may be a pastiche. The beginning perhaps made clear the *color*: apparently Ovid took the line that the speaker was impulsive by nature and love had been alternately hot and cold. Notice how he jumps back and forth addressing

Ovid rebelled against declamation: he probably disliked it as practical training for the world of affairs into which his father wanted to push him. Seneca says he disliked argumentation; though of course there is some argumentation in this declamation, there is no chain of arguments. Presumably *controversiae* did not appeal to Ovid unless they had certain specific qualities. What he liked was the opportunity declamation gave him for entering an imaginary situation, developing the characters involved, turning fine-sounding phrases, indulging perhaps in emotional appeal. Study in the rhetorical school did not make Ovid's poetry rhetorical in the first instance, though it practiced him in the use of rhetorical techniques. The schools allowed him, at a time when there was some check on his opportunity to compose verse, to indulge his creative instincts. It is surely significant that the one *controversia* of Ovid which Seneca remembers well is concerned with Ovid's favorite poetic theme of love.

Seneca's remarks about Ovid's ability, judgment, and lack of will power are very instructive. These are similar to qualities found in declaimers and rhetoricians and in the wider Roman public. They resulted when belief and hope of future achievements declined, while technique, training, and a rich cultural background persisted. Ovid is rhetorical in the sense in which Thomas DeQuincey

---

father-in-law, court, wife, and gods, and notice also the possibilities for dramatic delivery, especially of the final fierce *sententia*. The devices of rhetorical question, hyperbole, and amplification are evident; there is repeated use of the paradox of the too-loving father who would deprive his daughter of the right to love too much. There is no evidence that Ovid continued to declaim as an adult or maintained any close contact with rhetoricians, cf. T. F. Higham, "Ovid and Rhetoric," *Ovidiana*, ed. N. J. Herescu, Paris, 1958, 32-48. Higham takes too narrow a view of rhetoric, but rightly stresses Ovid's contributions to it.

used the word in his antithesis between rhetoric or "literary ingenuity," and eloquence or "urgencies of emotions and passion."[48] Ovid's choice of elegy marks him as unsympathetic to the serious hopes of the Augustan age as a renaissance of morals and letters. Elegy had a tradition of license, and writers of elegy had been political opponents of the regimes of Caesar and Octavian.[49] Conversely, Ovid rejected the moral position of the satirist (*Tristia* 2.563-68).

What Ovid lacked was a sense of direction or a call to persuade a wide popular audience to work toward some goal, both of which were present in Virgil and to a lesser extent in Horace. When he sets out to persuade in his early poems, as he often pretends to, it is for the fun of seeing what can be done, not out of concern for the goal. We may assume that Ovid accepted the empire (*Tristia* 2.51-60), that he felt no great regret for the republic (*Meta.* 15.762ff.). If pressed, he probably would have thought political freedom was incitement to faction. Even his own banishment for committing an unknown error and for writing the *Art of Love* he viewed as personal and unique, not as political or symptomatic. The truth is that the Roman government and its empire did not interest him. His praises of it, such as at the end of the *Metamorphoses* or in the second book of the *Tristia*, are flat and perfunctory, and in the early poems his tone in the few references to Caesar is snide or sarcastic.[50]

The purest Ovid is the early Ovid and it is in the early

[48] Cf. *The Collected Works of Thomas DeQuincey*, vol. 10, ed. David Masson, London, 1897, 21-133, esp. 94-95 and Hoyt H. Hudson, "DeQuincey on Rhetoric and Public Speaking," *Historical Studies of Rhetoric and Rhetoricians*, ed. Raymond F. Howes, Ithaca, 1961, 198-214.

[49] Cf. Brooks Otis, "Ovid and the Augustans," TAPhA 69 (1938) 188-229.

[50] Cf. T. F. Higham, "Ovid: Some Aspects of his Character and Aims," CR 48 (1934) 105-16, esp. 113.

Ovid that ancient poetry comes closest to being a successful response to a rhetorical challenge. Ovid's earliest poems are the *Amores* and the *Heroides*, though the exact date of publication is not known. The *Heroides* are imaginary love letters in elegiac verse, principally by forsaken women to their lovers or husbands. Since there is usually no way that the writer could get the letter to the addressee, the occasion is artificial, and the writer is imagined as giving vent to pent-up emotion.[51] The tone is, of course, highly pathetic, like the tone at the end of the declamation just quoted. It has often been said that the *Heroides* are *suasoriae* in verse,[52] but there are obvious differences: a true *suasoria* dealt with a matter of public significance even when, as in the case of Agamemnon and Iphigenia, private emotions were involved. In the case of the *Heroides* the private emotions are the object of interest even if the incident happens to have public significance. Slightly more accurately the *Heroides* are sometimes called *prosopopoeiae*, exercises assigned in the schools for which a student wrote a composition in the person of some mythological or historical figure and concentrated principally on the presentation of character.[53] Yet Ovid surely did not get the idea for the *Heroides* solely from the schools, since the verse epistle had antecedents. He has combined this with the love elegy, somewhat as Propertius did in one poem (4.3). There is further an important dramatic influence. Many

[51] Cf. Hermann Frankel, *Ovid: a Poet between Two Worlds*, Berkeley, 1945, 38.

[52] Cf., e.g., K. F. Smith, "The Poet Ovid," *Martial the Epigrammatist and Other Essays*, Baltimore, 1920, 72. For a more careful statement cf. Fränkel, *op.cit.* supra n. 51, 36-37 and Wilkinson, *op.cit.* supra n. 43, 95-96. A refutation has recently been attempted by Eberhard Oppel, *Ovids Heroides: Studien zur inneren Form und zur Motivation*, Erlangen, 1968.

[53] Cf. Quint. 3.8.49-54 where their relevance for history and poetry is noted and Theon, *Progymnasmata* 10.

of the heroines, Phaedra or Medea, for example, had been characters in Greek tragedy, and Ovid's approach is that of a rhetorical tragedian imagining what a character would have said under a given circumstance and how. Ovid himself felt attracted to tragedy and wrote one play, *Medea*, now lost. It probably had many of the qualities of tone and style evident in the *Heroides*.[54] Possibly the *Heroides* were even produced on the stage as mimes (*Tristia* 2.519-20).

Some of the techniques which Ovid had practiced in the rhetorical schools were adaptable to the *Heroides*, principally the creation of an emotional tone by personal appeal, amplification, hyperbole, rhetorical question, and other figures of speech and the composition of elegant *sententiae*. The basic similarity between the *Heroides* and declamation is the starting point, that is the imagining of a situation and the resulting question of what would be said under these circumstances. Ovid does not use the poems as a vehicle for philosophy or for alluding to personal or contemporary events or apparently even for picturing profound human experience, though his art is good enough that universality emerges from some of the pictures of the afflicted women. Since the women are all in an analogous position, he has posed for himself the additional challenge of achieving variety in sameness, as he was to do again in the *Metamorphoses*, and as the declaimers did in their constant reusing of the same theme.

The *Amores* belong to the tradition of the Latin subjective erotic elegy as written by Tibullus and Propertius, but with a difference which brings them closer to the viewpoint of the rhetorician. Tibullus and Propertius apparently drew their inspiration from personal experience

---

[54] Very little is known about the play. On its presumed rhetorical qualities cf. Tenney Frank, "Horace on Contemporary Poetry," *CJ* 13 (1917-18) 550-65, esp. 562-64.

and addressed their love poems to real persons. Ovid may occasionally draw on his own experience or feeling (e.g., *Amores* 2.4), but he makes it clear in the first poem that his inspiration is artistic and not erotic. He is not trying to win a girl, not trying to recount his love, but imagining what might be said by a lover at varying stages in a love affair: for example, when meeting his girl at a party with her husband (1.4), when pleading with the doorkeeper to let him in (1.6), when overhearing an old witch advising his girl (1.8), when confronted with a demand for money (1.10). Some of the themes are stock features of Ovid's repertory. For example, the idea that the gods laugh at the false oaths of lovers, which occurs in Ovid's declamation above (Sen., *Controv.* 2.2.10 *ad fin.*) is central in *Amores* 3.3 and shows up again in 3.11b. Some *Amores* (e.g., 1.8 and 3.2) experiment with materials which become part of the *Ars amatoria*.

Some of Ovid's achievements are brilliant. *Amores* 1.9 is a development of the simile between a lover and a soldier. "How are they alike?" Ovid may be imagined to have asked himself. They are both about the same age; they are both aggressive; they both keep watch all night; bad weather means nothing to them. There is nothing indolent about the lover, and this suggests to Ovid a moral ending to the poem. Perhaps he thought of Horace's *Roman Odes* and the martial virtues valued by Augustus. Certainly laziness is a vice; love must therefore be a virtue, for it was love that Ovid claims roused him from his bed of sloth. If you want to avoid idleness, the poem concludes, fall in love. If Augustus ever read this he surely thought it an insidious example of the rhetorical art of making the worse seem the better cause. Another excellent poem is 1.13, a mock attempt to persuade the Dawn to slow her horses and let Ovid dally longer with his mistress. He reminds the Dawn of all the toil she brings to the world, amplifying his list with specific examples: the soldier, the farmer, the schoolboy, the litigant, the spinner. But the Dawn is unslowed and Ovid loses his temper. The real reason the Dawn gets up so early is that she cannot stand the aged Tithonus who lies with her. Other gods have been more inclined to prolong the night. The Dawn heard him, asserts Ovid: she blushed as she rose. This charming elaboration of a conceit is what most rhetorical poets of the empire admired. Few of them ever did it better than Ovid or more frankly acknowledged that it was what to them made life worthwhile. In practice, many made the mistake of treating their particular conceit in a too serious tone. Ovid's rhetoric is acceptable to a large extent because it is tongue in cheek and whimsical rather than pompous and self-righteous.

Ovid's two masterpieces are the *Ars amatoria* in elegiac meter and the *Metamorphoses* in the dactylic hexameter of epic. The former is modeled on a handbook of the general type of the *ars rhetorica*. Just as rhetoric, grammar, poetics, surveying, and what not can be reduced to rules and precepts, so can the fine art of seduction. The influence of the rhetorical handbook does not, however, go beyond the general conception of the poem. Ovid is primarily interested in exercising his wits. Not only does he give advice both to men and (in the third book) to women, but he wrote also a *Remedies of Love* in which he shows how to break off a love affair grown wearisome. He thus poses as the detached professor ready with the arguments and techniques to gain any objective.

The *Metamorphoses* is a product of rhetorical challenge on a colossal scale. It is an epic of art and artistic creativity.[55] Ovid has chosen a theme which attracts him

[55] Cf. E. K. Rand, *Ovid and His Influence*, New York, 1925, Higham, *op.cit.* supra n. 50; Otis, *op.cit.* supra n. 43.

perhaps because it is a theme of constant re-creation. It offered him attractive opportunities to deal with his favorite topic of love. It offered the challenge both of achieving variety out of a very large body of often rather similar stories and of connecting these stories by inventive transitions.[56] Some declaimers were especially proud of elegant transitions from one part of a speech to another (Seneca, *Contr.* 1.1.25 and Quint. 4.1.76-77). It offered a rather free field for narration in individual stories and for elaboration of whatever incident most appealed to Ovid's imagination. It offered innumerable opportunities for writing imaginary speeches of persuasion or seduction and thus of course for *sententiae* and for all the devices of rhetorical style.

In the years preceding A.D. 8, while he was working on the *Metamorphoses*, Ovid also wrote the elegiac *Fasti*. Again he seems to have chosen a framework which he hoped might present imaginative opportunities. The *Fasti* is a versified calendar which begins in January and goes half-way through the religious and national holidays of the Roman year, describing their origins in varying degrees of detail as Ovid happens to be interested. The second half of the work was probably never completed. The initial composition was interrupted by Ovid's exile; subsequently he revised what he had done to make it more appealing to the imperial powers.[57] Perhaps his choice of a national theme was originally influenced by a desire to live in peace with the regime, for the original dedication was to Augustus (*Tristia* 2.551). But these

[56] Cf. F. J. Miller, "Ovid's Methods of Ordering and Transition in the *Metamorphoses*," *CJ* 16 (1920-21) 464-76.

[57] *Tristia* 2.549-52 may indicate that he had written all twelve books, but perhaps in rough form. There are no testimonia to the last six books elsewhere. Cf. Wilkinson, *op.cit.* supra n. 43, 251-54.

gestures did him little good; the lightning bolt of exile was hurled from the hand of the emperor infuriated at some unknown indiscretion on Ovid's part. Ovid later substituted a highly flattering dedication to Germanicus, Tiberius' heir, in hopes of getting at the good will of the court in this way. The *Fasti* may be taken to be the beginning of that fulsome flattery which is a standard ingredient of the literature of the empire.

Augustus' sudden order exiling the urbane Ovid to a semibarbarous village on the edge of the world at Tomi on the Black Sea was a crushing experience.[58] The poet never returned. The two collections of poems which he wrote there and which have survived (there were others which we do not have) might be compared to the fourth book of Horace's *Odes*, though their level of achievement is lower. Ovid's joy in life, inspiration, and even imagination are gone. What remains is his skill at versification and in diction. He wrote prose letters to friends in Rome (*Epist. ex Pont.* 4.2.5-6), but every once in a while he produced an epistle in elegiacs. It served to entertain himself (*Tristia* 4 1.29-40), though he feels that his standards are gone, for he no longer is willing to erase, rewrite, and edit (*Epist. ex Pont.* 1.5.5ff.; 3.9.7ff.).[59] More important, he hoped by his poetry to reach the emperor. The verse letters were largely addressed to influential people in Rome who were supposed to get them to the emperor's notice when he was approachable. Ovid is thus pleading his own case and the epistles aim at

[58] Cf. J. C. Thibault, *The Mystery of Ovid's Exile*, Berkeley, 1964, and Robert S. Rogers, "The Emperor's Displeasure and Ovid," TAPhA 97 (1966) 373-78.
[59] Cf. E. J. Kenney, "The Poetry of Ovid's Exile," PCPhS 11 (1965) 37-49. On Ovid's views of composition cf. R.E.K. Pemberton, "Literary Criticism in Ovid," CJ 26 (1930-31) 525-34 and Cunningham, *op.cit.* supra n. 46.

persuasion, but in a limited way only. Ovid does not attempt specific defense against the charge on which he was exiled (*Tristia* 1.1.25; *Epist. ex Pont.* 2.2.49-56; 3.1.147); he cannot even discuss the charge made against him without opening the imperial wound. His plea is for mercy, for forgiveness, for mitigation of his punishment as too severe for the faults he had shown. This is the way that appeal must be made to an absolute ruler, as Cicero had realized in his speeches before Caesar. A modern defender of Ovid might argue that his exile was a mistake in policy and that the basic principle was not what Ovid had done or said, but the need for freedom of speech. From Augustus' point of view it was not a case of responsible criticism or freedom of speech at all but of immorality. Ovid, after recommending license and decadence in the *Amores* and *Ars amatoria*, had apparently become involved in some particular example thereof. Against the general charge of preaching immorality Ovid repeatedly claims that he has not been so bad as the emperor thinks, that the intent of his poems was not immoral (*Tristia* 1.9.59-62; 2.353-58). This was not enough for Augustus, to whom it seemed clear that whatever the intent the effect had been immoral, and in the moral rearmament of the state there was hardly room for a major author who did not enthusiastically cooperate.

In one of his later poems (*Epist. ex Pont.* 2.5.65-70) Ovid discusses his view of the relationship between rhetoric and poetry. He is addressing his friend Salanus who is described as the rhetorical teacher of Germanicus:

> Our work differs, but issues from the same sources:
>   We both are students of a liberal art.
> You do not have the thyrsus, symbol of wild poetic
>   inspiration;
>   I have tasted the laurel. But both of us must be
>   inflamed.

And while your eloquence gives muscle to my verses,
Brilliance comes from poetry into your words.

These concepts are rather general, but in the case of
muscle (*nervi*) Ovid is probably thinking of the energy
and determination shown by the orator in arguing his
case and its manifestation in "proper" diction, pointed
sententiae, ethos, pathos, argumentation, and in vigor of
delivery. Brilliance, on the other hand, may be seen in the
choice of poetic words, in rhythmic construction, in
poetic figures, in ornamentation and amplified description. In his various attempts at imaginative fulfillment of
rhetorical opportunity or at appeal for recall, Ovid does
draw strength from rhetorical methods, especially those
of style, to a lesser extent those of arrangement or invention. Special studies of his rhetorical features, however,
tend to overemphasize them since, as we have said before, many are as poetic as rhetorical.[60] In fact, the most
important rhetorical quality of Ovid is his view of literature and society. He found rhetoric entertaining in a life
of graciousness and he tried to make it consoling in a life
of grief. He believed that life was mostly living and that
art was mostly art, and that both could be enjoyed.

[60] Other discussions of rhetoric in Ovid include C. Brueck,
De Ovidio scholasticarum declamationum imitatore, Giessen,
1909; R. Heinze, "Ovids elegische Erzählung," *Ber. Sachs. Akad.
Wiss.* 71.7 (1919); Hugo Magnus, rev. of N. Deratani, *Artis
rhetoricae in Ovidi carminibus, PhW* 42 (1922) 940-45; Ana-
cleto Cazzaniga, *Elementi retorici nella composizione delle lettere
dal Ponto di Ovidio*, Varese, 1937; Mary M. Avery, *The Use of
Direct Speech in Ovid's Metamorphoses*, Chicago, 1937; A. A.
Day, *The Origin of the Latin Love Elegy*, Oxford, 1938, 59-75;
E. O'D. Green, "The Speeches in Ovid's *Fasti*," *CW* 35 (1941-
42) 231-32; Paolo Tremoli, "Influssi retorici e ispirazione poetica
negli *Amores* di Ovidio," *Pubbl. dell' Istituto di filologia classica
di Trieste* 1 (1955); F. Arnaldi, "La retorica nella poesia di
Ovidio," *Ovidiana*, ed. N. I. Herescu, Paris, 1958, 23-31; E. J.
Kenney, "Liebe als juristisches Problem; ueber Ovids *Heroides*
20 und 21," *Philologus* 111 (1967) 212-32.

Livy

The only major Latin prose from the Augustan period is Titus Livy's enormous history of Rome from its foundation, a work closer in spirit to poetry than to modern concepts of historiography. Livy's motivation was rhetorical in some of the senses in which we have been using that word and his work shows powerful rhetorical characteristics.

Probably Livy had the usual rhetorical education, but we know nothing specific about it; indeed, we know very little that is specific about Livy's life except that he was born and died in Padua and spent some of his life in Rome.[61] According to Seneca (*Ep.* 100.9) he wrote, probably before turning to history, "dialogues, which one might list as historical rather than philosophical, and avowedly philosophical works." The dialogues may have been ethical discussions in an historical setting like Cicero's *De senectute*; the philosophical works mentioned were certainly Stoic.[62] Livy also wrote a letter to his son, which Quintilian refers to several times. It contained Livy's advice on the cultivation of a good literary style and possibly on other aspects of rhetoric, just as Cicero advised his son in the *Partitiones oratoriae*. Livy regarded Demosthenes and Cicero as the best models of style, followed by others who most resembled Demosthenes and Cicero (Quint. 10.1.39, cf. 2.5.20). He also cautioned against obscurity (Quint. 8.2.18). His admiration for Cicero as a writer was clearly enormous, and influenced

[61] The traditional dates for Livy's life are 59 B.C.-A.D. 17, though both may be too late, cf. Ronald Syme, "Livy and Augustus," *HSPh* 64 (1959) 27-87; P. G. Walsh, *Livy: His Historical Aims and Methods*, Cambridge, Eng., 1961, 1-19; R. M. Ogilvie, A *Commentary on Livy Books* 1-5, Oxford, 1965, 1-5.

[62] Cf. P. G. Walsh, "Livy and Stoicism," *AJPh* 79 (1958) 355-75.

his own style, which belongs in the Ciceronian rather than the Sallustian tradition.[63]

The historians Thucydides, Xenophon, Polybius, Sallust, and Tacitus all participated actively, though not always successfully, in the political affairs of their times. Perhaps the same is true for Herodotus, who in any event showed a restless energy for an active life of travel and inquiry. Livy had no part in the making of history and apparently no appetite for it. His industry is seen in the total size of the historical work which he left, not in the amount of research he performed in any particular part; his discipline, in his stylistic control and literary devotion, not in his mastery of his subject or its inherent problems. He lacked conspicuously the very qualities which the more scientific, if less artistic, Polybius required of an historian (12.25e): knowledge of documents, of geography, and of political affairs. Livy is clearly no scientific historian; he is a man of letters who happened to choose history as his principal subject. It was not a very unusual choice, for a tradition of literary history had existed since the time of Isocrates' pupils Theopompus and Ephorus. Cicero, whose work Livy so admired, had often considered writing literary history and had written, or encouraged others to write, the basic commentaries on events out of which a grand historical work could be created by ornamentation and amplification. Cicero regarded history, like philosophy, as an occupation for a great man robbed of opportunities in oratory by the infelicities of the times (*De legibus* 1.8) and he called it *unum hoc oratorium maxime,* the one thing closest to oratory (*ibid.* 1.5). In a famous sentence Quintilian cautioned the would-be orator from imitating the diction and

[63] Cf. Helen North, "Rhetoric and Historiography," *QJS* 42 (1956) 234-42; Walsh, *op.cit.* supra n. 61, 20-45; Leeman 168-97.

421

composition of the historian too freely (10.1.31): "history is very close to poetry, and in a sense a prose poem; the whole work is directed not to action and present contention, but to the memory of posterity and toward securing the reputation of the author's ability." This is history as Livy understood it, a literary product in between oratory and poetry with a touch of philosophy in the form of an emphasis on ethics and examples of moral purpose, both good and bad.[64]

The motives with which Livy turned to historical writing may be seen from the candid, but difficult, *Preface* which begins his work. The value of his achievement he will not assess, he says; there are too many rivals working on the same familiar material and trying to add some greater factual detail or some finer polish of style (like declaimers, we might add). He will find satisfaction, however, in contributing to the memory of the deeds of a great people. His subject is one of great scope and difficulty. Readers may be anxious to hurry on to the later part of the work, but Livy himself finds a reward for his labor in that study of the early years of Rome diverts his mind from the cares of his own age.[65] Then it was one saw those examples of virtue and character which made Rome great. Subsequently discipline failed, morality declined, and Livy's own generation has been brought to the point, he says, where it can bear neither its vices nor their remedies. Livy is thus attracted to history as a pub-

[64] Cf. H. A. Taine, *Essai sur Tite-Live*, Paris, 1874, 10: "il fut historien pour rester orateur."

[65] This does not mean that Livy unnecessarily amplifies early Roman history. In 9.17.1 he claims to have resisted digression as a refreshment of the mind. The digression there included (what would have happened if Alexander had attacked Rome) is perhaps adapted from a *suasoria*, cf. William B. Alexander, "The Study of the Ninth Book of Livy," *TAPhA* 39 (1908) 94-99.

lic service, predominantly a moral and philosophical
exercise to be practiced in retirement from the world
and as a private escape and diversion.

The question of Livy's attitude toward Augustus and
his age has often been raised.[66] It is material here only in
so far as it relates to the nature of Livy's rhetoric. Is he,
like Virgil, making use of a form of the new rhetoric to
show that the destiny of Rome will be fulfilled by Augustus? The answer is certainly no. He believed in the destiny of Rome, but a destiny which manifested itself in
the past when Romans lived in accordance with nature
and fate. In contemporary circumstances when neither
vices nor remedies can be borne, the republic has been
handed over to the care of one man, but Livy hardly
viewed this with satisfaction. Augustus was his personal
friend, and certainly read with satisfaction Livy's picture
of early Roman virtue. Livy had none of Ovid's moral
weaknesses in Augustus' eyes. At the same time, the emperor more or less humorously chided Livy for his sympathy with Pompey and the republic (Tac., *Ann.* 4.34).
We do not have Livy's account of contemporary history;
it was probably not the greatest part of his work, and he
certainly avoided any direct challenge to Augustus. For
example, his eloquent account of the death of Cicero,
which the elder Seneca preserves (*Suas.* 6.17),[67] attributes Cicero's proscription to the hostility of Antony and
avoids any implication that Augustus had sanctioned it.
The subsequent estimate of Cicero (*Suas.* 6.21-22) is
also politically impartial: Cicero, it is said, would have

[66] Cf. esp. Syme, *op.cit.* supra n. 61 and Walsh, *op.cit.* supra
n. 61, 10-18.

[67] Before this time it was unusual to quote in full a passage
easily available, but Dionysius does so repeatedly, and there are
many subsequent examples. The declamations quoted by Seneca
were of course unpublished; he may have quoted Livy simply
to conform to his other illustrations.

treated Antony in much the same way if he had had a chance. The leader of the constitutional senate and the violent triumvir are hardly quite so comparable.

In his usual moral and philosophical tone and in his habit of seeing ethical models for imitation in Roman heroes, that is, in his use of the commonplaces of Augustan rhetoric, Livy is comparable to Virgil. In his creation of an aesthetic realm where his imagination could explore the possibilities of rhetorical elaboration and perhaps forget the contemporary scene, Livy can be compared to Ovid. His method has been carefully studied, especially by comparing his account of incidents of speeches with those reported by Polybius, and it is clear that Livy's treatment of an incident was often rather free.[68] He likes to understand it in a dramatic and psychological way and to present it imaginatively and vividly. As a result his scenes sometimes lack historical possibility, but they attain dramatic probability. His speeches, of which there are over four hundred in the extant portion of the work, are so carefully polished as to suggest that he was, like many other Romans of the early empire, a frustrated orator.

Some of the speeches are reminiscent of the occasions of declamation. An example is the *controversia* of 40.8-15. The basic outline of the situation between King Philip of Macedon and his two sons, Perseus and Demetrius, is clear in Polybius 23.7. Though there is a lacuna in Polybius' text as we have it, he seems to have written a speech for Philip, but not to have developed the dramatic possibilities much further. Livy has developed them to the full in his presentation of the two young men and the sorrowful old king. The charge brought by Perseus

[68] Cf. K. Witte, "Ueber die Form der Darstellung in Livien Geschichtswerk," *RhM* 65 (1910) 270-305; A. H. McDonald, "The Style of Livy," *JRS* 47 (1957) 155-72.

against Demetrius is parricide, a favorite in the rhetorical schools. The speeches of the two brothers against each other are given in full as imagined by Livy in very much the style of the schools of declamation. Sentences are short and disconnected; there are many rhetorical questions; Perseus turns from father to brother. The tone throughout is emotional.

A fine example of a speech of a different sort is the great oration which Livy wrote for Camillus to close the first pentad of the history (5.51-54). It is a *suasoria* in which Camillus attempts to persuade the Romans by every argument he can muster not to abandon Rome for a new capital at Veii. One of his chief devices is an *a fortiori* argument of the type popular with the declaimers: the Romans had not abandoned Rome when being defeated by the Gauls; why should they abandon it now when victorious? Yet Livy realized that sophisticated oratory was not suitable in all occasions of early Roman history (3.56) and did not neglect the homely type of eloquence represented by Menenius Agrippa's speech on the war of the parts of the body against the belly as an illustration of the evils of civil dissension (2.32). All in all, his oratorical achievement is very considerable. Quintilian thought two aspects of Livy's work were most remarkable. One was his style.[69] Its *lactea ubertas*, or milky richness (10.1.32), achieved beauty rather than persuasion, though in narrative Livy had a wonderful charm and radiant clarity (10.1.101). The other is the eloquence of his speeches,[70] which Quintilian

[69] Cf. Norden 234-37; McDonald, *op.cit.* supra n. 68; Walsh, *op.cit.* supra n. 61, 245-70; Leeman 190-97. On Pollio's complaint about *Patavinitas* in Livy cf. supra 307.

[70] Cf. Taine, *op.cit.* supra n. 58, 249ff.; H. V. Canter, "Livy the Orator," *CJ* 9 (1913-14) 24-34 and "Rhetorical Elements in Livy's Direct Speeches," *AJPh* 38 (1917) 125-51 and 39 (1918) 44-64; Konrad Gries, "Livy's Use of Dramatic Speech,"

says in the latter passage is beyond praise, so effectively is everything fitted to the subject and to the characters, while no historian has better represented the tender emotions. Quintilian's words perhaps misrepresent the process of characterization, for in general Livy has not suited the speech to the character as known from a reconstruction of history, but created a character by writing a speech and then maintained it consistently. His creativity is that of a declaimer or dramatist with almost complete freedom, not that of one of the Attic orators seeking to present the character of a particular client in an appealing way.

The younger Pliny (*Ep.* 2.3.8) tells a story of a man from Cadiz in Spain who, moved by the fame of Titus Livy, walked all the way to see him,[71] and having looked upon him, departed. Livy is a monument, something apart from the realities of history, removed from the faction and dust of the arena, largely ignorant of war and sometimes of politics, perhaps superior to both, timeless and immortal. It is not clear whether Livy found complete pleasure in his work, but it may be doubted (31.1.1-5). He drove himself through 142 books to stop in the middle of the reign of Augustus. The elder Pliny quotes (*Hist. nat. pr.* 16) a sentence from a lost part of the work in which Livy says that he had already attained enough glory for himself and that he could have ceased to write if it had not been that his restless mind fed itself upon his work. It has usually been thought that death mercifully spared him from exhausting his material.

AJPh 70 (1949) 118-41; Walsh, *op.cit.* supra n. 61, 219-44; Ogilvie, *op.cit.* supra n. 61, 19-20. The rhetorical theory is unreliable in R. Ullmann, *La technique des discours dans Salluste, Tite-Live, et Tacite*, Oslo, 1927.

[71] Pliny does not say the man came to Rome, as Walsh assumes, *op.cit.* supra n. 61, 19. He may have found Livy at Padua, cf. Leeman 195-96.

During the reign of the emperor Augustus, several important genres of literature found themselves cut off from that aspect of life with which they had been practically connected. In oratory declamation became the dominant form. The epic of national achievement became, in the hands of Ovid, a narrative of fictitious adventure. Lyric poetry in the fourth book of Horace's *Odes* lost its personal inspiration. Elegiac poetry turned from real love affairs to imaginary love affairs and in the last poems of Ovid to flattery of the officials of state. History lost the political consciousness it had had in Sallust, was wary of contemporary events, and became a form of drama and poetry. Tragedy, despite the encouragement of Augustus and Horace and the single attempt of Ovid, did not revive. The Roman empire has been greatly admired by some historians for the stability which it achieved and for the institutions which it created. It has been severely criticized by others for repression of speech and ideas. Admiration of the empire should not be allowed to lead to deliberate imitation of it; acknowledgement of the repression of thought which accompanied it must not imply that there was at the time a better alternative. The empire may have become stable in part because of thought control, but it came to exist at all and in the first place because of the failure of freedom.

CHAPTER SIX

Eloquence in the Early Empire

The history of rhetoric and oratory in the first century A.D. is largely an extension of the tendencies of the Augustan age. The beginnings of an attempt to find new subjects and new opportunities for oratory can, however, be detected. In this chapter we will reconsider briefly the opportunities for oratory and then turn to the numerous discussions of the decline of eloquence, and to other developments in theory and application.

Any fair estimate would judge the early Roman empire as one of the most eloquent periods in human history. Rhetoric monopolized secondary education and in this period the crest was probably reached in the number of students trained in declamation and in the influence of rhetorical study on literary composition. The ideal orator continued to be an inspiration and a goal for thousands. Rhetorical theory was further elaborated and refined. Prose style continued to be a vital interest to the intelligentsia, and fashions swung back and forth within the various traditions of Latinity which we have seen before. For the would-be orator there continued to be some opportunities within the three traditional kinds of oratory as well as in adapting rhetoric to other literary forms. Though first century orators often published their better speeches, none of these have survived. Reports in Quintilian and Tacitus are our best sources of information about oratory at this time.

Oratory in the First Century A.D.[1]

Epideictic oratory, which had so far not been a very important form in Rome, continued to be represented

[1] There has been no collection of the fragments of imperial orators since Henricus Meyer, *Oratorum Romanorum fragmenta*,

primarily by funeral orations. Funeral eulogy, however, could be a delicate matter. Tiberius, in fear of political repercussions, apparently did not allow a panegyric of Germanicus in Rome, though one had been given at Antioch where he died (Tac., *Ann.* 2.73 and 3.5). Nero similarly avoided a funeral oration for his rival Britannicus (13.17); one was hardly appropriate for his mother Agrippina since it was clear that he was responsible for her death, but the notorious apologetic letter which Seneca composed rather took its place (*Ann.* 14.10-11). Seneca had also composed Nero's funeral speech for Claudius, perhaps the most polished literary work in this genre at Rome (*Ann.* 13.3). Another celebrated speech was Domitian's tearful, hypocritical eulogy of Titus (Dio Cassius 67.2.6). A few inscriptions take the form of simple *laudationes funebres*: best known is the *Laudatio Turiae* from the Augustan period (*CIL* VI. 1527.31670), but there is also the *Laudatio Murdiae* from the first century A.D. (*CIL* VI.2.10230) and the *Laudatio Matidiae* from the second (*CIL* XIV.3579).

An important new form emerged in the *actio gratiarum*, the speech of thanks to the gods and the emperor which a consul gave on assuming office. This practice seems to have begun under Augustus (Ovid, *Epist. ex Pont.* 4.4.35-42), though we hear little about it until Pliny's address to Trajan in A.D. 100, to be discussed in the next chapter. Many of the earlier speeches of this sort were probably quite short. More general flattery of course made its way into other kinds of oratory in the senate or the law courts and also into poetry, as seen in the poems of Ovid's exile or the *Laus Pisonis* or in the invocations of epic poets like Manilius, Lucan, and Valerius Flaccus.

Zurich, 1842. For discussion cf. Victor Cucheval, *Histoire de l'éloquence romaine depuis la mort de Cicéron jusqu'à la avénement de l'empereur Hadrien*, 2 vols., Paris, 1893; Clarke 100-108; Ronald Syme, *Tacitus*, Oxford, 1958, 322-39; Leeman 219-42.

All varieties of sincerity and taste can be found in this flattery: much of it is perfunctory and conventional, while when carried to extremes as it is by Lucan, the result seems almost satiric.

Deliberative oratory was most changed; the factionalism and bitter debates of the late republic were gone from the assembly and the senate. Indeed the assembly now existed only in name. The better emperors repeatedly encouraged the senate to take a responsible and constructive part in forming public policy, but they met with rather little success. We do hear about spirited debates under Tiberius on such matters as the authority of praetors to punish actors (Tac., *Ann.* 1.77) and on flood control (*Ann.* 1.79), but the senators easily panicked on matters relating to imperial authority or wishes. Tiberius began by trying to respect the independence of the senate (*Ann.* 1.11-15), but soon was driven to cry, "How ready these men are to be slaves!" (*Ann.* 3.65). Insecurity was so great as to overwhelm good judgment, as we have already seen in the case of Labienus and Cassius Severus. Tacitus (*Ann.* 2.34) describes a senatorial debate on limiting private extravagance where L. Piso railed against corruption, bribery, and informers. He said he was going to go to live in the country. Tiberius tried to persuade him to stay. But Piso was determined to show his independence and started a legal action against Urgulania, a close friend of the queen mother. In the reign of Claudius there were again lively debates, but the senators hesitated to come to a final decision without knowing the emperor's view (*Ann.* 13.26-27).

Emperors clearly had to have advice and alternative policies had to be discussed. If this could not be done in the senate, other mechanisms had to be found within the imperial court. Augustus formed a *consilium semestre*, a kind of executive committee of the senate (Suet., *Aug.*

35.3; Dio Cassius 53.21.4-5), but this too disappeared as the usefulness of the senate waned. Most emperors, like magistrates in the republic, convoked groups of friends for advice from time to time, often on judicial matters (e.g., Tac., Ann. 3.10 and 14.62), and in the later empire this tradition developed into a formal council or *consilium principis*.[2] A still more restricted group could be called from among the powerful prefects of the guard, the watch, the city, and the grain supply, who sometimes dominated administration, or from the emperor's personal staff of secretaries. One of the finest "debates" in Tacitus is that which opens the twelfth book of the *Annals* where Claudius is being advised by his staff of freedmen on the choice of a new wife. Quintilian (3.8.70) includes the advising of the emperor as one of the possibilities for deliberative oratory: the sophists were to develop the form considerably in the early second century. There continued to be opportunities for a military commander to use deliberative oratory in addressing his army (cf. Quint. 2.16.19; 12.1.28; Tac., Ann. 1.15ff.) or perhaps in addressing a provincial population, but the Romans made relatively little use of formal oratory as a way of promoting unity throughout the empire. The rhetoric of public works and coins, of bread and circuses, was more prevalent and perhaps more effective.

Among the orators of the early empire no names appear more frequently than those of the emperors themselves.[3] The *locus classicus* is the passage (*Ann.* 13.3)

---

[2] Cf. John Crook, *Consilium principis: Imperial Councils and Counsellors from Augustus to Diocletian*, Cambridge, Eng., 1955.

[3] Cf. Cucheval, *op.cit.* supra n. 1, 1.26-57, 294-312; 2.36-72, 133-50; G. Lienhart, *Tiberius, Caligula, Claudius, Nero quid extra munera imperatoria scripserunt et quomodo litteria faverint aut obtrectaverint fragmentis et testimoniis collectis demonstratur*, Frieburg, 1934; Henry Bardon, *Les empereurs et les lettres*

in which Tacitus reports the gossip among the Roman aristocracy when it appeared that Seneca was writing Nero's speeches:

"Nero was the first of those who had controlled the state to have need of another's eloquence. For the dictator Caesar was the equal of the greatest orators, while Augustus' oratory was ready and fluent, as befitted an emperor. Tiberius too understood the art by which he could carefully weigh his words, sometimes clear in meaning or else purposely ambiguous. Even the disturbed mind of Gaius Caesar did not destroy his power of speaking, nor in Claudius did one feel the lack of eloquence, as long as he spoke what he had planned ahead of time. Nero, even in his boyhood, twisted his vigorous mind into other channels: to carve, to paint, to practice songs or horsemanship. But occasionally in composing verses he showed that the basic elements of culture were in him."

Fronto (2.136-38 Haines) took an even more negative note. As will appear in the discussion of Domitius Afer, Gaius (Caligula) seems to have been very interested in oratory. Claudius was highly literate and had studied with Livy. A portion of one of his speeches, dealing with the adlection of Gallic senators, is preserved on a bronze tablet at Lyons.[4] It is hardly great oratory, but bears the

---

latines d'Auguste à Hadrien, Paris, 1940; O.A.W. Dilke, "The Literary Output of the Roman Emperors," *G & R* 4 (1957) 78-97.

[4] For translation and discussion cf. E. G. Hardy, "The Speech of Claudius on the Adlection of Gallic Senators," *JPh* 32 (1913) 79-95 and K. Wellesley, "Can you Trust Tacitus," *G & R* 1 (1951) 13-37. Also Vincent M. Scramuzza, *The Emperor Claudius*, Cambridge, 1940, 99-104; N. P. Miller, "The Claudian Tablet and Tacitus: A Reconsideration," *RhM* 99 (1956) 304-15; Syme, *op.cit.* supra n. 1, 317-19; Arnaldo Momigliano,

individual stamp of his pedantic and historically informed mind. Tacitus (*Ann.* 11.24) gives a version of the same speech, the best instance in ancient historiography for comparing what was actually said with an historian's presentation of it. Here Tacitus has not preserved Claudius' structure; he has much curtailed his meanderings and ineptitudes; but he has kept to the ethos of the speaker and the general character of his argument. Tacitus' version is a superior speech. In the case of Nero a speech in Greek delivered at Corinth in A.D. 67, after Seneca's death and thus certainly not his work, is preserved in an inscription, ending with a fine *sententia*, to the effect that other emperors had freed a city, but Nero a whole province.[5] The revolution of A.D. 68-69, with its succession of emperors seeking military and popular support, briefly produced conditions reminiscent of the late republic. According to Jerome's *Chronicle* Galba brought Quintilian to Rome, but for what purpose there is no hint. Galerius Trachalus, an able orator praised especially for his delivery (Quint. 12.5.5), supported Otho and was regarded as the author of some of his speeches including a very temperate appeal to the people in the forum (Tac., *Hist.* 1.90).[6] The three Flavian emperors were interested in oratory, witness their patronage of Quintilian, and apparently able speakers, though Domitian can hardly be said to have won men's sympathies.

Claudius the Emperor and his Achievement, New York, 1961, 74-79; U. Schillinger-Haefele, "Claudius und Tacitus über die Aufnahme von Galliern in den Senat," *Historia* 14 (1965) 443-54.

[5] Cf. William Dittenberger, *Sylloge inscriptionum Graecorum*, 3d ed., Leipzig, 1915-20, no. 814, and E. Mary Smallwood, *Documents Illustrating the Principates of Gaius, Claudius, and Nero*, Cambridge, Eng., no. 64.

[6] Cf. William T. Avery, "Roman Ghost Writers," *CJ* 54 (1958-59) 167-69.

There must have been a good deal of debate in the local senates of Greek and Roman towns throughout the empire, but for a Roman who was neither an emperor nor an adviser to emperors the most frequent opportunities for deliberative oratory were in school *suasoriae* or in speeches inserted in historical works or in epic or dramatic poetry, of which there was a great deal composed. The best are those in Seneca's tragedies and in Tacitus' various works. Both Seneca and Tacitus were great orators, perhaps the greatest orators of the ages in which they lived. We will return to consider their rhetorical achievements later.

The law courts were always the primary scene of ancient oratory and the arena for which rhetorical education offered preparation. In the early empire the number of cases increased, probably considerably;[7] the number of different courts also increased; advocates were still able to win great reputations. But constraints increased as well, both the more general constraint coming from the fear of official displeasure and more specific constraints resulting from changes in procedure, usually aimed at more efficient and equitable administration of justice.[8] With the exception of trials before the assembly, the republican law courts described in chapter one continued to function. As scenes of oratory the most important continued to be the criminal *quaestiones* and the centumviral court, largely concerned with issues of property

---

[7] Cf. E. Patrick Parks, "The Roman Rhetorical Schools as a Preparation for the Courts under the Early Empire," *Johns Hopkins Univ. Studies in Historical and Political Sciences* 63.2 (1945) 54-56.
[8] Cf. Theodor Mommsen, *Römisches Strafrecht*, Leipzig, 1899, 260-297; H. F. Jolowicz, *Historical Introduction to the Study of Roman Law*, Cambridge, Eng., 1952, 403-17; A.H.M. Jones, "Imperial and Senatorial Jurisdiction in the Early Principate," *Historia* 3 (1955) 464-88.

and inheritance. In the latter court the jury was enlarged to 180, though it often met in separate panels. Civil procedure under the formulary system continued as before. A new development was the emergence of the senate as a court, primarily for its own class on criminal or political charges, including extortion[9] and treason. Opportunity for eloquence existed in senatorial trials: M. Terentius, accused of complicity with Sejanus, saved himself by a moving speech according to Tacitus (Ann. 6.8-9). In addition to these courts a separate system of imperial courts developed. The emperor and his deputies, including his governors in the provinces and his prefects at home, could take original jurisdiction in almost any matter. At first the imperial courts were perhaps chiefly used in the provinces, but they gradually became the commoner scenes of both criminal and civil action everywhere. They could take cognizance of criminal charges for which the older courts made no provision; they were simpler in that a single judge could make prompt decision about both law and fact; they could draw on established procedures wherever suitable, including the formulary system; and from the point of view of litigants they had the unprecedented advantage of allowing for appeal to a higher authority, that is, to the emperor. It soon became possible in practice to appeal from any court to the emperor. Though dramatic addresses were sometimes made, and before some judges or emperors flattery could be effective, conditions in imperial courts ordinarily encouraged a businesslike presentation of the evidence rather than literary elaboration.

An excellent picture of the emperor's court in one of its best periods emerges from a letter of the younger Pliny (Ep. 6.31), who was invited to be a member of

[9] Cf. P. A. Brunt, "Charges of Provincial Maladministration under the Early Principate," Historia 10 (1961) 189-223.

435

Trajan's *consilium* at his seaside villa at Centumcellae. Several days were devoted to a variety of judicial hearings. Pliny describes three cases. In the first a nobleman from Ephesus was acquitted on an unspecified charge, probably sedition,[10] which Pliny was persuaded had been made by an informer at the instigation of the man's enemies. The next case, described in greater detail, was a charge of adultery against the wife of a military tribune which had been forwarded to the emperor by a provincial legate. The emperor had already ordered the tribune discharged and banished for his lenient treatment of the errant wife and now forced him to prosecute her for her crime, which the man did with great reluctance. She was found guilty and the emperor issued a judgment indicating that he regarded the decision as necessary for military discipline and that the case was to be a precedent for his legates to follow: he himself was not to be bothered by any similar cases again. In both of these instances Pliny gives the impression that the emperor had already made his decision and did not invite the opinion of the *consilium* or allow very much discussion by those involved. The third case, however, seems to have been handled with greater discretion; perhaps it involved more prominent Romans. It was the matter of the will of a certain Julius Tiro, part of which was allegedly forged, and had come to the emperor by a petition from the heirs. One postponement had already been granted and some of the heirs had withdrawn from the case, but two were present with their advocates. There was some discussion, but perhaps no formal oratory. This time the emperor asked the *consilium* what he should do and took their advice, which was to demand that the heirs collectively go on with the suit or that

[10] Cf. A. N. Sherwyn-White, *The Letters of Pliny*, Oxford, 1966, 392-93.

individuals should show their reasons for not proceeding. Otherwise all were to be found guilty of malicious prosecution. Pliny was very much impressed with Trajan's handling of the cases, and also with the comforts of his villa and the courtesies accorded the *consilium*. Most emperors took judicial duties seriously, but the setting was not always so pleasant. Domitian regularly heard cases at the rostrum in the forum (Suet., *Dom.* 8).

Even in the more traditional courts changes of procedure occurred which inhibited the grand oratory of the late republic (Tac., *Dial.* 38). The number of patrons was limited by the Julian law (Asconius, *In Scaur,* 18), apparently to two, and, more important, time limits, measured by a water-clock, were set for the speakers. Pliny was once allowed about seven hours in a speech before the centumviral court (*Ep.* 4.16.2), which perhaps represents the maximum, but minor cases might be limited to an hour or less (*Ep.* 6.2.5). To check abuses and to encourage poorer persons to undertake the role of advocates Claudius revoked the 250-year-old Cincian law and allowed payment of a fee to an orator up to a limit of 10,000 sesterces (Tac., *Ann.* 11.7).

Two related features of the judicial history of the first century need special mention: the treason trials and the role of informers. Both served further to undermine freedom of speech. Probably no emperor was opposed in theory to freedom of speech in the traditional Roman sense of the right of a man of dignity, family, and position to speak his convictions, limited by the right of another of greater dignity to enjoy respect. Even Tiberius said (Suet., *Tib.* 28) that in a free state the tongue and mind must be free. But the emperors' position was often insecure: we know of a succession of plots against each emperor, and plots against Gaius, Claudius, Nero, and Domitian ultimately succeeded. A corresponding inse-

437

curity and rivalry existed among the secondary level of officials and some senators and drove them to the point of seeking to remove their personal opponents from power and authority.

Tacitus and Suetonius represent treason trials as common in the early empire, but it has proved somewhat difficult to define the exact legal basis on which they were conducted or to discover the justice of the charges.[11] High treason in the form of armed rebellion (*perduellio*) had been a capital crime in the republic; it was the charge on which Cicero defended Rabirius. But events rarely went that far, and the republic had also prohibited conduct which diminished the authority (*maiestas*) of a magistrate (*lèse majesté*; cf. *Rhet. ad Her.* 1.21 and 25). Augustus passed a new *maiestas* law, but it was not until Tiberius' time that *maiestas* trials attained great notoriety. This resulted in part from his own failure to maintain satisfactory communications with the senatorial aristocracy and his feeling of resentment at his position. Much of the early litigation perhaps should be thought of as comprising test cases intended to define the scope of the law.[12] Tiberius consistently suppressed charges that seemed trivial (e.g., Tac., *Ann.* 6.5), but was apparently genuinely concerned about violations with religious implications, such as offenses against the cult of the deified Augustus, or real conspiracy against his own rule. The names of over a hundred defendants during Ti-

---

[11] Cf. E. T. Merrill, "Some Remarks on Cases of Treason in the Roman Commonwealth," *CPh* 13 (1918) 34-52; *CAH* 9.160-1; 10.626-34; Robert S. Rogers, *Criminal Trials and Criminal Legislation under Tiberius*, Middletown, 1935; B. Walker, *The Annals of Tacitus*, Manchester, 1952, 82-110 and 263-70; C. W. Chilton, "The Roman Law of Treason under the Early Principate," *JRS* 45 (1955) 73-81.

[12] Cf. Rogers, *op.cit.* supra n. 11, 130 and E. T. Salmon, *A History of the Roman World 30 B.C.-A.D. 138*, London, 1957, 132.

berius' reign are known, some of whom may have been charged with *perduellio*, others with *maiestas*. Some were certainly guilty. Convictions usually came in aggravated cases, but some innocent persons may have been convicted. Acquittals, however, were not infrequent and regular procedure was preserved.[13] The defendants were largely senators and thus tried in the senate. Not surprisingly, defendants sometimes had difficulty finding advocates to defend them (e.g., Tac., *Ann.* 2.29.1; 3.11). Charges might stem from actions or statements or both. The composition of slanderous poems was an acceptable ground for a charge, but there seems to be no clear case in which a person was punished for what he said in the senate or in a court of law.

Our major source on Tiberius' trials is Tacitus, and so great was his dislike of the emperors and so willing was he to seize upon the most tyrannic interpretations, that it is necessary to read his account of events with great caution and skepticism. For example, he describes eloquently (*Ann.* 4.34-35) the case of Cremutius Cordus, saying that he was accused on the unprecedented charge of praising Marcus Brutus and calling Cassius the last of the Romans in a historical work, and he puts in Cordus' mouth a splendid oration on freedom of speech. But the younger Seneca, who was alive at the time, says (*Cons. Marc.* 22.7) that Cordus committed suicide before his trial. It is thus likely that the real charges of treason were never brought forward, obviated by the death of the accused.[14] Treason trials remained a recurrent feature of aristocratic Roman life, especially under the more suspicious emperors. The later part of

[13] Cf. Rogers, *op.cit.* supra n. 11, 190-96.
[14] Cf. Frank Burr Marsh, *The Reign of Tiberius*, London, 1931, 290-93; Rogers, *op.cit.* supra n. 11, 87; Walter Allen, Jr., "The Political Atmosphere of the Reign of Tiberius," *TAPhA* 72 (1941) 1-25.

Domitian's reign proved a particularly difficult time.[15]
Greek and Roman constitutions did not provide for
the functions of a public prosecutor on a regular basis.
Magistrates could instigate prosecutions if they wished
to do so and this applied equally to the emperor and his
deputies. In theory criminal charges were made by an
injured person, a relative of a man murdered for example, or by his patron. If the injury were directed at the
state or society any citizen could take it upon himself
to bring an offender to justice. Such prosecutions were
a regular way to fame, wealth, and position. Private
prosecutors were needed by the state and were encouraged to act by laws which granted them the civil status
of their victims or financial reward in the event of success.[16] Tiberius insisted on the need to reward informers
if the laws were to survive (Tac., *Ann.* 4.30). Though
there were also penalties designed to prevent malicious or
speculative prosecution, the possible rewards were sometimes so enormous as to be difficult to resist. During the
early empire in particular a number of clever, unscrupulous men won position, wealth, and notoriety by feed-
ing on the suspicions of the emperor and his officials.
They are known as *delatores*, or informers. Tacitus (*Ann.*
1.74) takes Caepio Crispinus as a model of the type. He
had his first taste when in A.D. 15 he accused the pro-

[15] Cf. Chester G. Starr, *Civilization and the Caesars: the Intellectual Revolution in the Roman Empire*, Ithaca, 1954, 68-
88 and 114-46; D. McAlindon, "Senatorial Opposition to Claudius and Nero," *AJPh* 77 (1956) 113-32 and "Claudius and the
Senators," *AJPh* 78 (1957) 279-86; R. S. Rogers, "A Group of
Domitianic Treason Trials," *CPh* 55 (1960) 19-23; K. H.
Waters, "The Character of Domitian," *Phoenix* 18 (1964)
49-77.
[16] On acquisition of status cf. Lily Ross Taylor, *Party Politics
in the Age of Caesar*, Berkeley and Los Angeles, 1949, 113-14;
one-fourth the convicted man's estate usually went to the informer in treason cases, cf. Tac., *Ann.* 4.20.

consul of Bithynia of treason on the basis of "sinister remarks" about Tiberius. The prosecution failed, but Crispinus "entered on a way of life which the miseries of the times and the boldness of men later made familiar. Poor, unknown, and restless, he wormed his way by secret messages into the savage confidence of the ruler. Soon he was an object of danger to anyone of importance. By acquiring power with one, and hatred with all, he gave an example which others followed to become rich out of poverty, terrifying out of insignificance, and to achieve ruin for others and finally for themselves."

Who can justly be labeled an informer is a delicate question. Some able men were occasionally tempted; a few rose to fame through delation and survived to greater respectability. We shall consider the case of Domitius Afer shortly. A good example under Claudius was apparently P. Suillius Rufus (Tac., *Ann.* 11.1ff.); under the Flavians, Eprius Marcellus, Vibius Crispus, and M. Aquillius Regulus. Eprius became a kind of Judas figure in Rome because with Cossutianus Capito he was responsible for the prosecution and suicide of Thrasea Paetus in A.D. 66. (Tac., *Ann.* 16.21-35 and *Hist.* 4.6-8). Thrasea's house had become a center for Stoics and Cynics who were developing a philosophical opposition to the empire and to tyranny.[17]

Tacitus, when he discusses first century oratory in the *Dialogus*, and Quintilian, more guardedly, seem to have felt that the informers' oratory shared certain characteristics.[18] It was not ordinarily a product of careful rhetorical training, either in theory or declamation, but an expression of the character and opportunism of the speaker

[17] Cf. Starr, *op.cit.* supra n. 15, 135-42; Charles Saumagne, "La 'passion' de Thrasea," *REL* 33 (1955) 241-57; Syme, *op.cit.* supra n. 1, 555-61.

[18] Cf. Michael Winterbottom, "Quintilian and the *vir bonus*," *JRS* 54 (1964) 90-97.

and the raw emotions involved. The typical informer paid little attention to argumentation and less to style. A violent outpouring of words accompanied by excited delivery was his trademark. His immediate objective was to alarm the judge, to monopolize the attention of the court, and frighten his opponent into panic, a far remove from Cicero's conception of the three duties of the orator. We have already noted that Cassius Severus was commonly regarded as the first of the imperial orators (Tac., *Dial.* 19); the manner of the informers is clearly related to his bitter style.

Domitius Afer

The ablest orator of the second quarter of the first century A.D. was probably Gn. Domitius Afer;[19] Quintilian called him by far the greatest orator he had ever known (12.11.3). We can reconstruct the outlines of his career which may be taken as typical of one of the more successful orators of the early empire. Born in Nîmes, in Gaul, some time during the reign of Augustus, he was, so Tacitus characteristically puts it (*Ann.* 4.52) "of humble background and ready to shine by means of any crime." What Tacitus means is that Afer became an informer. He was praetor in A.D. 25, which suggests that he had secured some kind of influence already by that time, but his first big case came in the prosecution in 26 of Claudia Pulchra, a cousin of Agrippina the elder, who was now out of imperial favor. The charges included unchastity, adultery, and attempting to poison or bewitch the emperor; quite possibly she was involved in some conspiracy in Agrippina's interest which it was

---

[19] Cf. Meyer, *op.cit.* supra n. 1, 229-31; Cucheval, *op.cit.* supra n. 3, 214-35; *R-E* 5.1318-20 s.v. "Domitius" 14; Syme, *op.cit.* supra n. 1, 327-28; Leeman 240; George Kennedy, *Quintilian*, New York, 1969, 16-18.

inexpedient or impossible to unmask openly. Afer succeeded and had the satisfaction of hearing himself described by Tiberius as one who could claim to be "an orator in his own right" (Tac., *Ann.* 4.52). A prosecution of Claudia Pulchra's son Quintilius Varus the next year was less successful (*Ann.* 4.66). Under Tiberius' successor Gaius (Caligula) Afer ran into trouble. Gaius may have harbored some resentment from the Claudia Pulchra affair, since he was Agrippina's son, though Agrippina herself is said to have forgiven Afer (Dio Cassius 59.19). In any event, Afer was himself accused of treasonable insult to the emperor on the ground that he had set up a statue of Gaius with an inscription stating that he was consul for the second time in his twenty-seventh year. Since twenty-seven was too young to hold the consulship at all, it could be claimed that Afer was disloyally pointing to the unconstitutionality of the office, even though the erection of the statue was almost certainly an act of flattery. The charge could hardly have been made under Augustus or Tiberius, whose sense of values did not allow them to indulge in this kind of arbitrary suspicion, and the sequel suggests that Gaius' real motive was artistic jealousy. As he showed again in the case of the younger Seneca, Gaius was remarkably suspicious of anyone famous for eloquence. Yet so unstable and capricious was he that the fact of his inventing a capital charge did not mean with certainty that no escape could be found by a bold defendant. The emperor delivered in person a fancy speech against Afer, presumably before the senate sitting as a court on one of its own members. Dio's account continues as follows (59.19; the portions of Tacitus which dealt with this period are lost):

"But Afer then made no reply nor any defense, but pretending to be amazed and dumbfounded at the great

443

ability of Gaius and repeating over one by one the points of the accusation, as though he were a spectator rather than the accused, he praised the speech. When it was his turn to speak, he resorted to prayers and lamentations, and finally he flung himself down, and lying there on the ground he besought mercy from one he appeared to fear as an orator more than as emperor."

Afer's performance was just what Gaius wanted. With some encouragement from the freedman Callistus, whose friendship Afer had prudently cultivated, he graciously forgave Afer and subsequently (A.D. 39) made him suffect consul (Dio Cassius 59.20). Afer's fame increased, as did his fortune, which he invested at least in part in extensive brickyards near Rome (cf. *CIL* 15.979-86).

Under Claudius, Afer delivered the speech which Quintilian most frequently quotes, that in defense of Cloatilla, a kind of Roman Antigone earlier accused of illegally burying her husband who had taken part in a revolt (Quint. 8.5.16) and now brought to trial again perhaps in connection with a surety.[20] The quotations are mostly from the emotional peroration. Afer described Cloatilla as "a woman inexperienced in everything, unhappy in everything" (Quint. 9.3.66); he appealed to her brother and her father's friends who had brought the indictment (9.2.20), and he called upon her children to bury her even though she too became a convicted criminal: "Whatever may happen, sons, bury your mother" (Quint. 8.5.16). Throughout Claudius' reign Afer showed great security and independence, even to the extent of opposing several of Claudius' influential freedmen (Quint. 6.3.81).[21] Yet Claudius made Afer superin-

[20] Cf. Robert S. Rogers, "Domitius Afer's Defense of Cloatilla," *TAPhA* 76 (1945) 264-70.

[21] St. Jerome (*Ep.* 52.7.3) quotes "the orator Domitius" as saying "Should I treat you as emperor (*principem*) when you

444

tendent of the water supply (Frontinus, *De acqua.* 102).
He continued to handle cases, he wrote a work on proof
and evidence in oratory (Quint. 5.7.7), and he taught
rhetoric to, among others, Quintilian (10.1.86; 12.11.3;
Pliny, *Ep.* 2.14.10-11). Quintilian felt keenly the jests
made at Afer's expense when he continued to speak after
his powers were failing (12.11.3). He died in A.D. 59, "a
man who had held the highest offices and who demonstrated much eloquence" (Tac., *Ann.* 14.19).

The fact that Afer was so greatly admired by Quintilian suggests both that he had risen above the evil
reputation of his early career, if indeed that was ever
justified, for Quintilian was sensitive on moral issues, and
that his speaking was not in any extreme version of the
new style favored by the declaimers and the younger
Seneca, but in a somewhat more Ciceronian tradition.
Afer was a practicing orator throughout his career who
betrays no interest in declamation. According to Pliny
(*Ep.* 2.14.10) he spoke gravely and slowly. Quintilian
himself speaks of the "maturity" of his style (12.10.11)
and of his dislike of too much smoothness in the clausulae of sentences (9.4.31). Afer was famous for his wit,
and his best flashes were collected and published (Quint.
6.3.42). Quintilian quotes a number, some from
speeches, some from conversation. One which perhaps
shows some of the character of the man occurred one
day when he saw in the forum an ungrateful client who
pretended not to notice him. Afer looked away, but sent
his slave to say, "I hope you are grateful to me for not
seeing you?" (Quint. 6.3.93).

---

do not treat me as a senator?" If Afer ever said it, it must have
been to Claudius. Cicero (*De or.* 1.4) attributes a similar *sententia* to Crassus, with *consul* instead of *princeps*, and Jerome
may quote from memory, but literary imitation cannot be ruled
out.

In Afer's career the chief factors are perhaps the attractions of becoming an informer, the practical necessity of flattery, and the insecurity of fame. Words or actions could be twisted, and to many men saying nothing seemed the safest course. The virtues of the empire were real, but were only as strong as the character of the reigning emperor. Despite the efforts of the aristocracy to defame almost every prince after his death, seen by us best in the bitter portraits by Tacitus, it was only under a madman like Gaius that really intolerable conditions existed. Of course another tyrant might come at any time and did in Nero, Domitian, and some later emperors. We shall never know how many potentially great orators or writers in other genres were silenced by fear.

Discussions of the Decline of Eloquence

Many Greek and Latin writers of the first and early second centuries A.D. were concerned about a real or alleged decline in eloquence. We have a series of discussions of that topic, varying in length from short digressions to full scale works like Tacitus' *Dialogus de Oratoribus*.[22] These are important because they take us to the heart of the problem of the relationship between rhetoric and other aspects of civilization as the Romans saw it, including politics, philosophy, and literature, and because they bring out so clearly how rhetoric and oratory seemed to the Romans to be fundamental

[22] Cf. Norden 240-51; M. Dorothy Brock, *Studies in Fronto and his Age*, Cambridge, 1911, 13-24; Atkins 137-74; Henry Bardon, "Deux problemes de littérature imperiale," *Memorial des études latines offert à J. Marouzeau*, Paris, 1943, 232-40; Harry Caplan, "The Decay of Eloquence at Rome in the First Century," *Studies in Speech and Drama in Honor of Alexander M. Drummond*, Ithaca, 1944, 295-325, reprinted in *Of Eloquence. Studies in Ancient and Mediaeval Rhetoric*, Ithaca, 1970, 160-95; Donato Gagliardi, "Il dibattito retorico-letterario a Roma nel I secolo del impero," *Aevum* 40 (1966) 230-41.

to all literature. They help also to counterbalance the too easy assumption that changes in oratory and literature were entirely a result of the significant political changes which had occurred. Some general considerations should be kept in mind as background for these discussions.

In the early part of the reign of Augustus there had been optimism among some writers that literature might be entering a new age of creativity and purity of style. Dionysius of Halicarnassus expressed it most clearly in the introduction which he wrote to his study of the ancient orators.[23] This hope was probably bolstered by the belief which had occasionally been expressed in the past (e.g., Cicero, *De or.* 1.30 and *Brutus* 45-46) that the arts needed peace and leisure for their full development. Yet the hope did not outlive the generation of Dionysius and Virgil. In the previous chapter we saw the discouragement which came upon Horace, Ovid, and Livy. A discerning observer in the late years of Augustus might have pointed out that whereas early in the reign there were six or more writers of the first rank, now, with Ovid shattered by exile and the rest dead, only Titus Livy was left, while no new geniuses of the first order had been discovered.[24] Things doubtless seemed worse because they had first seemed better.

The pessimistic view was, however, not necessarily altogether a reflexion of actual conditions, for the common attitude of Greek and Roman antiquity toward the course of civilization was pessimistic. Nestor in the *Iliad* had seen a decline in his own lifetime; Hesiod canonized the golden age, the loss of innocence, and the progressive deterioration of morals, security, and happiness. Plato explained why even the best of states will in time

[23] Cf. APG 337 and supra 350-54.
[24] Cf. Leeman 225.

degenerate (*Republic* 8.545ff.) and lamented the invidious way in which the desire for wealth tended to undermine all other ambition and worthwhile activity (*Laws* 8.831c2ff.). Stoicism preached cycles of creation and destruction of the world and, as popularized among the Romans by Posidonius in the early first century B.C., renewed an interest in the golden age of the past and the deterioration of morality.[25] There was thus a literary commonplace about decline which might be adapted to many aspects of life. Ancient literature leaned heavily upon such traditional topics; they were used to order and interpret observed experience, and they could easily exaggerate what was observed.

Belief in decline of some sort was apparently especially congenial to Romans, conservative by nature and inclined to think that any change was change for the worse. The Romans had, in addition, a feeling of cultural inferiority to Greeks for which they compensated by idolizing certain Roman virtues and by representing Greeks as weak and degenerate. Since Greek culture obviously infiltrated Rome, the implication was that Rome was being corrupted. This Greek influence became marked in the second century B.C. and dominant in the first, the very time when the Romans were experiencing increasing difficulty in administering their political affairs. Hellenization was in part made possible by the great increase of wealth in Roman hands, wealth which could afford works of Greek art, Greek slaves, and opportunity for leisure, literature, and philosophy. Thus wealth, Greek influence, and political chaos are all parts of the same cultural complex which found expression in laments such as those of Sallust at the decline of Roman

[25] Cf. Seneca, *Epist.* 90.5 and E. Vernon Arnold, *Roman Stoicism*, London, 1958, 194-97.

morality. It is easy to belittle or dismiss Sallust's commonplace that gold is the source of evil: the matter is not so simple as he makes it and his terminology is not what a modern historian would choose, but the decline which he and other Romans felt had some reality; it is best seen in the inability to work out political solutions in the late republic, in the loss of a sense of common purpose among the Romans, in personal opportunism, in the inability to find meaning in life, in the search for luxurious ease, in the futile attempt of statesmen to impose sumptuary legislation and check extravagance. All of these manifestations of decline began well before the empire and continue under the empire with a few modifications. Romans did not suddenly become disgusted or indifferent to affairs in the empire; they had been wearying of them since the second century B.C. Informers did not suddenly appear; they were the successors of the republican opportunists. Conspiracy and plots against the government designed to secure the power of some one man were not sudden phenomena; they had occurred throughout the first century B.C. Roman history is a continuum and the empire may well be viewed as a way of living with the conditions of minds and heart which had come to exist among the Romans. What is remarkable is not so much the conditions of the empire as the remarkable achievement of the Augustan age which opened it.

Another factor which led the Romans to acknowledge and perhaps exaggerate decline in eloquence was the fact that to many, as to us, Roman oratory was overshadowed by the enormous figure of Cicero. Neither in historiography nor in lyric nor even in epic is a single man so dominant. Attempts to avoid comparison by repudiating Cicero's style could not obscure his achievement. Even

449

if the republic had continued, there would have been a void in literary history after the death of Cicero, just as English drama has never recovered from the death of Shakespeare. Cicero himself, never overly modest, anticipated the problem (*Tusc.* 2.5; *Brutus* 22 and 37-38).

Finally, Roman education was heavily directed toward oratory. It aimed at training a certain kind of man of public affairs whose abilities were especially suited to the Greek democracies or the Roman republic. But the practical need for this particular educational product declined in the empire, not directly because orators were suppressed by the government, but because problems were solved or obviated or better methods found for dealing with them. The educational system made little effort to adapt itself to the change. Like everyone else, educators had lost incentive and interest in intellectual activity. Their schools continued to produce orators who were told that rhetoric was important, that the orator could civilize the barbarous, reconcile the estranged, and console the bereaved. But the orators themselves lost faith in their commonplaces, by now too often repeated, and the tasks hardly seemed worth trying. The barbarous were either civilized enough for daily life or held in distant waste by Roman arms; no elegant orator wanted to talk to them. The estranged were dealt with by the orderly and rather mundane operation of Roman law where there was room for oratory indeed, but where novelty and imagination had to be restrained by practicality. And the bereaved probably found more comfort in mystery religions. But since speech was the distinctive attribute of man, the Romans had to speak, and they did, about pirates and ravished maidens, and they were not very satisfied with the result. Oratory ought to be concerned with greater things.

The earliest of the discussions is possibly that in the

forty-fourth chapter of the essay *On Sublimity*,[26] which may have been written in the later part of the reign of Augustus. "Longinus" here adopts a kind of dialogue form and reports a conversation between himself and an unnamed philosopher, who asks why it is that there are many men alive with ability to speak and a fine sense of style, but no longer or only rarely do there seem to be great geniuses. Must one, he inquires, accept the "trite" explanation that literature flourishes only under a democracy, which nourishes thoughts and hopes and produces rivalry and ambition? Now men are trained in a just servitude and become only great at flattery. Specific political oppression is not alleged; the tyrant is represented as a beneficent one. What is lost is incentive. "Longinus" replies that it is not the world's peace that causes the trouble. A great nature surely should be expected to rise above this, as above other inconveniences. Thus the political answer is superficial, and the real cause is the love of money and of pleasure which drowns the soul so that men never look up or care about fame.

Several features of this passage should be noted. The immediate political situation is easily associated with the Augustan age and its restoration of peace to the world, a peace now beginning to grow tiresome. On the other hand, the Roman republic was hardly a democracy and the whole passage is written from the Greek point of view. When he speaks of the political answer as trite, the author is thinking of explanations for the intellectual and literary decline in Greece, and especially in Athens, after the fourth century. We do not have such discussions, but their existence in the writing of historians or philosophers or rhetoricians would have been encouraged by the fact that Aristotle had directly associated the be-

[26] Cf. D. A. Russell, *"Longinus" On the Sublime*, Oxford, 1964, 185-87.

ginnings of rhetoric and oratory with the appearance of democracy in Syracuse.[27] The answer favored by "Longinus" is more philosophic than that proposed by the philosopher. It is perhaps Platonic in origin but is certainly congenial to Roman attitudes, and it would have been entirely acceptable even to Augustus himself who tried hard to spark a moral awakening. Finally, the passage should be read in the context of *On Sublimity* as a whole. In chapter four we stressed the fact that this was intended as a practical treatise: somewhat idealistically the author thought there was hope of creating great literature, oratory included, if writers had the requisite understanding of the art of writing and especially if they had a philosophical dimension or greatness of soul which could raise the substance to imaginative and insightful expression. The result is that although "Longinus" appears to agree with his philosophical friend that there is a dearth of great writers, he does not agree that conditions are such as to prevent great writers from appearing.

Another Greek discussion from about this time is one in the Jewish philosopher Philo, who lived in Alexandria in the early decades of the first century and came to Rome as an old man on an embassy to Caligula in A.D. 39-40.[28] We have his account of his embassy, a pamphlet rather oratorical in form attacking Flaccus the governor of Egypt,[29] and extensive writings on the Old Testament, interpreted under the influence of Greco-Roman

[27] Cf. *APG* 26-29; 58-61.

[28] Philo's works are edited with translation and notes by F. G. Colson and G. H. Whitaker, 10 vols., London, 1929-62. Cf. also Edwin R. Goodenough, *The Politics of Philo Judaeus*, New Haven, 1938; idem, *An Introduction to Philo Judaeus*, Oxford, 1962. The embassy is the only definite date in Philo's life. Other works of Philo mention moral decline, e.g. *Quod omnis probus* 62-74.

[29] Cf. Herbert Box, *Philonis Alexandrini in Flaccum*, London, 1939.

philosophy. Among the latter is an essay *On the Planting of Noah* in which mention of vines leads to a discussion of drunkenness and the thesis whether the wise man will or will not drink freely. Philo says that wise men in the past took wine, but most men today are not their equal in language or in deeds (156). Language has become depraved, diseased, and inflated. Actions are effeminate; few care for ancient ambition (158). But in ancient days, "Poets and prose writers and those interested in other liberal arts flourished; they did not sweeten and enervate the ears with rhythmical language, but they roused any part of the mind which was weak and broken down, and as much of it as was in tune they harmonized with the instruments of nature and virtue." The passage tells little about the literary attitudes in Rome for the reference is to Jewish writers and Greek philosophers, but it does show that the association of moral decline and literature was common among the Greeks in the first century and that discussions of decline did not always invoke political causes.

Among Latin discussions, that in the elder Seneca, because of the author's conservatism, can be taken to reflect a point of view during later Augustan or early Tiberian times even though it may not have been written until the fourth decade of the first century. Seneca was convinced that eloquence and all Roman life were not what they once had been.[30] Indeed, the belief that declaimers contemporary with his sons were inferior to those of his own youth afforded him the excuse for recalling the golden days of declamation. He wants his sons to realize "to what an extent native abilities sink every day lower and by some hostility of nature eloquence has abandoned us" (*Contr.* 1. *pr.* 6). Decline

[30] For further discussion of Seneca with bibliography cf. supra 322-30.

is thus a continuing process and part of the operation of a natural law. Though the declaimers of his own day showed a special vigor and polish (*Contr.* 10. *pr.* 5), "whatever Roman eloquence achieved to rival or excel Greek insolence reached its peak in the time of Cicero." "Since then, day by day, things have become worse, whether because of the luxury of the times (for nothing is so deadly to natural abilities as luxury), or because when the prizes to be won in this very honorable task became less, all ambition took itself to other areas more promising in fame and profit though less honorable, or whether by some fate, whose malign and eternal law it is in all things that whatever has been brought to the highest point falls again to the lowest more swiftly than it rose" (*Contr.* 1. *pr.* 7).

These are the three possibilities which Seneca sees. The third, fate, may be thought to embrace the first two, luxury and loss of incentive. It is the one against which there is no recourse but philosophical resignation and an explanation which suggests that such a vast trend is beyond the power of an individual man to alter. In his second cause, loss of incentive, Seneca seems to have in mind rewards in the form of office, prestige, and influence. Elsewhere (*Contr.* 10. *pr.* 5) he speaks of Labienus as "violentus et qui Pompeianos spiritus nondum in tanta pace posuisset," "a violent mind and one which in this time of overwhelming peace had not yet laid down the energies characteristic of the Pompeian party." Violent enthusiasms or ambitions were out of place in the Roman empire where the official attitude was that party strife had destroyed the republic.

Of the causes of decline which Seneca mentions, the one which most interests him and which he clearly regarded as most fundamental is the first, the luxury of the age. He thinks luxury works its poison by encouraging laziness. Thus, immediately after outlining the three possible causes of decline he goes on to say: "See how the abilities of the idle youth grow dull; there is no involvement in labor for any honorable end. Sleep and sluggishness and what is worse than sleep and sluggishness, an industry for evil, have invaded their minds. . . ." An enervated effeminacy has replaced early Roman vigor. Somewhat later (*Contr.* 1. *pr.* 10) he complains that no one is interested in memory, and that *sententiae* spoken in the past by the great can easily be represented as original thoughts by contemporary speakers, since the audience is too lazy to have studied them.[31] The point is that to become a good orator or even a good judge of oratory is hard work, and modern audiences and speakers are not willing to take the trouble. Seneca has learned Horace's lesson of the *labor limae*, but others have forgotten. Even Porcius Latro, Seneca's old friend and an able declaimer, shows some of the incipient laziness (*Contr.* 1. *pr.* 13-14), and it was laziness, and poetry, which ruined the youthful promise of Alfius Flavus (*Contr.* 1.1.22). Seneca apparently did not think things would get better if orators just tried harder. The evil was too deep-seated and he knew perhaps too well the aberrations of taste which trying for pointed epigrams in declamation could produce. He does not specifically blame declamation for contributing to the decline, but elsewhere, as we have seen, he does report some of the criticisms of declamation voiced by others which point out its stylistic artificialities and its inapplicability to the realities of the forum (e.g., *Contr.* 3. *pr.* 8ff. and 9. *pr.* 1ff.).

To sum up, Seneca seems to be in agreement with "Longinus" in noting the effect of political changes on eloquence, but in attributing major responsibility to a

[31] Cf. the story told by Vitruvius 7. *pr.* 5-7.

moral decline which he does not date but which must be presumed to reach back into the republic. But he differs from "Longinus" in that he betrays no inclination to hope for better things nor does he advance any program for reform.

A contemporary of Seneca who refers briefly to the history of oratory is Velleius Paterculus, author of a compendium of Roman history published about A.D. 30.[32] It is a significant, though not a great, work: the earliest surviving example of the kind of brief survey which furnished the maximum amount of historical reading many Romans of the empire could tolerate. Velleius writes in an elaborate style complete with apostrophe, digressions, commonplaces drawn from the rhetorical schools, and involved periodicity which is intended to be impressive and perhaps even stirring, but which has struck most readers as absurd. In other words, he is one of the earliest Latin examples of the possible bad effects of conventional rhetoric. Velleius is also important as an example of enthusiasm for the empire and especially for Tiberius, under whose military command he himself had served as an officer.

Although hardly a great authority on literary matters, Velleius unlike most ancient historians includes literary history in his work.[33] Homer gets a chapter (1.5) in the

---

[32] Velleius lived from c. 19 B.C. to c. A.D. 31. He was praetor in A.D. 15. For translation cf. Frederick W. Shipley, *Velleius Paterculus: Compendium of Roman History* (Loeb), London, 1924. For discussion of historical problems cf. G. V. Sumner, "The Truth about Velleius Paterculus," *HSPh* 74 (1970) 257-97.
[33] Cf. Friedrich A. Schoeb, *Velleius Paterculus und seine literhistorischen Abschnitte*, Tübingen, 1908; Francesco Della Corte, "I giudizi letterari di Velleio Paterculo," *RFIC* 15 (1937) 154-59; Italo Lana, "Velleio Paterculo della propaganda," *Univ. di Torino, Pubbl. della Fac. di Lett. e Filos.* 4.2 (1952); Leeman 248-51. The evidence does not seem adequate

account of legendary Greek history at the beginning, and Hesiod half a chapter (1.7.1). There is also a chapter (2.9) on Latin literature of the second century B.C. and a similar one (2.36) on writers of the Golden Age. These are mostly lists with some striking omissions such as the names of Ennius, Plautus, Horace, and Propertius. For all his admiration for the age in which he lived (cf., e.g., 2.126), Velleius believes there has been a moral decline at Rome (cf., e.g., 1.17; 2.1; 2.10). The passage which is most relevant to the state of rhetoric in the early empire is the literary-philosophical digression at the end of book one (chapters 16-18), which might roughly be described as Velleius' thoughts on the progression of the genres. He remarks that the great writers in each literary form are approximate contemporaries. Tragedy flourishes at one time, oratory at another. In Greece, for example (16), "what distinction was there among orators before Isocrates or after his pupils and their followers?"[34] The same phenomenon is observable in Latin where despite the work of Cato and a few others the greatest achievement came in the time of Cicero. Few before him and his contemporaries can delight a reader and none can arouse admiration (17). Velleius shrinks from saying specifically that eloquence has declined, but he clearly implies that it is no longer at the acme of the Ciceronian age. His explanation is rather hesitatingly advanced: namely, that while emulation and rivalry produce a series of good achievements in a particular form for a period of time, the effect of a great genius, if one does appear, is inhibiting on the other

---

to attribute Velleius' literary canons to any school, though Schoeb and Della Corte try, cf. also Schanz-Hosius 2.582-6.

[34] Isocrates is perhaps mentioned more for the length of his life which overlapped the other orators than because Velleius preferred him.

writers. They become discouraged at the possibility of surpassing an Isocrates or a Cicero and turn to other tasks. "This frequent and fickle jumping from one genre to another is the greatest obstacle to a perfected work of art" (17). Finally (18), Velleius wonders at but does not explain the fact that excellence is not shared by all cities: Athens had more eloquence than all the rest of Greece put together.

Thus Velleius, though a strong supporter of the empire, seems to believe that oratory has somewhat declined, that there is a general moral decline, and that literary achievements come in cycles, for which he has an explanation. Though he occasionally refers to fate and fortune in other parts of his work, he does not invoke fate to explain literary achievement. The theory of the progression of genres breaks down when studied in detail. The theory of the inhibiting effect of genius has greater merit. It would have been interesting if Velleius could have found information about the way earlier authors viewed literary tradition and opportunity in their own time. This might have included comments on the lack of suitability of some forms for some periods—Callimachus' attitude toward Greek epic, for example. Did fourth century B.C. Greek poets ever comment on their achievements and problems in comparison with those of Sophocles and Euripides? The other Augustan poets had no intention of competing with Virgil, but if he had not existed they might have been persuaded by Augustus to try. Emulation was of course a crucial factor in ancient and especially Roman cultural history. The Romans began by emulating the Greeks in a patriotic effort to create a literature of their own. They then moved on in many cases to emulation of their own classical writers. It is clear that within the narrow conceptions of traditional literary forms the effect of a great achievement might well be discouraging to other writers for a period of time, and many might prefer to aim at a different and perhaps lesser goal. Velleius' theory applies best in poetry, where the products are timeless, or in history, where a particular subject may be given an almost perfect treatment. It applies much less well in oratory, where each situation or case has unique features and demands a new speech, yet Cicero, as we have seen, did exercise an inhibiting effect on his successors. In the age of Nero, Stoicism gave some of the impetus to literature which "Longinus" had looked for. Two Stoics, Persius and Seneca, both have something to say about the decline of eloquence. In addition there are important references in a very different kind of writer, Petronius.

Encolpius, the roguish hero of Petronius' novel-like work, the *Satyricon*,[35] at one point (83) wanders into a picture gallery where he encounters an indigent old poet, Eumolpus, who tells him a racy story and then speculates on the reason for the decadence of painting. His explanation: obsession with making money and living for pleasure. Nobody cares about the discipline neces-

---

[35] Petronius is presumably the arbiter of elegance, suffect consul in A.D. 62, whose death is described in Tac., *Ann.* 16.18. In addition to works cited below the following discuss Petronius' criticisms of rhetoric: A. Collignon, *Étude sur Pétrone: la critique littéraire, l'imitation et la parodie dans la Satiricon*, Paris, 1892; R. B. Steele, "Literary Adaptations and References in Petronius," *CJ* 15 (1919-20) 279-93; Felix Scheidweiler, "Mitteilungen: drei Petronstelle," *PhW* 42 (1922) 1052-53; Atkins 2.159-66; J. K. Schönberger, "Nachmals Petron. c.1-5," *PhW* 59 (1939) 478-80 and 508-12 and "Mitteilungen zu Petron. c.3-5," *PhW* 60 (1940) 623-24; L. Alfonsi, "Petronio e i Teodorei," *RFIC* 26 (1948) 46-53; Gilbert Bagnani, *Arbiter of Elegance: A Study of the Life and Work of C. Petronius*, Toronto, 1954; H.L.W. Nelson, "Ein Unterrichtsprogram aus Neronischen Zeit," *Mededelingen der k. Nederlansche Akademie, Afdeeling Letterkunde* 19.6 (1956) 201-28.

sary for the arts or sciences or eloquence (88)! Later (118ff.) Eumolpus gives his views on epic poetry: it requires extensive training, a vast knowledge of literature, elevated poetic diction, and the full panoply of mythology and divine activity. He appears to intend a contrast with the epic of Lucan on the Civil Wars, which was being written about this time and dispensed with interventions by the gods. Eumolpus then illustrates his concept by a rather uninspired 300-line effort, also on the Civil Wars.

The most relevant passage in the *Satyricon*, however, is that with which the work as we have it begins.[36] Encolpius has been visiting a rhetorical school and after listening to declamations is discovered in the middle of an attack on the artificiality of declamation, which he claims is the cause of the decline of eloquence (1-2). Declaimers are insane, and their art, a world of pirates, tyrants, and immolated virgins, is entirely foreign to the forum, for which it pretends to train. The "honied globules of words and all the sayings and doings sprinkled with pepper or sesame" have corrupted style so that eloquence has lost all its force. Things were better in the days of Sophocles and Euripides, who had no need of training in declamation to find suitable words for speeches. In Pindar's time there was no academician to corrupt native good sense. So too in the time of Plato and Demosthenes. He goes on to say that Asianism has ruined everything. The advent of this corruption is described with the usual metaphorical contempt favored by the Atticists and it is said to have come "recently."

The rhetorician Agamemnon replies (3-5) with a defense of the schools. They have to teach the way they do or they would have no students. The real blame be-

[36] *Codex Parisinus Latinus* 7989 attributes the fragmentary surviving text to the fifteenth and sixteenth books of the work.

longs with the parents, who are in a great hurry to rush their children through school and out into the forum when still unprepared. Eloquence is a difficult study and needs a long period of training. The system is all right in theory, but the professors are not given a chance. Petronius' remarks need to be approached in different ways. First of all, his work is clearly intended to be naturalistic and what is said is therefore similar to what might be said under the dramatic circumstances described. Encolpius voices reasonable criticisms of the schools; Agamemnon gives tenable answers to these criticisms. The view that the ideas are commonplace is supported by the fact that the moral argument is substantially what we found in the elder Seneca and the criticism of declamation is also analogous to passages in his work. Furthermore, both the criticism and the answers foreshadow comments of Quintilian about conditions in the schools (2.4.10). Petronius is, however, the earliest author to associate the two topics of the evils of declamation and the decline of eloquence and to suggest that the former was one of the causes of the latter. Thus an educational explanation may be added to the moral, cyclical, and political explanations which we have met before. There is no sign of the latter two in Petronius, which may mean that they were not among the more generally voiced reasons.

Serious interpretation of Petronius is notoriously complicated by the form and style of his work.[37] For our purposes it is perhaps not essential to know whether Petronius himself agreed with what his characters say about eloquence and the arts; the chances are that he did fundamentally agree with it and the reason for thinking so is the very high literary standard of his work, the ab-

[37] The best discussion is that of J. P. Sullivan, *The Satyricon of Petronius*, Bloomington, 1968, 158-213.

sence from it of bombast and the declamatory style except for comic effect, and the generally conservative, classicist, and even Atticist tastes which he shows.[38] At the same time, though what the characters say is basically correct in Petronius' view, there is a humorous, tongue-in-cheek quality about *their* saying it. None has the ethos of a persuasive orator. Agamemnon in the portico and Eumolpus in the picture gallery seem to be semisatiric pictures of character types mouthing commonplaces, rather than serious attempts to convey a point of view. In the case of Encolpius' comments on declamation the reference to Asianism as "recent" probably is intended to indicate that he has taken over material from books he has read without entirely understanding the history of the subject. Yet Petronius allows the dramatic illusion to slip a little in giving an intensity of feeling to the criticism. The same happens in the passage on epic, where the long poetic composition can only have resulted from Petronius' personal interest in what he was doing.

A second Neronian author is the satirist Persius, who had studied with the great grammarian Remmius Palaemon and the well-known rhetorician Verginius Flavus, but clearly did not enjoy declamation (3.44-47).[39] His tastes were more for philosophy as taught by the Stoic Annaeus Cornutus, and he seems to have had contacts in the circle of Thrasea Paetus, whom we have met as the Stoic martyr of the age.[40] Persius' poetry is strongly Roman and characterized by obscurity, not the precious

[38] Cf. Evan T. Sage, "Atticism in Petronius," *TAPhA* 46 (1915) 47-57.
[39] Cf. the ancient life of Persius attributed by some manuscripts to Valerius Probus, otherwise to Suetonius, cf. J. C. Rolfe, *Suetonius* (Loeb), Cambridge, 1959, 2.494-99.
[40] Cf. supra 441.

obscurity of the Alexandrian or rhetorical poets, but an obscurity which comes from pungent abruptness of thought and allusion.

Of the six satires the first deals most directly with literature.[41] Persius has, he says (8), a secret he wants to tell; it comes out at the end of the poem (121): Who is there at Rome who does not have asses' ears? Everybody tries to write something grand (14), which they hope to recite impressively. The audience is then supposed to be overcome by emotion (19-20). Persius' imaginary interlocutor protests that there is no point in study unless you give expression to the powerful forces within you (24-25), but Persius will have none of that and proceeds to quote examples of the kind of overwriting he detests. The interlocutor points out that writers are trying hard to find a place in the mouths of men and to secure immortality (40-43). Persius does not object to enjoying praise, but doesn't think that praise should be the objective in writing (48-49). He criticizes obsession with smoothness (63-64), grand subjects (68), and Greek mythology instead of Roman life (71-75). Although poetry is primarily what Persius has in mind, there are references to oratory as well (83-87). Even in a serious trial the orator thinks first of being complimented for his speech! Answering a charge is less important than figures of speech. Writers would not produce the rot they do if they had any manhood (103-4); Lucilius and Horace had something worth saying in their attacks on vice (114-15); Persius himself wants as readers

[41] Cf. George L. Hendrickson, "The First Satire of Persius," *CPh* 23 (1928) 97-112; Felix Gaffiot, "La première satire de Perse," *RPh* 55 (1929) 271-80; William C. Korfmacher, "Persius as a Literary Critic," *CJ* 28 (1932-33) 276-86; Atkins 2.155-59; Kenneth J. Reckford, "Studies in Persius," *Hermes* 90 (1962) 476-504.

those who can stomach Old Comedy, not the pompous or the trivial (123-34).

This satire is clearly related to discussions of the decline of eloquence. Persius would attribute contemporary conditions to moral decline and to striving for effect, which recitation and declamation encouraged. Not only declamation, but the kind of literary effort which "Longinus" seems to be urging, could lead to the tasteless product which Persius protests in the hands of would-be writers who did not have "Longinus'" sensitivity.

Although Persius apparently had friends in the "philosophical opposition" to the empire there is nothing to suggest that he thought political conditions had removed the incentive to write or speak well. The ancient scholiast who wrote notes to his poems thought that the first satire was especially directed against the poetry written by Nero, and he even claimed that lines 99-101, where Persius ridicules verses on the bacchants, were quotations from Nero. And finally he claims that after Persius' death Cornutus suppressed a reference to Nero in line 121. Less direct reference to Nero might be seen in the fourth satire where Alcibiades is taken as the type of young man without self-control or self-knowledge. The critics have been uncertain about Cornutus' editing;[42] the less specific references have parallels in many imperial poets who seem to have been fond of writing about mythological or historical topics which could be, but did not have to be, applied to contemporary conditions and were therefore reasonably safe.

[42] Cf. E. Haguenin, "Perse a-t-il attaqué Néron?" *RPh* 23 (1899) 301-12; Alfred Pretor, "A Few Notes on the Satires of Persius," *CR* 21 (1907) 72-75; François Villeneuve, *Essai sur Perse*, Paris, 1918, 218-24; Leon Hermann, "L'empereur Néron et le roi Midas," *REL* 6 (1928) 313-19; Korfmacher, *op.cit.* supra n. 41, 281; Enzo V. Marmoreale, *Persio*, Florence, 1942, 212-26.

The Younger Seneca

The younger Seneca is an important figure in the history of rhetoric, in part because of his prose style, but also because he tried to use rhetorical devices of persuasion to secure practical fulfillment of certain philosophical and political ideals. The difficulty of Seneca's task is reflected in the severity of the judgments commonly made of him by modern writers: he has been labeled inconsistent, hypocritical, paranoiac, even loathsome.[43] But Tacitus, hardly an indulgent judge of political opportunism, put a generally favorable estimate on Seneca's intentions and career (*Ann.* 13.2), and he deserves more sympathetic consideration than he is sometimes given.

Seneca's life may be summed up as follows:[44] he was born in Spain about 4 B.C., came to Rome at an early age, and probably studied under some of the declaimers known to his father (*Contr.* 10. *pr.* 2, 9, and 12). Though sometimes critical of grammarians as pedantic (e.g., *Ep.* 108.29-35), he says nothing specifically against rhetoricians. Far more influential were his philosophical stud-

---

[43] Cf., e.g., J. D. Duff, *L. Annaei Senecae Dialogorum libri x, xi, xii*, Cambridge, Eng., 1915, xxvi; H. J. Rose, *A Handbook of Latin Literature*, London, 1949, 359 ("the loathing which his personality excites"); E. Philips Barker, *OCD* s.v. "Seneca 2" ("paranoiac abnormality"). The chief ancient detractor of Seneca was Dio Cassius (61.10). Syme, *op.cit.* supra n. 1, 550-51 shows Dio's prejudice and (552) pronounces Seneca's policy "the best available." Cf. also A. D. Nock in *CAH* 10.509: "a literary man with an ideal standard which was not the less real if it was at times inevitably compromised." Most sympathetic is Richard M. Gummere, *Seneca the Philosopher and His Modern Message*, Boston, 1922.

[44] The chief sources are his own works and the references in Tacitus, Suetonius, and Dio. Cf. Gummere, *op. cit.* supra n. 43; A. Bourgery, *Sénèque prosateur: études littéraires et grammaticales sur la prose de Sénèque le philosophe*, Paris, 1922; Italo Lana, *Lucio Annaeo Seneca*, Turin, 1955; *CAH* 10.702ff.

ies with Sotion, Attalus, and Fabianus. Some portion of his early life he passed in Egypt, where his maternal aunt was the wife of the governor, C. Galerius. His career at Rome began with the quaestorship in A.D. 32. By the end of that decade he was one of the best-known orators in the city, provoking the jealousy of Gaius Caligula, who called his speaking "show pieces" and "sand without lime" (Suet., *Gaius* 53), perhaps meaning that his style lacked strength and coherence.[45] Gaius considered executing Seneca, but allowed himself to be persuaded that Seneca was dying of consumption (Dio Cassius 59.19.8). Seneca thus survived, though perhaps in silence, only to be exiled to Corsica by Claudius in 41. The instigator was Claudius' wife Messalina, the charge adultery, the motive unclear (Dio Cassius 60.8.5). Seneca at first bravely consoled his mother Helvia from exile, but Corsica cannot be said to have grown upon his affection as the years passed. One of his most criticized works is that which he addressed to Polybius, the freedman secretary of Claudius, purportedly in sympathy for the loss of his brother, actually to try to secure his own recall by flattery of Polybius and Claudius, whose memory he later treated with a good deal of contempt in the *Apocolocyntosis.*[46]

It was perhaps while he was on Corsica that Seneca composed or at least planned his tragedies, for there seems little opportunity for them to be written later

---

[45] Cf. J. Stroux, "Caligulas Urteil über den Stil Senecas," *Philologus* 86 (1931) 349-55.

[46] Cf. Duff, *op.cit.* supra n. 43. Seneca is defended by Allen P. Ball, *The Satire of Seneca on the Apotheosis of Claudius*, New York, 1902, 31-37. Arnaldo Momigliano, *Claudius the Emperor and his Achievement* (trans. W. D. Hogarth), New York, 1961, 74-79, thought the *Consolatio* was fiercely ironic and had an inner consistency with the *Apocolocyntosis.*

and this was certainly the period when a tragic view of life most recommended itself to him. It is relatively easy to see contemporary political tyranny or Seneca's own discouragement and bitterness in the speeches of Seneca's characters and choruses. For all the strong rhetorical influences upon the style of the tragedies, there is a noteworthy failure of communication in them.[47] Each character tends to speak as though alone in the world, which is perhaps the way Seneca himself felt, and little persuasion is accomplished.

Claudius' domineering fourth wife, Agrippina, arranged Seneca's recall in 49. He was made praetor and appointed tutor to Agrippina's eleven-year-old son Nero, marked out for an imperial destiny (Tac., *Ann.* 12.8). Seneca could now be expected to be grateful to her and not particularly sympathetic to Claudius. Suetonius reports (*Nero* 52) that Agrippina was averse to Nero's studying philosophy, as an impediment to one who would be a ruler. Seneca's instruction included the areas of politics, maybe history, and certainly rhetoric (Tac., *Ann.* 13.2; 14.55). In the same passage Suetonius claims that Seneca kept Nero from studying the ancient orators out of jealousy of them. If the story has any truth it is

[47] Cf. Richard M. Smith, *De arte rhetorica in L. A. Senecae tragoediis perspicua*, Leipzig, 1885; H. V. Canter, "Rhetorical Elements in the Tragedies of Seneca," *Univ. of Illinois Studies* 10.1 (1925); E. Hansen, *Die Stellung der Affektrede in den Tragoedien des Seneca*, Berlin, 1934; Clarence W. Mendell, *Our Seneca*, New Haven, 1940, 111 (notes absence of debate); Giovanni Runchina, "Tecnica drammatica e retorica nelle tragedie di Seneca," *Annali dell' Univ. di Cagliari* 28 (1960) 163-324. D'Alton 459-61 fails to understand the problem. On political criticism in the tragedies, cf. Gaston Boissier, *L'Opposition sous les Césars*, Paris, 1909, 83-90. The tragedies seem to be a deliberately arranged series of philosophical dramas, cf. Berthe Marti, "Seneca's Tragedies. A New Interpretation," *TAPhA* 76 (1945) 216-45.

more likely that he thought an emperor should cultivate the contemporary style. He certainly regarded ability to speak well as an important quality in a ruler (*De ira* 1.6). The opportunity offered to Seneca by his relationship to Nero was not one to attract a nervous or unambitious man. At any moment he could only too easily be caught in court intrigue between some of the most ruthless opponents in history. As it was, after five years as tutor he had the pleasure of composing a funeral encomium for Claudius, which Nero delivered (Tac., *Ann.* 13.3); he was suffect consul in 56; he cooperated in Nero's removal of his mother in 59, and only after eight years as speechwriter, adviser, and minister of state did he find himself so hard pressed as to seek retirement (Tac., *Ann.* 14.53-54). It is customary to attribute most positive governmental policy in the early years of Nero's reign to Seneca.[48] Though there is little direct proof of this, his influence may have been considerable. The policy in effect was apparently designed to make Nero an enlightened despot, distributing benefits freely out of his own goodness to a grateful world. Seneca's treatise *On Clemency* was addressed to Nero and describes the virtue of a philosophical king.

After retirement Seneca spent three years in a rather precarious Indian summer devoted to philosophy before being implicated in the Pisonian conspiracy of 65. Like some other Stoics he seems to have wanted to bring his life to a significant close and accepted with dignity the

---

[48] Aurelius Victor, *De Caes.* 5.2 quotes Trajan's phrase *Neronis quinquennium,* often taken to mean "five golden years under Nero," and regarded as the first five years under Seneca's influence, cf. Syme, *op.cit.* supra n. 1, 262 and 550-52. Other interpretations have been suggested, cf. J.G.C. Anderson, "Trajan on the *Quinquennium Neronis,*" *JRS* 1 (1911) 173-79, answered by F. A. Lepper, "Some Reflexions on the *quinquennium Neronis,*" *JRS* 47 (1957) 95-103.

opportunity for a philosophical suicide. A splendid account of his final moments can be read in Tacitus (*Ann.* 15.60-64). Little is known about Seneca's speeches except that they were envied by Gaius and imitated by many (Quint. 10.1.125). He may have appeared in the law courts occasionally for his friends, and he doubtless spoke in the senate from time to time. It would seem out of character for him to have devoted much time to declamation after his schoolboy days. There are, however, some passages rather reminiscent of declamation in his writings, for example a discussion of the definition of crimes (*De constantia sapientis* 7), a passage on whether or not Caesar should have spared Brutus (*De beneficiis* 2.20), and a case involving two brothers who disagree (*ibid.* 5.20). *De beneficiis* 6.31 resembles a theme for a *suasoria*: "Should Xerxes begin war on Greece?" and actually includes a short speech written in the person of Demaratus the Spartan, dissuading Xerxes. Elsewhere Seneca occasionally inserts a speech into a dialogue almost as an historian might into a narrative, for example a speech by Claudius in the *Consolatio ad Polybium* (14-16), which preserves the pedantic manner of the emperor as known from Tacitus and Suetonius, and an imaginary speech of Augustus in *De clementia* (1.9).

The form which provided the model for much of Seneca's philosophical writing was the diatribe, an ethical lecture of a popular nature, often rather loosely put together out of commonplace arguments or examples. It originated among the Cynic and Stoic philosophers of Greece, Bion and Teles being among the first to use it. The first diatribes made little literary pretense and were not regarded as reaching the dignity of oratory, but they later exercised influence on more artistic philosophical writing such as the dialogues of Cicero or Dio or Lucian

469

and also on the satires of Horace and Juvenal. One of the commoner adaptations of the diatribe at Rome was the *consolatio*, a philosophical essay in the form of a letter of consolation for the loss of a relative.[49] Seneca's extant works (there were once many others) consist of thirteen prose treatises,[50] 124 letters, a Menippean satire on the deification of Claudius, and nine tragedies. There are also some epigrams which may well be his. A considerable number of these were certainly written at times when the author was debarred from public life, either during his exile on Corsica or after his retirement. In the Roman tradition so well represented by Cicero, Seneca felt a compulsion to make creative use of his leisure time. Many of his contemporaries did the same, but few of them were so deeply convinced of a particular point of view that almost their entire literary output is devoted, as Seneca's is, to its persuasive exposition. He wishes to expound his philosophy, which is basically Stoicism, though not narrowly doctrinaire (*De otio* 3.1), for he is anxious to find points of agreement with Epicurus and other philosophers, and he wishes

[49] On the diatribe and the *consolatio* cf. Henri Weber, *De Senecae genere dicendi Bioneo*, Marburg, 1895; A. Siegmund, *De Senecae consolationibus* I-III, Böhm.-Leipa, 1912-14; Charles Favez, *L. Annaei Senecae ad Helviam matrem de consolatione*, Lausanne, 1918, xxxviiiff.; M. Galdi, "Sulle *consolationes* di Seneca," *Athenaeum* 6 (1928) 220-48; E. Jacoby, "Composizione ed elementi costitutivi delle *Consolazioni* di Seneca a Marcia ed a Polibio," *Athenaeum* 9 (1931 243-59; idem, "Fonti retoriche delle *Consolazioni* di Seneca a Marcia e a Polibio," *Rendiconti del r. Istituto Lonbarda* 64 (1931) 85-96; Rudolf Kassel, *Untersuchungen zur griechischen und römischen Konsolationsliteratur*, Munich, 1958.

[50] Ten of these are called dialogues on the basis of Quint. 10.1.129. None have a dramatic setting, but Seneca sometimes argues with an interlocutor, as seen in *De tran. animi* discussed below. For translations cf. John W. Basore, *Seneca Moral Essays* (Loeb), 3 vols., Cambridge, 1958.

philosophy to be useful and appropriate in his own age. The specific purpose of individual works, of course, varies some. *De clementia* was addressed to Nero and intended to instruct and influence him. The three "consolations" are aimed at assuaging grief, though as has been said that to Polybius written during exile has also an important objective in currying favor at court. The tragedies have the least immediate objective, but all of them are imbued with Stoicism and present dramatically the horror of passion and violence and contravention of nature. A brief look at one of the treatises will illustrate Seneca's rhetorical purpose and introduce his literary theory.

De tranquilitate animi is addressed to Annaeus Serenus, a young protégé who served as Nero's go-between (Tac., *Ann.* 13.13) and prefect of the watch (Pliny 22.96). It cannot be exactly dated, but was probably written during the height of Seneca's power and influence, for Serenus' early death (from eating poisonous mushrooms, according to Pliny) is mentioned in the sixty-third letter. In the first section Serenus, who imitated Seneca not only in active participation in government, but in interest in Stoicism, confides his doubts about completely mastering some personal weaknesses. This is a subject which always interested Seneca, who liked to think of students of Stoicism, himself included, as travelers along a road with various stages leading to the happy state of the ideal wise man, attained by few. Serenus has convinced himself of the rightness of the simple life (1.5), but when he goes out he sometimes becomes dazzled by splendor and tempted by wealth (1.9). No problem was so great for Seneca himself as the question of what should be his attitude toward his own much-criticized riches, some of which he inherited but more of which were poured upon him by Nero. Serenus says (1.10) that he has followed the advice of his teachers to enter public life and stand for office in order to be useful to friends, relatives, citizens, and all men. Seneca himself had done the same and consistently presents it as the right course. But whenever disappointed or checked, Serenus says (1.11) he wants to throw away his ambition and turn to a life of tranquil contemplation. In literary studies he generally has taken the view which we associate with the elder Cato, that he should cling to the substance of what he wants to say and let the words follow as they may (1.13), but occasionally a noble subject has swept him to a style grander than his own (1.14). At this he feels some guilt. He fears in general that he may be losing ground in his philosophical growth (1.15) and appeals to Seneca for advice or reassurance. His situation is highly understandable for a thoughtful young man and is an interesting reflection of Seneca's own concerns.

Seneca's reply has been criticized for failing to answer the question posed.[51] It might be fairer to criticize it for failing to make clear initially that the problem of doubts and inner conflicts cannot be answered by learning some kind of easy tricks. What Seneca apparently tries to do is to answer the question in depth, though some of his material is commonplace. As can be seen also in the tragedies, Seneca is a very able student of psychology. He begins here by reassuring Serenus in a general way and tells him that essentially what he needs is self-confidence (2.2), which is based on what the Greeks called *euthymia*, but what may be called in Latin *tranquilitas*. While discussing how tranquility is attained Seneca hopes two other things will be accomplished. Human weakness will be dragged out into the light where a man can know his own part therein, and at the same time

---

[51] E.g., by Rose, *op.cit.* supra n. 43, 364 and Barker, *op.cit.* supra n. 43.

Serenus himself will be able to contrast the relative understanding he has achieved with the folly of others and find strength in this knowledge (2.5). Seneca then launches into an account of failure and frustration, particularly in active civic life, claiming that these have their origin in intemperance of mind and in unrealized desires, when men do not dare as much as they desire or do not achieve it and rely entirely on hope (2.7). "In aversion to the progress of others and in despair at their own, the mind becomes exasperated at fortune and querulous of the age" (2.11). Seneca believes that the best help is in a continual concern with practical and civic affairs, and he lists (3.3-6) many different opportunities open to all. Sometimes one must retreat, but as gradually as possible (4.1). Strength of mind comes from a just self-estimate, acknowledging both strengths and weaknesses (6.1). Here he does not ignore Serenus' concern about poverty and wealth: one advantage of living modestly is that it makes one less exposed to misfortune (8.9).

The greatest source of insecurity in Seneca's view is fear of misfortune, and the latter part of the work deals with defenses against it. The perfect wise man will have perfect confidence in himself and never yield to fortune (11.1). The less advanced should not try to get the impossible nor aim at the unworthy (12.1); he should be adaptable (14.1); he should regard the perversity of the crowd not as hateful, but as ridiculous (15.2). The misfortunes suffered by the good are better viewed as opportunities for bravery or immortality. Self-confidence comes from living honestly and simply (17). The mind which lives in accord with nature finds strength in contemplation, in amusement, even occasionally in intoxication, which brings release (17.8). The problem raised by Serenus of the appeal of the grand style is dealt with

473

by implication. Mention of intoxication suggests the madness of poetry, which Seneca accepts as an utterance of a mind fired by divine inspiration. "The mind must be borne off, must champ at the bit, must snatch its driver and carry him to where he would have feared to climb" (17.11). This kind of literary adornment is in accordance with nature; it is itself a virtue.

These ideas are basic positions of Seneca; most of them are repeated elsewhere. From the vantage point of history they seem particularly appropriate to the age in which Seneca lived and to the position of the Roman aristocracy. The Romans needed to retain their self-confidence, to find ways to participate constructively in public affairs while not abandoning all initiative to flattery or contempt of the emperor. Seneca himself in his attempt to work with the government and to mold and direct Nero set an example of flexibility and realism. The literary advice also was probably sound, though perhaps less realistic. It would have been good if Latin writers of the empire had something important and strongly felt, as Seneca believed he did, which they wanted to say and which they could have expounded clearly and naturally, allowing the subject itself to create its own literary excellence. It is what the author of the work *On Sublimity* also recommends. Stoicism temporarily provided him with a substance, but one which did not win enough deep popular belief to survive.

In one of the passages quoted above Seneca speaks of the mind becoming querulous of the age. This raises the question of his attitude about the decline of morals and of eloquence which we have been considering. From what has been said it might be expected that Seneca, despite his father's influence, would not be very insistent on this topic. He had preferred the new style not only for himself but also for Nero. He had been willing to

live with the realities of his time. Unlike some Stoics
he does not stress the role of fate in life. When he directly considers the subject of decline or progress his view
seems to be what might be expected. He expects progress
in the sciences (*Nat. quaest.* 7.30.5). No age, he claims,
is more or less wicked than any other, though there is a
kind of shifting around of the vices so that one prevails
at one time, another at another (*De ben.* 1.10; *Ep.* 97).
Divorce is mentioned as a vice particularly prevalent in
his own time (*De ben.* 3.16.2). A reference (*Ep.* 3.9.1)
to the decline of Latinity is slightly humorous in its context.

This is not quite the whole picture, however. The
Stoics generally believed in a golden age in the past
which had become corrupted into the world as we know
it. Seneca accepted this and discusses it at some length.
His view seems to be that of Posidonius, that in the
original golden age the world was ruled by wise men
(*Ep.* 90.5). This was followed (*Ep.* 90.37) by a period
in which men were not philosophers, but at least lived
in accordance with nature. Finally there came a third
period (*Ep.* 90.38) in which avarice appeared and began to corrupt men. It is this third age in which we live,
and presumably Seneca is thinking only about this age
when he claims that one time is about as virtuous as
another. Some passages, however, do not fit very well
with this picture. One problem is the important ninety-
fifth letter, parts of which may be concerned with deterioration from the golden age (e.g., section 18), but
others clearly indicate subsequent deterioration. Women
now lose their hair and get the gout, which they didn't
do in the time of Hippocrates (95.20), and perhaps most
specifically of all (95.23): "All study is at an end, and
professors of the liberal arts preside over deserted corners
without any audience." Possibly the letter was written

475

at a time of special discouragement; certainly the picture of rampant vice is influenced by the major theme of the letter, which is that precepts are not adequate for philosophical training without a real understanding of virtue. Seneca may have taken over more than he really believed from Posidonius' picture of decline. The one hundred and fourteenth letter has an account of the spreading evil of luxury which eventually infects style (114.9-10). Did Seneca believe that an age with this set of vices lacked others? One can appeal to the very specific statement of the ninety-seventh letter that the young men of his own time lived far more frugal lives than had the debauchees (e.g., Clodius) of the late republic. Seneca paints elsewhere (De const. sap. 2; Ep. 14.13) a very vivid picture of the moral, intellectual, and political collapse of the Roman republic. He regarded an emperor as necessary, and hoped for a good one (De clem. 1.4.1-2). Of Augustus in general he thought well. He noted, however, a marked loss of freedom of speech from Augustus to Tiberius (De ben. 3.26-27) and matters were worse under Caligula, when sponges were inserted into the mouths of the dying to choke their utterances (De ira 3.19). Since then, there has been some improvement. Perhaps this is his fundamental view, that sometimes things are better, sometimes worse, but that there is no clear, steady decline.

The attitude toward literature and speech implied in De tranquilitate animi is borne out by several other passages which deal with these topics more specifically.[52]

[52] Cf. Norden 306-13; Frank I. Merchant, "Seneca and his Theory of Style," AJPh 26 (1905) 44-59; G. H. Mueller, Animadversiones ad L. Annaei Senecae epistulas quae sunt de oratione spectantes, Weida, 1910; C. N. Smiley, "Seneca and the Stoic Theory of Literary Style," Univ. of Wisconsin Studies 3 (1919) 50-61; Bourgery, op.cit. supra n. 44, 73-91; A. M.

Most of what Seneca discusses is philosophical writing, which he carefully distinguishes from declamation; the latter teaches men to speak rather than to act (*Ep.* 20.2). Rhetoric is one of the rational parts of philosophy along with dialectic. It deals with words, meanings, and arrangements (*Ep.* 89.17). Seneca holds pedantic scholarship in contempt, but values the liberal arts as a way to prepare the soul for virtue (*Ep.* 88.20). His ideas on elementary education are very humane (*De ira* 2.21).[53] He thinks advanced students should engage in continually reading and writing (*Ep.* 84.1-2), but he distrusts discoursiveness: it is better to study thoroughly a small number of works (*Ep.* 2). Just because a subject for composition has been used by an earlier writer does not necessarily mean that it is exhausted; the latest writer actually has an advantage in that the words are ready before him (*Ep.* 79.6). This is a form of the doctrine of imitation. Writing can give immortality to writer and addressee (*Ep.* 21.5).

The substance of Seneca's ideas on style are contained in several discussions in the *Epistles*.[54] In the fortieth epistle Lucilius is told that the philosopher must neither rush headlong nor drag out his words: "speech which addresses itself to the truth should be simple and unadorned" (40.4). The style can rise at times, but it must maintain dignity and control (40.8). The forty-sixth epistle discusses the style of a new book by Lucilius and praises its eloquent smoothness. The seventy-fifth says (75.4) that the sum of the matter is this: "What we feel

---

Guillemin, "Sénèque directeur d'ames: III les théories littéraires," *REL* 32 (1954) 250-74; Leeman 260-83.

[53] Cf. C. Burnier, *La pédagogie de Sénèque*, Lausanne, 1914.
[54] For translations cf. Richard M. Gummere, *Seneca ad Lucilium Epistulae morales* (Loeb), 3 vols., Cambridge, 1953.

we should say, what we say we should feel." If it is possible to be eloquent too, so much the better. The one hundredth epistle deals with the style of Fabianus (cf. also 40.12), which is praised as not overcareful, but assured (100.5); the words are chosen, but not captured; the style in general is clear, smooth, elevated, but not violent (100.10). In philosophical writing Fabianus is outranked in Seneca's view only by Cicero, Asinius Pollio, and Livy (100.9). Finally, the one hundred and fourteenth epistle is devoted to the way in which style reflects character, or in which style is the man. "If a man is sound, self-controlled, serious, temperate, his artistic ability is also dry and sober; if the former is vitiated, the latter is also affected" (114.3). Seneca's example of decadent life and style is Maecenas (cf. also *Ep.* 19.19), whose speech and writing he criticizes for its improper use of metaphors, its degenerate word order, its carelessness, and its obscurity (114.4-8). When the mind has become accustomed to despising ordinary things it seeks also in speech something new (114.10). Speech has no fixed rules, Seneca claims (114.13), and therefore varies with the taste and vices of the times. In diction the excesses of archaists, of devotees of a humdrum style, and of an overwritten style are rebuked (114.13); in arrangement those who write excessively unrhythmical or excessively rhythmical sentences are equally at fault.

Seneca's theory of style is perhaps best summed up in a passage in the fifty-ninth letter (49.4-5): "You have the words under control. The language does not carry you off nor draw you further than you intended. There are many who are summoned by the charm of some pleasing word to write something which they had not planned, but this does not happen to you. Everything is compact and suited to the subject. You say as much as you wish and mean more than you say. This is an indication of a rather great subject. It is clear that your mind as well has nothing empty, nothing vainly puffed out." Seneca's theory of style is clearly influenced by Stoic theories of rhetoric.[55] It is equally well consistent with his general insistence on being in accord with nature and reason. Does his stylistic practice accord with his theory? Judgments on this vary somewhat; those who have studied the subject most carefully generally agree that it does.[56] Those who approach Seneca as a rich man who preached poverty and a philosopher who countenanced Nero, in other words as fundamentally hypocritical, have called his style rhetorical and even Asianistic, and cried "inconsistency" again. Certain points should be kept in mind. From Seneca's point of view a literary style like that of his contemporaries, if not given to any kind of excess, would be more "natural" than an imitation of an author of another period like Cicero or Livy. In writing in this new style he is not being affected. Furthermore, his education and that of his contemporaries was in the schools of the declaimers, and it is not a deliberate affectation if he is influenced by some of the features of the schools. The most striking is a tendency to write terse, epigrammatic *sententiae*. This inclination was probably strengthened by the fact that Stoicism had a tradition of seeking terseness and of coining moral maxims and paradoxes. The presence of these *sententiae* makes Seneca's prose style seem jerky, brittle, or perhaps mannered to many readers; that it is not extreme in this

---

[55] Cf. Smiley, *op.cit.* supra n. 52; APG 290-99; Leeman 277.
[56] Cf. Merchant, *op.cit.* supra n. 52, 58-59; Smiley, *op.cit.* supra n. 52, 61; Leeman 277-78. Norden 306-10 thought there was some inconsistency, as did D'Alton 332. An extensive and specific discussion of Seneca's style may be found in Walter C. Summers, *Select Letters of Seneca*, London, 1910, xv-xcv. Summers believed there was some inconsistency, lxxi.

mannerism may be judged by comparison with some of the expressions which he objects to in Maecenas or Pollio and by comparison with declaimers. Long, flowing periods seem affected to Seneca (*Ep.* 114.16) and did not, in any event, represent his manner of thought, which is not one of gradual development of a thought, slow elaboration, and careful structure, but one of a series of points deriving force from their bluntness and illustrated by examples. Perhaps most important to notice is that Seneca's preference is for common, sometimes even colloquial, words.[57] He is opposed to archaism, but he believes that Latin is poverty-stricken enough and that words should be found and used without undue concern for authority (*Ep.* 58).[58] The great majority of his metaphors are drawn from daily life, and though there are many of them, usage is rarely violent or frigid.[59] His style can hardly be called poetic and there are very few passages of amplification or descriptive writing. Distinctive as his writing is, only from the point of view of extreme classicism can his prose be called affected; from his own vantage point it is a natural middle course between the vices he criticizes. It is to be expected that his oratorical style would have been more indulgent of contemporary influences than is his philosophical style, and his poetic style in the tragedies is of course much more colored, though it avoids the extremes seen in Lucan.

Seneca was certainly not totally successful, either in writing, in politics, in philosophy, or in life. He claims (*Ep.* 10.8.15) that he began philosophically and, even when fully engaged in civic affairs, kept some of his re-

[57] Cf. Summers, *op.cit.* supra n. 56, xlii-li.

[58] Cf. Armand Pittel, *Vocabulaire philosophique de Sénèque,* Paris, 1937, 16-29.

[59] Cf. Charles S. Smith, *Metaphor and Comparison in the Epistulae ad Lucilium of L. Annaeus Seneca,* Baltimore, 1910, 181.

solves. The consistency which he best shows is a consistent effort to make the best use of opportunities, to do the best he can, not to turn away from life, to seek to serve. It cannot be denied that he indulged in flattery and went along with actions he disapproved, but regarded as unavoidable. His attempts to restrain Nero were evident (Tac., *Ann.* 14.14). Stoics believed that all vices were equal, and Seneca never claimed to be without vice. Some of his readers have labeled him self-righteous, but he has not very much to say about himself. The picture which he leaves is one of a man seeking to progress and seeing various opportunities in the present and various mistakes in the past (e.g., *Ep.* 6.1; 42.1). "Hoc mihi satis est, cotidie aliquid ex vitiis meis demere et errores meos obiurgare," he says in straightforward, natural Latin: "This is enough for me, daily to subtract something from my vices and to rebuke my mistakes." In the same passage (*De vita beata* 17) he candidly lists the faults that might be found with him, especially his wealth. The epistles, probably his finest works, were written during his retirement and gave him an opportunity to come to certain retrospective conclusions about life. They are surely addressed as much to himself as to Lucilius, especially in the repeated thoughts about death (cf. e.g., *Ep.* 26.4-7) and about ultimate philosophical peace. "In fretu viximus, moriamur in portu": "We have lived in the raging straits of life, let us die in the port" (*Ep.* 19.2).

The other writers of most importance for their views on the state of eloquence in the early empire are Quintilian, Tacitus, and Pliny the Younger, all of whom we will consider in the next chapter. Before moving to their period it is appropriate to consider those rhetorical theorists of the early and mid-first century who wrote in Latin.

481

Early Imperial Writers on Rhetoric

The extant portion of Suetonius' *Lives of the Rhetoricians* ends with a brief account of the Augustan declaimer Albucius Silus, whom we also know from the elder Seneca. The manuscripts preserve an index, however, and Suetonius apparently continued with the declaimers Cestius Pius and Porcius Latro, both also known from Seneca, and then went on to Q. Curtius Rufus, L. Valerius Primanus, Verginius Flavus, L. Statius Ursulus, P. Clodius Quirinalis, M. Antonius Liberalis, Sex. Julius Gabinianus, M. Fabius Quintilianus, and Julius Tiro.[60] These were presumably in Suetonius' view the most significant rhetoricians of the first century A.D. The list as a whole shows a preference for declaimers. Curtius Rufus is probably the author of the extant life of Alexander the Great, more an enormous declamation than a critical biography.[61] Julius Gabinianus was the most celebrated declaimer in Gaul in the time of Vespasian (Jerome, *Chron.* s.v. A.D. 76; Tac., *Dial.* 26.8). The others are little more than names save for Verginius Flavus and Quintilian.

Verginius Flavus was teaching rhetoric in Rome around A.D. 49, when the poet Persius studied with him,[62] and apparently continued to do so until he was exiled "because of the fame of his name" by Nero in 65 (Tac., *Ann.* 15.71). Quintilian refers to him with respect a half dozen times and may have known him personally in the period around 58 (11.3.126). What he knew best, however, was Verginius' textbook of declamation (7.4.40).

[60] Cf. Rodney P. Robinson, *C. Suetoni Tranquilli De grammaticis et rhetoribus*, Paris, 1925, 49-51.
[61] Cf. F. Heimreich, *Die Reden bei Curtius* (*Rhetorische Studien* 14), Paderborn, 1927; Schanz-Hosius 2.596-603.
[62] Cf. the life of Persius attributed to Suetonius. In general, cf. *R-E* 8A.1543-44.

It contained an extensive discussion of *stasis* theory (7.4.24), in which Verginius distinguished three kinds (conjectural, legal, and juridical). He also discussed Theodorus' rule that the exordium should mention the points to be made later in the speech, perhaps disagreeing. Quintilian says (4.1.23) that he misinterpreted Theodorus' requirement, which was only that the judge should be prepared for the chief questions. He treated definition as a species of legal *stasis* (3.6.45-46) and greatly restricted the concept of quality (7.4.40).[63]

In speaking of the history of rhetoric at Rome Quintilian (3.1.21) also provides a short list of important rhetoricians of the first century: Celsus, Laenas, Verginius again, Pliny, and Tutilius. Laenas was Popilius Laenas, possibly a descendant of the centurion who murdered Cicero. Quintilian (10.7.32) objects to his advice that declamations should be outlined in writing as an aid to the memory, but approves (11.3.183) his criticism of too much movement in delivery. Tutilius he never again mentions. The name occurs in Martial and the younger Pliny.[64] Celsus and Pliny are, however, more important.

Cornelius Celsus

A. Cornelius Celsus was the author of an encyclopaedia probably written in the time of Tiberius.[65] Quintil-

---

[63] Cf. Johannes Stroux, "Zu Quintilian: I. Das Lehrbuch des Verginius Flavus," *Philologus* 91 (1936) 223-26. The reference in Quint. 8.3.33 is not to Verginius but to Sergius Plautus, cf. Karl Barwick, "Quintilians Stellung zu dem Problem sprachlicher Neuschöpfungen," *Philologus* 91 (1936) 97-98.

[64] Martial's reference (5.56.6) is certainly to a rhetorician. Pliny's reference (*Ep.* 6.32.1) is contained in a letter to someone named Quintilian, but probably not the famous rhetorician. Cf. R-E 7A.1613-4.

[65] Cf. Fridericus Marx, *A Cornelii Celsi quae supersunt*, Leipzig and Berlin,1915, 411-21; Schanz-Hosius 2.722-27; Karl Bar-

ian says (12.11.24) that it included rhetoric, military science, agriculture, and medicine. Probably there were other parts as well, such as philosophy and jurisprudence. The books on medicine survive: they are a clear statement in excellent straightforward Latin of Greco-Roman medical knowledge drawn from a variety of sources. Celsus was probably not a physician himself and probably not a teacher of rhetoric either, but like the elder Seneca a man of leisure, taste, and intelligence. He has a great deal to say about medicine and doubtless his discussion of rhetoric was also extensive. Quintilian notes (*ibid.*) that he was a follower of Sextus, an eclectic philosopher of the early empire who combined doctrines of Stoicism, Platonism, and Pythagoreanism, describes him as *mediocri vir ingenio,* "a man of moderate intellectual ability" who wrote a creditable and learned work, and specifically refers to his treatment of rhetoric twenty-five times. Eighteen of these references disagree with specific teachings of Celsus. It is possible, of course, that where Quintilian does not otherwise say so he is following Celsus, and such a view leads to the conclusion that Celsus is Quintilian's major source.[66] But this is very unlikely; the fragments of Celsus suggest a narrow and technical viewpoint which is quite unlike Quintilian's own philosophy of education and rhetoric. More likely, Quintilian was trying to combat the influence of a widely available reference work with which he fundamentally disagreed: thus the polite firmness of his references. The only reference to Celsus' rhetorical books outside of Quintilian is one in the *Ars rhetorica* of the fourth cen-

---

wick, "Zu den Schriften des Cornelius Celsus und des alten Cato," *WJA* 3 (1948) 117-32 and *Philologus* 104 (1960) 236-49; Werner Krenkel, "Zu den Artes des Celsus," *Philologus* 103 (1959) 114-29.

[66] A position constantly taken by Jean Cousin, *Études sur Quintilien,* Paris, 1936.

tury Fortunatianus (3.2), which could come through the intermediary of Quintilian.[67]

Celsus' definition of rhetoric reminded Quintilian (2.15.22) of that of Theodorus: "to speak persuasively on doubtful matters of interest to a citizen." The orator's prize, Celsus said, is not a good conscience, but victory, to Quintilian a totally unacceptable position (2.15.32). Emphasis was put on the fundamental conflict which provoked a speech, on *stasis* theory (3.4.3; 3.5.13; 3.6.38), and on the proper arrangement of arguments (7.1.10); Quintilian does not mention Celsus when dealing with practical matters of evidence or the use of ethos or pathos through books five and six. Celsus' demand for strict relevance in the exordium (4.1.12) and for omission of the narration if the fact of the crime was denied (4.2.9-10) may reflect the influence of Theodorus; but his rejection of mutual accusation is compared to the view of Apollodorus (7.2.19). A number of the references involve style: neo-Atticism is suggested by the fact that Celsus forbade word coinage (8.3.35) and discouraged rhythmical effects in the exordium, quoting Asinius Pollio as a model (9.4.132), but in discussing figures he is said to follow Rutilius Lupus, whose examples were drawn from the Asianist, Gorgias of Athens. Like Caecilius, Celsus seems to have been very interested in figures. Quintilian generally thought that too many kinds of figures were being distinguished (9.1.19) and in one passage (9.2.104-5) lists nineteen devices which Celsus had unnecessarily tried to call figures.

We may conclude that Celsus' discussion of rhetoric, like his discussion of medicine, was drawn from a num-

[67] Thus it is not possible to reconstruct Celsus' rhetoric on the basis of other teachings of Fortunatianus, or of Isidore of Seville, as is done by J. Woehrer, "De A. Cornelii Celsi Rhetorica," *Dissertationes philologicae Vindobonenses* 7 (1903) 79-157.

ber of sources. It tended to take the form of more or less rigid rules, and though differing in details was in kind like the rhetorical precepts of Apollodorus or Theodorus. It was probably more adapted to declamation than to actual oratory in the courts, and it seems to have ignored deliberative and epideictic oratory completely.

Pliny the Elder

The remaining writer on Quintilian's list is another encyclopaedist, the elder Pliny. His *Natural History* alone survives, but his nephew, the younger Pliny, lists (*Ep.* 3.5) other works including an important history of Rome and of the German wars and a treatise entitled *Studiosus, The Student,* which he says educated and perfected the orator, beginning with the cradle. It was in three books, but published in six volumes because of their size, and like his work on grammar seems to have been written in the later part of the reign of Nero when historical subjects had become dangerous. According to Aulus Gellius (9.16) *The Student* contained a discussion of declamation with examples of argument. Quintilian seems to have it in mind in three passages. At the beginning of his own treatise on the education of the orator he says (1. *pr.* 4) that "almost all" who have written on rhetoric have ignored primary education, the inclusion of which is one of his own major contributions. The younger Pliny's description of *The Student* as beginning, as does Quintilian, from the cradle, suggests why the word "almost" was needed. Pliny furnished Quintilian with at least a formal precedent, but his work did not appeal. Quintilian specifically describes Pliny as pedantic (11.3.143) and elsewhere perhaps has his work in mind when he contrasts the practical orator at whom he aims with "the student of declamation" (2.10.15).

CHAPTER SEVEN

Quintilian and His Younger Contemporaries

M. Fabius Quintilianus, the greatest teacher of rhetoric at Rome, was born in Calagurris in Spain sometime around A.D. 40.[1] He was in Rome by the late fifties; possibly he studied there earlier with the grammarian Remmius Palaemon and saw in his school some of the moral evils which he later protests; certainly he attached himself to Domitius Afer. To Quintilian, Afer is not the informer, known from Tacitus, but a great orator and wise critic (10.1.86) whose only fault was a failure to recognize his declining powers and to retire before he spoke less than his best (12.11.3). Quintilian mentions Afer or has him in mind a couple of dozen times in the *Institutio*, and next to Cicero, Afer was probably the greatest influence upon him. As we have seen, Afer was a practicing counsel, a real-life orator, and Quintilian, though he taught declamation, never lost sight of a practical goal in education and maintained his own practice as long as he taught. Furthermore, Afer was never

---

[1] For a more extensive discussion cf. George Kennedy, *Quintilian*, New York, 1969, ch. 1 of which deals with Quintilian's life and times. Cf. also M. L. Clarke, "Quintilian: a Biographical Sketch," G & R 14 (1967) 24-37. The date of Quintilian's birth is deduced from the fact that he was *adulescens* at the time of the trial of Capito (6.1.14) in 57 (Tac., *Ann.* 13.32) and that he knew Domitius Afer "when he was old and I was young" (5.7.7). Afer died in 59 (Tac., *Ann.* 14.19). It seems reasonable to assume that Quintilian was studying rhetoric in Rome in the period 55-58 and he was 15-18 at the time. Cf. R-E 6.1845-64; Schanz-Hosius 2.745-60; Jean Cousin, *Études sur Quintilien*, Paris, 1936; idem, "Quintilien 1935-59," *Lustrum* 7 (1963) 289-331: Giuseppe G. Bianca, *La pedagogia di Quintiliano*, Padua, 1963.

a rebel, a revolutionary, or a radical. He got along as well as he could with the society in which he found himself, was ambitious, and not above flattery if that became necessary. Quintilian, too, is not a critic of the government; he accepted honor and advancement from the Flavians; he indulged in flattery when prudent (e.g., 4. *pr.*; 10.1.91-92). Like most Romans he criticizes moral faults, but apparently he did not believe that his age was one of decline or that all opportunity for greatness was gone. What little we know of Afer's prose style suggests maturity, gravity tempered with wit, naturalness.[2] These are not the common characteristics of the Neronian age, and admiration of them may have contributed to Quintilian's inclination to Cicero and the classics.

About the time of Afer's death Quintilian, his education complete, returned to Spain and lived there for nearly ten years. He probably practiced in the local courts, though he never mentions it. When the governor of Spain, Galba, was saluted emperor and marched home to supplant Nero in 68 he took Quintilian with him (Jerome, *Chron.* s.v. 68). This might well have proved disastrous for the young orator during the appalling year of the four emperors which followed when revolution shook Rome, and Otho, Vitellius, and Vespasian in turn succeeded Galba. Somehow Quintilian survived and turned to teaching. When, in the spring of 71 Vespasian's heir Titus returned to Rome at last from the capture of Jerusalem, Vespasian greeted him with all honor, and a program for a new world began to appear. One aspect of it was the appointment of Quintilian to a chair in rhetoric supported by the *fiscus*, or state treasury.[3]

[2] Quintilian's word for it is *maturitas*, cf. 12.10.11, also 9.4.31 and Pliny, *Ep.* 2.14.10.
[3] On the fact cf. Jerome, *Chron.* under A.D. 88. On the date cf. Zonaras 11.17 (Epitome of Dio Cassius 65.12).

The salary was a reasonable 100,000 sesterces a year, and of course was augmented by the fees Quintilian received from practicing in the law courts. He is likely to have doubled it.[4]

The Roman state had taken 163 years to move from an official policy of trying to prevent the teaching of Latin rhetoric to subsidy of it. In between, various tutors and teachers had been brought into the palace to train young members of the imperial family in rhetoric. The same period had seen the abandonment of the prohibition of fees for orators in court and vast sociological changes. Nero was the last ruler descended from an ancient Roman house; Vespasian came of respectable country stock. His administration brought a realism and a straightforwardness which not only swept out the decadent Neronian court, but reformed the finances, restored military discipline, and improved administration both at home and in the provinces. For the first time the government took cognizance, albeit a very limited cognizance, of higher education. It was not enough to expect aristocratic sons to learn how to perform in public life from aristocratic fathers; a broader path must be open to ability.[5] Thus the lectures of Quintilian. He did not, of course, compromise the traditional curriculum; he did not teach local government and economics, geography, money and banking, sanitary engineering, or public health.

---

[4] Martial 2.90 implies that Quintilian was not uninterested in position and money. Juvenal 7.186-89 perhaps confirms this, but exaggerates (receipt of the *ornamenta consularia* is not equivalent to a consulship) and should not be taken as evidence that he charged high fees while public professor. Juvenal may only use Quintilian's name to mean a famous rhetorician. Quintilian doubtless was well paid for serving as tutor to Domitian's heirs after his retirement and he may have had other special pupils.

[5] Cf. M. St. A. Woodside, "Vespasian's Patronage of Education and the Arts," *TAPhA* 73 (1942) 123-29.

He taught invention, arrangement, style, memory, and delivery and he criticized the *controversiae* and *suasoriae* written by his students. Occasionally he favored them with some literary remarks, and it is very likely that he gave them moral advice. What they gained was an ability to express themselves, self-assurance, a sense of the cultural tradition, some degree of taste. A modern liberal education is more ambitious, but not much more successful. It sometimes tries to train critics of society, which Quintilian would have thought a serious mistake.

Quintilian did not disapprove of large classes (1.2.9-15) and probably attracted considerable following. Presumably his lectures were free, but one might guess that he expected some kind of introduction or examined boys before admitting them as regular students. As in other rhetorical schools we should assume a steady stream of older auditors drifting in and out. The only person we can name as definitely a student of Quintilian was the younger Pliny, but there is perhaps a chance that Juvenal had at least attended some lectures.[6] Judging from the conditions of the time, most of the students would be sons of prosperous Italian or provincial families who had been sent to Rome by parents ambitious for them to rise socially and politically.

We know a little bit about Quintilian's methods: there was a preliminary course of lectures for boys who may have been fourteen or fifteen years old (1. *pr.* 7; 8. *pr.* 1-7). He complains that they were now coming at an older age than was necessary (2.1). This preliminary course gave an outline of the whole system of rhetoric in simple terms and inculcated the impression that there was only one right way to do things: the boy could learn later that what he thought was the only way was what

6 Cf. A. Kappelmacher, "Studia Juvenalia," *Dissertationes Philologicae Vindobonensis* 7 (1903) 159-99.

was usually the best way (8. *pr.* 4). For a while Quintilian experimented with reading and analysis of historical and oratorical texts with this group, but the study got in the way of the work of the more advanced students whose parents had sent them to study declamation, and was abandoned (2.5.1-2). Quintilian does not question declamation as the finest form of rhetorical exercise (2.10.2) and much of his time went to teaching it. He did, however, wish it to be a practical preparation for public life. He criticizes the use of bizarre subjects, swollen style, and unrealistic conventions.[7] To bring declamation back into line as a training for the law courts he suggests some modest reforms (2.10.9): use of proper names, more complicated cases, more normal diction, some sense of humor. Some of the examples of declamation scattered through his work show what he had in mind, but also suggest that he did not or could not push reform very far.[8]

Quintilian is an important figure in the history of education, but not as a reformer of the curriculum, which he largely accepts. His concerns are primarily with the point of view of the teacher, which must be practical, sensible, positive, and moral, and with the teacher-student relationship. The teacher is to regard himself as *in loco parentis* (2.2.4). He should, moreover, make learning seem natural and even fun. Quintilian's own students were almost entirely adolescents studying rhetoric, but he is filled with good advice for the elementary teacher about how to start young minds along the road to learning. Almost alone of ancient educators he is strongly opposed to flogging (1.3.13-14). Of course in

[7] Cf., e.g., 4.1.3; 4.3.2-3; 5.13.36 and 45-46; 7.2.17-23 and 54-56.
[8] Cf. 3.6.96-97; 5.10.111-12; 7.3.30-34; Kennedy, *op.cit.* supra n. 1, 50-52.

return the student develops duties to his master, whom he must not only obey, but love (2.9). Quintilian's ideal student as described in the *Institutio* (1.3.6-7) is rather too docile, too easily led for the advanced stages of education in the modern viewpoint.

While holding his professorship Quintilian continued to act as a pleader in the law courts. He mentions four cases specifically and in other passages refers more vaguely to his experience.[9] When appearing with another patron he ordinarily handled the statement of the case (4.2.86). His speech for Naevius of Arpinum was published (7.2.24), apparently his first successful case, probably to be dated during his first stay in Rome and spoken when he was around 20 years old. The most unusual case was that for Berenice of Judaea in a trial over which she presided, datable to her visit to Rome in A.D. 75 (4.1.19).

Quintilian says that after twenty years of teaching at a time when, unlike Afer, he hoped he would still be missed, he retired from his professorship and from the bar (1. *pr.* 1; 2.12.12). His motives may have been complicated by social pressures such as those seen in a poem which Martial (2.90) addressed to him or by political considerations. Domitian had been emperor since 81. The literary sources portray the latter part of his reign, especially from 89 on, as a period of terror. This may be somewhat exaggerated, but there was certainly a great deal of uneasiness among the upper classes with whom Quintilian associated, and in 90 or 91 he may have been glad to seek private life.[10] We do not know whether

[9] In addition to passages cited in the text cf. 6.1.39; 6.2.29; 7.2.5; 9.2.73; Kennedy, *op.cit.* supra n. 1, 20-22.

[10] For the standard view cf. *CAH* 11.22-33; for modifications cf. K. H. Waters, "The Character of Domitian," *Phoenix* 18 (1964) 49-77.

someone else was immediately appointed to his professorship.[11]

Quintilian's retirement turned out to be the most significant part of his career, for his friends, and especially Marcellus Vitorius,[12] to whom he dedicated his great work, prevailed on him to write a treatise on rhetoric based on his lectures. This work was begun within a few years after retirement; approximately two years went into research and writing, and Quintilian claims he would have spent more time on it, but his bookseller Trypho, whom he addresses in an introductory epistle, thought the market was pressing. The work was probably completed and published late in 94 or early in A.D. 95.[13] While writing, Quintilian was called back into quasi-official life and invited, or forced, to undertake the direction of the education of Domitian's two heirs, his sister's grandchildren (4 pr.). Their subsequent fate is unknown. We are also told (Ausonius 20.7) that Flavius Clemens, Domitian's cousin, was responsible for the award to Quintilian of the *ornamenta consularia*, an honorary tribute roughly analogous to the order of merit. It was probably granted late in 94 while Flavius was consul-elect or early in 95 when he was consul, certainly

[11] It might be guessed that the next rhetorician after Quintilian in Suetonius *De rhetoribus* would be a good candidate. This appears to have been Julius Tiro, about whom nothing is known unless he is the same person whose will is under discussion in Pliny *Ep.* 6.31.7.

[12] Suffect consul in 105, also patron of Statius (*Silvae* 4. pr. and 4.4) and probably of the grammarian Probus. Cf. *R-E Suppl.* 9.1744-45. Quintilian and Statius were probably not friends, cf. 10.3.17; *Silvae* 4. pr.; Kennedy, *op.cit.* supra n. 1, 26-28.

[13] Cf. Friedrich Vollmer, "Die Abfassungszeit der Schriften Quintilians," *RhM* 46 (1891) 343-48; J. Cousin, "Problems biographiques et littéraires relatifs à Quintilien," *REL* 9 (1931) 62-76; Italo Lana, "Quando fu scritta l'*Instituto oratoria* di Quintiliano," *AAT* 85 (1950-51); Kennedy, *op.cit.* supra n. 1, 26-30.

before September when he was disgraced and put to death on a religious charge which may have been inspired by his Christian leanings. Doubtless the award was in honor of the publication of the great treatise on rhetoric which might well be regarded as the finest product of Flavian patronage. Nothing is known of the rest of Quintilian's life and he may have died within a year or two. His wife and younger son had died in the 80's; his elder son died at the age of ten during the composition of the *Institutio*; all are memorialized in the preface to the sixth book.

Quintilian's published works consisted of the speech for Naevius, two sets of lecture notes taken down by his students and published without his authority, one short and based on the introductory course, the other longer and based on the major course (1. *pr.* 7), an essay *De causis corruptae eloquentiae, On the Causes of Corrupted Eloquence*, written about 89, and his great treatise *De institutione oratoria, On the Education of an Orator*. Only the latter survives. There are in addition two collections of declamations attributed to Quintilian: the *Declamationes maiores* are complete *controversiae*, the only such works surviving in Latin, but the approach is not at all like that of Quintilian. The *Declamationes minores* are 145 abbreviated declamations or parts of declamations and may somehow be derived from Quintilian's school. Most of the *Declamationes minores* are accompanied by *sermones*, or instructions on the treatment to be followed.[14]

Some of the contents of *De causis* can be seen from

[14] Cf. Constantin Ritter, *Die Quintilianischen Declamationen: Untersuchungen über Art und Herkunft*, Freiburg and Tübingen, 1881; A. Trabandt, *De minoribus quae sub nomine Quintiliani feruntur declamationibus*, Griefswald, 1883; Gerhard Fleiter, *De minoribus quae sub nomine Quintiliani feruntur declamationibus*, Münster, 1890; Gwynn 209-16.

the references to it in the *Institutio*.[15] Such an approach necessarily stresses similarities between the two works, but there were few radical changes in Quintilian's thought, and the *De causis* doubtless was a preliminary study of some topics later incorporated in the *Institutio*. The objective of the earlier work was apparently to counteract the declamatory style which had flourished throughout the first century and which Quintilian in the *Institutio* identifies especially with Seneca and his would-be imitators (10.1.125-31). This style seemed to Quintilian entirely unnatural, corrupted, and tasteless. References to the *De causis* do not seem to justify regarding it as a general assessment of the state of oratory like that in Tacitus' *Dialogus*. Though Quintilian saw corrupted literary style around him, his whole point of view is strongly against admitting any general decline in eloquence or literature. Great orators, he says, still speak in the forum (10.1.122), and doubtless Domitian was gratified to hear it. What Quintilian regarded as the corrupted style can be seen from a passage in book twelve (12.10.73):

"They are much deceived who think that the vitiated or corrupted style of speaking is popular or persuasive. It exults in license in the use of words or runs riot with childish epigrams, or swells with unrestrained pomposity or leaps about with empty commonplaces or glitters with adornment which will collapse if lightly touched or substitutes extravagance for sublimity or goes mad in a semblance of free speech."

Among specific subjects discussed were the use of hyperbole, which Quintilian approved in cases where the

[15] Cf. Augustus Reuter, *De Quintiliani libro qui fuit De causis corruptae eloquentiae*, Vratislaviae, 1887; Kennedy, *op.cit.* supra n. 1, 22-24.

thought outruns the ordinary power of words (8.6.76), and ways in which speech is corrupted, which Quintilian claimed were similar to the ways in which it is adorned (8.3.58). It is not surprising that some reference to the history of declamation was included (2.4.42), since the dangers of corruption were greatest there.

The twelve books *De institutione oratoria*[16] are the finest statement of ancient rhetorical theory. Quintilian had a respect for his subject which was lacking to Aristotle, and he benefited from over four hundred years of speaking experience. In comparison with Cicero he is more systematic and objective. The result is a work which has some of the features of the *Rhetoric*, and many of *De oratore* and the *Orator*, but certain other strong features as well. This does not mean, of course, that Quintilian's total achievement was comparable to that of Aristotle or Cicero. He is a scholar and teacher, a transmitter and refiner, not even a writer of the first rank. His writing is ordinarily straightforward and natural; his rare flights of eloquence tend to sink under their own weight, for example at the beginning of book twelve where he attempts an elaborate nautical metaphor, and

[16] The title in the best MSS is simply *Institutio oratoria*, but *De institutione oratoria* seems supported by *Ep. ad Tryph.* 1 and the models of *De oratore* and *De causis*. There are commentaries on book I by F. H. Colson, Cambridge, Eng., 1924; III by Joachim Adamietz, Munich, 1966; x by W. Peterson, Oxford, 1891; XII by R. G. Austin, Oxford, 1948. The best translation is by John S. Watson, 2 vols., London, 1856, though there is a translation in the Loeb series by H. E. Butler, 4 vols., London, 1920-22. Basic works on the *Institutio* include B. Appel, *Das Bildungs- und Erziehungsideal Quintilians nach der Institutio Oratoria*, Donauworth, 1914, Cousin, *Études cit.* supra n. 1, X. Gabler, *De elocutione M. F. Quintiliani*, Borna-Leipzig, 1910; Clarke 109-29; Leeman 287-310; Michael Winterbottom, "Problems in Quintilian," *Bulletin of the Institute of Classical Studies* 25, London, 1970.

occasionally he is unclear or confused, partly because in comparison with other rhetoricians he had little sympathy with technical terminology. His personality emerges clearly from his writing and the rather few references to himself: a sensible, prudent, strongly moral, down-to-earth Roman with a love for oratory and for young people, successful in his career, but afflicted by repeated tragedies in his private life. His work no longer brought him pleasure, but he wrote it with the same thorough determination to complete a task for the general good that a Roman commander might have displayed in pushing through the conquest of a province.

A satisfactory way to examine the *Institutio* may be first to look at its structure, which will reveal Quintilian's plan and intentions, then to consider his sources and relationship to the rhetorical tradition, and finally to assess his overall goal, the concept of the *bonus orator*.

The *Institutio* is made up of twelve books, seven of which have introductions, while in some other books the first chapter is introductory. The present chapter divisions, of which some represent logical units of thought, and the decision as to which books were to have separate introductions and which to start with chapter one seem to have been made by a later scribe, but the book divisions were made by Quintilian (cf. 1. *pr.* 21-22). The admirable prooemium to the first book is introductory to the whole work: first (1. *pr.* 1-8) Quintilian explains that he was urged to write by friends. It will not be possible for him to be original on many matters, but he will try to offer a judgment on conflicting views. This procedure is followed in varying degrees throughout the work and often produces an historical review of various parts of rhetorical theory. But Quintilian is not content with this and wants to do more:

497

instead of writing a rhetorical treatise he aims to produce a study of the whole education of the orator, taking him almost from the cradle and continuing the story up to retirement. Of course the great central part of the work is the body of theory which will be learned in rhetorical school, but this is prefaced with a discussion of elementary and grammatical instruction and amplified with a significant consideration of the adult career of the orator. As said in the last chapter, it is likely that the elder Pliny's *Studiosus* had a scope which included both elementary and advanced education, and Cicero's *De oratore* and *Orator* deal with the adult orator, but such a wide view of the subject was otherwise unusual. It resulted partly from practical considerations: Quintilian felt that primary and grammatical education was neglected and yet important for what followed, and as a retired pleader he himself was personally interested in the adult career of a practicing orator, but the plan resulted also from psychological reasons: Quintilian is a humanist and naturally inclined toward a view of the whole man; and it came also from idealism, the feeling that the orator was the greatest human type. Education will necessarily reflect the goal which it sets itself and the examination of that goal is a proper task of the educator. Quintilian throughout represents himself as an educator, not as a critic or declaimer. He wants to train great orators, not construct a great system of thought, and in this feeling he was in tune with his age which had begun to see human beings as individuals rather than as cogs in society.

The second part of the introduction (1. *pr.* 9-20) describes Quintilian's ultimate goal, the education of the perfect orator. What he seeks is a good man skilled in speaking, the tradition of Cato and the Stoics. Not in-

498

deed a philosopher; Quintilian is very distrustful of the rancorous and ill-kempt philosophers who had awakened the wrath of Vespasian and Domitian.[17] What is good in philosophy belongs by nature to the orator, and as we shall see, Quintilian has hope for a new philosophical eloquence.

The third part of the introduction (1. *pr.* 21-27) outlines the structure of the work which follows:

"The first book will contain those things which are prior to the work of the rhetorician. In the second book we shall consider the first lessons with the rhetorician and problems involving the nature of rhetoric. Five books will then be devoted to invention (for arrangement is a subdivision of it), four to style, in which part will also come memory and delivery. There will be one final book in which we must describe the orator himself, where we shall say in so far as our poor powers allow what ought to be his way of life, what his policy in undertaking, studying, and pleading cases, what his kind of style, what limit to his pleading, what studies after his retirement." (1. *pr.* 22)

This is, of course, the order of nature as the child grows and develops into a man. In the earlier books Quintilian tends to address parents or teachers, in the later books he speaks directly to the would-be orator. The concept of nature is important throughout: Quintilian wants to produce a natural style, he wants a speech to grow naturally and organically, and he wants to bring each speaker to his full natural development.

Later on (2.14.5) Quintilian introduces a different

[17] For Vespasian cf. Dio Cassius 65.13, for Domitian, Aulus Gellius 15.11. Cf. *CAH* 11.9 and 27 and F. G. Silher, "Quintilian of Calagurris," *AJPh* 41 (1920) 205-22.

structural principle which has been stressed by some critics:[18] this is the idea of *ars, artifex,* and *opus,* reminiscent of the *poiêsis, poiêtês, poêma* triad, a version of which is seen in Horace's *Ars poetica.* All of the *Institutio* except book twelve deals with *ars.* All of book twelve except chapter ten deals with *artifex.* Thus for eleven-twelfths of the *Institutio* the pattern is of no significance at all, and in book twelve its only significance is to explain the existence and position of chapter ten, which discusses the various styles to be found in the work of the orator. The pattern is thus of rather little importance in explaining the structure and proportion of Quintilian's work or his view of what he is doing.

A special problem in the structure and plan of the work is occasioned by the famous tenth book, which like books one, two, and twelve, is also something over and beyond the content of a rhetorical treatise. Its objective is to show how the orator can obtain facility through reading, writing, and speaking, which might be taken as a fulfillment of Quintilian's promise in the introduction to book one that he will try to nourish eloquence, not supply bare bones. This is especially true of the discussion of reading in chapter one, which aims at supplying a *copia rerum ac verborum* (10.1.5). Now this facility would logically be developed after the orator had learned the rudiments not only of invention, arrangement, and style, but also of memory and delivery. It seems rather strange, therefore, to find the whole discussion inserted into the middle of the account of style: books eight and nine deal with the virtues, defined by Theophrastus, of clarity, correctness, and ornamentation. The fourth traditional virtue, appropriateness, is dis-

---

[18] Cf. Adamietz, *op.cit.* supra n. 16, 14-16 and C. Joachim Classen, "Der Aufbau des zwölften Buch der *Institutio oratoria* Quintilians," *MH* 22 (1965) 181-90.

cussed in the first chapter of book eleven. In between comes the discussion of facility, with a Greek and more elaborate Latin reading list. On the other hand, the facility which Quintilian would like to develop will be seen primarily in style and within that category primarily in the use of the ornaments of style, so that book ten is by no means foreign to the discussion which immediately precedes. The jolt comes not so much in the transition from book nine to book ten as in the transition from ten to eleven. Book twelve, on the other hand, closely relates to many points in book ten and would follow ten easily. It is a well-known device of ancient rhetoricians to seek emphasis by hyperbaton, and book ten may be thought of in that way, a subject not integrated into the traditional outline of rhetorical theory which Quintilian desired to emphasize as the basis of style in particular and all good speaking in general. It thus seems unlikely that the placing of this book, a major part of the work, should be blamed on haste. Haste there was, however, according to the introductory epistle to Quintilian's bookseller Trypho. Possibly it may be seen in the hodgepodge chapter which ends book five or in the treatment of the *instrumenta* of the orator, in the earlier chapters of book twelve,[19] possibly in the lack of precision of some of the writing. The fairly extensive cross-references within the work, on the other hand, seem to be accurate for the most part and to have been carefully checked.

The direct sources of the *Institutio* may be grouped into two categories, first the lectures and discussions of rhetoric which Quintilian had given in his school before retirement and second the special research he did in composing the treatise itself, which he says (*Ep. ad*

[19] Cf. Gwynn 221-25; Austin, *op.cit.* supra n. 16 xxvii-xxxi; Classen, *op.cit.* supra n. 18.

Tryph. 1) took about two years.[20] The first category would be largely restricted to rhetorical theory and declamation as discussed from books three through eleven, though some of the point of view and opinions in books one and twelve may have found their expression in these lectures. The sources of the lectures in turn were of three sorts: first, the common tradition Quintilian had learned from his own study of rhetoric as a boy, which provided the framework of the subject and many of the commonplaces and examples and which were shared with other rhetorical teachers of the time. Of this he gives a very full and valuable exposition. Second were doctrines associated with particular individuals and regularly discussed in the schools. We cannot be certain how much to attribute to this group, but the dispute between the Theodoreans and Apollodoreans which had continued since the late first century B.C. is certainly an example. Another is probably the teaching of Caecilius on figures and variations of Hermagoras' *stasis* theory. Quintilian seems to have lectured on Plato's *Gorgias* (2.15.24-28) and thus the question of the relations between rhetoric and philosophy were part of the course. One might have expected the neo-Atticism dispute between Cicero and his friends to have entered into the picture, but it is discussed by Quintilian in book twelve (12.10.16ff.) rather than in the account of style and thus is not part of the exposition of rhetorical theory. The third source of the lectures was Quintilian's own belief and experience, both practical and theoretical. He mentions the problem he had in counteracting the stylistic influence of Seneca and it is possible that in the seventies he seemed rather

[20] Cousin's *Études, op.cit.* supra n. 1, are largely concerned with Quintilian's sources, but his conclusions are unreliable. Cf. also Merle M. Odgers, "Quintilian's Rhetorical Predecessors," *TAPhA* 66 (1935) 25-36 and Kennedy, *op.cit.* supra n. 1, 55-100.

unique in his views on style. Those views, however, were
largely derived from Cicero and in the course of the next
few decades they gained more currency, so that by the
time of the composition of the *Institutio* Quintilian's
discussion of style, though strongly felt, seemed less remarkable.

There are a number of passages in the rhetorical
theory of the *Institutio* where Quintilian claims or implies some originality and a number of additional places
where he advances theories which differ in varying degrees from what other writers say or are even unique.
Examination of some of these will contribute to an understanding of his objective and methods. For example,
in the latter part of book two, which constitutes a general
examination of the nature of rhetoric, Quintilian considers various traditional definitions and problems,
among them, "Is rhetoric a *virtus?*" By this he means
does the art itself have a moral quality, or does it take
its value from that of the user (2.20.1)? His answer is
that the rhetoric which he conceives is appropriate only
to a good man and is itself a virtue. The philosophers,
and he means the Stoics, have subtle arguments to prove
this; what is cited is the argument that the virtues are
qualities inherent in man which manifest themselves in
a rudimentary way even before training is given them.
Justice is an example, but so is speech. By this argument
even dialectic is a virtue, and rhetoric is so *a fortiori.*
The same conclusion can, however, be drawn from a
better proof which Quintilian regards as his own (*plani-
ore hac proprieque nostra probatione*) and which he
prefers because it is evident *ex ipsis operibus*, "from
the actual work of the orator." "For what can the orator
accomplish in laudation unless experienced in the honorable and shameful? Or in persuasion unless he sees
the expedient? Or in the courts if he be ignorant of

503

justice? Moreover, does not speech demand bravery since one must speak often despite the violent threats of the populace, often despite the dangerous displeasure of the powerful, occasionally, as in the trial of Milo, surrounded by armed soldiers? So that, if speech is not a virtue, it could never achieve perfection" (2.20.8). The argument tends to prove that the orator must have the virtues and that his speech will often exhibit these virtues. Those mentioned are prudence, justice, and fortitude, but the fourth traditional virtue of temperance is certainly needed, too, to judge from other passages. The argument does not prove that rhetoric, or the art of oratory, is itself a virtue, and it is not logically rigorous. All of this is characteristic of Quintilian: his point of view is moral, he does not sympathize with philosophy and logic, as a result sometimes falling into *petitio principii*, and he is far more interested in the concrete and the practical than in the theoretical. This exact argument does not seem to appear elsewhere, and his claim to originality may be admitted, but its assumptions run throughout Cicero's writings, and the argument which immediately follows in the context, that speech is the characteristic virtue of man, is a commonplace reaching back to the sophists.

A characteristic feature of Quintilian's teaching is the desire to give students practical advice in composition. Thus, in addition to a theoretical exposition of some rhetorical topic there is sometimes also a discussion with pedagogic purpose. For example, the first chapter of book four deals with the exordium, and at section fifty-two comes the remark: "Since it is not enough to demonstrate to learners what is contained in the theory of the prooemium, but one must say in what way prooemia may most easily be written, I add this remark. . . ." And there follows a series of practical suggestions in which

Quintilian repeatedly warns against a literal acceptance of rules and, as usual, pleads for naturalness and simplicity. The passage has clearly been influenced by his own experience and judgment as a teacher. An example of a practical pedagogical discussion from late in the work is that in the chapter on memory (11.2). After having discussed the traditional system, Quintilian expresses some doubts about practicability (23-27) and gives at length his own advice, which is of a simple and less technical sort.

His experience as an orator has influenced him as well. He refers to one of his own cases which could be only handled in a "figured" way (9.2.73), and his cautions against applying in the courts some of the techniques of the schools of declamation may come from this source. Several dangers are also pointed out in the chapter on refutation (5.13.42-52). After explaining how *visiones* can be used to produce a real and necessary emotion in the speaker (6.2.29-36) he adds, "I could not keep quiet about these matters by which I believe I attained whatever reputation for ability I have or have had; I have frequently been stirred so that not only have tears overwhelmed me, but pallor and apparently real grief."

The first part of the chapter which concludes with discussion of *visiones* contains Quintilian's treatment of ethos and pathos, presumably much as he dealt with them in his lectures. Basically the view is that they are degrees of the same thing: ethos is gentle and mild and demonstrates the speaker's moral character; pathos consists of strong emotions like anger, hate, fear, envy, or pity. We saw in the chapter on Cicero that this view was inherent in his discussion of the subject and follows from his concept of the three duties of the orator. Quintilian has developed and made more specific the teaching of Cicero, and this again is a regular feature of his work. Much the same is true of the chapter on humor.[21] The whole long account of style, taking up books eight, nine, and the first chapter of eleven, is based squarely on Cicero and organized around the four virtues of style as set forth in *De oratore* and *Orator*. Since we have not seen a steady tradition of Ciceronianism in the intervening century, we may conclude, though without certainty in individual cases, that resumption and development of Cicero's thought was a deliberate act on Quintilian's part. He is indeed the great Ciceronian of the rhetorical tradition and contributed to the canonization of the Ciceronian style. On the other hand, Quintilian is no blind worshiper of Cicero; he does not want an anachronistic revival of the pure style of Cicero. What he wants is an injection of the breadth, richness, imagination, and natural vitality of Cicero into the writing of his own day, retaining at the same time some of its own polish as seen, for example, in its taste for *sententiae*, overdone though this sometimes seemed to him to be.[22]

The second category of sources of the *Institutio* is the research which Quintilian conducted specifically in preparation for its composition. He discovered specific points in earlier writers which had not been part of his lectures; he expanded the subject considerably beyond what he had taught; and, as is regularly the case in scholarship, he was led to reexamine and revise his views as he wrote them down.

The best examples of discovery of specific points are probably to be found in the historical surveys of different questions which he inserts. We can be reasonably

[21] Cf. F. Kuehnert, "Quintilians Erörterung über den Witz," *Philologus* 106 (1962) 29-59 and 305-14.

[22] Quintilian's chief discussions of Cicero are 10.1.105 and 112; 10.2.25; 12.10.45-48. Cf. F. Sehlmeyer, *Beziehungen zwischen Quintilians Institutio oratoria und Ciceros rhetorischen Schriften*, Münster, 1912 and Kennedy, *op.cit.* supra n. 1, 110-12.

sure that they were prepared in connexion with composition of the *Institutio* since extensive discussions of this sort do not seem a normal part of rhetorical lectures and since Quintilian says specifically (1. *pr.* 2) that a purpose of his work is to help others decide between conflicting theories. Examples might be the survey of definitions of rhetoric in book two, chapter fifteen, or of different forms of *stasis* theory in book three, chapter six. The numerous references to disagreements among rhetoricians sprinkled throughout the work probably result from this same research.

Quintilian's greatest achievement was his expansion of a review of rhetorical theory into a whole program for the education of the orator. In this, as has been said, he apparently had the precedent of the elder Pliny. The additions which he made are of various sorts: first, the discussion of elementary and grammatical education preparatory to a rhetorical school. This part involved its own special sources, of whom the Stoics Chrysippus and Diogenes of Babylon are mentioned (1.1.4; 9; 16), but it has a highly personal tone. Although Quintilian never seems to have taught small children, he had strong views on how they should be treated. Second are additions to the body of rhetorical theory resulting from his attempt to be thorough and to deal with all aspects of preparation for actual speaking. Two of the most interesting and unique chapters are that in book five (7) on the examination of witnesses and that in book six (4) on *altercatio* or debate, which ordinarily concluded the presentation of a case. These discussions were mentioned in our first chapter as valuable sources of information on Roman precedure, but neither technique, as important as it was, was taught in the schools. It is his thoroughness that leads Quintilian to include them. Another addition is all of book ten which supplies the orator with facility. The literary critical portions, including the examination of imitation, are subjects which would ordinarily have been dealt with in monographs, but by Quintilian are made part of a greater whole, and the survey of Latin literature is probably his own addition to the survey of Greek writers he knew from Dionysius or other sources. The final addition is the twelfth book, the noble picture of the adult orator in all his powers. Despite Quintilian's protestations of originality (12. *pr.* 4) it has its antecedents in the *Phaedrus* and especially in *De oratore* and *De officiis*, but these are not, of course, rhetorical treatises, and the expansion is a real one.

Finally, the writing of the *Institutio* led him to certain changes in his own views. The change he himself points out is the revised *stasis* system which he sets forth (3.6.63-82). He warns his readers that he has come to regard his lectures as expounding a logical fallacy in treating legal *stasis* as a part of rational *stasis* and in including a *stasis* of exception or jurisdiction. Like Hippocrates, he is not ashamed to admit that he has been wrong. In his new system questions are either rational or legal. Rational questions can be divided into three kinds of *stasis*: fact, definition, or justice. Legal questions are divisible into various species, but at the same time each is reducible into one of the same three *staseis* as are rational questions. Exception—where, for example, the jurisdiction of the court is denied—is not a separate kind of *stasis*, but involves a rational or legal question and can be rephrased as one of the three kinds of *stasis*. The account is then followed by "an easier and more open road" (3.6.83), a practical way by which a student may approach the case at hand and in which the various parts are less rigorously stated: in legal questions, for example, three *simulacra*, or mirror images of *staseis* are accepted.

508

The goal of the *Institutio* is the training of the *bonus orator*. What did Quintilian mean by this concept, how may we assess its feasibility, and how much does his educational system contribute to its realization?[23] Although significant references are scattered throughout the work, the chief passages of interest in understanding the *bonus orator* are the preface to book one, the chapters in book three relating to the kinds of oratory, and the whole twelfth book on the adult orator. In broad outline Quintilian's perfect orator does not differ from the ideal of the latter part of Plato's *Phaedrus* or Isocrates' *Antidosis* or Cicero's *De oratore* and *Orator*, but just as those writings differ considerably in emphasis or detail, so Quintilian's goal has its own coloring. Rather heavy emphasis is put on the orator's personal morality and technical competence, rather less on his political and intellectual leadership. His role in the law courts seems more evident than in the council chamber or before the people. Such practical matters as delivery play considerable part in his success. Philosophy and law are tools and materials for him, not perfectly integrated into his cast of thought. In other words, the picture is much what one might have expected from a teacher of rhetoric who inherited a rich tradition and lived under an autocratic government. At the same time Quintilian's approach to most matters is positive and optimistic. He insists that a greater orator than Cicero or Demosthenes may yet appear; he stresses the good effects of trying.

The passages on the kinds of oratory in book three are important in understanding what Quintilian thought the possibilities of oratory were in his own time. He dis-

---

[23] Cf. Appel, *op.cit.* supra n. 16; Michael Winterbottom, "Quintilian and the *vir bonus*," *JRS* 54 (1964) 90-97; Kennedy, *op.cit.* supra n. 1, 123-35; Prentice A. Meador, Jr., "Quintilian's *vir bonus*," *Western Speech* 34 (1970) 162-69.

cusses epideictic first (3.7), equating it with speeches of praise and blame. At Rome, he says, it has practical adaptations, and he lists first funeral orations, secondly the praise or blame of witnesses or the accused in court, thirdly praise or blame of political opponents. There are also display speeches, such as the praise of Capitoline Jove which was a part of the Capitoline contest established by Domitian. This list is not entirely satisfactory. Funeral orations were certainly common, but highly traditional and often not much influenced by Greek epideictic. What Quintilian says about the praise of men in following sections could, however, be adapted to a funeral oration. A funeral speech must have been the only public address some Romans ever gave, and to a modern critic it seems illogical that teachers of public speaking did not specifically give attention to it. What is said about praise and blame in the law courts is valid enough, but Quintilian illustrates praise and blame of political opponents only from Cicero and it would be helpful to know how much of it went on in his own time. Certainly there was an opportunity for the ambitious to praise imperial officials and attack discredited functionaries. Strangest is perhaps the absence of any specific reference to the *gratiarum actio*, or speech of thanks to the emperor, which as we have seen had become a regular duty of each person entering on the consulship. The Capitoline contest is the only feature of the passage attributable to Quintilian's own time.

In the case of deliberative oratory, which is examined next, Quintilian makes an effort to enlarge its field (3.8.14). Greek writers, and Cicero too to a large extent, identify it, he says, with *contiones*. A considerable portion of the discussion is devoted to *suasoriae* in rhetorical schools, which perhaps were the commonest opportunity for deliberative speaking open to most Romans. There is also mention of deliberative oratory in historical writing (3.8.67). At the end of the chapter Quintilian returns to practical uses and sees them in counseling friends, in speaking in the senate, and in advising the emperor if he consults them, which certainly applied to those in the bureaucracy in Rome. In book two (16.19) and again in book twelve (1.28) addresses by an officer to his troops are mentioned in addition. But as in the case of epideictic, there is no specific consideration of the rhetorical problems posed by the conditions of imperial oratory.

Judicial oratory changed least from republic to empire. Quintilian is aware of certain differences in legal procedure (e.g., 3.10.1), but does not remark, as Tacitus and Pliny do, that the cases were less interesting. He almost certainly felt that it was a sign of peace and progress that the great political trials of the late republic no longer took place. The chapter (3.9) specifically devoted to judicial oratory is a short one, but in fact the following four books discuss judicial oratory and it is clearly the form which Quintilian regards as most reducible to rule.

The effect of reading book three is to conclude that opportunity for great oratory was limited. In book twelve Quintilian returns to the subject on a grander scale; he describes the *instrumenta* of the orator, which include knowledge of philosophy, law, and history, and in two passages he seems to catch a glimpse of something grander than anything described earlier in his work. One of these comes in the first chapter:

"For we are not educating a public workman nor a hired voice nor, to spare harsher terms, even a useful

511

advocate in litigation which men usually call a pleader, but an individual outstanding in natural ability who has thoroughly learned many liberal arts, some one to be a divine gift to human life, of the sort which no earlier age has known, unique and perfect in everything, perceiving the best, speaking the best. In the case of this man how small a part of his function will be the defense of the innocent or control of the crimes of the wicked or in financial transactions the aid of truth against fraud? Our greatest orator will take part in these actions too, but he will shine more brightly in greater matters when decrees of the senate are to be formed and public error is to be directed toward a better goal. Does not Virgil seem to have described such a man when he portrays one controlling the violence of a mob as it starts to throw torches and stones?" (12.1.25-27)

Quintilian goes on to quote the simile from the *Aeneid* applied to Poseidon as he quells the storm brewed by Juno, which we discussed in chapter five, and then to say that this same man will draw on his knowledge of philosophy to address his troops in time of war. It is difficult to think that Quintilian's great orator in the fullest sense can be anyone other than some future emperor, especially when we recall the picture in book one where the teacher is compared to Aristotle taking Alexander the Great upon his knee, or the fact that Quintilian had become tutor to Domitian's heirs. As Plato had longed for a philosopher-king, so Quintilian longs for an orator-emperor. His wish was shared by others. Given the role of rhetoric in ancient education, it must have been difficult to accept as lord a man who was not a good speaker. We have seen how Tacitus was appalled at the inadequacy of Nero, the first emperor unable to compose his own speeches. If speech was the greatest human art the emperor should be the greatest orator. In practice the fourth century emperor Julian probably came closer to this ideal than any of his predecessors.

The other passage comes in the second chapter (9-10) when Quintilian discusses the contribution of philosophy to oratory. In the preface to book one he had followed Cicero in seeing and lamenting a split in classical Greek times between the orator and the philosopher. Here he exclaims: "O may the day come when someone, the perfect orator whom we desire, will claim for himself this art which has become hated because of its arrogant name and the views of those who corrupt its benefits, and as though recovering stolen property will bring it back into the body of eloquence!"

This hope for a glorious philosophical eloquence is not unique to Quintilian. It was shared by others in his time and was one of the motivating factors in the movement known as the second sophistic, already well under way in Greece and destined to have some influence at Rome.[24] To it, and thus to the extent to which Quintilian's hopes were realized, we will turn in the next chapter. There remains one question already asked, but still unanswered. How much does Quintilian's educational system contribute to the realization of the perfect orator? He himself claims (2.19.2) that the *average* orator owes most to nature, but the *perfect* orator owes most to education. We have already stressed serious limitations in Roman education and said that Quintilian made no attempt to change the curriculum. But consciousness of these limita-

[24] Cf. Hans von Arnim, *Dio von Prusa*, Berlin, 1898, 134; Wilbur J. Greer, "Quintilian and the Declamation," CW 19 (1925-26) 27-31; F. Grypdonck, "Quintilianus Stoicijn of neosofist?" AC 35 (1966) 487-505.

tions actually grows out of a modern unwillingness to accept the orator as the goal. If for the moment we do accept that goal, many of the objections collapse. In any art the artist needs discipline, practice, and a demanding public. This Quintilian's orator certainly had. He should as much as possible be aware of technical possibilities, and to this all the rules of rhetoric contributed. But he must not be stultified by rules, and Quintilian repeatedly shows how rules do not always apply. He needs a self-consciousness, but not to the extent of inhibiting expression. The practice of declamation and Quintilian's enthusiasm for oratory would contribute to this, and so to a high degree would Quintilian's unusually nonrepressive educational system in which the fun of learning and speaking and the natural rivalry of a well-run classroom should lead to good results. The point of view was always moral, but not prudish and not oppressive. A great orator needs a vision of life, and the school could not itself give this, but Quintilian is careful to make clear at every point that the student is preparing himself for the dust of the forum: he will visit it often and he will know the weaknesses of academic seclusions. On one point there is doubt: How much genuine intellectuality must the orator have? Can he know a smattering of philosophy, law, and history which he will use as he needs or must he be genuinely philosophical, thoroughly learned in law and in history? Quintilian's sights are lower than Cicero's, Cicero's were lower than Plato's. This, in part, represents personal inclination and ability, in part the conditions of the times. Quintilian's world was more settled and legal and orderly and seemed to have less need of new ideas. It should be said in his behalf that he considered the problem and judged it as he saw it. Philosophy, law, and history have as many dangers as rhetoric ever had.

Tacitus

P. Cornelius Tacitus,[25] the greatest historian of the Roman empire and after Cicero the finest Latin prose stylist, was an orator of note in the late first and early second centuries. He was born around A.D. 55 and says (*Hist.* 1.1) that his public career was begun under Vespasian and continued under Titus and Domitian. He was praetor in 88 (*Ann.* 11.11). From 89 to 93 he seems to have served as a commander or governor in some province (*Agr.* 45) and to have returned to Rome in the last difficult years of Domitian's reign when Quintilian was publishing the *Institutio.* Domitian had probably approved the choice of Tacitus to be a suffect consul late in 97, though by the time he took office Domitian was dead and the more agreeable Nerva reigning in his place. The only event remembered from Tacitus' consulship was his eloquent funeral oration for the aged and respected Virginius Rufus (Pliny, *Ep.* 2.1.6). The following year saw Tacitus' publication of the *Agricola*, a biographical tribute to his father-in-law which shows some influence of oratorical forms,[26] and the ethnological monograph *Germania*. In January of 100 Tacitus collaborated

[25] Cf. Gaston Boissier, *Tacitus and Other Roman Studies*, London, 1906; B. Walker, *The Annals of Tacitus*, Manchester, 1951; Clarence W. Mendell, *Tacitus: the Man and his Work*, New Haven, 1957 (Mendell is, however, unreliable on the *Dialogus*); Ronald Syme, *Tacitus*, 2 vols. Oxford, 1958, to which the following account is often indebted.

[26] Though it is not best analyzed as a funeral oration as was once thought, cf. E. Hübner, "Zu Tacitus Agricola," *Hermes* 1 (1866) 438-48 and Jean Cousin, "Histoire et rhétorique dans l'*Agricola*," *REL* 14 (1936) 326-36. Alfred Gudeman saw influence of Greek sophistry, *De vita et moribus Cn. Julii Agricolae liber*, Berlin, 1902, 1-13. For more balanced views cf. Duane R. Stuart, *Epochs of Greek and Roman Biography*, Berkeley, 1928, 235-53; Syme, *op.cit.* supra n. 25, 125; R. M. Ogilvie and Ian Richmond, *Corneli Taciti De vita Agricolae*, Oxford, 1967, 13.

with Pliny in the prosecution of Priscus, the extortionist governor of Africa, in a celebrated trial in the senate over which the new emperor Trajan presided. Pliny says that Tacitus' speech was very eloquent and showed his customary sense of dignity (*Ep.* 2.11.17). Although Tacitus lived at least another fifteen years and clearly did not entirely withdraw from public affairs, since he became governor of Asia in 112-13, this is the last time his friend Pliny mentions hearing him speak.[27] Sometime after that successful trial of 100 he abandoned the art of oratory and in the *Dialogus de oratoribus* put on record his reasons for doing so.

Although most aspects of the *Dialogus* have inspired controversy at some time, there is no reason to question its authenticity and in the mid-twentieth century a consensus about its main features has emerged.[28] Date of publication is not definitely known, but is certainly later than was once thought. The point of view postdates Tacitus' last efforts at oratory and the accession of Trajan. A reasonable guess might be that it was issued in

[27] Pliny mentions (*Ep.* 7.20) reading drafts of books by Tacitus in 107 or 108, which the Melmouth translation rendered "oration," but the ref. is probably to the *Histories*, cf. A. N. Sherwin-White, *The Letters of Pliny*, Oxford, 1966, 427.

[28] Cf. K. von Fritz, "Aufbau und Absicht des *Dialogus de Oratoribus*," *RhM* 81 (1932) 275-300; A. Kappelmacher, "Zur Abfassungszeit von Tacitus' *Dialogus de oratoribus*," *WS* 50 (1932) 121-29; W. den Boer, "Die gegenseitigen Verhältnisse der Personen im *Dialogus de oratoribus* und die Anschauung des Tacitus," *Mnemosyne* 7 (1938-39) 193-224; Clarke 100-108; Syme, *op.cit.* supra n. 25, 100-120; Alain Michel, *Le Dialogue des orateurs de Tacite et la philosophie de Cicéron*, Paris, 1962; Leeman 320-23; Giuseppe Romaniello, *Il Dialogus de oratoribus nella definitiva soluzione della vexata quaestio*, Rome, 1968, tries again to argue for a somewhat earlier date. The chief commentaries are those of Alfred Gudeman, Boston, 1898 (expanded German edition, Berlin, 1914) and Alain Michel, Paris, 1962. For a translation cf. Herbert W. Benario (Library of Liberal Arts), Indianapolis, 1967.

101, when the man to whom it is dedicated, Fabius Justus, was consul designate. Apparent imitations of it occur in Pliny's *Panegyric*, originally delivered in the fall of 100, but extensively revised during 101 and 102. The letter of Pliny written about 107 contains a rather clear echo.[29] Tacitus begins in a way reminiscent of the opening of the *De oratore* or the *Orator* of Cicero. This Ciceronianism is persistent:[30] the prose style is quite unlike Tacitus' historical works and is much more like that of Cicero, and the dramatic use of the dialogue form is a Ciceronian reminiscence. But the Ciceronianism is ironic, for the question posed is: "Why is oratory dead?" In the course of the dialogue there is an examination into the truth of the assumption that oratory is in decline and one character, Aper, is made to deny it vigorously, but Tacitus himself clearly accepts the fact: he begins with direct assertion of it and the dialogue as a whole is directed toward explaining how it has come about. The views of Aper are not accepted by the other characters, with whom Tacitus associates himself, and the flourishing oratory which Aper vaunts is shown to be restricted to the attempts of informers. The most authoritative character in the dialogue is Curiatus Maternus, at whose

[29] Pliny, *Ep.* 9.10.2, addressed to Tacitus, resembles *Dial.* 9.6, cf. also 12.1. Opinions about the date of the *Dialogus* are collected by J. Frot, "Tacite est-il l'auteur du Dialogue des orateurs?" *REL* 33 (1955) 120-29. For the influence on the *Panegyricus* cf. Richard T. Bruère, "Tacitus and Pliny's *Panegyricus*," *CPh* 49 (1954) 161-79 and Rudolf Guengerich, "Tacitus' *Dialogus* und der *Panegyricus* des Plinius," *Festschrift Bruno Snell*, Munich, 1956, 145-52.
[30] Cf. R. Klaiber, *Die Beziehungen des Rednerdialogs von Tacitus zu Ciceros rhetorischen Schriften*, Progr. Bamberg, 1914; E. Kostermann, "Der Taciteische *Dialogus* und Ciceros Schrift *De Republica*," *Hermes* 65 (1930) 396-421; Michel's treatise, *op.cit.* supra n. 28.

home the conversation takes place. He it is who gives, at the end, the explanation of the decline which constitutes Tacitus' final answer. Though Tacitus claims to have been personally present at the discussion, he was "still a youth" (1.2) and takes no part in the conversation; in fact, his views are those of Maternus and this identification has further significance in that Maternus is presented as an orator of great ability who has recently decided to abandon oratory, as Tacitus himself seems to have done after A.D. 100. Maternus is severely criticized by some of his friends for betraying his trust and the dialogue is in part his apology. It serves as well for Tacitus himself. Their situations were, however, not quite identical. It makes rather little difference that Maternus has chosen to turn to tragic poetry from oratory, while Tacitus chose historiography. Clearly Maternus' poetry has a strong historical cast. But Maternus acted in the time of Vespasian when informers flourished, when the aristocracy was distrusted, and when freedom of speech was sometimes shaky. It is likely that he did not long survive.[31] Tacitus made his own apostasy in the reign of Trajan which he himself elsewhere refers to as characterized by "a rare felicity of the times when we may think what we like and say what we think" (*Hist.* 1.1). The restoration of relative liberty made it clearer than ever in Tacitus' view that there was no longer a need for the orator nor material for his eloquence.

---

[31] Dio 67.12.5 reports Domitian's execution of a "sophist" Maternus, possibly a confused report of the death of Tacitus' character, cf. Syme, *op.cit.* supra n. 25, 110-11 and 798-99. The analogy with Crassus in *De oratore* is attractive, but suggests that Maternus did not survive until Domitian's time, cf. Alan Cameron, "Tacitus and the Date of Curiatus Maternus' Death," CR 17 (1967) 258-61.

The dialogue is set in 75,[32] about thirty years before the date of composition and at a time when Tacitus was around twenty years old. Similarly, *De oratore* reported a conversation of Cicero's youth, thirty-seven years earlier. The literary imitation is deliberate, and in both cases the writer can create an effective dramatic dialogue between people who were conveniently dead at the time of publication. Both works are really about contemporary circumstances, but possibly Tacitus' attention was directed to the reign of Vespasian by his research for the *Histories* which began around this time.[33] In the *Dialogus*, Maternus is discovered by his friends revising his tragedy of Cato, which he had publicly recited the night before.[34] There are references to a *Medea*, a *Thyestes*, and a *Domitius* as well, all clearly containing criticism of contemporary conditions. Like that of Tacitus, Maternus' oratory is not being silenced by fear, but he has discovered that his point of view can find an expression in poetry, as Tacitus found in history.

The better part of the *Dialogus* is made up of five extensive speeches. First, Marcus Aper attacks Maternus' abandonment of oratory and attempts to demonstrate the overwhelming greatness of eloquence (5-10). He does not hesitate to allude to the oratory of his own age, including the informer Eprius Marcellus. Maternus replies briefly (11-13): he is weary of the labors of the orator, he finds a better defense in integrity than in eloquence, and he longs for the idyllic life of the poet. Clearly he is anxious to avoid any identification with

[32] On the basis of 17.3, cf. Syme, *op.cit.* supra n. 25, 670-71.
[33] "The *Dialogus* can perhaps be regarded as a by-product of the *Historiae*," Syme, *op.cit.* supra n. 25, 673.
[34] Cf. Tenney Frank, "Curiatus Maternus and his Tragedies," *AJPh* 58 (1937) 225-29.

informers. There is then an interlude, marked by the arrival of Vipstanus Messalla and a general discussion of the relative merits of the ancients and the moderns (14-16). Tacitus touches lightly (15) on the fact that Messalla was half-brother to the informer Regulus.[35] He had indeed defended him in a famous case a few years before (*Hist.* 4.42). Aper next delivers a second speech (16-23) which is a defense of the achievements of contemporary oratory. His first argument is rather trivial, that the term "ancient" is ambiguous, and that in a sense Cicero is a modern orator, but he goes on to attack orators down to Cassius Severus and to praise contemporary styles as briefer, clearer, more brilliant, and more graceful. Messalla replies to Aper (25-35) by praising the eloquence of the past and criticizing that of the present as more the art of an actor than an orator. Maternus urges him to get to the issue of the causes for the decline (27) and he promptly attributes this to the "laziness of youth, the neglectfulness of parents, the ignorance of teachers, and forgetfulness of ancient discipline" (28.2). We have met these complaints before. Messalla's ideal orator is reminiscent of Cicero's: a man who enters the forum armed with all the arts (32.2). Maternus again interrupts to ask for more detail about training (33), and we are given a brief picture of the contrast between old Roman education and the schools of declamation, with their subjects remote from all reality (35.4-5). Here there appears to be a sudden lacuna in the text. Messala apparently had something more to say and it is possible that Julius Secundus did as well, an adult figure who has not yet had his say.[36] The text as we have it continues

---

[35] Cf. H. Wagenvoort, "De Reguli in Taciti *Dialogo* partibus," *Mnemosyne* 54 (1926) 416-39.

[36] Cf. Will Richter, "Zur Rekonstruktion des *Dialogus de oratoribus*," NGG 1961, 387-414.

with what is apparently the middle of a final speech by Maternus running almost to the end of the dialogue (36-41).

It is unfortunate that we do not know the conversation which intervened between the speech of Messalla and the last speech of Maternus. The latter's interruptions may be taken dramatically to represent a slight, and very polite, impatience; presumably he agreed with much of what Messalla said, but still was unsatisfied with it as an explanation of the state of eloquence. Messalla presented in his own words substantially the same explanations which we have already seen in Seneca and Petronius: laziness, moral decline, the faults of declamation. But apparently Maternus regarded these more as symptoms than as causes. His own speech puts the blame primarily on the lack of materials for great oratory. The disorders and dissensions of the republic had naturally fanned the flames of political eloquence, but now this is no longer necessary under the orderly and peaceful government of the empire. At the same time the law courts are now more practical and just, but allow much less scope to the orator. Maternus repeatedly says that in most ways the change is an improvement and should not be regretted, but there is a note of nostalgia and toward the end (41.4) there is a distinct ironic note in the description of the senate as the best men, unanimous in policy, of the emperor as the wisest individual, and of the general absence of wrongdoing so that litigation is unneeded. Even if the empire does not actively repress freedom of speech, its nature even at its best tends to stifle discussion.

In discussing *On Sublimity* we saw that the political argument for the decline of eloquence was there rejected as trite and superficial in favor of the moral argument, and suggested that the political argument had chiefly been applied to Greek literature whereas its applicability at Rome was still not manifest. By the time of Tacitus the moral argument had been so commonly expressed that it in turn can be regarded as trite and the applicability of the political argument, not only under the repressive Flavians, but under the more liberal Trajan, has reemerged and become clear to Tacitus. There is no evidence that *On Sublimity* was known to him and the argument is largely his own thoughtful development, but some traces of it had, of course, lurked in earlier discussions, for example in Seneca's words *in tanta pace*.

The contrast between Quintilian's *Institutio* and Tacitus' *Dialogus* is inescapable and probably intentional.[37] A few references suggest that Tacitus had read the *Institutio*, and it is certainly likely that he would be familiar with the work of such an important person as Quintilian. But similarities between the two works are trivial and the authors' fundamental viewpoints are in direct conflict. This is carried to the point that none of the characters in the *Dialogus* is a spokesman for Quintilian's point of view or recognizes his objectives. The dramatic date of the *Dialogus* is twenty years before the publication of the *Institutio*, but it is four years after Quintilian's appointment by Vespasian and yet the opportunity is not seized to remark that some of the evils

---

[37] Cf. Guerngerich, "Der *Dialogus* des Tacitus und Quintilians *Institutio oratoria*," *CPh* 46 (1951) 159-61. Cf. also George Wormser, "Le *Dialogue des Orateurs* et l'*Institution oratoire*," *RPh* 36 (1912) 179-89; R. Dienel, "Quintilian und der Rednerdialog des Tacitus," *WS* 37 (1915) 239-71; Henry Bardon, "*Dialogue des orateurs* et *Institution oratoire*," *REL* 19 (1941) 113-31; Pasquale Smiraglia, "Il *Dialogue de oratoribus*: cronologia e rapporti con l'insegnamento di Quintiliano," *Annali della facoltà dell' Università di Napoli* 5 (1955); Michel, treatise *cit.* supra n. 28, 195-96; Leeman 320-23; Kennedy, *op.cit.* supra n. 1, 136-39.

in style or education noted by Messalla are being combatted by an influential teacher.

Tacitus' implied contempt for Quintilian may have a political or even a social element about it. Quintilian was a favorite of the Flavians, whom Tacitus hated, and Quintilian probably belonged to a class which was being advanced at the expense of those with whom Tacitus identified himself. His origin may have been no nobler than Quintilian's, but he became a senator and identified himself with senatorial interests when Quintilian was teaching children in the palace. More important, Quintilian's concept of the orator was viewed by Tacitus with contempt. Substantially Quintilian's view was the traditional one taken from Cicero. In this he is in agreement with Messalla and opposed to Aper. But unlike Messalla Quintilian refused to be discouraged: like Aper he thought there were orators of merit in his own time and he goes further to predict a glorious future for the traditional orator. Tacitus thought that contemporary oratory was only vigorous among the informers and he doubtless regarded Quintilian as, in practice, encouraging and compromising with informers. Quintilian certainly would have denied this, but it is true that the question was very delicate. Tacitus further thought that there was no hope for oratory and the entire concept and objective of Quintilian's *Institutio* under those circumstances became an empty delusion. Quintilian and his so-called educational reforms could thus be dismissed as creatures of Flavian propaganda. In the upshot the truth was somewhere between Tacitus' and Quintilian's position. Oratory and traditional rhetoric were not quite so dead as Tacitus thought nor did any orator as great as Cicero come again as Quintilian hoped. Tacitus' criticism, like his politics, was embittered and distorted.

523

In all of his historical writing Tacitus demonstrates a masterful control of rhetoric of all levels.[38] His object throughout is persuasion. "Without anger or partiality," as he somewhat insidiously puts it (*Ann.* 1.1), he would demonstrate to readers of all time his view of the principate as at heart a vicious and un-Roman tyranny which held power by threat and bribery but whose excuse for rule was the general moral collapse of Rome. Tiberius in particular, but all emperors, bureaucrats, and informers are presented with a subtle malice which does lip service to their official duty, but draws on the "color" of the rhetorical schools to discredit their motives and objectives.[39] The rhetoric of technique is further illustrated by Tacitus' remarkable style to which Sallustian brevity and Senecan *sententiae* have both contributed.[40] Tacitus is, however, never a rhetorical writer in the sense that Ovid or Q. Curtius is rhetorical: elaboration, meaningless amplification, artificial conceits had no attraction for him. His rhetoric is disciplined and austere.

Like other ancient historians Tacitus makes use of speeches at crises in his historical narrative or to present the reasons which influenced action or to help portray character in his actors.[41] Tacitus' speeches tend to be

[38] Cf. J. Mesk, "Zur Rhetorik bei Tacitus," *WS* 46 (1928) 233-34; A. Gunz, *Die deklamatorische Rhetorik in der Germania des Tacitus*, Lausanne, 1934; Cousin, *op.cit.* supra n. 26; Walker, *op.cit.* supra n. 25, 49-57 and 144-53; Syme, *op.cit.* supra n. 25, 304-63; Henry Bardon, "A propos des *Histories* de Tacite et la tentation de la rhétorique," *Hommages à L. Hermann*, Brussels, 1960, 146-51; Leeman 337-60.

[39] Cf. Thomas S. Jerome, "The Tacitean Tiberius: a Study in Historiographic Method," *CPh* 7 (1912) 275-76.

[40] Cf. Syme, *op.cit.* supra n. 25, 340-63; Leeman 337-60; Berend-Reiner Voss, *Der pointierte Stil des Tacitus*, Münster, 1963.

[41] Cf. Gustavus A. Harrer, "Senatorial Speeches and Letters in Tacitus' *Annals*," *SPh* 15 (1918) 333-43; R. Ullmann, *La technique des discours dans Salluste, Tite-Live et Tacite*, Oslo,

524

shorter than Livy's but often have a similarly moral impact. He claims (*Ann.* 3.65) that he chooses to include senatorial speeches only when they are illustrations of great virtue or vice. We have already referred to some of the more conspicuous speeches in the *Annals*, Tacitus' last historical work, covering the period from the death of Augustus to the death of Nero.[42] His earliest historical writing, the *Agricola*, contains his most remarkable oratorical effort, and the one closest to a school *suasoria*, a speech by the Scottish chieftain Calgacus to his troops on the eve of the battle of the Grampian mountains (30-32). Calgacus seeks to give nerve to his men by showing that there is no further refuge for them and by suggesting the moral weakness of the Romans, and he delivers one of the most memorable of Latin *sententia*: "To pillage, to slaughter, to rape they give the false name of empire; and where they make a desolation, call it peace." The grim irony with which Tacitus viewed his fellow countrymen made it possible for him to enter into the situation of his largely imaginary speaker and share his view of Rome.[43] The speech of Agricola which follows (33-34) is an entirely ordinary exhortation which does not touch upon the justification of empire and does nothing to counteract the force of Calgacus' remarks.

1927; N. P. Miller, "Dramatic Speech in Tacitus," *AJPh* 85 (1964) 279-96; R. H. Martin, "The Speech of Curtius Montanus: Tacitus, *Histories* 4.42," *JRS* 57 (1967) 109-14; D.C.A. Shotter, "The Debate on Augustus: Tacitus, *Annals* 1.9-10," *Mnemosyne* 20 (1967) 171-74. There is a discussion of the speech of Percennius, *Ann.* 1.16-17 and Tacitus' techniques in Erich Auerbach, *Mimesis: the Representation of Reality in Western Literature*, Garden City, N.Y., 1957, 29-37.

[42] For a list of the speeches cf. Walker, *op.cit.* supra n. 25, 259-62.

[43] Cf. Syme, *op.cit.* supra n. 25, 528-29 and W. Liebeschuetz, "The Theme of Liberty in the *Agricola* of Tacitus," *CQ* 16 (1966) 126-39.

The *Histories* contain, among other speeches, two spirited orations by the emperor Otho (1.37-8; 83-84) and two interesting scenes in the senate involving infamous informers, an exchange between Helvidius Pricus, son-in-law of Thrasea Paetus, and Eprius Marcellus, who had informed on him (4.5-8), and another between Messalla, the character in the *Dialogus*, speaking for his half-brother, the notorius Aquilius Regulus, and the outspoken Curtius Montanus (4.42-44). This occurred at the beginning of Vespasian's reign when his attitude toward the senate and toward informers was still in doubt. Vespasian tried to save face for the senate, but intervened on behalf of the informers as well. Tacitus was too young to have heard these exchanges in the senate, but he probably knew from good sources the substance of what was said.

One final speech in the *Histories* may be taken as illustrating the circumstances of some imperial oratory. This is the address of Mucianus to Vespasian, urging him to seek the throne (2.76-77). According to Tacitus the actual public address had been preceded by extensive private discussions. Only when the decision to make the attempt had been made was a scene arranged where Vespasian could be implored, first by Mucianus in a set speech and then by his officers, as though spontaneously (2.78).

Pliny the Younger

The younger Pliny was the nephew of Pliny the Elder, a pupil of Quintilian, a close friend of Tacitus, and the author of the *Panegyricus*, the first complete extent oration we have met since leaving Cicero.[44] He was born in

[44] For Quintilian, cf. *Ep*. 2.14.9; for Tacitus *Ep*. 1.6; 4.13; 6.9; 6.16; 6.20; 7.20; 7.33; 8.7; 9.10; 9.14. Despite criticism of prosopographical details by reviewers, the standard work on Pliny

A.D. 62 and belonged to a prosperous family of Comum in northern Italy. His public career was successful and rapid: probably quaestor in 90, tribune in 92, praetor in 93, suffect consul in September and perhaps also October of 100. He also held two prefectorships, was an augur, served as curator of the banks of the Tiber, and climaxed his career as special legate of the emperor to govern the province of Bithynia, where he probably died about 112.[45]

Pliny is chiefly known to us from his letters, ten books written between 96 and 108 and arranged in roughly chronological order, except that all the correspondence with the emperor Trajan is put together in book ten.[46] The letters are more artificial and less candid than those of Cicero: all are polished for publication, most deal only with a single subject, and Pliny exercised great care in their choice and arrangement (*Ep.* 1.1). They were, however, actually sent as letters to the addressee (*Ep.* 9.2), and they preserve a good deal of information about the public and private life of the time, including the political adjustment from the tyranny of Domitian to the greater freedom under Nerva and Trajan, with comments on the oratory and literary activities of Pliny and his friends.[47] We may first consider what is known about

---

is now A. N. Sherwyn-White, *The Letters of Pliny*, Oxford, 1966. Cf. also Santi Consoli, *De C. Plinii Caecilii Secundi rhetoricis studiis*, Catania, 1897; Clarke 106-8; J. Niemirska-Pliszcynska, *De elocutione Pliniana in epistularum libris novem conspicua quaestiones selectae*, Lublin, 1955; Jean Beaujeu, "Pline le jeune, 1955-60," *Lustrum* 6 (1961) 272-312; Leeman 323-28.

[45] On problems in Pliny's biography cf. Syme, *op.cit.* supra n. 25, 652-60 and Sherwyn-White, *op.cit.* supra n. 44, 69-82.

[46] Cf. Sherwyn-White, *op.cit.* supra n. 44, 20-41.

[47] Cf. A.-M. Guillemin, *Pline et la vie littéraire de son temps*, Paris, 1929; Atkins 303-8; J. Stinchcomb, "The Literary Tastes of the Younger Pliny," *CW* 29 (1935-36) 161-65.

Pliny as an orator and then his discussions of rhetoric in the letters.

Although he did not achieve anything like the quality of Demosthenes or Cicero, nor attain Quintilian's concept of the perfect orator, Pliny was certainly one of the two or three most famous Latin orators of his age, and his activities well illustrate the practical possibility open at the time. During much of his adult life he carried on an extensive practice as an advocate, especially property cases in the centumviral court which he refers to as "my arena" (*Ep.* 6.12.2); as a senator he participated in debate and was repeatedly asked to undertake public prosecutions for extortion. As consul he delivered a speech of thanks to the emperor for his appointment. As a public official at Rome or in Bithynia and as a leading citizen in Comum he spoke on various ceremonial occasions. Certain general characteristics run throughout his career: as Quintilian would have wished, he was a real-life orator whose responsibility was to his clients or the state. He shows little interest in declamation and may not even have practiced it as an adult, though he writes appreciatively of hearing the Greek sophist Isaeus (*Ep.* 2.3)[48] and had high artistic standards for oratory which led him to subject his actual spoken words to an exacting process of criticism and revision before they were ready for publication. He was scrupulous in his choice of cases and claims to have undertaken only four sorts (*Ep.* 6.29.1-3): those of his friends, those of people who were left helpless, those important as precedents, and those which could be called famous. The first three categories he claims to have derived from Avidius Quietus who got them from Thrasea Paetus, the famous Stoic hero. The categories rather fall short of Quintilian's moral advice

[48] Cf. P. Grimal, "Deux figures de correspondance de Pline," *Latomus* 14 (1955) 370-83.

on the subject (12.7.1-7), but the real point is that Pliny tried to avoid any activity smelling of the informer. He also usually avoided taking private briefs while holding public office (*Ep.* 1.23; 10.3A), unless special circumstances occurred. Pliny claims (*Ep.* 5.13.8) that he did not even accept the gratuity permitted by law for his services, and as he was a wealthy man this was consistent with Quintilian's teaching (12.7.8-12). A feature of his later activity at the bar was his custom of associating young men with himself and giving them practical training (*Ep.* 6.23).

Pliny's letters contain reference to at least eighteen specific speeches, of which he revised eight or more for publication.[49] There are in addition several references to unnamed cases which may be these or others. He says (*Ep.* 5.8.8) that he was only eighteen when he first appeared in court. That would be in late 79 or early 80. This first case was apparently not identical with his first great success, *For Junius Pastor* in the centumviral court (*Ep.* 1.18.3). An unfavorable dream the night before betrayed his nervousness and might be interpreted to mean that he felt, perhaps unconsciously, that his wife's family was opposed to his career. There are no references to specific cases from this point until 93, but this was surely the time in which hard work built Pliny's reputation as an able advocate; in the period of the letters Pliny was not at all anxious to stress his successes and advancement under Domitian and it comes as a surprise when we discover him cooperating in one case with Regulus, the most famous of the Domitianic informers

[49] R-E 21.447 says sixteen speeches; Schanz-Hosius 2.658-9 lists seven published and nine unpublished speeches. Cf. Henricus Meyer, *Oratorum Ronnorum fragmenta*, Zurich, 1832, 248-52 and Walter Menzes, "Pliny and the Roman Bar under Trajan," *Juridical Review* 36 (1924) 197-217.

(*Ep.* 1.20.14). Nor so far as we can see did he ever publish any of his speeches from the reign of Domitian. He does, however, mention specifically three from the later part of the reign: some points connected with his prosecution of the former governor of Baetica, Baebius Massa, for extortion are mentioned in a letter to Tacitus (*Ep.* 7.33), in the hope that the incident will be referred to in the latter's *Histories*. He also refers (*Ep.* 1.5.5) to his speech for Arionella in the centumviral court in opposition to Regulus and to a centumviral case in which he appeared with Satiricus Rufus. It was on this occasion that Regulus belittled him for imitating Cicero rather than being "content with the eloquence of his own age!" Proceedings in extortion trials had been simplified since Cicero's day by the *Senatusconsultum Passienum* or *Calvisianum*, passed under Augustus.[50] Prosecutors to represent complaining provincials were named by the senate and a jury of senators was chosen. In simple cases judgment could be given and damages assessed in less than a month, but if there were criminal allegations and an elaborate investigation had to be made in the province, the trial could be stretched out for over a year. The prosecution of Massa was successful, but seems eventually to have led to the conviction of Pliny's fellow prosecutor, Herennius Senecio, on a charge of treason.[51] In the letter which mentions Arionella, Pliny is at pains to show the ill will between himself and Regulus, which tempted him to try to get revenge after Domitian's death in something not unlike an informing on the informer. The specific incident he reports seems to come from the *altercatio*, or debate, which followed the formal speech in which Regulus tried to take advantage of Pliny's citation

[50] Cf. Sherwyn-White, *op.cit.* supra n. 44, 128.
[51] Cf. C. P. Jones, "A New Commentary on the Letters of Pliny," *Phoenix* 22 (1968) 134-35.

of a ruling by Modestus, whom Domitian had subsequently banished. Pliny refused to be trapped and told Regulus that it was illegal even to ask a question about a man who had been condemned.

Pliny's speech at the dedication of the library at Comum in 96 marks the beginning of a new phase in his oratorical career, for it was apparently the first of his speeches to be subjected to elaborate revision and prepared for publication. Although Domitian was very likely still alive at the time of delivery, publication occurred under Nerva when Pliny felt encouraged to take a longer-range view of his career. From the single letter (*Ep.* 1.8) which discusses the speech the following picture can be drawn.

Pliny presented to the city of Comum a public library which was valued at a million sesterces, together with an endowment of a 100,000 sesterces.[52] The idea of establishing libraries goes back to Asinius Pollio in the reign of Augustus, but is particularly suitable for a student of Quintilian, who had emphasized reading in his school far beyond what was done by most teachers in the empire. Presumably the library contained a carefully made collection of works, such as the list furnished in the tenth book of Quintilian, but unfortunately we have no information. Pliny came to the dedication of the library and spoke in the municipal council. From his description of his speech it appears to have contained an account of the previous philanthropic works of his family and gone on to announce an additional gift, an *alimenta*, or arrangement whereby he was to provide 30,000 sesterces a year for the support of freeborn boys and girls in the town by a kind of annual rent from his own prop-

[52] Known from the memorial inscription, *CIL* v.5262. Cf. E. de Saint-Denis, "Pline le jeune et l'éducation de la jeunesse," *Revue universitaire* 55 (1946) 9-21.

erty. This system had been tried by others and subsequently was practiced by the Roman government on a larger scale. Pliny's speech included a discussion of the *munificentiae rationem*, the purpose of his donation, apparently referring to the *alimenta*, not to the library. The letter does not indicate that he had much to say about the library on this occasion. Two rhetorical problems which he faced are remarked: one was how to avoid an impression of ostentation, which still bothers him considerably in the version he is preparing for publication. A partial answer was a very plain and simple style, which he describes in terms suggestive of Atticism. The other problem was that his new program would immediately benefit only a small part of the population and a major objective of his speech was to show that it was in fact directed to the general good of all. The speech, therefore, was by no means purely ceremonial; Pliny had a practical persuasive object, which in its ultimate goal was no less than the reversal of the decline in the Italian birthrate. In publishing the speech he hoped that other philanthropists would imitate his program.

The letter describing the library speech makes it possible to distinguish several stages in its literary development. First of all came Pliny's composition and revisions before delivery; here Pliny stresses the psychological and moral advantages of careful workmanship which caused him to think out what he was doing, insuring that it was not a hasty action soon to be regretted and at the same time accustoming his mind to generosity. At least in its planning stages the speech was thus in part addressed to Pliny himself. Of the actual affect of the speech on the audience at Comum Pliny says nothing at all. Subsequently he recited it to a group of friends, including Pompeius Saturninus, who made comments on it, "but of a general sort." Together with the letter, after the lapse of some time, Pliny sent Pompeius a written version to be corrected and criticized in detail. Pliny acknowledges that this procedure is a slow one, but it will either lead to the conviction that the speech is unsuited for publication or else the process itself will make the speech suitable for publication. The choice of this letter for publication can probably be taken as evidence that Pliny eventually found the speech worthy of publication.

Careful preparation, delivery, recitation, thorough revision for publication, this was the method followed by Pliny in the case of all of his subsequent major speeches (*Ep.* 7.17.7). His friends seem to have practiced something like it, and most Roman orators of the time would have felt that it was exceedingly rash to publish without subjecting a work to the whole procedure. Stylistic standards were exceedingly finicky, and there may well have developed a social convention by which a friend would feel insulted if he had not been consulted about a manuscript. Quintilian appears to have had reservations about extensive revision (12.10.49-57), but these were primarily directed against the custom of deleting popular passages from speeches to appease exacting critics of style. Pliny's request to Pompeius seems to make it clear that he did not think of his speech in a purely literary way: he was anxious to find the form of expression which would be most effective in carrying through his fundamental social and economic purpose, a view which Quintilian would probably have approved.

The simple style, in which at least a part of Pliny's library speech was composed, should not be regarded as a fundamental change in his stylistic inclinations. These always remain true to Quintilian's teaching that style should be suited to content, that Cicero was the best guide, but that style should change with the times. In Pliny's next major speech he says he took Demosthenes'

533

passionate attack on Midias (*Ep*. 7.30.5) as the object of his imitation. This was his speech *On Vengeance for Helvidius,* which was delivered in the senate early in the reign of Nerva when it seemed appropriate to Pliny to try to bring Publicius Certus to justice for activities under Domitian. The occasion of the speech is described in a long letter written some years later to a young man named Quadratus who was studying the published version as part of his rhetorical training (*Ep*. 9.13). All Pliny says about the contents is that he published the exordium as delivered and that he replied separately to the previous speakers in the senate who had tried to defend Certus. The speech was a success in the senate, but did not achieve Pliny's objective. The emperor refused to endorse Pliny's call for vengeance and quietly squashed the whole matter, though he also refrained from any new honors to Certus.[53] Pliny claims that he undertook the matter in the public interest, out of a feeling of indignation, and to establish a precedent. Publication might be taken to reflect persistence in these goals or a feeling that his success in the senate ought not to be forgotten, but Pliny had admired Helvidius and was a friend of his family, and it seems likely that genuine feelings were a part of the impulse to publication and also of course the usual desire to show again his opposition to conditions under Domitian. Publication could accomplish a real end in immortalizing Pliny's vengeance, and in that sense was as powerful as any action the emperor could have taken. A few days after the publication of the speech Certus was taken ill and died. Pliny heard reports that Certus imagined himself hunted down by Pliny, sword in hand.

[53] The problem is similar to that at the beginning of Vespasian's reign when the attitude of the new emperor was not yet known, cf. Tac., *Hist*. 4.6.

The second letter of the first book is another of Pliny's requests for revisions and corrections, but this time in reference to an unnamed speech. The success of his previously published works, Pliny says, has led him to be anxious to prepare another for publication. Since the date of the letter is apparently 97 or 98[54] there is a good chance that the previously published works are the library speech of 96 and that relating to Helvidius of early 97. The speech enclosed had already been subjected to extensive polish by Pliny and other friends: stylistic imitation has again played an important role. Pliny says that the models have been Demosthenes, Calvus, of whom he has recently become fond, and Cicero as always. The reference to Calvus should not be taken as a sign of Atticism on Pliny's part, especially when combined with Demosthenes and Cicero in this way. The most that the passage can be taken to mean is that the style of the speech varied considerably from part to part. The only hints as to content are the fact that the speech was on a controversial matter, that the main objective was vigor, but that there were opportunities for digression. The description suggests that this is probably the same speech of which Pliny a little later sent a completed portion to Lupercus in a letter (*Ep.* 2.5) published at the same time. The variations of style are dwelt on and the digressions had probably been expanded. The subject matter is still obscure, however, and the most that can be said is that it was judicial and involved in some way the defense of the rights and reputation of his native city. It has been given the name *Pro Patria* by modern critics. Nothing is known about specific motives for publication.

From the beginning of 98 until his consulship late in 100 Pliny held the office of prefect of the treasury of Saturn and did not practice as an advocate, except for

54 Cf. Sherwyn-White, *op.cit.* supra n. 44, 86.

535

one occasion. This was his prosecution of Marius Priscus, former governor of Africa, and his associates on an extortion charge, undertaken at the request of the senate and with the permission of the emperor (*Ep.* 10.3).[55] Tacitus was Pliny's colleague in the prosecution, which is described in a long letter (*Ep.* 2.11). Because of the criminal charges involved (including the killing of a Roman knight) Pliny and Tacitus refused to compromise the matter on a financial basis, and an investigation stretched out over about a year, with the final trial in the senate coming early in 100. The emperor, Trajan, who was consul at the time, presided. Such trials were very tense affairs, not only because of the specific issues involved, but because they were regarded by some senators as threats to privileges or even to the whole class. It was necessary to present the case in such a way as to minimize this aspect of the situation and to stress the specific charge and evidence. Pliny was nervous about his speech, and mentions the additional disadvantage that since Priscus had already been convicted on the lesser financial charges some senators felt he had been punished enough. Pliny was allowed to speak for twelve larger (twenty-minute) and four smaller (fifteen-minute) measures by the water clock, or a total of five hours. He says that the emperor was very kind and repeatedly had a freedman whisper that he should be sparing of his voice and strength. Possibly Trajan found five hours of Pliny's eloquence too much of a good thing. The first patron for the defense replied to Pliny the same day on behalf of Marcianus, charged with bribing Priscus. The second day was taken up by, first, a speech by Priscus, then Tacitus' accusation, "very eloquently" spoken, and finally Catius Fronto's

[55] Cf. Maria-Luisa Paladini, "Il processo di Mario Prisco nel *Panegirico* a Traiano di Plinio il Giovanie," *Rendiconti dell' Istituto Lombardo* 92 (1958) 713-36.

emotional peroration on behalf of the defendant. Priscus did not himself speak. On the third day the documentary and other evidence was produced and the decision reached. The latter took the form of an ordinary senatorial debate, as seen, for example, in the "trial" of the Catilinarian conspirators at which Cicero, Caesar, and Cato had spoken. There were two main positions expressed: restitution to the state of the money extorted in bribes and perpetual banishment from Italy, or restitution of the money without banishment. The emperor's influence seems to have carried the heavier sentence. Pliny and Tacitus received the thanks of the senate. There was less practical reason this time for the publication of Pliny's speech, and indeed we cannot be sure that it was published. He did apparently agree (*Ep.* 2.19) to recite it on at least one occasion, though hesitantly, on the ground that judicial speeches are really effective only in the actual circumstances of the courtroom. The description indicates that for all its length the speech was unadorned and to the point. The principal legal issue involved was Pliny's need to show that the law against extortion covered the actions of the defendant, which he did by analogy with the interpretation of other laws.

Chronologically Pliny's next speech was the *Panegyricus*, which we shall leave aside for the moment. Immediately after his term as consul he spoke at another extortion trial, this time against the associates of Caecilius Classicus. Classicus had been governor of Baetica, and the provincials approached Pliny because of his services to them in the case of Baebius Massa (*Ep.* 3.4). Although Classicus himself died before trial, the proceedings went ahead and are described in a letter to Cornelius Minicianus (*Ep.* 3.9). Pliny and his colleague Lucceius Albinus decided to proceed against Classicus' associates in three groups: first, the three more important individuals who

537

had profited from extortion, then against Classicus' son-in-law and a subordinate military commander, and finally against Classicus' wife and the other accomplices. The line of attack was first to prove the guilt of Classicus, which was not difficult since he had left incriminating documents, including a list of the money he got and an exultant letter to his mistress, then to prove that accomplices of Classicus were criminally responsible under the law (thus effectively forestalling the defense that they were ordered by their superior to do what they did), and finally to prove that individuals were in fact accomplices. As in the prosecution of Priscus there was thus need to extend the application of the law. Classicus' wife and son-in-law were acquitted and his daughter was not tried at all; the others were convicted. Pliny quotes the words he used in referring to the daughter: "Someone will say, 'Do you yourself then undertake to be her judge?' I by no means judge her, but I am mindful that I am an advocate appointed from among the judges." In the cross-examination Pliny was interrupted by friends of the defendant who thought he pressed too hard, and replied, "He will be no less innocent if I say all I have to say." One of the witnesses against Classicus' wife was accused of collusion with her, tried, and convicted during the course of the proceedings, but to Pliny's surprise this did not prove helpful in securing the conviction of the wife. References in later letters to the recitation (*Ep.* 4.5) and apparent publication (*Ep.* 9.4) of a very long speech consisting of separate parts probably mean that Pliny worked up his effort into literary form.

Pliny's fourth extortion case found him on the other side, speaking in late 102 or early 103 in defense of Julius Bassus, who had been governor of Bithynia. The speech is known chiefly from one letter (*Ep.* 4.9), at the end of which Pliny says that he plans slowly to revise it for pub-

538

lication. Although there were suggestions of more hei-
nous conduct, the actual charges were financial without
the criminal allegations made in the cases we have been
considering. Bassus had four advocates, of whom Pliny
and Lucceius Albinus seem to have been the chief and
were allotted nine hours between them. The prosecution
had six hours. Pliny spoke for three and a half hours the
first day and would have been content with that, but
was urged by Bassus to take advantage of an hour and a
half more the second day, which he did. There were three
advocates on the other side, one of whom was Theophanes, a delegate from Bithynia and presumably not a
senator, but allowed to plead in the senate. Pliny seems
always to speak first among the advocates on his side, as
Quintilian had also done. It was his duty here to speak
of his client's distinguished birth and unfortunate history, the conspiracy of informers against him, and the
reasons why he was disliked by Theophanes and others,
and to face the major charge which had been made.
Pliny makes no secret of the fact that Bassus was technically guilty; he had accepted money from provincials,
but in line with Quintilian's principles (12.1.34-45)
Pliny has considered the wider justice of the case and
concluded that his client is a good man who has acted
incautiously but deserves acquittal. In terms of *stasis* he
ruled out denial of the fact, which was too widely known
and would only provoke antagonism. He had to admit
also that the actions committed were prohibited by
law. To admit everything and throw his client on the
mercy of the court seemed imprudent. Pliny was thus
left with the *stasis* of quality, but here too he felt he
could not insist that what had been done had been
rightly done. In this dilemma he says he "thought it best
to hold a middle course." In the context what that would
seem to mean is a *stasis* of quality in which Pliny admit-

ted his client's actions had not been "right" but claimed that his intention had not been evil, he had acted unwittingly, and his real friendship with those from whom he received presents mitigated the wrong done. Thus Bassus' conduct was human and understandable, and justice would not be done by pressing the word of the law against him. Presumably the prejudices against him from previous incidents were brought out and the motives of his accusers questioned with the object of showing that the case was not a clear-cut matter of crime and punishment. Pliny's defense was successful, in large part because of the pity he was able to awaken for the misfortunes into which Bassus had fallen under Titus and Domitian.

After his consulship Pliny seems to have resumed practice in the centumviral court. He mentions (*Ep.* 4.16) a very successful speech which ran for seven hours and an occasion (*Ep.* 4.24) when he spoke before all four panels sitting as one. He also agrees (*Ep.* 4.17) to undertake a case on behalf of Corellia Hispulla but gives no details. Possibly some of these references are to the same case, though it seems unlikely that a letter promising to take a case would be put immediately after a letter describing the successful speech. He also spoke successfully before a judge, before a *quaestio*, and before a judge again in defense of some men accused of forging a will in their own favor and then poisoning the testator. Julius Servianus and Suburanus are named as judges and as they were prominent under Trajan the trial probably belongs in the period after Pliny's consulship.

Pliny's fifth and last extortion case found him defending Varenus Rufus in late 106 or early 107. Varenus was another governor of Bithynia whose defense took the form of various delaying tactics (*Ep.* 5.20.2; 6.5; 6.29.11).

This led to the Bithynians deciding to drop the matter (*Ep.* 7.6 and 10). Pliny's speech was delivered at the original hearing in the senate; apparently it was published, since he sends a finished copy to Cornelius Ursus (*Ep.* 5.20). Nothing is revealed about its rhetorical features.

Pliny played an important role in the improvement of provincial administration in his time. His own service in Bithynia was of course his most constructive contribution, but his involvement in five celebrated extortion cases is also remarkable. The two most flagrant cases were those of Priscus and Classicus, where he acted as a prosecutor. Both were governors under the weak Nerva, brought to justice under Trajan, who scrupulously enforced the law.[56]

Although Pliny clearly took satisfaction in the effectiveness of some of his earlier speeches, he reserves his greatest praise for his defense of Attia Variola in the centumviral court (*Ep.* 6.33). The action is probably to be dated in 106 or 107. As in the case described in an earlier letter (*Ep.* 4.24) all four panels of the court sat together, thus giving 180 jurors. The case involved prominent people and was somewhat sensational: Pliny's client was a daughter seeking to recover the estate of her father who at the age of eighty had acquired a new wife and then within eleven days was persuaded to change his will in favor of her and her son. The basilica was crowded and victory apparently only barely achieved. Pliny says, "We were victorious with two panels and defeated with two" (*Ep.* 6.33.5). Probably the separate panels voted on the cases of four separate individuals and Pliny succeeded in overturning the claim of the stepmother and her son, but

---

[56] Cf. Sherwyn-White, *op.cit.* supra n. 44, 414. Pliny sums up his experience in *Ep.* 6.29.8-11.

not others involved, such as other relatives or freedmen in the household.[57] The enthusiastic description of the speech continues as follows:

"Long as it is, I do not fail to hope that it will gain the favor of a very short speech, for there is refreshing variety in the abundance of matter, the adroit arrangement, the numerous short narrative passages, and the variation of the style. There are many elevated passages (something I would not venture to claim except when speaking to you), much determined argument, and much that is elegant. It often happened that the need for facts and figures and for all but calling for a counting table obtruded upon those ardent and noble parts so that the dignity of the centumviral court was suddenly transformed into the scene of a private case. We gave sails to indignation, to anger, to grief, and in the swell of this splendid case we were borne on as though on the high sea with many winds. In a word, some of my associates like to think that this speech (I shall say it again) is as it were the 'Ctesiphon' among my orations. . . ." (Ep. 6.33.7-11).

Except for the *Panegyricus*, Pliny's speech for Attia seems to be the only one of his orations referred to by a later writer. Sidonius Apollinaris (Ep. 8.10) in the fifth century says that Pliny won more glory for his defense of Attia in the centumviral court than by his "comparable" panegyric of the "incomparable" Trajan. Possibly the remark is based entirely on Pliny's own description.

In two letters of book six (6.12 and 6.18) Pliny promises to undertake the cases of Vettius Priscus and of the Firmani, but we do not know whether speeches were ever delivered. The letters of that book seem to relate to events of 106 and 107. The only other published speech

[57] Cf. Sherwyn-White, *op.cit.* supra n. 44, 399.

of Pliny of which we know is that for Clarius which is
mentioned in one of his last letters (*Ep.* 9.28.5) as having been revised and considerably enlarged, though the
client's name is not certain in the manuscripts. Possibly
the speech is the one meant in a letter to Tacitus (*Ep.*
7.20.2) or one to Maximus (*Ep.* 8.19) asking for comments and revisions before publication.

Two of Pliny's letters (3.13 and 18) discuss the extant
speech which has subsequently come to be known as the
Panegyricus.[58] Most informative is the second of these,
to Vibius Severus (*Ep.* 3.18). Briefly, Pliny says that at
the beginning of his consulship he delivered a speech of
thanks to the emperor in the name of the state in accordance with custom and the limits placed by the place
and the time available. There are few other references to
such speeches, but apparently beginning under Augustus
whenever a new set of consuls took office one of them
would deliver a *gratiarum actio* or speech of thanks, perhaps originally to the gods, but chiefly to the living god,
the emperor.[59] In ordinary years there should have been
six such speeches and there also seem to have been
speeches by consuls designate. These speeches often
must have been quite short (*Ep.* 3.18.6: *puncto tem-
poris*): senatorial proceedings under the empire were

[58] Cf. Josef Mesk, "Die Ueberarbeitung des Plinianischen
Panegyricus auf Traian," *WS* 32 (1910) 239-60 and "Zur Quel-
lenanalyse des Plinianischen *Panegyricus,*" *WS* 33 (1911) 71-
100; Marcel Durry, *Pline le jeune: Panégyrique de Trajan* (ed.
and comment.), Paris, 1938; Enrica Malcovati, *Il Panegyrico di
Traiano* (ed. and comment.), Florence, 1952; Syme, *op.cit.*
supra n. 25, 94-95. An English translation of the *Panegyricus* by
Betty Radice is available in the reissued Loeb edition, Cambridge, 1969.
[59] Cf. Ovid, *Epist. ex Pont.* 4.4.35-42 and Maria-Luisa Pali-
dini, "La *gratiarum actio* dei consoli attraverso la testimonianza
di Plinio," *Historia* 10 (1961) 356-74. On the influence of
Pliny on later writers of panegyrics cf. Josef Mesk, "Die anonym
überlieferten lateinischen Panegyriker und die Lobrede des
jüngeren Plinius," *WS* 34 (1912) 246-53.

boring enough without unnecessary additions, and it is impossible to imagine hardheaded rulers like Tiberius, Vespasian, and Trajan sitting and listening to artificially fulsome accounts of their own virtues. It is also possible that the speeches were omitted or replaced by a letter if the emperor was absent, which would cut down the number considerably.

Pliny's speech must be regarded as somewhat special: no previous consul is known to have revised and expanded a speech of thanks as he did for recitation and publication. The special circumstances relate both to Pliny and to Trajan. The former was one of the leading orators of the age; more than usual interest could be expected in his treatment of his subject. Unfortunately his consulship fell in the early fall at a time when only senators chosen by lot were required to attend sessions (Suet. *Aug.* 35.3). One of the excuses for recitation and publication was thus the fact that some senators had missed the speech. Further, there was in Pliny's mind clearly an intention to give greater significance to the speech than was customary, and for this purpose enlargement and publication were almost essential. This brings us to Trajan. He had begun well as emperor in the view of Pliny and his friends, but so had other emperors including Nero and Domitian, who had both ended badly. Enough time had elapsed so that some uneasiness had begun to build up about the difficulty of maintaining the felicity of the times: Tacitus' *Dialogue* and *Histories* betray a little of the same feeling. Both in the speech itself (e.g., 45.6; 73.6; 75.3-5) and in his letter about it Pliny does not disguise his fundamental purpose: "that the virtues of our emperor be reinforced by sincere praise of them and secondly that future emperors be admonished, not as by a teacher, but in the form of example, by what road they best might attain the same glory" (*Ep.*

544

3.18.1-2). Pliny's confidence was not misplaced, and his speech may have contributed to the fact that Trajan remained true to his liberal principles and was honored throughout the empire as the best of rulers.

After the original delivery Pliny amplified the speech and circulated it among his friends for their comments (*Ep.* 3.13). He also delivered some or all of it before a large audience in three sessions of recitation (*Ep.* 3.18.4). Finally it was published. We do not know how long the polishing took: the first of the letters refers to the speech as "recent." The recitation could have been sometime during the winter of 100-101 (the weather was bad) or even later. We have no references to publication and it is impossible to fix the date accurately. The most troublesome passage is one (16-17) which prophesies victory in the Dacian war and a triumph which did not actually come until late 102 or early 103, but it is possible to take the passage for what it is, prophecy of future victory, and to date it, if not to the original delivery in 100, at least to a revision of early 101.[60] The published version, as has been said, also seems to show the influence of Tacitus' *Dialogus*, which we have dated around 102.[61]

The *Panegyricus* as we have it consists of nearly a hundred pages of Latin text. If recited in an imposing manner, with pauses for effect, it could easily take five hours to deliver, whereas the original form may well have taken less than an hour. It is impossible to be certain about what constituted the original speech and what is later addition, though the passages prophesying a triumph and those showing influence from the *Dialogus* presumably belong in the latter category. The document is usually thought of as falling into six main parts:[62] a

[60] Cf. Marcel Durry, *Pline le jeune* IV, Paris, 1959, 13.
[61] Cf. Bruère and Guengerich, *op.cit.* supra n. 29.
[62] Cf. Durry, *op.cit.* supra n. 60.

short introduction (1-3), an account of Trajan's career before he became consul for the third time at the beginning of 100 (4-24), a list of Trajan's services to Rome as emperor (25-55), a description of his third consulship (56-80), an account of the virtues of his private life (81-89), and finally Pliny's private expression of thanks to him (90-95). These six parts were probably all represented in the original speech, and the introduction and conclusion may be much as delivered. The middle portions are those where amplification is most likely. They consist of a large number of individual points about things Trajan has done or qualities he has demonstrated, each elaborated into a paragraph. Many of these points could have been made in the original speech, but much more briefly.

As a political and historical document, the *Panegyricus* is important and even interesting. It would have been even more interesting at the time when the direction of Trajan's development was a crucial matter for all Romans. Judged as a piece of oratory the *Panegyricus* is tiresome in the extreme. Its length now mitigates against its interest, but the fundamental objection is the homogeneity of tone. There are no emotional high points, no abrupt changes of speed or style, no sudden flashes of passion or of wit, none of the charm of variety which marks the great efforts of Cicero. Some of this quality results from the subject and the occasion, which doubtless debarred joking, but Pliny has not sought variety. Throughout he maintains the same highly worked out flow of noble *sententiae*. Even the exclamations and the rhetorical questions do not ruffle the surface of his paean. It is a fitting tone for the oratory of a glorious, but static, empire.

Pliny certainly regarded literature and especially oratory as an important feature of civilized life. We have already considered his references to his own speeches and their revision and publication. He specifically discussed his custom in one letter (*Ep.* 7.17), revealing that the practice was criticized by some persons. Of course he revised for publication not only his speeches but also his letters.

Several of Pliny's letters touch upon questions of prose style.[63] The principles which emerge are largely consistent with Quintilian's teaching: style must be suited to subject and will vary within a speech; it can best be learned by imitation of writers like Demosthenes, Cicero, and Calvus (*Ep.* 1.2). Writing to a young friend, Pliny lists specific exercises in imitation and composition (*Ep.* 7.9). Corrupted eloquence once flourished, but taste has now been reformed to more austere standards, without debarring the florid where it is appropriate (*Ep.* 3.18.8-10). The true orator must venture to rise above pedestrian discourse and be willing to risk a fall to attain what is great, as Demosthenes did (*Ep.* 9.26.8ff.). One of the most interesting of the letters on style is a rather long communication urging the superiority of copiousness over brevity upon the deaf ears of Tacitus (*Ep.* 1.20). Fullness, however, suggested the tradition of Cicero and Quintilian and had a moral tone about it; Regulus, Pliny notes (*Ep.* 1.20.14), contrasted this kind of elaboration with his own inclination to aim at the jugular vein of the victim.

Pliny was anxious for posterity to know of his friendship for Tacitus, even it must be remembered when the *Histories* and *Annals* had yet to be written. There were, however, great differences between the two orators. Tacitus' chief Latin stylistic model is Sallust, Pliny's is Cicero. Tacitus abandoned oratory; Pliny rewrote his speeches for the ages. Tacitus' *Dialogus* views the state of

[63] Cf. Leeman 323-28.

eloquence with gloom. Pliny, like Quintilian, stresses the achievements of his contemporaries, in which he shared. Since he clearly knew the *Dialogus* it seems possible that he was waging a quiet campaign to prove that the diagnosis of Tacitus and other prophets of gloom was wrong. "If ever our city flourished with liberal studies, it does so now," he exclaims (*Ep.* 1.10.1). He calls the oration of Pompeius Saturninus the equal of any of the ancients; people should not look down on him because he is a contemporary (*Ep.* 1.16.8). The abilities of the sophist Isaeus also evoke enthusiasm (*Ep.* 2.3). He does complain of the dullness of much of the work of the centumviral court and of the hired audience to be found there (*Ep.* 2.14), but his words are more an indictment of the legal profession than of the general state of eloquence. When he himself appears, the honor accorded to oratory becomes clear (*Ep.* 4.16), and the court was jammed when he gave his great speech for Attia Variola (*Ep.* 6.33). Toward the end of the collection he can still express satisfaction in his own eloquence (*Ep.* 9.23.1). Pliny's enthusiasm is not entirely convincing and some of it results more from polite manners than good criticism, but it offers some counterbalance to the view of Tacitus, strongly prejudiced as always. During the happy years of Trajan the decline of eloquence, the decadence of rhetoric, and the decay of taste were not universally evident. The law courts were busy, the senate met and occasionally discussed, albeit gingerly and sometimes inconclusively, matters of moment. And it was possible, under favorable conditions, to use the art of persuasion in a speech to the emperor.

Juvenal

Juvenal, the only important poet of the second century A.D., was writing satires during parts of the reigns of Trajan and Hadrian. He was not only strongly influenced by rhetoric, but specifically refers to rhetoricians on several occasions. For example, he mentions Quintilian by name four times, and scholars have speculated that he may have studied in Quintilian's school, which is at least chronologically possible.[64] The references are not complimentary, however, and if Juvenal ever did attend Quintilian's school his memory of it was rather bitter: Quintilian is presented as a lucky political and economic opportunist.[65] The question cannot be definitely settled, but whether or not Juvenal studied with Quintilian he was certainly thoroughly familiar with the concepts and techniques taught in similar schools of the late first century. The impact of rhetoric on Juvenal is not primarily a matter of his writing poetry in the form of declamations or theses, though he will sometimes argue a point, such as the disadvantages of marriage in the sixth satire.[66] There is, moreover, no need to draw a sharp line between sincerity of emotion and artificiality of expression, or between poetry and rhetoric in his work. Juvenal has found what is for himself and his contemporaries a natural form of expression for his indignation within the tradition of the Roman invective as we know it from speeches like

[64] Quintilian is mentioned in *Sat.* 6.75 and 280 and 7.186 and 189. Juvenal was born probably around A.D. 60 and began to publish around 110, cf. Gilbert Highet, *Juvenal the Satirist: A Study*, Oxford, 1954, 5. In addition to works cited below on Juvenal's rhetoric cf. H. F. Rebert, "The Literary Influence of Cicero on Juvenal," *TAPhA* 57 (1926) 181-94 and Inez Scott (Ryberg), "The Grand Style in the Satires of Juvenal," *Smith College Classical Studies* 8 (1927).

[65] Cf. esp. A. Kappelmacher, "Studia Juvenaliana," *Dissertationes philologicae Vindobonensis* 7 (1903) 159-99.

[66] The influence of declamation on Juvenal is most stressed by Josué De Decker, *Juvenalis declamans: étude sur la rhétorique declamatoire dans les Satires de Juvenal*, Gand, 1913; cf. also Highet, *op.cit.* supra n. 64, 93 and 96.

Cicero's *In Pisonem* or the discussions in Quintilian.[67] It seems possible that Juvenal was for some time a conventional user of rhetoric; the anonymous ancient biography says that he practiced declamation until middle life to develop his mind rather than as a preparation for school or forum, and Martial (7.91) addressed him as "eloquent." But, like Tacitus, early in the second century he experienced a kind of revulsion at what he was doing and turned to satire to express his bitterness. The first poem is the declaration of this conversion, and the famous line "si natura negat, facit indignatio versum/ qualecumque potest" is his keynote: "If nature fails, indignation makes what kind of verse it can."

The passage in Juvenal most directly relevant to the history of rhetoric comes in *Satire* seven (106-243).[68] The poem deals with the remuneration of poets, historians, and orators, taken up in that order, which is also the order of Quintilian's discussion of the genres (10.1.93-122). All appear to have fallen into a decline because the writers are not appreciated. Orators include both speakers in the courts and rhetoricians: but fees from cases are not great enough to pay for the impressive clothes and jewelry which really make the crucial impression, since eloquence itself accomplishes nothing, and the teacher of rhetoric, for all the tedium of his profession, has great difficulty collecting his fee. Men will squander great sums on buildings and dinners, but not on education. It almost sounds as though Juvenal had had some experience trying to live as a teacher, but he enters into other pictures with comparable vigor. The passage contains a picture of schoolroom routine, but one slightly confusing

[67] Cf. William S. Anderson, "Juvenal and Quintilian," *YCIS* 17 (1961) 3-93.
[68] Cf. Charles Knapp, "Juvenal VII, 150-68" *CW* 18 (1924-25) 65-68.

to the modern reader.[69] It is also this passage which refers to Quintilian as the lucky exception to the rule of poverty.

Suetonius

During the reigns of Trajan and Hadrian, C. Suetonius Tranquillus composed a number of works, most in Latin but some in Greek, which drew together a great deal of historical, biographical, antiquarian, archaeological, and literary information.[70] His methods and point of view were those of a grammarian in the wide sense of that word current in his time.[71] That is, he was not primarily interested in language, but in knowledge which might elucidate specific details in all kinds of literary studies. Although his only well-preserved work is his *Lives of the Caesars*, other writings are known in part from a list in the Greek encyclopaedia called the *Souda*, references in later grammarians, and especially from the use made of them by St. Jerome. The earliest[72] and one of the most ambitious of these works was *De viris illustribus, On Famous Men*, of which most of the book on grammarians and rhetoricians is preserved. We have had occasion to refer to it several times. The brief section on the

[69] E.g., is it the pupil or the teacher who has to go over everything twice? Favoring the teacher is M. L. Clarke, "Three notes on Roman education," *CPh* 63 (1968) 42-44.

[70] The most complete edition of the fragmentary works is still Augustus Reifferscheid, *C. Suetoni Tranquilli praeter Caesarum libros reliquiae*, Leipzig, 1860. For *De gramm. et rhet.* cf. Rodney P. Robinson, *C. Suetoni tranquilli De grammaticis et rhetoribus*, Paris, 1925 and the Teubner edition edited by G. Brugnoli, *C. Suetoni Tranquilli opera*, vol. ii, part 1, Stuttgart, 1963.

[71] Cf. Alcide Macé, *Essai sur Suétone*, Paris, 1900, 53-59.

[72] It was not known to Suetonius' friend Pliny, but was apparently published before Trajan's death, which would probably date it between 112 and 117, cf. Macé, *op.cit.* supra n. 71, 69 and 244.

rhetoricians discusses the attempts to prevent the teaching of Greek rhetoric in the second century and Latin rhetoric in the first century b.c. and then briefly outlines the careers of a number of rhetoricians from Plotius Gallus to the Augustan age, where the work now breaks off. Originally the discussion of rhetoricians went down to the end of the first century a.d. through Quintilian and Julius Tiro, just as that on the grammarians ends with Probus and that on the Caesars with Domitian. Suetonius seems to have been especially interested in teachers of declamation and to have said little about rhetorical theory. Some portions of the book, or books, on poets survive in revisions by later grammarians. There were also sections on orators, historians, and philosophers. Part of the discussion of Passienus Crispus from the account of orators is preserved by a scholiast on Juvenal, and from the brief notices in St. Jerome's *Chronicle* it seems likely that Suetonius covered the main orators from Cicero to Domitius Afer, including Calidius, Asinius Pollio, Messalla, Cassius Severus, and other more minor figures. As far as we can see he did not discuss Pliny or Tacitus. These accounts like the others were anecdotal and personal and did not attempt much in the line of criticism, nor was Suetonius interested in proving or disproving a decline in eloquence.

The history of Latin rhetoric in the early empire has been seen to involve a consciousness of decline, most marked in Tacitus and Juvenal, coupled with attempts at revitalization as seen, for example, in "Longinus," Seneca, Quintilian, and Pliny. We may now turn to the situation as seen by Greek orators and writers in this same period, some of whom worked in Asia or Greece, but many of whom visited or lived for a time in Rome.

CHAPTER EIGHT

The Age of the Sophists

Greek rhetoric was less affected than Latin by the transition from republic to principate. The civic life of the Greek cities went on in a semiautonomous manner, political freedom was not noticeably reduced below the level at which it settled after the original Roman conquest of the East, and in many locations internal peace and security stimulated intellectual life and opportunities for speech.[1] Rhetorical schools flourished everywhere and often the rhetoricians seem to have overshadowed the philosophers. For the Greeks the early empire was primarily an age of eloquent discourse rather than of analysis or reexamination, though attempts were made, as they were by Latin writers, to find new uses for rhetoric and new materials for oratory. Two movements dominated the rhetorical history of the period: Atticism, in diction and style, and sophistry, virtuoso public declamation by professional orators. The two movements are closely intertwined; sophists were generally Atticists in style and spread Atticist standards, and the study of Attic models helped enrich the contents of sophistic oratory and create philosophical Hellenism.

Atticism is the more specific and limited of the movements. We have already seen its beginnings in the time of Dionysius of Halicarnassus and Caecilius of Calacte. Apparently under Roman influence Greek rhetoricians

---

[1] On the history of the period cf. Frank Frost Abbott and Allan Chester Johnson, *Municipal Administration in the Roman Empire*, Princeton, 1926; M. Rostovtzeff, *Social and Economic History of the Roman Empire*, Oxford, 1926; *CAH* 11; A.H.M. Jones, *The Greek City from Alexander to Justinian*, Oxford, 1940; Harold Mattingly, *Roman Imperial Civilization*, London, 1957.

sought to return to the standards of diction and composition known in the fourth century B.C. They chose certain writers as approved models and rejected others.
Xenophon and Plato had their admirers, but the cult
of Demosthenes grew steadily. Viewed historically Atticism is a form of archaism, viewed critically, a form of
classicism. It is logically to be identified with the doctrine of imitation as the source of creative excellence.
Though Atticism purifies language and style, it can also
stultify, for the virtue of correctness is everything: innovation in style is discouraged and innovation in thought
or manner deemphasized; only in *sententiae* is novelty
pursued. The result is a highly competent literary technique with little significant content. How the more important Greek writers of the early empire conform to
the diction and syntax of fifth and fourth century prose
has been studied in considerable detail.[2] This conformity reaches a climax in the mid-second century, especially in Aelius Aristides. During the same period a number of *lexica* of Attic words were compiled varying in degree of strictness; the strictest lexicon is apparently that of
Moeris. On the other hand the anonymous *Antiatticista*
tried to counteract the tide and broaden the base of
word choice.[3]

The greatest Greek writer of the early empire is doubtless Plutarch, but he is not a major figure in rhetorical
history. He writes in a simple, not particularly Attic
style;[4] in his biographical works he does not compose for-

[2] Cf. esp. Wilhelm Schmid, *Der Atticismus in seinen Haupt-
vertretern von Dionysius bis auf den zweiten Philostratus*, 4 vols.,
Stuttgart, 1887-96. For literary history of the early empire cf.
Maurice Croiset's section "Période de L'Empire," in *Histoire
de la littérature grecque* 5 (Paris, 1901) 317-859.
[3] Cf. H. E. Erbse, "Untersuchungen zu den attizistischen
Lexika, mit Text der Fragmente und Indices," *ADAW* 1949, 2.
[4] Cf. *R-E* 2.926-38 ("Plutarch und Rhetorik"); also Norden
392-94; R. Jeuckens, *Plutarch von Chäronea und die Rhetorik*,

mal orations, and he does not much exploit oratorical forms for the exposition of his philosophical and moral ideas in the *Moralia*, though two early works on vegetarianism are labeled "speeches." He is much less rhetorical in instinct than either Dio or Seneca, two self-proclaimed "philosophers" with whom his life overlaps, and though he admires eloquence, his sympathies, like those of Plato, were with philosophy as opposed to rhetoric. Among the *Moralia*, however, there are a number of essays which expound a thesis in the traditional sense of the schools: "Can virtue be taught?" "Is water or fire more useful?" Several relate to education, but ordinarily Plutarch has philosophical education chiefly in mind, and in his treatise *On Listening to Lectures* (41) he gently warns against the appeal of the showy sophists. It is the speaker's character which is most important in true persuasion, he explains in discussing the role of oratory in his treatise *On Precepts of Statescraft* (801c-804c). The most specifically rhetorical work contained in the *Moralia* is the *Lives of the Ten Orators*. This is not by Plutarch at all, but was probably written during the second century by someone who drew extensively from Caecilius of Calacte.[5]

Our knowledge of Greek oratory from the time of Demosthenes, Hyperides, and Dinarchus throughout the Hellenistic period is very scanty. No complete speech

---

Strassburg, 1908; F. Kraus, *Die rhetorischen Schriften Plutarchs und ihre Stellung im plutarchischen Schriftenkorpus*, Munich, 1911; K. M. Westaway, *The Educational Theory of Plutarch*, London, 1922; Friedrich Bock, "Plutarch und die Schrift *De educandis pueris*," *PhW* 42 (1922) 66-71; E. G. Berry, "The *De liberis educandis* of Pseudo-Plutarch," *HSPh* 63 (1958) 387-99.

[5] Cf. Ernestus Ofenloch, *Caecilii Calactini Fragmenta*, Leipzig, 1907, xxi-xxv and Harold North Fowler, *Plutarch's Moralia* 10, London, 1960, 342-457.

survives. Beginning in the later part of the first century after Christ the situation improves: we have a considerable number of speeches or works in the form of speeches by several authors of the first, second, third, and fourth centuries, some of them among the most influential and admired men of their day. These works are perhaps not really worthy of comparison with those of Demosthenes or Cicero, but a few rise almost to the level of Isocrates. Furthermore we have two literary surveys of the orators: Philostratus, writing in the 230's, discusses sophistic orators from Gorgias and Protagoras to those of his own age, while Eunapius does something similar for philosophers and sophists of the second half of the third and first half of the fourth century. Though not comparable in historical information or critical acumen to Cicero's *Brutus*, these works, and Philostratus in particular, do much to bring alive the great imperial sophists, to re-create the atmosphere in which they worked, and to make it possible for us to understand them. Though maddeningly casual or deliberately coy about many details, Philostratus is highly readable and as good a *raconteur* as many about whom he writes.

Philostratus

Philostratus was a member of a well-known literary family of Lemnos and lived there, in Tyre, and in Athens in the late second and early third centuries; he is not known to have visited Rome, but he addressed his work to an elderly senator who probably became the emperor Gordion I, saying that he had discussed sophists with him in Antioch.[6] He does not define a sophist, but he

---

[6] Cf. Karl Münscher, "Die Philostrate," *Philologus, Suppl.* 10 (1907) 469-560; Wilmer Cave Wright, *Philostratus and Eunapius, The Lives of the Sophists* (Loeb), London, 1922; R-E 21.125-74. On the identity of Gordion cf. G. W. Bowersock, *Greek Sophists in the Roman Empire*, Oxford, 1969, 6-8.

does distinguish different kinds and different historical periods of sophistry. "Ancient" sophistry was begun by Gorgias of Leontini in the fifth century B.C. and flourished for a hundred years or so. "Second" sophistic began with Aeschines when, exiled from Athens in 330 B.C., he gave oratorical demonstrations in Rhodes and Asia Minor. According to Philostratus, the older sophists discussed topics like courage, justice, heroes, gods, and the nature of the universe, and aimed at demonstrating the probability of their position. The younger sophists presented character types like the rich man, the poor man, nobles and tyrants, and historical hypotheses involving proper names. They did not care about convincing the audience of their position, but about treating the material artistically (1.481). What this appears to mean is that the younger sophists practiced declamations somewhat like those discussed by Seneca, though from the examples Philostratus subsequently gives there was perhaps more interest in *suasoriae* than was common at Rome: the rich man, poor man, tyrant, and the like are the characters of declamation and the historical hypotheses are the themes of *suasoriae*. A declaimer of course had no judges to persuade of his case but was praised or blamed for his treatment by the bystanders. The older sophists like Gorgias used a much wider variety of themes and to some extent cared about what they said: they were not entirely satisfied unless the audience went away convinced of the position they had defended.

Another kind of distinction which Philostratus draws is between the pure sophist and the sophistic philosopher. In the case of old sophistry, he says (1.481), a sophist expounded a subject of which he claimed a knowledge: for example, he knew what courage is and explained it at length. A philosopher, and Philostratus is thinking of writers of Socratic dialogues, had no cause to plead but sought the truth, which he pursued by asking and answering a series of questions. On the other hand, in the second sophistic the Socratic philosopher has apparently disappeared and we are left with a philosopher who uses oratory to expound his theories, much like the older sophist, and a pure sophist who has no particular theories, but is interested in declamation (1.484). These categories seem generally valid and might be represented by Isocrates, Plato, Dio Chrysostom, and Herodes Atticus respectively.

Philostratus' historical divisions present certain problems of interpretation. He deals with the sophistic philosophers first, starting with Eudoxus in the fourth century B.C. and going through Carneades to Dio and Favorinus. Though only eight speakers are discussed, they are evenly distributed up to the mid-second century after Christ, then silence. The ensuing period may not have produced any good examples. The discussion of pure sophists is much more extensive. Philostratus associates the beginning of the second sophistic with the Attic orator Aeschines, Demosthenes' opponent in the fourth century B.C., but then jumps (1.511) to Nicetes, who lived in the late first century after Christ, saying that Nicetes found oratory at a low ebb. Three intervening sophists are named and dismissed as of no ability, but there is no mention of important Hellenistic declaimers, not even of Demetrius of Phaleron. Quintilian (2.4.41) thought that declamation began in the time of Demetrius, which would only be a few years later than that of Aeschines, and seems to indicate that there was something of a controversy on the point. Possibly we should think of two views among rhetoricians, one which looked to Aeschines and one to Demetrius, in which case Philostratus has accepted one and rejected the other. Kayser thought that there might be a lacuna in the text of Philostratus;[7] Wright believed that biographies of Hellenistic sophists were already in existence and that Philostratus passed over them because he had nothing to add;[8] Schmid noted that there were in fact only a few important sophists in the later centuries B.C.[9] This is probably what Philostratus believed, whether or not it was really true. Philodemus, writing in the mid-first century, has much to say about the art of sophistry but not about particular sophists. Philostratus himself names Ariobarzanes of Cilicia, Xenophron of Sicily, and Peithagoras of Cyrene as belonging in this time, but they are totally unknown to us.

As a classicist and Atticist Philostratus is interested in sophists of the fifth and fourth centuries and anxious to associate sophistry as he knows it to the great age, through Aeschines or through juxtaposition. He cares little about Hellenistic oratory of any sort and ignores it as he ignores details about later sophists when they do not interest him, for he has no conception of scholarly responsibility. As we have said, the association of Aeschines and sophistry was probably not his own invention: a logical jump from Aeschines to Nicetes is also implied by Tacitus (*Dial.* 15). Philostratus bases his view that Aeschines began the second sophistic on the latter's "inspired extemporization" (1.509). In origin the idea may have been influenced by the fact that Aeschines, always a writer of colorful style, went from Athens to Rhodes and to Asia and could thus be regarded as beginning Asianism. Philostratus, however, is not personally interested in this and never mentions Asianism. It would have been inconsistent with his association of sophistry with Attic writers. Yet, as Wilamo-

---

[7] Cf. C. L. Kayser, *Flavii Philostrati Opera* 2, Leipzig, 1871, viii-ix.
[8] Cf. *op.cit.* supra n. 6, xiv.   [9] Cf. *op.cit.* supra n. 2, 1.27ff.

witz pointed out,[10] we can probably accept a continuous, if sometimes slender, historical tradition from fifth century sophists through orators of Asia and Hellenistic declaimers, to the second sophistic. A final way in which Aeschines and sophistry might be connected is that Aeschines was known to have been an actor (1.507) and was always theatrical in manner, while tragedy was later called the mother of sophistry (2.620).

From Philostratus' account it seems clear that declamation was regarded as the most important activity of the later sophists. His citations suggest that *suasoriae* from classical Greek history furnished the commonest themes, but *controversiae* occur. Since the theme was usually chosen by someone in the audience (1.529), much emphasis was put on extemporaneity, though a few sophists like Aristides achieved great reputations without it (2.583). Philostratus rejects (1.523) the possibility of an art of memory and thought it entirely a gift of nature. We have seen that extemporaneity was not stressed in Roman schools, which sometimes did try to teach memory systems, but the sophists of course were not schoolboys learning to speak; they were adult and accomplished orators showing off their powers. Many of them were teachers of declamation, hopeful of attracting high-paying pupils. The charging of fees by the early sophists had been a subject of contention, but Philostratus defends the practice in his day (1.494-95), and it was certainly a reasonable thing to do. His own teacher in Athens, Proclus of Naucratis, charged a hundred drachmas a course and allowed students to use his library (2.604). Philostratus does not indicate whether sophists gave lectures on rhetorical theory to their stu-

[10] Cf. U. von Wilamowitz-Moellendorf, "Asianismus und Atticimus," *Hermes* 35 (1900) 13-14.

dents or not; they certainly declaimed before their students and discussed the treatment of the theme, and doubtless also listened to students' declamations and criticized them. Holders of official chairs may have given a series of lectures on the art, as Quintilian did, and some sophists, Hermogenes and Apsines, for example, published works on rhetorical theory. The greater sophists may have expected students to master the basic system of rhetoric with a less prestigious master before applying to themselves.

In addition to declamation sophists engaged in other forms of oratory. Many of them sometimes spoke in the law courts for fees. Polemo, for example, was paid two talents to go from Smyrna to Sardis and plead a case before the centumviral court of Lycia (1.524-25), and at the time of his death he had just been chosen as public advocate to plead a case on behalf of Smyrna before the emperor (1.539-40). Judicial oratory was regarded as less honorable than declamation: it was practical and did not allow for the same colorful treatment (2.599). The appropriate style was regarded as rather different (2.606).

A third form of sophistic oratory is in the grander tradition, reminiscent of Isocrates. This is the careful composition of large-scale oratory for a special ceremony or as a panegyric or in connection with an embassy. Polemo's speech at Hadrian's dedication of the temple of Olympian Zeus in Athens is a good example (1.533). The sophists lived chiefly in the major cities of Asia, especially Smyrna and Ephesus, which were rivals; in later times Antioch became an important center, and there were sophists in Egypt. The chief Athenian sophist was Herodes Atticus, who lived at Marathon. Most sophists, however, traveled either on lecture tours to enhance their reputation or to appear in a court or to speak by invitation in some other city. Many visited Athens, some came to Rome, Nicetus went "beyond the Alps and the Rhine" to defend himself against charges made by Verginius Rufus (1.512), while Dio went to southern Russia and also wandered along the Danubian boundary in exile, speaking to anybody who would listen. Sophists often engaged in politics in their home cities and were regularly sent on important embassies, much as Gorgias had been sent to Athens by Leontini in 427 B.C.[11] Usually the embassies were to the emperor. Philostratus mentions several, including one by Scopelian to Domitian to persuade him to rescind an order against planting vines in Asia (1.520) and an embassy to Hadrian by Polemo which secured a million drachmas for public works in Smyrna (1.531). Aristides' extant lament for Smyrna after its destruction in earthquakes is said to have moved Marcus Aurelius to tears and led to the rebuilding of the city (2.582). His most famous speech, *On Rome*, was delivered in that city, but on a private visit rather than a public embassy and it seems to have no specific immediate objective.

In several passages Philostratus gives a picture of what it would be like to listen to a great sophist. Polemo, for example, would arrive in a litter because of his arthritis, radiating confidence. After the theme was chosen he would withdraw briefly to consider it, and then return to declaim. Apparently he began sitting down, but would leap up as his excitement increased. He would round out his periods with a smile, to show how easy it was for him to achieve the *clausulae*, or he would stamp the ground, "not unlike the horses in Homer!" (1.537). Another fine passage (2.572-73) describes a performance

[11] Cf. Bowersock, *op.cit.* n. 6, 43-47.

by Alexander of Seleucia in the theatre of Agrippa in Athens when he passed through on his way to answer a summons from Marcus Aurelius, who was in Pannonia. He delivered first a miniature Panathenaic oration praising Athens and apologizing for not visiting it before. Then the theme is chosen: "Recall the Scythians to their earlier nomadic habits on the grounds that they are losing their health by living in cities." During the middle of the speech the great resident sophist and philanthropist Herodes Atticus arrived dressed in a traveler's costume, and Alexander repeats what he has said before, but shows his cleverness by varying each *sententia* slightly: "Even water when stagnant becomes ill" in the first version turns in the second into "Of waters too the sweeter are those that course." We must assume a high degree of sophistication in some of the audience; they knew the themes and the commonplaces and could appreciate nuances of variation, classical allusions, gestures.

There seem to have been at least two schools or traditions of style among the sophists.[12] All were Atticizing as far as vocabulary went, all were given to *sententiae* and figures, but some were considerably more restrained than others. Philostratus calls the elaborate and ornamented style "dithyrambic" (1.511) and "Ionian" and says it flourished especially at Ephesus (2.598). He quotes an extreme example of it from Onamarchus of Andros, speaking a declamation about a man who, like Pygmalion, fell in love with a statue (2.598-99):

"O enlivened beauty of a lifeless body, what divine spirit inspired your development? Some god of persuasion or of grace or Love himself, the father of beauty? In truth, everything is evident in you: the form of your

12 Cf. Norden 407-16.

face, the flower of your flesh, the shaft of your eye, gracious smile, blushing cheek, hints that you hear. And too, you have a voice ever about to speak. . . ."

Various degrees of this artificial style could be seen in Nicetes, in his pupil Scopelion, and in Polemo who had studied with Scopelion and others (1.536). A tradition of a much simpler style (*apheleia*) was to be found in Isaeus, his pupils Dionysius and Marcus, and especially in Herodes Atticus (2.564). Philostratus uses a kind of technical terminology which apparently developed among the sophists to describe qualities they valued.[13]

In discussing sophistry Philostratus stresses only its artistic side: how splendid the sophist sounded, how clever his *sententiae*, how excited his audience. He does not consider the intellectual, political, or social impact of sophistry nor does he say much about the subject matter of the orators. What is preserved includes some of the declamations, such as two by Polemo disputing the right to give a funeral oration on those who fell at Marathon and one by Herodes Atticus in the person of a Theban urging war on Macedon,[14] and also a number of grander efforts by Dio Chrysostom, Aristides, and from the fourth century by Libanius and Themistius. These suggest an attempt to fulfill some of the hopes for great and philosophical oratory such as those we have seen expressed by Quintilian at the end of his work. We will consider some of Dio's and Aristides' speeches shortly, but taken as a whole they may be said to sum

[13] Wright, *op.cit.* supra n. 6, 567-75 provides a glossary of some of these terms.
[14] On Herodes cf. infra n. 31. Polemo was edited by Hugo Hinck, Leipzig, 1873. Cf. also Hugo Jüttner, "De Polemonis rhetoris vita, operibus, arte," *Breslauer Philologische Abhandlungen* 8.1 (1898).

up the moral and historical achievement of Hellenism and to project it in a splendid panorama before the Greco-Roman world. The sophists thus contributed to unifying and expounding the culture of their age in somewhat the same way that the emperor Hadrian unified and amplified the arts of architecture and sculpture. Sophistic oratory at its best is a verbal counterpart of the villa at Tivoli. In the last great period of peaceful, prosperous classicism the sophists, like the emperor, strolled through the world enjoying and expounding its achievements and its glories.

The Chairs of Rhetoric

Philostratus reports the appointment of several of the sophists to state professorships in Athens and Rome.[15] He says, for example, that a certain Theodotus was the first incumbent of a chair with a salary of 10,000 drachmas and was chosen personally by Marcus Aurelius. Professors of Platonism, Stoicism, Aristotelianism, and Epicureanism were appointed at the same time, the choices being made by Herodes Atticus. Since many of the incumbents, like poet laureates of England, were not, in Philostratus' opinion, worth mentioning (2.566-67), we cannot compile a complete list of them. There was a chair of rhetoric at Athens before this time, but perhaps supported out of municipal funds; the sophist Lollian was the first incumbent (1.526). Philostratus also speaks of "the political chair" at Athens which carried a salary of one talent (6000 drachmas). It was held by a certain Apollonius (2.600) at the time when Heracleides seems to have held the other chair. There were also chairs of

[15] Cf. Corrado Barbagallo, *Lo stato e l'istruzione pubblica nell' impero Romano*, Catania, 1911; John W. H. Walden, *The Universities of Ancient Greece*, New York, 1912, 130-94; R-E 23.110-12; Marrou 405.

Greek and Latin rhetoric at Rome, continuations of those established by Vespasian at the much greater salary of 100,000 sesterces (Suet., *Vespasian* 18). Sophists sometimes went from the chair of Athens to the "higher chair" of Rome, greater in salary and prestige (2.589, 594). We do not know who first held the Greek chair in Rome: Nicetes might be a possibility since Pliny the Younger mentions him in the same breath with Quintilian (*Ep.* 6.6), but it is strange that Philostratus does not mention this if it is true. Instead he certainly gives the impression that Nicetes stayed in Smyrna except for the trip to plead against Rufus, which we have mentioned. Philostratus never mentions the Latin chair and we do not know the names of Quintilian's successors unless one was Julius Tiro, who seems to have followed Quintilian in Suetonius' account of rhetoricians.

Dio Chrysostom

The best example of a sophistic philosopher among those cited by Philostratus is Dio of Prusa, in Bithynia, who by the time of the third century rhetorician Menander (*RG* 3.390 Spengel) had become known as Chrysostom, or the Golden Tongued.[16] We have a corpus of eighty "orations" attributed to him, of which the thirty-seventh is usually thought to be the work of Favorinus and the sixty-third and fourth are probably also spurious.[17] Dio was born around 40 of a good family, was well educated, and became famous as an orator in his home province. The forty-sixth speech seems to date from this

---

[16] Cf. Hans von Arnim, *Leben und Werke des Dio von Prusa*, Berlin, 1898; *R-E* 5.848-77; Schmid-Stählin 2.361-67; E. D. Phillips, "Three Greek Writers on the Roman Empire," *C & M* 18 (1957) 102-19.

[17] The most useful edition is the Loeb in five volumes with intro., notes, and trans. by J. W. Cohoon and H. Lamar Crosby, Cambridge, 1939-51.

period and gives us some information about Dio's family and activities; it was delivered in an assembly held after a mob had attacked Dio's house because of grievances over the high price of grain. Apparently he was regarded as having exploited the grain shortage for his own advantage (46.8). Bithynia already suffered from social and economic tensions which later led the emperor Trajan to send Pliny to straighten out the province's affairs. Subsequently Dio went to Rome where he was nearly ruined through friendship with a member of the imperial family who fell from influence and lost his life. Dio alludes to the circumstances at the beginning of his thirteenth oration, but does not identify his patron. It is likely to have been Flavius Sabinus, executed by Domitian in 82.[18] Dio's own punishment was exile from Italy and Bithynia. He describes in the same speech (9-10) how he consulted the Delphic oracle and was advised to go on doing what he was doing until he came to the end of the earth. This he interpreted to mean that he should follow the life of a wandering philosopher of the Stoic or Cynic style, going from place to place with virtually no possessions, earning his way as a servant, and talking about philosophy. His course took him around Greece and far into Europe to the Danube and beyond into Russia. At the time of Domitian's death he was in a Roman army camp where, on receipt of the news, according to Philostratus (1.488) he stripped off his rags, like Odysseus fighting the suitors, jumped on an altar, and delivered an invective against the tyrannical emperor and an exhortation to the troops to responsible action. Under Nerva and Trajan he was allowed to resume a position as a leader of society in Bithynia and to travel where he wished; he visited Rome where he addressed the emperor and indeed seems to have become

---

[18] Cf. von Arnim, *op.cit.* supra n. 16, 230-31.

a friend of Trajan. We last hear of him in the letters of Pliny from Bithynia (*Ep.* 10.81 and 82) about 111 when he was meeting opposition in trying to complete a program of public works in his native city. Philostratus' picture of Dio is that of a moral philosopher who is eloquent and makes use of oratorical forms. Synesius, a Greek writer of the early fifth century, admired Dio and has left a short essay on him which makes a thorough-going distinction between his career before exile and after exile. According to Synesius, Dio was at first a sophist and strongly antiphilosophical. He mentions a work *Against the Philosophers*, a *Reply to Musonius*, and several sophistic speeches: one on the vale of Tempe, one on Memnon, and a *Eulogy of the Gnat*. Philostratus mentions also a eulogy of a parrot, but none of these speeches survive. In the period in question, roughly A.D. 60-80, the showy public declamation of *suasoriae* or *controversiae* which we have been considering had probably not yet become common in Greek cities; doubtless Dio declaimed, but probably only in rhetorical schools. The speeches we have suggest that Dio always had some philosophical inclination and that exile did not create such a sharp break in his intellectual development as Synesius seems to imply.

The effect of exile, however, was to convince Dio that the rewards of life which he had been pursuing, power, wealth, fame, and pleasure, were idle and to turn him in the direction of moral philosophy. Though he scorns sophistry, he never rejects eloquence and he continues to make use of oratorical forms. Probably his style was always in the relatively restrained tradition. Philostratus says it was unique, but reminiscent of Demosthenes and Plato. Dio also seems to have admired Xenophon to an unusual extent (18.14-17).

The extant speeches can perhaps best be thought of

in four main groups. A few probably antedate his exile and can be regarded as products of his sophistic period, though already somewhat philosophical in cast. A couple of dozen seem to date from his exile, among them several in dialogue form. The speeches dating from his return can be classified into those relating to matters in Bithynia and those which include his most ambitious works, delivered elsewhere and dealing with grander themes. A number of speeches cannot be classified with any certainty, primarily the shorter philosophical works which might date from his exile or might be later.

Dio is an interesting and appealing figure. He lacks the pomposity and meretricious quality of many sophists; he has something to say which he presents in a simple but elegant manner. Though not fond of specific historical details, he often gives a picture of life in the empire, especially in his much-admired *Euboeic Discourse*, which is a parable about a man shipwrecked on the island of Euboea and saved by simple but virtuous peasants whose way of life is charmingly told.[19] Dio is not an original philosopher and his interests are chiefly ethics and aspects of metaphysics with ethical significance. In the original sense of the word "sophist," a teacher of practical wisdom, Dio well deserves the name. He draws on a variety of Academic, Stoic, and related sources, much as Plutarch did about the same time, but he is less the scholar than Plutarch, and considerably less interested in history; at the same time he is more the orator, more anxious to persuade an audience. As seen in the speeches from the later part of his life, during the principate of Trajan, he seems to have visualized a kind

[19] Cf. J. Day, "The Value of Dio Chrysostom's Euboean Discourse for the Economic Historian," *Studies in Roman Economic and Social History in Honor of Allan Chester Johnson*, Princeton, 1951, 209-35.

of orderly, virtuous, more or less static society in which each man performed his allotted role and did not rebel against his duty. At the top is the emperor, intent on the interests of all, at the bottom the industrious and virtuous peasant, in between citizens and craftsmen of all sorts. Political union and cooperation is to be a part of the whole, and the cities are to be made healthful and beautiful. The Homeric poems in particular, and other classical writers like Plato, are taken as the texts which lead man to a fitting imitation of the gods and nature and thus to happiness.

The most thoroughly sophistic work of Dio to be preserved is the *Encomium of Hair*, which Synesius incorporated into his own *Encomium of Baldness*. As such things go the work has charm: it is very short and is simply expressed. It has, too, a logical coherence: Dio awakens in the morning after an extended illness, notices the neglected state of his hair, which he presumably wore fairly long, and as he tries to do something about it reflects on the way hair can greatly contribute to or greatly detract from appearance. From himself he turns to contemporaries who give too much attention to appearance, and then characteristically jumps back to classical times, to the Spartans combing their long hair before the battle of Thermopylae and then to Homer. About half the text is devoted to references to hair in Homer, just as more serious later works often draw liberally from Homer.[20] In discussing Homer Dio mentions first men, then gods, ending with Zeus, a progression seen later in his great Olympic speech. There is thus a general "upward" movement in the course of the little work, but it carries no meaning beyond its own modest cleverness.

[20] Cf. W. A. Montgomery, *Dio Chrysostom as a Homeric Critic*, Baltimore, 1901 and C. Affholder, "L'exégèse morale d'Homère chez Dion de Pruse," *BFS* 45 (1966-67) 287-93.

Other works of a sophistic sort are the encomium of law (75) and of custom (76) and the eleventh or *Trojan Discourse*, which is a *tour de force* demonstrating the "falsehoods" of Homer and showing that the Trojans must have won the war. The sixtieth speech is a mythological exercise in dialogue form reconstructing the story of Nessus and Deinaria. It is more sophistic than philosophical and might be taken as evidence that Dio had interested himself in the dialogue form before his exile. The twenty-eighth and twenty-ninth belong together and are also perhaps relatively early works. Twenty-eight, also in dialogue, describes Dio's arrival in Naples (4) where he sees a handsome athlete named Iatrocles and learns about the death of the boxer Melancomas. Dio offers the conventional consolation that it is fortunate to die while still young, strong, and handsome. Twenty-nine is a funeral oration for Melancomas to be delivered by an unnamed official, but since according to twenty-eight Dio did not arrive in Naples until two days after the funeral, it is presumably a literary exercise. Melancomas' ancestry and physical and moral qualities are dealt with in a rather general way, and it has thus been thought by some that he was an imaginary, ideal athlete.[21] The real interest of the speech is Dio's celebration of Greek athletics as superior to the arts of war. Thus the speech is perhaps one of the earlier instances of his theme of Hellenism. Another speech which seems to have sophistic qualities is the Rhodian discourse (31).[22] It purports to have been delivered in the Rhodian assembly in an attempt to get the city to give up the habit of voting a

[21] Cf. L. Lemarchand, *Dion de Pruse, Les Oeuvres d'avant l'Exile*, Paris, 1926, 30ff.

[22] Cf. von Arnim, *op.cit.* supra n. 16, 210-22. He dated the speech to the end of A.D. 70 on the basis of the references (112) to the city's freedom and distinguished it from later speeches of advice to cities such as the Alexandrian and Tarsic discourses.

statue in honor of a foreign dignitary and then simply putting his name on one of the many statues standing in the city. Dio examines the legal, moral, and religious implications of this policy, certainly revealing his own philosophical assumptions, but the whole thing is so enormously developed that it can hardly have been delivered in its present form. Possibly as Pliny did with the *Panegyric* and other speeches, Dio has revised and amplified an actual speech into the fullest possible form.

Special interest attaches to Dio's eighteenth speech, an open letter to an unnamed, probably Greek, statesman whose general literary education seems to have been neglected and who wants to acquire greater eloquence. The chief reason for giving the work an early date is the very slight role that the philosophers are given in the program (13). Dio explains (5) that he would outline a different course for a boy or for one who intended to speak in the law courts; there is thus no attention to the theory of rhetoric, and the objective is a general literary background for cultured speech, a knowledge of character, a sense of style, and a few models for particular occasions. Dio is clearly anxious not to discourage his pupil by making the course too difficult, and probably for this reason starts with comedy. Writers recommended are Menander, Euripides, Homer, Herodotus, Thucydides, Theopompus, Demosthenes, Lysias, Hyperides, Aeschines, Lycurgus, and especially Xenophon, but there is also a short passage in which the recipient is recommended to read some orators from "a little before our time":

"For the abilities of these orators would be useful to us in that we would not encounter them with our judgment enslaved, as we would the ancients. Through feeling able to criticize something of what is said, we will most take heart to attain the same results ourselves. . . ."

572

Recent orators recommended are Antipater, possibly the
father of Nicolaus of Damascus and thus a figure of the
first century B.C., Theodorus, presumably the rhetorician
from Gadara, Plution, who is mentioned by Seneca
(*Suas.* 1.11), and Conon, an Augustan writer known
from Photius. Fundamentally Dio's position is classicizing and moderately Attic, despite these few later names.
The speech as a whole, of course, invites comparison
with the tenth book of Quintilian, chiefly to Dio's disadvantage. He says even less than Quintilian does about
the writers he mentions except for Xenophon, and even
there treatment is rather eccentric: no work is referred
to except the *Anabasis*, the speeches in which are suggested as good practical models for the recipient. He
also differs from Quintilian (10.3.19-21) in recommending that the recipient dictate rather than write his own
compositions (18).[23]

A couple of dozen of Dio's speeches seem datable to
his exile. He had adopted the way of life of a wandering
cynic philosopher, and it is not surprising to find several
speeches which are really diatribes relating to the life
and teachings of Diogenes. The sixth, on tyranny, the
eighth, on virtue, the ninth, which describes Diogenes'
teaching at the Isthmian games, and the tenth, on servants, are of this sort. Stoicism furnishes the inspiration
for other speeches such as the fourteenth and fifteenth,
which relate to slavery and freedom; both of them make
some use of dialogue, and there is a set of a dozen dialogues between Dio and a pupil. The twenty-third, on the
Stoic paradox that the wise man is always happy, is an
example.

[23] Christ thought the addressee might be Nerva, cf. Schmid-
Stählin 2.363, but this is very uncertain, cf. von Arnim, *op.cit.*
supra n. 16, 140-41. On Xenophon cf. Karl Münscher, "Xenophon in der griechisch-römischen Literatur," *Philologus, Suppl.*
13.2 (1920), esp. 115-16.

From the period after Dio's return from exile we have a collection (numbered chiefly in the forties and fifties) of speeches relating to public matters in Bithynia. These are of considerable historical interest and in fact are the only surviving examples of what might be called the day-to-day political oratory of the Roman empire.[24] An interesting example is number forty-five, delivered in the assembly in Prusa early in the reign of Trajan (2-3) and primarily directed toward defending the role Dio has played in negotiations between the city and the emperor. Dio seems continuously to have been an object of envy in Prusa; here he tries to win sympathy by reference to his exile (1) and appreciation by reference to the privileges he has acquired for the city from Trajan when he could have sought honor for himself (3). At the same time he tries not to flaunt his own role and attacks no one by name. The key is low; there is no pathos, little ornamentation save for one comparison between himself and Odysseus (11), a role we have seen him play before. The worst feature of the speech from the point of view of a modern reader is the vagueness of detail: there is none of the sharp and specific clarity of Lysias or Demosthenes, but of course Dio's audience already knew the circumstances. He outlines (12-13) a rather imaginative program for the beautification and political development of Bithynia, including a synoecism of the cities like that which Theseus was supposed to have accomplished in Athens. This is one of the best examples of how he attempts to draw on the traditions of Hellenism to enrich the life of his own time.

Dio's noblest works are the four speeches on kingship (1-4) and his speech at the Olympic games (12). Of these

[24] Cf. von Arnim, *op.cit.* supra n. 16, 308-92 and C. Vielmetti, "I discursi bitinici di Dione Crisostomo," *SIFC* 18 (1941) 89-108.

the Olympic speech is the earliest, apparently delivered at the first Olympic festival after his return from exile, which would place it in the summer of A.D. 97.[25] Gorgias and other sophists of the classical period had frequented the Greek games, and the tradition was carried on by philosophers and orators of the empire. Possibly those in charge sometimes invited famous speakers to appear, but most sophists did not need an invitation or excuse to speak. Dio does not justify his appearance; it is, however, symbolic of his reemergence into full public life in the year following Domitian's assassination.

The speech may be regarded as falling into five main parts. Some of these parts could have been used in other contexts and perhaps were. Furthermore, it is always possible that Dio has elaborated the published text beyond what he actually said at Olympia, though we need not doubt an actual delivery. As the speech now stands there is first an introduction (1-20) which develops a bird metaphor: Dio is the owl, the philosopher bird, reticent of speech, with no special cause to plead, in which he resembles Socrates, a bird who attracts other birds to himself. The showy sophists are like peacocks. Dio refers to his exile and says that his speech will wander as he has (16), but this is deliberate self-deprecation, for the structure is all quite deliberate. This kind of indirect introduction was usual in epideictic—it can be seen, for example, in Isocrates' *Helen*—but a passing reference to Phidias is made (6), foreshadowing what comes later.

The second part of the speech is a *propositio* (21-26). In the sophistic manner Dio asks his audience what he

---

[25] Cf. B. F. Harris, "The Olympian Oration of Dio Chrysostom," *JRH* 2 (1962) 85-97. On the speech as a prose hymn cf. Theodore C. Burgess, "Epideictic Oratory," *Univ. of Chicago Studies in Classical Philology* 3 (1902) 178.

should speak about. He does not indeed request a theme to declaim, but suggests first that he might describe the lands and people he has seen in exile, something he does in part in his thirty-fourth speech, or alternatively he might discuss the nature and power of divinity, a topic suggested by the great temple of Zeus with its statue by Phidias there before him. Since no opportunity for choice is given, the passage is really a rhetorical device to introduce his subject and allow him once more to allude to his exile, which might be expected to win him sympathy. He asks also (23) if he should not invoke the Muses, as Hesiod did, quoting the first eight lines of the *Works and Days*. This is reminiscent of sophistic invocations of gods such as those found among the works of Aelius Aristides. Dio uses the invocation to lead to his real subject, which is not the nature of deity in the abstract, but the specific question of how man's conception of deity has come to him, including the contributions of poets and sculptors.

Dio is now ready to move on into the main body of the speech. There is first an analysis, drawing on Platonic and Stoic writers (27-46), of the sources of man's conception of deity. Dio identifies two kinds of sources and subdivides the second into three species, thus creating a total of four sources. The first source is inborn and comes through man's perception of the order and beauty of the universe. A digression attacks the blindness of the Epicureans, hardly a potent force in Dio's time. The other sources are acquired or engendered: the conception presented by the poets, that enforced by lawgivers, and that envisioned in the plastic arts. As he turns to this fourth source Dio inserts a brief exhortation to attention (43): he has come to the heart of his speech and his real subject.

The second half of the main body of the speech claims

(47) to examine the contributions of various interpreters of divinity to man, but the lawgiver is immediately passed over (48) and attention is primarily given to the sculptor with comparisons to the poet. Phidias is imagined before a tribunal of the Hellenes and is questioned about his statue of Zeus (49-54): "Has he achieved a suitable presentation of the god?" Dio then makes Phidias reply in his own defense (55-83), claiming basically that he has achieved as much as is possible in his difficult medium. Various qualities of Zeus which Phidias has tried to portray are mentioned. The passage is one of the better pieces of art criticism from antiquity and may even have some originality.[26] It is, however, reminiscent of sophistic descriptions of works of art, such as the *Imagines* of Philostratus, and in form both the question to Phidias and his reply are *suasoriae*. Phidias seems to have been a frequent character in declamation, but here Dio has set his piece into another speech, thus creating an enormous artistic frame of philosophy and religion. The final part of the Olympic speech is a short peroration (84-85), recapitulating the questions with which Dio has dealt and ending with a brief address by the god to the Greeks: they carry out their rites beautifully, but they neglect themselves.

The Olympic speech of Dio is perhaps the finest oration surviving from the time of the Roman empire and worthy of comparison with work of the Attic orators. It is beautifully organized, and it deals with cosmic subjects and noble art. Man and god, Homer and Phidias are brought together on the field of Olympia for the edification of Dio's contemporaries. The philosophy and criticism are perhaps not truly profound, but they seem deeply held and valued. They are certainly presented with considerable art and imagination. There are con-

[26] Cf. Cohoon, *op.cit.* supra n. 17, 2.2.

ceits and artificial transitions, but all handled with restraint and without pomposity. If the ending is somewhat unexpected, it is perhaps intended to try to bring home philosophy to the individual and to end on a striking note. This it does: Zeus quotes the very Homer who has contributed to his own conceptualization! The total effect of the speech to a modern reader is doubtless more sophistic than philosophical: the speaker certainly utilizes many of the techniques of the sophist and declaimer, but his subject is given a seriousness and universality beyond that of any ordinary declamation. There is virtually no political implication to the speech and no immediate course of action which Dio is recommending, but yet he is actively interested in persuasion: the work is not an exercise in verbal wit; Dio cannot be imagined taking an opposed theme and arguing it with equal fervor. What we are witnessing is the transition of oratory into the sermon: Dio is preaching the faith of Hellenism, its gods, its poetry, its art, and its culture as a whole. This theme became the noblest materials of oratory from his time to the end of pagan antiquity.

Dio knew several Roman emperors: probably Vespasian, Titus, and (to his sorrow) Domitian, certainly Nerva and Trajan. The forty-fifth speech, discussed above, refers to Nerva as deceased and reports a successful embassy to Trajan. At the time of its delivery Dio was apparently about to set off again for Rome and the emperor. We have four works on kingship which appear to have been addressed to the emperor, and possibly were delivered before him in person. Though they are printed as a set in modern texts, the first seems earlier and implies less of an acquaintance with the emperor than the third. Von Arnim thought the second and third belonged to the same period, but that the fourth was earlier.[27]

[27] Cf. von Arnim, *op.cit.* supra n. 16, 393-410.

Comparison with the *Panegyric* of Pliny naturally suggests itself and is instructive. Dio is less flattering than
Pliny, less personal and specific, far more philosophical
and concerned with setting forth classical models for
imitation drawn from Homer, Socrates, and Diogenes.
Pliny speaks as a Roman aristocrat and member of the
government with immediate personal political involvement; Dio speaks as a Greek intellectual of some independence with philosophical and moral convictions.
Pliny's occasion was formal and official, Dio's much less
clear. Possibly he addressed Trajan on his birthday.[28]

The four speeches differ considerably. The first and
third take an oratorical form and have something of the
structure of the Olympic speech. This is especially true
of the first, which starts with an epideictic prooemium—
this time Timotheus the flute player and Alexander (1-9)
—goes on to consider what subject to discuss (9-10),
mentioning again the wanderings of Dio and invoking
persuasion, the Muses, and Apollo, then proceeds to the
body of the work which has again two major parts: a
theoretical one on the nature of kingship, based chiefly
on Homer (10-36), and a second part which starts out
to examine the administration of Zeus, but gives it up as
an impossible task (48-49) and tells instead the story of
the choice of Heracles, which Dio interprets as a myth
showing how Heracles, having demonstrated his moral
excellence, received the gift of kingship over man. The
myth, like the Phidias declamation, is a rather showy
sophistic piece whose history goes back at least to the
sophist Prodicus of Ceos in the fifth century. There is
no real peroration, but the recipient (Trajan, though he
is not named) is addressed in the second person at the
very end.

[28] Cf. von Arnim, *ibid.* On kingship speeches in general cf.
Burgess, *op.cit.* supra n. 25, 136-37.

In the third speech the opening theme is Socrates' judgment of the king of Persia, but there is a long passage on the evils of flattery before the main topic is announced (3-24). The body of the speech again has two parts, but the more artificial part, a Socratic dialogue, comes first (29-41) and the long theoretical part on the virtues of a king follows (42-138). The other two "speeches" are actually dialogues on the same general subject of kingship, number two between Alexander and Philip of Macedon, number four between Diogenes and Alexander. In all of the speeches the same elements are present, though in different proportions: Homer, Socratic philosophy, Diogenes and Cynicism, Stoicism. As we have said the thrust is moral and general, not specific or political. If Trajan could come to understand virtue, Dio was content to have confidence in his political judgment. We have already noted that the giving of advice to the emperor was suggested by Quintilian as a possible subject of great oratory.[29] The possibility was developed by a number of more imaginative orators, including Pliny, Dio, and Aristides. Of them all, Dio demonstrates both the greatest independence and the greatest intellectual depth.

Trajan seems to have developed an admiration for Dio, though we need not believe Philostratus' story (1.488) that the orator was invited to ride in Trajan's triumphal car. The emperor certainly honored his requests in Bithynia, and von Arnim thought that in the speech to the people of Alexandria (32) Dio was speaking as a representative of the emperor, trying to calm the unruly inhabitants of that volatile city.[30] This is possible, for the speech for all its length has few declamatory features and makes a practical effort to win sympathetic attention. It

[29] Cf. supra 510.
[30] Cf. von Arnim, op.cit. supra n. 16, 437-38.

is, however, like several other speeches of Dio in trying to convince the inhabitants of some city to give up a persistent local foible, and thus to be associated with one of his regular themes. The Rhodian speech is an early example of the type; two other instances are the addresses to the people of Tarsus (33 and 34) who had developed an objectionable snort!

Roman critics like Quintilian and Tacitus probably would not have regarded Dio as an entirely satisfactory realization of their ideal orator, if only because he was a Greek, but he comes closest to the goal of anyone in his time. His work demonstrates what was then possible in oratory: he values eloquence enormously and though he came to distrust sophistry, he did not discard epideictic forms. His conversion to philosophy, unlike Tacitus' conversion to oratory or Juvenal's to satire, did not lead him to deny oratory. He was for much of his life an effective public speaker in his own country and used his oratory to help her with those abroad, though his mind is less instinctively political than moral or cultural. He did not speak to be clever, but discovered a code of values and a meaning in life which he tried to spread throughout the world by preaching. He is never precious, rarely bombastic, artificial only with restraint. His worst faults are a general vagueness about details, which sometimes passed for good manners, and a tendency to labor the obvious, as he does to some extent in the myth of the choice of Heracles. He deserves to be read and remembered.

In his own time the most famous sophist of the second century was Herodes Atticus.[31] Only one oration survives,

---

[31] Cf. *R-E* 8.921-54; Schmid-Stählin 2.694-96; Paul Graindor, *Un milliardaire antique: Herode Atticus et sa famille*, Cairo, 1930; Harry C. Rutledge, "Herodes the Great, Citizen of the World," *CJ* 56 (1960-61) 97-109.

a *suasoria*, *On the Constitution*, based on the old speech by Thrasymachus with the same name, which we know from Dionysius' essay on Isaeus. The style is so Atticizing that some scholars have been convinced the work is not by Herodes, but an actual late fifth century product![32] To posterity it is not oratory, but the philanthropy made possible by enormous wealth which has given Herodes Atticus his fame, and especially the buildings he built for Athens. More famous as an orator to later antiquity and better known today is Aelius Aristides.

Aelius Aristides

Aristides was not good at extemporization, but liked to think out the contents of his declamations carefully. Philostratus, who refers to a number of these declamations, claims that his strengths were his learning, his force, and his ability to portray character, and that he was the most disciplined artist of all the sophists (2.584-85). Most of his life was passed in Asia, where he was born in a small city in Mysia, probably in 117 and lived principally in Smyrna, but he traveled in Egypt and Greece, and came to Rome. He died in 189.[33] Fifty-five carefully

[32] Cf. Engelbert Drerup, *Ein politischer Pamplet aus Athen 404 v. Chr.*, Paderborn, 1908, answered by Frank Adcock and A. D. Knox in *Klio* 13 (1913) 249-57, who regarded it as a work of a pupil of Herodes. Edition by H. Hass, Leipzig, 1880.

[33] Cf. *R-E* 2.886-94; Schmid-Stählin 2.698-708; Hermann Baumgart, *Aelius Aristides als Repräsentant der sophistischen Rhetorik des zweiten Jahrhunderts der Kaiserzeit*, Leipzig, 1874; André Boulanger, *Aelius Aristide et la sophistique dans la province d'Asie au IIe siècle de nostre ére*, Paris, 1923; U. von Wilamowitz-Moellendorff, "Der Rhetor Aristides," *SPA* 1925, 333-53; Roger Pack, "Two Sophists and Two Emperors," *CPh* 42 (1947) 17-20; Phillips, *op.cit.* supra n. 16; Friedrich W. Lenz, *Aresteidesstudien*, Berlin, 1964 (and many other works on the text and scholia); C. A. Behr, *Aelius Aristides and the Sacred Tales*, Amsterdam, 1968; Bowersock, *op.cit.* supra n. 6, esp. 36.

worked orations attributed to him survive; the diction is prime Attic. The subjects include addresses to the gods to be used as prologues at sophistic displays (1-7), a strange series of holy discourses (23-28) about his long illness and recovery, and a considerable number of *suasoriae* drawn from events in Greek history. The most significant works are probably the encomium of Rome (14), the monody for Smyrna (20), and the speeches or, better, treatises, *On Rhetoric* (45) and *On the Four* (46).[34] Writings on rhetorical theory attributed to Aristides are not genuine, and will be considered in the next chapter.

The encomium of Rome was delivered in 143, probably in the lecture hall which Hadrian built in Rome called the Athenaeum. Possibly the speech was connected with the celebration of the birthday of Rome on April 21 in the *templum Urbis*.[35] Aristides says that it is a thank-offering for reaching Rome safely. He seems to have come as a sophist rather than an ambassador; his friend Herodes Atticus was consul in Rome the same year. The speech is entirely encomiastic and consists largely of comparisons between Rome and previous great cities, to Rome's advantage. The peace which she has brought and the way she has shared her citizenship are particularly stressed. Though somewhat informative to

---

[34] There is no complete English translation of Aristides. A Loeb volume of some speeches has been announced. For trans. of the encomium of Rome cf. infra n. 35. Cf. also James H. Oliver, "The Civilizing Power: A Study of the Panathenaic Discourse of Aelius Aristides against the Background of Literature and Cultural Conflict," *Trans. of the Amer. Philosophical Soc.*, 58.1, Philadelphia, 1968.

[35] Cf. Saul Levin, *To Rome*, Glencoe, 1950 and James H. Oliver, "The Ruling Power: A Study of the Roman Empire in the Second Century after Christ through the Roman Oration of Aelius Aristides," *Trans. of the Amer. Philosophical Soc.*, 43.7 871-1003, Philadelphia, 1953.

an historian of the empire, and beautifully finished in diction and composition, the oration lacks the significance of both Pliny's *Panegyric* and the speeches of Dio *On Kingship*. Aristides does not appear to be trying to accomplish anything except an eloquent expression of his admiration for Rome: he is not trying to make her better, or give her new models, or influence her rulers in any way. There is no indication that he even regarded himself as helping to unify patriotic sentiment. His objective is entirely verbal. His materials, however, are similar to those used by Dio for nobler ends and include the whole tradition of Hellenism. Literary sources seem to be chiefly Isocrates and Plato.[36]

The *Monody for Smyrna* is a prose poem in the form of a short lament for the city's destruction in the earthquake of 178. It seems to have become part of a program for the city's reconstruction which ultimately attained the support of Marcus Aurelius (cf. Philostratus 2.582). Aristides also wrote a *Palinode for Smyrna and her Reconstruction* (21), a *Smyrnaicus* (15), and a *Letter to the Emperor on Smyrna* (22).

The old dispute between rhetoric and philosophy, begun in the time of Plato, Aristotle, and Isocrates, occasionally rekindled. It was a burning issue in second century Greece, but we saw that in Cicero's time, and particularly in his own *De oratore*, a restatement was attempted which sought to merge the figures of the eloquent philosopher and the philosophical orator. This is still largely true in Quintilian. Dio's conversion to philosophy did not lead him to break with oratory. In the second century, however, philosophy again becomes more vigorous and seeks followers, and a tension develops.

[36] Cf. Oliver, *op.cit.* n. 35, 884-85. In general cf. Harry M. Hubbell, *The Influence of Isocrates on Cicero, Dionysius, and Aristides*, New Haven, 1911.

Juvenal's conversion to satire already foreshadows what is to come, but the most striking battle was that for the soul of Marcus Aurelius in which Fronto pleaded the cause of the rhetoricians. Two of Aristides' most important works contributed to this dispute. The long treatise *On Rhetoric* (45) is intended to be an answer to Plato's *Gorgias* and to show that rhetoric is important and is, in the technical sense, an art. Plato's objections could equally be turned against philosophy. Aristides treats the subject very seriously, claiming that he has a responsibility to defend rhetoric as one would a parent and invoking the aid of Hermes, Apollo, and the Muses. Although he draws on Plato in many works and admired him as a writer, he cannot accept Plato's views of rhetoric or of statesman in whose lives rhetoric played a role and who are heroes of the classical age. His equally long speech *On the Four* is his answer to Plato's criticism of Miltiades, Cimon, Themistocles, and Pericles. The *Souda* contains a statement that Porphyry, the neo-Platonist philosopher, attempted a reply to Aristides' *On Rhetoric*, which would seem to indicate that his attack was regarded by philosophers as a serious matter. Although to a modern reader Aristides falls far short of Plutarch, Dio, and Lucian in the interest of what he has to say, the style in which his bland orations were composed represented the ideal of imperial Atticism. He is the only imperial writer accepted by the later rhetoricians on a par with the Attic orators.

Lucian

Lucian was born in Samosata in Syria about 120 and died sometime after A.D. 180.[37] Three of his works can be

[37] Samuel Chabet, *L'Atticisme de Lucien*, Paris, 1897; Emily J. Putnam, "Lucian the Sophist," *CPh* 4 (1909) 162-77; Roy J. Deferrari, *Lucian's Atticism, the Morphology of the Verb*,

used to reconstruct an outline of his life. First is the *Twice Accused,* a dialogue in which Zeus sends Hermes down from heaven to settle a number of lawsuits. Among them are the Academy vs. Intemperance, the Stoa vs. Pleasure, and especially two prosecutions of "the Syrian," or Lucian himself, one by Oratory, one by Dialogue. Oratory (27-28) accuses Lucian of ingratitude and desertion and describes him as a Syrian who spoke Greek with an accent, who came to Ionia to study rhetoric, became a successful speaker, traveled, apparently as a sophist in Ionia, Greece, Italy, and Gaul, and who then fell into the clutches of Dialogue, the son of Philosophy, with whom he now leads a shameless life. Lucian confesses to the charge (30-32), but justifies his conduct on the ground that Oratory is no longer "modest" (31), and he describes her in terms reminiscent of Dionysius of Halicarnassus' characterization of Asianism in the introduction to *On the Ancient Orators.* Dialogue complains of wrongs and insults (33): Lucian has destroyed her dignity. In reply (34) he claims that the real objection to him is his unwillingness to engage in philosophical quibbles.

Lucian's work as a whole seems to confirm the picture of a man with rhetorical training who composed sophistic works, but in time reacted to some of the excesses of sophistry and turned toward moral philosophy, which he expresses through diatribes and dialogues. A comparison

Princeton, 1916; André Boulonger, "Lucien et Aelius Aristide," *RPh* 47 (1923) 144-51; Jacques Bompaire, *Lucien écrivain: Imitation et création,* Paris, 1958; Jacques Schwartz, *Biographie de Lucien de Samosate,* Brussels, 1965. The *Encomium* of Demosthenes is probably a fourth century imitation, but its authenticity as a genuine satiric work by Lucian was defended by A. Bauer, *Lukians Demosthenous encomion,* Paderborn, 1914.

to Dio's "conversion" is evident, and the two authors are alike in using the diatribe and dialogue forms, in drawing on Platonic, Cynic, and Stoic sources, and in a persistent classicism: Lucian not only writes in a highly Attic style, but often as far as the contents go he could have been living in the fourth century B.C. But Lucian differs from Dio and all other sophists in that he is instinctively a satirist, apparently alienated from the society of his time and with none of Dio's, or Aristides' admiration for the empire. The impression which his works leave is one of wit and irritability. He does not seem to have been greatly admired in his own time. Doubtless most sophists and philosophers took themselves too seriously to appreciate him.

Lucian mentions that he was about forty years old at the time of *Twice Accused* (32), so that his "conversion" to satiric philosophy must be dated earlier than that. We do not know of any particular incident which set it off, as we do in the case of Dio. *The Dream* gives a picture of Lucian's youth. His father had arranged for him to learn to be a stonecutter with his uncle, but his first attempts are disastrous. He has a dream, rather like the choice of Heracles, in which Sculpture and Education both appear and plead with him. Education wins, chiefly by showing him the appeal of the sophist's life (15). She will open to him all the world and its people and give him fame and fine clothes. Perhaps she did so. In the *Apology*, the third of the semiautobiographical works, he claims that his fees for sophistic demonstrations were as high as those charged by anyone (15), though perhaps he did not find so many occasions as he hoped for. The speech results from his acceptance of a state position in Egypt in the later part of his life. His duties were rather like those of a court recorder (12), so that in a sense he has remained in a position related to oratory, though of a rather humdrum sort. He claims that the salary is "many talents," which seems unlikely, and boasts about his future prospects. Apparently he was accused of inconsistency in accepting this office since he had earlier published a vigorous attack *On Those Serving for Pay*. At the time he meant chiefly grammarians and rhetoricians and the like serving as private tutors, but Egypt was technically regarded as the property of the emperor and his post made him a member of the imperial household. In practice he probably accepted the position because he needed the money.

Lucian's chief subjects are philosophy and religion, the opportunists who exploited them, and the hypocrites who practiced them. His most famous works are his dialogues, including the *Dialogues of the Dead, of the Gods,* and *of Courtesans.* He also wrote in the diatribe form, his *Slander* may be taken as an example, and in the form of the epistle, as for example in the critical work *How to Write History* which attacks contemporary rhetorical history of the kind we shall find Fronto composing. The *True History* is a satire of a work of travel and adventure, in which the speaker pretends to have reached the moon. All of these works were probably delivered as lectures. The more strictly sophistic works are mostly to be dated early in his career. They include *controversiae* (*The Tyrannicide* and *Disowned*), *suasoriae* (*Phalaris*), *prolaliae*, or introductory prose hymns (*Dionysus* and *Heracles*), and encomium (*In Praise of the Fly*). Significantly there are no examples of serious major speeches such as Dio's *On Kingship* or Aristides *On Rome* or the speeches of advice to cities which those orators delivered. That role of rhetoric did not appeal to Lucian or he was incapable of it. Instead he adapted rhetorical techniques to the elaboration of a world of satiric fantasy, thus once again extending the realm of rhetoric.

Of all of Lucian's works the one most specifically relating to the rhetoric of his time is the ironic lecture called *The Teacher of Orators* or, in the Loeb edition, *A Professor of Public Speaking*. Here Lucian affects to be demonstrating to a student that an easy royal road can be found to the glorious and honored name of sophist. He himself took the laborious old road (8) which involved study and imitation of the classics (9), but the footprints of Demosthenes and Plato are now almost indiscernible. A fancy and effeminate sophist is introduced to explain the new way to win rhetoric as a bride; possibly Lucian means him to be a caricature of the rhetorician Pollux (cf. Philostratus 2.592) since he claims to be a namesake of the sons of Zeus and Leda (24). The secrets of the new easy road to rhetoric, wealth, fame, and influence are, of course, ignorance, boldness, daring, and shamelessness, plus a loud voice, a singsong delivery, fancy clothes, and attendants (15). Outward appearance is most important, but fifteen or twenty characteristic Attic words help give the color of credibility (16). Demosthenes and Plato may be forgotten, but recent orators should be read (17). Don't prepare, but speak extemporaneously whatever comes to mind; never stop talking; bring in all the old commonplaces (20). Laugh at all the other speakers. Live a notorious private life. The sophist admits he generally fails in court, but everyone points him out, and that is what really matters (25).

This picture of sophistry is unfair as a criticism of Dio or even Aristides. It is only a reasonable exaggeration of the conduct of lesser sophists known from Philostratus, and it is most interesting if viewed as a confession by Lucian, the sophist who has turned satiric philosopher.[38]

Later Greek Sophists

From the later second century the best known sophist-philosopher is Maximus of Tyre, of whom forty-one *Dialexeis*, or philosophical lectures survive.[39] For example, "Whether Socrates Did Rightly in not Answering to His Critics." The form is that of the diatribe, the manner that of a sophist, the material is Platonism and Cynicism. Though Philostratus demonstrates the interest in sophistry in the early third century, the unsettled conditions of the middle of that century worked against the orator, and especially the wandering display orator seeking rewards in the cities of Greece and Asia. It is a general period of literary decline save for philosophy, which found converts in the disillusioned and depressed. Neo-Platonism gradually became a leading intellectual force. The later third and fourth centuries, however, were a renaissance of classicism and great sophists again flourished, the most eminent being Libanius, Themistius, and Julian, the sophist emperor. The circumstances of their time and the quality of their oratory are complex matters which are beyond the scope of our present study.[40] It is more relevant here to return to the second

[38] For a somewhat negative assessment of the period cf. B. A. van Groningen, "General Literary Tendencies in the Second Century A.D.," *Mnemosyne* 18 (1965) 41-56.

[39] Cf. Hermann Hobein, *De Maximo Tyreo Quaestiones philologicae selectae*, Jena, 1895; Schmid-Stählin 2.767-69; R-E 14.2555-62; Guy Soury, *Aperçus de philosophie religieuse chez Maxime de Tyr*, Paris, 1942.

[40] The best general introduction to the writers of the fourth century is T. R. Glover, *Life and Letters in the Fourth Century A.D.*, New York, 1924. Cf. also Walden, *op.cit.* supra n. 15; Glanville Downey, "Themistius' First Oration" *GRBS* 1 (1958)

century and inquire what was the influence of the second sophistic on Latin letters.

The second sophistic influenced Latin letters only to a limited extent. There were no great Latin sophists who traveled to the intellectual capitals and enthralled audiences; there were no Latin speeches of advice to kings and cities. Favorinus, the best known western sophist, was a Greek-speaking Gaul. Latin, as we have seen, did not much develop epideictic forms, but there were the speeches of thanks on achieving the consulship, there were funeral orations, and in the age of Fronto some of the minor sophistic forms were practiced for exercise or entertainment. Apparently the feeling continued that what was appropriate in Greek was not necessarily appropriate in Latin. The distinction between being a Greek and being a Roman was still strong in Roman minds in the earlier part of the second century, as seen in Tacitus or Juvenal, but thereafter began to break down. Hadrian's philhellenism accelerated a process already begun which brought Greeks into Roman political life at high levels. Although the Greek sophist Herodes Atticus and the Roman orator M. Cornelius Fronto were both consuls in A.D. 143, Herodes had the greater distinction of being *consul ordinarius* and giving his name to the year, whereas Fronto had to be content with a suffect consulship in the later summer when Rome was deserted. The teaching of rhetorical theory and Latin declamation continued vigorously, but no important new Latin theorists appeared and no professional rhetorician achieved the influence of the great Greek sophists. The Atticism movement in Greek did not cause a revival of Latin neo-

---

49-69 and A. F. Norman, *Libanius: Selected Works* (Loeb), Cambridge, 1969.

Atticism, but did contribute to the archaism fad which found preferred models for literary imitation in second century B.C. Latin writers like Ennius and Cato. Perhaps the major features of Roman rhetorical history in this period can be brought out if we consider three authors, Fronto, Aulus Gellius, and Apuleius.

Fronto

M. Cornelius Fronto was born in Cirta in North Africa shortly after A.D. 100, passed through the *cursus honorum* to the consulship in 143, and apparently survived to at least 175.[41] He does not seem to have been very influential politically, and the one position where he might have exercised power, the proconsulate of Asia, he refused because of poor health. But he was definitely an influential literary lion and regarded as the greatest Latin orator of his time (Dio Cassius 69.18). We know him chiefly from a collection of letters discovered in the early nineteenth century in palimpsest. That is, the codex in which the letters were originally written was broken up, an attempt made to erase the writing, and the material reused for Christian works, which became part of two

[41] The standard text of Fronto has been that of S. A. Naber, Leipzig, 1867, now replaced by M.P.J. Van den Hout, *M. Cornelii Frontonis Epistulae*, Leiden, 1954. References in the discussion here are, however, to vol. and pages in the Loeb Library edition by C. R. Haines, *The Correspondence of Marcus Cornelius Fronto*, Cambridge, 1919, since that is the only readily available edition in American libraries. Cf. works cited below and M. Dorothy Brock, *Studies in Fronto and his Age*, Cambridge, Eng., 1911; Felicitá Portalupi, "Marco Cornelio Frontone," *Pubbl. Fac. Magist. Univ. di Torino* 18 (1961) 1-134; H. G. Pflaum, "Les correspondants de l'orateur M. Cornelius Fronto de Cirta," *Melanges Bayet*, Paris, 1964, 544-60; René Marache, "Fronton et A. Gellius (1938-64)," *Lustrum* 10 (1965) 213-45. On the date of Fronto's death cf. Bowersock, *op.cit.* supra n. 6, 124-26.

codices, one at Milan and one in Rome. The surviving pages are difficult to read and out of order, and many are not preserved at all. Yet a great deal of sense has been made of the material, and Fronto has been rescued from the darkness as a distinct literary personality.

Some would say not entirely to the advantage of his reputation. The letters disappoint as historical sources, especially considering the fact that they are addressed to and include replies from such important people as Antoninus Pius, Marcus Aurelius, and Lucius Verus, but in fairness to Fronto it must be noticed that the imperial letters are as unsatisfactory in this respect as his own. What we have is a collection devoted to personal and literary matters. To modern readers the most objectionable, but one of the most interesting, interchanges is the correspondence between Fronto, Verus, and Marcus on the encomiastic history of Verus' Parthian war which Fronto composed (2.194-98 Haines). Verus supplied information and Fronto was to work it up into the desired form. Verus admits that his deeds are only "what they are," but says that they will seem what Fronto wishes them to be. Nobody involved seems to have thought that historical veracity was a significant factor. From Fronto's work there survives only the highly artificial *Preface* (2.198-218), largely based on rhetorical commonplaces and literary imitations and well illustrating the faults of the historiography of the time which Lucian denounced in *How to Write History*.

Fronto was neither morally nor intellectually in advance of his age, but a sympathetic and extensive reading of the letters can lead to a good deal of affection for him. He was certainly a much more sensible and sensitive man than Aristides, more amiable and constructive than Lucian, and more modest and restrained than Herodes. His letters reveal a highly sophisticated, literate society, pre-occupied with physical ailments, real or imaginary,[42] and putting a very high value on personal friendship. Marcus Aurelius clearly had great affection for Fronto, to the extent that their letters to each other are sometimes almost embarrassing for a third party to read (cf., e.g., 1.30-33; 2.120-26). Fronto complains (2.154) that warmth of affection is not characteristically Roman and seems to have felt a compulsive need of intimate acquaintances which he candidly expresses. Possibly inner tensions of loneliness and boredom should be viewed as a feature of the age, also reflected in the prevalence of hypochondria or in the introspection of Marcus Aurelius or in the growth of Christianity. Fronto's general personality and attitude toward the government is somewhat reminiscent of Quintilian's, though he had less interest in education than did Quintilian. His most personal letter, that on the death of his grandson (2.222-32), also recalls in tone Quintilian's pathetic remarks on the death of his own children (6. pr.). Fronto never mentions Quintilian by name in the extant letters.

Fronto was not a sophist, not a rhetorician, nor a professional teacher but a Roman orator who was interested in sophistry and rhetoric and became a tutor. His Roman quality must be stressed since it has been denied.[43] In fact, though he certainly felt Greek influences, his most admired models of life and speech are the old Romans: Cato especially, Plautus, Ennius, and Roman historians down to Cicero and Sallust. Again, like Quintilian, he disliked Seneca; he has rather little to say about Greek literature; his conception of an orator's duty is quite Roman and involved speech in the lawcourt and the senate and guarding the purity of the Latin language.

[42] Cf. Bowersock, op.cit. supra n. 6, 71-75.
[43] By Clarke 131.

Fronto refers to his activity as a patron (e.g. 1.232)[44]
and mentions several specific actions such as that involving his speech *For the Bithynians* (2.88 and 98-100)
which was published, but was not up to Cicero's *Pro
Sulla* in his own opinion. It was probably a judicial
speech in the senate on a charge against a governor. A
long letter to Arrius Antoninus (2.176-86), judge for
Transpadine Italy, deals with the legal affairs of a municipal senator in Concordia, near Venice, named Volum-
nius, who was being denied his seat after a brief banishment. It is really a speech in the form of a letter, with
exordium, narration, discussion of the legal situation,
and an emotional appeal based on the advanced age of
the client. The longest fragments of Fronto's judicial
oratory are pieces of his speech *On Foreign Wills* preserved in a highly flattering manner in a letter by Marcus
Aurelius when still Caesar (1.154-62). Marcus describes
how he himself had declaimed Fronto's speech (with appropriate gestures) to the emperor Antoninus Pius, who
had been unable to hear Fronto deliver it originally.
Marcus then quotes back to Fronto five passages which
he especially admires. They seem to represent the better
part of the speech and to have been copied out by Marcus by his own hand, which was a compliment (1.168).
The language is excellent: crisp, vigorous, straightforward, reminiscent of Cato. Fronto demonstrates with
reasonable probability that requiring the wills of Romans
who lived abroad to be proved in Rome would result in
inconvenience and injustice. In another legal action
Fronto found himself about to attack Herodes Atticus
without, he claims, realizing that he was a friend of
Marcus. Marcus appealed to Fronto tactfully and the
latter apparently modified the severity of his attack, but
did not give it up entirely (1.58-79). Subsequently he

[44] Cf. *R-E* 4.1327-30 where eleven speeches are listed.

595

and Herodes became friends, though the original charges were severe, including manslaughter. It seems likely that Fronto was pleading for Demostratus and that Herodes, though involved in the case, was not actually on trial himself.[45] Very possibly Fronto was not so ignorant as he pretended of the relationship between Marcus and Herodes; a suggestive letter on envy among Marcus' friends (1.70-74) may be dated to this time.

A speech about which we would willingly know more is one which the Christian apologist Minucius Felix quotes (*Octavius* 9.8, cf. 31.1), but which is not referred to in any of Fronto's surviving letters, most of which are probably earlier. It appears to have attacked the rites of the Christians, which are referred to as involving lust and drunkenness of the wildest sort.[46]

Fronto often mentions the senate, but we do not have any good example of his oratory there. He does quote two sentences from his speech of thanks on the consulship, delivered in the senate on the Ides of August 143 (1.118). The quotations are obscure but seem to have something to do with the social class from which senators have come at different times. One remark met with applause, the other with "murmur," and Fronto's point in quoting them is that an orator must keep the attitude of his audience in mind. He goes on to define the greatest virtue of an orator (*summa illa virtus oratoris*) as a path between what he wants to say and what his hearers want to hear, stressing the speaker's need to preserve his dignity.

The other oratorical works of Fronto of which we can form some judgment are short epideictic or sophistic *paignia*. These include an *Eroticus* in Greek

[45] Cf. Bowersock, *op.cit.* supra n. 6, 95-99.
[46] Cf. P. Frassinetti, "L'orazione di Frontone contro i cristiani," *GIF* 2 (1949) 238-54.

(1.20-30) inspired by the speeches in Plato's *Phaedrus*. Marcus Aurelius said that in his opinion it equalled the *Attici* in the close-packed thought, the subtle argument, and the felicity of the whole (1.30). But he seems to say this at least as much out of affection for Fronto as out of real admiration for the speech. Elsewhere (1.116) he describes a declamation of Polemo as rather the opposite: something one could praise, but hardly love. We also have, this time in Latin, the introduction to Fronto's *Praise of Smoke and Dust* (1.38-44) and some of his *Praise of Negligence* (1.44-49). He says (1.40) that no compositions of this kind existed in Latin, except what could be found in early comedians: the requirements are abundance of *sententiae* and finish of style, and the object is *suavitas*, "sweetness." We have seen Dio's *Encomium of the Gnat* and other Greek examples of this genre were common, but Fronto apparently first brought this form of sophistry to Latin oratory. Still another sophistic work by Fronto is his *Arion* (1.54-58), a rhetorical narrative about the lyre player from Lesbos.

We have said that Fronto was not a rhetorician, in the sense that Quintilian, for example, was. But he did have opportunities to expound views about language and style, the aspects of rhetoric which interested him. Aulus Gellius reports five conversations of Fronto on linguistic matters, claiming (19.8.1) that he himself often attended Fronto and learned much from him. The matters discussed are the names of the colors in Greek and Latin, which was the subject of a conversation between Fronto and the sophistic philosopher Favorinus (2.26), the use of the expression "many mortals" by the first century B.C. historian Claudius Quadrigarius (13.29), the meaning of the phrase *praeter propter* (19.10), Latin words lacking a singular or plural (19.8), and the

Latin for "dwarf" (19.13). The latter was a conversation between Fronto, the grammarian and orator Postumius Festus, and a certain Sulpicius Apollinaris which took place at the entrance to the imperial palace in Rome. These conversations are, of course, somewhat reminiscent of the literary discussions of Crassus and Antonius, or Afer and Quintilian, but show the great emphasis which Fronto put on matters of diction. As sources Fronto here cites Ennius, Pacuvius, Cato, Varro, Nigidius, and Virgil, and mentions Cicero's name.

A letter which well summarizes Fronto's attitudes toward style is that which Haines regarded as the earliest extant and therefore put first in his collection.[47] It takes the search for unusual or unexpected words as the most important feature of stylistic study. Cato, Sallust, Plautus, Ennius, and a few other authors are praised for their skill at this, while Cicero's neglect of it is criticized, though his many other virtues are granted. Various words for "wash" are considered, also the position of epithets. Fronto is doubtless wrong if he thought early Latin writers chose their words with greater care than later writers did. The Augustan poets, of whom he is not very fond, really deserve the palm here, but by Fronto's time their language seemed trite. In fact, though the principle on which Fronto based his theory of style was the search for the exactly "right" word, readers have always recognized that he was attracted by the flavor and novelty of archaism; genuine old Latin words which are no longer in use had for him a special literary distinction, just as fourth century Attic diction, even more remote in time, had special appeal to his Greek contemporaries. But the predilection is not carried beyond good taste: Fronto's Latin is not a pastiche

[47] Cf. also Leeman 367-68.

of archaic words and phrases and in practice seems hardly more artificial than does the Latin of Sallust.[48]

Fronto is regularly addressed as *magister*, or teacher, by Marcus Aurelius and also by L. Verus (e.g., 1.274) and is described in an inscription as "teacher of the emperors Lucius and Antonius."[49] The details of the appointment are not known, but it certainly antedates Marcus' designation as Caesar at the age of eighteen in 139, the earliest year definitely assignable to any extant letter in our collection. Possibly Fronto was asked to help Marcus gain facility in oratory following his adoption by Antonius Pius and the death of Hadrian in 138, but he certainly speaks as though he had guided his education from an earlier time.[50] If a salary was involved, allusions to it are discreetly veiled. In the early years Fronto provided Marcus with assignments (*materia*) in reading and composition. For example, he sent a piece of Coelius Antipater to be studied and a topic for composition, possibly related to it (1.18). Maxims (1.12), commonplaces (1.54), and similes (1.34) were also assigned. Fronto was inordinately fond of similes and often mentions them in writing to Marcus. He also furnished Marcus with topics for declamation (1.210 and 214).

[48] For Fronto's stylistic views cf. Brock, *op.cit.* supra n. 41, 95-261; René Marache, *Mots nouveau et mots archaïques chez Fronton et Aulu-Gelle*, Rennes, 1957, and *La critique littéraire de langue latine et le développement du gout archaïsant au IIe siècle de notre ère*, Rennes, 1952. Marache connects archaism in Fronto and Gellius with Latin stylistic traditions rather than with Greek Atticism.

[49] *CIL* x.1.6334 = Dessau 1129.

[50] *R-E* 4.1314 dates Fronto's direction of Marcus Aurelius to about 130 on the basis of *pueritia* in 2.124 Haines, but the reference is a vague compliment and need imply no direct knowledge of Marcus at the time. Cf. 2.74 (*De eloq.* 3.3): *incunabula studiorum tuorum mihi cognita sunt.*

Although Fronto's specific teaching function faded as time passed, in later years he occasionally still advised Marcus in the voice of a master (e.g., 2.100). Fronto's teaching was apparently almost totally limited to matters of style, and he never discusses technical aspects of invention, arrangement, memory, or delivery, which Marcus presumably had studied earlier with a professional Greek or Latin rhetorician.[51]

To judge from the letters, Marcus was for a time a willing and appreciative pupil, and he always seems to have been genuinely fond of Fronto, but he had reservations about the study of rhetoric which ultimately led him to reject eloquence as an object of pursuit. In the opening passage of the *Meditations* (1.11) he thanks Fronto for teaching him the danger of envy and other vices and for pointing out the lack of affection among the Roman nobles. This is not inconsistent with Fronto's advice, but it overlooks Fronto's real objectives. One letter by Fronto (1.100-102) appears to be answering Marcus's complaints about insincerity in speech, citing Socrates as an example apt to appeal to Marcus. When twenty-five (i.e., between April 146 and 147) Marcus wrote to Fronto (1.214-18) confessing the appeal that the works of the Stoic philosopher Ariston had for him, his moral dissatisfaction with himself, and his neglect of his literary studies. He promises to read some Cicero and to write an exercise, but declines to plead on both sides of a case any longer. In the *Meditations* (1.7) he gives the credit to his teacher Rusticus for leading him away from sophistry, oratorical display, and rhetoric.

Fronto attempted to rescue Marcus Aurelius for rhet-

---

[51] The life of Marcus in the *Historia Augusta* 2-3 lists Marcus' teachers. Fronto is the only teacher of Latin oratory named; Aninius Macer, Caninius Celer, and Herodes Atticus are the Greeks.

oric, partly by the influence of his friendship, partly by flattering his oratorical abilities, partly by argument. The chief documents, and most extensive exposition of Fronto's rhetorical ideas, are the four letters *On Eloquence* (2.52-84) to which may be added another long letter known as *On Speeches* (2.100-114).

The first letter *On Eloquence* is found in folia 389-404 of the Ambrosian palimpsest, though the pages have been disarranged as usual. As arranged by modern scholars the letter discusses two subjects whose relationship to each other is not entirely clear. One is diction: Fronto flatly opposes word coinage, urges an exhaustive search for the best word, and approves the deliberate accumulation of approximate synonyms in one sentence (2.53-54). The other part is a philosophical exhortation of Marcus to pursue eloquence as something useful and necessary to a ruler. The most interesting section (2.62) tries to answer Marcus' complaint that when he has said something brilliant he feels pleased and that this feeling is wrong. Chastise yourself if you must, he says, for self-satisfaction, but why chastise eloquence any more than you would a quality like good judgment which might also give you self-satisfaction.

The second letter *On Eloquence* is almost entirely lost; the third stresses Marcus' ability at oratory, his desertion of it for philosophy, but his continuing need of rhetoric to express his thought. The fourth letter is a critique of a recent speech by Marcus, which Fronto says was not entirely characterized by *elocutione novella*. This has been taken as a technical term, the "new style" of Fronto and his friends,[52] but since the phrase occurs only here it would probably be better simply to take it

[52] Cf. J. W. Mackail, *Latin Literature*, London, 1895, 233-46. *Nostrae sectae* in 2.36 does imply that Fronto regarded his teaching as having certain characteristics.

to mean "novelty of expression," the use of a peculiarly appropriate but unusual word such as Fronto regularly urges. His tastes doubtless were shared, but there is little reason to formalize them into a school with a specific jargon. Similarly, there is little reason to invent an African school of Latin which had kept alive vocabulary otherwise archaic and which then emerges into literature in the second century.[53] Fronto, Apuleius, and Tertullian were Africans by birth, but this is probably only a coincidence. The stylistic tastes of the second century, like the artistic tastes of the time, are best thought of as an extreme form of classicism analogous to the Greek Atticism then flourishing.

Fronto's views on style are again summed up in a later letter to Marcus entitled *De orationibus, On Speeches*. Here (2.102) he strongly castigates the hectic, trivial style of Seneca or (2.104) the empty repetitions of Lucan, and rebukes the choice of words in a recent edict of Marcus as inappropriate. "Keep to the old mintage," he says (2.112), but make it current and alive. "Seek some word, not coined by you, for that would be absurd, but employed more neatly, more suitably, more appropriately." (2.114). This may be taken as Fronto's permanent and final view of style.

Aulus Gellius

Aulus Gellius' *Attic Nights* is important in the history of rhetoric chiefly for the information about and quotations from early Latin writers which it presents.[54] Gellius was an antiquarian, interested in history, law, religion, medicine, philosophy, and above all in grammar, who

[53] Cf. Brock, *op.cit.* supra n. 41, 161-261.
[54] The best translation is that of John C. Rolfe in the Loeb Library, *The Attic Nights of Aulus Gellius*, 3 vols., London, 1960-61. On Gellius as a critic cf. E. Yoder, "A Second Century Classical Scholar," *CJ* 33 (1957-58) 280-94; Marache, *La critique littéraire*, cit. supra n. 48, 183-317.

started a miscellany during his student days in Athens and continued it at Rome to the length of forty books. He seems to have been an approximate contemporary of Fronto, whom he knew and whose literary tastes he somewhat shared. He served as a judge in Rome (14.2), but he was not particularly distinguished as an orator. Although he has no rhetorical theories of his own, he does comment on rhetorical matters, such as the doctrine of the three styles (6.14), or compare passages of Cato, Gaius Gracchus, and Cicero (10.3). His views on diction (11.7) are more moderate than Fronto's, but his practice is rather similar; he makes less use of archaism, more use of new words;[55] and he shares Fronto's distaste for Seneca (12.2). The Latin authors he prefers are the orators and historians of the second and first centuries B.C. down to Sallust. We are especially indebted to him for preserving such fragments of Cato as the better part of the speech *For the Rhodians* (6.3). He listened to sophists and sophistical philosophers like Herodes Atticus and Favorinus, and he shares the sophistic reverence for Hellenism as seen in Homer and the classics, but not the sophist's craving for rhetorical creativity, and he does not discuss Atticism. Ordinarily, his method is to report a conversation or opinions on a disputed point, without giving much stress to his own judgment. As seen, for example, in his treatment of *For the Rhodians* and Tyro's criticism thereof, he can be precise, reasonable, and just, but he is often content with trivialities.

Apuleius

Apuleius was born in Madauros in north Africa around A.D. 125.[56] He studied in Carthage and Athens, visited

---

[55] Cf. René Marache, *Mots nouveaux et mots archaïques chez Fronton et Aulu-Gelle*, Rennes, 1957.

[56] Cf. Ben E. Perry, "The Literary Art of Apuleius in the *Metamorphoses*," TAPhA 54 (1923) 196-227 and "An Interpretation of Apuleius' *Metamorphoses*," TAPhA 57 (1926) 238-

Rome, and eventually returned to Africa where he lived the rest of his life, dying perhaps around 170. Apuleius is best known as the author of the Latin romance *Metamorphoses*, sometimes called the *Golden Ass*, written in a highly artificial prose style, reminiscent of Greek sophists in the tradition of Gorgias and also of the literary fashions of the mid-second century as seen in Fronto and Aulus Gellius: archaism, word coinage, and a search for novelty abound. There is primary rhetoric in that the work is apparently intended to encourage the worship of Isis, and a good deal of secondary rhetoric, not only in the style, but in episodes reminiscent of declamations (e.g., the story of the cruel stepmother in book ten) and in the trial scenes of books three and ten, but the overall impression is not one of rhetorical sophistication. Far more significant rhetorically are two other works by Apuleius, his *Apology* and his *Florida*.

The *Apology* is a complete Latin oration, the published and thus doubtless somewhat amplified version of what Apuleius said in his own defense during a trial held at Sabrata in Africa before the proconsul Claudius Maximus.[57] The date cannot be set with certainty, but is probably in the later 150's. The charge is the use of magic to gain the hand and estate of Pudentilla, widow of Sicinius Amicus of Oea, near Tripoli. An additional charge mak-

---

60; Elizabeth H. Haight, *Apuleius and his Influence*, New York, 1927; Max Bernhard, *Der Stil des Apuleius von Madaura*, Stuttgart, 1927; E. Paratore, "La prosa di Apuleio," *Maia* 1 (1948) 33-47; L. Callebat, "L'archaisme dans les *Metamorphoses* d'Apulée," *REL* 42 (1964) 346-61; B. C. Dietrich, "The Golden Art of Apuleius," *G & R* 13 (1966) 189-206. There are numerous translations of the *Metamorphoses*; for the oratorical works cf. H. E. Butler, *The Apologia and Florida of Apuleius of Madaura*, Oxford, 1909.

[57] Cf. Rudolf Helm, "Apuleius' Apologie, ein Meisterwerk der zweiten Sophistik," *Altertum* 1 (1955) 86-108.

ing Apuleius responsible for the death of his stepson Pontianus was dropped in the early stages (*Apol.* 2). We are obviously on an entirely different intellectual level than in Cicero's or Pliny's speeches—for one thing Apuleius' oration has no apparent political significance—but the world which appears is reminiscent of the background of Horace's epodes and satires or Petronius or, of course, Apuleius' own *Metamorphoses*.

In rhetorical technique the *Apology* does not represent a radical break with tradition, but like other able orators Apuleius has adapted argument and arrangement to the particular needs of the occasion. His exordium (1-3) is drawn from the opponent, the judge, and the case. He defends himself and tries to generalize the issue as Cicero might have done: it is not only himself but philosophy which is on trial (1 and 3). Taken together with the title and a number of references to Plato this suggests that Apuleius would like to present himself as a kind of Socrates, on trial for his beliefs and ways of life, and in one passage he emotionally presents neo-Platonism as a mystical religious creed. The Socratic analogy is not very convincingly maintained, since most of the speech deals with the details of the charges and their refutation. Apuleius seeks first (4025) to refute what his opponent has used to raise prejudice against him: his beauty, his eloquence and poetry, his use of a mirror, his poverty, and his place of birth. These slanders he shows to be mutually contradictory (25). Then he goes on to the charge of magic, giving first a preliminary refutation (25-27) and then a more detailed treatment of the whole matter. Section twenty-eight contains a *partitio* in which he promises first to refute the arguments against him, second to show that even if he were a magician he has not engaged in any evil practices, then to deal with the motivation and circumstances of his marriage, and finally to show how his stepson Pudens has been turned against him.

This promise is not literally followed through: refutation of the arguments seems to run from sections twenty-nine through sixty-five, while sixty-six begins the matter of the marriage, thus overlooking specific treatment of the second topic. In practice, Apuleius thus relies on *stasis* of fact, rather than quality, though the total effect of the speech, as of Apuleius' other writings, is certainly to reveal a fascination with the possibilities of magic.[58] The passage from sixty-six through ninety-six is a persuasive presentation, beginning with a *narratio*, of the circumstances under which Apuleius married Pudentilla, of the resulting events, and of the various characters involved. Most convincing is the matter of Pudentilla's letter (81-83) which the opposition has quoted out of context to try to show that Pudentilla regarded her husband as a magician. This part of the speech ends with a digression on the eloquence of Lollianus Avitus, the former proconsul. The fourth topic, the matter of Pudens, is then briefly treated (98-101) and the speech ends with a brief peroration (102-3). Of the whole, critics have well observed that Apuleius rather plays with his adversaries in the first two-thirds of the work and then springs on them the trap of evidence and argument.[59] We do not, however, know whether or not Apuleius won his case; he seems to have moved to Carthage.

Apuleius calls his work *On the God of Socrates* an oration (4). We may regard it as a piece of sophistic oratory, suitable to be recited or read aloud, and compare

[58] Cf. Adam Abt, *Die Apologie des Apuleius von Madaura und die antike Zauberei: Beiträge zur Erläuterung der Schrift De magia*, Giessen, 1908.

[59] Cf. Haight, *op.cit.* supra n. 56, 59-60.

it to speeches of Aristides or Maximus of Tyre on subjects related to Plato. Most reminiscent of the sophists, however, is the *Florida*, a collection of twenty-six short rhetorical pieces of considerable variety. The origin of the collection is debated: was it put together by Fronto or by some later admirer? Are the passages taken out of larger works, or are they rhetorical exercises?[60] Two of them could be regarded as complete short speeches on particular occasions: number nine, in which he compares himself to the sophist Hippias and praises the proconsul Severianus, and sixteen, which thanks Aemilianus Strabo and the senate of Carthage for a statue which has been ordered in his honor. Others certainly could be parts of speeches of the type given by traveling sophists or intended for special occasions. There are comparisons, descriptions, and fables which could be parts of speeches or exercises. The style varies greatly with the subject. The twenty-six pieces are divided into four "books" in the manuscripts. Since these "books" are so small, it seems tempting to believe that someone has cut out a series of admired passages, including two complete short speeches, from a collection of four large books of sophistic speeches by Apuleius. In any event, the collection is adequate to show that Apuleius came closer than any other Latin writer we know to several kinds of epideictic oratory being practiced by Greek sophists.

Christian Rhetoric[61]

We have seen that rhetoricians like Quintilian and orators like Dio or Aristides in Greek and Fronto or

[60] Cf. Karl Mras, "Apuleius' *Florida* im Rahmen ähnlicher Literatur," AAWW 86 (1949) 205-23. Mras reviews the various possibilities and concludes that the *Florida* is made up of extracts from four larger books of *prolaliae*.

[61] Cf. Henri-Irénée Marrou, *Saint Augustin et la fin de la culture classique*, Paris, 1958, esp. 505-40; Clarke 148-57. Anto-

Apuleius in Latin sought a wider field for rhetoric. In terms of content the most satisfactory areas to which they turned were the cultural heritage of Hellenism, which they perhaps hoped would give greater meaning and unity to the life of their times, and philosophy, as seen in the diatribes of Dio, the Platonic orations of Aristides, and the Platonism of Apuleius. Belief in Hellenism or in a philosophical school helped give the orator a positive and practical goal of persuasion: his work becomes more than declamation, exercise, or entertainment. This aspect of rhetoric was much enlarged by the success of Christianity, which had become a serious intellectual influence of international dimensions by the mid-second century A.D. Greeks and Romans educated in rhetoric and philosophy were converted to Christianity, and though they often rejected the mythical and pagan literature in which they had been trained, and sometimes forswore literary values as a whole, they were apt to continue to draw on the concepts of philosophy or employ the devices of rhetoric in support of their new enthusiasm. Pagans occasionally replied with rhetorical attack upon Christianity, though the ultimate Christian victory has suppressed much of what they said. We have already seen that Fronto spoke against the Christians on at least one occasion. The best-known attack on Christianity in Greek in this period is the work of a Platonist named Celsus, known through the refutation of the Christian Origen. The most eloquent and pro-

---

nio Quacquarelli, *La retorica antica al bivio* (*L'ad Nigrenum e l'ad Donatum*), Rome, 1956; *Rhetorica e liturgia antenicena*, Rome, 1960; Christine Mohrmann, "Problèmes stylistique dans la littérature latine chretiènne," *VChr* 9 (1955) 222-46; Jacques Fontaine, *Aspects et problèmes de la prose d'art latine au III* *siècle. La genèse des styles chrétiens*, Torino, 1968.

found reply to Christianity is found in the work of the sophist emperor Julian in the fourth century.

There are, of course, rhetorical techniques evident in the New Testament; if the Sermon on the Mount is hardly a typical Greek oration, Paul's address on Mars' Hill or his defense before Agrippa can be analyzed in terms of argument, ethos, and pathos as taught in the schools.[62] Beginning in the second century there is a corpus of apologetic works, designed to answer charges of immorality, to persuade educated pagans of the truth of Christianity, and to differentiate Christianity and gnosticism.[63] The earliest complete example in Greek is the first *Apology* of the Syrian convert Justin Martyr, composed in Rome about A.D. 150.[64] This is an open letter to Antonius Pius, his heirs, the senate, and the Roman people on behalf of men of all sorts who are unjustly hated for their religion. Justin was quite familiar with Greek philosophy, which he regarded as preparation for the truth of Christianity, and his tone is more that of the exhorting philosopher than of an orator pleading a case. He does not aim at stylistic adornment or literary finish, and he does not seem to have imitated

[62] Cf. Eduard Norden, *Agnostos Theos: Untersuchungen zur Formengeschichte religiöser Rede*, reprint Stuttgart, 1956, and A. N. Wilder, *The Language of the Gospel: Early Christian Rhetoric*, New York, 1964.

[63] Cf. M. Pellegrino, "L'elemento propagandistico e protrettico negli apologetti greci del II secolo," *RFIC* 19 (1941) 1-18 and 97-109 and R. M. Grant, "The Chronology of the Greek Apologists," *VChr* 9 (1955) 25-33.

[64] Cf. Basil L. Gildersleeve, *The Apologies of Justin Martyr*, New York, 1877; Edgar J. Goodspeed, *Die ältesten Apologeten*, Göttingen, 1914; P. Keresztes, "The Literary Genre of Justin's Apology," *VChr* 19 (1965) 99-110; H. Chadwick, "Justin Martyr's defense of Christianity," *BRL* 47 (1965) 275-97; L. W. Barnard, *Justin Martyr, his Life and Thought*, Cambridge, Eng., 1967.

the structure of an oration. Only the first part of the work (1-12) is actually a defense of the charges of atheism, immorality, or disloyalty, made against the Christians. The bulk of it (13-60) is a demonstration of the truth of Christianity, followed (61-67) by a description of Christian worship. The trial of a Christian named Ptolemaeus subsequently moved Justin to compose a shorter second *Apology* in which (3) he prophesies his own martyrdom. Other important Greek apologists of the second century are Tatian and Athenagoras.

More oratorical than Justin is the earliest Latin apology, the *Apologeticum* of Tertullian.[65] Tertullian was another African, born in Carthage about the middle of the second century. His numerous writings, at first orthodox, then heretical, date from the reign of Septimius Severus and Caracalla (193-216); all bear the stamp of his sarcastic, argumentative intelligence. He was not a man to compromise or conciliate pagans or other Christians, and he pursued his convictions wherever they led. We do not know what his education was like, but he was certainly familiar with Greek and Latin philosophy and literature which he often draws on for his arguments, and he is a skilled rhetorician who could have pleaded any cause with distinction.

The *Apologeticum* has a force unheard in Latin rhetorical literature since the *Philippics* of Cicero, a fiery

---

[65] For a translation cf. the Loeb edition (with Minucius Felix) by G. H. Rendall, London, 1960. Cf. also Christine Mohrmann, "Observations sur la langue et style de Tertullien," *ND* 4 (1950-51) 41-54; Carl Becker, *Tertulians Apologeticum, Werden und Leistung,* Munich, 1954; Jean-Pierre Waltzing, *Tertullien, Apologétique,* Paris, 1961; R. Braun, "Observations sur l'architecture de l'*Apologeticum,*" *Hommages à J. Bayet,* Brussels, 1964, 114-21; P. Keresztes, "Tertullian's *Apologeticum,* a Historical and Literary Study," *Latomus* 25 (1966) 124-33; Richard Klein, *Tertullian und das römische Reich,* Heidelberg, 1968.

defense of the life and belief of the Christians against the slander and legal restrictions of Rome, but accompanied by an effective statement of the political loyalty of the Christians. The materials out of which it is constructed are those already used by Justin, whose work Tertullian certainly knew, but they are sharpened into a more rhetorical form. The exordium (1-3) addresses the rulers of Rome as though seated in the law courts. The primary point is that Christianity is being condemned unheard: "Hatred is deserved only when known to be deserved." Various "signs" in the rhetorical sense are introduced as basis for argument from probability: those who become acquainted with Christianity cease to hate it; hatred throws a veil of shame over evil, but the Christian feels no shame, hence his creed is not an evil. Trajan's advice to Pliny not to seek out Christians, but to uphold the law if they refused to recant is reduced to its absurd implications: Christians are tortured to make them deny rather than confess.

The fourth chapter begins the heart of the work with a *partitio* in which Tertullian announces that he will deal first with the legal standing of the Christians (4-6) and then with the crimes alleged against them. Chapters seven to nine refute charges of murder, cannibalism, and incest, ten to twenty-nine deal with the Christians' attitude toward paganism. A section explaining the Christian god and religion falls in the real center of the work and is reminiscent of the symmetry favored by Demosthenes.[66] In Justin's *Apology* this aspect of the subject constituted the bulk of the work. Then Tertullian takes

[66] Otto Schönberger, "Ueber die symmetrische Komposition von Tertullians *Apologeticum*," *Gymnasium* 64 (1957) 335-40, sees a symmetry of length in the development of the parts of the work.

up the more difficult matter of Christian loyalty to the emperor and the state (30-45). His work concludes with a peroration comparing Christianity to philosophy, to the advantage of the former, and leading in the last chapter to an emotional contrast of pagan and Christian martyrs.

Tertullian writes in a peculiarly twisted, occasionally obscure, ironic, epigrammatic, Latin style which well fits his strong personality. He is capable of being unforgettably vivid as in this passage in which he is seeking to refute the rumor that the Christians at communion killed and ate small children and then proceeded to orgies of incest:

"To invoke the evidence of nature herself against those who presume that such acts can be believed, come see the reward offered these crimes: they are supposed to promise eternal life! Believe it for the moment. Then tell me whether one who believed would yet think it worth the price to attain immortality with so guilty a conscience. Go ahead, bury your knife in a child guilty of nothing, enemy of no one, child of all. Or if that act is to fall the lot of another, come you and stand behind a human creature dying before he has lived, watch his young soul slip away, catch his healthy blood, sop your bread in it, devour it with gusto. Meanwhile your mother or your sister are seated so that when the lights go out you won't fail to get them. It would be a sin, if it weren't incest! When you are initiated and instructed in these rites you attain immortal life. I want you to tell me: is eternity worth it? For if it is not, surely these crimes cannot be believed . . ." (*Apol.* 8.2-4).

Tertullian marks the limit of our study of Latin oratory. His force is reminiscent of Cato or Gaius Gracchus, but his thought is something new. In the following

612

centuries a Christian rhetoric is indeed developed, finding perhaps its full theoretical expression in the second part of Augustine's *De doctrina Christiana*. It remains for us to round out our picture of classical rhetoric with examination of those later treatises which belong solely to the classical tradition.

CHAPTER NINE

Greek Rhetoricians of the Empire

From the imperial and later periods there is preserved a considerable body of Greek writing on rhetoric. Some of this had already been collected in Byzantine manuscripts, for example in what is now *Parisinus Graecus* 1741, written in Pergamum about A.D. 1000 and containing Aristotle's *Rhetoric* and *Poetics*, Demetrius' *On Style*, various works by Dionysius, the *Aristides Rhetoric*, and also the treatises of Menander, Alexander, Apsines, Minucianus, and Maximus.[1] The first printed collection of Greek rhetorical works was made in 1508 and 1509 by Aldus Manutius in Venice, based on a similar manuscript. In the early nineteenth century Christian Walz undertook to amplify this into a collection of all Greek discussions of rhetoric in one vast edition, omitting only Aristotle and Dionysius who were easily available elsewhere. His *Rhetores Graeci* was published in nine volumes between 1832 and 1836 and has recently been reprinted.[2] It begins with treatises on *progymnasmata*, or introductory exercises, such as those of Theon, Hermogenes, and Aphthonius, then goes on to Hermogenes and other writers on rhetorical theory, followed by introductions, scholia, and commentaries by later rhetoricians like Syrianus and Sopater. In volume eight are printed treatises on figures and style, in nine the remaining general treatises such as those of Apsines and Menander as well as indices and a full table of contents. The more important later Greek rhetorical works, with the addition of Aris-

---

[1] Cf. Hugo Rabe, "Rhetoren-corpora," *RhM* 67 (1912) 320-57.

[2] Osnabrück, 1968.

totle, were again edited in three volumes published by L. Spengel between 1853 and 1856;[3] a revised edition begun by C. Hammer in 1894 led to publication of only one volume which contains Anaximenes, Longinus, Apsines, the *Anonymous Seguerianus*, and a few other works. Between 1892 and 1931 Hugo Rabe edited several important additional writers in individual volumes of the *Bibliotheca Teubneriana*: Hermogenes (1913), Syrianus' commentary thereon (1892-93), Aphthonius (1926), John of Sardis' commentary thereon (1928), and the *Prolegomenon Sylloge* (1931).

In this chapter we will consider chronologically some of the rhetoricians of the first, second, and third century whose influence was greatest and longest felt. The principal areas of interest were *stasis* theory, figures of speech and "ideas" or forms of style, and rules for epideictic oratory, which had not been spelled out in great detail before but were comparatively more important in this age of sophists. Indeed, all of the developments in rhetorical theory should be viewed as directed primarily to the needs of declaimers and sophists or as a contribution to rhetorical criticism of the classics. The great model of style in this period is Demosthenes, whose works were the subject of many commentaries. Plato, however, was much admired and in the third century and later there develops a tie between rhetoric and neo-Platonism.

Aelius Theon

Progymnasmata were introductory exercises in composition as practiced in the grammatical and rhetorical schools. The *Rhetores Graeci* collection contains three treatises describing how these are to be composed and there is also some discussion of the subject in Quintilian

[3] Reprinted Frankfurt, 1966.

(2.4) and other writers. The earliest treatise on *progymnasmata* is apparently that by Aelius Theon of Alexandria, perhaps written in the first century after Christ.[4] There were several writers named Theon and they are difficult to sort out and to date. This author may, however, be the "Stoic" rhetorician whose *stasis* theory and discussion of stylistic figures is mentioned by Quintilian (3.6.48 and 9.3.76). The *Souda* attributes to him grammatical and rhetorical works and commentaries on Xenophon, Isocrates, and Demosthenes. His *Progymnasmata* describes fifteen exercises designed to prepare a student not only for declamation, but also for the writing of history and poetry. The author is clearly a classicist and Atticist who most often takes Demosthenes as his model, but also admires Lysias, Aeschines, Herodotus, Thucydides, Homer, Plato and other earlier writers. To judge from the introduction, the work has been rearranged by a later editor, and it breaks off incomplete.

The *Anonymous Seguerianus* and His Sources

In 1843 Seguier de St. Brisson pointed out the existence of an anonymous treatise on the parts of an oration, unknown to Walz, but preserved in a Paris manuscript (1874); from him the author has acquired the epithet of the *Anonymous Seguerianus*.[5] The treatise refers fre-

---

[4] *RG* 1.145-257 Walz; 2.60-130 Spengel. Cf. G. Reichel, *Quaestiones progymnasmaticae*, Leipzig, 1909; Schmid-Stählin, 2.1.564; *R-E* 5A.2037-54; Italo Lana, *I progimnasmi di Elio Teone*, 1. *La storia del testo*, Turin, 1959. Lana's speculation that Theon was the author of *On Sublimity*, though unproved, is no more improbable than other such speculations, cf. *Quintiliano, il "Sublime," e gli "Esercize Preparatori" di Elio Teone*, Turin, 1951.

[5] *RG* 1. 427-60 Spengel; 352-98 Spengel-Hammer, Cf. *R-E* 1.2328-30. The attribution of the original treatise to a certain

quently to the views of the Apollodoreans, still a vital
force, and counteracts or supplements them with citation
of three other sources: Neocles, Alexander son of Numenius, and Harpocration. Alexander and Harpocration
can be securely dated in the mid-second century A.D.
and this is a likely date for composition of the original
on which our treatise is based. Because of the austere
presentation of the material most critics have felt that
what we have is probably an epitome, perhaps made
fifty years or so later. The concepts and terminology
bring together Aristotelian, Stoic, and other materials
stretching over the entire history of rhetoric, but the
author's point of view is the classicizing Atticism of the
first and second centuries. His examples are taken from
the great Attic writers, and he does not specifically apply
his theory to declamation as Hermogenes was soon to do.
The four standard parts of an oration—prooemium, narration, proof, and epilogue—are each given a chapter,
but the treatment is novel in that, with the partial exception of the prooemium, the writer considers invention, arrangement, and style as applied in turn to each of
these parts.

Of the three major sources of the *Anonymous Seguerianus* Neocles is possibly the earliest, but the least
known.[6] It is possible that his work was known to Quintilian.[7] Here he is cited twelve times and there are also
a few citations in the work of the Byzantine scholar
Maximus Planudes. Apparently Neocles disagreed with

Cornutus has not been accepted. It was advanced by J. Graeven,
Cornuti artes rhetoricae epitome, Berlin, 1891.

[6] Cf. *R-E* 16.2416-22.

[7] Cf. Karl Aulitzky, "Apsines περὶ ἐλέου," *WS* 39 (1917) 44-
45. The passages in question are Quintilian 5.11.36 and *Anonymous Seguerianus* 384 Spengel-Hammer (sec. 181).

Apollodorus, but perhaps not so strongly as Alexander did, and from the references one might hazard the guess that he had considerable interest in *kairos* and in the emotions.

Alexander was the son of Numenius, an official under Hadrian, and must have lived through the middle of the second century.[8] He wrote what was apparently the best known treatise on figures of speech after Caecilius, on whom he drew; an epitome of it survives, and signs of its influence are clear on most later Greek and Latin discussions of figures.[9] He also wrote a more general treatise on rhetoric which is the source for the *Anonymous Seguerianus*. Alexander's views are here repeatedly contrasted with those of the Apollodoreans. It appears that Alexander's great appeal rested on his command of earlier sources, his ability to give a clear and perhaps succinct description of rhetorical rules or figures, and his reasonable viewpoint about rhetorical conventions, which many people found it possible to accept. Alexander's influence has much to do with making the *Anonymous Seguerianus* one of the more attractive writers on the subject.

Harpocration, the third source cited, appears to be a rhetorician mentioned in the *Souda* as author of works on Hyperides, Herodotus, and Xenophon, a treatise on stylistic "ideas," and an art of rhetoric.[10] The stylistic "ideas" suggest the time of Hermogenes, and this is confirmed by a later scholiast who reveals that Harpocration attacked Hermogenes in discussing *stasis* theory (*RG*

[8] Cf. *R-E* 1.1456-59.
[9] *RG* 8.421-246 Walz; 3.1-40 Spengel. Cf. B. Steusloff, *Quibus de causis Alexander Numenii liber . . . qui vulgo genuinus habetur putandus sit spurius et quae epitomae ex deperdito Alexandri libro excerptae supersint, demonstratur*, Breslau, 1861.
[10] Cf. *R-E* 7.2411-12. He is not identical with the grammarian who compiled the *Lexicon of the Ten Orators*.

7.349-50 Walz). His own views on that subject were eccentric, for example, he put *paragraphe* first (cf. Syrianus 2. p. 60 Rabe).

Hermogenes, Minucian, and the *Aristides Rhetoric*

During later antiquity, Byzantine times, and the Renaissance Hermogenes was probably the most read and most influential Greek rhetorician.[11] He has generally been assumed to be identical with a sophist, Hermogenes of Tarsus, described by Philostratus (2.577) as a young prodigy who, at the age of fifteen, was honored by a visit from Marcus Aurelius. This event took place when Marcus was in the East in A.D. 176 (Dio Cassius 71.1) and suggests that Hermogenes was born around 161. But after an early flowering his oratorical powers suddenly waned—his winged words had molted, as his rivals put it—and though he apparently continued to speak until old age, he lost all claim to distinction. He was certainly dead by the time Philostratus wrote.

Philostratus makes no mention of Hermogenes' teaching rhetoric nor of his technical works; according to the scholiasts these also were written in his youth, between his fifteenth and twenty-third year.[12] Dio Cassius' reference might be taken to mean that Marcus Aurelius at-

[11] For the text cf. Hugo Rabe, *Hermogenis opera* (*Rhetores Graeci* 6), Leipzig, 1913, reprinted Stuttgart, 1969, also RG 3.1-445 Walz, 2.133-456 Spengel. For discussion L. Radermacher in *R-E* VIII. 865-78 (also published in 1913), and Schmid-Stählin 2.2.780. Influence in later antiquity is seen in the extensive body of commentary on Hermogenes as collected in Walz. Cf. Stephanus Gloeckner, "Quaestiones rhetoricae. Historiae artis rhetoricae qualis fuerit aevo imperatorio capita selecta," *Breslauer Philologische Abhandlungen* 8.2 (1901). For the Renaissance cf. Annabel M. Patterson, *Hermogenes and the Renaissance: Seven Ideas of Style*, Princeton, 1970.

[12] Cf. Hugo Rabe, "Nachrichten über das Leben des Hermogenes," *RhM* 62 (1907) 247-62.

tended Hermogenes' rhetorical lectures rather than declamations, but a teenage oratorical sensation is easier to
imagine than a teenage professor. Hermogenes' rhetorical writings are not simply student notebooks, like
Cicero's *De inventione*, and it is tempting to believe that
they were products of the period after his oratorical collapse.

Five works survive under Hermogenes' name. The
Progymnasmata are brief descriptions of twelve preparatory exercises in rhetorical composition: myth, narration,
chria, etc. On grounds of *testimonia* and style Rabe
sought to show that Hermogenes did not write this
work.[13] His arguments have had some acceptance, but
no one of them is very strong and it remains possible
that this is a genuine if minor work by Hermogenes, perhaps epitomized or edited by a later student of rhetoric.
The three major works attributed to Hermogenes are
On Staseis in one book, *On Invention* in four books, and
On Forms in two books. Cross-references from one to the
other[14] and the general direction of the argument suggest that the three may constitute a kind of unity or art
of rhetoric intended to present those features of the subject which interested Hermogenes. He expressly assumes
at the outset of *On Staseis* much of the traditional material of rhetorical theory, and other topics he ignores or
abandons, such as the five parts of rhetoric. Though he
discusses invention, it is not something coordinate with
arrangement, style, memory, and delivery, and it becomes
an art of division and amplification. Style interests him
greatly, but only certain aspects of it. He has no political

---

[13] Cf. *op.cit.* supra n. 11, iv-vi. For a translation of the *Progymnasmata* cf. Charles Sears Baldwin, *Medieval Rhetoric and
Poetic*, New York, 1928, 23-38.

[14] Cf., e.g., *On Invention* 3.4 and 4.6; *On Forms* 2.9 p. 378
Rabe.

interests and never mentions Rome or the Romans. Once (*On Inv.* 3.4 p. 132 Rabe) he claims that victory is the goal of an orator, but elsewhere his reader is never expected to plead in court or in senate: Hermogenes is in fact totally concerned with training a declaimer. One of the first logical divisions made in *On Staseis* is the distinction between persons and actions, and the author soon reveals that by "persons" he means the common types who appear in declamation. The subjects of oratory which he discusses—he calls them problems—are the traditional themes of judicial or deliberative declamation, the latter chosen from Greek history of the fifth and fourth centuries B.C.

It is the interest in declamation which has doubtless dictated the basic approach to the subject which Hermogenes seems to follow. A declaimer must decide first what is to be his treatment of his problem. This means he must decide the *stasis* of his speech, and it is that subject with which Hermogenes begins. The declaimer can then go on to consider what he is going to say and finally can consider the stylistic qualities which he wishes to impart, the subject of the two books *On Forms.*[15] Hermogenes, however, is no Quintilian and does not express himself in such a direct or pedagogic way. A passage from the end of the first chapter of *On Staseis* shows how he viewed his task and gives an indication of his style and manner of thought.

"As for the kind and form of causes, it would be superfluous to discuss these at present, for surely we learn the kinds and forms in order that we may practice causes making use of the proper forms of speech: judicial judicially, deliberative deliberatively, epideictic epideictically,

[15] Some writers of *Prolegomena* divide rhetoric into *noēsis* (including *stasis*), *heuresis*, and *diathesis* (including style), cf. p. 199 and 235 Rabe.

and each as is proper, suitably to the subject. But it would be useless to know well any of the aforesaid matters if one had not yet considered basic division of questions into headings and did not know this matter at hand of the so-called *staseis* of causes. Thus to teach the theory of forms first is altogether senseless, and if we should somehow try to say something about them now, we would expend more discussion on side issues than on the subject. For discussion of the forms of discourse and the use of each of them is a specialized business and no small one, but rather great and consummate. As a result, we should now consider the division I have mentioned, that into headings. A person will make the right division if he understands the difference and import of persons and things and also the so-called *stasis* of the question. I leave to others to inquire whence the term *stasis* comes, whether from the conflict of the contestants or from some other derivation, but dismissing the name as accepted or implicit in all questions and preferring as the topic of discussion how we shall come to an understanding of these matters, I necessarily start my account of division of headings from *stochasmos*, as will become clear, and in due course will speak about other headings."

Hermogenes' concept and terminology of *stasis* is basically that of Hermagoras.[16] He is, however, not very interested in the stages leading to determination of *stasis* (*kataphasis, apophasis, synechon, aition*), and he has

[16] Cf. Gloeckner, *op.cit.* supra n. 11; Gualtherus Jaeneke, *De statuum doctrina ab Hermogene tradita*, Leipzig, 1904; Radermacher, *op.cit.* supra n. 1, 870-71; *R-E Suppl.* 7.1135-37; Georgius Kowalski, *Hermogenes De statibus*, Warsaw, 1947; Ray Nadeau, "Classical Systems of Stases in Greek: Hermagoras to Hermogenes," *GRBS* 2 (1959) 53-71; Dieter Mathis, "Hermagoras von Temnos 1904-1955, *Lustrum* 3 (1958) 102-4; Raymond E. Nadeau, "Hermogenes' *On Stases*: A Translation with an Introduction and Notes," *SM* 31 (1964) 361-424.

adopted Theodorus' word *kephalaia*, "headings," which he uses to mean all the different categories involved in his subject, including not only the different *staseis*, but the subdivisions thereof. Hermagoras had listed four kinds of cases in which no *stasis* could be found; Hermogenes elaborates this in his first chapter to eight headings and adds three more which are almost asystatic. Most striking of all, under the apparent influence of Stoic categories, Hermogenes or some source which he follows has departed from the concept of four coordinate kinds of *stasis* and substituted an arrangement in which each kind is subordinate to the one previously discussed. A matter under litigation (*to krinomenon*) is either uncertain or certain. If uncertain, the *stasis* is one of conjecture or fact ("Did it happen or not?"), which Hermogenes, like Hermagoras, calls *stochasmos*. If certain, the matter is either undefined, which then requires *stasis* of definition (*horos*), or defined ("Is it murder or homicide"). If defined, it is qualified or explained in some way (*poiotês*) or it is not ("Is it just?"). If it is not qualified, it is not or it is subject to the jurisdiction of the addressee (objection, *metalepsis*). Whenever the first half of one of these statements applies, the *stasis* has been found. Whenever the second half applied, the next stage of subdivision is required. Hermagoras had made an overall contrast between rational *staseis*, in which argument plays the main role, and legal *staseis*, in which the interpretation of a law is the heart of the matter; Hermogenes applies this distinction only to *stasis* of quality. At the outset Hermogenes seems interested in all forms of oratory, but as usual *stasis* is mostly applicable to judicial speeches. One deliberative problem is cited in connexion with *stasis* of quality (2. p. 38 Rabe).

It is not Hermogenes' custom to name other technical writers, but in a number of passages he seems to be tacitly

623

criticizing some well-known source. His refusal to speculate on the etymology of *stasis* is probably an example. Fortunately the scholiasts frequently give us the name of Hermogenes' chief opponent in *stasis* theory: he is Minucian, an Athenian of the time of Antoninus Pius, famous as an orator, but not apparently a sophist since he is not discussed by Philostratus.[17] The *Souda* attributes to him, in addition to speeches, a treatise on *progymnasmata* and an art of rhetoric. There was apparently also a commentary on Demosthenes.[18]

Minucian's art of rhetoric can be partially reconstructed.[19] It began with a glance at rhetoric as a whole, the various parts, the duties of an orator, and the parts of an oration.[20] Minucian's own experience as a practicing orator may have given him a wider interest in his subject than existed in the declamation-oriented Hermogenes. Yet the bulk of the work was entirely devoted to *stasis* theory.[21] Thirteen different kinds of *stasis* were distinguished by promoting some subdivisions to equivalent rank. During the third and fourth centuries Minucian was apparently somewhat more influential than Hermogenes; this may have been partly because he had a series of very distinguished descendants living in the intellectual capital of Greece.[22] His son Mnesaeus was an orator, his grandson Nicagoras a famous sophist, his great-grandson Minucian the Younger again an orator and rhetorician in the mid-third century. The latter may

---

[17] Cf. *R-E* 15.1975-86.

[18] Cf. John Doxapatres in *RG* 6.111 Walz.

[19] Cf. Gloeckner, *op.cit.* supra n. 11, 22-50 and Otmar Schissel, "Ein Minukianzitat in der Redelehre des Rufus," *PW* 47 (1926) 828-31.

[20] Cf. Georgius Pletho in *RG* 6.585-87 Walz.

[21] Cf. Marcellinus in *RG* 4.684 Walz.

[22] Cf. Otmar Schissel, "Die Familie des Minucianus," *Klio* 21 (1927) 361-73.

be the Minucian who wrote the extant work *On Epi-cheiremes*.[23] The elder Minucian's overall view of rhetoric and a superiority in definition may have recommended him to neo-Platonists like Porphyry, who according to the *Souda* wrote a commentary on his art of rhetoric. Hermogenes clearly felt that his own work was superior to Minucian's in judgment, arrangement, and clarity; he probably does go more directly to the heart of *stasis* of theory and illustrates it better than his rival had done, though his definitions are sometimes poor. These may have been the qualities which appealed to students in the fourth century and later when Minucian was increasingly neglected and ultimately lost, while Hermogenes was constantly studied.[24]

An older contemporary of Minucian and Hermogenes who adopted Minucian's theory of thirteen types of *stasis* was Telephus of Pergamum.[25] Telephus was primarily a grammarian, interested in Homer. He wrote an influential treatise *On Rhetoric in Homer*, which apparently examined Homeric instances of all kinds of rhetorical topics, including *stasis*.

The second major work attributed to Hermogenes is *On Invention* in four books. Books one and two are short and deal with the prooemium and narration of a speech, respectively. There are no introductions and no attempt is made to state the traditional functions or objectives of these various parts of an oration, but a kind of structural formula is examined in each case. Hermogenes' discussion of the narration has chapters on the transplanting of cities, on the introduction of laws, and on

[23] RG 9.601-13 Walz; 340-51 Spengel-Hammer; Prentice A. Meador, Jr., "Minucian, *On Epicheiremes*: an Introduction and a Translation," *SM* 31 (1964) 54-63.

[24] Cf. Gloeckner, *op.cit.* supra n. 11, 113-15.

[25] Cf. R-E 5A.369-71 and Hermann Schrader, "Telephos der Pergaminer," *Hermes* 37 (1902) 530-81.

war and peace, matters which apply to deliberative oratory.

Books three and four are each about three times the size of books one or two. Further, book three begins with a brief introduction claiming that the heart of the subject, the introduction of headings and epicheiremes, has been reached, and there is a dedication to an unknown Julius Marcus, something otherwise unprecedented in Hermogenes. Throughout the book the author is not interested in proof in the way Aristotle was, but in amplification and the arrangement of material. In the manuscripts some of the chapters seem to be out of logical order. The fourth book begins with the statement that since the epicheireme and related matters have been discussed it is now necessary to consider figures of speech, and the author never returns to the remaining part of the oration, the epilogue. As in *On Staseis* the interest throughout the work is in declamation; the author is again not very clear in his definitions, but liberally illustrates with examples from declamatory subjects or from classical authors, especially from Demosthenes.

As has been stated, we have a considerable body of commentary on Hermogenes from late antiquity and Byzantine times. These include *prolegomena* to the various works by named or anonymous writers,[26] as well as running commentaries such as that of Syrianus to *On Staseis*, apparently the most read of the works of Hermogenes. Several commentators omit *On Invention* when discussing works by Hermogenes; several others,

---

[26] Edited by Hugo Rabe, *Prolegomenon sylloge*, Leipzig, 1931. For discussion of these *prolegomena* cf. APG 59-60; Ludwig Radermacher, "Timäus und die Ueberlieferung über die Ursprung der Rhetorik," *RhM* 52 (1897) 412-19; Klaus Schöpsdau, *Antike Vorstellungen von der Geschichte der Griechischen Rhetorik*, Saarbrücken, 1969.

however, mention it.[27] There are two *prolegomena* specifically attached to *On Invention*, one by John of Sardis, who lived in the tenth century, and one by John Doxapatres, who lived in the eleventh. John of Sardis seems to have no doubt that *On Invention* is a genuine work, but he either has a different version of it or has not read it very carefully, for he claims (p. 358 Rabe) that it contains discussion of *prooemium, diêgêsis, pistis,* and *epilogos.* John Doxapatres knows that there is no account of the epilogue (p. 372 Rabe) and discusses the question of authenticity (pp. 364-65 Rabe). He thinks the work is genuine for five reasons: everybody says so; there is a reference in it to *On Staseis; On Staseis* foreshadows it; without it the unified *Art of Rhetoric* which the triad composes would be incomplete; and the material and classifications are similar to those used by Hermogenes in other works. Most of the commentators discuss the applicability of the general title (epigraph they call it) *Art of Rhetoric* to one or all of the works of Hermogenes.

John Doxapatres' first point may be restated to say that the manuscripts support attribution to Hermogenes; the third and fourth points are weak, but the second and fifth have some force. Rabe, pointing out that Syrianus and Lachares quote something resembling statements in *On Invention* as coming from Apsines, and feeling that the style was not that of Hermogenes, denied the work's authenticity.[28] Others have contented themselves with concluding that we have at best a considerably altered form.[29] The first two books are certainly not unlike Her-

---

[27] *Prolegomenon sylloge* pp. 203, 290, 302, and 337 Rabe omits; pp. 257 and 308 includes.

[28] *Op.cit.* supra n. 11, vi-ix.

[29] Cf. L. Radermacher in *R-E* 8.873-77.

mogenes in thought and style; peculiarities come mostly in books three and four where some student or some later rhetorician may have added material, as was also done to the *Aristides Rhetoric*, or perhaps some copyist confused the order. Possibly a final book or section on the epilogue is lost.

On Forms is the longest, the most polished, and the most interesting of Hermogenes' works. In order to understand it, however, we must go back to a slightly earlier treatise and consider the history of the so-called virtues of style.

Rhetoricians in the time of Isocrates and Aristotle had shown an interest in various qualities or virtues which were given definitive expression by Theophrastus in his treatise *On Style*. We have seen that the four Theophrastan virtues of correctness, clarity, ornamentation, and propriety reappear in Cicero and Quintilian, and we have also seen that Dionysius of Halicarnassus modified the theory into three necessary, and a varying number of additional, virtues, which are subdivisions of ornamentation.[30] Quintilian (8.3.49) seems to have known a concept of ornamental virtues which included *acutum, nitidum, hilare, iucundum,* and *accuratum*.

In the later second century A.D. under influences of Atticism and classicism the theory of the stylistic virtues developed into what were called the "ideas" or "forms" of style as discussed in a small work attributed to Aelius Aristides[31] and in Hermogenes' *On Forms*. Presumably the central concept is derived from Platonism, which was becoming more popular at this time. What we

[30] Cf. supra 349.
[31] Cf. Guilelmus Schmid, *Aristidis qui feruntur libri rhetorici II*, Leipzig, 1926. Also André Boulanger, *Aelius Aristide et la sophistique dans la province d'Asie au IIe siècle de notre ère*, Paris, 1928, 239-49; Schmid-Stählin 2.2.688; *R-E Suppl.* 7.1126-27.

may call the *Aristides Rhetoric* bears little resemblance to other writings of Aristides, but in two passages (1.141ff. and 174ff.) draws on him without mentioning his name, which may have been noticed and become the source of the attribution in later antiquity. Actually the *Aristides Rhetoric* is a conflation of several works.[32] There is first a treatise *On Political Discourse* which expounds the theory of the "ideas" or virtues of style. Twelve are listed in the first section: *semnotês, barytês, peribolê, axiopistis, sphodrotês, emphasis, deinotês, epimeleia, glykytês, saphêneia* (and *katharotês*), *brachytês* (and *syntomia*), and *kolasis*.[33] The method is to discuss each in terms of *gnômê* or thought content, *schêma* or figures, and *apangelia* or expression. Illustrations are taken chiefly from Demosthenes, and the author's objective seems to be to create an understanding of style which will allow a student to become a sophist like Aristides or the others described by Philostratus. If we wish to give a name to this author the best possibility is not Aristides himself, but Basilicus of Nicomedia.[34] Basilicus was a rhetorician to whom the *Souda* and Tzetzes attribute a variety of rhetorical works similar in nature to those of Hermogenes. Syrianus (p. 13 Rabe), commenting on Hermogenes' *On Forms*, says that the latter's sources were Basilicus and Zenon, and that Basilicus' account was inferior to Hermogenes' in judgment and arrangement. This is not specific enough to point to the first book of the *Aristides Rhetoric*, but is a perfectly reasonable statement about it.

[32] Cf. W. Schmid, "Die sogenannte Aristidesrhetorik," *RhM* 72 (1917-18) 113-49 and 238-57.

[33] These might be roughly translated dignity, gravity, amplification, sincerity, vehemence, directness, force, diligence, sweetness, clarity, brevity, and prudence.

[34] Cf. Schmid, *op.cit.* supra n. 6, 244. On Basilicus cf. also Gloeckner, *op.cit.* supra n. 11 and *R-E* 3.97-98.

The concluding portions of the treatise seem to have been edited by someone who summarized some parts (1.132-40), added material on other aspects of style (1.141-74), summarized the twenty-ninth speech of Aristides (1.175-81), and paraphrased portions of the *Iliad* and *Odyssey* (1.182-86). There follows a second book, *On the Simple Style*, of which Xenophon is taken as the canonical model. A number of the same "ideas" are discussed in terms of content, figures, and expression. Schmid suggested that this second book might be the work of the Zenon mentioned in Syrianus as having written on this subject, but we cannot be certain.[35]

We may now return to Hermogenes' treatise *On Forms*, which is somewhat more elaborately developed than the *Aristides Rhetoric* and as usual with Hermogenes is well and fully illustrated.[36] At the outset (p. 213 Rabe) Hermogenes explains that an understanding of the "ideas" or forms of discourse is necessary for criticism of classical and contemporary writers and in the creation of works which are worthy to stand beside the classics. Imitation, even if supported by great native ability, is not enough if understanding is lacking. Although it is his intention to discuss the forms themselves first and leave the style of individual authors until later, it soon emerges that Demosthenes is in Hermogenes' opinion the one great artist who exemplifies all styles and all mixtures of styles (pp. 215-16 Rabe). Previous writers on forms of discourse have been confused and uncertain, he says, a reference which the commentator Syrianus

[35] Cf. *op.cit.* supra n. 32, 244.
[36] Cf. R-E 8.871-72 and *Suppl.* 7.1127-28; G.M.A. Grube, *The Greek and Roman Critics*, London, 1965, 338-39; Wladyslaw Madyda, "Ueber die Voraussetzungen der hermogenischen Stillehre," *Deut. Akad. Wissens. Berlin Sekt. für Altertumswissens,* 13 (1959) 44-51.

(p. 13 Rabe) applies to Basilicus; writers on Demosthenes have concerned themselves only with individual problems and not with such overall characteristics as dignity or simplicity (p. 217 Rabe); Syrianus again cites Basilicus and adds Zenon as among those who wrote running commentaries. The *Aristides Rhetoric* had, of course, drawn its examples largely from Demosthenes, but the author, whether Basilicus or someone else, had not started from an assumption of his preeminence or treated the forms as manifestations of his art the way Hermogenes does.

The forms which characterize Demosthenic style are stated (pp. 217-18 Rabe) to be *saphêneia, megethos, kallos, gorgotês, êthos, alêtheia,* and *deinotês.*[37] The order appears to have been influenced by that traditional in discussion of the virtues, with *deinotês* representing an appropriate utilization of other qualities.[38] Of the seven forms only *deinotês* and *saphêneia* appear in the list of the *Aristides Rhetoric,* though the two lists are more similar than they appear at first, for in the ensuing discussion Hermogenes subdivides these forms, identifying some fourteen others, of which seven have names common to the *Aristides Rhetoric* and others are somewhat similar in fact if not in name. There is also some difference in the treatment of the forms, which in the earlier work consisted of considerations of *gnômai, schêmata,* and *apangeliai* in each case. Hermogenes again substitutes a more elaborate scheme, considering *ennoia* or thought, plus figures of thought, and *lexis,* style, which is broken down into choice of word, figures of speech, and composi-

---

[37] These may be roughly translated clarity, greatness, beauty, brevity, character, truth, and force.

[38] Cf. Ludwig Voit, *Deionotes: ein antiker Stilbegriff,* Leipzig, 1934, 53-68.

tion, which is in turn a matter of *kola* and of rhythm.[39] It is generally agreed that Hermogenes had the first book of the *Aristides Rhetoric* before him as he wrote and made conscious "improvements."

The account of the forms takes up all the first book and over two-thirds of book two. A fitting conclusion for the whole, following up suggestions made at the beginning of book one, is then provided in a consideration of "political discourse," the various degrees of effective combination of the forms. Hermogenes is not thinking about composing actual political oratory, but about school oratory made up of political materials from the classic days of Greece. In deliberative and judicial oratory the best model is said to be Demosthenes; in panegyric it is the "Platonic" style (pp. 386-87 Rabe), in poetry it is Homer. The victory of rhetoric over poetics may be seen in Hermogenes' treatment of all poetry as a subdivision of epideictic (p. 389 Rabe). At the end of the work there is brief consideration of the forms as manifested in Lysias, Isaeus, Hyperides, Isocrates, Dinarchus, Aeschines, the two Antiphons, Critias, Lycurgus, and Andocides in political discourse, of Plato, Xenophon, Aeschines Socraticus, Nicostratus, Herodotus, Thucydides, and Hecataeus among the panegyric writers. History, like poetry, is thus a subdivision of epideictic. The writers cited are entirely classics, but we should not overlook the fact that in earlier portions of the treatise Hermogenes does cite one orator of his own age, albeit apologetically (p. 353 Rabe), Aelius Aristides.

Twenty-three times in the course of *On Forms* Hermogenes promises to discuss something in a later treatment of *deinotês* or of the "method" of *deinotês*. The promises are not fulfilled in the chapter on *deinotês* in

[39] Cf. H. Becker, *Hermogenis Tarsensis de rhythmo oratorio doctrina*, Münster, 1896.

book two and are presumably references to a separate work.[40] An essay entitled *On the Method of Deinotês* exists, bearing Hermogenes' name. It does not, however, fulfill most of the promises either and is a series of disconnected chapters on figures and other aspects of style.[41] Since the contents and terminology are not unlike what Hermogenes elsewhere says, it is possible that the treatise contains genuine pieces of his theory loosely put together by some editor to supply a work whose existence was promised but not fulfilled.

Apsines

In addition to the *Anonymous Seguerianus* there survive from this general period two other rhetorical handbooks concerned primarily with parts of the oration. One is a very abbreviated work, little more than a series of definitions, by Rufus of Perinthus.[42] He is known from Philostratus (2.597-98) as a sophist and pupil of Herodes Atticus and therefore can be dated to the second half of the second century. The other is the more extensive work of Valerius Apsines of Gadara.[43] Apsines was a student of Basilicus, whom he mentions in high terms in his introduction, and settled as a sophist in Athens. Philostratus calls him his friend and praises his memory and precision (2.628). This gives us a date in the first half of the third century.

Apsines himself refers (e.g., p. 299 Spengel-Hammer)

[40] Cf. Emil Bürgi, "Ist die dem Hermogenes zugeschriebene Schrift περὶ μεθόδου δεινότητος echt?" *WS* 48 (1930) 187-97 and 49 (1931) 40-69.

[41] Cf. Hagedorn, *op.cit.* supra n. 36, 84-85.

[42] RG 3.447-60 Walz; 1.463-470 Spengel; 399-407 Spengel-Hammer. Cf. *R-E* 1A.1207.

[43] RG 9.467-542 Walz; 1.331-414 Spengel; 217-339 Spengel-Hammer. *R-E* 2.277-83. On the name Valerius cf. James H. Oliver, "Wife of the Sophist Apsines," *Hesperia* 10 (1941) 261.

to a separate discussion of figures and we have mention
also of his Demosthenes commentary (Maximus Planudes 5.517 Walz). His extant work, however, is an *Art
of Rhetoric* primarily adapted to the needs of would-be
declaimers. Prooemium, *prokatastasis* or preparation for
the proof, narration, enthymemes, "headings," and epilogue are discussed. Previous writers, Apsines says at the
beginning of the section on "headings," have adequately
discussed *staseis*. He may have Hermogenes or Minucian
in mind, but he does not betray their direct influence.
The section on the epilogue has an interesting extended
discussion of pity.[44] To the end of the treatise is appended a short essay *On Figured Problems*, probably a
genuine fragmentary work by Apsines on the treatment
of the subject in certain difficult kinds of declamation.
The topic is considered in the *Dionysius Rhetoric* as well.

The *Dionysius Rhetoric*

Among the writings of Dionysius of Halicarnassus is
preserved an *Art of Rhetoric*[45] which is, however, not a
general rhetorical handbook at all. The first seven chapters deal with varieties of epideictic oratory, the eighth
and ninth are devoted to figured themes in declamation,
the tenth to mistakes in declamation, and the eleventh
explains how to criticize characterization and style. It
seems likely that the chapters on epideictic are the work
of a single author; the other chapters are probably by
somebody else, perhaps by several separate rhetoricians,
and the total work is thus a conflation in much the sense

[44] Cf. Aulitzky, *op.cit.* supra n. 7.
[45] Cf. Hermann Usener, *Dionysii Halicarnasei quae fertur Ars
rhetorica*, Leipzig, 1895; Hermann Usener and Ludwig Radermacher, *Dionysii Halicarnasei quae exstant* vi, Stuttgart, 1965,
xxii-xxvi and 295-387; R-E 5.969.

that the *Aristides Rhetoric* is. None of the parts can be attributed to Dionysius, and it is even clear from a scholion that the attribution in the manuscript is nothing more than a guess, based on the statement in the tenth chapter (10.6, p. 364 Usener-Radermacher) that the writer planned to compose a treatise on imitation, which Dionysius did. The various writers admire Plato more than Dionysius ever did, and the subject matter discussed comes closest to the interests of rhetoricians in the period A.D. 150-250. The style is the standard Atticizing Greek of the Roman empire.

The chapters on epideictic are dedicated to an unknown young man named Echecrates. The name is rare in the empire and its associations with the *Phaedo* of Plato suggest that the family had an interest in philosophy, perhaps with the neo-Platonism which developed in the third century. The forms of epideictic discussed are, first, panegyric, by which is meant an encomiastic speech to be delivered at a festival; second, gamelion, a speech at a marriage, often making some use of the old "thesis" "Should a man marry?"; third, genethliac, or speech on a birthday; fourth, epithalamion, or speech at the arrival of a bride at her new home; fifth, prosphonetic, or ingratiating address to a ruler; sixth, epitaphios, or funeral oration, public or private; and seventh, athletic protreptic, or speech of exhortation before the games. These are probably all ancient forms, often existing side by side in poetic and prose versions. In the time of the second sophistic the prose hymns seem largely to replace the verse, and many of these forms became popular as declamations.[46] What we have in effect is a treatise on

---

[46] Cf. Theodore C. Burgess, "Epideictic Literature," *University of Chicago Studies in Classical Philology* 3 (1902) 89-261 and *R-E Suppl.* 7.1131-35.

aspects of sophistry: Dio's *Olympic Discourse* is a panegyric, the tenth oration of Aristides is a birthday speech for Apollo, there is an epithalamion by the fourth century orator Himerius, the prosphonetic is a variety of the royal address such as Dio's or Aristides' speeches to the emperors, and the epitaphios is of course a well-known form.

As described in the *Dionysius Rhetoric* each epideictic form is a collection of commonplaces with content and organization prescribed in considerable detail. The panegyric, for example, is to begin with praise of the god who presides over the festival, listing his attributes. Then comes praise of the city where the festival is located: its location, origin, founder, history, size, beauty, power, public buildings, rivers, legends. The next theme is the festival itself, its origin, legends, and history. Other festivals may be compared unfavorably. Then comes the program of the festival: topics are suggested for a festival which includes music and literature and one which is purely athletic. The prize is then described and praised and can also be compared with other prizes. Finally there is to be praise of the emperor or king or others in charge. These topics are found in various odes of Pindar, which are the general models for the type; no extant speech conforms very closely to the outline, but a student or would-be sophist who wished to compose a speech finds his subject matter nicely laid out for him here and can concentrate on what was most valued: diction, composition of periods, *sententiae*, and delivery.

Menander

A more extensive treatise on epideictic oratory is that which is attributed to Menander of Laodicea, a rhetorician of the third century who, according to the *Souda*, composed commentaries on Hermogenes and on Minucian's *progymnasmata.*[47] The work we have is actually two treatises, one incomplete, entitled Menander's *Division of Birthday (Genethlion) Epideictic,* or possibly (!) Genethlion's *Division of Epideictic,* while the second larger work is headed Menander *On Epideictic.* Whether Menander wrote only one or both is not agreed. Among the forms discussed in the second treatise are royal discourses and the *lalia,* an informal style of demonstrative speech with no fixed rules. Menander's work is useful in studying the structure and commonplaces of the sophists down through the Byzantine period.[48]

Longinus

The third century rhetorician closest to the neo-Platonism movement was Cassius Longinus (c. A.D. 213-73),[49] the "Sublime Longinus" as Gibbon calls him, thinking he was the author of *On Sublimity.*[50] Porphyry (cf. Eunapius, *Lives* 456) was his student in Athens and preserves part of a letter from Longinus inviting him to come to Palmyra and bring copies of Plotinus' works.[51] The letter reveals that Longinus when young had traveled widely with his parents and met many of the philos-

[47] Cf. *RG* 9.127-330 Walz; 3.331-36 Spengel. The best text is that of Conrad Bursian, "Der Rhetor Menandros und seine Schriften," *Academie der Wissen. Munchen: Abhandlungen der philosophisch-philogisches Classe* 16.3 (1882). Cf. also Burgess, *op.cit.* supra n. 45 and *R-E* 15.762-64.
[48] Cf. L. Previale, "Teoria e prassi del panegyrico bizantino," *Emerita* 17 (1949) 72-105 and Roger Pack, "The Roman Digressions of Ammianus Marcellinus," *TAPhA* 84 (1953) 181-89.
[49] Cf. *R-E* 13.1401-15; Schmid-Stählin 2.889-91; Emil Orth, "De Longino platonico," *Helmantica* 6 (1955) 363-71; J. M. Renaitour, "Un auteur oublié, Longin," *BAGB* 24 (1965) 502-15.
[50] Cf. supra 370.
[51] Porphyry, *Life of Plotinus* 19, available in the Loeb Library translation of Plotinus, by A. H. Armstrong, vol. 1, Cambridge, 1966.

ophers of the time. He eventually settled in Athens, but about 268 moved to the court of the remarkable Queen Zenobia at Palmyra in Syria. Here he became involved in her opposition to the emperor Aurelian and was put to death when Aurelian captured the city. Porphyry (*Life of Plotinus* 14) describes Longinus as a philologist, not a philosopher, but makes clear his deep interest in philosophy and quotes the preface to one of his philosophical works (*ibid.* 20). Others are named in the *Souda*, as are grammatical works, all lost. Finally, but not mentioned in the *Souda*, there were the *Philological Homilies*, a collection of lost treatises on literary subjects.[52] The rhetorical treatises may have been a part of this collection or may have been separate works.

Three fragmentary rhetorical treatises survive under Longinus' name.[53] The first was part of a short general *Art of Rhetoric*. Whatever introduction originally existed is lost, as is the discussion of invention applied to prooemium and narration. The extant part begins in the middle of a discussion of materials for examples and enthymemes useful in the proof; *stasis* is not brought in. This part of the treatise is then concluded with consideration of the epilogue, which Longinus presents as primarily an opportunity for amplification. There then follow about two pages on the arrangement of material within each of the parts of an oration and about six pages on style. The chapter might be described as a revision of Aristotle's discussion; the "ideas" of style are ignored and two qualities are sought: clarity in expounding the subject and charm, which is treated in terms of diction,

---

[52] Cf. M. J. Boyd, "Longinus, the *Philological Discourses,* and the *Essay on the Sublime,*" *CQ* 7 (1957) 39-46.

[53] Cf. *RG* 1.299-328 Spengel; 179-216 Spengel-Hammer; A. O. Prickard, *Libellus De sublimitate Dionysio Longino fere adscriptus,* Oxford, 1947.

figures of speech, and composition, tropes and figures of thought being ignored. The treatise ends with discussion of delivery and memory.[54] Longinus claims that his treatise is adequate for an able person to use in becoming a "perfect orator." Taken as a whole Longinus' handbook is more elegant than other treatises of the third century; it is also somewhat less technical. In the discussion of style some illustration is given, and Plato, Xenophon, Aeschines, Antisthenes, Isocrates, and others are mentioned, but the extensive examples of Hermogenes are lacking. The really remarkable feature of the treatise is that the author seems seriously to believe that he is dealing with an art of persuasion. The whole objective of style in his view is to make a speech more persuasive (559 Walz); the same is true of delivery (9.567 Walz), and at no point does he imply that he is writing an art of declamation. This point of view might be taken to reflect opportunities for real persuasion which Longinus found at the court of Zenobia, but those opportunities were restricted to the final years of his life. It is much more likely that the sources are the discussions of persuasion in Plato and Aristotle, which were reinvigorating the tradition as represented by Longinus in both rhetoric and philosophy, and his own experience with exposition of ideas among the philosophers of the time.

A three and a half page summary of rhetorical theory purports to be an epitome of the *Rhetoric* of Longinus. The first part may represent the lost contents of the work just discussed, for the middle section does reproduce Longinus' theories about the epilogue, arrangement, and style, but the epitomizer goes on to a strange conclusion in which he says that "the rhetor," presumably Longinus, set up seven models of every virtue: Aeschines (Socrati-

[54] The section on memory is omitted in Prickard's text, supra n. 53.

cus) and Plato from among philosophers, Herodotus and Thucydides from among historians, and Isocrates, Lysias, and Demosthenes from among the orators, but that he criticized Thucydides as labored and Plato as "artless in his mixture of the ideas of style," a judgment with which the epitomizer does not agree. Since artlessness can be the greatest art, the epitomizer may not have understood his text.

The third work is a collection of twenty-five short quotations, *From the Writings of Longinus*. Plato and Thucydides are here praised without reservation, as are also Demosthenes and Aristides. The title suggests that more than one source has been used and no logical order seems to be followed. Seven of the quotations relate to matters of invention, two to matters of arrangement, fourteen to style, all mixed in together. The remaining two are of a general nature and quite interesting: of these the fifth says: "That Demosthenes being the cleverest in replies did not always abide by the rules of art, but he often became an art unto himself. Much of the same is true of Aristides." It is encouraging to find, near the end of ancient rhetoric, a rhetorician who sees the superiority of the great creative artist to the rules of the pedant. It is this attitude which continues to leave the slight suspicion that for all the historical objections maybe Cassius Longinus could have written *On Sublimity* after all!

Another observation, the last in the collection, takes us back to the world of Gorgias and the sophists of the fifth century B.C.: "That the function of rhetoric is to say small things grandly, grand things cutely, novel things antiquely, and antique things novelly." This view continually lurked in the subconscious of even the noblest rhetoricians and orators. It was almost totally suppressed in the time of Cicero and Dionysius, but as rhetoric lost some of its practical concerns the bombast, cuteness, archaism, and striving for novelty gradually worked their way again to the surface. The sincere efforts of the greatest rhetoricians of the Roman empire to find new subjects of serious persuasion were partially successful and had some influence in the long run, but they were not widely imitated by the masses. That the rhetorical handbook we have just discussed, the work of a later Greek who recognized the persuasive object of rhetoric, should conclude in this way is ironic, but represents the conviction of most of his contemporaries. Classicism, Atticism, archaism, the revival of philosophy, and the wide dissemination of learning produced among the greatest of minds a breadth of vision, a sense of balance, and a unified concept of Hellenism, but for most the appeal of rhetoric was in style and *sententiae*.